CW00544580

30127074479200

THE CIVIL PLEAS OF
THE SUFFOLK EYRE OF 1240

SUFFOLK RECORDS SOCIETY

President
Norman Scarfe

Vice-Presidents
James Campbell
David Dymond
Peter Northeast
Joy Rowe
William Serjeant

Chairman
John Blatchly

Co-ordinating Editor
David Sherlock

Secretary
Claire Barker
Westhorpe Lodge
Westhorpe
Stowmarket, Suffolk IP14 4TA

website: www.suffolkrecordssociety.com

THE CIVIL PLEAS OF
THE SUFFOLK EYRE OF 1240

Edited by

ERIC JAMES GALLAGHER

General Editor

DAVID SHERLOCK

The Boydell Press

Suffolk Records Society
VOLUME LII

© The Trustees of the Suffolk Records Society 2009

All Rights Reserved. Except as permitted under current legislation
no part of this work may be photocopied, stored in a retrieval system,
published, performed in public, adapted, broadcast,
transmitted, recorded or reproduced in any form or by any means,
without the prior permission of the copyright owner

A Suffolk Records Society publication
First published 2009
The Boydell Press, Woodbridge

ISBN 978–1–84383–433–5

Issued to subscribing members for the year 2008–2009

| Suffolk County Council |
| Libraries & Heritage |
| ꭰoɴ | 08/09 |
| | | |

The Boydell Press is an imprint of Boydell & Brewer Ltd
PO Box 9, Woodbridge, Suffolk IP12 3DF, UK
and of Boydell & Brewer Inc.
668 Mt Hope Avenue, Rochester, NY 14620, USA
website: www.boydellandbrewer.com

A catalogue record for this book is available
from the British Library

This publication is printed on acid-free paper

Printed in Great Britain by
CPI Antony Rowe, Chippenham and Eastbourne

CONTENTS

ILLUSTRATIONS

PREFACE

The purpose of this volume is to provide an edition of the civil, or common, pleas in the plea roll of the justices in eyre in Suffolk, which opened in Ipswich on 30 April 1240. It does not cover the criminal and crown pleas. It is hoped that these will be the subjects of a subsequent study for the Suffolk Records Society. The eyre was a visitation of royal justices through a group of counties commissioned to hear all types of plea, criminal and civil. It also carried out inquiries into, amongst other things, the rights of the crown.

The roll records all the pleas heard by the judges, as well as any other business in a particular county. It also provides evidence of amercements levied by the justices on individuals, which the sheriff would be expected to collect, and pay in and account for at the Exchequer.

This eyre took place at a time of relative tranquillity in England with Henry III almost at his most powerful before the balance of power between the barons and the king began noticeably to shift. The close examination of the plea roll of any eyre is of value in its own right and as an addition to the available canon of published eyre rolls. However, the Suffolk eyre of 1240 is of particular interest as it is the first from Suffolk to be edited and is also from one of the most populous and economically prosperous parts of England at that time. The roll is also the earliest to survive in full. There is a roll from the Suffolk eyre of 1228 but unfortunately only its civil pleas survive.

The choice of the Suffolk eyre was dictated by the fact that I lived in Suffolk and that nobody had edited a Suffolk eyre roll before. Much of the research for this edition was done as part of a doctoral thesis and depended on the staff of The National Archives (formerly the Public Record Office) and I give them my thanks for providing me with advice and help. I am also grateful to a number of members of the Suffolk Records Society who provided particular help on the place names of Suffolk, namely, John Blatchly, Peter Northeast and David Dymond. I am also grateful for the support of the Institute of Historical Research, both in its facilities and for help freely given by those who attended some of the regular seminars held there. The support, interest and encouragement of my fellow postgraduate students and the staff of King's College London and of those in the King's College Library in Chancery Lane have been much appreciated.

I have made every effort to translate the text correctly. Naturally, any errors are my responsibility but I would like to express my thanks to Christopher Whittick and Lesley Boatwright for helping me to keep such errors to a minimum. I am also most grateful to Professor David Carpenter of King's College London for the constructive enthusiasm with which he supervised the thesis on which this edition is based.

I would like to dedicate this book to my wife Julia and both of my late parents. My wife, in particular, has encouraged me in my historical studies through the years and she has helped enormously in the production of my thesis on which this book is based.

Eric Gallagher
Norwich
2008

INTRODUCTION

THE GENERAL EYRE AND SUFFOLK

By 1240 the general eyre visitations sent out by the central government from West-minster into the counties had become a regular mechanism for linking central and local government and had developed administration, bureaucracy and records to a high degree.[1] These visitations were carried out by groups of itinerant justices, often in well defined circuits covering the whole country. The king used the general eyre to deliver his justice, both civil and criminal, throughout the kingdom, to oversee the performance of the local officials, to ensure that royal rights were not impinged on, to raise revenue and to determine if there were any special local difficulties within the county that ought to come to his attention. The money raised and the information received were important for the working of kingship in the twelfth and thirteenth centuries.

Local inquests by royal officials were not new. Domesday Book was compiled from local inquests made by travelling commissioners. The origins of the eyre system are obscure but they certainly date back at least to the reign of Henry I. A large degree of judicial activity took place around 1130, which is recorded in the pipe roll of that year. It indicates that a number of judges were splitting up the country between them to hear pleas. Richard Basset, for example, is shown as covering Sussex, Leicestershire, Norfolk and Suffolk.[2] However, it seems these eyres were ad hoc arrangements, which were not part of any general circuit. There is also little or no indication of what types of plea – other than crown pleas – they actually heard.

It was really in 1176 that the first chronicled general eyre took place in its complete form with its groups of itinerant justices appointed to defined circuits that covered the whole country. These justices were commissioned to hear all pleas[3] (*omnia placita*) according to defined *capitula itineris*, or articles of the eyre, set down for the eyre. As time went on the *capitula* were revised and expanded and had probably risen to about thirty-six by 1240.[4] The juries of presentment, formed from the leading freeholders of each hundred or borough in the county, responded to these *capitula* at the opening session of the eyre.[5] The *capitula* in general covered the hearing of the crown pleas, that is both the criminal pleas which had arisen since the last eyre and the investigations into royal rights. The impositions connected with

---

1   For a description of the increase in bureaucracy and records see Clanchy 1993, pp.62–78 and pp.81–98 for the types of records.
2   See Reedy 1966, pp.688–724 on the eyres of Henry I. See *Pipe Roll 31 Henry I*, pp.10, 34, 59, 70, 88, 94, 98 and 106 for all the counties covered by this 'eyre'. Also see Green 1986, pp.106–110 for the debate on the start of the eyre system.
3   See *Bracton* ii, p.308.
4   This estimate is based on the lists as defined in *1249 Wilts Crown Pleas*, pp.27–33 where Meekings provides a probable date when each of the individual *capitula* were introduced. By 1272 the number of *capitula* had risen to 69 according to Cam 1930, p.30.
5   See *Bracton* ii, pp.329–333.

criminal pleas were highly unpopular. The localities would often have amercements for tiny infractions of procedure, while the murdrum fine had simply become a way of raising money.[6] In addition the chattels of all convicted criminals and outlaws went to the king. The eyres gathering information on the king's rights in the localities and ensuring that his rights were protected were not particularly popular as they may have impinged on the perceived, or actual, rights of a local magnate. For example, in this eyre there is a jury investigating whether the king or the lord of the manor had rights of wreck in Wrentham.[7] The other major business of the eyre was to hear all outstanding civil pleas, and it is these which form the subject matter of this edition. This part of its function was far more popular and less contentious.[8]

During the reign of Henry III generally there were growing intervals between the holding of the general eyre in the counties so other commissions, justices of assize for civil pleas, and of gaol delivery[9] for the criminal pleas, were sent out and sometimes these commission justices consisted of knights of the shire.[10] The assizes of novel disseisin and mort d'ancestor proved particularly popular as the plaintiffs could attempt to obtain redress outside the normal terms of the eyre without going to the Bench[11] at Westminster. But, this may be more costly to the plaintiff as the writ *de cursu* was probably only sixpence compared with the cost of a writ for a special commission for a specific judge on an assize. There were about twenty-four cases of possessory assizes heard by justices in Suffolk on at least twelve separate occasions in the year 25 Henry III, or from 28 October 1240 to 27 October 1241.[12] There are naturally many more for the other counties, which is a good indicator of the popularity of the possessory assizes in the localities.[13]

There are two known visitations of general eyre justices in Suffolk during Richard's reign: 1194–1195 and 1198–1199; and two in John's: 1201–1203 and

---

6   Murdrum was the killing of someone who was not of native English ancestry, that is probably of French or Norman descent. For the Englishry and the murdrum fine and accidental death see *Bracton* ii, pp.378–382. See *1248 Berkshire Eyre*, p.305, no. 746 where the justices imposed a murdrum fine upon a vill when it was obviously an accidental death. For the latest discussion on murdrum see Brand 2003, pp.77–80.

7   See p.xx and **265** below.

8   See Appendix F(ii) where the relative popularity of the main possessory assizes at an eyre can be seen for around the period of 1240. It can be seen that they constituted almost half the cases. These assizes are explained below, pp.xxxv–xli.

9   The assizes and gaol deliveries were often performed together by the justices of assize. See *Close Rolls, 1237–1242*, p.442 where all assizes and gaol deliveries were expected to be heard by the archbishop of York and William de Cantilupe in Suffolk.

10 See Patent Rolls – Meekings Notes, in the shoebox in the strong room at TNA, 22 Henry III, C66/48, nos. 822 and 926 where Thomas de Hemmegrave acts as an assize judge at Ipswich on an assize of novel disseisin and in 25 Henry III, no. 990 where he acts as a judge at Bury St Edmunds. He was also a *curialis*, or household knight of the king. A number of other knights shown as jurors or electors of a grand assize are also evident in these possessory assizes, for example Hugh Burt.

11 The Bench in this case is shorthand for the court of Common Pleas or the court *coram rege*. The court *coram rege* could meet anywhere in the kingdom depending upon where the king was at the time. The Bench always met at Westminster.

12 See Patent Rolls – Meekings Notes, in the shoebox in the strong room at TNA, 25 Henry III for the Suffolk cases.

13 For the development of the four knights system of assizes see Musson 2004, pp.97–110. For the popularity of the possessory assizes between eyres see *1235 Surrey Eyre* i, p.67 where he demonstrates that there were nearly 800 commissions between the years 1232 and 1238. There is also the evidence shown in this paragraph when even though the eyre of 1240 is over in Suffolk there are still twenty-four cases of possessory assizes taken in one year.

1208–1209.[14] The number of eyres in Suffolk launched during the reign of Henry III was eight, which matches the number of visitations, or almost complete visitations in this reign.[15] Eyres were held in Suffolk in 1219, 1228, 1234–5, 1240, 1245, 1251, 1257–8 and 1268–9. This means that there is, on average, a visitation every seven years of Henry's reign, which by the 1260s was regarded as the customary frequency.[16] However, during the period 1234 to 1258 there were four eyres in Suffolk of which the first three occurred every five years.[17] The business of the eyre must also have increased given the number of days taken by the eyre in Suffolk.[18] In the eyre of 1208–1209 the eyre court sat in Suffolk for only eighteen days whereas in the final eyre of Henry's reign in 1268–1269 it sat for eighty-one days.[19] In this 1240 eyre it sat for a total of twenty-three days.[20]

The eyre system was also becoming more organised and bureaucratic during the reign of Henry III, and in 1240 the eyre judicial process was perhaps at its height. During the rest of Henry III's reign there were many innovations, small in themselves, but which improved the record keeping and the follow up to what was one of the main purposes of the eyre: the raising of money for the king. The innovations made to the plea roll included the separation of the roll into separate parts for foreign pleas (those relating to counties other than that being visited),[21] amercements, essoins and attorneys. These helped the sheriff and the justices to keep on top of their increasing administrative load and the sheriff to keep track of the payments owed to the king.

Money was raised from a variety of sources in both the criminal and civil pleas. For the criminal pleas it might come, as we have said, from penalties imposed on hundreds, vills or tithings[22] in the form of murdrum fines and a variety of other amercements. It might also come from the sale of chattels of outlaws and convicted criminals. In respect of civil pleas it came from amercements for false claims, for non-prosecution of the plea by the plaintiff, for withdrawal from a plea after the case had started and for losing the case. Money could also be raised from payments for final concords made at the court, which recorded agreement between plaintiffs and defendants.

Norfolk, Suffolk, Yorkshire and Lincolnshire were counties visited most frequently by the justices in eyre, precisely because they contributed the most money to the king's treasury. The eyre in Suffolk in 1240 alone contributed more than 3 per cent

---

14 See Crook 1982a, pp.47–48 for the visitations in these reigns.
15 See Appendix D for the dates the eyre met in Suffolk and Crook 1982a, pp.48–51 for the visitations in Henry III's reign for all the counties.
16 See Cam 1921, pp.83–88 where she indicates that this requirement was part of the list of barons' reforms, although Treharne 1971, pp.188–189 appears to indicate that although this was an unwritten norm it was not written into the demands of the barons.
17 See 'The issues of the Suffolk eyre' below p.lv where the reason for this increased frequency is discussed.
18 See Crook 1982a, pp.242–243 for the increase in the business transacted at the eyre, in particular after 1278.
19 See Crook 1982a, pp.70 and 135. The number of days calculated excludes Sundays and appropriate feast days. See footnotes 40 and 41 on p.xiii below as to why Sundays are excluded from the sitting days.
20 See p.xiv below.
21 Probably from 1247 onwards. See *1249 Wilts Crown Pleas*, p.21.
22 The tithing was in some counties a sub-division of the hundred, or in effect a lord's 'view of frankpledge'. See *Fleta* ii, 1953, pp.174–176 for a list of wrongdoings which the sheriff can ask the tithing about from the head of the tithing at the sheriff's tourn at the Hundred Court.

of the total raised by an eyre visitation through all the counties, as will be seen later.[23] It was essential for the king to maximise his revenue from this source, given that Henry III did not manage to persuade his magnates to grant him taxation after 1237. Among the objections raised to Henry's request for an aid in 1256 for his intervention in Sicily was 'the impoverishment of the kingdom by eyres'.[24]

The Suffolk visitation of 1240

The Suffolk eyre of 1240 was part of a general visitation which took place in the middle of a relatively stable period in the personal reign of Henry III, which is dated from 1234 after Henry's dismissal of his great ministers, Hubert de Burgh in 1232 and Peter des Roches in 1234.[25] The mandate for the visitation, of which the Suffolk eyre of 1240 formed part,[26] was probably issued in the early part of 1239.[27] A mention is made of the visitation of 1239–41 by Matthew Paris as he considered the reason for calling the eyre was 'to get plunder for the king's coffers under the guise of administering justice'.[28] Given that Henry III seems to have had difficulty in raising money from his magnates this might be why his government perfected the eyre process and used it as often as they did.[29] It was just over five years since the last eyre in Suffolk,[30] which is less than the convention of seven years between eyres within a county referred to in the 1260s.[31]

The eyre visitation of 1239–1241 consisted of two circuits and each has come to be known as the circuit of the chief professional justice within the circuit, Robert de Lexington and William of York.

---

[23] See 'The issues of the Suffolk eyre' pp.lv–lvi below, where the amounts from Suffolk as shown on the amercement section at the end of this plea roll, JUST1/818 membranes 56–62 are shown. The civil plea amercements and agreements are also shown at the end of the transcribed text below.

[24] Annals of Burton in *Ann. Mon.* i, p.387. See Maddicott 1984, p.48 for the influence of the activities in the eyre on the grievances of the barons in 1258.

[25] For the downfall of Hubert de Burgh see Carpenter 1996, pp.45–60. For the fall of Peter des Roches see Vincent 1996, pp.434–455.

[26] See Appendix D.

[27] This is an assumption as there are no surviving Patent Rolls for 1238–1240 and the Close Rolls are lost from 1238–1239. It is a reasonable assumption because there is a mandate in the Patent Rolls for the eyre of 1234–1235. See *Cal. Pat. Rolls 1232–1247*, pp.76–78.

[28] This quote is from *1249 Wilts Crown Pleas*, p.7. It was an amalgam of two thoughts by Matthew Paris who wrote of the justices of the 1239–1241 eyre visitation that 'under the pretence of justice, they collected a huge sum for the use of a King who squandered everything' and similarly in a reference during the visitation of 1252–1258 where he referred to the money raised by Henry III as 'whatever he could extract from the rapines of the itinerant justices'. See *Chronica Majora* iv, p.34 and v, p.458.

[29] The king's request for an aid on movables was refused by the magnates after 1237 on six separate occasions: 1242, 1244, 1248, 1253, 1257 and 1258. See Harriss 1975, p.29. Also see pp.lv–lvi for further information on this topic.

[30] This assumes that the visitation of Adam the son of William in September 1235 is not taken into account. The roll of the proceedings of Adam son of William survives (see JUST1/1173 in TNA) and his name is used as a heading in the pipe roll from Michaelmas 1236. It is still there in the first pipe roll immediately after this eyre at Michaelmas 1240. Adam's visitation took place at Thetford and covered both Norfolk and Suffolk. He dealt with crown pleas, in particular those indicted in the 1234–1235 eyre for Norfolk and Suffolk but who had fled and had since returned.

[31] See above, p.xi, where it is suggested that Norfolk, Suffolk, Lincolnshire and Yorkshire were more frequently visited at this time to obtain greater revenue for the king. I agree with Stacey 1987, p.213 where he argues that the king had become financially dependent upon the eyre as a source of revenue and these were his most populous counties and from which he derived most financial benefit.

Each of the two teams of justices began its circuit at a slightly different time. Robert de Lexington began his in Northamptonshire in October 1239, completed it in January 1240 and then moved on to Leicestershire later that month.[32] William of York, who led the second circuit, began his work in Norfolk in January 1240 because he had remained on the bench at Westminster until the end of the Michaelmas term in 1239.[33] York and his team were in Norfolk, at Norwich, from 19 January until 16 February. It looks as though the team then split up for the remainder of the pleas at King's Lynn and Great Yarmouth as the feet of fines (the records of the agreements made before the eyre, which refer to both the return date of the concord and the justices before whom it was made) shows only three of the justices taking the pleas – William of York, Roger of Thirkelby and Jeremy Caxton.[34] So it is assumed that the other three; Ranulf the abbot of Ramsey, Henry of Bath and Gilbert of Preston took the session at King's Lynn.[35] The justices would have been commissioned to make the visitation to all the counties in the circuit, but occasionally changes were made to justices in the circuit with for example one or more detached from the circuit to hold eyres in other counties. Thus Henry of Bath was detached from York's circuit to take the eyre in Hampshire as the senior justice.[36]

From Norfolk the justices went to Suffolk and probably opened the eyre at Ipswich on Monday 30 April.[37] The date, found on the earliest dated fine and on the heading to the earliest essoin section in this roll, is shown at Ipswich as the quindene of Easter (Sunday 29 April).[38] Crook indicates that the eyre also started in Ipswich on Sunday 29 April,[39] but I have taken the view of Cheney,[40] that the court would not normally sit on a Sunday, although it could do so in an emergency.[41] The crown

---

[32] The dates of the early part of the eyre as shown in Crook 1982a, pp.97–100 for Lexington's circuit were mostly taken from the feet of fines for each county. The later county eyres of 1242–1244, which consisted of those counties left out of the main visitation of 1239–1241, can be followed in the *Cal. Pat. Rolls, 1232–1247* or the *Close Rolls, 1242–1247*.

[33] See Crook 1982a, p.97.

[34] See 'The documents of the Suffolk eyre of 1240', and in particular the sub-section on Feet of fines, pp.xxvii–xxviii which explains the form of the concord and what is the 'foot'.

[35] See Crook 1982a, p.100. It is also evident from the feet of fines where those shown for Great Yarmouth only show the three justices named, even though the King's Lynn equivalents show all the justices. The fact that both places were being visited at the same time indicates that they must have split up.

[36] See *Close Rolls, 1237- 1242*, p.345.

[37] As Meekings indicates in his book on the Wiltshire eyre 'it is on Final Concords, essoins and foreign pleas that we depend for estimating the duration of the Eyre'. See *1249 Wilts Crown Pleas*, p.21. In the case of Suffolk a separate portion of the roll for foreign pleas is not present because the system had not yet been developed by the clerks to do so. According to Meekings the system of separate rolls for foreign pleas was only started in 1247 and they tended to indicate a set of return days when the hearing of the foreign pleas began in a separate heading on the roll from which the dates could be determined. The Suffolk foreign pleas are spread throughout the civil plea roll for the 1240 eyre in Suffolk in JUST1/818. Therefore they cannot be used for dating.

[38] See CP 25(1) 213/17/85, which indicates the date of the agreement as the quindene of Easter and the plea roll JUST1/818, membrane1, which also has a heading indicating that the essoins were taken at Ipswich on the quindene of Easter. Easter in 1240 was on Sunday 15 April. The quindene of Easter is therefore Sunday 29 April 1240.

[39] See Crook 1982a, p.101.

[40] See Cheney 1996, p.66.

[41] G.O. Sayles argues that Sunday was a normal day for business unless it was for one of the major feasts, such as Easter. See *Sel. Cases King's Bench* ii, p.lxxvi. It is possible that the eyres did so due to the limited time to hear all pleas. As both civil and criminal add up to nearly 1,400 pleas in this Suffolk plea roll of 1240, it is possible it may have done so in this case.

pleas were only started at Ipswich on Monday 7 May,[42] the date given in the heading on the roll, and probably ended on Tuesday 15 May when the civil pleas may have also ended.[43] The court moved to Cattishall and probably began to hear pleas on Monday 21 May and closed its session there on Thursday 31 May. According to the surviving feet of fines there was also a session at Cattishall on Monday 4 June as there are some thirteen final concords surviving with this date. The session at Dunwich opened and closed on 11 June. The total number of sitting days of the court was probably as follows at the three venues:

Ipswich	12[44]
Cattishall	10[45]
Dunwich	1.

The participants in the 1240 Suffolk eyre

The participants in this Suffolk eyre were many and varied. There were the justices, clerks and ushers, as well as the jurors and the litigants themselves, or their attorneys, directly involved in the pleas. Some of the litigants may also have had serjeants or *narratores*,[46] who would act and speak for them as a sort of barrister in their pleas.

There would also be other people present some of whom would be used to enforce the will of the court and others who would answer to the 'articles of the eyre'. These would include the sheriff, the previous sheriffs since the last eyre in Suffolk who were still living,[47] the existing sheriff's constables etc. and also the leading men and freeholders in the hundreds, towns and vills from whom the jurors of the hundred would have been elected. It would be the jurors of the hundreds and the boroughs that would answer to the 'articles of the eyre'.[48] Unfortunately in the roll only one kalendar of juries has survived for one of the towns, Dunwich. It names the twelve jurors, three bailiffs, two coroners of the town and the two electors.[49] There would

---

[42] See the heading on membrane 45 of JUST1/818, which is the start of the crown pleas. It indicates that the crown pleas *a die Pasche in tres septimanas*, which would normally be on Sunday 6 May 1240, but for the same reason above it is likely that the pleas actually started on the Monday. For all the relevant dates for the Suffolk eyre of 1240 see Appendix D.

[43] There are twenty-three chirographs with the date of Tuesday 15 May 1240 made at Ipswich. I would argue that it is probably the date of completion of the eyre at Ipswich and not Sunday 13 May as shown in Crook 1982a, p.101. See Appendix E for the dates of the chirographs made at the eyre. This evidence gives a total of thirty elapsed days from the start date of the eyre.

[44] This assumes that no business was done on the feasts of SS Philip and James (1 May 1240) and the feast of the Invention of the Holy Cross (3 May).

[45] No business was done on Ascension Day (24 May 1240). See Cheney 1996, p. 65 for feast days when the courts would not sit.

[46] See Brand 1992a, pp.6–7 where he indicates that 'by 1239, then, there was a group of presumably professional lawyers able to specialise in the functions of the serjeant and in practice in the Bench, though also perhaps available for employment elsewhere'. There are two cases of men amerced *pro stultiloquio*, false and frivolous pleading, in the amercements. See **1643** for *Johanne Rouland* and *Willelmo Angot* and **1645** for *Thoma Geremy*, who may have been serjeants pleading on somebody else's behalf. Unfortunately the pleas, in which they may have appeared, are not known.

[47] There were three such sheriffs in Suffolk – see Appendix C.

[48] See *1235 Surrey Eyre* i, pp.24–26.

[49] See membrane 44, **1143–1146**. The jurors of Dunwich appear to be specific to Dunwich. They certainly take no part in any grand assizes but they probably took part only in the crown pleas. The electors, who also acted as jurors, were probably chosen to elect the remaining jury by the bailiffs, who then would answer the queries from the justices as part of the 'articles of the eyre' and which were normally shown in the plea roll under the crown pleas. The jury also presented the crown pleas

have been a similar set of people, for each hundred or borough present at the eyre, except for the coroners. The number of jurors for each hundred or borough is indicated in the crown plea membranes, but not their individual names. I have calculated that the number of jurors comes to 384.[50] The number of coroners was four for the county of Suffolk and a variable number for the boroughs.[51] There were also the bailiffs to the ten boroughs and to the twenty-four hundreds.[52] I therefore calculate that there would have been approximately 450 men involved as jurors, coroners, electors and bailiffs from the hundreds and boroughs.[53] Those mentioned above as officers of the hundred, borough or vill were at the eyre to answer on the crown pleas and to the 'articles of the eyre'. This number would be in addition to the number of people having a direct involvement in the eyre as litigants etc.

Appendix I(i) below indicates that the total named individuals in the civil pleas of the roll was 5,852, but some of these would not need to attend or even be able to attend.[54] If such are excluded it is estimated that this is reduced to 5,364. The largest proportion of this number is the litigants or those vouching for them: 1,383 plaintiffs, 2,026 defendants and 918 vouchers to warranty or sureties. If duplicated names are excluded I have calculated the total in attendance, and actively involved in the civil pleas only, at all three venues, as approximately 4,000.[55] It has been calculated that, excluding duplicates, there were 146 attorneys, 395 jurors in the cases, including 180 knights who selected, or were selected as jurors of a grand assize. Of these administrative knights, fifty-six were asked to select a jury for a grand assize.[56] The remainder of the 4,000 is made up principally with the plaintiffs, defendants and sureties.[57] In respect of the crown pleas there were probably the 450

---

to the justices. See Harding 1993, pp.84–85. See Pollock and Maitland 1968, ii, p.645 for the election of the jury by the electors, who would be knights. This is also implied in *Bracton* ii, pp.327–329.

[50] This might be increased to 387 if the number of jurors for the vill of South Elmham, which in the crown pleas is shown as *vj* in membrane 49d, but is indicated as *venit per tres* (3) in the amercement section for the crown pleas in membrane 57. South Elmham was deemed to be a quarter of Wangford Hundred and it came by *ix*, so I think the *venit per tres* a more likely figure.

[51] Ipswich had four after King John had chartered them in 1200. See Pollock and Maitland 1968, i, p.658. The coroners, electors and bailiffs for the hundreds and boroughs are not enumerated in the roll but can be estimated by using a similar number as Dunwich.

[52] Ipswich had two bailiffs, who were taken from the four coroners, but this is not the case for Dunwich, so it cannot be assumed the other boroughs followed Ipswich. See Pollock and Maitland 1968, i, p.658. There appears to be one bailiff for each of the hundreds.

[53] This assumes that each of the hundreds, boroughs etc. will endeavour to produce the same numbers and types of office holders as Dunwich, plus the numbers indicated as jurors in the crown pleas. I make the number of officers to be brought for Suffolk to about 450. However, there may be some duplication of the people who are named as jurors in the civil pleas. On top of this number would be the judges, clerks and officers of the court who travelled with the justices and also communicated with the king when necessary, or his other offices of state. We do not have any named individuals of this type other than it is likely that Robert of Whitchester attended the eyre as the clerk to William of York.

[54] For example, those named in the assizes of mort d'ancestor as having been seised of the land in question by the plaintiff would almost certainly be dead. Appendix I(ii) is included to obtain the numbers of certain officers used in the calculations here and below.

[55] I have calculated a total of 3,936 named individuals attending the eyre and involved in the civil pleas.

[56] There was an overlap between these knights and the jury in that sometimes they were asked to select a jury and sometimes they served on a jury of the grand assize. Appendix I(i) indicates that there were 104 named knights used to select a jury in the grand assize. After taking into account those named more than once as a selector of a jury the number is reduced to 56. The 124 knightly jurors in the grand assize are included in the figures given for jurors or recognitors in Appendix I(i).

[57] This indicates that 33 per cent of the people attending appear more than once in the pleas. Some

jurors of presentment for the eyre from the hundreds and boroughs. This brings the total to approximately 4,450. On top of this would be the twelve burgesses from the boroughs and the reeve and four men from each of the significant vills in the county – about 440 in Suffolk[58] – so a further 2,250 men, or thereabouts, may have attended at one or more of the three venues. Even if we assume the hundred jurors, bailiffs etc. were included within this total, this still brings the total to approximately 6,250.[59] This moreover excludes those directly involved in the crown pleas, as for example, criminals brought to justice, appellees and their sureties, and the first finders of dead bodies.[60] And, on top of these numbers would be the justices, clerks and the other officers of the court.

On the first day of the eyre at Ipswich the town's population must have almost doubled or even trebled, although not everybody indicated above would be there as some of the litigants would have been instructed to attend at Cattishall or at Dunwich.

The sheer numbers involved in movements around Suffolk are quite remarkable and indicate the level of sophistication of the judicial process in thirteenth-century England. These numbers and the time taken to complete the business of the eyre may also be reasons for the suspension of the general eyre at the end of the thirteenth century.[61]

The justices[62] and other officers

The justices mentioned above, who had taken the Norfolk eyre, also opened the proceedings at Ipswich, the only exception being Jeremy Caxton who left after the Norfolk eyre.

As the senior professional justice William of York was responsible for the conduct of the eyre and also for reporting to the Exchequer, via the estreat roll, the amount of money being raised.[63] He is named on the pipe roll in the heading under which are listed the debts arising from the eyre. The heading is shown as *De Amercia-*

---

appear considerably more of course, for example Hubert of Braiseworth, who appears seventeen times in the rolls, twelve of which are as a juror.

[58] See *1249 Wilts Crown Pleas*, p.17, and *Feudal Aids* v, pp.33–48 for the equivalent *Nomina Villarum* of 1316 for Suffolk and which is used for the number of vills and boroughs in the calculation above. The list in *Feudal Aids* is incomplete as there is no reference to the hundred of Loes, so I have taken the number of vills within this hundred from the index in *Domesday Book Suffolk*, Part Two. This brings the total to 440 plus the burgesses from four boroughs. Meekings also indicates that there may have been a larger number of 'towns' or 'vills' in 1249, as is shown in the *Nomina Villarum* of 1316. This is born out for Suffolk. I have counted 560 vills in *Domesday Book Suffolk*, Part Two, *Index of Places*. There is also indirect evidence in *1249 Wilts Crown Pleas*, p.225, of non-attendance and what it could mean as shown in **383** where the tithings of Bechampton and Monk's Wynterburn did not attend and so were amerced for default.

[59] As a comparison, Meekings in *1249 Wilts Crown Pleas*, p.20 estimated the total attending the eyre for both civil and crown pleas etc. as between four and five thousand.

[60] When the Suffolk crown pleas are published it will be possible to arrive at a more complete figure.

[61] For these and other reasons for the end of the eyre see Burt 2005, pp.1–14.

[62] For a general outline of some of the justices' careers see Turner 1985, pp.191–258. He has a reasonable amount of detail on William of York throughout the chapter, but only scattered references to the other judges shown here.

[63] See *Close Rolls, 1237–1242*, p.201 where William of York is urged to send his estreat to the Exchequer without delay. Perhaps another indication that Matthew Paris was correct on the money making aspect to the eyre system and also that this system was a well oiled machine.

mentis per Willelmum de Eboracum et Socios Suos.[64] However, the titular head of the eyre was not William but Ranulf, abbot of Ramsey, it being sometimes the case for the professional justices to be headed by someone of a higher social status.[65] Thus Ranulf's name is listed above that of William of York on the final concords made at Ipswich and is shown as 'Ranulf the abbot of Ramsey'. The abbot only sat at Ipswich as his name appears on the final concords for those made at Ipswich, but not on those at Cattishall or Dunwich.

The abbot was one of the clerics used as a royal judge to whom Robert Grosseteste objected strongly as he wanted to see ecclesiastics completely withdrawn from secular office.[66] However, it did not do any good as Ranulf continued occasionally to be a justice in eyre, as did other clerics. William of York is shown first on all the agreements made at Cattishall and Dunwich and is shown as the leading justice on the heading of the crown pleas.[67]

William of York was the most senior justice in the king's employ at this time, with the possible exception of Robert de Lexington. William had probably been a Chancery clerk from 1219 and also acted as a clerk in the first part of Martin Pattishall's circuit in 1226–1227. He also acted for the first time as a justice in the Cumberland eyre of 1227.[68] He served as a junior justice in a further five counties, and then from 1234 to 1241 he visited some thirty-two counties as the senior justice.[69] Evidence of his value to the king was his appointment to head the court *coram rege* in November 1241. He also played a leading part in assisting those appointed to be in charge of the kingdom when the king was in France in 1242.[70] He was subsequently rewarded with the bishopric of Salisbury in 1246.[71] Even while bishop he continued to act occasionally as a justice.[72] Matthew Paris's view of William was not positive as on his death he indicated that William introduced the 'evil custom' of forcing every tenant to attend at the court of their overlord 'to the great loss and damage of the subjects and little or no gain of the overlords'.[73]

According to the order in which they appear in the feet of fines, the next most important justice was Henry of Bath. At the time of the 1240 eyre in Suffolk, Bath was only starting out on his career as a justice. As far as we know his appointment

---

[64] See p.lv below in 'The issues of the Suffolk eyre of 1240' for more on this topic.

[65] See Crook 1982a, p.16.

[66] See *Letters Grosseteste*, pp.105–108, *epistola* xxvii.

[67] The abbot would not normally take part in the judgement given in a crown plea where a punishment of blood was involved, as laid down at the Lateran Council of 1215. However, many prelates took part in the judicial process up to the moment when judgement was given. The prelates would not take part in any execution either. Bishop Robert Grosseteste objected to the abbot of Crowland taking part in Robert de Lexington's circuit. So perhaps the clerks knew to ensure that the prelates were not mentioned in the crown pleas.

[68] See Meekings 1950, pp.499–500, reprinted in his *Studies in 13th Century Justice and Administration*.

[69] See Crook 1982a, p.17 for a review of his career. He appears in this roll in **525** as a lender of money. Presumably he had it recorded in the roll to indicate that the sheriff could distrain the debtors from their lands if they had not paid the debt by the day specified in the roll.

[70] In fact in the *Ann. Mon.* iii, p.159, that is the *Annales de Dunstaplia*, William of York, Walter Gray, the archbishop of York, and William de Cantelupe are all entrusted with the custody of the realm. However, in other sources William of York is not mentioned as a regent, the only regents being the archbishop of York and William de Cantelupe. See *Close Rolls, 1242–1247*, p.12.

[71] See *Flores Historiarum* iii, p.321 and *Cal. Pat. Rolls, 1232–1247*, p.494 where the king assented to William's election as bishop.

[72] He took the pleas in 1251 of the City of London. See *Cal. Pat. Rolls, 1247–1258*, p.110.

[73] See *Chronica Majora* v, p.545.

to York's circuit of 1239–1241 was his first appointment as an itinerant justice. He obviously rose rapidly up the career ladder as he was a senior justice by the time of the Hampshire eyre of 1241[74] and was the senior justice of the Bench by the Hilary term of 1245.[75] He was apparently highly valued by the king as a sheriff because he held Yorkshire from 1242 to 1248, although he had deputies after his appointment to the Bench. He also held many lands in Yorkshire from appointments to ecclesiastical livings.[76] He was also senior justice of the court *coram rege* in October 1249 moving there from the Bench before he suffered a short term disgrace in February 1251, when according to Matthew Paris he was removed from the court *coram rege* for corrupt practices.[77] He was fined a massive 2,000 marks payable at 200 marks a year, and if he was to die before payment had been completed his executors were to continue to pay his debt.[78] However, according to Matthew Paris, his wife and Richard, earl of Cornwall, helped him recover the king's favour. He was re-appointed as senior justice *coram rege* in 1253 and remained so until his death in 1260.

Roger of Thirkelby was in a similar position to Henry of Bath in the 1239–1241 eyre of William of York, that is a junior justice just starting out on his judicial career. He was in charge of his own circuit by 1243–1244 and was the senior justice in thirty-eight eyres until 1258. He died in 1260.[79] He also appears as a litigant in the roll as Roger had Norfolk interests through his wife Letice de Roscelin, who was the heiress of her father, Peter de Edgefield. It is likely that he was defending his wife's interest for the advowson of the church at Walcott in Happing hundred in Norfolk in the grand assize noted in **149** and subsequently adjourned to Chelmsford in **784** in this roll.

Finally, the last junior justice on our list, Gilbert of Preston, proved to be the busiest of these justices in the eyre courts. He took part in over fifty-five eyres as a junior justice from 1239 to 1254 and there were a further twenty-nine of which he was the chief justice of the eyre from 1254 to 1272. This circuit under William of York was his first eyre as a junior justice.[80]

The justices brought with them a staff of clerks and other court officials who kept the records and acted as ushers in the court hearings. The clerks kept a record of the pleas on the plea rolls, a copy of which would be made for each justice, and also issued chirographs for those who came to an agreement in the eyre. They may have had access to copies of some of the plea rolls of the previous eyres for reference in case a litigant asked for the rolls to be examined to settle a dispute.[81] The clerks would also make a separate record of any money to be collected for the king on the

---

[74] See Crook 1982a, p.102.
[75] See Meekings 1981, 'Robert of Nottingham, Justice of the Bench, 1244–6', p.134.
[76] See Meekings 1981, 'Alan de Wassand (†1257)', p.471.
[77] *Chronica Majora* v, pp.213–214.
[78] See *Cal. Pat. Rolls 1247–1258*, p.101.
[79] See Crook 1982a, pp.17–18 for a review of his career.
[80] See Crook 1982a, p.19.
[81] See Crook 1982a, pp.12–20 on the survivability of the rolls, and that copies of the rolls were probably originally kept by the justices for whom the copy was made, so William of York may have had all his rolls available from his previous eyres. Also see *Sel. Cases Proc. w/o Writ*, pp.clxxxi–clxxxiii where they indicate the difficulty of obtaining rolls for consultation, especially when the justice had died and passed on his rolls to another justice. See **493** where the rolls of the previous eyre, probably the one made in 1235, were asked to be examined to settle a point. If the roll required was from the 1235 Suffolk eyre they must have obtained it from a justice not at this eyre as none of the justices at the previous eyre was a justice at this eyre. This may also be the reason for the obvious addition to the

estreat roll. This roll would be a copy of the amercement section at the end of this plea roll. The estreat roll would be sent to the Exchequer on completion of the eyre in the county, so it knew what money to collect.

One of the clerks is known and he was Roger of Whitchester, who was at this time the clerk of William of York, the chief justice in this eyre. He had been William's clerk since around 1230 and he was to continue in this position until 1246 when he became the keeper of the writs and rolls of the Bench.[82] He subsequently became a junior justice himself in 1251 in three assizes in Kent and then he went on an eyre circuit for the first time in 1254 in Essex under Gilbert of Preston. He was also busy as a justice in the Bench from 1251 to his death in 1258.[83]

The sheriff of the county, in this case two counties, as the sheriff administered both Norfolk and Suffolk, would also appear with his staff. The holders of the sheriff's office since the last eyre were also required to attend to answer for certain 'articles of the eyre' during their office. The sheriff at the time of this eyre was John de Ulecote and there would also have been three other ex-sheriffs in attendance, as all were still living.[84] The previous sheriffs would, no doubt, have answered any matters arising from their terms of office since the last eyre and according to the articles of the eyre. The current sheriff also gave notice to all those who should attend the eyre and, through his team of summoners the sheriff would have sent personal summonses to those of higher rank. He was also responsible for summoning or securing those involved in the crown and common pleas. For crown pleas these included juries of presentment, those accused of crimes, their sureties and bailees, first finders of dead bodies and neighbours, tithing heads whose members had committed crimes, those who had already attended at a county court to make or defend appeals, and any who had committed serious crimes and were in the gaols located in the county. For common pleas the participants would probably have been summoned by the sheriff to appear at the 'first assize of our justices when they come to those parts' by an original writ obtained from the Chancery by the plaintiff, and which would have been served by the sheriff on those named in the writ. The current sheriff executed the orders of the court, for example to distrain defaulting litigants to appear before the court. For those cases adjourned from a previous county or cases adjourned from one venue to another the sheriff would be responsible for ensuring that his fellow sheriffs knew the venues for the people concerned in their respective counties. It is interesting to note that cases are heard in the common pleas from as far away as Cornwall, Worcestershire and Wiltshire. The sheriff was also responsible for ensuring that the venue of the next eyre was publicised in the hundred courts and in other public places so that all interested parties had notice to attend. Finally, the sheriff was responsible for executing all the verdicts produced in the eyre.[85]

The coroners of the county and the boroughs[86] would have with them their own

---

end of the plea indicating they had examined the rolls because they had to await the delivery of the roll, or the information from the justice whose roll it was, after he had examined it on their behalf.

[82] See *Cal. Pat. Rolls, 1232–1247*, p.480.

[83] See Meekings 1957a, pp.100–128 for a relatively detailed summary of his career.

[84] See Appendices C and D for the sheriffs and eyres in Suffolk.

[85] See Table 3 below, which indicates that a total of 331 verdicts were reached for the plaintiff or the defendant in the civil pleas of this eyre. The number of verdicts for the crown pleas will only be known after further research.

[86] Unfortunately none of them are known except for the coroners of Dunwich. See above p.xv. See Hunnisett 1961 for the role of the coroner and in particular pp.2–4 for the reason for establishing the role of coroners and how they would serve the eyre.

clerks and their rolls, which were documents of record for the justices to see who had died in suspicious circumstances since the last eyre and what had been done to find the possible suspects. They were also responsible for ensuring that those who were sentenced to abjure the realm did so and to ensure that those who found the body attended the eyre by attachment. They would present what had happened since the last eyre from their rolls in the crown pleas.

The first day of the eyre at Ipswich must have generated a great buzz of excitement and on such occasions the justices of an eyre might be feasted or offered gifts by some of the local magnates.[87] Not all the 6,000 plus participants would have been at Ipswich on the opening day as no doubt some of the litigants expected to appear were given a later day and others were told to go to Cattishall or Dunwich, possibly depending upon which was nearest to their tenement. Litigants from the hundreds within the liberty of St Edmund would come to Cattishall, as that was the nearest place to the town of Bury St Edmunds, but outside the town's boundary as the abbot had always ensured that the eyre and any other of the king's assizes were held outside its *banleuca*.[88] There may also be some litigants from Norfolk and Essex who started their plea in Suffolk, possibly because their vill was nearer to a Suffolk eyre venue than a Norfolk or Essex one.[89] It is also possible that the sheriff, who was responsible for both Norfolk and Suffolk and considered them as an administrative whole, decided where they would appear when serving the litigants with the summonses to appear.

It looks as though the first three weeks after the preliminary proceedings and the swearing in of the jurors were given over to the common pleas, and then it is likely that the justices split; two or probably three taking the remainder of the civil pleas, and two to take the crown pleas.[90] The abbot of Ramsey no doubt avoided taking the crown pleas to ensure that he was not responsible for the shedding of blood. At Cattishall and Dunwich they would no doubt also have split the justices to cover each type of plea, civil and crown, as the abbot had left the eyre after Ipswich. All of the liberty of Bury St Edmunds crown pleas were heard at Cattishall, but the dates on which they were heard or not are given in the roll. Both civil and crown for Dunwich were held at Dunwich in the one day – 11 June.

The contents of the eyre roll reflect the comparatively tranquil state of the kingdom at this time. The routine of the eyre proceeded as normal. Hundred by hundred the juries of presentment appeared for the crown pleas. There is also nothing in the common pleas to indicate that the king was having difficulties with his magnates. The king only brought one action against a magnate, Simon de Pierpont, over the right of wreck in Wrentham, and this he lost (**265**). However, there is a marginal

---

[87] See *1249 Wilts Crown Pleas*, p.13 where he has indicated that one of our justices, Henry of Bath, was a recipient of the largesse of the bishop of Winchester. He provides a list of some of the items of food and money spent on them from the Winchester manorial accounts of Bishop Ralegh.

[88] The town of Bury St Edmunds lay outside the jurisdiction of the eyre as the abbot of Bury St Edmunds had his own court that had jurisdiction in the town for both civil and criminal cases. It also acted as an honorial court for the rest of the liberty of St Edmund. The eyre justices could hear cases raised from the rest of the hundreds of the liberty at the eyre, but any money raised in amercements etc. went to the abbot and not the king. See *William of Hoo*, p.61n where Antonia Gransden indicates the extent of the jurisdiction of the eyre system within the liberty.

[89] See **641** where the plea started in Suffolk at Ipswich but it is almost certainly for a tenement in Wix in Essex, which happens to be nearer to Ipswich than Chelmsford.

[90] On membrane 45, the start of the crown pleas, the heading indicates that they probably started on Monday 7 May 1240 and carried on until Saturday or Sunday 12 or 13 May 1240.

reference made to it at the end of the plea, possibly indicating that the case was to continue in the court *coram rege*. The king was obviously not satisfied with this answer![91] Litigants, both local and those adjourned from other counties, pursued their pleas in apparent calm. Their actions were focused on their local disputes and not on any wider political issues.

THE DOCUMENTS OF THE SUFFOLK EYRE OF 1240

The principal documents produced by the eyre court were the plea rolls compiled by the justices' clerks during its sessions, there being one set for each justice. The plea roll edited here contains the following: civil pleas, including foreign civil pleas from counties other than Suffolk; essoins; the amercements and the final concord agreements. The civil pleas from Suffolk and the foreign civil pleas are not separated from each other in any way. This is unlike the surviving plea rolls from the visitations from 1246 onwards when the civil and foreign pleas were completely separate. The same applied to the attorneys. The crown pleas and the amercements of crown pleas are not included in this volume. The civil and the crown pleas are in the same roll, but are in separate blocks and are differentiated from each other by separate headings, with the crown pleas starting at the top of a new membrane.

The clerks of the eyre courts had the task of writing up the plea rolls and therefore putting on record the names of the litigants, the type of action being taken, the essentials of the dispute, any jury verdict, and the details of the judgement. Court procedures such as the issue of judicial writs, may be noted on occasion as well, and also the imposition of amercements and the award of damages. The plea roll is therefore a record of the business of the court and can be used to analyse the types of actions, processes and decisions.[92] Later,[93] the treasurer and barons of the Exchequer were ordered to recover all plea rolls from the itinerant justices and also those from the court *coram rege* and Bench for safekeeping at the Exchequer.[94] It is not likely to be the roll of the senior justice because it lacks the marginal annotations in connection with amercements usual with such rolls.[95] Since a good many of Roger of Thirkelby's later rolls survive it seems likely the surviving roll for this eyre was his also. This could be warranted with the fact that Roger died while sitting as a

---

91 Wreck is the right to seize objects cast on the shore. See Plucknett 1948, pp.422–423.The case did not actually proceed to the court *coram rege* because it looks as though Simon de Pierpont died in 1241 as there is an order to the sheriff to take his lands into the king's hands in the *Cal. Pat. Rolls, 1232–1247*, p.267. However, Copinger in *Manors of Suffolk* ii, p.211 indicates that the Pierpont family still held Wrentham with the right to wreck. The information he indicates comes from the Hundred Rolls of 1274–1275 and the Quo Warranto inquiries from 1278 onwards.

92 See Table 3 below for an analysis of the Suffolk civil pleas indicating the types of action encountered at this eyre.

93 On 8 December 1257. See *Close Rolls 1256–1259*, p.281.

94 Many later plea rolls survive as a result of this edict, sometimes more than one for an eyre. In the Suffolk eyre of 1286–1287 there are four judges' rolls surviving plus a *rex* roll; that is a roll that contains the word *Rex* instead of the justice for whom they were made. They are JUST1/826 and JUST1/827 for the 'Rex' roll, JUST1/828 and JUST1/829 are Richard Boyland's rolls, JUST1/830 and JUST1/831 are Walter Hopton's rolls, JUST1/832 and JUST1/833 are Solomon Rochester's rolls, JUST1/834 and JUST1/835A are Master Thomas Siddington's rolls.

95 See *1249 Wilts Crown Pleas*, p.23 for the marking up of the plea roll and pp.109–112 and Meekings 1957c, pp.229–231 on marking up the estreat roll and the sequence of the estreat sent to the Exchequer.

judge on the Bench at Westminster in 1260 and, as David Crook has said, 'relatively little effort would have been needed by the Exchequer to secure them'.[96] Many of these rolls survived once they were in the safekeeping of the Exchequer. This plea roll is now kept safely in The National Archives at Kew and is number 818 in the class of Eyre Rolls, Assize Rolls, Etc. (JUST 1).

The 1240 Suffolk eyre roll

The surviving roll JUST1/818 in The National Archives has sixty-two membranes and an outer wrapper or cover (membrane 63) which has been stitched into the roll after membrane 2. All the membranes have been stitched together at the head. The wrapper must have come loose over the years and subsequently been stitched into this position to save it. It is now impossible to read any markings or the title of the roll on this cover, which can be done on other eyre rolls. The dimensions of the roll are typical of eyre rolls of the period (1240s). The membranes are of approximately uniform width (18.2 cm) but of varying length (averaging 58.3 cm), the longest being membranes 12 and 21 (69 and 68.7 cm respectively) and the shortest membranes 62 and 5 (35.5 and 44.6 cm respectively). One membrane has additional pieces of parchment attached at the foot by stitching; thus membrane 21 is 57.38 cm long with an additional piece of 11.32 cm attached. The membrane is a total of 68.7 cm long and is the second longest of the membranes.

As the wrapper is totally illegible it is impossible to determine beyond doubt if the roll was provided with an Agarde's index number. This was the collection of plea rolls and concords of the time of Henry III sorted and stored by Arthur Agarde, deputy chamberlain 1569–1615, in the chapter house of Westminster Abbey.[97] But it is possible to tell that it almost certainly was as he provided a general description of the roll. The membranes are numbered 1 to 62, and it appears that the roll has been numbered on three separate occasions. The first numbering of the membranes was probably done at the time of Agarde. The second may have been done when the roll was stamped 'Public Record Office' with a crown in the middle of the stamp.[98] Membranes 22 to 62, on the second renumbering, contain a mistake when the enumerator renumbered membrane 22 as membrane 23. All subsequent membranes contain a similar mistake. The third numbering was probably done around 1950 by Meekings,[99] when he reverted to the original numbering at the time of Agarde and crossed out this mistaken numbering from membranes 22 to 62.[100]

The condition of the roll is generally good and it is almost completely legible except for a few damaged edges or rubbing at the extremities, particularly at the end of the membranes and on the dorsal side. It is written clearly, on the whole, and mostly by one hand, although there is evidence of up to eight other hands being

---

[96]   Crook 1982a, p.18. Also see Crook 1982a, pp.17 and 100 where he discounts that the roll could be for William of York, because of the lack of process mark margination, indicative of a senior justice's roll and pp.19–20 where he discounts the roll as being for Gilbert of Preston. I would argue that Henry of Bath had no material interest in keeping his roll, whereas Roger did. See **149** and **784** below.

[97]   For recognisable Agarde indices see *1249 Wilts Crown Pleas*, p.24, and *1263 Surrey Eyre*, p.xxxix.

[98]   This was probably in 1838 when the eyre records were moved to a repository at Carlton Ride by Palgrave, the deputy keeper shortly after the Public Record Office was set up.

[99]   See *1248 Berkshire Eyre*, p.liii. A note on the front cover of the document indicates that it was repaired on the 24 April 1950.

[100]   Clanchy describes a similar situation in the 1248 Berkshire eyre. See *1248 Berkshire Eyre*, p.lii.

involved. The essoins taken at Ipswich and Cattishall are certainly written by a different hand than the majority of the roll. The other hands are usually additions to a plea or interlinear additions. But, in one case, taking up approximately a third of membrane 10, the roll is written by another hand and may be the hand that wrote the majority of the essoins. It is very distinctively more cursive and loopy than the main clerk's hand. In one other case a very small and neat hand writes two consecutive pleas on membrane 36. It looks as though the more loopy hand reappears at the end of the dorsal side of membrane 36 and also in a number of other places for a complete plea but then the roll reverts to the main hand. The membranes are written on both sides with the exception of membrane 62, the amercements and agreements for Dunwich, because there are insufficient amercements and agreements to continue on to the dorse side of the membrane.

There is a heading at the beginning of the essoins taken at Ipswich on membrane 1 but because there is no heading at the start of the civil pleas at Ipswich, which would be the norm, similar to that shown in membrane 26 for the civil pleas taken at Cattishall, there may be a missing membrane before membrane 3. The wrapper for the roll was placed after membrane 2 by the Public Record Office and possibly contained these details, but it is now, as has been said, so worn that it is impossible to read.[101] The first membrane for the crown pleas at Ipswich does contain a proper title heading indicating the justices and the starting date of the crown pleas heard there. There is no equivalent heading for Cattishall except to indicate the start of the crown pleas for the hundreds of the liberty of Bury St Edmunds. The membrane for the civil pleas made at Dunwich (membranes 44–44d) does not have a proper heading, only the word 'Dunwich' and the whole membrane is in a different hand. The crown plea membrane for Dunwich is written in the same hand as the civil pleas.

I have found two instances where the clerk has used a process mark to indicate that the paragraph opposite the mark is the continuation of another plea later in the roll. **329** on membrane 11d continues at the end of membrane 11. There is at the end of membrane 11d an indication that the rest of **329** is in effect over the page at the sign of the cross, but apart from the process mark, a cross, there is no other indication that this paragraph on membrane 11 belongs to the same plea.[102] It is obvious that the clerk could not complete the text on the dorse side, but there was sufficient space on the front side of the membrane to complete the plea. In the other instance, see **450** and **1096** below, the process mark is shown as a 'Q' with a very long straight tail and with two dots on either side of the tail. The process mark is shown in the margin at the end of **450** and is shown again in the margin at the beginning of **1096**. In this instance the pleas are on membranes 17 and 42 respectively.

The membranes have the usual marginalia, county if a foreign plea, hundred or liberty if a civil plea as well as notes of amercements and damages etc. Marginalia were also used for process marks, which were designed to provide a guide for the

---

[101] See *1248 Berkshire Eyre*, where the details of the wrapper have survived. However, its wrapper contains the information that it covers both crown and assize pleas. There appears to be no heading as such on membrane 1 of this eyre for the start of the civil pleas at Reading. In the *1256 Shropshire Eyre* Harding has indicated that there is a heading for the civil pleas on membrane 1.

[102] The scribe uses the words *Verte rotulum et quere ad crucem in fine rotuli* at this point at the very end of membrane 11d. So a clerk may be looking for a cross, but crosses are used by the clerks for other reasons than to signal the continuation of a plea on the other side of the membrane. See *1256 Shropshire Eyre*, p.lix for another reason.

clerks of what had happened in the plea and whether further action was required. For example, the sign standing for *est* (÷) indicates where the court has taken some action. The amercements for the crown pleas are arranged by hundred or borough, and there is a separate sub-section for the civil plea amercements and for money to be raised from agreements at the end of the amercement section. The amercement section of the roll has survived relatively unmarked at the end of the roll. This is another indication that the roll was for a junior justice because a senior justice's roll should have been crossed out once the copy had been made on the actual estreat. The actual estreat, or the copy of these amercements and money to be raised from agreements sent to the Exchequer, is missing. The estreat would not, of course, survive with the roll unless put back with it by a modern editor.

There is no surviving jury kalendar for the hundreds and boroughs in the crown pleas, except for Dunwich, where oddly it forms part of the civil pleas. It may be that the same justice heard both civil and crown pleas at Dunwich and because there was not much business the clerk wrote down the jury at the start of the proceedings. The kalendar is laid out in two parts with the names of the bailiffs, and coroners at the top of each part followed by the electors and jurors respectively. The names of the jurors are also laid out in two parts, six in each part.

There does not appear to be a fixed layout that the clerks follow at every eyre. For example, essoins, if they have survived, often appear in the roll, either prior to or after the civil pleas, for each place where the eyre is held within the county. It does appear that where both civil and crown pleas survive the civil pleas appear first, through all the locations where the court sat, followed by the crown pleas. This roll is no exception.

The plea roll is laid out through the membranes as follows:[103]

Table 1. *Analysis of membranes*

Membrane number	Contents	Dates mentioned (if applicable)
1–2d	Essoins taken at Ipswich	Sun. 29 April
		Wed. 2 May
		Sun. 6 May
		Tues.15 May
		Thurs. 17 May
		Sun. 20 May
3–25	Suffolk civil and foreign civil pleas taken at Ipswich[104]	None
25–25d	Essoins taken at Cattishall	Sun. 20 May
26–43d	Suffolk civil and foreign civil pleas taken at Cattishall	From Mon. 21 May
44–44d	Suffolk civil pleas taken at Dunwich,[105] including a kalendar of jurors and officers for the crown pleas	None
45–52d	Crown pleas begun at Ipswich	Mon. 7 May
53–55	Crown pleas for the liberty of Bury St Edmunds taken at Cattishall[106]	None

---

[103] See Crook 1982a, p.101 for the general layout of the Suffolk eyre roll of 1240.

[104] Foreign Pleas are included in the civil pleas at Ipswich, Cattishall and Dunwich and are scattered throughout the pleas, and not separated out into a discrete section.

[105] There are no foreign civil pleas at Dunwich. The marginalia do differentiate between the pleas that relate to Dunwich and those that relate to other hundreds in Suffolk.

[106] There are other hundreds and vills shown in membranes 53–55 but they are all part of the liberty. See below.

Membrane number	Contents	Dates mentioned (if applicable)
55d	Crown pleas for Dunwich.	None
56–58d	Amercements from the crown pleas	
59–60d	Amercements from the civil pleas	
61–61d	Money raised from agreements, including some amercements from civil pleas interspersed	
62	Amercements from crown and civil pleas from Dunwich plus an agreement	
63	Cover, actually stitched into the roll after membrane 2	

The total number of separate items that can be transcribed and translated is 1666, made up as follows:

Table 2. Number of separate items in the roll

Plea type	Number of items
Essoins	105
Attorneys	97
Suffolk civil pleas	821
Foreign civil pleas	137[107]
Crown pleas	441[108]
Amercements from crown pleas[109]	41[110]
Amercements from civil pleas	19[111]
Agreements	5[112]
Total	1666[113]

The fiscal documents and financial reckoning

Towards the end of the civil and crown pleas two or more of the justices, some of the clerks and the sheriff and his officers held a session to deal with fixing the money to be raised from the amercements and agreements generated by the eyre during its sessions. The procedure at the end of the eyre is hinted at in the eyre in Rutland in 1253 where the two colleagues who took the civil pleas were 'in a certain chamber where they were amercing the county'.[114] A more detailed account of the procedure, but produced considerably later (1290s), is to be found in the legal treatise known as *Fleta*. It states that the amercements are determined according to the litigants'

---

[107] The 97 attorney items and the 137 foreign pleas are intermingled with the Suffolk civil pleas, unlike later rolls where there were separate sections for these items.

[108] These cover items **1161** to **1601**.

[109] For convenience of indexing, the amercements and agreements have been divided into groups of 20 items, where there are no smaller natural groups. Occasionally I have extended the number beyond 20 items if the end of the section or a side of a membrane is within a small number of items.

[110] These cover items **1602** to **1641** and **1665** for the crown plea amercements for Dunwich.

[111] These cover items **1642** to **1659** and **1666**, which is for the amercements and agreements for Dunwich.

[112] These cover items **1660** to **1664**.

[113] There is no Kalendar of Juries of Presentment for the crown pleas unlike in the eyre rolls for Berkshire (1248) and Shropshire (1256). See *1248 Berkshire Eyre*, pp.291–297 and *1256 Shropshire Eyre*, pp.301–306 for examples of these.

[114] See Meekings 1956, p.617 for the detail on this process. This article is also reprinted in his *Studies in 13th Century Justice and Administration*. There are specific references to the issues of the eyre in chapter 5.

ability to pay by way of assessments 'by the oaths of knights and other reputable men of the same county'. It is also interesting that each amercement is, according to *Fleta*, determined by the relevant peer group; that is earls and barons amercements by other earls and barons, and 'serjeants, as serjeants, by serjeants' etc.[115] Meekings indicates that for the barons it was likely that the barons of the Exchequer were held to be equivalents who could assess them for an amercement.[116] It is also possible that many of the amercement amounts were determined by custom, as many in cases of a similar nature are of the same value. The same applies for the amount charged to have a chirograph of an agreement.[117] The justices might pardon amercements at this session, such pardons being formally noted in the plea roll. A total of forty-six plaintiffs and fifteen defendants were pardoned in fifty cases for poverty and the result noted in the plea roll. In a further twenty-eight cases poverty was merely noted in the plea but apparently in these cases too the amercements were pardoned as the names do not appear in the amercement section.[118]

The amercement and agreement sections and the estreat

The plea roll JUST1/818 contains an amercement and agreement section for both the crown and civil pleas.[119] This includes all the issues owing from the eyre for Suffolk. As each of the amercements and amounts for the final concords were settled a copy would be entered on the amercement and agreement membranes. The individuals named as being amerced were obtained from the plea roll where an indication in the margin of the plea roll indicates if an amercement was due to be collected or an amount of money was due for an agreement.[120] Sometimes the amercement amounts are also mentioned in the margin of the plea roll.[121] The amercement and agreement display the crown and civil plea amercements separately and in different formats, the crown pleas by hundred or *villata*, whereas the civil pleas in this roll are listed in no particular order. One can see a general pattern of listing the amercements for the lowest numbered plea items transcribed moving through to the higher numbered pleas, but this is not consistent. Once the amercement section was completed for the senior justice's roll a copy of this would then be made and sent to the Exchequer. The so-called estreat roll for the Suffolk eyre has not survived.[122] It was probably the

---

[115] See *Fleta* ii, Book I, c. 46, pp.103–104.

[116] See *1249 Wilts Crown Pleas*, p.109.

[117] It would appear that for certain types of minor offence the court ordered the same amercement. See **839** and **843** for amercements of half a mark for non-prosecution of the plea, and **468** and **472** for the same amounts for a licence to agree, and this appears to be the customary rate for the amercement of this type of offence or for a final concord. There are a number of examples where these values differ. See **215** for an example of a non prosecution where the amercement is one mark.

[118] **198**, an assize of novel disseisin, is a good example of the plaintiff being pardoned for poverty. **813** is a good example of the defendant this time being pardoned for poverty in another assize of novel disseisin. Of the twenty-six cases where poverty is merely noted, the first example in the text is **324** where Richard of Hopton, his wife and her sister did not prosecute and the poverty was noted, as they had no sureties, except their faith, because they could not afford sureties. Their names do not appear in the amercement section.

[119] The civil pleas amercements from this plea roll are transcribed at the end of the civil pleas text. See below, membranes 59 to 62.

[120] That is *misericordia*, or *misericordie* if plural amercements.

[121] See **160** where the plea indicates the size of the amercement on a collective and on a separate basis. The separate items are shown in the amercement but not the size of the collective amercement.

[122] Crook 1982a, p.44 indicates that only three estreat rolls survive, and two of them are fragmentary. None of them relate to Suffolk.

estreat roll that was amongst those asked to be sent 'without delay to the Exchequer' in a letter to William of York on 1 July 1240.[123]

Once the estreat roll was in the Exchequer a copy of it would then be made and sent to the sheriff to inform him of the money he needed to collect. Occasionally, if the king had an urgent financial need, the estreat could go direct to the sheriff who would then bring it to the Exchequer when he came to account.[124] The amounts collected would be entered on the pipe roll, which should also show how much the sheriff has failed to collect. The first pipe roll after the Suffolk eyre was that for 24 Henry III recording the audit begun at Michaelmas 1240 and is shown under the classification at The National Archives as E372/84.[125] The section of the pipe roll relating to this Suffolk eyre is on rotulo 8d, but it is almost impossible to determine the amount collected because the sheriff accounted for both Norfolk and Suffolk and neither the clerks of the sheriff nor the Exchequer differentiated between the two counties.[126]

Feet of fines

Many of the pleas in the text below have been cross-referenced in this edition to their appropriate feet of fines.[127] The plea roll and the feets of fines are preserved in The National Archives and were organised in their current form in about 1880–94.[128] Unfortunately they were rearranged by county rather than by the eyre or the bench or assize where they were originally produced. It is therefore occasionally a problem to locate all the feets of fines, which relate to a particular eyre because some of the final concords made at this eyre related to a different county as a result of a foreign plea.[129] In total I have located 127 chirographs which relate to agreements made during the Suffolk eyre of 1240, of which fifty-five were made at Ipswich, sixty-nine at Cattishall and three at Dunwich.[130]

As many of the feet of fines have survived they are often used by modern historians to determine the dates of an eyre where no dates are shown on the plea roll. The feet of fines found in The National Archives are mostly the third section of a chirograph on which the agreement was written three times on one piece of parchment, one copy for each litigating party and one for the Exchequer, which was at the foot of the parchment, hence the name.[131]

Of these chirographs, twenty-seven relate to foreign pleas, one of which relates

---

123 See *Close Rolls 1237–1242* (HMSO, 1911) p.201.

124 The sheriff accounts for the money whenever the Exchequer gives him a date to appear, which might be at any time between Michaelmas and the following summer. The actual date of the Suffolk account by the sheriff is shown in the Memoranda Rolls and is for 24 Henry III on the feast of St Edmund in year 25, that is Tuesday 20 November 1240.

125 See Stacey 1987, pp.204–205 for his ideas on the workings of the Exchequer throughout the year.

126 For the issues of the eyre and for a discussion on the problems in determining an amount collected, see pp.lx–lxii below.

127 See Appendix J for a typical example of a feet of fine along with its transcription and translation.

128 See *Guide Contents PRO* i, pp.123–126.

129 I located a number of mistakes made by the compilers in the nineteenth century, of which one involved the feet of fines for Suffolk in CP 25(1) 213/16 where there is no chirograph number 75. This also means that there are two chirographs for Suffolk that are numbered '81', one in this book of chirographs and one in CP 25(1) 213/17.

130 See Appendix E for a breakdown of these agreements and when they were made.

131 See **1100** where all three sides of the chirograph have survived – CP 25(1) 213/15/9, CP 25(1) 213/15/14 and CP 25(1) 213/17/102.

to lands in Suffolk, Essex, Kent, Surrey and Sussex,[132] two for Wiltshire[133] and twenty-four for Norfolk,[134] Norfolk is not considered as one administrative unit with Suffolk when it comes to eyres, as they are when the sheriff of Norfolk and Suffolk accounts for the money raised by the eyre in both counties. I have also located a further sixteen chirographs made later, but relating to pleas adjourned from this eyre, of which ten were made at Chelmsford, four at Canterbury and one each at Hertford and Westminster.[135]

The fines were dated by a return day, which helps us to mark the progress of actions made before the justices of the common pleas, and also provides a check for the dates and duration of the eyre.[136] The permission to make a final concord appears to vary in cost. It is clear from the amercement and agreement part of the plea roll that almost half were priced at half a mark (6s. 8d.), while 22 per cent were priced at one mark (13s. 4d.). The average cost price is calculated from the licence to concord figure in Appendix G, Summary of Fines and Amercements, and is 14s. 6d. This is because there are a number of agreements, which are considerably above the norm.[137] The heaviest cost for the parties is shown as one hundred shillings, or five pounds, in **264** below, but this may be because the defendants, Robert de Grimilies, Richard Cook and Nigel, his groom, had illegally entered the warren of William the Breton and beaten up his serjeant. Robert also owed to William twenty marks (£13 6s. 8d.). Perhaps the justices and juries decided that Robert and his associates needed to pay a considerable sum because of their violent behaviour.

The number of concords made at an eyre varied: the eyre of 1228 in Suffolk produced 152 fines, of which 148 related to Suffolk, whereas the eyre of 1234–1235 in Suffolk produced a similar number to this eyre, 125. The reason for this may be that there was a longer interval between the eyres. There was an interval of over nine years from the eyre held in 1219 and that in 1228, whereas there was one of only six years between the eyres of 1228 and 1234–1235 and just over five years between the 1234–1235 and 1240 eyres.

Other relevant documents

The writ file, which has survived from a small number of eyres, has not survived from this eyre. According to Clanchy these documents were of two types, writs and jury panels. The writs are also divided into two types, original writs and judicial writs. The original writs were those that 'originate litigation in royal or other courts

---

[132] See CP 25(1) 283/11/156. See **754** for the agreement made in the roll. This feet of fines indicates that John de Say had lands in Brandeston in Suffolk, Gosfield in Essex, Hatcham in Surrey, Cocking in Sussex and Shipbourne in Kent. They are in fact held by Sarah the wife of Roger de Bavent – and John de Say gets to keep Shipbourne for a rent of 60s. per year payable at three terms. But if she defaults she can distrain him by his chattels etc. held in his tenement in Shipbourne.

[133] See CP 25(1) 250/11/14 and CP 25(1) 282/6/78, which relate to the same Wiltshire plea and are in effect the left and right hand chirographs of the same final concord.

[134] They are all in the final concord series for Norfolk CP 25(1) 156/61, nos. 694–695, 697; 156/66, nos. 803–804, 806–810, 812–813, 816–817, 820–824; and 156/67, nos. 833–836, 840.

[135] The eyre visitation of William of York moved to Chelmsford after Suffolk from 17 June 1240 to 10 July 1240, then to Hertford for 15–26 July. Kent was only visited from 2–25 June 1241. The chirograph made at Westminster was on the octave of St Martin, or probably on Monday 19 November 1240. See **731** below.

[136] See Appendix E for the return days shown on the feet of fines.

[137] The cost of 6s. 8d. for a licence to concord is also the norm in the Derbyshire eyre of 1281 with an average of 8s. 6d. See *1281 Derbyshire Eyre*, pp.221–228 and p.249.

or evoke it to royal courts or other courts'.[138] Judicial writs were those 'issued by a judge in the course of litigation begun by an original writ as defined above'.[139] The jury panels, as is implied by the name, are lists of jurors empanelled to judge the plea. These were usually written on separate pieces of parchment.[140] Only four eyre writ files survive according to Crook from the reign of Henry III. These are from the Berkshire eyre of 1248,[141] the Lincolnshire eyre writ file of 1256–1257,[142] the Kent eyre of 1262–1263[143] and the Cambridgeshire eyre of 1272.[144] It is certain that a file would have been available to the justices as all writs originating pleas had to be returned to them. They could also have been used as a reference document by the justices during the eyre as to what the case was about. Why so few have survived can only be guessed at, but it is probably because the writ was but a transient document it could be discarded once it had served its purpose.

CIVIL PLEAS OF THE SUFFOLK EYRE OF 1240

Henry II introduced his legal reforms in the civil area of the law for a variety of reasons, but one of the main purposes was to provide a quick remedy for freeholders who had been wrongly disseised of their properties and denied succession to their inheritance without judgement.[145] The remedies he introduced, notably those of the assizes of novel disseisin and mort d'ancestor, occupy the major part of the pleas contained within the plea rolls, and this Suffolk eyre plea roll of 1240 is no exception. A total of 44 per cent of the civil cases brought by Suffolk plaintiffs in front of the justices at Ipswich, Cattishall and Dunwich in 1240 were of these two types of assizes. Novel disseisin pleas were normally begun and completed within the visitation and the complete record is contained in the plea roll. The Suffolk eyre is no exception to this. For the mort d'ancestor pleas and the other actions, delaying tactics were often used by the litigants but only that part of the process which took place in Suffolk is available in this roll. At least 12 per cent of Suffolk pleas and 43 per cent of the foreign pleas managed only a stage in the process at this eyre and were then adjourned elsewhere. You can get a flavour of the delaying tactics from the foreign pleas from other counties and the fact that 60 per cent of these pleas are adjourned to the next county, Essex, or to other counties in the eyre, or to the court at Westminster. See Table 4 for a full analysis of adjournments and foreign pleas.[146] The only way to follow the pleas that are adjourned to another county is to follow them from adjournment to adjournment and from plea roll to plea roll until the case is resolved in one way or another. Other pleas were not prosecuted or were

---

138 See *Early Registers of Writs*, p.lxiv.
139 See *Early Registers of Writs*, p.lxvi.
140 For a good description of these writs and the writ file see *1248 Berkshire Eyre*, pp.lx–lxiii. Clanchy transcribes the surviving writ file for this eyre, with occasional translations, on pp.401–499.
141 See Crook 1982a, pp.37–39. The writ file for the Berkshire eyre is JUST4/1/1.
142 See JUST4/1/3.
143 See JUST4/1/5, part 1.
144 See JUST4/1/6.
145 See Hudson 1996, pp.131–132 for the introduction of the assizes of novel disseisin and mort d'ancestor, and for a general discussion of these procedures together with the writ of right and the grand assize see pp.192–204. There is a good analysis of the development of the assizes during the reign of Henry II in Biancalana 1988a, pp.431–536.
146 See p.liii below.

withdrawn at the eyre, and others reached agreements (22 per cent of Suffolk and 31 per cent of foreign pleas), often with only the barest outline of the case being presented. I have estimated, taking account of all these items, approximately 62 per cent of all pleas are concluded by these processes.

The opening of the action by the plaintiff

The eyre court either enabled litigants to gain satisfaction (or otherwise) at the eyre itself or was merely a stage in the process through which they could do so. A free-holder, claiming his or her right to land, could start the process of litigation at his or her lord's court, the county court, or even at the Bench at Westminster.[147] There are a number of cases in the roll where there is evidence of the case starting at the lord's court. Such a case is that between Hubert of Braiseworth against Hugh of Cotton, who started the process in the court of the liberty of Bury St Edmunds for twenty-one acres of land, **938**. William of Cotton was asked at the court of Bury St Edmunds to vouch for Hugh of Cotton, but for some inexplicable reason he decided to do it at the eyre. The sheriff was ordered by the eyre court to distrain William to go back to the court at Bury St Edmunds and warrant Hugh there. It is unfor-tunate that the plea and the result of the case at the court of Bury St Edmunds are not extant. A similar case to that above is **997**, which had also started in the court of Bury St Edmunds, where Benedict de *Twamill* had been sued by a Thurston the son of Reynold. It appears that Benedict must have produced a charter by Roger de *Twamill* at the court of Bury St Edmunds and called a William the son of Simon de *Twamill*, the grandson of Roger de *Twamill* and his heir, to warrant the charter. However, William turned out to be under age so the steward of Bury St Edmunds was ordered not to proceed in the case until William was of full age, and presumably the resumption would be at the court of Bury St Edmunds.

However, freeholders could seek redress immediately in a royal court if they had been disseised of their possession, unjustly and without judgement, by obtaining a writ of novel disseisin.[148] This is but one of many types of writ available to the litigant from the Chancery. Writs, therefore, determined the form of the action, outlined its scope and determined its limitations. The litigant initiating such an action had to go to the Chancery and pay an amount of money for the writ, which was an order to the sheriff of the county to perform the action indicated in the writ. Writs of this 1240 Suffolk eyre have not survived, but one can see how the system operated from the surviving writ file from the Berkshire eyre of 1248.[149] A consid-erable proportion of the litigants would probably have obtained their writs within five weeks of the beginning of the eyre, so they probably knew when the eyre was going to appear in their locality and obtained writs accordingly. This could possibly

---

[147] See Lapsley 1935, pp.299–325 for a discussion on whether the county court was a court of record and the usefulness of obtaining a judgement there. See Milsom 1969, pp.6–8 on the fact that the county court would be the regular court for any normal litigation. Also see Palmer 1982, pp.315–317 for the writs that could be pleaded in the county court. For the manorial courts see *Sel. Cases Manor Courts*, pp.lxxiii–clxvii where they investigate the benefits of pleading in the manorial court for land held by customary tenure by villeins, and even free tenants. They look in particular at cases involving inheritance of customary land, conveyancing the land from one 'owner' to another, admin-istration of estates, guardianship, marriage etc.

[148] See *Bracton* iii, pp.18ff.

[149] See *1248 Berkshire Eyre*, pp.lx–lxxx and pp.401–499, which transcribes and in certain cases trans-lates the writs. Also see 'Documents of the Suffolk eyre', pp.xxviii–xxix above.

indicate that the knowledge of the eyre circuits and its timetable had been effectively communicated throughout the country.

When the eyre was proclaimed the sheriff and his officials would have to process a large number of these writs in a short time. Some litigants arrived at the eyre ready to settle out of court, often by not prosecuting, or to withdraw from the prosecution of their plea, or to reach an agreement for which they would pay a fine.[150] These fines, or agreements, can often be seen either recorded in the plea roll or on a document produced by the clerks – a chirograph. Other litigants may have defaulted from a plea; that is not turned up without giving a reason, and this may not have been their first default. The missing litigant may also have failed to appoint another person to stand in their place, for example an attorney.

Essoins

Litigants might not have been able to arrive at the eyre locations for a variety of valid reasons and they would send essoiners to make their excuses and hopefully to receive a new date for the postponed case. This can also be seen as a delaying tactic, particularly by the defendant if he had a weak case. However, the material contained in this eyre roll illustrates the operation of the rules on essoins as outlined in *Bracton*.[151] For example, there are no essoins allowed for assizes of novel disseisin and only limited essoins are allowed in the assize of mort d'ancestor.[152] The roll also indicates the careful regulation of essoins by the court in accordance with the rules.

There are a total of 105 essoins in the roll with eighty-three essoins taken at Ipswich, and the remaining twenty-two essoins being taken at Cattishall. Of the eighty-three essoins taken at Ipswich, twenty-three relate to foreign pleas, and some of these state that the litigants could not travel from their home, possibly from the county to which the plea relates. Similarly, there are five essoins related to foreign pleas at Cattishall. The county of origin of the plea is shown in the margin of the roll. Most of the foreign pleas which were delayed by an essoin came from Norfolk, fifteen, or 54 per cent, but there were also litigants coming from as far afield as Wiltshire and Gloucestershire, who also essoined.

Most essoins, where identified, are of the type *de malo veniendi*, which means that the litigant, who is usually the defendant, could not appear because of sickness, or had had an accident on his or her way to the court. In the roll, the first sixty-nine essoins[153] cannot be exactly determined as to what type of essoin they are because there is no heading on the first membrane to tell us the type. It is probably safe to assume that these sixty-nine essoins are *de malo veniendi* because the types of plea identified in the essoin are by no means all of the 'right' group of pleas. The clerks may have assumed that the judges and other readers of the roll would understand what was in this first section. The remaining essoins are grouped under a heading

---

150   See *1235 Surrey Eyre* i, pp.40–41 for his argument that often a withdrawal or non-prosecution of a plea is in fact an out of court settlement especially after the expense of getting a writ and attending the court.

151   Essoins and the reasons allowed for them are covered in detail in *Bracton* iv, pp.71–146. Also see *Glanvill*, pp.169–170 for the rule that no essoin is allowed in an assize of novel disseisin. This is in accordance with its aim of giving swift justice.

152   See *Bracton* iii, p.208, and pp.252–253 for the limits on the assize of mort d'ancestor.

153   These are numbered **1–69** in the roll.

indicative of their essoin type and the date that the essoiner was to make an appearance. The other type met in this roll is *de malo lecti*, or bed sickness; they are always identified separately with their own headings and are also in a date sequence. This excuse could only be used in actions of the 'right' group, although there is an action of dower in this roll in which a litigant has used this type of essoin.[154]

The entry recording the essoin normally indicates first the name of the litigant claiming the essoin followed by the name of the opposing litigant, the type of plea, the name of the essoiner and the place and time for the parties to appear. Sometimes this roll only provides the place if it is to be at the next session; for example at Cattishall in **26** where the essoiner, Ralph the son of Roger, essoined the litigant Simon Peche. The essoiner also pledged his faith (*affidavit*), that his essoinee will be at the session mentioned. In **6** the essoiner pledged his faith that Alice the wife of John Blench will be at Ipswich in a month after Easter.

The litigant also sometimes pledges to be at the court in the same session, but at a later date; for example in **15** the abbot of Battle agreed to be at Ipswich via his essoiner, William the son of John, on a day one month after Easter concerning a plea of utrum against Adam the Fleming. Later in **120** they reached an agreement via a chirograph. Sometimes you can see delay from one session to another. In **10** and **654** the probable brothers, Ralph and Robert Blund, essoined against the same litigant Hugh de Vere, earl of Oxford, on a plea of land, once in Ipswich and once in Cattishall. It is even remarked on in the roll that both are now essoined in **654**. One can see that this type of essoin is becoming a delaying tactic on the part of the defendant. The litigant being essoined could also delay matters to a later county in the eyre circuit or even to a specified later time altogether. In **78** the litigants were asked to be at Chelmsford in Essex, which is the next county in William of York's circuit, whereas in **914** the litigants were given a year and a day to get themselves to the Tower of London and the Bench at Westminster.

If the litigant essoining was a baron, or he was involved in a trial by battle, sureties were taken by the court and identified in this roll. It is assumed that the sureties in both cases were to ensure that the litigant appeared as they would be responsible and the sureties could be amerced if the litigant did not appear on the date specified.[155] For example, the abbot of Bury St Edmunds essoined in **1** on the surety of Peter de *Bruniford* on a plea of land to appear at Cattishall five weeks after Easter.[156] There are two essoins involving a trial by battle, **52** and **70**. They are both Norfolk pleas. In **70** Warren de Montchensy essoined from a trial by battle against Brian the son of Alan on the surety of Roger of Boyland. Later in the eyre they reached an agreement in **708**.

The essoin type *de malo lecti* meant that the litigant could not even start on the journey to the eyre session, having proved he was sick and confined to his bed. It was therefore less used as an excuse. If a court decided to go through this procedure then a writ *mitte* was issued by the court to the sheriff to send four knights to visit the litigant and to check that he was as ill as he had indicated. There is one essoin

---

[154] See *Bracton* iv, p.97 where he indicates by the type of writ when a litigant may use an essoin *de malo lecti*. He also indicates that in an action of dower the litigants should not be able to plead *de malo lecti* because in the action of dower the grand assize or trial by battle is not possible, but see **80**.

[155] It is not certain if this is a general legal rule but it does appear to be the case and applied by the justices in this roll.

[156] Probably on Monday 21 May 1240.

in the roll which demonstrates the appointment of knights to go to the litigant and the result of their visit. It is shown in **914** that four knights have gone to see John of Freston, who had previously essoined *de malo veniendi* in **21**, where he was supposed to appear one month after Easter in Ipswich. He subsequently essoined *de malo lecti* with two sureties, William of Felsham and Richard of Herringfleet, and was scheduled to appear at Ipswich[157] on Friday 25 May, **76**. He had not arrived so the court, in the interim period[158] between Ipswich and Cattishall, had the four knights visit him and they confirmed a new date for him to be present in a year and a day and that he should be at the Bench in Westminster.[159]

There are five other essoins *de malo lecti* in the plea roll, three of which were postponed to the Essex eyre at Chelmsford, of which one is further postponed to Kent where an agreement is made.[160] Of the other two essoins, **79** has no further plea shown in the roll even though a chirograph of an agreement exists indicating that the agreement was made at Cattishall during the eyre.[161] The final essoin *de malo lecti*, **82**, is unfinished, although the protagonists are shown, but there is no plea in the roll with the people named in the essoin nor can any chirograph be found. In all the cases, with the exception of one,[162] where an essoin has occurred, it is impossible to say whether the subsequent delay achieved by the essoin was for a genuine reason or was the result of clever tactics by the essoiner.

As well as essoins the defendant could produce a voucher to warranty, someone who is basically going to become the defendant if he vouches the case of the original defendant. Naturally, if he loses he suffers the consequences of amercement, damages and possibly remand into custody. He may also have to hand over some of his land to the original defendant to the value of the land originally asked for by the plaintiff. But, the voucher can, of course, exercise all the delaying tactics again of essoins or defaulting. He could even claim his age; that is that he is not of full age,[163] so the plaintiff would have to await the voucher's full age before the case could proceed.[164]

---

[157] In fact by this time the eyre had moved on to Cattishall.

[158] 17 May 1240 according to **914**.

[159] Apparently he suffered from *languor*. *Bracton* iv, p.91 indicates that a delay of a year and a day is the norm for *languor*. For the writ of *mitte* see *Bracton* iv, pp.113–115 and for how the knights judge the bed sickness see *Bracton* iv, pp.107–108. Also, p.125 for the knights' lack of flexibility in determining how long, and where the litigant has to take his case; that is the Tower of London, but in fact the Bench. I can find no reference to this case in *Curia Regis Rolls, 1237–1242*, vol. XVI edited by C. Hector.

[160] See **908** where Henry of Caldecott eventually makes an agreement with Master Robert de L'Isle at Canterbury although it was not made in the Kent eyre. See the footnote at the end of **908** and the feet of fine CP 25(1) 213/17/87. He had previously made an essoin *de malo veniendi* in **9** in the plea roll.

[161] See CP 25(1) 213/16/78. I would have thought that the agreement was noted in the roll even if it was only to record the amount of money to raise from the production of the chirograph.

[162] See **76** where the essoiner may have subsequently died.

[163] See *Glanvill*, pp.82–83 or *Bracton* ii, p.250 where the idea of full age is laid out. It identifies that a son and heir of a knight's fee is of full age when the heir is twenty-one, if the heir is of a sokeman then the full age is fifteen and if of a burgage tenant when the heir is able to count money, measure cloth and 'perform other similar paternal business'.

[164] See **280**.

Attorneys

Attorneys were appointed by many of the litigants to act on their behalf. Their role was to appear in place of the litigant, not to speak for them. Relatives and depend-ants were often appointed as attorneys.[165] As an example, in **139** Matilda of Newton appointed her husband Nicholas de Alneto. A husband could also appoint his wife, the only example in this roll being in **728**, where Richard the barber appointed his wife Basilia to stand as his attorney. Sons could also be appointed as attorneys by their mothers (presumably widows), as for example Felicity the wife of Simon de Blogate appointed her son Henry in a plea of land against Gilbert the son of William of Carlton in **312**. There are a total of 144 separate and formally appointed attorneys named in 154 pleas or essoins in the roll. The number must be higher as there are many instances of unnamed attorneys for litigants in the pleas. I have calculated that there are a total of 59 pleas where an attorney is mentioned as standing in for a plaintiff, defendant or voucher to warranty but no name is mentioned in the plea nor can it be found in the list of attorneys. Forty-six of the appointments of attorneys in the list of attorneys appointed in the roll cannot be shown to have elicited any further action in the roll. It is possible that they were settled out of court, or that they were adjourned to another eyre but not shown in the roll.[166] Unfortunately the eyre roll of Essex, the next county in the circuit, is not extant to be able to follow up some of these pleas. The use of attorneys was obviously an established practice, but it had not yet become a profession, as there are very few attorneys who appear more than once in the roll, a total of seven. There is only one attorney that is appointed for three different people but all in the same plea.[167] As already explained if a litigant wanted somebody to speak for them they appointed a serjeant or *narrator*.[168] None are readily identified as such in the roll.

Analysis of the pleas

The headings shown in Table 3, p.xxxvi and in the Index of Pleas are those estab-lished by Maitland.[169] They analyse numerically the actions and illustrate the number of pleas by type of action and the results. This table only analyses the Suffolk pleas. For the equivalent tabular analysis of foreign pleas see Appendix F(i) below.

Forty-four per cent of the actions brought before the justices in this eyre at its three locations by the litigants of Suffolk were those initiated by the possessory assizes of novel disseisin, 25 per cent (together with that of nuisance) or mort d'ancestor, 19 per cent. These have been compared with those figures published for the 1235 eyre in Surrey, 1248 in Berkshire, 1249 in Wiltshire, 1256 in Shropshire, 1263 in Surrey and 1281 in Derbyshire.[170]

---

[165] See Brand 1992b, pp.24, 43–45 and 49–50 for the origins of attorneys in English courts and what they could or could not do in the court, and also on the increasing professionalism of attorneys.

[166] The concord between William the son of Rainer and Ivetta the wife of Adam of Cretingham, Beatrix the wife of Herbert Welaund, Christine the aunt and Matilda the daughter of Stephen de Wynesham is possibly an example of settling out of court. See **130** and the feet of fines CP 25(1) 213/16/79.

[167] See **205–207** for the appointment of Edmund de Wymundhall as the litigants' attorney and **464** for the case. It does not get very far as it is adjourned for a voucher to warranty to be presented.

[168] See p.xiv above.

[169] The Index of Actions is taken from Maitland, *Bracton's Note Book* i, pp.177–187 and it shows twelve main headings under which actions can be classified.

[170] See Appendix F(ii). I think this analysis confirms Susan Stewart's conclusion in the *1263 Surrey Eyre*, p.l, n. 34 that more analysis is required of the plea rolls for counties to confirm trends in the

In seventy-one cases of novel disseisin, including nuisance, where there was a clear decision either way, the judgement favoured the plaintiff compared with seventy-seven for the defendant. By contrast in cases of mort d'ancestor the plaintiff won in only twenty-three cases compared with forty-two for the defendant. This does not take into account the cases agreed between the litigants. In thirty-five cases of mort d'ancestor the litigants made an agreement, which might be shown in the plea roll as a simple statement that the two parties have agreed and that one of the litigants has offered a sum of money to have a chirograph made to record the details of their agreement.[171] Of the other types of action, dower (6 per cent of Suffolk pleas) and the plea of entry *cui in vita*, where Suffolk widows sought redress after their husbands had alienated the dower or other land 'whom she could not contradict in his lifetime' form 7.1 per cent of Suffolk pleas (fifty-eight cases), with just 40 per cent of the widows winning their pleas, or reaching an agreement.[172] Other writs of entry (6 per cent), actions of right (12 per cent), personal actions (13 per cent), and a wide variety of other actions make up the rest of the business of the civil pleas. A total of 147 Suffolk actions (22 per cent) ended with an agreement of sorts, and a further forty-two foreign plea cases ended in agreement, 219 pleas out of a total of 924 pleas.[173] Out of these 219 agreements, chirographs have survived for 127.[174] In a further seventy cases the agreement was enrolled in the plea roll, of which thirteen were both enrolled and a chirograph produced. Of the pleas that do reach a conclusion 40 per cent of the Suffolk pleas are decided for a defendant or a plaintiff. Neither the plaintiff nor defendant fared better than the other did.

Novel disseisin

Two hundred and four assizes of novel disseisin were brought before the court by Suffolk litigants who claimed that they had been unjustly and without judgement disseised of their lands, pasture, common rights or rents or that their neighbours had caused them a nuisance, which stopped the plaintiff from enjoying the use of his land. There was a time limit put on the plaintiff before which he could not sue by this writ, a time limit that moved over time. At the time of the Suffolk eyre of 1240 the limit was established as 'after the first crossing of Henry III to Brittany', which

---

use of these assizes. The addition of some of the later eyres' figures for these assizes, as well as this eyre, tends to buck the trend she hints at, which is that the total percentage of the two most popular assizes of novel disseisin and mort d'ancestor as a proportion of all actions lie between 45 and 50 per cent. Even this Suffolk eyre percentage figure for these two assizes is marginally less than this percentage range, 44 per cent. I also think that further analysis is required of the assizes of novel disseisin and mort d'ancestor taking place between eyres as well as those of other types of plea. Perhaps this analysis could provide a trend on the relative popularity of these types of action until the end of the eyre process.

[171] See **227** where Peter of Burgate reaches an agreement with Thomas of Gedding. There is no information in the plea as to what land was in dispute; for that it is necessary to obtain the information from the surviving chirograph (if there is one). In this case see CP 25(1) 213/15/35 where Thomas had sued Peter for 50 acres of land in Burgate. In fact it is more complicated than that because Peter was vouched to warranty by four other people for a total of 13 acres of the 50. So it is possible that originally Thomas had writs out against these others. However, it is only when one reads the agreement that one realises that Peter, the defendant, won the case as he kept the land although it cost him 4 marks plus 10s. for the chirograph.

[172] See chapter 7 in Gallagher 2005 for a fuller analysis of the problems of women in these types of pleas.

[173] This is 23 per cent of all pleas, excluding the void items identified.

[174] See pp.xxvii–xxviii.

Table 3. Suffolk civil pleas

Void items have been included in this table because, for those that do contain information, they relate to Suffolk. 'Total conclusions' are shown because some cases came to more than one conclusion.

Form of action	Adjourn-ments	% of total cases in action	Agreed	% of total cases in action	Not pros-ecuted	% of total cases in action	With-drawn	% of total cases in action
Actions of dower	15	32	4	9	6	13		0
Actions of entry	9	15	8	13	16	27	3	5
Miscellaneous actions, land (unspecified)	4	7	43	74	4	9		0
Actions of right	28	29	41	43	6	5	3	3
Actions on limited descents (mostly mort d'ancestor)	12	8	35	22	40	25	4	3
Appellate proceedings		0	1	25	1	25	2	50
Assizes of novel disseisin	1	1	3	2	41	22	11	6
Nuisance		0		0		0	1	7
Assizes utrum	3	8	7	19	2	3		0
Assizes of darrein presentment		0		0		0		0
Miscellaneous actions (others)	6	11	6	11	9	19		0
Personal actions	20	19	29	28	35	33	3	3
Total outcomes	98	12	177	22	160	19	27	3

Judged for plaintiff	% of total cases in action	Judged for defendant	% of total cases in action	Void	% of total cases in action	Total conclusions	Total cases in action	% of total cases
14	30	8	17		0	47	47	5.72
11	18	14	23		0	61	60	7.31
3	5	1	2	2	3	57	57	7.06
5	5	12	13	1	1	96	96	11.57
23	15	42	27	2	1	158	158	19.24
	0		0		0	4	4	0.49
62	33	72	38		0	190	189	23.02
9	60	5	33		0	15	15	1.83
15	42	8	22	2	6	37	37	4.38
	0	1	100		0	1	1	0.12
8	15	3	6	20	38	52	52	6.46
7	7	8	8	3	3	105	105	12.79
157	19	174	21	30	4	823	821	100

was in May 1230.[175] Most disseisins on the Suffolk eyre appear to be very recent and it was the nature of this action for judgement to be swift; delay was not allowed. Even essoins were not allowed in this action.[176] Judgement was also speeded up by the fact that the jurors had already inspected the land beforehand and in many cases they were ready to give a verdict by the time of the court. The effectiveness of the assize of novel disseisin as a fast means of remedy can be found in the fact that all but one Suffolk novel disseisin action at the court were brought to a conclusion.[177] There is also another adjournment in a case of novel disseisin in a foreign plea from Norfolk to the court *coram rege*, **309**. The clerk indicated that the case was originally heard by Robert de Lexington, possibly at the court *coram rege* prior to the start of this general eyre. The litigants, John of Gaywood (plaintiff) and Earl Warenne (defendant), were supposed to appear to hear the judgement of the ordinary jury. However, neither litigant appeared so William of York adjourned the judgement to when he was sitting *coram rege*. It was not until late in 1241 when William was appointed the senior justice *coram rege*, because he played a full role as the senior justice in his eyre circuit until that time, that this case could be heard in front of him and his fellow justices at court *coram rege*. Earl Warenne almost certainly never heard the verdict as he had died before this date.[178]

In over 25 per cent of the cases of novel disseisin the threat of the action may have been enough to resolve the dispute for either the writ was not prosecuted or the case was withdrawn at the court. Sometimes the defendant does not have to make any plea and the jury immediately indicates who has won, plaintiff or defendant, and the court amerces the litigant who has lost. In eighteen cases one or more of the defendants do not turn up and of these eight are won by the plaintiff and eight by the defendant. On the face of it this would disprove the claim that when the litigant does not turn up he loses the plea.[179] However in all the cases where a defendant has not turned up, another defendant in the plea, or the bailiff of the defendant, has turned up to represent his or her interests. Where none of the defendants turns up the plaintiff, or plaintiffs, in the action wins.

In some cases the issues were complex and contradictory so the jury was called upon to use its local knowledge of the plaintiffs and defendants, as well as of the property in dispute and the result of their enquiries, to decide the truth of the matter.

---

[175] See **160** where, although it is not actually mentioned in full in the roll, it is implied by the shorthand method the clerk used; that is *post primam etc.* It is also shown in a writ of novel disseisin for which see Clanchy *1248 Berkshire Eyre 1248*, pp.423–424 for loss of a tenement.

[176] See *Bracton* iii, p.64.

[177] See **333**. Although the clerk does not complete the plea, it is obvious from the marginalia that it may have been adjourned to await the age of the defendant. This is very unusual as normally there were very few instances of adjournment of a novel disseisin plea. See Sutherland 1973, pp.19–20 and 129–133.

[178] The case was first heard *coram rege* at Thetford on Tuesday 19 July 1239 in front of Robert de Lexington (*Curia Regis Rolls 1237–1242*, vol. XVI, pp.217–218, no. 1173). What is also interesting about this case is that there is a tit for tat disseisin by John of Gaywood's lord, John Marshall, and his men, and Earl Warenne and a number of his men. The reason was that John of Gaywood had disseised his brother's four daughters and his brother had been Earl Warenne's man. When John disseised the daughters he went and paid homage to John Marshall. Earl Warenne and his men then disseised John on behalf of one of the daughters and then John Marshall seized the messuage on behalf of his man John. The case according to the jury was in effect lost to John as the jury found for the daughters. In the court *coram rege* Lexington gave a date of the quindene of St Michael, 13 October 1239, to hear judgement, but by then Lexington had just started on his eyre at Northampton. No subsequent judgement at the court *coram rege* can be found for this case.

[179] See *1263 Surrey Eyre*, p.li.

Sutherland indicated that it is not uncommon for disseisins to be committed by a large band of supporters.[180] For example, in **348** the plaintiff, Robert Figge and Avelina his wife, named twenty-four defendants in his writ; the jury decided that fourteen defendants disseised him unjustly of his common pasture but the plaintiff was in mercy for a false claim against ten innocent parties. In **795**, another plea of novel disseisin, there were sixty defendants but this time the jury decided the case in favour of all the defendants and the plaintiff was in mercy for a false claim. Sometimes the jurors provided detailed information in their verdicts, which gives additional insight into the case. For example, in **160** the jurors identified those persons who had sold the various amounts and types of land that were the subject of the plea to the plaintiff's father Thomas Luton, to William Luton and Alice his mother, the plaintiffs. This was done to show how long the plaintiffs had enjoyed the identified lands before the twenty-five defendants had disseised them. The jurors indicated that Thomas Luton had held the majority of this land for ten years and that William had held it, presumably after Thomas's death, for six months. The remainder of the land, which William had bought, he had held for over three years. *Bracton* indicated that within the law the tenant could resort to a large measure of self help to evict a disseisor but that such a remedy should be taken '... while the disseisin is fresh, that the *injuria* of disseisin does not grow cool by acquiescence, dissimulation, negligence, weakness, despair, or negligent impetration ...'.[181] There is no indication that any tenant took such timely action in this roll.

Awards of damages were assessed by the court, payable to the winning plaintiffs by the losing defendants. The damages covered the profits the land would have realised if it had not been lost to the plaintiff, and the value of any chattels consumed or destroyed; and the assessments were on the whole in proportion to the size of the tenement. In **160** the court was also quite imaginative in its award of damages by indicating that the twenty-five defendants would pay 8 marks in common and 1 mark separately, a total of 33 marks for the 25 acres in dispute. William Luton and his mother were lucky in that it looks as though they received all the damages but in other pleas the plaintiffs sometimes did not receive a penny as it all went to the clerks. In **382** the damages of 5s. 6d. were all assigned to the clerks. The award of any, or all, the damages to the clerks may have been in accordance with some rule and scale, as Meekings implies, but the evidence of this plea roll and of the various other printed plea rolls does not bear this out. *Glanvill* and *Bracton* appear not to provide any evidence on what basis the clerks are awarded the damages. Meekings implies that there may have been an arrangement between the sheriff's office and the officers of the court, but that it was probably an ad hoc arrangement. Harding, however, argues that the clerks were '... maintained largely from the damages (one mark or half a mark a time) awarded to successful plaintiffs, which were diverted automatically to the clerks in whole or in part'. I do not think that the marginalia of this roll bear out this argument, certainly not for this time in Henry's reign. Perhaps it was more systematically applied later in the reign, or in the reign of Edward I as the Statute of Westminster II of 1285 c. 44 implies, where specific fees are laid out, for example 4s. for the making of a chirograph. In addition to damages someone convicted of disseisin may be remanded in custody, and they would almost certainly be amerced as well. The disseisor who lost the action would also owe the sheriff an

---

[180] See Sutherland 1973, pp.118–125.
[181] See *Bracton* iii, pp.19–23.

ox or 5s.[182] At the assize in Suffolk the sheriff would have collected £17 15s. (or 71 oxen) if the rule had been enforced.[183]

The defendant or plaintiff in an assize of novel disseisin could appeal an outcome if they were dissatisfied. They could bring an action of attaint, by which a jury of twenty-four reviewed the verdict of the assize, and reversed it if they disagreed with it. Although there are two examples of where the attaint proceeds and a jury was appointed, out of the eleven items in the roll where attaint processes are mentioned, none of them produced a decision for either the plaintiff or the defendant at this eyre. In the two cases concerned, **774** and **776**, both resulted in an agreement. In **774** the agreement between the prior of Shouldham and Roger the son of Hermer concerning his common pasture and the restoration of the ditches is spelt out in the roll. In the other nine instances, where the case did not get as far as a jury, the roll only indicated that either an agreement was made, or the plea was withdrawn or the plea was not prosecuted.

Mort d'ancestor

The assize of mort d'ancestor had been introduced as part of the reforms of Henry II and its purpose was to allow an heir of a deceased father, mother, sister, uncle or aunt to sue for the recovery of an inheritance held as of fee from which he or she had been unlawfully excluded.[184] Sutherland suggests that the assize of mort d'ancestor was often an instrument against the lord if the heir was refused entry into his ancestor's holding.[185]

There was a specified time before which heirs could not sue using this writ and for which they would have had to use a writ of Right to gain redress, and which from 1237 had been set as the last crossing of King John from Ireland in 1210. Alongside the normal writ of mort d'ancestor there were two other writs; one of which allowed for the cases where the degree of kinship was outside the limits of the assize, such as inheritance from grandfather or cousin and was called *cosinage*,[186] and the other, used by parceners claiming their inheritance and was called *nuper obiit*.[187] The process followed by the sheriff, on receipt of the writ of mort d'ancestor, was similar to that of novel disseisin, that is he sent recognitors to view the property to find out if the ancestor named in the writ held it in demesne as of fee on the day he or she had died, and to check if the claimant was the next heir. The

---

[182] See *Bracton* iii, pp.18, 76 for the rules on assessment of damages for the plaintiff, and the ox or 5s. to the sheriff; and see *1235 Surrey Eyre* i, pp.25, 32, 84–85 and 95–96 for his arguments on the clerks' share of the damages. See Harding 1973, p.72 on his arguments on damages going to the clerks. In other eyres there may be an arrangement that if damages are assigned to the clerks they are either all assigned or only half the damages. But there are occasions where specific amounts from the damages are assigned. As to why some plaintiffs have their damages assigned and others not, it is difficult to provide an explanation. Perhaps, it was also done on ability to pay.

[183] There is no evidence in the roll that the rule was enforced.

[184] See *Bracton* iii, pp.245–246 for his reasons when a disseised heir may plead this assize. *Bracton* ii, pp.296–297 indicates the order by which a disseised person may use the various writs open to them to obtain satisfaction, as *Bracton* says 'from possession to property'. This indicates that the plaintiff can sue from novel disseisin, to mort d'ancestor, to entry, to the writ of Right in sequence but not at the same time.

[185] See Sutherland 1973, p.31.

[186] Just as Robert of Boyton did to the land of his kinsman, Thomas de Blunville, the late bishop of Norwich, in **182**.

[187] Just as Millicent the daughter of Alice Shire did in **1149** against her sister Margery and her husband. She probably did not really want the land as she quitclaimed her share for twenty shillings.

defendant would then be summoned to the court; but in contrast to novel disseisin pleas the defendant could exercise many of the delaying tactics that could be used in the other types of plea and thus caused the adjournment of the plea in 8 per cent of the Suffolk mort d'ancestor cases.[188] There are also seven instances of essoins in mort d'ancestor pleas in the roll. Twenty-two per cent of the cases concluded with an agreement, twenty-two by chirograph and thirteen by an enrolled agreement. Three cases are also concluded by a licence to render the land to the plaintiff, see **380**, **554** and **750**. In forty of the cases the plaintiff did not prosecute and in four cases the plaintiff withdrew from the plea after it had started and thus faced amercement.

After a case had commenced in the court, there were numerous exceptions and claims that the defendant could make to rebut the plaintiff's plea. For example: that the ancestor did not die seised in demesne as of fee (in **316**, **372**, **377** and **850**); that the plaintiff was not the nearest heir, often he had an elder brother (in **223**, **394** and **853**); that the plaintiff was a bastard (in **381** and **800**); that the plaintiff had sold the land to the defendant (in **384**); that the plaintiff, or even the defendant, was a villein (in **362** for plaintiff, or in **385** for the defendant); that the assize had been taken before, perhaps at a previous eyre or assize (in **329** and **493**).[189] The jurors were then called upon to give their judgement based on the arguments put forward. Out of sixty-five judgements (41 per cent of all Suffolk mort d'ancestor cases) only twenty-three, or 35 per cent of the judgements, were for the plaintiff and forty-two for the defendant. Some verdicts indicate the depth of knowledge required of juries, particularly in relation to who had held the land from whom and what was the relationship of the descendants to the ancestor mentioned by the plaintiff. In **329**, for example, there are seven defendants, and the jurors indicated that the plaintiff, John the son of William Dosi, was the son of the man who had died seised of the land, which one of the defendants, Richard the son of Simon, currently held. The jury went into the detail of how the land passed from the grandfather of the defendant Richard back to the lord of the fief, while his daughter Edith was under age. The lord then sold it to the father of the defendant Simon. Simon realising that if he and his issue were to hold on to the land he would have to marry the heiress to the land, as she was the daughter of the defendant's grandfather.[190] However, the jury then pointed out that Simon died, that the heiress subsequently married for a second time and that this husband sold the land to the plaintiff's father, who died seised of the land. The jury also indicated the amounts of land of two other defendants that the plaintiff was also entitled to hold as his father was also in seisin of that land at the time he died, so the plaintiff recovered his seisin. But the jury then proceeded to show that the plaintiff's father had not died seised of the land of two other defendants, Roger Habanc and Matilda his wife, because the land was the dower of Matilda's sister. For this false claim the plaintiff was amerced.

Amercements were imposed on the losing parties in the normal way but no damages were imposed on this type of plea. In order to recover damages if a lord had made waste of the land, while acting as the guardian of an heir, then a relative or friend could bring a separate action for waste on the heir's behalf and assessment was then made of any damages incurred.[191]

---

[188] See Table 3 on pp.xxxvii–xxxviii.
[189] For a complete list see the index of pleas.
[190] She is Edith and the mother of Richard the son of Simon.
[191] See *Bracton* iii, p.328.

Dower

The writ of dower was mostly used by a widow when she had not received her dower from her husband's estate by the heir.[192] A wife's dower was not always safe from alienation and as the writer of *Glanvill* pointed out it was at the disposal of the husband, even against her will. After all, he or his family provided the dower, but a woman could not alienate her dower during the lifetime of her husband.[193] After she had entered into possession of the dower on her husband's death she was also restricted to what she could do, as she had to seek agreement of her husband's heir to any alienation of the dower land.[194] In **1157** Clarice, the widow of Gerard the son of Walter, lost her claim for her dower of half a messuage against Richard Pery, and also lost in a case for another half of a messuage against Constantine Woodmouse, because her husband had sold a half messuage to them both, and with her consent in the local court of Dunwich. Her consent was required in this instance as this was the local customary law of the town of Dunwich as is shown in the plea. But, if she had lived elsewhere in Suffolk where a similar custom was not practised, after her husband's death she would have been able to reclaim her dower land by obtaining the writ of entry, *cui in vita*, and pursuing the plea in court even if she had consented at the time of the disposal of the land.[195]

There is no particular order for the actions of dower being taken in the plea roll. They do not often come consecutively but they are occasionally taken in groups. In the plea roll there is a total of sixty-three actions of dower involving widows litigating on their own, and in eleven of these pleas wives pursued their dower from their previous husband with their second (or subsequent) husband. These are the plaintiffs in these actions. In twenty-four of these pleas they achieve a favourable result by agreement (six), or by judgement (eighteen). Nine cases were dismissed in favour of the defendant as false, of whom five were women, and twenty-four cases adjourned, of which six cases are adjourned to Cattishall and thirteen are adjourned to the next county in the eyre, Essex.

A good example will draw attention to some of the problems encountered by a widow in the course of her actions to recover her dower and why a potentially richly dowered widow was a good catch if she could recover her dower. Alina, the wife of Geoffrey de Say, brought three writs for her dower from her dead husband Hubert de Vallibus. Two are foreign pleas from the Norfolk eyre, and one began in this Suffolk eyre. In the first plea, **153**, she was claiming the advowson of the church of Cringleford, located just outside Norwich, from Alexander de Vallibus and also

---

[192]   See *1235 Surrey Eyre* i, pp.60–63.
[193]   See *Glanvill*, p.60.
[194]   See Biancalana 1988b, p.268.
[195]   *Glanvill*, p.60 also indicates that the husband can 'sell or alienate in whatever way he pleases his wife's dower during her life' and it is also stated that a woman cannot then reclaim the dower from the purchaser. However, Biancalana argues in 1988b, p.284 that by the mid-thirteenth century the law on dower had changed and that the widow could sue for her dower as being a third of the land that a husband had when he married plus a third of later acquisitions. He also argues that the widow had her writ of entry, especially the writ, *cui in vita*, if her husband granted the land away. The writ's name, translated as 'whom in life' is contained within the wording of the writ, *cui ipsa in vita sua contradicere non potuit*, and which can also be seen in **453**, the first entry plea in the roll of this type, where dower is involved. This indicates that while her husband was alive he had the complete authority to do anything with his wife's lands that came with her when she married him, or which was given her in dower when she married. See *Early Registers of Writs*, p.99, no. 211 for the wording of the writ. Also see below in the next section on Entry.

nine acres in Rockland from the abbot of Langley. She met her first delay because Alexander vouched to warranty Thomas of Moulton, the son of Thomas of Moulton, and the abbot claimed a view, which was given to him. She then had to wait until the court met at Cattishall. In the second plea, **475**, for a rent of 72s. 6d. and twenty-two acres of land in Cringleford as part of her dower she suffered another delay against a further four defendants. The defendants were Simon Peche and his wife Agnes for the rent, and William Mauclerc and William Stute for the land in Cringleford. The delay was caused by the claim for a view by the defendants. This was given to them. The final plea, **526**, was the Suffolk plea, and was perhaps the most interesting of the three. Alina was claiming one and a half carucates of land and 40s. rent with appurtenances in Denham and the advowson of Denham church as her dower against the same Thomas of Moulton[196] and his wife Matilda, who was a descendant of Edward de Vallibus. Alina was also claiming that the land was contained within the manor of Surlingham which belonged to her husband Hubert and which was given to him by Robert de Vallibus, his father, as her dower. At least they received a decision in this plea, but Alina and Geoffrey would not have liked it, as judgement was given for Thomas and Matilda to retain control of the vill of Denham and the one and a half carucates and rent as the jury considered that the manor of Denham had never belonged to Surlingham since it was a *capitalis* manor.[197]

In **727** the court now took up again the pleas outlined in **475** and Alina suffered further delay when, through a series of vouchers to warranty, three of the defendants vouched Thomas of Moulton and his wife Matilda, who was conveniently absent, but whom Thomas indicated that without her he could not vouch. This could just be an indication that some of the land might be Matilda's dower, *maritagium* or inheritance.[198] There was yet further delay and the case was referred to Chelmsford in the next county in the eyre. The abbot of Langley also vouched Henry of Barford for six of the nine acres and Thomas and Matilda for the remaining three acres. One of the defendants, the abbot of Langley, vouched Henry of Barford and it was in the final plea, **1038**, that Alina received nothing for her trouble, because she and Geoffrey did not turn up and in fact had already been given a day at the Bench in Westminster.[199] Unfortunately, there was no indication of a settlement in any of the feet of fines to any of these pleas and their litigants or anything further in this plea roll. Through all these pleas Alina and Geoffrey have won precisely nothing. Alina must have been a good catch to Geoffrey de Say with potentially all these lands and rents.

However, both Alina and Geoffrey were persistent in trying to recover some of the lands in question. There is evidence in the Curia Regis rolls that Alina and Geoffrey eventually won one of the pleas against those mentioned in **475**. The reason is that Thomas and Matilda took it in turns not to show up at the court of the Common

---

[196] This is the same Thomas vouched to warranty by Alexander de Vallibus.

[197] That is the vill of Denham has always been a chief manor in its own right. The vill of Denham is in the Hoxne hundred and, according to *Feudal Aids 1284–1431* v, p.37, the main holders of the hundred were the bishops of Norwich. The vill of Surlingham cum Rokelund and Brandon is in the hundred of Henstead in Norfolk. According to *Feudal Aids 1284 – 1431* iii, pp.428 and 430, Surlingham's main tenant was Hubert of Moulton. The Vallibus family is also mentioned on these pages as having holdings in the vill. The Moulton family continued to have an interest at least to 1431. So it looks as though Alina lost in Surlingham as well. It is probable that this was the son of the same Thomas of Moulton who had been the chief judge in the Norfolk and Suffolk eyre of 1234–1235. See *Cal. Pat. Rolls 1234–1247*, p.77; also Crook 1982a, p.90.

[198] It is possible that she was the daughter and heir of Hugh de Vallibus. See Pitcairn 2000, p.5.

[199] In fact as far as I can see the cases were transferred to the Bench. See below.

Pleas and it looks as though the judges in that court finally decided that Matilda was in default. The result of all this was that Alina and Geoffrey got seisin of the land indicated in **475** and Thomas and Matilda had to compensate the others for their lost land.[200] However, in the plea **727** where the abbot of Langley had vouched Henry of Barford to warranty it does not appear to be taken in the court of Common Pleas until 1244. Further delay can only be expected as Henry then vouched Thomas of Moulton and Matilda his wife.[201]

Entry

The actions by writs of dower and entry formed 6 per cent and 7 per cent respectively of the Suffolk pleas. Of the 107 pleas in these two categories eighty-four were actions pursued or defended by women litigants.[202] In pleas of entry eleven were pursued by women using the writ *cui in vita* when the dower or part of it, that is the specific land that has been assigned as dower to the wife; or any other inheritance or *maritagium* had been transferred to others without her consent by her husband.[203] The writ of entry was therefore useful to a widow to gain her dower or *maritagium* if it had been transferred to others without her consent.

Once a woman was married she gave up her relative independence, in comparison with her status as a widow or even as a single spinster, because all her property and possessions were in the control of her husband. There is one plea in the roll which exemplifies this, see **646**, where Golder Hagen, the son of Edmund, and Bella his wife, tried to recover Bella's right to a third part of one messuage by means of a writ of entry, *sine assensu viri*. The case shows Bella had demised it to Clement the son of Roger without her husband's assent. Unfortunately, this plea did not proceed to a conclusion. As Judith Bennett indicates 'Femaleness was defined by the submissiveness of wives who are expected to defer to their husbands in both private and public.'[204]

There is one situation, however, where a wife is able to plead on her own behalf and that is where she has in effect lost her husband because he has been outlawed. There is one such case in the roll. **300** contains cases of entry for Agnes the wife of Adam the son of Robert, one of which indicates that her husband has been outlawed. She wins one of those pleas because the land was her own *maritagium*.

---

[200] See *Curia Regis Rolls 1237–1242*, vol. XVI, p.398, no. 1950 and *Curia Regis Rolls 1242–1243*, vol. XVII, ed. Alexandra Nicol, p.131 no. 650, where further delay takes place for vouchers to warranty of Thomas and Matilda; also p.287, no. 1476 for delay where Thomas and Matilda do not come but their lands are distrained for them both to appear at the court; and p.426, no. 2131, where Thomas appoints an attorney; finally, pp.479–480, no. 2353, where Geoffrey and Alina finally win one of their pleas. Matilda fails to appear yet again, so Geoffrey and Alina get Alina's dower lands and rents and the others can claim from lands distrained from Thomas and Matilda.

[201] See *Curia Regis Rolls 1243–1245*, vol. XVIII, p.212, no. 1026, where Alina and Geoffrey are still trying to get a portion of her dower, the 6 acres vouched for by Henry of Barford. It looks as though Thomas of Moulton was once again vouched to warranty by Henry of Barford for 5 acres of land, 3 perches and 2s. 6d. rent in Surlingham, and he failed to appear. So by this time it was nearly five years beyond the end of the Norfolk/Suffolk eyres of 1240 and it was still not over. I have also looked in the two latest published *Curia Regis Rolls*, vols XIX and XX, and there is no mention of this case or any other involving Alina and Geoffrey de Say. This takes us to Michaelmas 1250. However, there is a gap of three to four years in the Curia Regis rolls between 1245 and 1249.

[202] There are a total of forty-seven actions of dower and sixty actions of entry in the Suffolk pleas.

[203] See *Bracton* iv, pp.21–34. See **635**, as an example of a dower or part of a dower which Agnes the wife of William de *Bruniford* says her husband gave away and which she is fighting to have returned.

[204] See Bennett 1987, p.6.

There is another obvious type of entry plea involving 'alienation by villein'. The common law did not allow villeins to alienate their land. There are four pleas of entry in the plea roll, one of which is a foreign plea from Norfolk, and in two of the cases the defendant won even though the person who gave him or her entry is stated by the plaintiff to be a villein. This is because the jury agreed with the defendant that the person was not a villein and in fact was a free man or woman.[205] In the other two cases, one was adjourned until a ward comes of age. The plaintiffs, Adam Bullok and Margery his wife, had indicated that Adam of Tuddenham held the land in villeinage from them, and claimed that the defendant, Matilda, who was the wife of Adam of Tuddenham, only had entry into the land because she was the wife of Adam of Tuddenham. Matilda claimed she held nothing in the land except the wardship of John the son of Adam, presumably the son and heir of Adam of Tuddenham her late husband. John, who was present in the court, claims his age, which means that Adam Bullok and Margery will have to wait until he is of age to sue him for the land, **1006**. The other plea, **323**, is interesting in that the plaintiff, Alice the wife of Roger of Burgh, tried to sue Oliver of Burgh for the land held in villeinage by a Philip the clerk from Alice. It looks as though Alice believed that Philip had granted the land to Oliver when Philip held it in villeinage and had no right to do so.[206] Oliver won because he proved he did not hold the land when Alice obtained the writ. Alice therefore sued the wrong man. She was allowed to sue the correct man, William Chauceden, if she wished. This also begs the question whether William Chauceden had granted the land to Oliver before Alice knew what was happening. It does indicate that the justices were intent on applying the law as shown in *Bracton*.

Other forms of the writ of entry were available for the recovery of land which had been demised to another for a term which had expired – in **157, 300, 471, 955, 958, 986, 991, 1003, 1016, 1030, 1035, 1036, 1044** and **1053**, or if the land had been transferred to another by a guardian during a minority, in **175, 345, 601, 992** and **1011**. Only in **157, 175** and **300** are the issues between the litigants provided in detail.[207]

Villein cases

Villeins, or those that appear in a plea where they are accused of being villeins or those that appear because the land is held in villein tenure, appear in sixty-eight out of the total of 958 pleas.[208] Villeins can also be seen in two essoins out of a total of 105 essoins in the roll. This accounts for 6.6 per cent of the total plea items excluding attorneys. It compares with 5.2 per cent in both the Berkshire eyre of 1248[209] and the Wiltshire eyre of 1249.[210] Of the sixty-eight pleas sixty-one are Suffolk pleas, the remainder being foreign pleas. I think these figures are indicative of how inferior villeins are in relation to the law and the royal courts. Villeins must

---

[205] See **412** and **560** below.

[206] See *Bracton* iv, p.36 where he indicates the writ of entry in which a villein has alienated the land held in villeinage. This is the one which Alice would have raised against Oliver.

[207] For all types of the writ of entry see the index of pleas.

[208] See Appendix B for the total number of items in the roll.

[209] See *1248 Berkshire Eyre*, calculated from the number of pleas indicated in the 'actions' in its index of pleas and writs and where villeinage is mentioned with a plea number in its index of subjects in comparison with the total pleas, civil and foreign, on p.cviii. My calculation for the Suffolk pleas is performed on a similar basis.

[210] See *1249 Wilts Civil Pleas*, calculated as above for the Berkshire eyre.

after all have been a sizeable proportion of landholders in Suffolk, even if lower than in the country as a whole given the number of freeholders already referred to.

Christopher Dyer and other recent historians, who have commented on villeinage in England in the thirteenth century, have defined the consequence of being a villein, as 'a person denied access to the royal courts' for all the various types of civil plea writs that can be exercised there.[211]

Bracton indicates that *omnes homines aut liberi sunt aut servi*,[212] but this does not indicate what constitutes a *servus*, that is a serf, a *villanus* or a *nativus*, as the unfree are described in our roll.[213] *Bracton* indicates that the criminal law protects the villein from being killed or maimed by his lord.[214] Villeins can also be identified by the obligations and services they must perform to their lord and also by the rights that lords have over their villeins. Villeins are seen as owing specific obligations, such as heavy labour service to their lord, the payment of tallage and the payment of merchet and heriot, the former to obtain leave to marry off a daughter, the latter the death duty paid to the lord. Both *Glanvill* and *Bracton* indicated that villeins have no right to alienate the land they hold in villeinage. In fact *Glanvill*, the earlier tract by about forty to fifty years, indicates that a villein may only go into the royal court on two separate occasions; one to prove that he is a free man, and two if a lord seeks to have his villein returned to him, probably after his villein has become a fugitive and left the lord's lands.[215] In the latter case the lord would have taken out a writ *de nativo habendo*, which orders the sheriff to seek out the villein and his household in his jurisdiction and to have them at the court where the matter would be decided. Perhaps a good example here is what happened to the villein Clianus the son of Olive de *Bruniford* and his household in **527**. Thomas had brought a plea of *naifty* against Clianus, who is described as his 'naif and fugitive'. Clianus came and acknowledged that he was the villein of Thomas whereupon he and his entire household were handed over to Thomas. Thomas de Greley had obviously had enough of him as he then gave Clianus and his entire household to a new lord, Peter de *Bruniford*. The commitment of Clianus and his household to Peter is then noted in the court record. It is not known if Thomas de Greley sold Clianus to Peter or whether he was part of some other transaction, perhaps the sale of a manor of which Clianus is tied. If Clianus the son of Olive de *Bruniford* had been able to establish his freedom this transaction would not have been possible. This is one of the most notable differences between the free tenant and the villein. As is shown in the London eyre of 1244, 'Earls, barons and free tenants may lawfully ... sell their serfs (*rusticos*) like oxen or cows ...'.[216]

There is another agreement covering the foreign pleas **356**, **982** and **1017**, which is of interest because the plea is first adjourned in **356** to allow the sheriff, the

---

[211] See Dyer 1996, p.278. Dyer also provides a clear definition of what being a villein meant in terms of being circumscribed by the customs of the manor and of the various taxes and conditions that applied to a villein. Also see Vinogradoff 1892, pp.43–88; R.H. Hilton 1965, pp.10–13; Miller and Hatcher 1978, pp.112–117; and Hyams 1980, pp.49–65 on the insecurity of villein tenure.

[212] See *Bracton* ii, p.29.

[213] The terms used in these court rolls include *nativus* for a 'naif' or *villanus* for villein, not *servus* for serf. These are considered to be interchangeable terms for a villein. For other definitions and other terms for the *villani* see Hilton 1965, pp.6–10.

[214] See *Bracton* ii, p.438.

[215] See *Glanvill*, pp.53–58 on villeins having a writ to prove they are in effect free, and pp.141–142 on the writ for the lord to order the sheriff to effect the return of his villein.

[216] See *1244 London Eyre*, no. 346. Also see *Casus Placitorum*, pp.78–79 no. 20.

royal officer, to get the villein, John Grim, from the liberty of Freebridge in Norfolk after the bailiff of the liberty had failed to do so. He obviously managed it as in **982** John Grim and Hamo of Narborough reached an agreement by mutual payment for the concord.[217] In fact John Grim, the defendant, acknowledged he had made previous covenants, as well as the chirographs, with Hamo of Narborough (see **1017**), concerning his freedom and his household and it appears that Hamo is acknowledging John's free status. But, the plea implies that in the chirographs John had to agree to his younger son Walter and his household remaining with Hamo, and whom Hamo retained as his villeins. Unfortunately the chirographs have not survived to record in full this agreement. This is an excellent example of the sort of decisions villeins occasionally had to make if they were to buy their freedom. John Grim was obviously a fairly wealthy ex-villein if he actually paid to Hamo the ten marks for the privilege of purchasing his freedom. It is also indicative that John Grim acts as the surety for Hamo of Narborough for the chirograph raised in **982**. This action would normally be performed by a free man as John Grim had now become.

The royal courts had been used for a long time by lords to recover runaway serfs, but the corollary was also allowed by the accused villein to prove his free status.[218] The specific writs of villeinage, *de nativo habendo* and *de libertate probanda*, are fifteen in number in this roll. In the first the writ is taken out by the lord claiming a person is his villein and that he has fled from him; in the second the villein is trying to prove he is a free man. The writs *de libertate probanda* and *de nativo habendo* can be interlocutory. In proceedings against a claimed villein when a writ *de nativo habendo* is brought against a 'free man' demanding his arrest and handing over to his lord as a villein, the 'free man' may obtain the counter writ *de libertate probanda* to prove that he is indeed a free man.[219] Until the matter is decided the writ *de libertate probanda* appears to take precedence as *Glanvill* indicates that the villein shall enjoy free status until it is proved that he is a villein.[220] The writ *de libertate probanda* may also be used by a man of apparent villein status claiming to be a free man on his own initiative. *Glanvill* indicates that in this case the person must obtain leave to have the case heard in the royal court and if this is granted the man appears also to enjoy free status until the case is proved in the royal court.[221]

The greatest detail about how the pleas of *de nativo habendo* and *de libertate probanda* are processed is shown in **1108**. Although it does not contain any references to how a villein wins the plea of *naifty* it does contain the essence of the process itself. Hubert of Braiseworth claimed Edmund the son of Robert the Noble as his villein and provided the family tree of Edmund, amazingly scrutinising his lineage by going back four generations. Hubert indicated that three of those named relations of Edmund were present in the court, Richard son of Cecilia, Hubert son of Agnes and Stephen son of Gunnilda, and all three acknowledged that they were villeins of Hubert. Hubert of Braiseworth also indicated that all the people named in this extended family, fourteen in all, had been villeins, including Edmund's mother

---

[217] See *Early Registers of Writs*, p.315 for the probable writ, *non omittas propter libertatem*, used by the sheriff to get the villein 'John Grim' out of Freebridge. Also see Cam, *Liberties and Communities*, pp.191–192 for the use of this process if the steward of the liberty failed to take action, which he obviously has done in **356**.

[218] Glanvill's treatise has both of the following writs, so they had been in existence for over fifty years and the writ *de nativo habendo* might be older than this. See Van Caenegem 1959, pp.340–343.

[219] See Van Caenegem 1959, pp.336–344 on these two writs and their process in the king's courts.

[220] See *Glanvill*, p.55.

[221] See *Glanvill*, p.56.

Juliana the daughter of Edric. Edmund replied that though his mother was a villein she had been freed and married to his father, Robert the Noble, who was a free man. However, Hubert produced witnesses that he had been born before the marriage, that is Edmund was a bastard, and therefore was still Hubert's villein. In the judgement of this court it was considered that Edmund had been born to an unfree mother before she was married to his father. *Bracton* identifies the specific situation as shown in this case, of an unfree woman having a child by a free father. *Bracton* indicates that so long as the child was born in wedlock and outside the villein tenement the child will be considered as of free status. But, Edmund's parents were not married when Edmund was born, so the court came to apply the law correctly.[222] The court could not give any other answer and Edmund was then considered to be the villein of Hubert.

The lord might also try to obtain a judgement that the defendant is in effect a villein by the fact that he used to perform certain identified 'villein' customs and services. The best method of getting back these ancient rights of labour services was to plead previous seisin of these customs and works. In **332** the prior of Weybourne is trying to seek the re-imposition of villein customs and services which he says had been withdrawn from him for two years and more. What is particularly interesting about this plea is that it provides a complete list of what the prior considers to be the villein services of Thomas Oldherring. They include three ploughings in the winter, six shillings rent and food at various times of the year, including one hen at Christmas and five eggs at Easter, and furthermore twelve carrying services in the autumn. Unfortunately it does not provide the amount of the customary aid or the amount he would have to pay as a merchet for the marriage of his daughters and sisters but all other services are detailed. Thomas wins the plea after producing a charter proving that these services were never performed by himself, or his father or grandfather, but in fact the land had been enfeoffed to his father Nicholas for 8s. rent to cover all services. Afterwards, a jury decided in Thomas's favour that he and his ancestors had never performed the customs and services set out by the prior, but only paid the money rent of 8s. a year as indicated by Thomas.

As has been pointed out in the possessory assizes section above, if a defendant is proved or acknowledges that he/she is a villein of a lord then the plaintiff may no longer proceed against him. As the author of the *Mirror of Justices* says, the villein, '… holds fees of their lords, it must be understood that they hold only from day to day at the will of their lords and by no certain services'.[223]

Ancient demesne was the land in the hands of the king at the time of Domesday and which may have passed out of the king's hands since Domesday but to which the tenant sokemen still held the same rights and privileges that they had when the lands passed out of the king's hands.[224] If the lords tried to impose increased rents or services then the villeins on these 'ancient demesne' manors were protected by the king and the victims of such demands could obtain aid in the king's courts by means of the writ *monstraverunt*. This writ is an instruction to the bailiff of the manor to do full right to the demandant 'according to the custom of the manor'.[225]

There is one ancient demesne dispute in this roll, **1118**, which involved the claim

---

[222] *Glanvill*, v, 6, p.58. Also *Bracton* ii, p.30 and iii, p.92 in an assize of novel disseisin implies the same.

[223] See *Mirror of Justices*, p.79.

[224] See Pollock and Maitland 1968, i, pp.383–406.

[225] See Pollock and Maitland 1968, i, p.388.

that the lord was trying to impose extra customs and services on his villein tenants. This case is, I believe an additional piece of evidence of where peasants attempt to use the writ *monstraverunt* to restrain their lord and reduce their labour services or taxation to their lords, even though, as it transpired, there is no valid claim to ancient demesne.[226]

In **1118** some of the peasants of the manor of Stradbroke had attempted to claim 'ancient demesne' to restrain their lord from claiming pannage, or the right to tax his villeins for allowing their pigs to feed on his woodland, even though in this case the wood was no longer in existence but had in fact been turned into arable land. Their lord and the defendant, William le Rus, quite rightly claimed that the land was not 'ancient demesne'. The manor of Stradbroke had originally been part of the honour of Eye of Robert Malet[227] and it appears to have been given to the Rus family sometime around 1125.[228] William le Rus had succeeded to the manor in 1234 from Hugh, William's father.[229]

William claimed that all of the plaintiffs were his villeins and that he could organise their payment of pannage as he wished and that they had all paid him and his ancestors suit at his manorial court. Six out of the eight eventually gave up their claim after William had offered five marks to the court to inquire into the matter. However, what is of particular interest is that the other two indicated that they were free men and that they did not owe William the villein customs, and that they also wanted a jury of sokemen rather than a jury of free men and knights. It is possible that they felt that they would not get anywhere with the normal jury of free men and knights at the royal court. As William le Rus had in effect no case to answer the two 'free' men would have to try a different route to get out of the customs and services that William was exacting from them. The eyre court appears not to countenance the idea of a jury of sokemen, and William 'went without day'; that is William had no case to answer.[230]

The last plea I shall mention concerning villeins, **1104**, is for a trespass and for breach of the king's peace. This was an action the villein could bring before the court but the case demonstrates in its narrative that villeins can be turned out of their property at the whim of their lord. Nicholas Felage, who was the plaintiff, is named in the plea as the villein of the abbot of Bury St Edmund. Nicholas complains that he was robbed of his barley to the value of 40s. and that he and his wife were badly beaten by the defendant, Adam the son of Hervey. Adam denies the robbery and the beating. Adam does say that Nicholas was turned out of his house by the sergeant of the abbot of Bury St Edmunds and his house and his crop demised to

---

226 As Dyer 1996, p.280 indicated, such use can be seen as a 'valuable insight into peasant attitudes'. Dyer's idea is that peasants on such 'ancient demesne' land claimed this status to their land as they looked back to some time when the peasants had been subject directly to the king and perhaps when their services had been relatively light compared with their existing service load from their current lord.

227 *Domesday Book Suffolk* Part One, section 6, no. 308.

228 *Cal. Chart. Rolls* i, 47, when Ernald the son of Roger, sometimes known as Ernald 'Ruffus', a name form of the family 'Rus', was given the manor of Stradbroke. In plea **448** 'Ernald' is shown as 'Ernulf'.

229 *Cal. Pat. Rolls 1232–1237*, p.43 appears to suggest Hugh was his younger brother, but three pleas in this roll indicate that he is William's father and that he succeeded to Hugh's lands. See **384, 407** and **448**.

230 It has not been possible to determine in what court a jury of sokemen would be involved. See Miller 1951, p.225 where he indicates that sokemen had 'continued to attend its court – indeed, became burdened with the duty of doing so'. It is possible that this is the court to which the plea refers.

him after Nicholas had refused to withdraw from his land and had uprooted trees. This was all apparently done on the abbot's orders. Nicholas obviously had felt sufficiently strongly to stay on with his wife given the work he had probably put in on the holding. It also looks as though he was trying to improve his land holding by assarting some of his land by uprooting trees, but the abbot was adamant that the land be demised to Adam. The villein also fell foul of the legal procedure that the plaintiff should first have taken his complaint before the coroner, in the court of the liberty at Bury St Edmunds. He was offered the option of taking his case before the country, that is the jury, but it looks as though he did not fancy his chances there and so made an agreement with the defendant for the crops that were taken. Nicholas made the best of a bad case badly presented, but still ended up falling foul of the eyre for having come to this agreement with Adam for the crops, probably because the court now considered that the crops belonged to Adam after they had been given to him by the abbot. He, that is Adam, subsequently made a fine for 10s.

Right

There are two other actions that account for almost a quarter of all the actions. They are actions of Right (12 per cent) and personal actions (13 per cent). In some respects it is of significance that the numbers of the actions of Right are out of line with some other eyres. The Berkshire eyre of 1248 only has 5 per cent of its cases as actions of Right and the Wiltshire eyre of 1249 has 7 per cent.[231] Sutherland indicates that during the thirteenth century the possessory assizes became more popular than the older writs, such as that of Right, and this appears to be borne out by the figures in Table 3 above. However, he also implies that the actions of Right dwindled in use during this century[232] but the number of actions of Right (ninety-six) in this eyre appears to indicate that it was still reasonably popular in Suffolk at this time. However, there is evidence that other and speedier remedies, particularly the writs of entry, which often covered the same ground for the recovery of possessions and property, become more popular than the old writ of Right.

Actions of Right could be used to pursue claims of land, advowson, customs and services and wardship. Many freeholders, like William Cook of Livermere, opted as the defendant to use the process of the grand assize as part of the action of Right, **1067**. This was a process, introduced as part of the reforms of Henry II, as an alternative to a trial by battle to determine who has the final right to the property in dispute.[233] It did not do away with the trial by battle, in fact battle was offered in six pleas in the roll, but both methods of action pursued the matter to its root, that is who had the greater right to the land.[234] This was unlike the possessory assize of novel disseisin where it was only necessary to determine if somebody had disseised the plaintiff, even if the plaintiff had no right to the land in the first place. The jury in the grand assize was used to determine the truth of the matter. In the case of Peter de Grenville and Isabella of Saxham against William Cook the plea

---

[231]   See *1248 Berkshire Eyre*, p.cviii and *1249 Wilts Civil Pleas*, p.28.

[232]   See Sutherland 1973, p.43.

[233]   See **151**. This is the only plea in the roll where the jury in a grand assize is seen to provide a verdict. In all the others where the parties come to an agreement no mention is made of what the jury said. It looks as though they came to a private agreement, which may also be the case where the plaintiff did not prosecute.

[234]   See *Glanvill*, pp.180–181; Pollock and Maitland 1968, ii, pp.632–634; Hudson 1996, p.134 for its introduction and pp.203–205 for its operation; and Warren 1987, pp.117–118 for the introduction and idea behind the grand assize and trial by battle.

indicates the process of the selection of the jury; that is four knights are selected by the court and agreed with the litigants, who will go to the neighbourhood of the land in question and choose a number of local knights to inquire into the truth of the matter.[235] This process of inquiry might take a long time to determine and there are a number of instances in the roll where the jury is named and then the case is adjourned to later in the eyre.[236] In fact, in the case of Peter and Isabella against William Cook the jury is named but they did not need to adjudicate since Peter and Isabella came to an agreement with William Cook and a chirograph was made detailing the agreement.[237] The roll has thirty-two instances of a grand assize being used of which twenty, or 63 per cent, come to an agreement, which implies that this type of action fulfilled one of the intentions of Henry II to obtain an agreement between the parties to the action. Of the other twelve grand assizes five were not prosecuted by the plaintiff, six were adjourned and one other went to trial.

The plea roll also indicates the procedure if a trial by battle was to be used to determine the outcome of the case. In all the cases shown in the roll the litigants chose a champion, who is often named, and who would do battle. Whichever champion won meant that their litigant would have the right of the land etc. Unfortunately only one of the pleas in the roll, **797**, indicates the outcome of the battle, or even if the battle took place. More often the plea is adjourned so that they can prepare the champions to come armed to proceed to the battle.[238] In **797** the procedure is explained as to what the sheriff must do in re-assigning the land to the successful litigant after the battle was fought. It explains that Brian the son of Alan is being assigned a third of the land of William le Blund except for the advowson of the church and the chief messuage and other named appurtenances and it has to be valued by the sheriff and a jury. The results of this valuation are to be made known at Chelmsford on the next eyre. Battle may also be offered for an appeal of felony and there are two examples in the plea roll, **192** and **213**, which both end with a fine being paid to the king, one of ten marks and of one mark respectively.

Many actions of Right must have been decided in lower courts, either county or seignorial, for which records are sparse. In **476** it is implied that the original trial was in the county court of Suffolk and that because the eyre intervened the case had been adjourned there to enable a warrantor to arrive, probably because the warrantor would almost certainly be at the eyre. The warrantor having arrived, the court indicated that the case should be concluded at the county level warranting the litigant there.

Personal actions

Litigants could transfer their cases from the county court to the eyre or to the Bench by means of a writ *pone*, but there is only one identifiable example in the roll

---

[235] In **1067** eighteen knights are chosen to determine the right of Peter de Grenville and Isabella of Saxham against the abbot of Bury St Edmunds and William Cook of Livermere, but probably only twelve were actually used by the court.

[236] See **149** where the jury is chosen and then the case is delayed until the court meets at Cattishall when the twelve are expected to appear.

[237] See CP 25(1) 213/17/121 where William acknowledges the land to be the right of Peter and Isabella, but they agree that William can have half the land in question for a money rent of twenty pence per annum payable at four terms.

[238] See **755** where Roger de Mortimer and Hugh de Albanico the litigants choose their champions, John Punchard and Adam the son of William respectively and then they are asked to be at Chelmsford for the battle.

where a fine was made at the Bench and then the case transferred to the eyre court whereupon an agreement was made, as in **1075**.[239] In fact this plea also relates to a personal action plea, **1106**, where two of the same litigants, Thomas the son of Ranulf, the plaintiff, and William the son of Sefrey, the defendant, are involved in a *de fine facto* plea for eight acres of heath pertaining to ten acres of land. The fine being asked to be enforced was made originally at Westminster in the Bench, but there was another fine mentioned and made in front of Robert de Lexington at the previous eyre in Suffolk in 1235. What is interesting here is that the rolls of Robert de Lexington were examined in this eyre to see if the fine could be found. Presumably, the clerks would have to locate them first, possibly with Robert on his eyre or even at his home.[240] There was a fine found in Lexington's roll, but not for the heath land, only for his common of pasture that pertained to the ten acres of land. So Thomas lost his case, but the amercement for a false claim was pardoned because he was poor. This is confirmed by the fact there is no mention of any amercement against Thomas in the amercement section for this eyre.

The other personal action pleas of warranty of charter, debt, annual rent, *de fine facto*, detinue of charters or chattels, covenant, trespass and replevin can be located through the Index of Pleas.[241]

Other actions

For all miscellaneous types of plea in the common pleas business at the eyre see the Index of Pleas below. These include pleas on fishery, waste, escheat, exaction of service for mesne tenants, franchise or on liberties, homage and hunting rights.

Adjourned actions and foreign pleas

Adjournments happened frequently and for a variety of reasons on most types of pleas, except for those of novel disseisin where only one is recorded. An analysis of where they were adjourned to (where known) is shown below in Table 4. It shows that 69 per cent of the Suffolk pleas that were adjourned became foreign pleas by being adjourned to the next venue on the circuit, Chelmsford in Essex.

Ninety-eight Suffolk pleas (12 per cent) and fifty-nine foreign pleas (43 per cent) were adjourned.[242] Cases already adjourned were likely to continue to be adjourned again and again, usually because of the default of one or more parties to the dispute. 61 per cent of adjourned cases heard in Suffolk were adjourned to the next county (Essex) in William of York's circuit by indicating that the adjournment was to Chelmsford. Others are shown as being adjourned to the other locations in the county where York made a visitation during the eyre – Cattishall and Dunwich. Sometimes they would be adjourned to the county where the case should really have taken place or to the Bench at Westminster.

---

[239] The chirograph is CP 25(1) 213/17/113.

[240] Robert of Lexington was taking the Lincolnshire eyre at this time. It is unlikely that the rolls would have been at the Exchequer as the edict collecting all extant plea rolls had yet to be issued. Unfortunately Lexington's plea roll for Suffolk in 1235 does not survive.

[241] The writ detinue of charter is where a person is wrongfully detaining a charter, which might help a person's case. Replevin is the action to recover lands or goods that have been distrained, perhaps by the sheriff on the orders of the court.

[242] See Table 3 for the Suffolk adjournments and Appendix F(i) for the numbers of foreign pleas adjourned.

Table 4. Adjournment locations

Court or county (if known)	Total adjour. pleas	% total adjour. pleas	Adjour. Suffolk pleas	% adjour. Suffolk pleas	Adjour. foreign pleas	% adjour. foreign pleas
Assize[243]	4	3	1	1	3	6
Bury St Edmunds	9	7	9	12		
Cattishall	29	23	16	21	13	25
Chelmsford	77	61	46	61	31	60
Coram rege	2	2	1	1	1	2
Dunwich	1	1	1	1		
Hampshire	1	1			1	2
Hertfordshire	2	2			2	4
Kent	1	1			1	2
Suffolk	1	1	1	1		
Total	127[244]	100	75	100	52	100

The tactic of delay by a variety of reasons is one of the tactics used by litigants to forestall a decision being made against them and it is often the case that the adjourned actions are adjourned again and again to different counties. Twelve of the Norfolk pleas are adjourned to Chelmsford, so they have probably already been adjourned from Norfolk, through Suffolk to Essex. Unfortunately we cannot follow them there to see how well they do. However, we can follow some cases where they are eventually adjourned to the Bench at Westminster in the printed volumes of Curia Regis rolls. As we have seen in the case of Geoffrey de Say and his wife Alina against the abbot of Langley for nine acres in Rockland in Norfolk the case was adjourned three times in Suffolk, once for a view and the other two times to await the vouchers to warranty. The vouchers to warranty were Henry of Barford for six of the acres and Thomas of Moulton and Matilda his wife for the other three acres. There may have been an adjournment at Chelmsford as well but there is an indication in **1038** that it went straight to the Bench. The case can be followed in the Bench, although it appears to proceed in a languid manner there. The abbot claimed another view in the Bench and still has Henry of Barford as his voucher to warranty, but when the case proceeded against Henry in 1244[245] it is delayed yet again as he vouched to warranty the same Thomas of Moulton and his wife Matilda. Thomas of Moulton, and Matilda his wife, who appear to be perpetually absent from all the proceedings in the Bench, are to be summoned to the Bench in the court in the county of Suffolk by the sheriff and to are appear at the Bench on the octave of

---

[243] This indicates that the plea was adjourned to the first assize that would come into that county.

[244] The other thirty cases are largely 'adjourned to await the age' of one of the litigants or vouchees to warranty.

[245] This is the first instance of this case appearing in the Curia Regis rolls, so it took four years from the eyre in Suffolk to get there. See *Curia Regis Rolls, 1243–1244*, vol. XVIII, p.212, no. 1026. It was probably adjourned to Monday 6 June 1244. Also see pp.xlii–xliv above where this case and another two made by Geoffrey and Alina are discussed in relation to how women may take pleas before the royal courts and how they fared.

Holy Trinity Sunday. This case and others like it could go round in circles for many years, and it had still not reached a conclusion in 1245 and maybe even later!

In total, foreign pleas came to over 14 per cent of all the items shown in the plea roll. They may involve places and litigants far from Suffolk.[246] They also add to the knowledge of how the process was operated by the various court systems and how they interrelated with each other. One hundred and three foreign pleas taken in Suffolk were the cases from Norfolk and account for 75 per cent of the foreign pleas. Norfolk is the nearest county to Suffolk and the preceding county in the eyre circuit of William of York. It is likely that many were adjourned cases from the Norfolk eyre, although it is possible that some of the Norfolk pleas were started in Suffolk because of their proximity to Suffolk. Other foreign pleas from counties near to Suffolk account for a further 9 per cent of which nine cases are from Essex, which is the next county in the circuit, and three cases from Cambridgeshire. Some of the places in dispute in Essex were located near to Suffolk, so it is understandable that the litigants went to Ipswich rather than down to Chelmsford.[247] The remaining 18 per cent were spread across fourteen counties most of them far from Suffolk. Fifty-nine (43 per cent) of the foreign pleas were adjourned of which fifty had an adjournment venue.[248]

The pardon of amercements

There are a total of 457 civil plea amercements in the amercement section of the roll. Amercements were made for a variety of offences, for example non-attendance of jurors and recognitors, for disseisin of a property, for a false claim for trespass, for an unjust detention, non prosecution of a case or withdrawal from a case after it has started, and others.[249] Occasionally the amercement was pardoned by the justices, usually for poverty or youth. As already indicated above a total of fifty cases, or 9.6 per cent of all amercements mentioned in the roll, end with the amercement being pardoned for poverty.[250] Three amercements were pardoned for youth.[251] A further eleven amercements were pardoned for no given reason, one was pardoned for being a scholar, **326**, and one was pardoned for the queen, **651**. It looks as though the queen, Eleanor of Provence, was using her intercessory patronage to ensure that Alice Biccernut did not have to pay her amercement for a false claim.[252] Unfortunately, we do not get any idea as to why the queen interceded on Alice's behalf.

The analysis of the progress of the legal cases has demonstrated both the variety and the complexity of the cases brought before the justices in Suffolk in 1240. They illustrate the complexity of the tenurial relationships and how the various

---

[246] See, for example, those pleas from Cornwall, Gloucestershire, Worcestershire and Wiltshire. Of course they may have used an attorney so they did not need to travel to Suffolk.

[247] See Appendix F(iii) for where the foreign pleas are from and **255** for an example of an Essex plea where it is logical for the litigants to go to Ipswich rather than Chelmsford. Great Maplestead is in Hinckford hundred in Essex, which is next to the Suffolk border. It is also close to the river systems giving easier access to Ipswich than the journey overland to Chelmsford.

[248] See Table 4.

[249] See Appendix G for the complete list of reasons for the amercement.

[250] See p.xxvi.

[251] See above in pp.xxv–xxvi for the process of the fiscal session at the end of the eyre.

[252] See Parsons 1997, p.147 where he argues that Eleanor of Provence was very active in this regard and 'could make her wishes known to officials'.

legal remedies open to the litigants depended upon these relationships. They also demonstrate the many means available to the litigant to delay the process if it was in their best interests. Analysis throws light on the sophistication and intricacy of the various royal courts and their processes that had developed since the time of Henry II. It also indicates in a few instances the activities of the lower courts at the county, liberty and seigneurial level. It is not surprising that the litigants pursuing or defending the claims when faced with the complexity of the rapidly developing legal system began to depend on professional lawyers to help them through the maze of the legal processes.[253]

The royal justices with their clerks and records moving from place to place within the county for its eyre and then proceeding to the next county in the visitation must have been seen by the county's gentry and other levels of the county society as a demonstration of royal power and justice in their localities. It must on occasion have helped to foster co-operation between the king and the local community. It is also no surprise that sheriffs in response to royal writs outlining the cases often failed to produce the litigants, witnesses, vouchers, recognitors and jurors at the right place and the right date. However, it can be seen as a demonstration of the relative success of royal justice in Suffolk when 177 cases of Suffolk litigants reached an agreement, or in 157 cases plaintiffs, and in 174 cases defendants won their respective cases. That is 62 per cent of the Suffolk civil pleas. It is also a demonstration of delay or possibly litigants being put to meaningless trouble and expense in the ninety-eight cases of adjournments, sixty-seven of which would mean travelling to another county.

At the time of this Suffolk eyre, the eyre system was at its height and probably more flexible compared with later eyres. I think that can be seen by the level of detail in the roll compared with those of the Suffolk eyre of 1286. First is the volume of membranes in the 1286 eyre compared with this 1240 eyre. The clerks have physically to write, handle, store and access sixty-two membranes of parchment for all types of plea for one justice in this eyre, compared with the 112 membranes for one justice – Solomon Rochester – in the 1286 eyre; an 80 per cent increase. Second, Rochester's roll is divided not just into essoins, civil and crown pleas, Suffolk civil and crown plea amercements and agreements as in 1240, but also includes separate rolls for attorney and sureties, foreign amercements, gaol delivery, quo warranto pleas and plaints.

THE ISSUES OF THE SUFFOLK EYRE OF 1240

The collection of money from the eyre visitations to the counties was a major source of revenue for the king. It has been estimated that upwards of £24,000 could be raised from a nationwide visitation in the 1240s. This money would be collected over a number of years depending upon how long the visitation took and how long it took the sheriff to collect the money.[254] The money collected from an eyre proved to be more than a lay subsidy calculated as a thirtieth on movables, although, of

---

253   See Brand 1992b, pp.33–42.
254   In *1249 Wilts Crown Pleas*, pp.112–113 Meekings attempted a calculation of the issues of the eyre visitation of 1246–1249 where he obtained a figure of around £24,000 of which £22,000 was for the crown and £2,000 for the lords of liberties that were entitled to the profits of royal justice. He also attempted a similar calculation in *1235 Surrey Eyre* i, p.135 for the visitation of 1234–1236 where

course, the bulk of the subsidy money came into the Exchequer within a year.[255] It has been calculated that the financial contribution from the eyres between 1240 and 1243 accounted for between 7.9 per cent and 20 per cent of the royal cash receipts in any one year.[256]

It is not possible to provide a reasonably accurate figure from the pipe rolls for the contribution from Suffolk in this eyre, unlike other counties. But, the plea roll does provide separate amercement and agreement sections within the roll for both the crown and civil pleas,[257] and these indicate that the amount expected to be collected by the sheriff was around £650, or about 2.7 per cent of the estimated total revenue from an eyre.[258] The amercement rolls indicate that the crown pleas contributed almost twice as much as the civil pleas.

This compares with £220 for Surrey in 1263, and approximately £700 for Wiltshire in 1249. I suspect that the figure of £650 is a considerable understatement of the Suffolk account given the actual amount raised for the counties of Norfolk and Suffolk of over £2,000 on the pipe rolls.[259] It is certainly puzzling that Suffolk produces less revenue than Wiltshire. A reason why the £650 is an understatement is that there are a number of amercements in the roll which do not have a value shown against them, and which probably mean that the amercement had still to be assessed or the clerk has made a mistake.[260] It is also possible that the clerks did not complete all the amercements because this roll was probably only for a junior justice and did not merit the care taken for that of the senior justice.[261] There are also examples of pleas where the plaintiff has not prosecuted the plea and there is no indication of an amercement, either in the margin of the plea or in the list of amercements at the end of the roll, for example **330**. This section will attempt to describe the collection of and accounting for the issues for Norfolk and Suffolk where possible and also to explain the difficulties in the way of such an analysis given that the sheriff reports in the pipe rolls for both Norfolk and Suffolk as one administrative unit and not two.

Revenues from justice

In civil pleas litigants were amerced for a variety of reasons. Amercements consisted overwhelmingly of small penalties given to those unsuccessful litigants who made a false claim, those who did not prosecute the case and anyone convicted of an offence, including those who committed a disseisin or a trespass. The justices also had discretion to pardon the amercement of poor persons.[262] For those amerced the justices could order a remand into custody of the losing litigants to put pressure

---

he obtained a figure of £22,000. But it has to be noted that this potential revenue was raised in up to four years in one eyre and three years in the case of the other.

[255] See *Red Book* iii, p.1064 where it records the total receipts from the thirtieth of 1237 as 33,811 marks 2s. 1d., or £22,540 15s. 5d.

[256] See Stacey 1987, p.206, table 6.1.

[257] See JUST1/818, membranes 56–62.

[258] See Appendix G for the summary of the amercements of the civil pleas. The total of the crown pleas is shown in this appendix for completeness. This percentage depends upon the Meekings figure being accepted as relatively accurate.

[259] See p.lix below and Appendix H(i).

[260] In membrane 60 Thomas de Hemmegrave is amerced *pro pluribus transgressionibus* but no amount is shown. However in the pipe roll he is shown as having been amerced twice for the same reason but with two different amounts, one of 2 marks and the other for 20s. See Appendix H(iii).

[261] See p.xxiv above for the arguments for believing this is the roll of a junior justice.

[262] See p.xxvi above for amercements pardoned for poverty.

on them to find sureties or to make a fine.[263] The value of the fine may or may not be in addition to an amercement. This pressure appears to have been placed more on defendants than on plaintiffs on an analysis of this roll. Some twenty defendants are remanded in eleven cases and fourteen plaintiffs in thirteen cases. With the exception of a single case of Right all the other cases are from the possessory assizes – fourteen of which are novel disseisin. Only two of these cases end with a compound of the amercement and a fine, **192** and **758**. Other people involved in the case as sureties could also be amerced if the original litigant did not prosecute.[264]

The crown pleas produced even more money for the king. There could be collective fines on a community, that is a hundred, tithing or vill, for murdrum. Murdrum is a fine levied on a district where a person has been killed in that district, and the dead person could not be proved to be English and the killer could not be produced for justice to be given to him, or her.[265] There are a number of instances of murdrum that can definitely be assigned from the plea rolls: the hundreds of Carlford and Colneis are fined a total of £2 each for murdrum and Plomesgate is fined four marks.[266] In addition to this fine other collective amercements could be made for concealment, for mistakes or for not making suit;[267] or, if the hundred, vill or tithing responsible failed to arrest those accused of crimes and allowed them to escape. The king also received the profits of the chattels confiscated from those found guilty and the profits of the chattels of those who abjured the realm. *Bracton* indicates that the chattels of most suicides were also forfeit to the crown.[268]

The amercement section of the roll and the estreat

The amercement section that has survived displays both the crown and civil plea amercements as explained earlier and there would have been the estreat roll used by the sheriff to help in the accounting of the amercements in the eyre.[269] Amercements for disseisin, false claim and withdrawing from an action are shown as generally being 6s. 8d. (½ mark) or 13s. 4d. (1 mark) although they could go as high as £3 6s. 8d. (5 marks) if the litigants were more wealthy. For example, the amercement of five marks was the imposition on Robert des Eschaleres[270] for his disseisin of Emma the daughter of Geoffrey in **763**, although his partner in crime, Martin

---

263 See *1235 Surrey Eyre* i, p.86 for the process of remanding into custody in the eyre.

264 See **426** where the sureties Roger Auket of Yaxley and Gilbert the Carpenter de *Raudeston* are amerced with the litigants, Andrew Tabbard and Avice his wife, who did not prosecute.

265 See *Bracton* ii, pp.379–382 for when murdrum can be levied on the community and how it can be discharged.

266 See JUST1/818, membranes 48, 48d and 49 for the imposition of the murdrum fine on Plomesgate, Carlford and Colneis respectively and membranes 56d and 57 for their appearance on the amercement section of this eyre. These items only appear on the pipe roll for the Michaelmas following the year in which the Suffolk eyre was completed, that is Michaelmas 1241 and not 1240. See E372/85, membrane 10.

267 The vill of Laxfield in Hoxne hundred is amerced £2 for not making suit; see JUST1/818, membrane 57 for the amercement and membrane 50 for the plea details concerning a killing not pursued.

268 See *Bracton* ii, pp.423–424. He does indicate that if a man committed suicide and was not accused of a criminal offence, his heirs would not lose his chattels, but if he was accused the chattels would be confiscated. *Bracton* also indicates that his goods would be confiscated if he committed suicide because of 'weariness of life or because he is unwilling to endure further bodily pain' but his heirs could inherit his property. The chattels confiscated from suicides went to charity.

269 See pp.xxvi–xxvii above.

270 There is a Robert de Eschales shown in the *Book of Fees* ii, p.915 as having a fee in Wetherden in Stow hundred and there is a knight 'Robert of Scole' shown as a juror in the grand assize of

of Middleton, was shown in the amercement section with no actual amercement against his name. It maybe that Robert was paying for them both, or that the scribe had omitted the amercement for it to be decided later at the Exchequer. A surety is mentioned for Martin of Middleton which would normally imply that the surety was responsible for the payment if Martin failed to make payment so it is possible that the scribe has made a mistake and just omitted the amount. I suspect the latter.

There is no whole county imposition shown in the amercement section, nor any mention of one in the crown pleas section of the roll. These could include a fine or amercement for an unjust outlawry or for not pursuing thieves and concerning civil pleas that the men of the county shall not be troubled (*ne occasionentur*).[271] However, there is an imposition shown in the pipe roll for fifty marks *ante judicium*, or before judgement, for the men of the county of Suffolk, but this county imposition does not appear in the amercement section of the roll.[272] This was a common fine made before the start of the eyre and was commonly known as *beaupleader*. It was obviously paid off in the following year because it does not reappear in any subsequent pipe roll.[273] The amercements for crown pleas are shown hundred by hundred and follow in turn. The lands belonging to any liberty, but located within those hundreds, which were not part of the liberty and whose lord was not the lord of the liberty, were exempt from paying a share of the amercement. Vills and individuals were each amerced in the crown pleas for one sum 'for many faults' to cover the times they had been amerced.

The collection and accounting of the issues

John de Ulecote, in his account as the sheriff of Norfolk and Suffolk for the year ending at Michaelmas 1240,[274] accounted for £1,067 5s. 8½d. for both the Norfolk

---

the Norfolk plea in **369** below. There is no indication that these people had an interest in Lackford hundred, which is the hundred shown in the margin in **763**.

[271] Meekings indicates that these fines were often made against the men of the county for a general or specific reason; for example 'for being kindly treated', perhaps an agreement made by the men of the county and the justices at the beginning of the eyre, or perhaps 'for a false or wrongful judgement' for a specific case in the crown pleas. See *1249 Wilts Crown Pleas*, p.113 for the various reasons that have appeared for these common fines.

[272] See E372/84, membrane 8d for this common fine. There is a similar common fine in the Surrey eyre of 1263, although there is not a Surrey amercement roll to check if there is an entry in the amercement roll. See *1249 Wilts Crown Pleas*, pp.113–114. It was not a popular exaction. It was subsequently banned in the Provisions of Westminster in 1259 and subsequently in the Statute of Marlborough in 1267.

[273] It must have formed part of the general lump sum payments by the sheriff. Unfortunately, there is no receipt roll to identify these payments.

[274] This does not necessarily mean that the sheriff actually accounted for this money at Michaelmas (Saturday 29 September) but when the Exchequer arranged for him to pay it. It all depended upon the schedule set by the Exchequer. The memoranda roll indicates when the sheriff actually accounted for the year ending at Michaelmas. See E368/13, membrane 18 where it indicates that the sheriff accounted for the 24th year of Henry III in the feast of St Edmund in year 25, that is Tuesday 20 November 1240. As Stacey indicates, the Exchequer was open all the year round by this time and it could be any time up to the summer of the following year before the sheriff actually accounted for the year. The sheriff also had to pay in money at the Easter proffer and possibly some of the money collected from the eyre would be included. The Easter proffer need not necessarily be paid by the sheriff in person but could be paid in by a servant or even a relative. According to the memoranda roll E368/13, membrane 13, the Easter proffer was paid in by William de Ulecote, the sheriff's son, at the close of Easter 1241. Stacey 1987, pp.204–205 indicates that the proceeds from the eyre were usually paid promptly.

and Suffolk eyres. From this sum a total of £80 was deducted for authorised payments to four of the judges officiating at the eyres of Norfolk and Suffolk. See Appendix H(i) 1, below.[275] The payment is shown under the heading *De Amerciamentis per W' de Ebor' et socios suos* on the pipe roll and the sheriff presented tallies as proof of payment.[276] The actual amount paid into the Exchequer was £989 7s. 1½d.

Some of the issues appeared as lump sum payments by the sheriff; others appeared as specific payments, or debts outstanding, for which named individuals, hundreds, or vills answered. The sheriff was also responsible for the collection of these specific debts. A considerable number of unpaid debts were never entered on to the pipe roll but were resummoned from the record of outstanding debts that the sheriff accounted for on the estreat roll.[277] Any payments from these debts by the individuals on the estreat roll would appear on the receipt roll in the Exchequer and would subsequently appear in the pipe roll as part of the lump sum payments made by the sheriff. As already indicated, there is no receipt roll extant for this period for Suffolk. The amounts paid into the treasury by the sheriff are shown below in Appendix H(i) for the six years following for both counties and amount to a total of £1,510 4s. 2d. To obtain a total for the eyres of Norfolk and Suffolk the individual amounts also need to be added. These are identified in Appendix H(iii)[278] for the first six pipe rolls after the first mention of the amercements produced from the eyres of William of York for Norfolk and Suffolk. The total for both the amount paid in as lump sums and the individual payments is £2,005 10s. 3½d. for Norfolk and Suffolk. So, although the eyre took place in Suffolk in April to June 1240 the king continued to receive revenue from the eyre for a considerable time thereafter,[279] although, as will be seen below, there are many difficulties in giving precise figures about the flow of money.

Some of the individual amounts on the pipe roll can be identified from this plea roll as belonging to Suffolk pleas. For example, Peter of Beccles is shown in this

---

275 See pipe roll E372/84, membrane 8d for the revenue received into the Treasury and also separate deductions made to the named judges. These are the authorised payments of £20 or 30 marks (same value) to the judges in the *Cal. Lib. Rolls*, p.463 for Henry of Bath, p.477 for Jeremy Caxton, who did not officiate in Suffolk, and p.487 for Gilbert of Preston and Roger of Thirkelby. These payments would have been made to judges by the sheriff before he attended his session on the warrant made in the writ indicated in the liberate rolls. There is a supplementary amount of £2 1s. 5d. paid in by the sheriff and shown in the roll as 'allocated to the same', which brings the total to that paid in by the sheriff. The supplement is therefore an item to be allocated by the sheriff to the same judges as an addition to their expenses. Presumably when they submitted their account for payment to the sheriff they had this additional amount which the king had not had an account of when he made the order for the payment. However, it looks as though authorisation for payment had not been received by the sheriff or in the Exchequer, hence the amount actually paid in.

276 The first time the number of tallies is mentioned is in pipe roll E372/87, membrane 8 for this heading when a total of 21 tallies are indicated.

277 There is a note, normally at the end of the entries relating to the eyre, showing that wholly owing debts and debts from the liberties were not listed: *debita et libertates huius itineris non sunt in rotulo*. The complete process of accounting from the pipe rolls is described in Meekings 1957, pp.222–253.

278 There are no additions from the Receipt Rolls as shown in Appendix H(ii).

279 Stacey 1987, p.213 indicates that the king received £1,500 in 1242–1243 when no eyre was sitting. I have shown in Appendix H(i) that the sheriff of Norfolk/Suffolk contributed £56 14s. 10½d. This figure excludes the amount contributed by individuals from the Norfolk/Suffolk eyres, which I calculate as being £107 1s. 1d. for the same period. Of course Stacey's figure is for all judicial receipts and would have included some money raised from amercements from those imposed on the Bench or at the court *coram rege*.

plea roll[280] as owing twenty-five marks for having a jury of twenty-four after he brought an action of attaint against a jury on an assize of novel disseisin. Peter was to pay five marks for the jury of appeal, and an amercement for withdrawing from this action. He is also shown as having to pay twenty marks for a fine with four sureties. None of these are found in the amercement or agreement sections of this plea roll. In the pipe roll, E372/84, Peter is shown as owing fifteen and a half marks for three debts; five marks for a jury of twenty-four for the appeal, ten marks for withdrawing from the plea and half a mark for an unknown debt. It also reveals that he was supposed to pay five marks a year. He paid nothing as shown in the pipe roll E372/84 (Michaelmas 1240), which would have been the first opportunity to pay part of the debt. He did make a payment of five marks in the next pipe roll (Michaelmas 1241) as planned.[281] In the following pipe roll[282] he pays off the remaining debt of ten and a half marks.[283]

Sometimes an individual appears not to pay off his debt in full and it remains on the pipe roll for years, even though the amount is trivial. A good example is that of Gilbert Maunce, who did not start paying off his debt of only a half mark until the year after the eyre. In 1241 he paid 40d. and in the following two years he did not pay anything, but in the year 1244 he paid a further 20d. The remaining amount of 20d. is not indicated in the pipe rolls as ever having been paid. It was still on the roll in the pipe roll of 1261–1262, over twenty years after the eyre.[284]

Problems identified in accounting for the issues in the pipe rolls

The sheriff accounts for both Norfolk and Suffolk revenues in the pipe rolls as though they are one entity and this continues throughout the medieval period. However, it is likely that the sheriff relied on separate summonses and estreat rolls for the two eyres in helping him collect the money in the two shires. This is unlike other sheriffs who had responsibility for more than one county. William le Zuche, for example, was responsible for Surrey and Sussex but he accounted for the counties separately in the pipe rolls.[285] It is therefore impossible to differentiate the revenue between the counties collected by the sheriff for Norfolk and Suffolk and paid by him as a lump sum without the receipt rolls. The sums shown in Appendix H(i) are for the lump sum amounts paid in by the sheriff for Norfolk and Suffolk from the eyres in both counties. To obtain the total revenue from the eyre for both counties it is necessary to add in the amounts paid by the sheriff for the individuals in both counties where debts were noted separately outside the lump sum.[286] The total from the amercement section shown in Appendix G is the only indication of the size of the revenue to be expected from the Suffolk eyre but as already remarked this seems a lot smaller than the probable figure.

---

280   See **758** or JUST1/818, membrane 29.
281   See E372/85, membrane 10.
282   See pipe roll E372/86, membrane 10.
283   It indicates that he had paid and is shown as *Quietus est*, which is usually indicative of him having paid the amount he is supposed to owe.
284   See E372/105, membrane 5.
285   See E372/111, membrane 23d and membranes 4d–5d respectively for the first time the Surrey and the Sussex eyre of 1263 is accounted for in the pipe rolls. This is also discussed in *1263 Surrey Eyre*, pp.ciii–cvi.
286   See Appendices H(iii) for the individual debts and payments into the treasury and K(i) for the total revenue below.

The individual amounts shown in the pipe roll are for both counties and it would only be possible to assign the individuals and their amounts to their relevant counties if there were an estreat, or amercement section and a plea roll for both counties and an extant receipt roll for both counties.[287] Unfortunately, there is only a plea and amercement section for the Suffolk eyre of 1240, those for the Norfolk eyre not surviving. In addition, because there is a considerable overlap in the personnel taking part in both county eyres it is not always possible to identify to which of these counties the amercement or fine was written in the pipe roll. It has been possible to link a few amercements and fines in the pipe roll with the Suffolk amercements and the plea roll relating to the civil pleas and the plea numbers from the text below are shown in Appendix H(iii).

A further problem with the pipe rolls, which makes it more difficult to determine the debts that are relevant to this eyre, is that the clerks have placed certain other debts with the debts raised from this eyre. These extraneous debts were originally reported under separate headings in the pipe rolls, but the debts are eventually combined under the heading *Amerciamenta per W. de Ebor*,[288] although sometimes, but not always, they are identified with a sub-heading.[289]

To add to the confusion there was a separate visitation to Norfolk and Suffolk by Walter de Grey, archbishop of York, and William de Cantilupe in 1242 when they were acting as regents while the king was overseas in France. The sheriff was ordered to bring all outstanding assizes before the archbishop at his first coming.[290] The pipe roll for 26 Henry III (E372/86) indicates that a separate estreat was prepared for these sessions in Norfolk and Suffolk as the sheriff accounted for a lump sum of £157 15s. 10d. under the heading *Amerciamenta per Archiepiscopum W. Ebor'* as well as showing fourteen individual amounts below. This separate heading for the archbishop continues until the pipe roll E372/89 (29 Henry III), but some of the items for the visitation of the archbishop begin to be shown under the heading for the 1240 eyre in the roll E372/88. From the roll E372/90 the entries for the archbishop's visitation are all included under the heading *Amerciamenta per W. de Ebor'* but with the first item being a note explaining that the lump sum return of 26s. 8d. has been paid into the Exchequer by the sheriff for the eyre of Walter, the archbishop of York.[291] This also indicates that the estreat has been marked up by the clerk for those amercements for which a payment has been made.

However, by the time of this combination the amounts being paid into the Exchequer for the items recognisable from this eyre are negligible. The sheriff paid in as a lump sum only £5 13s. 4d., and the amount paid in by individuals, or by the sheriff on their behalf, was only £1 7s. 8d. None of these items extraneous to the 1240 Suffolk eyre has been included in the summary of the payments shown in the

---

287   Crook indicates that this may be possible for the visitation of 1278–1289 where there appears to be a relatively complete set of rolls for both counties. See Crook 1982a, pp.166–168. There is a receipt roll for the eyre of 1278–1289.

288   This is William of York, the leading judge of this eyre.

289   For example in the pipe roll E372/85, membrane 10d for 25 Henry III there are debts under the heading *De Debitis Judeorum Inventis in Arca Cyrographorum*, that is the debts of the Jews found in the Chest of Jewish Bonds, which are eventually combined with the items from this eyre in the pipe roll E372/88, membrane 4, but under a sub-heading *Debiti in dorsa sicut continentur in rotulo xxv. Rotulo xxv* relates to the pipe roll for 25 Henry III.

290   See *Close Rolls, 1237–1242*, p.442.

291   See pipe roll E372/90, membrane 14d.

list of individual items in Appendix H(iii), or included in the totals in Appendix H(i) 10, below.

The revenue from the Suffolk eyre of 1240 would have been greater had there not been the two great liberties of Ely and Bury St Edmunds in the county. Their lords could claim the issues of the eyre within their own liberties. A total of £23 was collected by the sheriff in 1242 for the liberty of Ely. This would have been paid back to the lord of the liberty.[292] However, the total value of the issues for Norfolk and Suffolk is a significant portion of the total revenue raised by the complete eyre visitation – approximately 8.4 per cent of the £24,000 total to be expected at this time. Even if the amercement section total shown in Appendix G for the Suffolk eyre was the same figure on the estreat roll, and as we have seen it is likely to have been smaller, then Suffolk contributed about 32 per cent of the total raised from Norfolk and Suffolk.

Like all kings, Henry III required money to fulfil his ambitions. He had an ambition to recover the lands lost by King John, his father, while retaining the lands he still held in Gascony. Henry III made a number of attempts to recover the lost lands, one in 1230 and another in 1242–1243 both failing dismally. These and other wars in Wales during this period required a lot of money and one of the most lucrative methods to raise money were the visitations of the general eyres. The justices also seemed to boast about how much they raised for the king; back in the 1220s William of York boasts to the Chancellor that he is raising 40 marks a day for the king.[293] It can therefore be stated that the eyre system was a relatively easy way to raise money for the king while still providing justice in the shires. The eyre proved to be relatively popular with the local populace, as far as the civil pleas were concerned, but the crown pleas were becoming burdensome to the local community. This is particularly so for the general amercements made on vills, tithing and hundreds. The eyre also allowed the king to monitor what was happening in these shires as well as to investigate his property rights by means of the interrogations of the juries of presentment of each hundred.

CONCLUSIONS

Effectiveness of the eyre

Henry Summerson indicated that the eyre was 'the last, grandest and most public of a series of courts, an occasional extension of a system in operation all the time ... which it served to regulate and to supervise'.[294] He was commenting, in particular, on the crown pleas in a Devon eyre, which is beyond the scope of this edition, but I think the comment relates to eyres in general.

By 1240 it has been shown that the eyre had overarching jurisdiction as the king's court and could hear all types of plea. It was also proving to be an effective way of achieving speedy results for the litigants once an issue was put to the court.[295] As can

---

[292] See Meekings 1957c, pp.230–231 for how liberties are dealt within the pipe roll.

[293] See Meekings 1950, p.499, no. iv.

[294] See Summerson 1979 and *Devon Eyre*, pp.xv–xx for Summerson's views on how he saw the eyre as the culmination of a series of presentments in a variety of local courts.

[295] See above for a variety of delaying tactics used before the issue was even put to the court, particularly pp.xxxi–xxxiii on essoins. But there could also be delays by taking the issue through other courts, from the lord's court to the county court as well as the other King's courts at Westminster.

be seen from the analysis of the Suffolk civil pleas[296] most of the pleas reached some form of conclusion, 62 per cent, that is for the plaintiff, defendant or the litigants reached an agreement. What can also happen is that the record of an agreement is entered into the plea roll, sometimes in addition to a chirograph being produced. There are forty-seven such enrolled agreements for Suffolk in this plea roll along with the 127 chirographs identified as being made for pleas made in this eyre.[297] It has been argued that in the majority of the pleas where the litigant did not prosecute or withdrew from the plea it was because of some sort of settlement out of court rather than an error by the plaintiff.[298] In that case the measure of a result in this 1240 Suffolk eyre court rises by possibly a further 22 per cent for Suffolk pleas, or 84 per cent overall.

The civil plea side of an eyre continued to be popular in Suffolk as can be seen by the volume of civil pleas in this eyre. There were a total of 821 taken at the eyre for Suffolk alone, almost twice as many items as in the crown pleas. This was pretty quick and efficient justice given that the eyre in Suffolk sat for only twenty-three days.[299] Of course, if a litigant wanted to settle a dispute he or she had to go to the eyre at this time as the central royal courts of the Bench or *coram rege* suspended their sittings until the eyre visitations had been completed. However, from 1249 the importance of the eyre for civil pleas was diminished partly because the central courts continued to sit while the eyre was in progress. Therefore litigants had a choice as to where they took their plea but, perhaps more importantly, the litigants needed only to go to the one court and not to travel around the country chasing the eyre if there were significant delays and adjournments in their case. This eventually led to the decline and disappearance of the foreign pleas in the counties as the judges were no longer allowed to adjourn a plea outside the county where the property in dispute lay.

The eyre may be seen as a point of focus for the local community given that over 6,000 people probably attended the eyre at one or more of the three locations in the county where the justices sat. It would also be a demonstration of royal supervision over many in the county. Also, almost 4,000 people were actively involved in the civil pleas in attempting to find a solution to their various problems concerning their lands.[300] The sheer number of litigants must be seen as measure of the eyre's popularity in the thirteenth century. The plea roll shows how the assizes were used for litigation over very small pieces of land and although it is an impossible task to establish the social position of litigants there is an impression that many were small landholding freemen. Therefore the common law was now also bringing wider sections of society into the royal courts.

The eyre did have the virtue of being a royal court, and the thoroughness with which it reviewed and examined all criminal activity in the county since the last eyre, made it a court of public record. There tended to be another aspect of the eyre, which appeared to predominate, that is its concentration on errors and omissions as

---

[296] See Table 3 above for the analysis.
[297] Occasionally the details of the agreement are shown in both the plea roll and the chirograph; for example see **909**.
[298] See p.xxxi above.
[299] See p.xiv above for the calculation of the total number of sitting days at the eyre. I calculate the justices were dealing with, on average, thirty-six cases a day.
[300] See pp.xiv–xvi above for the calculation of these figures.

grounds for amercements of the various levels of community: tithing, hundred or even the county. The heavy exaction on the hundreds, boroughs and tithings, sometimes for relatively trivial offences, was not popular in the localities but it made an excellent contribution to the king's coffers, often through the years when the eyre was not sitting.[301]

Decline and end of the eyre judicial system

The major reason for the decline of the eyre on the civil pleas side is similar to that of the crown pleas, namely that other legal processes had developed to take its place. The introduction of judges who could hear the possessory assizes locally between the eyres led eventually to hearing all types of civil pleas and litigation at regular and relatively frequent assize circuits.[302] These were originally established in 1273, and although the arrangement gradually fell apart, a new system was set up by the statute of Westminster II in 1285 and by the statute *De justiciariis assignatis* in 1293.[303] By the end of the thirteenth century these more frequent processes had become accepted by the local seigneurie and knights in the counties mostly because they could obtain faster redress of their concerns.

The eyre as an event was being replaced by other structures for criminal and civil litigation that were more frequent than the eyre process and had eventually become more acceptable to local society. This removed the need for a general eyre *ad omnia placita* in the provinces; and in fact made it 'inessential to the functioning of legal administration in England'.[304]

The eyre during the reign of Henry III had become a regular occurrence for the counties, the only exception to its regularity being around the time of the Barons' War. Even then, however, there was a special set of eyres sent out to redress the grievances of local society, which were set out in their council of November 1259.[305] This eyre was postponed and a general eyre put in its place, the uncompleted eyre of 1261–1263, when the breaking of the customary seven year rule for holding eyres in a county and the outbreak of the war caused it to be abandoned.[306] The eyres resumed after the war for what became Henry III's last eyre of 1268–1272 with Suffolk being visited by the eyre justices in 1268 and 1269 on four separate occasions.[307] It had the most comprehensive programme, no doubt to inquire into

---

[301] See Crook 1982b, p.247.

[302] See Musson 2004, pp.101–102 for numbers of commissions of assizes and gaol deliveries at various dates in the reign of Henry III, and pp.97–110 for the development of the 'four knights' system as an additional judicial process to the eyre system.

[303] See *Cal. Close. Rolls 1272–1279*, p.52 for the start of regular assize circuits, and *Cal. Close Rolls 1288–1296*, pp.318–319 for reference to the new system introduced in 1293.

[304] See Crook 1982b, p.248 and references in footnote 302 above.

[305] See R.F Treharne 1971, pp.199–202 for the enquiries to be made and the articles to be considered by the judges, and the different mode of raising issues – the *querelae*.

[306] See *Close Rolls 1261–1264*, pp.134–135 for the protest by Norfolk to being made to have another eyre within the seven-year customary time, which was scheduled to open in October 1262; and p.311 for the revocation of the summons of the eyre in Norfolk. Suffolk had also been informed of their eyre. There is no separate revocation for Suffolk or any evidence that it was visited by the eyre justices. The eyre itself petered out and was subsequently abandoned.

[307] See Appendix D.

the problems thrown up by the war and because of this each session of the eyre took longer on the whole to complete.[308]

After the eyre of 1268–1269 Suffolk was next visited in a general eyre in November 1286 and it lasted until 13 February 1287 except for a month over Christmas, a gap of over thirteen years between eyres.[309] It sat for fifty-four sitting days, compared with the twenty-three sitting days for 1240.[310] This eyre of 1286–1287 was the last time any general eyre took place in Suffolk.[311] A general eyre was planned and had begun its work in 1293–1294, but it was suspended by Edward I because of the war with France. The eyre visitations were never fully resumed after this disruption.

The eyre became even more complicated and protracted in the reign of Edward I when seventy-two additional *capitula* were added to the articles of the eyre. None of the existing *capitula* were excluded, and the *quo warranto* enquiries were added to the list making it a 'rather ponderous institution'.[312] Although there were other eyres in the fourteenth century, they were individual eyres to a specific set of counties, for example the London eyre of 1321; but in all of these can be shown to be for specific reasons.[313] A full eyre programme was planned to start in 1329 to cope with the lawlessness and disorder in the counties but although a few counties were completed it fizzled out with the demise of Mortimer in 1330 when Edward III began to exercise his authority. At that point another change took place to the system that had existed prior to 1305, when the link between the assize and the gaol delivery system was revived with increased powers for the latter to deal with the lawless. This development, with increase in powers of the keepers of the peace and by occasional visits of the King's Bench armed with trailbaston[314] and gaol delivery powers, provided the machinery for the more flexible use of the king's justice in the counties.

In the thirteenth century the eyre had become a 'nice little earner' for the king. A full programme of eyres might bring in as much revenue as all his other sources put together, albeit over a period of years.[315] However, as the eyre system began to be

---

[308] The eyre in Suffolk in 1240 took a total of twenty-three sitting days whereas for Suffolk in the 1268–1272 eyre it took eighty-one sitting days. Although the previous eyres in Suffolk took less sitting days than the Suffolk eyre of 1268–1269, there is one that came close to it, namely the Suffolk eyre of 1251, which took in total sixty-nine sitting days but I think this is explained by the unusual circumstance of the leading judge, Henry of Bath, being removed in disgrace. See *Chronica Majora* v, pp.213–214. The remaining cases were adjourned to 30 April 1251 and were to be heard by Gilbert of Preston and Master Simon of Walton. See *Close Rolls 1247–1251*, pp.430 and 529. There are no extant civil plea rolls for the Suffolk eyres of 1251 or 1268–1269.

[309] Although the eyre started in November 1278 in Cumberland it was interrupted for two years in 1282 because of the Welsh war. See Crook 1982a, pp.144–146 for the general progress of this eyre.

[310] See p.xiv above.

[311] This seems to bear out the argument by Burt 2005, pp.1–14, who argues that a general increase in the business of the eyre – hence the increase in the sitting days shown above – and most importantly the growing infrequency of the eyre, and that the eyre is seen as no longer the main form of justice in the localities, are the main reasons for the demise of the eyre system.

[312] See Cam 1930, p.230. She indicates that the Statute of Westminster I in 1275 alone added thirty-three *capitula* and thirty-nine from the *Quo Warranto* inquests; see Sutherland 1963, pp.25–26 and pp.186–188.

[313] The London eyre of 1321 may have been called to punish the city for siding with the opponents of the king, and resulted in the city not having a freely elected mayor until after the king was replaced in 1327. See *1321 London Eyre* i, pp.xv–xxii.

[314] Trailbaston proceedings were set up specifically to deal with and to enquire into the spate of armed gangs in the localities after 1305.

[315] See pp.lv–lvi above for the financial significance of the eyre in the reign of Henry III.

superseded by other and more frequent mechanisms of justice it would be obvious to the Exchequer that the revenue from an eyre was falling and being replaced by the new arrangements. Also, the crown was beginning to develop new more lucrative ways of raising revenue to fund its wars, examples being taxation in the form of lay or clerical subsidies, customs on wool and loans by Italian bankers. These innovations were to fund Edward I's wars in Wales, France and Scotland[316] and became more reliable than the potential revenue from an eyre.

---

[316] For a general discussion on the financial innovations of Edward I's reign see Carpenter 2003, pp.470–477.

Appendix A

Suffolk Hundreds at the time of the 1240 Eyre

Hundred or villata	Lord of hundred	No. of civil pleas (location identified)
Babergh	Abbot of Bury St Edmunds	74
Blackbourn	Abbot of Bury St Edmunds	30
Blything	The king	61
Bosmere	The king	47
Bury St Edmunds	Abbot of Bury St Edmunds	1
Carlford	Prior of Ely	23
Claydon	The king	14
Colneis	Prior of Ely	7
Cosford	Abbot of Bury St Edmunds	36
Dunwich	The king	6
Exning	The king	7
Hartismere	The king	38
Hoxne	Bishop of Norwich	44
Ipswich	The king	15
Lackford	Abbot of Bury St Edmunds	14
Loes	Prior of Ely	27
Lothingland[1]	The king	38[2]
Mutford	The king[3]	14
Plomesgate	Prior of Ely	29
Risbridge	Abbot of Bury St Edmunds	49
Samford[4]	The king	43
Stow	The king	21
Thedwestry	Abbot of Bury St Edmunds	27
Thetford[5]		2
Thingoe	Abbot of Bury St Edmunds	8
Thredling	Prior of Ely	6
Wangford	¾ The king ¼ bishop of Norwich	20
Wilford	Prior of Ely	4
Total civil pleas		705

---

[1] Henry III later gave this to the Balliol family.
[2] This includes one plea, **322**, where the scribe has in the margin 'Lothingland', but the place is probably in Norfolk.
[3] The king held this in 1240 but from 1243 onwards the hundred was in the hands of the Hemmegrave family.
[4] This hundred was later given to Ralph de Ufford by Henry III.
[5] These pleas are shown in the roll as being in Babergh hundred. Sometimes cases for Thetford were taken in Suffolk and sometimes in Norfolk.

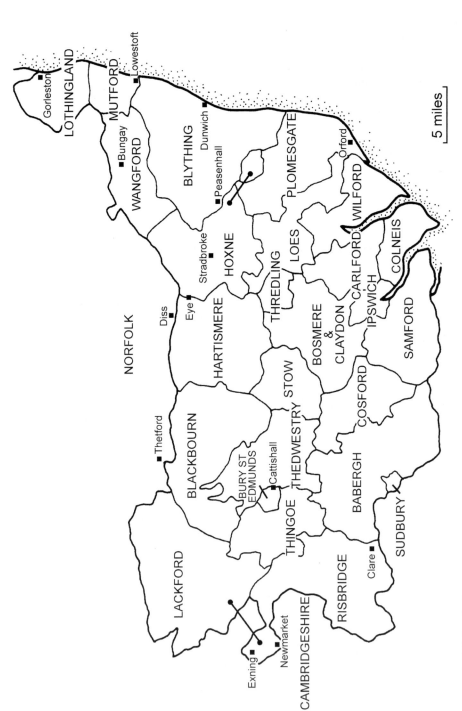

Fig. 1. Suffolk hundreds

Carlford, Colneis, Loes, Plomesgate, Thredling and Wilford constitute the five and a half hundreds of the liberty of the priory of Ely in Suffolk. Loes was shared with the Bigod family, the earls of Norfolk. In fact Plomesgate is classed as one and a half hundreds, the half hundred being the Domesday hundred of 'Parham'. Thredling is really an addition to the five and a half hundreds and, as its name implies, is classed as a third of a hundred.

Babergh, Blackbourn, Cosford, Lackford, Risbridge, Thedwestry and Thingoe constitute the eight and a half hundreds of the liberty of the Abbey of Bury St Edmunds. Babergh and Blackbourne are classed as a double hundred and Cosford as a half hundred.

Wangford belonged three-quarters to the king and one quarter to the bishop of Norwich.

Appendix B

Size and Nature of Tenements in Dispute in the Suffolk Eyre of 1240

The land in the 468 pleas where a size is mentioned is shown mostly in acres, 88 per cent, but other measures are also used, all of which have been recalculated into acres for the purpose of this analysis, except for those indicated below. The size of the land in acres for each type of unit of measurement is also shown:

1. In Table 5 below there are two pleas for which, although an amount of land is stated, it is not possible to provide a grouping. In one plea, **1082**, where units of 'rengate' are used for a Norfolk plea, it has not been possible to determine a length or width of a rengate and in the other, **333**, the width and length are shown but the square footage calculated is so small that it is not worth including.[1] Both of these have been included in the pleas showing no area of land in dispute.

2. Roods are mentioned in 30 pleas, 6.5 per cent, and are one quarter of an acre.

3. The carucate in Suffolk is equal to 120 acres in 14 pleas.[2] It is also seen as equal to one hide.

4. The virgate is shown as being equal to 30 acres; that is one quarter of a carucate.[3]

5. There are 9 pleas where a knight's fee or portion of a knight's fee is mentioned as being claimed. Its measurement has not been determined in terms of acreage, as it has not been possible to equate acreage to a knight's fee.[4] There are 4 other pleas

---

[1]   It is only 80 square feet in area, so it is less than 0.002 of an acre.

[2]   In Suffolk it is normally assumed that a carucate is 120 acres. See Maitland 1897, p.483 for his reasons for believing that to be the case in Norfolk and Suffolk. Also, see Douglas 1927, p.50 and Darby 1952, pp.163–164.

[3]   There are three pleas where virgates are mentioned, all foreign pleas: Gloucestershire, Surrey and Cambridgeshire. In **95** the plea contains more than one type of area of land so the virgates are incorporated as a fraction of a carucate. In **389** the amount of land is shown, as one sixth of a knight's fee less 3 virgates of land, and the knight's fee cannot be determined so I have left this amount of land out of the lands in dispute. The virgate is not a measure used in East Anglia, where carucates and acres tend to be used.

[4]   What appears to be common is that a knight was supposed to be maintained by whatever the measure is of a knight's fee. In Suffolk the knight's fee may have been equal to a five hide unit or 600 acres.

Table 5. *Size (in acres) and nature of tenements in dispute by type of action*

60.7 per cent of holdings in dispute, where the size of a tenement is known, are in Group A, that is they are less than or equal to 9 acres of land. A further 24.8 per cent are between >9 and 33 acres inclusive and then a further 11.4 per cent are between >33 acres and one carucate. This leaves 3.0 per cent of land in dispute in tenements over 120 acres. The land in dispute is very often not the only holding that the suing freeholder owns, or is suing for. Even if he is suing for land from one lord, he may hold more land from another lord, or lords.

Action type	Group A < or = 9	%	Group B >9 to 33	%	Group C >33 to 120	%	Group D >120	%	Total A to D	% of pleas with size of land	Pleas with no land shown	Total pleas
Actions of dower	20	47.6	12	28.6	5	11.9	5	11.9	42	9.1	21	63
Actions of entry	36	83.7	5	11.6	2	4.7	0	0.0	43	9.3	26	69
Actions of right	36	40.0	30	33.3	21	23.3	3	3.3	90	19.4	36	126
Actions on limited descents	78	70.9	27	24.5	5	4.5	0	0.0	110	23.8	50	160
Appellate proceedings	0	0.0	0	0.0	0	0.0	0	0.0	0	0.0	11	11
Assizes of darrein presentment	0	0.0	0	0.0	0	0.0	0	0.0	0	0.0	3	3
Assizes of novel disseisin	71	75.5	18	19.1	4	4.3	1	1.1	94	20.3	119	213
Assizes utrum	15	65.2	4	17.4	4	17.4	0	0.0	23	5.0	14	37
Miscellaneous actions	11	42.3	10	38.5	4	15.4	1	3.8	26	5.6	121	147
Personal actions	14	40.0	9	25.7	8	22.9	4	11.4	35	7.6	90	125
Prohibitions to courts Christian	0	0.0	0	0.0	0	0.0	0	0.0	0	0.0	4	4
Total	281	60.7	115	24.8	53	11.4	14	3.0	463	100.0	495	958

where a portion of knights' fees is mentioned but only for service; the land in these 4 pleas are separately identified by one of the other measures above.

Size of tenements in actions

In order to show the frequency of different sizes of holding in the litigation of the civil pleas the pleas have been grouped into the following four bands.[5] The number of pleas where no amount of land is shown is also provided by the various types of action.

A Holding of up to 9 acres.
B Holding of between 10 and 33 acres and all those called either half or one virgate (in Suffolk 30 acres).
C Holding of between 34 acres and up to one carucate (120 acres).
D Holding greater than one carucate.

Tenements in dispute in the main assizes and other pleas

The following graph indicates the number of holdings by the main assizes.

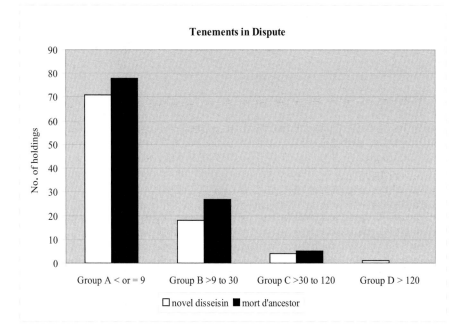

Tenements in Dispute

☐ novel disseisin ■ mort d'ancestor

See Keefe 1983, pp.20–24 for a view on the possible relationships between the size of the land and a knight's fee; also see Warner 1996, pp.144–145. However, as their arguments are not conclusive I have left them out of the calculations below. All but one are Suffolk pleas, the one exception being from Norfolk, **893**.

5 It has been decided to use the same four bands as in *1263 Surrey Eyre*, App. VII, pp.clxi–clxiii. The only difference is that Group C is shown as land up to the Suffolk carucate in area.

The following graph indicates by group size the number of holdings by the main types of action.

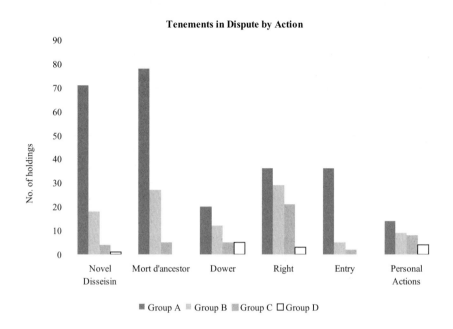

Table 6. Average size of tenements in dispute in the main assizes and other pleas

Action type	Amount of land in plea in acres	Number of pleas in dispute	Number of pleas with land	Average acreage of land for pleas with land	Average acreage of land for all pleas
Actions of dower	1525.575	63	42	36.323	24.215
Actions of entry	310.775	69	43	7.227	4.504
Actions of right	2616.425	126	90	29.071	20.765
Actions on limited descents	1195.800	160	110	10.871	7.474
Appellate proceedings		11	0		
Assizes of darrein presentment		3	0		
Assizes of novel disseisin	1012.825	213	94	10.775	4.755
Assizes utrum	277.400	37	23	12.061	7.497
Miscellaneous actions	1042.700	148	26	40.104	7.045
Personal actions	1805.775	125	35	51.594	14.446
Prohibitions to courts Christian		4	0		
Total	9787.275	959	463	21.139	10.206
Total acreage in Suffolk	945,414				
% of land in dispute in Suffolk	1.035				

Appendix C

Sheriffs of Norfolk and Suffolk during the Reign of Henry III

Date appointed	High sheriff	Knight/ curialis etc.	Deputy	Date appointed
25 June 1215	John Marescallus	Knight, *curialis*		
10 Sept. 1217– April 1227	Hubert de Burgh	Knight, *curialis*	Richard de Fressingfield	29 Sept. 1220
			Richard Wuket	29 Sept. 1221
			Thomas de Ingoldesthorp	29 Sept. 1223
			Thomas de Ingoldesthorp	29 Sept. 1224
			Hugh Ruffus	June 1225
29 April 1227	Herbert de Alencun	Knight, *curialis*		
12 June 1232	Robert de Cokefeld	Knight, *curialis*		
11 July 1232	Peter de Rivall'	Knight, *curialis*		
24 June 1232	Robert de Briws	Knight, *curialis*		
22 May 1234	Thomas de Hemmegrave	Knight, *curialis*		
21 April 1236	Thomas de Ingoldesthorp	Local knight		
7 Dec. 1237	Robert de Briwes *or* le Brus	Local knight		
29 Sept. 1239	John de Ulecote	Local knight		
29 Sept. 1241	Henry de Neketon	Local knight		
4 May 1242	Hamo Passelewe	Local knight		
18 April 1249	Robert le Sauvage	Local knight		
5 Nov. 1255	William de Swyneford	Local knight		
26 Oct. 1258	Hamo Hauteyn	Local knight		
9 Jan. 1260	Hervey de Stanho	Local knight		
9 July 1261	Philip Marmyun	Local knight		
26 Feb. 1262	William de Hecham	Local knight		
8 Oct. 1262	Nicholas de Espigornel	Local knight		
18 Dec. 1263	John de Vallibus	Local knight		
27 June 1264	Hervey de Stanhou	Local knight		
28 Aug. 1265	John de Vallibus	Local knight		
25 Oct. 1265	Nicholas Spigornel	Local knight		
12 Aug. 1266	Roger de Colevill	Local knight		
17 Oct. 1267	Robert de Norton	Local knight		
7 Aug. 1270	William Giffard	Local knight		

Appendix D

Eyres held in Suffolk during the Reign of Henry III[1]

2345

Eyre no.	Eyre dates	Chief judge	Places eyre held in county	Date started	Date completed
1	1218–1222	Geoffrey Buckland	Ipswich	2 May 1219	22 May 1219
			Dunwich	23 May 1219	24 May 1219
			Bury St Edmunds	5 June 1219	22 June 1219
			Thetford	28 June 1219	2 July 1219
2	1226–1229	Martin Pattishall	Ipswich	22 Sept. 1228	13 Oct. 1228
			Dunwich	6 Oct. 1228	10 Oct. 1228
			Cattishall	20 Oct. 1228	29 Oct. 1228
3	1234–1236 and 1238	Robert de Lexington	Ipswich	10 Nov. 1234	20 Nov. 1234
			Cattishall	24 Nov. 1234	14 Dec. 1234
			Cattishall	14 Jan. 1235	14 Jan. 1235
3a[2]	1235	Adam son of William	Thetford	9 Sept. 1235	Unknown
4	1239–1241 and 1242–1244	William of York, provost of Beverley	Ipswich	30 April 1240[3]	15 May 1240[4]
			Cattishall	21 May 1240[5]	31 May 1240
			Cattishall	4 June 1240	4 June 1240
			Dunwich	11 June 1240	11 June 1240

---

[1] For the information in this table see Crook 1982a, pp.75, 83, 90, 101 (this eyre), 106, 116 and 135.

[2] According to Crook 1982a, p.90 there was an extra session to the eyre held by Adam son of William for those people who had fled the eyre but had now returned. An assize session was also held. The eyre roll, JUST1/1173, survives and the entries in the pipe roll for this session are shown separately from those of Robert de Lexington as 'Amercements by Adam the son of William and his allies'.

[3] See Appendix E, which shows that the earliest agreements were made on the quindene of Easter, which would almost certainly have been Monday 30 April 1240. The crown pleas were only started on Sunday 6 May 1240, as shown on the heading of the roll, JUST1/818, on membrane 45, but probably actually started on Monday 7 May 1240. See p.lxxv.

[4] The date entered by Crook is 13 May 1240. See footnote above for the page number, but the more likely date of completion is Tuesday 15 May 1240 as Easter Day was on Sunday 15 April 1240, as the feet of fines is shown as *Pasche in unum mensem*. There are also chirographs from this eyre with this date. See Cheney 1996, p.66 for her arguments on sitting days.

[5] This is shown as *Pasche in quinque septimanas*, which would normally be the Sunday 20 May, but for reasons above it probably started on Monday 21 May.

Eyre no.	Eyre dates	Chief judge	Places eyre held in county	Date started	Date completed
5	1245	Henry of Bath	Ipswich	1 July 1245	1 July 1245
			Cattishall	15 July 1245	22 July 1245
6	1250–1252	Henry of Bath	Ipswich	14 Jan. 1251	3 Feb. 1251
			Cattishall	3 Feb. 1251	9 Feb. 1251
			Cattishall	3 April 1251	1 June 1251
			Great Yarmouth[6]	3 or 10 Feb. 1251	3 or 10 Feb. 1251
7	1252–1258	Gilbert of Preston	Ipswich	18 Nov. 1257	25 Nov. 1257
			Ipswich	14 Jan. 1258	3 Feb. 1258
			Cattishall	25 Nov. 1257	9 Dec. 1257
			Cattishall	14 Jan. 1258	14 Jan. 1258
8	1268–1272	Nicholas Tower	Ipswich	3 Nov. 1268	7 Dec. 1268
			Ipswich	3 May 1269	20 May 1269
			Dunwich	25 Nov. 1268	25 Nov. 1268
			Cattishall	2 June 1269	22 July 1269
			Cattishall	15 Sept. 1269	15 Sept. 1269

Appendix E

Number and Dates of Chirographs made during the Suffolk Eyre of 1240

Date in feet of fine	Actual date	Where made	No. of chirographs
Quindene of Easter	Monday 30 April	Ipswich	9
Easter, plus 3 weeks	Monday 7 May	Ipswich	23
Easter, plus 1 month	Tuesday 15 May	Ipswich	23
Easter, plus 5 weeks	Monday 21 May	Cattishall	6
Morrow of Ascension	Friday 25 May	Cattishall	48
Octave of Ascension	Friday 31 May	Cattishall	2
Morrow of Pentecost	Monday 4 June	Cattishall	13
Morrow of Trinity	Monday 11 June	Dunwich	3
Total			127

---

6 Only essoins were held here although Crook indicates that the justices may also have taken the crown pleas at Great Yarmouth. See Crook 1982a, p.116.

Appendix F
Civil and Foreign Pleas

Appendix F(i) Foreign pleas taken in the Suffolk eyre of 1240

Form of action	Adjournments	Agreed	Not prosecuted	Withdrawn	Judged for plaintiff	Judged for defendant	Void	Total conclusions	Actual total	Total per cent
Actions of dower	9	2			4	1		16	16	11.7
Actions of entry	1	2		1		5		9	9	6.6
Miscellaneous actions, land (unspecified)	3	11					1	16	16	11.7
Actions of right	22	5	1	1	2	1		31	31	22.6
Actions on limited descents (mostly mort d'ancestor)		1	1					2	2	1.5
Appellate proceedings	3	3	1					7	7	5.1
Assizes of darrein presentment	1						1	2	2	1.5
Assizes of novel disseisin	1	3	1	1	2			8	8	5.8
Nuisance			1					1	1	0.7
Assizes utrum	1	1						2	2	1.5
Miscellaneous actions, others	9	3	1			2	2	17	17	12.4
Personal actions	6	11			3	2		22	22	16.1
Prohibitions to courts Christian	3					1		4	4	2.9
Total outcomes	59	42	6	3	11	12	4	137	137	
Total per cent	43	31	4	2	8	9	3			100

Appendix F(ii) Comparison of novel disseisin and mort d'ancestor as a percentage of all pleas for counties shown (excluding foreign pleas)

County and year	% novel disseisin	% mort d'ancestor	Total %
Surrey 1235	29.7	18.4	48.1
Suffolk 1240	24.8	19.2	44
Berkshire 1248	30	15	45
Wiltshire 1249	23	24	47
Shropshire 1256	32.5	17	49.5
Surrey 1263	23	27	50
Derbyshire 1281	16.9	19.1	36
Northamptonshire 1329	17.0	8.0	25

Appendix F(iii) Provenance of foreign pleas

The county already visited by William of York's eyre is shown in italics.

County	Number of pleas	% of total
Bedfordshire	1	0.73
Buckinghamshire	1	0.73
Cambridgeshire	3	2.19
Cornwall	2	1.46
Essex	9	6.57
Gloucestershire	1	0.73
Hampshire	2	1.46
Hertfordshire	3	2.19
Kent	3	2.19
Lincolnshire	1	0.73
Norfolk	*103*	*75.18*
Somerset	1	0.73
Surrey	3	2.19
Sussex	2	1.46
Wiltshire	1	0.73
Worcestershire	1	0.73
Total	137	100.00

Appendix G

Summary of Amercements and Fines in the Suffolk Eyre of 1240 Plea Roll

Civil pleas	Number of items		£	s.	d.
Appeal	2		7	6	8
Attaint	4		6	0	0
Disseisin	55		29	6	8
False claim	74		28	13	4
False declaration	8		2	6	8
False pleading	3		1	6	8
Jury	7		10	0	0
Licence to concord	82		59	6	8
Non-prosecution	121		41	0	0
Not come	22		7	6	8
Nuisance	8		3	16	8
Other	12		5	16	8
Trespass	9		4	0	0
Unjust detention	31		11	6	8
Withdrawal	19		6	13	4
Total from civil pleas	457	*Total issues*	224	6	8
Total from crown pleas	488	*Total issues*	418	14	10
Total from crown and civil amercements and fines in the plea roll	945	*Total issues*	643	1	6

Appendix H

Sheriffs' Payments and Individual Debts arising from the Eyre of 1240

Here is a summary of issues of the Norfolk and Suffolk eyres of 1240 as recorded in the pipe rolls and Exchequer records. It is not possible to separate out the financial records for the counties of Norfolk and Suffolk in the pipe rolls as they are accounted for as one county, although the membrane contains the words 'Norff Suff' at the end of the membrane on the dorse side. I have tried to identify what belongs to Norfolk and to Suffolk as individual amounts come in. See 'Issues of the Suffolk eyre 1240' above, pp.lx–lxii, for the problems encountered and why it is very difficult to differentiate between the two counties.

Appendix H(i) Sheriffs' payments as recorded in pipe rolls

1. Michaelmas 1240 (E372/84, membrane 8d)

Amercements by William of York and his fellows

	£	s.	d.
John de Ulecote, sheriff, from amercements of men, vills, hundreds and tithings	1067	5	8½
From which Jeremy Caxton was paid 30 marks[1]	20	0	0
From which Roger of Thirkelby was paid £20	20	0	0
From which Gilbert of Preston was paid £20	20	0	0
From which Henry of Bath was paid £20	20	0	0
Supplement	2	1	5
Paid into the treasury £989 7s. 1½d.			

2. Michaelmas 1241 (E372/85, membranes 10–10d)

Amercements by William of York and his fellows[2]

	£	s.	d.
John de *Ulecote*, sheriff, from amercements of men, vills, hundreds and tithings	242	1	11
Paid into the treasury £243 6s. 4d.			
From surplus on Norfolk/Suffolk account	1	3	5[3]

---

[1] For expenses approved by the king see *Liberate Rolls*, pp.437, 463, 477 and 487 for the order to the sheriff to pay the four judges their expenses out of the amercements collected from the eyres. It looks as though the sheriff needed a reminder for Henry of Bath as he was originally told about his expenses on p.437 and then was reminded on p.463 on 28 April in the *Liberate Rolls* to pay the money to Henry. The sheriff accounted for all payments to the four junior justices in the pipe roll.

[2] On the membrane there are two headings – the one shown above and 'The above mentioned amercements by William of York'. The sheriff's account shown here is in the latter.

[3] The roll shows this amount but I calculate it as £1 4s. 5d., a difference of 1 shilling.

3. Michaelmas 1242 (E372/86, membranes 10–10d)

	£	s.	d.
1. Henry de *Neketon* and Hamo de *Passelewe*, sheriffs, account for many debts whose names are shown with the letter '.t.' in the roll preceding in the dorse until the title 'List of Debts in *Arcis Cyrographorum* by 22 tallies'	139	1	8

Paid into the treasury. Quit   £139   1s.   8d.

	£	s.	d.
2. Henry de *Neketon* and Hamo de *Passelewe*, sheriffs, from amercements of men, vills, hundreds and tithings	40	16	8

Paid into the treasury. Quit   £40   16s.   8d.

4. Michaelmas 1243 (E372/87, membranes 8–8d)

	£	s.	d.
Hamo de *Passelewe*, sheriff, from debts of many in roll preceding in the dorse by 21 tallies	56	14	10½

Paid into the treasury   £56   14s.   10½d.

5. Michaelmas 1244 (E372/88, membranes 4–4d)

	£	s.	d.
Hamo de *Passelewe*, sheriff, [from debts] shown with letter 't'	2	16	8

Paid into the treasury   £2   16s.   8d.

6. Michaelmas 1245 (E372/89, membranes 2–2d)

	£	s.	d.
Hamo de *Passelewe*, sheriff, [from debts] shown with letter 't'	39	0	10

Paid into the treasury (in 3 payments)   £32   7s.   6d.

Sheriff owes £6 13s. 4d. (shown as 10 marks)

7. Michaelmas 1246 (E372/90, membranes 14–14d)

	£	s.	d.
Hamo de *Passelewe*, sheriff, from amercements of men, vills, hundreds and tithings with letter 't..' and letter 'd..'	2	16	8
Hamo de *Passelewe*, sheriff, from amercements of men with letter 't.' letter 'd.'	2	16	8

Paid into the treasury. Quit   £5   13s.   4d.

8. Total paid into treasury from pipe rolls (1–7 above)

	£	s.	d.
Total paid by sheriff for Norfolk and Suffolk[4]	1,510	4	2

---

[4]   This does not include the £24 paid to the liberty of Ely.

9. See App. H(ii). As recorded in receipt roll of Easter 1240 and 1241 (E401/14)

	£	s.	d.
Total of payments recorded in receipt roll			
Total paid into treasury to Easter 1240 on receipt roll for Norfolk and Suffolk. There is nothing recorded on the receipt roll.	0	0	0

10. See App. H(iii). As recorded as individual debts on pipe rolls

	£	s.	d.
Total of payments recorded as individual debts on pipe rolls			
Total paid into treasury by individuals on pipe rolls E372/84–90	495	6	1½

	£	s.	d.
11. Total of 8–10 above	£2,005	10	3½

Appendix H(ii) Individual debts arising from the Norfolk and Suffolk eyres of 1240: from receipt rolls

There is nothing surviving on the receipt rolls for the period of either the Suffolk or the Norfolk eyre of 1240.

Appendix H(iii) Individual debts arising from the Norfolk and Suffolk eyres of 1240: from the pipe rolls

Name	Civil case (if known)	Reason	F/A[5]	Amount	1st year	Payments
Sheriff, John de Ulecote		year and day, waste	A	40s.	1240	1243, in full
Richard Mauduyt		trespass	F	100s.	1240	1240, in full
William de Sculham		nuisances	F	20 marks	1240	1243, in full
Hugh de Albinaco		trespass	A	£10	1240	1242, in full
H. of Clacklose – Norfolk		murdrum	A	40s.	1240	1242, in full
H. of Clacklose – Norfolk		no coroners	F	30 marks	1240	1240, £17 12s. 8d.; 1241, in full
Nicholas de Stuteville		many injustices	A	40 marks	1240	1240, 10 marks
John de Ulecote, sheriff		year and day, waste	A	18s.	1240	1240, in full
Roger de Cressy		year and day, waste	A	£1 11s. 10d.	1240	1240, in full
City of Norwich		before judgement	A	20 marks	1240	1240, £8 18s. 2d.; 1242, £4 8s. 6d. in full
Abbot of Bury St Edmunds		year and day, waste	A	20 marks	1240	1243, in full
Whole county of Suffolk		before judgement	A	50 marks	1240	1241, in full
Thomas de Hemmegrave'		keeping chattels	A	£6 19s. 8d.	1240	1242, pardoned
Simon Waleran, Philip de Engate and allies		trespass	F	£3	1240	1240, £2 10s. 0d.
John de Hodeboville		concealment	A	100s.	1240	1240, 90s.; 1242, in full
Stephen of Reedham		withdrawal	A	10 marks	1240	1240, 40s.
Peter de Beccles	758	jury and withdrawal	A	15½ marks	1240	1241, 5 marks, 1242, in full
John de St Denis	898	trespass	A	30 marks	1240	1240, £10, 1241, 73s. 4d.

5 F = fine, the amount being entered in the plea roll. A = amercement.

Name	Reason	Civil case (if known)	F/A[5]	Amount	1st year	Payments
John de Fleg	trespass and keeping chattels		A	5 marks, 14s.	1240	1243, in full
Heirs of Robert de Vallibus	two debts	**526**	A	3 marks	1240	1243, in full
Henry de Ver'	debt		A	£29 19s. 0½d.	1240	1240, possibly £10 18s. 0½d.; 1243, in full
Prior of Thetford	loans		F	40 marks	1237	1240, 40 marks, in full
William Talebot	debts		F	£17 15s. 1d.	1237	1243, in full
William Talebot	debts		F	5 casks of wine	1237	1243, in full
Roger le Bigod	loans, scutage		A	£36 3s. 4d.	1240	1240, in full
Whole county of Norfolk except for the liberties	before judgement		F	160 marks	1240	1240, £90 13s. 4d.; 1241, £8 13s. 7d.; 1242, £7 6s. 5d. in full
Hubert de Burgh, Earl of Kent	agreement		F	100s.	1240	1241, in full
Vill of Tilney (Norfolk)	concealment		A	12 marks	1241	1241, 113s. 4d.
Vill of East Walton (Norfolk)	not making suit		A	2 marks	1241	1241, 1 mark
Vill of Wiggenhall (Norfolk)	for harbouring		A	20 marks	1241	1241, £9 11s. 0d.
John de Ulecote, sheriff	keeping chattels		A	61s. 4d.	1241	1241, 1s. 4d.
Henry son of Peter of Heacham and Robert of Sedgeford	concealment		A	½ mark	1241	1241, 40d.
Robert son of Gilbert of Walpole and Osbert son of Henry	concealment		A	½ mark	1241	1241, 40d.
Vill of Sinterlee'	not making suit		A	20s.	1241	1241, 10s.
William son of John	trespass etc.		A	100s.	1241	

Name	Reason	Civil case (if known)	F/A[5]	Amount	1st year	Payments
Ralph le Fol' of Burnham and Thomas son of Walter	non habet		A	½mark	1241	1241, 40d. 1243, in full
Robert son of Richard of Docking and Henry Louerd'	non habet		A	½ mark	1241	1241, 40d.
Ralph son of Orm' in Felthorpe (Norfolk) and Jordan Cliture	non habet		A	½ mark	1241	1241, 40d. 1242, in full
Nicholas of Scratby and Ralph Serich of Filby (Norfolk)	non-attendance		A	½ mark	1241	1241, 40d. 1243, 20d. by Ralph
(Norfolk) Ralph Warinete' of Filby and Ralph son of Alan	non-attendance		A	½ mark	1241	1241, 40d. 1242, in full
Thomas de Hemmegrave	trespass		A	2 marks, 30s.	1241	1241 10s., 1242 pardoned
Ralph Carter and allies	false appeal		A	40s.	1241	1241, 10s.
H. of Tunstead (Norfolk)	murdrum		F	3 marks	1241	1241, 1 mark
John le Gros' and Richard of Westgate (Norfolk)	false claim		A	½ mark	1241	1241, 40d.
Hugh of Antingham, Roger Ruffus' and Roger Bacun'	false claim		A	10s.	1241	1241, ½ mark
Gilbert Burhard of Thetford and his allies	trespass		A	5 marks	1241	1241, 40s. 1244, 1 mark
Raymond Pann'	agreement		F	1 mark	1241	1241, ½ mark, 1242, ½ mark
William de Melewude'	trespass		A	40s.	1241	1241, 20s., 1243, in full
Walter de Leonibus'	agreement		F	1 mark	1241	1241, ½ mark
John Bond de Bedesham' and Thomas dictis [Bond] de Belham' (Norfolk)	non habet		A	½ mark	1241	1241, 40d.

Name	Reason	Civil case (if known)	F/A[5]	Amount	1st year	Payments
Thomas son of Michael de Thirkleshall' and Thomas son of William of Shingham (Norfolk)	non habet		A	½ mark	1241	1241, 40d.
Thomas son of Philip of Thetford	false claim		A	½ mark	1241	1241, 40d.
Nicholas son of William of Repps and Roger Colston of Bastwick	non-prosecution		A	½ mark	1241	1241, 40d.
Alex' Ketill de Stow and William son of Ralph de Posford'	non habet		A	½ mark	1241	1242, 40d.
(Ely) Geoffrey Carbonell, William son of Humphrey son of William of Claydon	trespass		A	40s.	1241	1241, 20s.
H. of Plomesgate	murdrum		A	4 marks	1241	
H. of Carlford	murdrum		A	40s.	1241	1244, 30s.
Ermis of Kettleburgh	?		F	32s.	1241	
H. of Colneis	murdrum		A	40s.	1241	1244, 36s.
H. of Lothingland	having coroner		A	20 marks	1241	1241, £7 16s. 8d. 1242, 4 marks, 1243, in full
William M---', Richard le Rede and Robert le Red'	non-attendance		A	½ mark	1241	1241, in full
Hugh son of Kamille	trespass		A	2 marks	1241	1241, 20s.
Thomas Garneys, John Norman of Elmham	non habet	500	A	½ mark	1241	1241, 40d., 1243, in full
(Ely) Roger of Chilton and Osbert his brother	disseisin	831	A	40s.	1241	1241, 30s. 1242, 5s.
William Sket	appeal	210, 776	F	40s.	1241	1241, 2½ marks, 1242, in full

Name	Reason	Civil case (if known)	F/A[5]	Amount	1st year	Payments
Loretta of Gedding and Winneriis Vis de Lu	agreement	**491**	F	1mark	1241	1241, ½ mark
Gilbert Maunce	agreement	**512**	F	½ marks	1241	1241, 40d., 1244, 20d.
William son of Robert	agreement	**904**	F	1 mark	1241	1241, 5s., 1242, in full
Roger le Bigod	trespass, agreement		A	110 marks	1242	1242, 25 marks 1243, 56 marks
Robert son of Robert of Newton and Peter son of William of Sproughton	withdrawal		A	10s.	1241	1241, 40d.
Roger of Stratton and Roger le Veyse'	trespass		A	10s.	1241	1241, 6s. 8d.
H. of Wilford	murdrum		A	60s.	1242	
Bailiff of Ipswich	trespass		A	40s.	1243	
sheriff for various litigants	disseisin etc.		A	3 marks 10s.	1243	1243, in full
Thomas Tolle	non-prosecution		A	½ mark	1244	1244, 2s. 2d.
Total paid into treasury in this period excluding items pardoned and the casks of wine						£495 6s. 1½d.

Appendix I

Analyses of Types of Persons and Office Holders named in the 1240 Suffolk Eyre Roll

Appendix I(i) Analysis by role in the judicial process

Type of person	Total named individuals
Acts for defendant or plaintiff	4
Attachee	46
Attorney	158
Champion in trial by battle	4
Defendant	1,959
Defendant and surety in the same plea	34
Defendant and voucher to warranty in same plea	33
Essoiner	115
Guardian	6
Juror	407
Knight in view, grand assize, witness	104
Lord of the fief	6
Office holder	125
Person named and seised of property at one time, probably dead	311
Plaintiff	1,368
Plaintiff and defendant in same case	3
Plaintiff and surety in the same case	10
Plaintiff and voucher to warranty	2
Recognitor	45
Saint	42
Suitor with plaintiff or defendant	50
Sureties or pledges	722
Unknown	145
Villein	17
Voucher to warranty	117
Ward	4
Witness	15
Total named individuals in the roll	5,852
Total named individuals excluding king, saints, or dead persons etc.	5,364[1]

---

[1] This total includes two of the guardians that appear to have attended the eyre. Those excluded are the four other guardians, six lords of the fiefs, the 125 office holders, who are accounted for as not attending but mentioned in the text, namely the 311 persons seised of the land in dispute at one time but now probably dead, and finally the forty-two references to named saints. It is assumed that the remaining person types attended at one or more of the locations in the Suffolk eyre. This total includes multiple occurrences of the same individual.

Appendix I(ii) Analysis of those in the roll indicated as holding an office

Office holder	Total named individuals	Office holder	Total named individuals
Abbot	34	Lord	2
Archdeacon	1	Marshall	2
Attorney	151	Master	23
Bailiff	12	Member of the king's wardrobe	1
Bishop	23	Monk	1
Brother in a religious house	4	Parker	4
Butler	3	Parson	41
Chancellor	1	Patron of church or other body	6
Chaplain	16	Priest	2
Clerk	10	Prior	55
Constable	2	Prioress	11
Coroner	2	Rector	2
Dean	8	Reeve	4
Earl	18	Sacristan	2
Elector	2	Seneschal or steward	2
Forest officer	2	Sergeant	8
Judge	11	Sheriff	13
Keeper	2	Vicar	1
King	71	*Total individuals with office*	*943*
Knight	390		

Appendix J

Transcription and Translation of Chirograph CP 25(1) 213/17/108

This is the foot of the chirograph made between the prior of Chipley and Sarah of Hawkedon and others named in the chirograph, but not in the plea, made at Cattishall on Friday 25 May 1240. See **950**. This was chosen as a typical agreement made at the eyre.

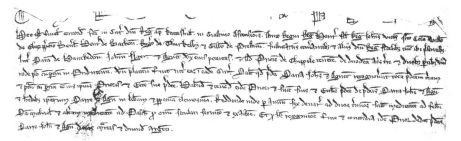

Fig. 2. Chirograph CP 25(1) 213/17/108, reproduced by permission of The National Archives

Transcription

Hec est finalis concordia facta in curia domini Regis apud Katteshill', in Crastino Ascensionis, Anno Regni Regis Henrici filii Regis Johannis vicesimo quarto coram Willelmo de Ebor' preposito Beverl', Henrico de Bathon', Rogero de Thurkelby et Gilberto de Prestun' Justiciariis itinerantibus et aliis domini Regis fidelibus tunc ibi presentibus Inter Saram de Hauckedon, Johannem Ilger et Agnetem uxorem eius petentes, et Adam Priorem de Chippele tenentem, de duodecim acris terre et duobus partibus unius rode prati cum pertinenciis in Pridintun', unde placitum fuit inter eos in eadem curia, Scilicet quod predicti Sarra, Johannes et (Agnetem[s]) recognoverunt totam predictam terram (5)et pratum cum pertinenciis esse ius ipsius Prioris et Ecclesie sue predicte, habendam et tenendam eidem Priori et successoribus suis et ecclesie predicte de predictiis Sarra, Johanne et Agnete et heredibus ipsarum Sarre et Agnetis in liberam et perpetuam elemosinam, Reddendo inde per annum sex denarios ad duos terminos, scilicet medietatem ad festum Sancti Michaelis et alteram medietatem ad Pascham pro omni seculari servitio et exactione. Et pro hac recognitione fine et concordia idem Prior dedit predictis Sarre, Johanni et Agneti duas marcas et dimidiam argenti.

Translation

This is the final agreement made in the court of the lord king at Cattishall on the morrow of the Ascension [Friday 25 May] in the twenty-fourth year of the reign of Henry the son of King John in front of William of York, provost of Beverley, Henry of Bath, Roger of Thirkelby and Gilbert of Preston, itinerant justices, and other faithful men of the lord king then present there between Sarah of Hawkedon, John Ilger and Agnes his wife, plaintiffs, and Adam the prior of Chipley, defendant, concerning twelve acres of land and two parts of one rood of meadow with appurtenances in *Pridinton*, in respect whereof there was a plea between them in the same court, namely that the said Sarah, John and Agnes acknowledged all the aforesaid land and meadow with appurtenances to be the right of the prior and his successors and of his said church, to be had and held by the same prior and his successors and the same church of the said Sarah, John and Agnes and the heirs of Sarah and Agnes in free alms, six pence a year to be paid at two terms, namely half at the feast of St Michael [29 September] and the other half at Easter for all secular service and payment. And for this acknowledgement, fine and agreement the same prior gave to the said Sarah, John and Agnes two and half silver marks.

Appendix K

Samples of Transcription and Translation of Civil Pleas in the 1240 Suffolk Eyre Roll

Line numbers in the membrane are shown in brackets.

1. Assize of Novel Disseisin (*Membrane 5d*). Plea **160**

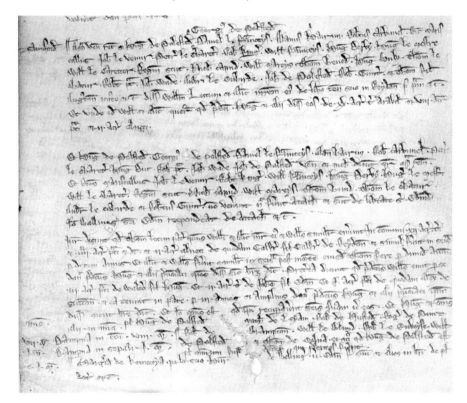

Fig. 3. Plea 160 from the 1240 Suffolk eyre roll, reproduced by permission of The National Archives

Transcription
(*Saunford*) Assisa venit recognitura si Hugo de Polested', Georgius de Polsted', Daniel le Fraunceys, Alanus Hairun, Robertus Carbunel', Ricardus Mariscallus, Johannes le Venur, Petrus le Chareter, Robertus King', Willelmus Fraunceys, Hugo Derby, Hugo le Mestre, Willelmus le Caretter, Reginaldus Scut, Nicholaus Capud, Willelmus Mareys, Thomas Heved', Hugo Buk, Thomas le Chacur, Robertus Prat, Johannes Wade, Aubri le Cuhirde, Johannes de Polested', Robertus Gunter, et Thomas filius (5)Augustini injuste etc [et sine judicio] disseisiverunt Willelmum Lutun et Aliciam matrem eius de libero tenemento suo in Reydon' post primam [transfretacionem domini Henrici Regis in Britannem] etc. Et unde idem Willelmus

et Alicia queruntur quod predicti Hugo et alii disseisiverunt eos de xv acris terre arabilis et viij acris prati et ij acris alneti.

Et Hugo de Polested', Georgius de Polsted', Daniel le Frainceys, Alanus Hairun, Robertus Carbunel', Petrus le Chareter', Hugo Duc', Robertus Prat, Johannes Wade, Johannes de Polsted', veniunt et nichil dicunt quare assisa remaneat. (10)Et Ricardus Mariscallus, Johannes le Venur, Robertus King', Willelmus Frainceys, Hugo Derby, Hugo le Mest', Willelmus le Chareter, Reginaldus Scut, Nicholaus Capud, Willelmus Mareys, Thomas Hund, Thomas le Chacur, Aubr' le Cuhirde et Robertus Gunter non venerunt nec fuerunt attachiati et sunt de libertate Sancti Edmundi. Ideo ballivus Sancti Edmundi respondeat de attachiamento etc.

Juratores dicunt quod Thomas Lotun pater ipsius Willelmi, et Alicia mater eius et Willelmus simul emerunt in communi xij acras terre (15)et iiij^{or} acras prati et dimidiam et ij acras alneti de quodam Galfrido filio Galfridi de Reydon' et simul fuerunt in seisina per decem annos. Et Alicia et Willelmus fuerunt similiter in seisina post mortem eiusdem Thome fere per dimidium annum donec predictus Hugo et alii prenominati ipsos disseisiverunt sicut breve dicit. Preterea dicunt quod predictus Willelmus emit pro se iij acras prati de Waltero filio Hugonis, et ij acras terre de Johanne filio Edmundi et j acram prati de quodam Alexandro de Sutton' et ea tenuit in pace per iij annos et amplius donec predictus Hugo et alii prenominati ipsum (20)disseisiverunt sicut breve dicit. Et ideo consideratum est quod ipsi recuperaverunt seisinam suam versus eos. Et Hugo et omnes alii in misericordia (*misericordie*). Plegii Hugonis de Polsted': Mathias de Leyam, Robertus de Nusted', Rogerus de Punz (Robertus de Brampton', Willelmus le Blund, Robertus le Envoyse, Willelmus de Polsted' et Thomas de Calna. Et sciendum quod Hugo de Polsted' est plegius (25)omnium supra dictorum qui presentes fuerunt.[i]) Dampna: in communi viij marcarum (*viij marce*). Dampna: in separali j marce (*j marca, et j marca*).

Translation

(*Samford*) An assize comes to declare if Hugh of Polstead, George of Polstead, Daniel le Franceys, Alan Heron, Robert Carbunel, Richard Marshall, John le Venur, Peter the carter, Robert King, William Franceys, Hugh Derby, Hugh le Mestre, William Carter, Reynold Scutt, Nicholas Capud, William Mareys, Thomas Heved, Hugh Buck, Thomas le Chace, Robert Prat, John Wade, Aubrey le Cuhirde, John of Polstead, Robert Gunter and Thomas the son of Austin have unjustly disseised William Lutun and Alice his mother of their free tenement in Raydon after the first [crossing of the king into Brittany] and in respect whereof William and Alice complain that the said Hugh and the others disseised them of fifteen acres of arable land, eight acres of meadow, and two acres of alder grove.

Hugh of Polstead, George of Polstead, Daniel le Franceys, Alan Heron, Robert Carbunel, Peter Carter, Hugh Buck, Robert Prat, John Wade, John of Polstead come and say nothing to stay the assize. Richard Marshall, John le Venur, Robert King, William Franceys, Hugh Derby, Hugh le Mestre, William Carter, Reynold Scutt, Nicholas Capud, William Mareys, Thomas Heved, Thomas le Chace, Aubrey le Cuhirde and Robert Gunter have not come nor were they attached and they are of the liberty of Bury St Edmunds. Therefore let the bailiff of Bury St Edmunds answer concerning the attachment etc.

The jurors say that Thomas Lotun, the father of William, and his mother Alice and William together bought in common twelve acres of land and four and a half acres of meadow and two acres of alder grove from a certain Geoffrey the son of Geoffrey of Raydon and they were in seisin together throughout ten years. Alice and

William were similarly in seisin, after the death of the said Thomas, for nearly half a year until the said Hugh and all those named before disseised them as the writ says. Meanwhile, they [the Jurors] say that the said William bought for himself three acres of meadow from Walter the son of Hugh and two acres of land from John the son of Edmund and one acre of meadow from a certain Alexander of Sutton and he held it in peace for three years and more until the said Hugh and the others named before disseised him as the writ says. So it is adjudged that they have recovered their seisin against them. Hugh and all the others are in mercy (*amercements*). Sureties of Hugh of Polstead: Matthew of Layham, Robert de Nusted, Roger de Punz, Robert of Brampton, William le Blund, Robert le Envoyse, William of Polstead, and Thomas de Calne. Note: that Hugh of Polsted is the surety for all of the said [defendants] above who were present.

Damages: in common 8 marks (*eight marks*).
Damages: separately 1 mark (*one mark, and one mark*).

2. Assize of Mort d'Ancestor (*Membrane 3*). Plea **94**

Fig. 4. Plea 94 from the 1240 Suffolk eyre roll, reproduced by permission of The National Archives

Transcription

(*Hertesmere'*) Assisa venit recognitura si Walterus pater Radulfi fuit seisitus in dominico suo etc [ut de feodo] de novem acris terre et dimidia et una acra prati cum pertinenciis in Thorendon' die quo obiit et si [obiit post ultimum redditum domini Johannis Regis patris nostri de Hibernia in Angliam], et si [ipse] Radulfus [propinquior heres eius est] quam terram et quod pratum Robertus Passelewe et Petrus filius Walteri tenent. Qui veniunt, et Robertus dicit quod nichil inde tenet set Petrus totum tenet etc. Walterus non potest hoc dedicere. Ideo Robertus inde sine die et Walterus in misericordia. Et Petrus dicit quod assisa non debet (5)inde fieri quia fratres sunt et de uno patre et una matre. Et preterea dicit quod alias implacitavit eum in curia de Eye per breve de recto. Et ideo consideratum est quod assisa non fiat inter eos et sit in misericordia et perquirat sibi per breve de recto si etc. Misericordia perdonatur pro paupertate.

Translation

(*Hartismere*) An assize came to declare if Walter the father of Ralph was seized in his demesne [as of fee] of nine and a half acres of land and one acre of meadow with appurtenances in Thorndon on the day he died, and if [he died after the last return of the lord king John, our father, from Ireland into England], and if Ralph [is the nearest heir], which land and that meadow Robert Passelewe and Peter the son of Walter holds. They come, and Robert says that he holds nothing in respect thereof but Peter holds all and Walter is not able to deny this. So Robert [is] to go without day and Walter [is] in mercy. Peter says that the assize should not be taken on this because they are brothers of one father and one mother. Moreover, he said that he impleaded him at another time in the court of Eye by a writ of right. So it is adjudged that the assize is not to be taken between them and he is in mercy and may proceed [against] him by a writ of right, if [he wishes]. The amercement is pardoned for poverty.

3. Exaction of Services (*Membrane 43d*). Plea **1118**

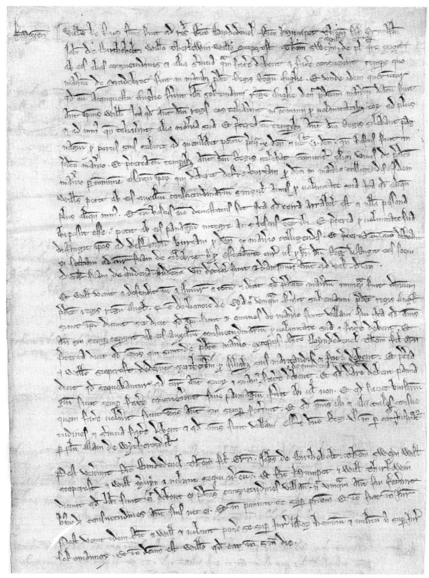

Fig. 5. *Plea 1118 from the 1240 Suffolk eyre roll, reproduced by permission of The National Archives*

Transcription

(*Hoxene*) Willelmus le Rus summonitus fuit ad respondendum Ricardo Bindedevel, Ricardo Hunipot, Thome filio Ernulphi', Johanni de Bircheholt, Willelmo Therlewin, Willelmo Stopcroft, Thome Sweyn [et] (Willelmo Mervyn[i]) de placito quare exigit ab eis alias consuetudines et alia servicia quam facere debent et facere consueverunt tempore quo manerium de Stradebroc fuit in manibus predecessorum Regis regum Anglie. Et unde idem queruntur (5)quod cum a conquestu Anglie fuerunt liberi sokemanni regum Anglie donec predictum manerium datum fuit antecessoribus ipsius Willelmi, ita quod antecessores domini Regis eos taliaverunt in communi pro voluntatibus eorum ad plus et ad minus quando taliaverunt alia maneria sua. Et preterea cum temporibus antecessorum domini Regis solebant pagnagium [solvere] pro porcis suis, scilicet ad quemlibet porcum precii x denariorum et ultra j denarium quando boscus fuit in predicto manerio. Et preterea cum temporibus antecessorum domini Regis solebat communiter eligi unus de predicto (10)manerio per communem assensum ipsorum qui deberet deferre bursam pro denariis in manerio colligendis, idem Willelmus petit ab eis auxilium consuetudinarium singulis annis pro voluntate sua ita quod aliquando plus aliquando minus, et cum boscus (omnino[il]) devastatus sit, ita quod terra arrabilis est et nulla pessona ibi possit esse petit ab eis (panagum[s, e]) integre ac si boscus esset ibi. Et preterea pro voluntate sua distringit ipsos ad deferendum bursam pro denariis in manerio colligendis. Et preterea cum non debeant (15)ei sectam ad curiam suam de Stradebroc nisi pro efforciamento curie vel pro brevi domini Regis distringit eos sequi ad curiam suam de quindena in quindenam unde deteriorati sunt et dampnum habent ad valenciam d. marcarum.

Et Willelmus venit et defendit vim et injuriam et totum et dicit quod predictum manerium numquam fuit dominicum predecessorum Regis Regum Anglie, quia est de honore de Eya nec umquam fuerunt sokemanni predecessorum Regis Anglie sicut ipsi dicunt, set dicit quod ipsi sicut et (omines[s]) de manerio sunt villani sui, ita quod omnes (20)antecessores sui semper ceperunt ab eis auxilium consuetudinarium pro voluntate sua et facere debent. Et preterea dicit quod omnes qui sunt de predicto manerio, exceptis Ricardo Byndedevel, Thoma filio Ernulfi et Willelmo Stopcroft, dederunt merchetam pro filiabus suis maritandis et facere debent. Et preterea dicit quod sequebantur ad curiam antecessorum suorum et suam (et[i]) facere debent (de quindena in quindenam[i]), et quod dare debent pannagium sicut semper facere consueverunt sive pannagium fuerit ibi vel non, et quod faciet bursarium (25)quem facere voluerit sicut omnes antecessores sui semper fecerunt, et quod omnes isti et alii tales consuetudines et servicia facere debent et quod omnes sunt villani, offert domino Regi v[que] marcas per sic (quod[i]) inquiratur per plegium Alani de Wytheresdal'.

Post venerunt Ricardus Bindedevel, Thomas filius Ernulfi, Johannes de Bircheholt, Thomas Sweyn, Willelmus Stopcroft et Willelmus Mervyn et nolunt sequi versus eum. Et Ricardus Hunipot et Willelmus Thirlewin (30)dicunt quod liberi sunt nec debent ei predictas consuetudines villanas, nec umquam antecessores sui fecerunt huiusmodi consuetudines antecessoribus suis nec ei. Et inde ponunt se super patriam. Et ideo fiat inde jurata.

Post (venit[s]) idem Ricardus et Willelmus et nolunt ponere se super juratam liberorum hominum et militum nisi super juratam sokemannorum. Et ideo dictum est Willelmo quod eat inde sine die.

Translation

(*Hoxne*) William le Rus was summoned to answer to Richard Bindedevel', Richard Hunipot, Thomas the son of Ernulf, John de Bircheholt, William Therlewin, William Stopcroft, Thomas Sweyn and (William Mervyn[i]) concerning a plea why he exacts from them customs and other services other than those which they should do and have become accustomed to do in the time when manor of Stradbroke was in the hands of the predecessors of the king, the kings of England. The same claim in respect whereof that from the conquest of England they were free sokemen of the kings of England, until the said manor was given to the ancestors of William, so that the ancestors of the lord king taxed them in common at their will, for more or for less when they have taxed their other manors. Moreover, in the time of the ancestors of the lord king they were accustomed [to pay] the pannage for their pigs, namely for each pig a price of ten pence and a further one penny when there was wood in the said manor. Moreover, in the time of the ancestors of the lord king it was a common custom to choose one from the said manor, by their common assent, who would carry the purse for the money collected in the manor. Despite all of this, the same William claims from them customary aid for each year at his will so that sometimes it is more, some time less, and though the wood is entirely devastated so that the land is arable and no pig food is able to exist there, he claims from them the pannage in full as if the wood was there. Moreover, at his will he distrains them for carrying the purse for the money collected in the manor. Moreover, though they do not owe suit to him at his court of Stradbroke except for afforcement of court, or for a writ of the lord king, he distrains them to pay suit at his court from quindene to quindene, in respect whereof they have suffered and have damage to the value of five hundred marks.

William comes and he denies force and injury and everything and he says that the said manor never was the demesne of the predecessors of the king, the kings of England, because it is of the honour of Eye, nor were they ever the sokemen of the predecessors of the king of England as they say, but he says that they and everybody from the manor are his villeins, so that all his ancestors always took from them customary aid at their will, and rightly so. Moreover, he says that all who are from the said manor, excepting Richard Bindedevel, Thomas the son of Ernulf and William Stopcroft, gave merchet, for their daughters to marry, and rightly so. Moreover, he says that they were paying suit at his ancestors' (and[i]) his court, and rightly so (from quindene to quindene[i]), and that they should give pannage as they have always been accustomed to do, whether the pannage was there or not, and that he will appoint as purse carrier whoever he wishes, as all of his ancestors have always done, and that they ought to do all of these and other such customs and services, and that they are all villeins, he offers to the lord king five marks on condition (that[i]) it is inquired into, on the surety of Alan of Withersdale.

After, Richard Bindedevel, Thomas the son of Ernulf, John de Bircheholt, Thomas Sweyn William Stopcroft and William Mervyn have come and they do not wish to proceed against him. Richard Hunipot and William Therlewin say that they are free [men], nor do they owe to him the villein customs, nor have any of their ancestors done customs of this kind to his ancestors or to him, and then they put themselves on the country. So let there be a jury thereon.

After, the same Richard and William come and they do not wish to put themselves on a jury of free men and knights, but on a jury of the sokemen. So it is said to William that he is to go without day on this.

NOTES ON THE TEXT, TRANSLATION AND
EDITORIAL METHOD

Text

The roll is divided into separate items by the clerks and these were usually specifically identified with a form of paragraph mark at the beginning of each item. The closest symbol identifiable to this mark is ¶. The items can also be identified by the gap placed between them and often by separate marginal annotation, often the name of a hundred or county. In my text the items have been serially numbered in **bold** type and where the number is referred to in the introduction, or I have used it in a footnote, it is also shown in **bold**.

The enrolled items in the text of the civil pleas on the plea roll have been numbered successively from **1** to **1160**. The amercements of the civil pleas and the final concords follow the crown plea amercements and they are numbered from **1642** to **1659** and **1666**.[1] The enrolled records of money due for final concords are numbered from **1660** to **1664**.[2] The civil plea amercements and final concords have been divided into blocks of twenty items and each block given a number. I have chosen to start with a new number at the beginning of a new side of a membrane; therefore there may occasionally be fewer than twenty items if there is a smaller group at the end of a side of a membrane. This method of numbering has been chosen for the amercements for the purposes of ease of indexation in accordance with the customary practice developed by Harding.[3]

All abbreviations in the manuscript except 'etc' and some terminations of proper names have been extended without special indication in the translated text. Suspension marks at the ends of surnames and place names are uniformly shown thus: Battesford', Buk'.

The manuscript's use of capitals and punctuation has not been followed, but has been standardised to modern English convention throughout to make the reading clearer in accordance with the normal practice in editions of eyre rolls. An unfinished entry is indicated by '... [unfinished]'.

Irregularities in the manuscript are put between round brackets and indicated as follows:

    (*abc*)   word or words in the margin. The clerk in an eyre roll normally places marginalia alongside the place in the plea where the content of the marginalia is mentioned in the text. The marginalia are shown in the translated text, within brackets and in italics, at the end of the sentence

---

[1]   This number is for the amercements for Dunwich, which follow the final concords of the civil pleas.

[2]   There are some amercements included in these items and there are some agreements included in the amercement items **1642–1659**, but these are limited. See p.xxv, Table 2, which identifies the number of items by the various types of plea and n.110 above, which indicates the plea numbers of the crown pleas.

[3]   See *1256 Shropshire Eyre*, pp.310–341.

in the text to which the marginalia refers. Marginations whose content is not identified in the text are shown within brackets, italicised and placed at the beginning of the translated text. There are also marginations near the start of an entry where the clerk has indicated the hundred or county, to which the case belongs, or an amount of money offered for an agreement or chirograph. I have placed these at the beginning of the text and translation within brackets and in italics. I believe that this method gets closer to what the clerk's methods were than the conventions adopted by other editors to date.[4] All damages noted in the margin, or partly in the margin, are shown separately in the text after the sentence to which they occur. They are not italicised.

(abc^c) word or words deleted, or cancelled by being crossed through by the clerk,

(abc^e) word or words erased; i.e. scraped off the surface of the manuscript but some still visible,

(abc^i) word or words interlined,[5]

(abc^r) word or words repeated in error; e.g. 'attornatus attornatus' in MS is shown as (attornatus^r) to indicate the mistake made,

(abc^s) word inappropriate or unusual in form; e.g. should be plural form when singular or eccentric spelling,

(abc^{il}) indicates illegible words, and words supplied from the context.

There are occasions when one or more of the above apply in which case the appropriate superscripts are shown as in the following example: (abc$^{e, i}$) indicates the word was erased and interlined.

Words in square brackets [abc] have been supplied to clarify the sense.

Words in **bold** type are headings in the manuscript and they are not numbered.

The method of rendering numbers used by the clerk has been followed, using 'j' for single minims and final minims, for example, 'xij'.

Other comments on the text, for example regarding marks in the text, change of hand or unusual layouts are supplied in footnotes where they apply.

---

4   Clanchy in *1248 Berkshire Eyre*, p.cxx indicates that the words in the margin of his roll are placed at the beginning of the text, italicised and in brackets, wherever in the margin they occur. It is therefore not always possible to identify quickly to what the marginal note in the text refers; nor does it indicate the position in the margin where the marginal note occurs. It is odd that Clanchy adopted a different approach when dealing with the crown pleas in that he used the method of italicising the words in the text to show they were also marginated text. He only put marginated text at the beginning of the crown plea if he could not find the appropriate word or words in the actual text.

Harding adopted a different approach. Words or phrases in the text which are repeated as marginations are italicised in both his Latin transcription and translation. There are no separate identifiable marginations as in Clanchy and also in the roll except if there were any marginations whose words were not contained in the body of the text. In this case he placed them at the beginning of the plea in a similar manner to Clanchy. See *1256 Shropshire Eyre*, p.lix for his methodology.

Editions of eyres where only an English version is provided have adopted a similar method to Harding except, for the marginalia whose words are not contained in the body of the text, they have placed the marginalia in the translated text in italics and in brackets in a place in the text where it was reasonable to place them in the context of the plea. See *1249 Wilts Crown Pleas*, p.151; *1249 Wilts Civil Pleas*, pp.30–31; and *1281 Derbyshire Eyre*, p.lxvii.

5   The clerk often uses interlined abbreviated text to indicate a number, e.g. iiij^{to} for quarto. The 'to' has been rendered as superscripted text as here. Other numbers are often interlined with abbreviated text and they have been similarly rendered as superscripted text.

Translation

The English version keeps closely to the Latin, including the translation of many of the repetitive words (*predictus*, *inde*, *unde*, *idem*) where they would add to the understanding of the plea.

Marginated words are given in italics in round brackets in a similar method to that indicated for the transcription above.

Etc is often used by the clerks where common form legal phrases have been omitted. I have supplied them in full within square brackets on the first occasion when they occur but not subsequently. For example in plea **94** (above, p.xciii), the first mort d'ancestor plea, the text is shown as follows: *Assisa venit recognitura si Walterus pater Radulfi fuit seisitus in dominico suo etc [ut de feodo] de novem acris terre et dimidia et una acra prati cum pertinenciis in Thorendon' die quo obiit etc. Et si etc [obiit post ultimum reditum domini Johannis Regis patris nostri de Hibernia in Angliam], et si [ipse] Radulfus [propinquior heres eius sit] etc.*

Communia pasture is rendered 'common pasture' rather than 'common of pasture'.

Place names have usually been given their modern form. Where they cannot be identified the Latin version has been repeated in italics. An apostrophe at the end of the Latin place name indicates that there is a suspension ending that cannot be determined. Place names that are indicated in the text but which are not found in the hundred shown in the margin, or if no hundred is mentioned in the margin, are identified where possible in a footnote on the first time the place is encountered, but not afterwards.

Latin names (Christian and surnames) are rendered by standard forms and have been translated where possible. Forenames have been modernised, with some personal preferences used, such as 'Matilda' (not 'Maud'). Where a second name is occupational, it has been translated where possible, otherwise the Latin form has been kept. For other surnames, if there is an obvious translation it is used, e.g. 'Nicholaus Crawe' becomes 'Nicholas Crowe'.[6] Otherwise, they are left in standard-ised medieval form, for example the surname 'Aguillon' is used in the translation whatever Latin variation of this surname is written by the clerk.[7] If no standardised medieval form can be found then the Latin form is kept in the translation. Where a second name is indicative of an identifiable place it has been translated, e.g. 'of Stradbroke'; where the second name cannot be reliably identified as a place the Latin *de* followed by the Latin place name is used, e.g. Roger de Brautton' in **28**. The only exception to this is where a Latin name has entered into the historical record, e.g. 'Thomas de Hemmegrave' instead of 'Thomas of Hengrave'. The use of *de* is also kept for those names of French origin, e.g. 'de Beauchamp'. Other well known family names have been given their historical or modern equivalents: Beauchamp for *Bello Campo*, Beaumont for *Bello Monte* etc. The main variations in spelling of a second name or of a place in the manuscript are shown in the index of people and places and cross referenced. All identified places and toponymic surnames are indexed under their modern forms. All other surnames are indexed under the form found in the translation.

Jur has been extended to *Juratus* and translated as 'Sworn'.

---

6 See Reaney 1997, p.118.
7 This person's name appears in a variety of forms in the text, for which see the index under 'Aguillon' which is the name that Meekings uses for this surname in the *1235 Surrey Eyre* iii.

Sums of money have been translated from the Latin in the form they are shown in the Latin, e.g. *xiv denarios* is shown as 'fourteen pence', not 1s. 2d. Note: 12 pence (old pennies) = 1 shilling; 20 shillings = one pound (£1); one mark = 13 shillings and 4 pence; half a mark = 6 shillings and 8 pence.

The samples in Appendix K above show the transcribed text with the corresponding translation and a copy of the membrane on which it appears. The pleas are selected to illustrate the various types of plea found in the roll and the formulaic nature of the text.

The lists of amercements and final concords have been translated. Where possible they are cross referenced to the number in the main text. The amounts and type of money indicated in an amercement or final concord have been translated as shown in the text, e.g. *di'm'* is shown as 'half a mark' and subsequently shown alongside in £ s. d. for clarity. Christian names have been modernised but not surnames to highlight differences between the amercement and the text.

CIVIL PLEAS OF
THE SUFFOLK EYRE OF 1240

(The National Archives, JUST1/818)

ESSOINS TAKEN AT IPSWICH ON THE QUINDENE OF EASTER[1] IN THE COUNTY OF SUFFOLK IN THE TWENTY-FOURTH YEAR IN THE REIGN OF KING HENRY THE SON OF KING JOHN BEFORE WILLIAM OF YORK AND HIS FELLOWS.

[1] Sunday 29 April. This agrees with Crook 1982a, p.101 as the start date of the eyre at Ipswich. However, it is possible that they met on Monday 30 April if Cheney 1996 is accurate about not sitting on a Sunday except in an emergency.

1. The abbot of Bury St Edmunds against Richard de Grey and Lucy his wife concerning a plea of land by William the son of Adam in five weeks from Easter day by the surety of Peter de *Bruniford'* at Cattishall.[1] [*chirograph* CP 25(1) 213/16/78]

[1] See **79** for another essoin by this trio but by a different essoiner and the plaintiff and defendants are to appear at a different time.

2. (*It is a new essoin, by pone*) (David of Laxfield against Roger of Hawstead concerning a plea of land by[c]) Thurstan de *Mentemore* (in five weeks[c]) from Easter day (at Cattishall[c]).

3. (*It is an old essoin, by pone*) (The prioress of Thetford against the same concerning a plea of land by John the son of Alexander[c]) to the same term.

4. (*Norfolk*) Hamon Chevere, plaintiff, against Ernald de Mounteney and Peter de Mounteny concerning a plea of land by William the son of Adam of Southwood at the assize in one month from Easter day [Tuesday 15 May]. He pledged his faith.

5. (*It is a new essoin, others are in the writ*) Henry de Colville against Hawise of Hopton concerning a plea of land by Daniel of Barnwell in one month from Easter day.

6. (*It is an old essoin*) Alice the wife of John Blench against Robert the son of Reynold de Bonevito concerning a plea of land, whereupon a grand assize by William the son of Robert in one month from Easter day at Ipswich. He pledged his faith.

7. (*It is a new essoin*) Margery de Bluville[1] against Roger of Shotford concerning a plea of land whereupon a grand assize by Halex[2] of Heckingham in one month from Easter day. He pledged his faith. [**533**]

[1] Margery in **533** is shown with the name *Bleville* rather than *Bluville*.
[2] His first name might be Alexander.

8. (*It is a new essoin, by pone, others are in the writ*) John the son of Robert of Mendham against Gilbert of Mendham concerning a plea of land by Thomas the son of Walter in one month from Easter day. He pledged his faith.

9. (*It is a new essoin*) Henry of Caldecott against Master Robert de L'Isle concerning a plea of land by Henry the son of Henry in one month from Easter day. He pledged his faith.

[1] See the essoin in **75** where Henry indicates that he is sick in bed and **908** for the conclusion of the plea.

10. (*Norfolk, It is an old essoin*) Ralph le Blund whom Robert vouched to warranty against Hugh de Vere the earl of Oxford, concerning a plea of land by Walter the son of Richard in five weeks after Easter at Cattishall. He pledged his faith. The same day is given to Ralph whom Robert vouched in the Bench.

¹ *vetus est* indicates this is an old case possibly raised at the Norfolk eyre, which preceded this county and postponed to Suffolk. It is also possible that it is from the previous eyre at Suffolk or Norfolk in 1234.

11. (*Norfolk, it is an old essoin from the eyre, by the lord Robert de Lexington*¹) James Lenveise who vouched John Lenveyse to warranty against Ralph, the parson of Kirstead, concerning a plea of land whether it is free alms by William Page in five weeks after Easter at Cattishall. He pledged his faith. The same day is given to John le Cuner whom James le Enveyge vouched to warranty against him. [**802**]

¹ Robert de Lexington was the chief judge on the Norfolk eyre of 1234. It is probably a leftover from this eyre.

12. (*It is a new essoin*) Humphrey of Naughton¹ against William Thalebot concerning a plea of naifty in one month from Easter day. [**483**]

¹ Whatfield-cum-Naughton are in Cosford hundred.

13. Thomas of Moulton,¹ the son, against Geoffrey de Say and Alina his wife concerning a plea of dower by John the son of Robert.

¹ This might be Moulton [St Michael] in Depwade hundred in Norfolk or Moulton in Risbridge hundred as these are the nearest Moultons to Hoxne hundred. However, if he is the son of the judge Thomas of Moulton then it might also be the Moulton in Lincolnshire. See **526** where this Thomas is shown as the son of Thomas of Moulton, not 'the younger' as the Latin indicates.

14. Matilda the wife of the same Thomas against the same and for the same plea by Clement the son of Gilbert in five weeks after Easter at Cattishall.

15. (The abbot of Battle against Adam the Flemingᶜ) concerning a plea of land by [the assize of] utrum by William the son of John on a day in one month from Easter day.

16. Beatrice Brunman against William of Ramsholt on a plea of naifty by Baldwin Tyrel.

17. Henry de Cotinton against William de Alencon on a plea of mort d' ancestor by William son of Henry.
Robert de Cotinton concerning the same against the same by William Underwood in one month from Easter day.

18. The prior of the Hospital of St John of Jerusalem in England versus Robert de Aula Arsa concerning a plea of rent by Maurice de Gondingh'.

19. (*It is a new essoin, others are in the writ*) William de Acr' has a wife Alice against Margery who was the wife of Henry de Kemesek concerning a plea -------¹ by William of Chadacre in one month from Easter day. He pledged his faith. The same day is given to Alice.

¹ The plea is missing and there is a space for it to be inserted in the roll.

20. The abbot of Bury St Edmunds against Peter de Grenville and Isabella of Saxham concerning a plea of land by Walter the son of William. [**1067**]

21.¹ (*It is a new essoin*) John of Freston against Master Ralph de L'Isle concerning a plea of land² by Henry of Freston in one month from Easter day. He pledged his faith.

1   See **914** where there is a further essoin by John of Freston after the visit of four knights.
2   It is smudged on the membrane, but it appears to be *terre*.

22. (*It is a new essoin, by pone, others are in the writ*) William of Newton against Richard of Newton concerning a plea of land by William de Botonhal in one month from Easter day. He pledged his faith.

23. (*Cambridgeshire*) Ralph of Soham against Stephen Turpin concerning a plea of *de fine facto* by Richard Hampton in five weeks after Easter at Cattishall. He pledged his faith. [**816**]

24. (*[It is a] new essoin*) Ralph le Bigod against Walter of Shipmeadow concerning a plea of fishery by John the son of Stephen on a day in one month after Easter. The same Ralph against William the Master of Mettingham[1] concerning a plea of fishery by John of Newport in one month from Easter day. The same Ralph against Hugh the son of Ralph concerning a plea of fishery by Henry de Rodes. [*chirograph* CP 25(1) 213/17/90[2] and CP 25(1) 213/17/89[3] and CP 25(1) 213/16/71[4]]

1   It is unlikely that William was a Master at Mettingham College, supposedly founded in 1382, unless there was a previous college in Mettingham. See *VCH Suffolk* ii, pp.144–145 for Mettingham College. However, he might just be Master William of Mettingham, that is he has gone through the schools and become a Master. Normally the clerk writes the title *magister* before the name unlike in this case when it comes after the Christian name.
2   This chirograph was made at Canterbury. It relates to Walter of Shipmeadow and Ralph Bigot.
3   This agreement with Hugh the son of Ralph was also made at Canterbury on the octave of St Michael.
4   This is the agreement between William of Mettingham and others and Ralph Bigot.

25. Ralph le Bigod against Walter Hart concerning a plea of fishery by William the son of Gilbert in one month from Easter day.

26. (*It is a new essoin*) Simon Peche against Geoffrey de Say and Alina his wife and Mabel the sister of Alice by Ralph the son of Roger in five weeks after Easter at Cattishall. [**475** and **727**]

27. Henry the son of Wuner against Richard of Hopton concerning a plea of mort d'ancestor by Alan the son of Wuner. [**324**]

28. Idonea (she has a husband Ralph[i]), the wife of Ralph de Colville against Stephen of Stratton and Anna his wife concerning a plea of dower by Roger de Brautton in one month from Easter day. [**634**]

29. William Auten against Ralph de Blund concerning a plea of the assize of mort d'ancestor by John the son of Henry etc in one month from [Easter] day.

Membrane 1d

30. Hugh de Albanico earl of Arundel against Roger de Mortimer concerning a plea of land by Richard Pic'. [**755**]

31. (*No ----*[il]) The prior of Ely against Walter de Hadford concerning a plea of land by Roger of Newton.
    The same prior against the abbot of Bury St Edmunds concerning an unjust seizure of livestock by Geoffrey of Bath.
    The same abbot against the same concerning the same [plea] by Roger the son of Ralph.

32. (*It is a new essoin*) Thomas Balaunc against Richard of Cransford concerning a plea of land by Richard the son of Thomas in one month from Easter day. [**474**]

33. (*Norfolk*) Thomas of Whimpwell against Godfrey de Miliers concerning a plea of land by Richard the son of Richard. [**694, 937, 1029**]

34. (*It is a new essoin, by pone*) Agatha of Happisburgh against the same concerning the same [plea of land] by John of Happisburgh on a day in five weeks after Easter at Cattishall. [See **33**]

35. Roger Bennet against the same concerning the same [plea of land] by Geoffrey of Hingham. [See **33**]

36. Peter the son of Andrew against the same concerning the same [plea of land] by Roger Gigg. [See **33**]

37. (*Suffolk, it is an old essoin from the eyre*) Thomas de Lascelles against Idonea de Beche concerning a plea of land by Elias of Hornes on a day five weeks after Easter at Cattishall. [**255**]

38. (*Norfolk*) William of Kerdiston against Roger of Kerdiston concerning a plea of warranty of charter by William de Grene. [**402**]

39. (----*il* [1], *It is a fresh summons*) Ralph Guyun, the attorney of Thomas de Lascelles, against Idonea de Beche concerning a plea of land by John Pannel on a day five weeks after Easter at Cattishall. [**255**]

   [1]   The left hand side of the membrane is eaten away at this point.

40. The abbot of Bury St Edmunds against the bishop of Rochester concerning a plea of *de fine facto* by Richard of Tivetshall. [**745** and **1117**]

41. The same bishop against the same concerning the same by Thomas of Freckenham.

42. The abbot of Bury St Edmunds against Matthew de Luvaynes[1] concerning a plea of replevin by Thomas the son of Stephen. [**656**]

   [1]   This might be Louvain in France. See Reaney 1997, p.286.

43. The same abbot against the bishop of Ely concerning a plea of liberties by Robert the son of Geoffrey.

44. Alexander the parson of Fressingfield against Matilda of Fressingfield and Robert the son of Hubert concerning a plea of land by utrum, by William of Clopton. [**411**]

45. Robert of Shelfhanger the attorney of Eudo the clerk against Walter the son of Gilbert of Shelfhanger concerning a plea of land by John the son of Robert.

46. Matilda the wife of Ralph de *Trelly* against Hugh Burch and Margery his wife concerning a plea of measure of dower by Hubert of Bedingham in one month from Easter day. [**462**]

47. The same Margery against the same Matilda concerning the same [plea] by William Vissop (to the same term[i])[1].

   [1]   This phrase is shown on the membrane as common to **47**, **48** and **49** by means of lines drawn to these items.

48. The same Matilda against Simon Bolt concerning a plea of land by Hugh the son of Simon [to the same term].

49. The same Matilda against Hugelina who was the wife of Richard de Vel by Adam Hareward [to the same term].

50. Thomas Russel against Richard Picot concerning a plea of land by Thomas the son of Ranulf. [**530**, **615** and **1051**]

51. (*Gloucestershire*) Ralph of Wilton against the bishop of Worcester concerning a plea of land by Robert le Sauvage.

52. (*Norfolk, Trial by Battle*) Roger de Quessy against William de Stuteville concerning a plea of land, whereupon a judicial combat, by John the son of Hugh on the quindene of the Saints Philip and James [Tuesday 1 May] by the surety of Roger of Boyland. [**460**]

53. (*Gloucester*) John the Monk attorney to the abbot of Bruern[1] against Walter the bishop of Worcester concerning a plea of land by Thomas of Newmarket.

   [1]   This is Bruern Abbey, a Cistercian house in Oxfordshire founded in 1147.

54. Philip de Crunihal attorney of Walter the chamberlain and Mabel his wife against the same concerning the same [plea] by William the son of Henry.
   William the son of David attorney against the same concerning the same [plea] by Hugh of Yate.

55. (*Norfolk*) William Mauclerc against Geoffrey de Say and Alina his wife concerning a plea of land by Robert the son of William in five weeks after Easter.

56. Hugh de Augeville against Ivo of Stockton concerning a plea of an assize of mort d'ancestor by Angod de Squireton.

57. Gilbert the son of Thomas against Walter of Sibton concerning a plea of covenant by Adam the son of Hugh.

58. (*Wiltshire*) Waleran of Blunsdon against Master Richard de la Wyke concerning a plea (to keep the fine[i])[1] by Ralph the son of Walter on a day five weeks after Easter [21 May] at Cattishall.

   [1]   There is a writ crossed out here in the text, which is *quare impedit*. This is a writ used if darrein presentment was not possible. See Pollock and Maitland ii, 1968, p.139. The Latin translates as 'of why he prevents'.

59. Gilbert of Birchleys[1] against Benedict the son of Alwin and Christine his wife concerning a plea of an assize of mort d'ancestor by William de Benham. [*chirograph* CP 25(1) 213/16/70.[2]]

   [1]   Birchleys, Essex, now just a small group of houses and possibly a farm etc.
   [2]   This is the correct chirograph even though the tenant is shown as 'Gilbert of Belstead' and the land in question is in 'Great Belstead' in Samford hundred.

60. (*Norfolk*) Robert Russel of Wiggenhall against Walter the archbishop of York[1] concerning a plea of custody by Richard the son of (----[ii]) on a day five weeks after Easter at Cattishall.

   [1]   This is Walter de Grey, archbishop from 1215 to 1255.

61. Richard of Akethorpe against Stephen of Akethorp and John his brother concerning a plea of land by Henry the son of William in one month from Easter day.

62. The prior of Thetford against Hugh le Franceys[1] is concerning a plea of warranty[1] by Bartholomew of Diss.

   [1]   This could be translated as Francis, or 'the Frenchman'. See Reaney 1997, p.176.
   [2]   This is warranty of charter.

63. Thomas Stute[1] against Geoffrey de Say and Alina his wife concerning a plea of land by Walter the son of Richard. [See **727**, notes 1 and 4.]

   [1]   This could be the name Stout according to Reaney 1997, p.430.

64. Richard the English against Baldwin le Rus[1] concerning a plea of land by Richard the son of William.

   [1]   This is possibly the name Rous. See Reaney 1997, p.384.

65. The prior of Broomholm[1] against Ralph the dean of Westerfield concerning a plea of land by John of Mendlesham.

   [1]   This was a Cluniac house in Norfolk. Its motherhouse was Cluny itself. See also **892**.

Membrane 2

THE ESSOINS TAKEN ON THE QUINDENE OF EASTER CONTINUED

66. (*It is a new essoin*) Gerard de Oldingeshole against William de Oldingesole, the prior of Hertford, William the son of Peter of Fenstead, Gilbert Golding, Gilbert le Newman [and] Gilbert the Miller[1] concerning a plea of land by William Quopin in one month from Easter day.

   [1]   See **748**.

67. William de Oldingesole against the same concerning the same [plea] by Elias Fader'.

68. (*It is a new essoin*) The same Gerard [de Oldingesole] against Adam of Bedingfield, Henry of Hastings, Robert Mauduyt and Margery his wife concerning a plea of customs and services by Robert the son of Walter, in one month from Easter day. [**976**]

69. The same Gerard against Nicholas de *Sanford* concerning a plea of trespass by William de Parcun. [**886**]

ESSOINS OF SICKNESS PREVENTING TRAVEL AT IPSWICH ON THE NEXT WEDNESDAY AFTER THE QUINDENE OF EASTER [Wednesday 2 May].

70. (*Norfolk, Trial by Battle*) Warren de Montchensy against Brian the son of Alan concerning a plea of land, in respect whereof a trial by battle by Geoffrey Crowe on the nearest Monday before the Ascension [21 May] at Cattishall by the surety of Roger of Boyland. [**702**, **797**]

ESSOINS OF SICKNESS PREVENTING TRAVEL AT IPSWICH IN THREE WEEKS AFTER EASTER [Sunday 6 May].

71. (*Norfolk*) William the prior of Walsingham against William Dacun concerning a plea of prohibition[1] by Bartholomew of Walsingham.

   [1]   That is a plea of prohibition to Court Christian.

72. (*Norfolk*) Emma of Hockham against Adam of Rockland[1] concerning a plea of ward by Adam Guatte. [**931**]

> 1   There are four possibilities in Norfolk: Rockland All Saints and St Andrew in Shropham hundred, Rockland St Mary in Henstead hundred, and Rockland St Peter in Wayland hundred.

73. (*Surrey*) William de Waterville against Roger de Bavent and Sarah his wife concerning a plea of land by Robert of Sampford.

74. (*Essex*) Henry de Merk against Matthew of Peyton and Rose his wife concerning a plea of dower by Richard the son of Richard. [**752**]

ESSOINS OF BED-SICKNESS AT IPSWICH IN ONE MONTH FROM EASTER DAY.

75. (*By pone, on the morrow*) Henry of Caldecott at Wheatacre in the county of Norfolk against Master Robert de L'Isle concerning a plea of land by Stephen of Loudham and Eustace of Stoke on the morrow of the Ascension of the Lord [25 May] at Cattishall. [**908**]

76. John of Freston at Freston in the county of Suffolk against the same and concerning the same [plea] by William of Felsham and Richard of Herringfleet, on the morrow of the Ascension of the Lord at Ipswich.[1]

> 1   That is Friday 25 May. By this time the eyre had moved to Cattishall. However, see **914** where John of Freston is shown as being too ill to attend, which is probably the reason why this case cannot be found in the roll.

ESSOINS OF SICKNESS PREVENTING TRAVEL AT IPSWICH IN ONE MONTH FROM EASTER DAY.

77.[1] (*Surrey, it is a new essoin, by pone*) William de Waterville against Roger de Bavent and Sarah his wife concerning a plea of land by Robert of Sampford (in octave of Holy Trinity[r]) [Sunday 17 June] at Chelmsford.[2]

> 1   See **73**. This appears to be a repeat of the essoin. See **404** for the appointment of an attorney.
> 2   This is in different handwriting as though it was added later, perhaps when the clerks knew that they would be in Chelmsford in the octave of Holy Trinity.

ESSOINS OF SICKNESS PREVENTING TRAVEL AT IPSWICH ON THE NEAREST THURSDAY BEFORE THE ASCENSION OF OUR LORD.[1]

> 1   Ascension was on Thursday 24 May, which suggests this was the Thursday prior to Ascension, that is 17 May when the court was not sitting at all but was probably on its way to Cattishall.

78. (*Essex*) Alice the wife of Stephen of Langdon against Nicholas de Beauchamp concerning a plea of land by Laurence of Plumberow at the arrival of the justices at Chelmsford. He pledged his faith. The same day is given to Stephen the husband of Alice.

ESSOINS OF BED-SICKNESS AT [IPSWICH] ON A DAY FIVE WEEKS AFTER EASTER.[1]

> 1   Sunday 20 May 1240. Crook 1982a, p.101, indicates that the eyre was at Cattishall from Monday 21 May. Note that there were also some essoins at Cattishall on this date. Could the judges have split up and one or more arrived at Cattishall later than the rest?

79. (*Suffolk*) The abbot of Bury St Edmunds at Chevington against Richard de Gray and Lucy his wife concerning a plea of land by Roger the son of Ralph and Warren de Wadeshill.[1] If not etc. [*chirograph* CP 25(1) 213/16/78][2]

¹ There is a Wadgell's Hall, Wood and Farm near Great and Little Thurlow in Risbridge hundred. There is a Wade Hall near Leiston in Blything hundred. However, the former is the most likely, for which see **826**.

² See **1**, another essoin by the same trio of plaintiff and defendants. However the agreement does not appear to be in this roll although the chirograph indicates that an agreement was made at the time shown at the heading for this essoin, that is 5 weeks after Easter. The chirograph indicates that an agreement was made at Cattishall with the abbot of Ramsey present as a justice. Crook 1982a, p.100 indicates that he did not appear at Cattishall, although it has to be said that this is the only chirograph I can find with his name on from Cattishall. This suggests the clerks may have made a mistake, or the abbot was called away from Cattishall almost at the start of the proceedings. The land in question in the agreement indicates it is in Mildenhall in Lackford hundred not Risbridge hundred where Wadgell is located.

80. (*Kent*) The keeper of the priory Church of Christ at Canterbury against Burga who was the wife of Peter of Benden concerning a plea of dower by Hamo of Chartham, in the octave of the Holy Trinity at Chelmsford. He pledged his faith.

81. (*Norfolk*) Walter de Evermue against William of Reedham concerning a plea of land, whereof a trial by battle, by William Syfteby in the octave of the Trinity at Chelmesford. He pledged his faith. William appoints as his attorney Robert of Stokesby or William (Gr----^{il}).

82. (*Surrey*) Walter de Frewyc against Burga who was the wife of Peter of Benden ...¹

¹ It finishes here with no further information, but see **80**.

Membrane 2d

ESSOINS OF SICKNESS PREVENTING TRAVEL AT THE SAME TERM.

83. (*-rff*^{'il})¹ Robert Blund, against Hugh the earl of Oxford concerning a plea of land by William the son of Adam in the octave of the Trinity at Chelmsford, pledged his faith. The same day is given to Ralph [le] Blund whom the said Robert vouched to warranty. Note: that they are both now essoined.

¹ This is probably *Norfolk* as this essoin is exactly the same as **654**.

Membrane 3

84. (*Essex*) Giles de Argentan appoints as his attorney William the palmer against Hugh de Heddeng and his co-parceners concerning a plea of land etc. [**255**]

85. Margery his wife appoints as her attorney Richard de Coveneye against the same concerning the same [plea] etc. [**255**]

86. Thomas of Poynings appoints as his attorney Hugh Burhard against the same concerning the same [plea]. [**255**]

87. Ela his wife appoints as her attorney Adam of Poynings against the same concerning the same [plea] etc. [**255**]

88. Anna the wife of Thomas of Sutton appoints as her attorney Gerard of Sproughton or Gilbert of Sutton against Agnes of Cretingham concerning a plea of covenant etc and against Ralph de Colville and others named in two writs concerning a plea of dower etc.

89. The prioress of Redlingfield[1] appoints as her attorney William of Redlingfield against Matilda Bacon concerning a plea of the assize of mort d' ancestor.

> [1] Redlingfield was a house of Benedictine nuns in Hartismere hundred.

90. The abbot of St Osyth[1] appoints as his attorney Geoffrey Clement or Richard the clerk or Richard of Tuddenham.

> [1] A house of Augustinian canons in Essex.

91. (*Essex*) The agreement between John de Neville on the one part and Henry of Necton[1] on the other [part] as regards the manor of *Tuddenham*,[2] namely: that John demised the said manor to Henry with a wood of the manor (which is called *Sudhow*[i]),[3] and the other appurtenances until the end of three years. Namely, on condition that the same John would be able to request from the lord king (within five weeks after Easter[i]) that the same Henry would be able to sell the said wood and to do what he wanted with it within the said term, then the agreement made between them is to remain [in force] according to the purport of their chirograph. If not however, the same Henry will render an account with the said John concerning those issues, which in the meanwhile he will take from the said manor and has taken thus far, and similarly concerning the costs[4] that he has paid. As a result hereupon it satisfies both of them.

> [1] Henry of Necton is probably the same person who was the sheriff of Norfolk and Suffolk 1241–1242 and who also was the warden of Orford and Norwich castles. The family also had land in Great Barford in Thedwestry hundred in Necton Hall.
> [2] There is a Tuddenham in Carlford and Lackford hundreds and also a Tuddenham in Mitford hundred in Norfolk but none as far as I can find in Essex.
> [3] I can find no wood called this near either of the Tuddenhams in Suffolk.
> [4] This is the cost of getting him to pay his money or money to be paid by him for not doing so.

92. (*Essex, Suffolk*) Roger of Essex appoints as his attorney either John de Heddeng, Roger de Essewell[1] or Warren Grapinel against Sara the daughter of Margery de *Pridington* and others named in the writ concerning a plea of land and against the prior of Chipley.

> [1] This might be Eriswell in Lackford hundred.

93. (*Suffolk*) Hugh de Hendeng appoints as his attorney John de Heddeng against Idonea de Beche concerning a plea of land etc. [**255**]

94.[1] (*Hartismere*) An assize came to declare if Walter the father of Ralph was seized in his demesne etc [as of fee] of nine and a half acres of land and one acre of meadow with appurtenances in Thorndon on the day he died, and if [he died after the last return of the lord King John, our father, from Ireland into England],[2] and if Ralph [is the nearest heir], which land and that meadow Robert Passelewe and Peter the son of Walter holds. They come, and Robert says that he holds nothing in respect thereof but Peter holds all and Walter is not able to deny this. So Robert [is] to go without day and Walter [is] in mercy. Peter says that the assize should not be taken on this because they are brothers of one father and one mother. Moreover, he said that he impleaded him at another time in the court of Eye by a writ of right. So it is adjudged that the assize is not to be taken between them and he is in mercy and may proceed [against] him by a writ of right, if [he wishes] etc. The amercement is pardoned for poverty.

    1   See Appendix K for a full transcription and translation.
    2   This was in 1210 as determined in the Statute of Merton in 1236, four years prior to this eyre. See *EHD* III, pp.351–354. See *1249 Wilts Civil Pleas*, p.30 for the full text of the formula for a plea of mort d'ancestor.

95. (*Gloucestershire*)[1] W[alter] the bishop of Worcester by his attorney claims against Olympias, who was the wife of Richard of Willington, two and a half carucates of land with appurtenances in Yate, and against Simon de Belvr' one virgate of land with appurtenances in Alvington, and against Andrew de Aqua one virgate of land with appurtenances in the same vill as the right of his church of Worcester etc.

    Olympias and the others come and claim a view. They are to have it. A day is given to them at Chelmsford on the octave of the Holy Trinity and meanwhile etc. Simon and Andrew appoint Hugh of Yate as their attorney.

    1   This may have been a left over from a previous eyre or the bench.

96. Matthew de Luveyn and Muriel his wife appoint as their attorney Ralph of Norton or Ralph de Manville against Adam de Hulino concerning a plea of land and against Geoffrey of Badley concerning a plea of warranty of charter etc.

97. (*Buckinghamshire*) Walter of Morton, Reynold the baker, Richard of Barton, Walter Durendeyc, Robert the son of Peter of Morton and Nicholas le Sumenter[1] of Morton presented themselves on the fourth day against Peter de Molendino and John his brother as regards the peace of the lord king having been broken, whereupon they appealed them etc. Peter and John have not come and they were the plaintiffs. The same Walter and the others then appealed without day. Peter and John are to be taken [into custody] and their sureties [are] in mercy (*amercements*). Let the names of the sureties be sought in the writs of the Michaelmas term in the twenty-fourth year.[2]

    1   A sumpter was the driver of a packhorse.
    2   24 Henry III, that is 1240.

98. (*Surrey*) A day is given to Richard of Clare and Alice his sister, Robert of Walton, William de la Garston, Odo of Crowhurst, plaintiffs and Roger of Clare and Alice his wife concerning a plea of warranty of charter at the arrival of the justices in the county of Surrey.[1] Note: that the said Alice, wife of the said Roger,

12

readily grants that all the defendants may hold in peace all their tenements and that those tenements according to the contents of their charter are to be the subject of a chirograph. Roger appoints as his attorney Roger the son of Roger of Leybourne, and Robert of Walton and Odo of Crowhurst appoint as their attorney William de la Grafton.

1   According to Crook 1982a, p.102 the justices sat in Surrey in May 1241, so they had a long time to wait to sort out the chirograph.

99. The lord king has commanded by his writ to the eyre justices in the county of Suffolk that the plea, which was placed before them in their aforesaid eyre, between Matilda de Iarpenville, the plaintiff, and Adam of Wiggenhall, whom the bishop of Carlisle[1] vouched to warranty, or whoever else had afterwards been vouched to warranty concerning the deforcing of the reasonable dower of Matilda in Garboldisham should be adjourned until the arrival of the justices at the first assize in the county of Essex. Note: that a day is given to them at Chelmsford in the county of Essex[2] in the octave of the Holy Trinity[3] [17 July] etc.

1   The clerk wrote *Carol' Episcopus* which stands for *Caroliensis Episcopus*, that is 'bishop of Carlisle', but see **154** where the clerk uses *Karoliensis*.
2   No plea roll is extant.
3   According to Crook 1982a, p.101 this was the first day of the eyre in Essex.

100. (*Sussex*) Lucy the wife of Robert de Senges appoints as her attorney Thomas de Senges against Walter Bulrich concerning a plea of the assize of mort d'ancestor.

101. Ralph the merchant appoints as his attorney Geoffrey of Wetherden against Robert Clenchemere and Matilda his wife and Sarah Clenchemere concerning a plea of land etc. [**129** and **1119**]

102. Isolda of Hastings appoints as her attorney William de Wendlesworth against Roger of Hastings and others in the writ concerning a plea of dower etc.

103. Alexander de Vallibus appoints as his attorney Richard of Bungay against Geoffrey de Say' and Alina his wife concerning a plea of dower etc.

104. Richard of Freston appoints as his attorney William of Brantham against Simon the son of Robert concerning a plea of land etc.

105. The lord king has commanded the justices by his writ that Richard de Revers has appointed as his attorneys Walter of Merton, Walter of Rudham and Adam Payn to gain or lose in the plea which is between the said Richard and Godfrey, the parson of the church of Landepar-',[1] that the same Godfrey draws the parishioners of the said church of Kenwyn into the court Christian against the [king's] prohibition etc. [**125**]

1   This place cannot be found. In **125** it is shown as *Landegeith*, but this cannot be found either.

106. The plea between Matilda of Lothingland and Agnes her sister, the plaintiffs, and Richard de L'Isle, the defendant, concerning forty acres of land in Gorleston, is stayed without day because Richard has died etc.

107. (*Norfolk, one mark*) Jordan Bunewastel gives one mark for licence to agree with William Wyat concerning a plea of land by the surety of Stephen of Brockdish and Richard Beard. [*chirograph* CP 25(1) 156/66/808]

108. Geoffrey de Say and Alina his wife appoint as their attorney Roger Hovel against Alexander de Vallibus and other named in the writ concerning a plea of dower. Alina removed Geoffrey her husband whom previously[1] etc.

[1] Probably acted as her previous attorney.

109. (*Cambridgeshire*) A day is given to the abbot of Sawtry, the plaintiff, through his attorney and Lesuine of Lynn through his attorney, concerning a plea of taking his chirograph as regards the plea of one messuage at the arrival of the justices in the county of Cambridgeshire.[1]

[1] This case is being adjourned to Cambridgeshire, which according to Crook 1982a, p.101 started in Cambridge on 30 September 1240 and was completed on 20 October 1240.

110. Hawise, the wife of Henry Wymer, appoints as her attorney Henry her husband against Richard of Hopton and Avel' his wife and others concerning a plea of mort d'ancestor. [**324**]

111. James of Playford appoints as his attorney Ernulf of Playford against Alan of Witnesham concerning a plea of warranty of charter.

112. Amabil the wife of Richard le Noreys appoints as her attorney her husband Richard against William Beche concerning a plea of warranty of charter etc.

113. John the chaplain of Hickling appoints as his attorney John the clerk of Rishangles concerning a plea of land etc.

Membrane 3d

114. (*Somerset*) W[alter] the bishop of Worcester presented himself by his attorney on the fourth day against Robert de Gurney, who essoined in the county of Gloucester concerning a plea of land on the grounds of bed sickness.
Robert has not come etc nor have the knights who made a view of him, namely: James de Bayeux, William of Thorney, William of Easton,[1] and Jordan le Warre. So they are attached to be before the eyre justices at Chelmsford in the county of Essex in the octave of the Holy Trinity to bear witness to etc. (*Chelmsford*). The same day is given to the abbot of St Augustine's at Bristol who vouches to warranty the said Robert concerning a certain mill pertaining to that land etc.

[1] There is an Easton in Somerset to the east of Westbury, but there is also an Easton, now Easton Bavents, in Blything hundred. It added Bavents in the time of Edward I. As it is a Somerset plea I suspect it is the former.

115. (*Norfolk, half mark*) Ernald de Munteny gives a half mark for licence to agree with Stephen of Brockdish concerning a plea of land (of two acres with appurtenances in Burston[i]) by the surety of Roger of Boyland. The agreement is such that Ernald hands over the said land with appurtenances to the said Stephen, and Stephen gives to the same Ernald twenty shillings.

116. The abbot of Sibton[1] appoints as his attorney his monk Friar Walter or Laurence of Blythburgh against Alice who was the wife ... [unfinished]

[1] Sibton Abbey was a Cistercian house founded by William de Cheney c.1150. Traces of it still stand.

117. Alice the wife of Thomas of Worlingham appoints as her attorney her husband Thomas against Hugh Slaywricte concerning a plea of assize of mort d'ancestor.

118. The prior of Blythburgh[1] appoints as his attorney Laurence of Blythburgh against William la Pes concerning a plea of land.

  [1]   A priory of Augustinian canons founded in 1135.

119. (*Hartismere*) Robert the son of John who brought an assize of novel disseisin against Roger the chaplain and others for a tenement in Finningham has not prosecuted. So he and his sureties for prosecuting [are] in mercy, namely: William Navel of Sutton and Walter the constable of Mendlesham. The sureties for Roger's amercement [are]: Richard of Barnham and Roger the chaplain of Finningham.[1]

  [1]   This is probably a mistake by the clerk as it should be the sureties for Robert's amercement, not Roger, who are in trouble as the assize was not prosecuted by Robert.

120. (*half a mark*) The abbot of Battle gives half a mark for licence to agree with Adam the Fleming concerning a plea to investigate whether etc by the surety of the same Adam. [*chirograph* CP 25(1) 213/17/85]

121. Master Thomas of Wymondham, who brought an assize of novel disseisin against Godfrey de Miliers concerning common pasture in Wymondham, comes and seeks licence to withdraw from his writ and he has it and Godfrey [is] then without day etc.

122. (*two and a half marks*) William Garnoyse gives two and a half marks for licence to agree with John of Stradbroke concerning a plea of land by the surety of Alexander of Chippenhall and Hubert of Horham. [*chirograph* CP 25(1) 213/16/69]

123. (*two and a half marks*) John of Stradbroke gives two and a half marks for licence to agree with the same William concerning the same by the surety of Adam of Bedingfield and Geoffrey of Barham. [*chirograph* CP 25(1) 213/16/69]

124. (*Hartismere*) An assize comes to declare if Hubert of Eye the father of Thomas was seised in his demesne etc of two roods of meadow with appurtenances in Eye on the day he died etc and if etc which meadow Geoffrey the vicar of Eye holds. He comes and by licence he returns [it] to him. So he is to have his seisin. The amercement is pardoned by the lord Jeremiah.[1]

  [1]   This might be Jeremy Caxton, the justice, who did not sit in Suffolk. He left the circuit after the Norfolk eyre.

125. (*Cornwall*) Richard de Redvers presented himself by his attorney on the fourth day against Godfrey the parson of *Landegeith*[1] concerning a plea why the same [Godfrey][2] draws into the plea in Court Christian the parishioners of the church of Kenwyn and *Trenery*[3] against [the king's prohibition]. The sheriff has sent word that the same Godfrey has no lay fee by which he can be distrained. So the bishop of Exeter is ordered to make him come to Chelmsford on the octave of Holy Trinity [Sunday 17 June] (*Chelmsford*). **[105]**

  [1]   This place cannot be located in Cornwall. In **105** it is shown as *Landpar--*. Obviously Godfrey is the same person mentioned in **105**.
  [2]   I have assumed that Godfrey is the correct name and that *Galfridus* for 'Geoffrey' written by the clerk was a mistake.
  [3]   This place is obviously in Cornwall but I cannot locate it. It is possibly part of Truro as Kenwyn is near Truro.

126. (*half mark, Mutford'*) Robert de Boys of Carlton gives a half mark for licence to agree with Roger the son of Thomas by surety of the same Roger. [*chirograph* CP 25(1) 213/15/28]

127. (*half mark*) Henry the son of William gives half a mark for licence to agree with the same Roger concerning a plea of land by the surety of Robert de Bosco. [*chirograph* CP 25(1) 213/15/33]

128. Master Robert of Coddenham appoints as his attorney Hugh de Arderne or William of Felsham concerning a plea of the assize of novel disseisin against the prior of the Hospital of St John of Jerusalem in England[1] and others named in the writ etc.

    [1]   Probably the Hospital of St John of Jerusalem in England at Ipswich.

129. Sarah [Clenchemere] of Wetherden and Matilda wife[1] of [Robert Clenchemere[2]] appoint as their attorney Robert Clenchemere against Richard the merchant concerning a plea of land etc. [**101** and **1119**]

    [1]   The clerk actually wrote *uxor eius*, that is, that Matilda was the wife of Sarah – unlikely!
    [2]   In the plea **1119**, Matilda is shown as the wife of Robert Clenchmere and *Sarr de Wetheresdon* is shown as Sarah Clenchmere in **101** and **1119**. The clerk may have made a few mistakes here. One possibility is that Sarah was indeed called Clenchemere and perhaps she came from Wetherden, so the clerk in one item called her one name and in the other plea called her by the other name. I have assumed that the plea information is more likely to be correct. The plaintiff is shown in **101** and **1019** as Ralph the merchant.

130. Ivetta the wife of Adam of Cretingham, Beatrice the wife of Herbert Welaund, Christine the [aunt][1] and Matilda the daughter of Stephen de Wynesham appoint as their attorney Adam, the husband of Ivetta, against William the son of Rainer concerning a plea of mort d'ancestor. [*chirograph* CP 25(1) 213/16/79][2]

    [1]   The clerk actually wrote *avunculus*, uncle.
    [2]   There is no follow up in the roll of this mort d'ancestor plea, only this chirograph indicating the agreement. It looks as though William won. The chirograph also indicates that it is indeed Christine the aunt and not Christian the uncle who is involved.

131. (*Norfolk*) A day is given to Richard de Gray, plaintiff, by his attorney and the prior of Weybourne,[1] defendant, concerning a plea of right[2] on a day five weeks after Easter at Cattishall by prayer of the parties. The prior appoints as his attorney Roger the clerk against the same Richard and similarly against Thomas Aldaring concerning a plea of naifty.[3]

    [1]   Weybourne, Norfolk, a priory of Augustinian canons.
    [2]   Plea **489**, between a Richard de Grey and the prior of Weybourne, is a plea of common pasture.
    [3]   This is a plea of personal freedom. See **332** for the naifty plea detail, although the plea **332** looks more like a plea of customs and services by means of a plea of right.

132. William the son of Martin appoints as his attorney Roger of Culford or Roger de Hill against Godfrey de Phalesh' concerning a plea of novel disseisin.

133. Simon of Sutton appoints as his attorney William of Henham against John of Easton concerning a plea of land etc.

134. Warren the falconer appoints as his attorney Robert the son of Warren against the earl Roger Bigod concerning a plea of replevin.

135. (*Norfolk*) Roger of Dickelburgh and Matilda his wife presented themselves on the fourth day against Nicholas Crowe concerning the sureties for a jury of twenty-four to attaint the twelve. Nicholas has not come [but] was seen in the court and was the plaintiff. So it is adjudged that Roger and Matilda [are] then without day and Nicholas and his sureties for prosecuting [are] in mercy, namely Geoffrey and Richard of Gooderstone (*amercements*).

136. (*Southampton*) Eva de Clinton presented herself on the fourth day against Stephen the sacristan of St Mary in Southampton [and] Robert the dean of Southampton why they held the plea concerning a plea [demanding] why they have prosecuted in Court Christian concerning chattels. Stephen and Robert have not come and they had a day by their essoiners at Norwich on this day. So the sheriff is ordered that he produce Stephen in court with better sureties, that he is at Cattishall on a day five weeks after Easter[1] and to show why he has not kept the day given to him by his essoiner. The sheriff has sent word on this day that Robert the dean has no lay fee by which he can be distrained. So the archdeacon of Winchester is ordered to have him [before the court] on this day (*Winchester*).

  [1] Monday 21 May because Easter Day was on 15 April that year.

137. Parnel the wife of Louis de Gerardville appoints as her attorney Martin the son of Gater against William Spendeluve and others in the writ concerning a plea of dower. [**649**]

138. Roger de Marisco and Macelina his wife, Robert the miller and Margery his wife, Mariota of Alton, Richard the son of William and Leinna his mother, [and] Matilda the daughter of Richard of Alton appoint as their attorney William the son of John against Richard Grant concerning a plea of land etc.

139. Matilda of Newton appoints as her attorney her husband Nicholas de Alneto against Richard of Newton concerning a plea of land etc.

140. (*one mark*) The abbot of Bury St Edmunds gives one mark for licence to agree with Theobald of Leiston concerning a plea of land etc. [*chirograph* CP 25(1) 213/16/49][1]

  [1] Note in this chirograph written at Ipswich that Ranulf the abbot of Ramsey is absent from the list of justices. Crook 1982a, p.100 indicates that the abbot was only present at the Ipswich pleas.

141. (*one mark*) Theobald of Leiston gives one mark for licence to agree with the same abbot concerning the same [land] by the surety of Philip of Freston etc. [*chirograph* CP 25(1) 213/16/49]

142. (*two marks*) The prior of Ely gives two marks for licence to agree with Walter of Hatfield concerning a plea of land by surety of Matthew Christian. They are to have a day to levy their chirograph at Cattishall (*Cattishall*). [*chirograph* CP 25(1) 213/17/93][1]

  [1] There is no mention of Matilda, Walter's wife, in this plea but there is in the chirograph. See **705** where the prior appoints his attorney at Cattishall in this plea, where Matilda is mentioned. However there is no mention of the chirograph to be made at the pleas below at Cattishall.

143. William the parson of Dennington appoints as his attorney Geoffrey of Badingham against William Gosewold concerning a plea of land etc.

Membrane 4[1]

  [1] There is a fault in the parchment in the first plea, which the clerk has written around.

144. (*Norfolk*) Andrew of Hingham, Roger de Muystroyl, William of Hingham and Jordan of Shelton four knights, [summoned to choose twelve jurors] etc to make a recognition of the grand assize between William the Earl Warenne,[1] demandant, and John of [Horsham] St Faith, the tenant, concerning thirty-three acres of land and one messuage with appurtenances in Edingthorp, whether John has the greater right of holding the land and messuage from the said earl, or the same earl of holding it in demesne, have come and chosen these: Roger of Calthorpe, Brian of Hickling, Stephen of Stoke, John de Curton, Sampson Talebot, Richard of Whitwell,[2] William de Ages, Geoffrey of Snoring, Rayner of Burgh, Reynold le Gros, Richard the butler of Rougham, William Luvel of Barton, Hubert Hacon, William de Senges, Hugh de Dunedal and Richard de Curton.[3]

A day is given at Cattishall on a day five weeks after Easter (*Cattishall*).

[1] I can find no indication that William the Earl Warenne had any interest in Edingthorpe.
[2] This could either be Whitwell in Eynsford hundred in Norfolk or the Whitwell in Rutland. I assume the former.
[3] Note this makes fourteen jurors not twelve. The court kept two in abeyance in case two did not turn up. There is a 10 cm gap between this part of the plea and the final sentence.

145. Matthew of Peyton, Richard Mauduyt, Adam of Eleigh and Adam of Mendham, four knights summoned to make a recognition of the grand assize between Roger of Shotford, demandant, and Alan of Withersdale, tenant, concerning one mill and two carucates of land with appurtenances, except for fifty-five acres in Weybread and the advowson of the church of Weybread, as to which of them has the greater right in the said mill etc have come and chosen these, namely: Ralph of Cookley, John the son of Robert of Ubbeston, Thomas le Latimer, Osbert of Bawdsey, William de Alneto, Robert de Emeseye, Walter of Hatfield, John of Brantham, Giles of Wattisham, John de Hodeboville,[1] William the son of Robert of Reydon, William of Stratford, Robert de Wykes, John de Crammaville.[2]

Later they have agreed and Alan of Withersdale gives five marks for licence to agree by the surety of Herbert de Alicon,[3] and Robert de Bosco[4] (*5 marks*).

A day is given to them on the next Monday after the [feast of the] Invention of the Holy Cross at Ipswich [Monday 7 May]. [*chirograph* CP 25(1) 213/16/47] [See **147**]

[1] *Hodebovill* is in Acton in Babergh hundred according to the *Book of Fees* (vol. III), p.104.
[2] There is a gap of about 2 cm at this point in the membrane.
[3] This is probably Herbert de Alencon an ex-sheriff. Herbert de Alencon (or Herbert de Alicon as shown here) is the highest scoring witness for Roger Bigod III's surviving charters, scoring 6 out of 10. See Morris 2005, p.69. He was for a time sheriff of Norfolk and Suffolk in 1227–1232. See Appendix C. He was born between October 1181 and January 1182. The last reference appears to be 1255, so he lived into his mid-seventies. For more on him and his family, see *Eye Priory* ii, pp.57–8, 64, 67–8. See also a description of the Alencon family in *Sibton Abbey* i, pp.28–29.
[4] There is a gap of 6.5 cm at this point in the membrane.

146. William de Colville[1] Adam of Mendham, Thomas le Latimer, William de Alneto, four knights, summoned to choose [the twelve] to make a recognition of the grand assize between Brian the son of Anselm, demandant, and the prior of Bricett,[2] tenant, concerning twenty acres of land with appurtenances in Ringshall, as to which of them has the greater right in the said land, have come and chosen these, namely: Hubert Gernegan, William de Ciresy,[3] Philip of Winston, Richard Mauduyt, William de Havil, William the son of Rainer, William of Cotton, Hubert of Braiseworth, Roger Sturmey, William the son of Robert of Reydon, Matthew of Peyton, Robert le Enveyse, Stephen of Stratton, Walter of Hatfield, John Cordebof [and] Ralph of Weston. Note that the prior gives half a mark in return for having a mention of a year and a day from when Henry the old king was alive and dead (*half a mark*).

Afterwards, they are agreed and Brian gives ten shillings for licence to agree with the prior of Bricett by the surety of the same [prior][4] (*10 shillings*).

The prior gives ten shillings for licence to agree with the same Brian concerning the same by the surety of the same Brian[5] (*10 shillings*).

A day is given to them at Ipswich on the Monday after the [feast of the] Invention of the Holy Cross. [*chirograph* CP 25(1) 213/15/8]

1   The family originated in 'Colleville' in Normandy and held lands in Carlton Colville in Mutford hundred as well as elsewhere.
2   The priory of Augustinian canons at Great Bricett, Bosmere hundred, was founded in 1114–1119.
3   There are a number of towns in France called 'Cerisy', three of which are in Normandy.
4   The clerk crossed out the word 'prior' but I think it makes more sense to leave it given the next sentence.
5   There is a gap of 3.25 cm at this point in the membrane.

147. William the son of Robert, Robert of Boyton, William de Ciresy and Hubert Gernegan, four knights, summoned to choose twelve etc to make [a recognition] of the grand assize between Alan of Withersdale, demandant, and Roger of Shotford concerning two shillingsworth of rent with appurtenances in Weybread, whether he Roger, who is the tenant, has the greater right of holding that rent of the said Alan, or the same Alan of holding that [rent] in demesne, have come and chosen these, namely: Ralph of Cookley, John the son of Robert of Ubbeston, Philip of Winston, Thomas Latimer, Gilbert the son of Thomas of Ilketshall, Osbert of Bawdsey, William de Cauxto, Robert le Enveyse, Walter of Hatfield, John of Brantham, Giles of Wattisham, John de Hodeboville, William the son of Robert of Reydon, William of Stratford, Robert de Wykes and John de Crammaville.

Later they have agreed as is shown above.[1]

A day[2] is given on the Monday next after the Invention of the Holy Cross [Monday 7 May] at Ipswich and the twelve are to come then. [*chirograph* CP 25(1) 213/16/47][3]

1   See **145**. There is a gap of 6.6 cm between the end of this sentence and the next.
2   This paragraph is shown as a separate paragraph on the membrane – it has a paragraph/section mark in the margin – whereas the previous three pleas are shown as having a day given to them as part of the plea. It is likely that this paragraph belongs to this plea however.
3   According to the chirograph the agreement was made on the morrow of Holy Trinity, that is Monday 11 June 1240, at Dunwich. On the reverse of this chirograph it is indicated that 'Philip Burdun and Christiana his wife and John de Mireus lay their claim', presumably laying their claim to the rent.

Membrane 4d

148. (*Suffolk*) Thomas of Stratton appoints as his attorney Edmund his brother or Robert de Welhelin against Master Ralph de Rauneston and many others named in the writ concerning a plea of novel disseisin etc.

149.[1] (*Norfolk*) Geoffrey Tregoz, Andrew of Hingham, Thomas Bacon and Adam of Tivetshall, four knights, selected to choose the twelve etc to make a recognition [of the grand assize] etc between Roger of Thirkelby[2] and Letta his wife, demandants, and Thomas of Walcott, deforcer, concerning the advowson of the church of Walcott whether he Roger and Letta have the greater right in the said advowson or the said Thomas, have come and chosen these, namely: Thomas de Valeynes,[3] William Ruston, Robert de Curton, Brian of Hickling, Roger of Calthorpe, Robert the son of Ralph of Thorpe, Godfrey de Miliers, Roger of Suffield, Robert Malet, Henry of Stratton, William de Ages, William de Senges, Hamon Chevere, Hugh de Dunedal, William of Reedham and Bartholomew of Creake.

A day is given to them at Cattishall on a day five weeks after Easter and the twelve are to come then.

1   There is a gap of 5.5 cm between this plea and the previous one.
2   One of the judges on this circuit.
3   This is the same Thomas de Valeynes as in **151**.
4   There is a gap of 7.6 cm at this point in the membrane between here and the next paragraph.

150.[1] (*Blything*) Robert the son of Reynold claims against Oliver the son of Drogo twenty-four acres of land with appurtenances in Chediston as his right, and in respect whereof a certain Robert his ancestor was seised in his demesne as of fee and right in the time of Henry, the grandfather of the current lord king by taking profits therefrom to the value of half a mark, and from the same Robert the right to that land descended to a certain Reynold as son and heir, and from the same Reynold to this Robert, who now claims as son and heir, and that such is his right he offers to prove etc.

Oliver comes and denies his right, but he readily grants the seisin of the said Robert his ancestor[2] and says that the same Robert gave that land, which he claims against him, to a certain Drogo, the father of that Oliver whose heir he is, by his charter, which he proffers and which attests to this. Thus, that same Robert, on whose seisin this Robert prosecutes, did not die seised as he says, and that it is so he puts himself on [the verdict of] the witnesses named in the same charter and on the country, and Robert likewise. So let there be a jury thereon, whether the said Robert, the ancestor of this Robert who now claims, gave the land to the said Drogo by his charter and put him in seisin, so that he did not die seised as Oliver says or not.

The jurors say that the said Robert gave the land to the said Drogo by his charter and put him in seisin, so that he was in full seisin for four years before the said Robert set out for the Holy Land. So it is adjudged that Oliver holds [the land] in peace forever and Robert is in mercy. He made a fine for half a mark by the surety of Robert of Bocking (*half a mark*).

1   There is a gap of 4.7 cm between this plea and the previous one.
2   That is Robert the ancestor of Robert son of Reynold not Oliver's ancestor.

151. (*Blything*) Adam of Mendham, William the son of Robert of Reydon, Ranulf de Blything and Adam of Eleigh, four knights, selected to choose on oath etc the twelve etc to make a recognition of the grand assize between Roger of Felthorpe, demandant, and Andrew of Westhall, tenant, of fifty acres of land with appurtenances in Westhall, whether the same Andrew has the greater right in the said land or the said Roger, have come and chosen these, namely: Thomas le Latimer, Robert de Grimilies, John Cordebof, Reynold the son of Osbert, William of Reedham, Thomas de Valeynes,[1] Richard Mauduyt, Hubert Gernegan, John of East Henham, Hubert of Braiseworth, William de Alneto, William of Haughley, William of Cotton, Hugh of Gosbeck, William the son of Rainer, and William de Colevill. They [the jurors] say on their oath that the said Andrew, who is the tenant, has the greater right in the said land than the said Roger. So it is adjudged that the said Andrew and his heirs may hold the said land in perpetuity without any claim that the same Roger or his heirs may be able to claim in the said land. Roger [is] in mercy (*amercement*). Robert de Grimilies, Reynold the son of Osbert, William of Reedham and Thomas de Valeynes have not come, so [they are] in mercy (*amercement*).

1   See Reaney 1997, p.464 where the name may now be 'Vallins'.

152.[1] Richard the English appoints as his attorney Wyncencius[2] le Rus against Baldwin le Rus and others named in the writ concerning a plea of land etc.

   [1]   There is a gap of 11 cm between this plea and the previous one.
   [2]   This might be Vincent but it is not certain.

Membrane 5

153. (*Norfolk, at Cattishall*) Geoffrey de Say and Alina his wife claim against Alexander de Vallibus the advowson of the church of Cringleford, and against the abbot of Langley[1] nine acres of land with appurtenances in Rockland[2] as the dower of Alina etc. Alexander comes and then vouches to warranty Thomas of Moulton the son of Thomas of Moulton. He is to have him by the aid of the court on a day in five weeks after Easter at Cattishall. The abbot comes and claims a view. Let him have it. A day is given to them at Cattishall in the same term.

   [1]   The Premonstratensian canons' house at Langley, Lodden hundred in Norfolk, founded in 1195.
   [2]   Probably Rockland St Mary in Henstead hundred as Cringleford is nearer to this Rockland than any other.

154. (*Wangford, Chelmsford*) Matilda who was the wife of John de Iarpenville by her attorney claims against Waleran de Muncy a third part of five shillingsworth of rent with appurtenances in Weston, a third part of eighteen penceworth of rent with appurtenances in Lidgate, a third part of five shillingsworth of rent with appurtenances in Worlingham, a third part of four shillingsworth of rent with appurtenances in *Cote*,[1] a third part of five shillingsworth of rent with appurtenances in Stoven, a third part of ten shillingsworth of rent with appurtenances in Kessingland, a third part of three shillings and nine and a half pence worth of rent with appurtenances in Gisleham, a third part of two shillings of and six penceworth of rent with appurtenances in Rushmere, a third part of six shillingsworth of rent with appurtenances in Pakefield and a third part of twenty-two penceworth of rent with appurtenances in Kirkley as her dower etc and in respect whereof the said John her late husband dowered her on the day etc.

Waleran came and vouched to warranty John the son of John de Iarpenvill who is under age and in the guardianship of W[alter Mauclerc], the bishop of Carlisle. So the guardian is to be summoned that he be [there] at the arrival of the judges at Chelmsford in the county of Essex and he may have the said John there etc.

   [1]   *Cote* cannot be found in Wangford or any other hundred in Suffolk.

155. (*Hertfordshire*) Maria who was the wife of Alexander de Alneto claims against Adam de Hilling half of one carucate of land with appurtenances in Brickendon and Hoddesdon[1] and a third part of fifty acres of land with appurtenances in Brickendon as her dower etc and in respect whereof the said Alexander, her late husband, dowered her on the day etc.

Adam comes and says that it is not possible to answer her without Lauretta de Creding and Wymesa who was the wife of Walkelin Visdelu his co-parceners (who[s])[2] are present. They answer together and say that she ought not to have the dower because the said Alexander was not seised in his demesne as of fee of the said land on the day that he married her or ever afterwards, so that he could dower her, because a certain Gillian, who was the wife of William de Alneto, held that land in dower on the day that etc and similarly after the death of Alexander, so that he never was seised of the said land. And that it is so he puts himself on the jury of the country, and she [does] similarly. So let there be a jury thereon. The sheriff of

Hertfordshire is ordered that he makes come the twelve [jurors] at Chelmsford in the octave of Holy Trinity [Sunday 17 June] etc by whom [the truth can best be known] and who have no [affinity with either party] to ascertain whether the said Alexander was seised of the said land in his demesne as of the fee on the day that he espoused her, so that [he could dower] her, as she says or not, because both[3] etc (*Chelmsford*). It has been conceded here that the inquest may proceed whether they come or not. Lauretta and Wymesa appoint as their attorney this Adam etc. (Afterwards, they have agreed and Adam gives one mark for licence to agree[i].)

[1]   I cannot find these vills in Herefordshire, which appears to be what the clerk has written, but Brickendon and Hoddesdon exist in Hertfordshire. I understand that the 't' in 'Hertford' was often missing. See Reaney 1997, p.228.
[2]   The clerk wrote *qui* instead of *que* as both of these co-parceners are women.
[3]   The clerk wrote *eam* but I think he has made a mistake here and it should be *tam* translated as 'both' as the standard phrase appears to translate as 'both parties put themselves on the inquest'.

156. Robert Aguillon appoints as his attorney Robert Gravenel against Henry de Wyntermed.

157. (*Hoxne*) Thomas le Buck claims against William of Gislingham one quarter of one knight's fee with appurtenances in Bedingfield as his right etc and in which the same William has no entry except by Robert of Gislingham to whom Gilbert de Buck the father of Thomas and Ascelina his mother, whose heir he is, demised it for a term,[1] which has expired etc.

William comes and denies force and injury and says that in fact he had entry by Robert his father. But Robert had no entry except by the said Gilbert and Ascelina, as Thomas says, because Robert, his father, impleaded in the court of the lord king a certain Sylvester, the brother of the said Gilbert, concerning half of one knight's fee with appurtenances in Badingham,[2] so that at length a fine was made in the same court between them in this form, namely, that the same Sylvester, who held everything, acknowledged the said half to be the right of that Robert. For this acknowledgement the same Robert granted to the same Sylvester a quarter [of a knight's fee][3] and the other half[4] remained to the same Robert and he was in seisin all his life, so that then he died seised (*on the morrow*).[5]

Thomas says that his fine ought not to harm him because after the fine [had been] made, the same Sylvester came and enfeoffed the said Gilbert of that half[6] [of the fee] which remained to him by that fine by his charter which the same Thomas proffered, and which attests to this. As a result the said Ascelina, who held that land in dower, was answerable to the same Gilbert as warrantor of her dower. Afterwards, the said Gilbert and Ascelina, by common agreement, demised to the said Robert the said land for the life of that Ascelina for six marks, and she proffers a certain covenant sealed with the seal of that Robert, the father of that William, which attests to this.

Afterwards, they are agreed and William gives one mark for licence to agree by the surety of Sampson of Battisford (*one mark*). [*chirograph* CP 25(1) 213/15/25][7]

[1]   See Pollock and Maitland ii, 1968, pp.106–117 for what is a 'term' and a 'termor'.
[2]   The clerk made a mistake here with *Bedingham*, which is in Loddon hundred. Badingham is in Hoxne hundred.
[3]   This is what is shown in the chirograph.
[4]   That is a quarter remaining to Robert.
[5]   There is a gap of 2.4 cm between this paragraph and the next one in this plea.
[6]   That is the quarter which Sylvester still had.

7 Thomas won from the agreement but then rented it out to William and his heirs for 6 marks a year payable at two terms.

Membrane 5d

158. (*Norfolk*) William of Reedham claims against Walter de Evermue fifty acres of marshland with appurtenances in Runham as his right etc and in respect whereof a certain Gerard his ancestor was seized in his demesne as of fee and right in the time of Henry the grandfather of the present king by taking profits therefrom to the value of half a mark. From that same Gerard descended the right to a certain Matthew as son and heir, and from the same Matthew to that William who now claims as son and heir, and that such is his right he offers to prove by the body of a certain free man of his, Thomas the son of Ernulf, who is prepared to prove this just as the court considers, as by the command of Ernulf his father,[1] and if, as regards him, [he shall fall ill] etc by another etc.

William of Ditton and Adam de Blukeville,[2] who made themselves answerable for the said Walter and who avouched them in the presence of Richard Mauduyt, Thomas de Hemmegrave, Thomas le Latimer and William of Cotton before whom he appointed them in his place, come and deny the right etc and the seisin of the said Gerard and everything etc by the body of a certain free man of his, named Clement the son of Sampson, who offers to deny this by his body etc and if [not] by him etc by another etc. So it is adjudged that there be a duel between them (*judicial combat*). Clement gives a pledge for denying and Thomas gives a pledge for proving. The sureties for Clement [are]: Thomas de Hemmegrave,[3] Roger the son of Osbert, Robert of Boyton.

The sureties for Thomas [are]: Walter of Ingham, Robert of Stokesby, Adam of Burlingham knight, Reynold the son of Gervase of Stokesby. A day is given to them on Monday before the ascension of our Lord [Monday 21 May] at Cattishall, and then let them come armed (*at Cattishall*).

1 That is the father of Thomas.
2 See **536** where these two possible attorneys are removed by Walter.
3 Thomas Hemmegrave was a household knight (*curialis*) of Henry III at this time and would have been one of the administrative knights acting as a juror on some of the grand assize pleas.

159. (*Blything*) A jury chosen by consent of the parties comes to declare by Roger the son of Osbert, Robert de Grimilies, William of Hingham, John of Brantham, Robert de Bosco, Richard of Glemham, William the son of Robert of Reydon, Hubert Gernegan, Hugh of Gosbeck, William of Reedham and Robert de Wykes if Simon de Pierpont and his ancestors, from the conquest of England to the nineteenth year [1235] of Henry the current king, had his warren in Wrentham, both in the land of Thomas of Poynings and in Simon's land,[1] so that the said Thomas and his ancestors had no warren there, nor could they hunt for foxes and hares in the district of Wrentham as of right, just as the same Thomas and his ancestors were accustomed to hunt for foxes and hares in their [own] land in Wrentham, and whenever in the land of Simon, for this reason that the said Simon and his ancestors hunted in the land of Thomas and his ancestors in Wrentham as the same Thomas says.[2] They [the jurors] come and say on their oaths that from the conquest of England all the vill of Wrentham, was both the fief of the ancestors of Thomas of Poynings and the fief of Simon, with the exception of a certain park of Thomas in which Thomas can hunt foxes and hares, so that no one [else can hunt there][3] without his permission, and it[4] was always the warren of the predecessors of Simon. As a result neither

Thomas nor his ancestors were able to hunt foxes and hares in the territory of the same Simon, nor also in the district of the same Thomas outside the enclosure of that park without the permission of Simon and his ancestors. So it is adjudged that the warren throughout Wrentham, outside the park, remains to the same Simon and his heirs forever without any claim of [Thomas and] his heirs. Thomas [is] in mercy (*amercement*). Because Simon claimed warren throughout Wrentham, both in the enclosure of Thomas, and elsewhere, he is in mercy for a false claim (*amercement*). Because the jurors testified that after the park was not enclosed the same Simon used to hunt in that enclosure just as each free man of the neighbourhood, it is said to the same Simon that he may use the same seisin hereafter, if he wishes, until the park has been enclosed.[5]

1   The fact that this case goes back to 1235 is confirmed in the Curia Regis rolls where it appears that a 'Margery de Puningg' was bringing the case against Simon. It obviously did not reach a conclusion then because Margery, later in the Curia Regis rolls, is appointing an attorney. See *Curia Regis Rolls* xv, 1233–37, nos. 1731 and 1757. So it looks as though Thomas (her son?) took over the case at this eyre. There is no further reference to this case in the Curia Regis rolls before 1235, or after this result in this eyre in the Curia Regis rolls which follow this eyre.

2   I have translated what is there up to this point but it is difficult to see the complete sense of this sentence. Perhaps the clerk has made some omissions; perhaps the words *vel non* after 'Thomas says' would help, or perhaps the details of what Simon's claim is meant to be could be clarified by indicating after *ut de jure* the words *sicut idem Simon dicit, vel*, which would translate 'as the same Simon says or'. There might also be some mistakes in his Latin, or there might be some clerical shorthand which I have been unable to translate. I think what the clerk wants to say is that Thomas is claiming warren throughout Wrentham, including having warren on Simon's land as a sort of quid pro quo, and that Simon has stopped him and his predecessors from hunting anywhere in Wrentham, including on Thomas's own land, because Simon considers he has sole right to hunt throughout Wrentham, including on the land of Thomas. The jury below appears to put this interpretation on events, with the one proviso about the park.

3   I think the clerk has missed out a phrase here which would give the passage more sense.

4   That is the whole vill of Wrentham was the warren of Simon and not Thomas, except for this park on Thomas's land.

5   On the whole Thomas lost in this plea. Although I can find reference in the amercement section to Thomas's amercement (see **1642**) I can find no reference to Simon's.

160.[1] (*Samford*) An assize comes to declare if Hugh of Polstead, George of Polstead, Daniel le Franceys, Alan Heron, Robert Carbunel, Richard Marshall, John le Venur, Peter the carter, Robert King, William Franceys, Hugh Derby, Hugh le Mestre, William Carter, Reynold Scutt, Nicholas Capud, William Mareys, Thomas Heved, Hugh Buck, Thomas le Chace, Robert Prat, John Wade, Aubrey le Cuhirde, John of Polstead, Robert Gunter and Thomas the son of Austin have unjustly disseised William Lutun and Alice his mother of their free tenement in Raydon after the first [crossing of the king into Brittany],[2] and in respect whereof William and Alice complain that the said Hugh and the others disseised them of fifteen acres of arable land, eight acres of meadow, and two acres of alder grove.

Hugh of Polstead, George[3] of Polstead, Daniel le Franceys, Alan Heron, Robert Carbunel, Peter Carter, Hugh Buck,[4] Robert Prat, John Wade [and] John of Polstead come and say nothing to stay the assize. Richard Marshall, John le Venur, Robert King, William Franceys, Hugh Derby, Hugh le Mestre, William Carter, Reynold Scutt, Nicholas Capud, William Mareys, Thomas Heved, Thomas le Chace, Aubrey le Cuhirde and Robert Gunter have not come nor were they attached and they are of the liberty of Bury St Edmunds. Therefore let the bailiff of Bury St Edmunds answer concerning the attachment etc.

The jurors say that Thomas Lotun, the father of William, and his mother Alice and William together bought in common twelve acres of land and four and a half acres of meadow and two acres of alder grove from a certain Geoffrey the son of Geoffrey of Raydon and they were in seisin together throughout ten years. Alice and William were similarly in seisin, after the death of the said Thomas, for nearly half a year until the said Hugh and all those named before disseised them as the writ says. Meanwhile, they [the jurors] say that the said William bought for himself three acres of meadow from Walter the son of Hugh and two acres of land from John the son of Edmund and one acre of meadow from a certain Alexander of Sutton and he held it in peace for three years and more until the said Hugh and the others named before disseised him as the writ says. So it is adjudged[5] that they have recovered[6] their seisin against them. Hugh and all the others are in mercy (*amercements*). Sureties of Hugh of Polstead: Matthew of Layham, Robert de Nusted, Roger de Punz, Robert of Brampton, William le Blund, Robert le Envoyse, William of Polstead and Thomas de Calne. Note: that Hugh of Polsted is the surety for all of the said [defendants] above who were present.

Damages: in common 8 marks (*eight marks*).

Damages: separately 1 mark (*one mark, and one mark*).

1 See Appendix K for a full transcription and translation.
2 The date was May 1230. See Sutherland 1973, p.55 for the table of limitations of the assize of novel disseisin. He also indicates that this date was set in June 1237 by the king. This statement will be missed out in future unless specifically stated in the roll. This is the year from which novel disseisins may be initiated. If the claim went back prior to this date the plaintiff would have to use a different writ, such as a 'writ of right'.
3 There is a fault in the membrane at this point, which the clerk has worked around. See Fig. 3.
4 The clerk has actually written *Hugo Duc* at this point. However, it is assumed that it should be *Buck* as Hugo Duc was not mentioned in the original list in the first paragraph.
5 There is a fault in the membrane here that runs down the membrane almost to the end. It has been stitched and the clerk has worked around it.
6 I would have expected a present or future tense here as surely they would recover their seisin after the judgement. However, he is consistent throughout the roll so I have translated it as shown because it might be the clerk's way of indicating that they have won the case that they have put forward.

161.[1] Margery de Kemesec appoints as her attorney Henry de Bellinger against Edmund her son and others in the writ concerning a plea of dower etc.

1 This is a duplicate of **187**.

Membrane 6

162. (*Bosmere*) An assize comes to declare if John of Aveley, William de Ciresy, Robert Blund and Geoffrey Nogard have unjustly disseised Robert the son of Gilbert de Mara of his free tenement in Creeting after the first etc and in respect whereof he complains that they have disseised him of one messuage.

John and the others come and readily grants the assize.

The jurors say that the said John and the others did not disseise him of any free tenement because the same Robert was never in seisin. So it is adjudged that John and the others [are] on this without day and Robert is in mercy (*amercement*).

163. (*Bosmere*) An assize comes to declare if Gilbert de Mara the father of Robert was seised in his demesne as of fee of six acres of land and eighteen penceworth of rent with appurtenances in Creeting St Mary on the day etc and if etc (of which land and rent[s])[1] John de Hauville was in full seisin, and thereupon he puts himself on the assize. So let the assize proceed.

The jurors say that the said Gilbert did not die seised of that land nor of the rent as in demesne etc. So it is adjudged that John [is] without day and Robert [is] in mercy (*amercement*).

> [1] The clerk has made a mistake here and it should read *cuius terre et cuius redditus* not *quam terrram et quem redditum*.

164.[1] (*At the feast of St Michael*) The lord king has commanded [his] justices that they [adjourn] all the pleas moved before them against the prior of Thetford after he has set out going on his embassy to the Roman Court,[2] which journey he began at the feast of the purification of St Mary [2 February] in the year twenty-four and similarly, it extends to those pleas which [are] still to be brought. They may adjourn [them] until the octave of St Michael [Saturday 6 October].

> [1] This is not a plea as such but is more of an instruction to the justices to hear the pleas that would normally be heard in the moot court at Thetford. This is more of a one-off article for this eyre. I would have expected this normally to appear in the Patent Rolls.
> [2] That is the papal court.

165. (*Norfolk*) Roger the son of Robert Bosse claims against Roger the son of Bartholomew of Calthorpe four acres of land with appurtenances in Erpingham, and against Bartholomew the son of Roger ten acres of land with appurtenances in the same vill, and against Roger Gray one and a half acres of land with appurtenances in the same vill, and against John the son of Ralph three acres of land in the same vill, and against Robert the son of John three acres [of land with appurtenances in the same vill], and against Robert of Hastings three acres of land in the same vill, and against Agnes Wilf of Ingworth three and a half acres of land with appurtenances in the same vill, and against Reynold her son one and a half acres of land with appurtenances, and against Reynold the son of Simon one acre of land with appurtenances in the same vill, and against Robert the son of Simon Payn one acre of land with appurtenances in the same vill, and against Alice who was the wife of Richard Pixton two acres of land with appurtenances in the same vill, and against Robert the son of Eudo one and a half acres of land with appurtenances in the same vill, and against Agnes, Botild and Heloise the daughters of Ralph Bricun three roods of land with appurtenances in the same vill as his right, and in respect whereof a certain Roger his ancestor was seised as of right and fee in the time of King Henry the grandfather of King Henry the current king, by taking profits to the value of half a mark etc. From the same Roger, who died without an heir, the right to that land descended to a certain Hugh as brother and heir, and from the same Hugh to a certain Robert as son and heir, from the same Robert to that Roger who now claims, and that such is his right he offers [to prove].

Robert the son of Eudo, Agnes, Botild and Heloise[1] come and are under age and they say that their ancestors in respect thereof died seised and they claim their age and they have [it], because Alice who was the wife of Ralph Brictmere, and Agnes Botild and Heloise who are under age, are being joined together in the writ.

Richard the son of Bartholomew and all the others come. Bartholomew the son of Roger and all the others come and vouch to warranty Roger the son of Bartholomew, who is present and he warrants them. He says that he ought not to answer to the said Roger on this writ because the said Roger, of whose seisin Roger the son of Robert Bosse who claims, is speaking, obtained that land and had a certain brother, a certain Hugh mentioned before, [and] the first born [brother] named Adam, from whom issued a certain Bartholomew, from whom issued this Roger, who is the tenant. Inasmuch as the said Roger who obtained that land died without heirs from him, and he[2] did not hold that land from his first born brother and that Roger, who

26

is the tenant, is [descended] from the first born brother, and Roger,[3] who claims [is descended] from the younger [brother], it does not seem to him that he should, nor could, claim that land.

Roger Bosse says that the said Roger, of whose seisin he speaks, obtained that land from Roger his father and the father of the said Adam and Hugh, and did homage to him. Afterwards, [he did homage] to Adam the first born and heir of Roger, and afterwards to Bartholomew the son and heir of Adam. He seeks judgement as the said Roger obtained the said land and held that from the ancestor of the said Roger, who is the tenant, and that Roger the son of Bartholomew is descended from the brother of the first born and he Roger Bosse of the younger brother.

Afterwards, Roger Bosse came and withdrew [from the plea], so [he is] in mercy. He made a fine for half a mark by the surety of Roger of Calthorpe (*half a mark*).

1   *Hawis* was written by the clerk.
2   That is Roger the son of Robert Bosse, the plaintiff.
3   That is Roger the son of Robert Bosse, the plaintiff.

166.[1] (*Bosmere*) Assize comes to declare if Robert de la More has unjustly levelled a certain dyke in Creeting to the nuisance of John de Hauville's free tenement in the same vill after the first etc. Robert comes and says nothing to stay the assize.

The jurors say that the said Robert unjustly knocked down the certain dyke to the nuisance of John. So it is adjudged that the dyke be raised and it is to be as it ought to be and is accustomed to be and Robert [is] in mercy (*amercement*).

1   There is a gap of 7 cm between this plea and the last.

167. (*Blything*) An assize comes to declare if Ranulf de Cravene, the father of John of Easton, was seised in his demesne as in fee etc of one carucate of land with appurtenances in Henham on the day on which he died, and if etc and if he died after the last return etc and if the said John etc. Whereof Thomas de Cravene holds two parts except for two parts of twelve acres and of one rood of land, and Matilda his mother holds one third part except a third part of twelve acres and of one rood of land, and Walter of Hingham holds twelve acres of land, and Thomas de Sinterton holds one rood of land. They come and say nothing to stay the assize.

The jurors say that the said Ranulf died seised in his demesne etc of the said land and that the same John is his nearest heir but they say that he died before the term. So it is adjudged that John is to take nothing by this assize and is in mercy for a false claim and all the others [are] without day. He may proceed against them if he wishes by a writ of right etc (*amercement*). [*chirograph* CP 25(1) 213/16/74][1]

1   The chirograph indicates that the agreement came about after this assize of mort d'ancestor.

168. (*Blything*) Lena, who was the wife of William of Sutton, who brought a writ of entry against William Wilger and others named in the writ, claims a licence to withdraw her writ and she has [it].

169. (*one mark*) Thomas of Risby gives one mark for licence to agree with Giles de Munpincon concerning a plea of trespass by the surety of the same Giles.

170. Ada the wife of John of Stanton appoints her husband John as her attorney against Alice and Katherine le Walesch[1] concerning a plea of land etc. [**518**]

1   See **1097** for similar spelling of their surname. It is also assumed that these two sisters are the same as those in **186**, **450** and **1096** as the opposing litigants in **170** and **186** are shown as litigants in **450** and **1096** even though their surname is shown as *le Waleys* in the text. Katherine's surname

is also shown as *le Waleys* in the amercement and agreement section of this roll. See **1663**. I have indexed them under 'Waleys' as that is the surname in the plea and in the agreement.

171. Katel the wife of John Marshall of Bury St Edmunds appoints as her attorney her husband John against the same concerning the same.

172. Amabil, who was the wife of John of Horringer, appoints as her attorney John de Wymundhall against Henry of Caldecott and against Henry the son of John of Horringger concerning a plea of dower etc.

173. Robert Figge and Avelina his wife appoint as their attorney John de Wymundhall against Henry of Belton and others named in the writ concerning a plea of novel disseisin. [**348**]

Membrane 6d

174. (*Hertfordshire*) Parnel, who was the wife of Alan Buy, was attached to answer Richard de Buxe concerning a plea [demanding] why she made waste, sale etc of the woods which she holds in dower from the inheritance of the said Richard in Hoddesdon. Richard, through his attorney, complains that she assarted against the prohibition five carucates of the said woods, in respect whereof he has suffered damage, and he has damage to the value of twenty-one marks and thereon he produces suit.

Parnel comes and denies force and injury and waste etc and she says that in fact she assarted one acre of a certain thicket and she made it arable land, so that he assuredly, as regards that assart, will not be able to have any damage. She then puts herself on [the verdict of] the country, and he likewise. So let there be a jury thereon, and they are to come at the arrival of the justices at Hertford.[1]

[1] The court moved to Hertfordshire and was in session from 15 to 26 July 1240.

175. (*Kent*) Stephen de Forest and Heloise his wife claim against John of Wootton eight acres of land with appurtenances in Wootton as the right and inheritance of Heloise and in which the same John has no entry except by Avelina de Celar' who demised that to him while the same Heloise was under age and in her wardship etc.

John comes and denies force and injury and such entry and says that he had entry by the same Heloise who sold that land to him when she was of age and in her full power and without a husband by her charter, which he proffers and which attests to this. And that it is so he puts himself on the jury of the country, and upon the witnesses named in the charter, and she likewise. So the sheriff has been commanded that he summons to Chelmsford on the octave of the Holy Trinity, Ralph the son of Robert de Metega, Theobald de Cumbe, Alexander de Waddington, Rayner de Camp and Adam his brother, the witnesses named in the charter (*Chelmsford*). Besides those eight, both knights and the other free and law worthy men [are to be summoned] by whom etc and who [are] neither etc to ascertain etc if the said Heloise, after she was of full age and without a husband and in seisin of the said land, sold the said land to that John by her charter as the same John says, or if the same John entered into the said land by the said [Avelina] while the same Heloise was under age and in wardship etc as the same Heloise says, because then etc.

176. (*Sussex*) A day is given to John of Gaddesden by his attorney, plaintiff, and Ralph del Brak, defendant, concerning a plea of debt and a plea of warranty of

28

charter on the octave of the Holy Trinity at Chelmsford by prayer of the parties as of the day etc (*Chelmsford*).

177. A day is given to the prior of Lewes[1] by his attorney, plaintiff, and Adam de Bested, defendant, concerning [a plea of] customs and services on the octave of the Holy Trinity at Chelmsford (*Chelmsford*).

> [1] Lewes was the first Cluniac house in England, founded by William de Warenne in 1077.

178. Andrew of Hingham appoints as his attorney Bartholomew the son of Henry against Philip of Flegg concerning a plea to hear judgement etc. [**262** and **1114**]

179. (*Lincolnshire*) John of Gaddesden by his attorney presented himself on the fourth day against Ralph of Rochford concerning a plea that he keep the covenant made between them concerning two carucates of land with appurtenances in *Clipstead*, together with the marriage of his first born son John. Ralph has not come and has made many defaults, so that the sheriff was ordered that he distrain him by [all his] lands etc that he may be [here] on this day. The sheriff has done nothing thereon nor has he sent the writ. So as before, the sheriff is ordered that he distrain [him], etc that he is at Chelmsford on the octave of the Holy Trinity, and that the sheriff is to be there to hear judgement on him because he has not sent the writ etc as etc (*Chelmsford*).

180. (*Worcestershire*) A day is given to Thomas of Brampton, by his attorney, the plaintiff and William the son of Warren, by his attorney, the defendant to levy their chirograph in the octave of the Holy Trinity at Chelmsford (*Chelmsford*).

181. (*Norfolk*) The prior of Lewes[1] by his attorney presented himself on the fourth day against William the son of William and Thomas the son of Richard concerning a plea that they do him the customs and right services, which they ought to make to him etc. William and Thomas have not come. At another time the sheriff was ordered to distrain them by [all their] lands etc [and] that they be [here] on this day, and the sheriff has done nothing thereon. So as before the sheriff is ordered to distrain them by [their] lands etc so that he has their bodies at Chelmsford on the octave of the Holy Trinity etc (*Chelmsford*).

> [1] It is assumed that the attorney of the prior of Lewes in Sussex came originally to the Norfolk eyre. The plea was then postponed to Suffolk and is now being postponed to Essex.

182. (*St Etheldreda*)[1] Robert of Boyton claims against the prior of Eye one messuage and five acres of land with appurtenances in Playford as his right, and in respect whereof Thomas de Blunville, formerly the bishop of Norwich his kinsman whose heir he is, died in seisin etc.

The prior came and on another occasion in respect thereof [i.e. the land], he vouched to warranty James of Playford, who comes now by his attorney and says that he is not bound to warrant him because after Fulcher, his ancestor, had given that land by his charter to the monastery of Eye, a certain prior of the same monastery and convent had given that land to a certain Hervey the son of Peter, who was in seisin by his[2] feoffment and he died seised. After him [Hervey] the said Thomas held the said land through all the days of his life and that it should be inquired into by the country he offers twenty shillings to the lord king. They are received (*twenty shillings*).

The prior says that the said Hervey was never enfeoffed of the said messuage and land, by any prior of his monastery nor by any former prior has he entry into the land and that messuage, but if he had any entry (then[i]) he says [it was] by his trespass and not by the consent or will of any prior and convent of his monastery, and then he puts himself on the jury. So let there be a jury thereon, namely if the said Hervey was enfeoffed by the prior and monastery of Eye as regards the said land and messuage as the same James says or not.

The jurors, chosen by the consent of the parties, say that the said Hervey had entry in the said land by a certain prior and the convent of Eye and he held it all his life and died seised. After the death of the same Hervey, Thomas de Blunville entered into that land and then did homage to a certain prior, but a long time after he had held that land. Because it has been proved incontestably that the ancestor of that prior enfeoffed the said Hervey and Thomas after the ancestors of that James had enfeoffed the priory of Eye of the said land and messuage, it is adjudged that James is quit of that warranty, and the prior is in mercy. Robert is to recover his seisin against the same prior. Afterwards, the prior came and made a fine for one mark (*one mark*).

1   This indicates that the plea involves land within the liberty of the priory of Ely.
2   That is by the previous prior of Eye.

183. William Prior appoints as his attorney Henry de Cumpegnyo against Margery who was the wife of Henry de Kemek concerning a plea of dower etc.

184. The abbot of Leiston[1] appoints as his attorney Brother Matthew or Hubert of Redlingfield, members of his chapter, against Aurelia of Leiston concerning a plea of land etc.

1   Leiston Abbey, a house of Premonstratensian canons founded by Sir Ranulf de Glanvill in 1183.

185. Anselm the parson of Rendham appoints as his attorney Ralph Swan against William of Rendham and others in the writ concerning a plea of land etc.

186. Selena, the wife of Robert of Alderwood, appoints as her attorney Robert her husband against Catherine le Walesche and Alice her sister concerning a plea of land etc.

187.[1] Margery de Kemesec appoints as her attorney Henry de Bellinger against Edmund her son and others in the writ concerning a plea of dower etc.

1   This is a duplicate of **161**.

Membrane 7

188. (*Bosmere*) An assize comes to declare if Terence, the prior of the Hospital of St John of Jerusalem in England, and Richard the dean of Coddenham unjustly etc disseised Robert the parson de Byry[1] of his free tenement in Hemingstone, Coddenham and Baylham after the first etc and in respect whereof the same Robert complains that they disseised him of two carucates of land with appurtenances.

The bailiff of the prior and Richard the dean come and say nothing to stay the assize.

The jurors say that the said Richard, always in all his purchases and his acquisitions, which he made to the benefit of the said Robert and his brothers, his wards, in his charters and chirographs, set himself up with them as the chief (lord and did homage to the lords[i]),[2] and always was in continuous seisin until that time when the said Richard gave that land to God and the Hospital of St John. As a result neither the said Robert, nor any of his brothers, had separate seisin of the said land, nor enjoyed his separate part. They [the jurors] say precisely that the said Terence and Richard have not disseised him as he says. So it is adjudged that Terence and Richard [are] without day. Robert [is] in mercy for a false claim, by the surety of Hugh de Arderne, clerk, and William of Haughley, knight (*amercement*).

1 I have not seen Bury St Edmunds in this roll written like this, and can find no reference to a 'Byry' in Bosmere hundred or in the rest of Suffolk. According to Reaney 1997, p.41 it might also be a manor house, so Robert might be a parson of a manor house.

2 Interlined on two separate lines but they belong together.

189. (*Hertfordshire*) Richard Ruffin was summoned to answer Andrew le Goz concerning a plea that he keep to his covenant made between them for sixty acres of land with appurtenances in Throcking. In respect whereof the same Andrew complains that the same Richard by that covenant ought to have demised[1] to him all his land from Throcking for fifty-three marks, of which he paid him eleven marks cash down, with the residue evidently due to the same [Richard] at a certain place and day. And when the same [Andrew] came at that day and place with the money, according to the covenant made between them, the same Richard, acting maliciously against his covenant, withdrew himself [so] that he broke that covenant and kept the eleven marks which he [Andrew] has given him cash down. As a result he has suffered damage to the value of twenty marks, and he then produces suit etc.

Richard came and by licence they have agreed. The agreement is such that the said Richard owes to the same Andrew sixteen marks, and Andrew relinquished to him all right and claim that he had in the said land by reason of the said covenant if he could have any in the same because of it. Note: that the same Richard will pay to the same Andrew, the said sixteen marks at two terms, namely: on the day of the Nativity of St John the Baptist at Bury St Edmunds, eight marks, in the year twenty-four [24 June], and eight marks on the day of St Michael [29 September] in the same year. If he does not do [this] he grants [that] etc. The costs etc.

1 The clerk wrote *dimisse* instead of *dimisisse*. I have not come across *dimisse* in any Latin dictionary.

190. (*Stow*) An assize comes to declare if Hubert Gernegan, Walter de Baldegrim and Richard Fuctedame unjustly disseised Reynold the chaplain of Battisford of his free tenement in Thorney after the first etc and in respect whereof he complains that they disseised him of five acres of land etc. Hubert and the other comes and says nothing to stay the assize. Richard has not come and he was attached by William the reeve of Stonham.

The jurors say that the said Hubert and Richard[1] disseised him as the writ says. So it is adjudged that he [Reynold] is to recover his seisin against them. Hubert and the others [are] in mercy for disseisin. They are remanded in custody (*All[to the clerks], amercements, remand in custody, to the clerks*).

Damages: two shillings.

1 The clerk obviously forgot about Walter!

191. (*Norfolk, void here because [it is] elsewhere*)[1] (Simon of Whatfield presents himself on the fourth day against Margery de Rivers[2] concerning a plea that she warrants to him sixty acres of land with appurtenances and one messuage in Stoke which he holds etc. Margery has not come and was summoned etc. The sheriff of Norfolk is commanded to make a survey and appraise the value of the said land and the survey to be made known etc. The sheriff of Hertford will take [into his hands] to the value of etc. She is to be resummoned etc.ᶜ)

¹ This plea is crossed out by means of crossing through all the lines of the plea in the figure of an
'N'. See **226** for the actual plea.

² Margery de Rivers had an honorial fief in at least Suffolk and Essex, see *Book of Fees* i and ii,
pp.579, 914 and 918. She is also shown as *Margery de Ripariis* in a number of other pleas. See
index of people and places for a complete list.

192.[1] (*Norfolk*) Stephen of Reedham who appealed William Grim concerning the
breaking of peace of the lord king, whereon there was waged a trial by battle. The
same William came and placed himself in the mercy of the lord king. He is remanded
in custody. Afterwards, he came and made a fine on payment of ten marks, by the
surety of William of Reedham and Robert of Stokesby (*ten marks*).

[1] This looks like a crown plea left over from the Norfolk plea roll.

193. Thomas the son of Hubert, who brought a writ of customs and right services
against Andrew Porthoro and Reynold the Potter, comes and seeks licence to withdraw from his writ. Let him have it.

194. (*Blything*) The prior of Wangford[1] was summoned to answer Katherine, who
was the wife of Ralph the son of Hugh, concerning a plea that he warrants her ten
acres of land with appurtenances in Frostenden which she holds etc and she says
that the same prior ought to warrant her on account of [the fact that] he is in seisin
of her homage and service namely of thirty pence per year. Asked why she brought
that writ, she said that Agnes of Frostenden impleaded her in the county [court], so
that in respect thereof she vouched the prior to warranty.

The prior comes and says that he willingly warrants her. So he is told that he
must go to the county [court] and warrant her there etc.

[1] Wangford was a Cluniac house founded in 1159.

195. (*Blything*) An assize comes to declare if Robert Malet unjustly etc disseised
Margery of Poynings of her common pasture in Benacre which pertains to her free
tenement in Wrentham, and in respect whereof she complains that he disseised
her of six and a half acres of pasture. Robert comes and says nothing to stay the
assize.

The jurors say that he disseised her as the writ says. So it is adjudged that she is
to recover her seisin against him. Robert [is] in mercy (*amercement*).

Damages: sixpence.

196. (*Lothingland*) An assize comes to declare if Nicholas of Fritton and William de
Camelesfeud unjustly disseised the prior of St Olaf[1] of his free tenement in Fritton,
and in respect whereof the same prior complains that they disseised him of one acre
of land with appurtenances in the same vill.

Nicholas and William come and say nothing to stay the assize.

The jurors say that they disseised him [the prior] as the writ says of the said land.
So it is adjudged that the prior is to recover his seisin and they [are] in mercy for
disseisin, by the surety … [unfinished] (*amercements, remand in custody*).

Damages: twenty pence. All to the clerks.

[1] The Augustinian priory of St Olave's, Herringfleet, in Lothingland hundred, founded near to the
accession of Henry III.

197. (*Bosmere*) William de *Ryoucestr*'[1] was summoned to answer Geoffrey Tregoz
concerning a plea that he do him customs and rightful services, which he should do
him for his free tenement that he holds from him in Coddenham.

William comes and says that he holds no tenement from him, for which neither the customs and services ought to be made to him nor does he claim any tenement there. It is adjudged that William is without day and Geoffrey [is] in mercy for a false claim (*amercement*).

    1   I cannot find such a place. It might be Rochester in Kent.

198. (*Samford*) An assize comes to declare if William of Holbrook and Walter Butresleye unjustly disseised Hamon of Dodnash and Avice his wife of their free tenement in Bentley, and in respect whereof they complain they disseised them of three acres of land with appurtenances in the same vill.

    William and Walter come and say nothing to stay the assize. Roger de *Bruniford*[1] [is] in mercy for a manifest trespass (*amercement*).

    The jurors say that Walter and William did not disseise them as the writ says. So it is adjudged that they [are] without day. Hamon [is] in mercy and is pardoned for poverty. It is said by William that he is to render them henceforth two pence per year. The prior of Leighs,[2] the lord of that fief, is present and he agrees this.

    1   This is an odd plea of novel disseisin that suddenly introduces a new person who has no apparent connection with the plea.
    2   Almost certainly the priory of Leighs, Essex, a house of Augustinian canons founded in the late twelfth century by Ralph Gernun.

199. R. the bishop of Rochester appoints as his attorney Bernard of Freckenham or Baldwin de Mordon against the abbot of Bury St Edmunds concerning a plea of *de fine facto*. [**745** and **1117**]

200. Thomas de Greley appoints Edmund Cook as his attorney before Robert de Lexington and his fellow judges against Cliandus de *Bruniford* concerning a plea of naifty. [**527**]

201. (*Stowe*) An assize comes to declare if William of Onehouse unjustly disseised Ralph Swan and Denise his wife of their free tenement in Onehouse since the first crowning etc and in respect whereof they complain that he disseised them of two and a half acres of land with appurtenances. William comes and says nothing to stay the assize.

    The jurors say that the said William did not disseise them as the writ says because Denise is a villein nor does she have any free tenement. So it is adjudged that they are to take nothing by this assize, and they are in mercy for a false claim by the surety of William of Holbrook (*amercements*).

202. (*Blything*) Alpesia who was the wife of William the son of Theobald gives half a mark for licence to agree with the abbot of Leiston concerning a plea of land by the surety of the abbot (*half a mark*). [*chirograph* CP 25(1) 213/15/24] [**288**]

203. The prior of Hickling[1] ... [unfinished]

    1   This is in Norfolk and was a house of Augustinian canons.

204.[1] Margery the wife of Simon of Gorleston appoints as her attorney Simon her husband against Stephen the son of Roger concerning a plea of land.

    The[2] prior of Castle Acre appoints as his attorney William of Dunham or Simon of Weasenham against Robert the son of Humphrey of Bury St Edmunds concerning a plea of arrears of the annual rent.

    1   See **351** for the conclusion of an agreement concerning the plea of this first appointment of an attorney. The second plea of the arrears of annual rent has no end in this eyre.
    2   There is no separate paragraph mark here so no separate item number.

205. [----ⁱˡ]¹ appoints as his [or her] attorney Edmund de Wymundhall against Mabel of Browston concerning a plea of dower.

¹ The name could not be deciphered. This probably relates to **464** where this person is probably Laurence of Newton, but it is not obvious from what remains legible.

206. Thomas of Wheatcroft appoints as his attorney that Edmund against the same and concerning the same [plea].

207. Roger the son of Thomas appoints as his attorney that Edmund against the same [and] concerning the same [plea].

Membrane 7d

208. (*Hartismere*) An assize comes to declare if Richard the chaplain of Yaxley, the uncle of Henry the son of Simon, was seised in his demesne as of fee etc of thirty acres of land with appurtenances in Yaxley on the day he died, and if he died after the last return etc and if etc which land Hugh the son of William holds. He comes and says that the assize should not be taken on this because the said Richard was the uncle of the same Hugh and Henry and brother of their fathers from the [same] father and mother. Henry cannot deny this. So it is adjudged that the assize may not be taken between them. Henry is in mercy, and he may proceed [against] him by writ of right if he wishes. The amercement is pardoned.

209. (*Hartismere*) An assize comes to declare if John the son of Benedict, brother of Matilda the daughter of Benedict, was seised in his demesne etc of eight acres of land with appurtenances in Redlingfield on the day [he died] etc and if etc which land the prioress of Redlingfield¹ holds. She comes by her attorney and says that the assize should not proceed upon her because she [Matilda] impleaded her elsewhere concerning the same land by a writ of right in the county [court] and she sought judgement. Matilda cannot deny this. So it is adjudged that the prioress is to go without day on this. Matilda [is] in mercy. It is pardoned because [she is] poor.

¹ This was a Benedictine nunnery founded in 1120.

210. (*Norfolk, forty shillings*) William Schec¹ gives forty shillings to have a jury of twenty-four to attaint the twelve [jurors] by the surety of William de Auberville, John (the son of Robertⁱ) of Ubbeston and Hugh de Arderne the clerk.

¹ See **776** for the end of this plea.

211. (*Norfolk, twenty shillings*) Roger the son of Robert of Dereham¹ gives twenty shillings to have a jury of twenty-four to attaint the twelve by the surety of Nicholas of Lynn and Thomas of Grimston.

¹ There are two Derehams in Norfolk, East Dereham in Mitford hundred and West Dereham in Clackclose hundred. I think the latter is the likely one as East Dereham was in the liberty of Ely and the clerk may have made a reference to this in the margin.

212. (*Norfolk, twenty shillings*) Thomas of Grimston gives twenty shillings to have a jury of twenty-four to attaint the twelve by the surety of Adam of Rockland and Roger of Boyland. [**775**]

213.¹ (*Norfolk*) Geoffrey le Despencer who appealed John de Bosco concerning the peace of the lord king [broken] etc whence a duel by battle etc has not prosecuted. He is in gaol, and all his sureties [are] in mercy, namely: Matthew of Waxham, Thomas Youle of Waxham, John the son of Peter of Ingham, Bartholomew of Horsey,

Goscelin the son of Peter of Waxham, William the son of Goscelin of Ingham (*amercements*). Afterwards, Geoffrey came and made a fine for himself for one mark by the surety of Walter of Ingham knight (*one mark*).

> [1] This plea looks as though it is the result of a crown plea rather than a civil plea. See **1661** for the agreement.

214. (*Norfolk*) Baldwin de Freville who brought a writ of entry against Richard of Pattesley for six acres of land with appurtenances in Wellingham, has not prosecuted. So he and his sureties for prosecuting [are] in mercy, namely: Robert the son of Henry de Cressinghall, and Peter de Peleville, knight (*amercement*).

215. (*Norfolk*) The same Baldwin who brought a writ of entry against Alan Nodel and others named in the writ, has not prosecuted. So he and his sureties for prosecuting [are] in mercy. He made a fine for himself and his sureties for one mark by the surety of Thomas of Ingoldisthorpe (*one mark*).

216. (*Exning*)[1] An assize comes to declare if Robert Dobel, the father of Amice, Agnes and Matilda, was seised in his demesne as of fee of one and a half acres of land with appurtenances in Exning on the day he died, and if he died etc and if etc whose land Henry de Cumpenye holds. He comes and then vouches to warranty Edmund de Kemesec. He is to have him at Cattishall on the morrow of the Ascension of the Lord [Friday 25 May] by help of the court. He is to be summoned in the county of Essex (*Essex*).

> [1] Exning is in Suffolk and was classed as a hundred. See Cam 1930, p.279. In Domesday it was in Staploe hundred in Cambridgeshire.

217. (*Exning*) An assize comes to declare if Henry Modi, the father of Ralph was seised in his demesne etc of fifteen acres of land with appurtenances in Exning on the day he died, etc and if etc and if etc which land Geoffrey Beivin holds. He comes and then vouches to warranty the same Edmund. He is to have him at Cattishall on the morrow of the Ascension of the Lord [Friday 25 May] by help of the court. He is to be summoned in the county of Essex (*Cattishall, Essex*).

218. (*Exning*) An assize comes to declare if Robert the servant, Martin Gyle, Godwin le Snur, Ralph the son of John, Adam Wenedell, Nicholas Newman, John Grey, and Peter Starling unjustly disseised Rainer de Lagwode of his free tenement in Exning after the first etc.

John de Langwath of Exning and Alexander Steppere[1] of the same.[2]
Robert and all the others come and say that the assize should not be taken on this because he is a villein of Thomas de Hay.

He acknowledged the same. So he [is] in mercy for a false claim (*amercement*). He is remanded in custody, The others [are] without day. [Sureties] of Rainer ...[3] [unfinished].

> [1] According to the Reaney 1997, p.426 he was a bleacher of cloth or flax.
> [2] These are the sureties of Rainer as shown in **1642**. It is likely that their names were added later from the amercement section of the roll but the clerk did not write them in the correct place.
> [3] This is where the clerk should have put the two sureties shown above.

219. (*Hartismere*) Matilda, who was the wife of Reynold of Finningham, claims against Alphesia of Bacton half of one acre of land with appurtenances in Finningham as her dower etc.

Alphesia comes and then vouches to warranty the prior of Bricett who is present and he warrants her. He then vouches to warranty Robert de Somers. He is to have him at Cattishall on the morrow of the Ascension of the Lord [Friday 25 May] by the aid of the court (*Cattishall*). He is to be summoned in the county of Suffolk (*Suffolk*). **[1020]**

220. (*Mutford, half a mark*) Walter Craske gives half a mark for licence to agree with Thomas le Latimer concerning a plea of warranty of charter by the surety of Simon le Daveys. [*chirograph* CP 25(1) 213/16/54]

221. (*Norfolk*) Leunia, who was the wife of Peter le Franceys, who claimed her dower against Hugh the son of Ralph Curlew, comes and acknowledges that they have given satisfaction to her. So all [are] without day.

222. (*Hartismere*) Agnes, who was the wife of Robert de Furnell, claims against Ralph de Furnell half of thirty-four acres of land with appurtenances and three shillings and two penceworth of rent with appurtenances in Bacton, and against William the son of Simon half of six acres of land with appurtenances in the same vill, and against Simon the baker and William his brother half of two and a half acres of land with appurtenances in the same vill, and against William Mutred half of four acres of land with appurtenances in the same vill as her dower etc.

Ralph and the others come and vouch to warranty, for the half of the said thirty-four acres of land and of three shillings and two penceworth of rent with appurtenances, Roger de Furnell, who is present, and warrants them. All the others similarly then vouch that Roger to warranty, who is present, and he warrants them. He answered for all and says that she ought not to have half but a third part because it is knight's fee and not socage, and she cannot deny this, and she holds herself satisfied. So she is to have her seisin etc. Roger makes an exchange to them to the value [of their holdings] etc.

223.[1] (*Stow*) An assize comes to declare if Godwin de Ponte, the father of Mabel, the wife of Ernulf Smackinger, was seised in his demesne etc of one and a half acres of land with appurtenances in Creeting [St Peter][2] on the day he died etc and if etc and if etc which land Adam de Ponte holds. He comes and says that the assize should not be taken on this because a certain William the brother of Mabel, who was the rightful heir of Godwin after the death of Godwin, quitclaimed all right and claim that he had in the said land to this Adam by a certain charter, which he made on this, and which he proffers, and which attests to this. But, in fact he says that he never was seised of the said land. Afterwards, the same Adam comes and says that the said Godwin died before the term. Afterwards, he grants that he died within the term, and she is to recover her seisin against him. He [is] in mercy for an unjust detention (*amercement*).

[1] There is a gap between this plea and the previous one of approx. 4.5 cm.
[2] This is in Stow hundred. Creeting St Mary is in Bosmere hundred.

Membrane 8

224.[1] Margery, who was the wife of Henry de Kemesec, by her attorney claims (against[i]) William Meyner two acres of land with appurtenances in Exning, and against Ralph Cook two acres of land with appurtenances in the same vill, and against Godwina, who was the wife of Rainer of Newmarket, six acres of land with appurtenances in the same vill, and against Martin Young two acres of land with appurtenances in the same vill, and against Walter the son of Ivetta four acres of land in the same vill, and against Geoffrey Hole six acres of land with appur-

36

tenances in the same vill, and against William Notting three acres of land with appurtenances in the same vill, and against Gilbert of Burwell four and a half acres of land with appurtenances in the same vill, and against Stannard Smith three acres and three roods of land with appurtenances in the same vill, and against Alexander Chapp fifteen acres of land with appurtenances in the same vill, and against John Landwathe sixteen acres of land with appurtenances in the same vill, and against Peter the merchant one acre and one messuage with appurtenances in the same vill, and against Simon Gyrim[2] fifteen acres of land with appurtenances in the same vill, and against Henry de Kumpenye[3] forty-seven acres of land with appurtenances in the same vill, and against Millicent Russel fifteen acres of land with appurtenances in the same vill, and against Ralph Cissor[4] one messuage with appurtenances in the same vill, and against Simon Gerard ten acres of land with appurtenances in the same vill, and against William Prior[5] two acres of land with appurtenances in the same vill, and against Walter Thekewald nine acres of land with appurtenances in the same vill, and against Martin Fish one acre of land with appurtenances in the same vill, and against Thomas le Sumeter three roods of land with appurtenances in the same vill, and against Geoffrey Chaplain one and a half acres of land with appurtenances in the same vill, and against Elias le Beyt one and a half acres [of land] with appurtenances in the same vill, and against John Godfrey one acre of land with appurtenances in the same vill, and against Richard Gyrdemere two acres of land with appurtenances in the same vill, and against Agnes Pyring one and a half acres of land with appurtenances in the same vill, and against Ralph Mody one acre of land with appurtenances in the same vill, as her dower in respect whereof Henry Kemesec, her former husband, expressly dowered her. William Meyner and all the other tenants come in person except for William Priur who comes by his attorney, Henry de Kumpenye, and they claim a view. They are to have it.

A day is given to them on a day five weeks after Easter at Cattishall, as from the day in the day (*At Cattishall*). They all appoint Henry de Kumpenye (or[i])[6] Walter the son of Ivetta as their attorney.[7]

[1]   The hand changes here to one that is more decorated with flourishes.

[2]   This is probably the name Grim. See Reaney 1997, pp.206–207.

[3]   This might be the name Compain. See Reaney 1997, p.107.

[4]   He was a cutter of cloth, or tailor.

[5]   See **183** for the appointment of an attorney where he is shown as 'William Prior'.

[6]   The clerk had crossed out *et* and inserted *vel*.

[7]   This adds up to 172 acres and two messuages, a sizeable dower. The original holding would have been three times this in acreage with one third to the widow and two thirds to the heir.

225.[1] The same Margery presented herself on the fourth day by her attorney against Warren the carter concerning a plea [for] one rood of land with appurtenances in the same vill, and against Hervey the clerk concerning a plea of one messuage with appurtenances in the same vill, and against Peter de Hauville concerning one messuage with appurtenances in the same vill (which she claims as her dower etc.[i]) Warren, Hervey and Peter have not come etc and [were] summoned etc. Judgement: the land shall be taken [into the hands of the king] etc and the day etc and they are to be summoned to be there at the same term [of the court] etc. Afterwards,[2] Edmund de Kemesec comes and warrants all the above mentioned. He has nothing to say why [she should not have] her dower both of the manor of Exning and of the manor of Chilbourne with all its appurtenances in respect whereof she was expressly dowered. So it is adjudged that she is to recover her seisin against him.

Edmund [is] in mercy, and is to make an exchange to the value for all, and similarly [to pay] damages[3] (*amercement*).

1 There is a line from the previous plea from in front of *Datus est* … to the start of this plea to show the clerk that they are connected and that the clerks possibly should not place anything in the gap of 6 cm left after the previous plea.
2 There is a change of clerk here so this postscript must have been put in later, possibly at Cattishall.
3 This now gives Margery another one rood and two messuages.

226. (*Norfolk*) Simon of Whatfield presented himself on the fourth day against Margery de Rivers concerning a plea that she warrant him sixty acres of land and one messuage with appurtenances in Stoke which Robert de Curton claims as his right against him and in respect whereof the same Simon vouched to warranty the same Margery. Margery has not come etc and was summoned etc. So it is adjudged that the land of Margery be taken [into the hands of the lord king] etc to the value [of that claimed] etc. The day [of confiscation is to be told to the justices] etc [and on that day] she is to be summoned [to be here] etc but, because it is not known concerning the value of the said land and messuage, a survey and valuation is to be made. The survey etc he [the sheriff] is to make known at Cattishall on the fifth week after Easter [Monday 21 May][1] by letters etc and by two [of those who made the inquest]. When the sheriff has made known the survey [and value] of the land then let the sheriff of Hertford be commanded that he may take etc to the value [remaining] etc the day etc and she is to be summoned [to appear] (*Hertford*).

1 This should be Sunday 20 May. According to Crook 1982a, p.101 the eyre started at Cattishall on Monday 21 May.

227. (*ten shillings*) Peter of Burgate gives ten shillings for licence to agree with Thomas of Gedding concerning a plea of the assize of mort d'ancestor by the surety of Adam of Tivetshall and John Talchot. [*chirograph* CP 25(1) 213/15/35]

228. (*10 shillings*) The same Thomas gives ten shillings for licence to agree with the same [Peter of Burgate] concerning the same plea by the surety of the same Peter. [*chirograph* CP 25(1) 213/15/35]

229. (*Blything, 40 shillings*) Godfrey the parker[1] gives forty shillings for licence to agree with Theobald of Leiston by the surety of Theobald of Leiston. [*chirograph* CP 25(1) 213/15/22]

1 A parker was a park keeper. For cases involving parks see **159** and **856**.

230. Ralph de *Thonny* by his attorney claims against Herbert Alicon two hundred marks, which he owes to him and which he unjustly holds back. The same Ralph complains in respect whereof that since by his charter he should have paid in full to the same Ralph or his attorney, one hundred pounds within the octave of Easter in the nineteenth year of the reign of King Henry [Sunday 15 April 1235], and fifty marks within the next octave of St Michael following in the same year [Saturday 6 October], the same Herbert held back from him the said two hundred marks, in respect whereof he has suffered loss and damage to the value of fifty marks, and he produces the charter of Herbert which attests to this.

Herbert comes and a day is given to them at Chelmsford in the octave of the Holy Trinity by prayer of the parties etc. (*Chelmsford*).

231. (*Blything*) A jury comes to declare whether nineteen acres of land with appurtenances in Henstead are free alms pertaining to the church of Henstead whereof

Robert de Henford is parson, or the lay fee of Robert of Blundeston, Robert of Aveley, Alan de Marisco, Robert the son of Alexander, and Alan Grinnel, and in respect whereof the said Robert of Blundeston holds fifteen acres, and Robert two acres, Alan de Marisco half an acre, and Robert one acre, and Alan half an acre. Robert of Blundeston and Alan Grinnel and Robert the son of Alexander come [to the assize]. Robert of Blundeston acknowledges that the said fifteen acres of land with appurtenances are free alms of that church. So it is adjudged that Robert the parson has recovered his seisin, and Robert of Blundeston [is] in mercy by the surety of William de Lech of Wrentham. Alan says nothing to stay the jury, and all are to come on Thursday (*amercement, Thursday*).

Robert the son of Alexander comes and then vouches to warranty Walter Legat [and] he is to have him by help of the court on Thursday. Afterwards, Robert the parson of Henstead comes and acknowledges that all have satisfied him except Alan de Marisco who has not come and he was re-summoned etc. So let the assize be taken against him by default.

The jurors[1] say that that the half acre is free alms pertaining to the church of Henstead. So it is adjudged that Robert the parson is to have his seisin and Alan is in mercy for an unjust detention (*amercement*).

> 1 This paragraph is written in different ink and may also be in a different hand.

232.[1] (*Norfolk*) Ismania, who was the wife of John Costentin claimed against Jacob of Barking a half of two acres of land with appurtenances in Terrington, and against Reynold le Walsch and Stephen the son of Godwin a half of one and a half acres of land with appurtenances in the same vill, and against Walter of Terrington a half of one and a half acres of land with appurtenances in the same vill as her dower etc. Jacob and all the others come and by licence they render [the lands] to her. She is to have her seisin etc.

> 1 There is a 6.5 cm gap between this plea and the previous one.

233. John de Hauville appoints as his attorney Walter Bruse against Alice de Mara concerning a plea of dower etc. [**349**]

234. Avelina, the wife of Henry Prat, appoints as her attorney her husband Henry Prat against Roger the son of Gilbert concerning a plea of land etc.

Membrane 8d

235. (*Norfolk, half a mark*) Peter of Pickenham gives half a mark for licence to agree with Simon the son of Ernald concerning a plea of land by the surety of the same Simon. [*chirograph* CP 25(1) 156/66/824]

236. (*Blything*) An assize comes to declare if Roger of Carlton, Roger of Runham, Peter his brother, Simon Marshall, Edmund of Brundish, Roger Calf, John of Carlton, William de Releshal, Roger of Carlton, William Bachelor, Richard Potekine, Thomas Lenebaud[1], Nicholas le Sol, Osbert Gas, Frebert Kins, William Lenebaud, Roger his son, Austin Bleriwas, Hugh Bekecot, William the son of Roger, Alan Hard, William of Framlingham, William Capel, William de Fremigham[2] and Geoffrey the hosier unjustly etc disseised William of Cotton and Joan his wife of their free tenement in Bruisyard and Peasenhall after the first crossing etc and in respect whereof the same (William[i]) and Joan complain that they disseised them of twenty acres of land with appurtenances in Peasenhall and eight acres of land with appurtenances in Bruisyard.

None (of those[i]) disseisors has come except Roger of Carlton, the first named in the writ, and Thomas Lenebaud who say nothing to stay the assize. Of those who have not come, they were not found nor attached because all [are] unknown and the men of R. Bigod the earl of Norfolk.

The jurors say that Roger and all the others disseised them as the writ says. So it is adjudged that they have recovered their seisin against them, and Roger and all the others [are] in mercy (*amercements*). Sureties of Roger and Thomas: Herbert [de] Alicon,[3] and Ralph le Bigod the uncle of the earl R. Bigod. Afterwards, Roger of Carleton came and made a fine for forty shillings for himself and all the others by the surety of the above mentioned (*forty shillings, to the clerks*).

Damages: three shillings.

[1]   Thomas Lenebaud was a clerk and seems to have been very important in the Bigod administration. He witnesses five out of the ten surviving charters for Roger Bigod III, and the witnessing occurs right down to this earl's death in 1270. See Morris 2005, pp.69–70. He was one of the executors of Roger Bigod III's will, and seems to have fallen out with the next earl over its execution. He died *c*.1283. If this is he, which seems likely given the fact that he represents the accused with Roger de Carleton, then this is his earliest Bigod related appearance.

[2]   This is probably 'Framlingham' as well.

[3]   See **145** n.3 for the relationship between Herbert de Alicon and the Bigods.

237. (*sixteen marks*) William of Gislingham recognises that he owes to Thomas de Buck ten silver marks[1] of a fine made between them, which he will pay to him on the feast day of St Michael in the twenty-fourth year [29 September]. If he does not do [this] as he grants that he may be distrained etc while etc and concerning the cost etc.

[1]   I presume that the debtor originally owed 16 marks and now owes 10, unless 10 marks of silver equals 16 marks in other metal.

238. (*Blything*) An assize comes to declare if Agnes Aylwy, the mother of Alice and Agnes, was seised in her demesne as of fee of two messuages with appurtenances in Southwold on the day of which she died etc and if she died etc and if the said [Alice and Agnes are her next heirs] etc which messuages John de Balye and Richard Tacun hold. They have not come and they have been resummoned. So let the assize be taken against them by default.

The jurors say that the said Agnes did not die seised of the said messuages as of fee because she was a villein of the abbot of Bury St Edmunds and she held that land in villeinage. So it is adjudged that they are to take nothing by this assize, and they are in mercy for a false claim. The amercement is pardoned because they are under age and poor.

239. (*Bosmere*) A jury comes to declare whether one and a half acres of land with appurtenances in [Steeple] Barking[1] is free alms pertaining to the church of Adam the parson of [Steeple] Barking or the lay fee of Robert the son of Ivo, Roger le Grey and Alice his wife, and in respect whereof the said Robert holds half and the said Roger and Alice the other half. They come and acknowledge that the said land is the free alms of the said church and they have entry into that land by a certain Ralph, who was the [previous] parson of the same church, and that they have nothing from the ordinary of the place nor of the [parsons'].[2] So it is adjudged that the said Adam is to recover his seisin and they [are] in mercy for an unjust detention (*amercements*).

[1]   The clerk has written *Stepelberching*. I believe that this place must be the Barking in Bosmere hundred but I cannot find such a place as Steeple Barking in Bosmere hundred.

² I think this should be *personis* to keep it in context. The clerk wrote *pranis.*

240. (*Mutford*) An assize comes to declare if Alan the son of Richard unjustly etc disseised Richard the son of Thomas of his free tenement in Kessingland after the first etc and in respect whereof the same Richard complains the said Alan disseised him of about two acres of land etc.

Alan has not come and he was attached by Robert of Mutford, the serjeant. So Robert [is] in mercy and the assize may be taken against him by default.

The jurors say that the said Alan disseised the said Richard as the writ says. So it is adjudged that the same Richard is to recover his seisin against him and Alan [is] in mercy for disseisin (*amercement*). Remand in custody.

Damages: four shillings.

241. (*Norfolk one mark*) William Malerbe give one mark for licence to agree with Ranulf of Cringleford concerning a plea of land by the surety of Ranulf of Cringleford. [*chirograph* CP 25(1) 156/67/836]

242. (*Norfolk, one mark*) Ranulf of Cringleford gives one mark for licence to agree with the same concerning the same [land] by the surety of the same William. [*chirograph* CP 25(1) 156/67/836]

243. (*twenty shillings*) William of Darsham gives twenty shillings for licence to agree with Robert Snow concerning a plea of land by the surety of William the son of Simon of Hempnall and the same Robert Snow. [*chirograph* CP 25(1) 213/16/68]

244.¹ (*Stow*) An assize comes to declare if Richard Caiphas unjustly etc disseised Ralph the son of William of his free tenement in Creeting [St Peter] after the first crossing etc and in respect whereof that he disseised him of one acre of land with appurtenances in the same vill.

Richard comes and says nothing to stay the assize.

The jurors say that the said Richard disseised the said Ralph as the writ says. So it is adjudged that Ralph is to recover his seisin against him. Richard [is] in mercy for disseisin (*amercement, forty pence*). He is remanded in custody (*Remand in custody*).

Damages: half a mark.

Afterwards, Richard Caiphas (comesⁱ) and gives forty shillings to have a jury of twenty-four to attaint the twelve etc. (*forty shillings*).

¹ The amount to have the attaint is shown again in **779**.

245. (*Hartismere*) Geoffrey of Hickling who brought an assize of novel disseisin against Hubert Gernegan and others named in the writ has not prosecuted. So he and his sureties for prosecuting [are] in mercy, namely William the son of Robert of Rishangles and Hubert Hacon knights (*amercements*).

246. (*Ipswich*) A jury comes to declare whether eight acres of land and one messuage with appurtenances are free alms pertaining to the church of Stoke, in respect whereof Master William of Massingham is the parson, or the lay fee of Reynold the clerk. He came and by licence they have agreed. The agreement is such that the same Reynold acknowledges that the said land and messuage are the free alms of the said church and he [Reynold] hands it over to him [William]. For this return the same William gives to the same Reynold six marks. So he is to have his seisin etc. The prior of Ely places his claim etc. [*chirograph* CP 25(1) 213/15/30.¹]

[1] On the reverse of the chirograph it indicates that the prior of Ely laid a claim for the land in his demesne and for villein services. The chirograph also indicates that Agnes de Presteshey also laid a claim on the reverse.

247. (*Samford*) An assize comes to declare if Geoffrey the son of William unjustly etc disseised Richard Wygeyn of his free tenement in Chattisham after the first etc and in respect whereof the said Richard complains that the said Geoffrey disseised him of a certain quickset hedge in the same vill.

Geoffrey comes and says nothing to stay the assize.

The jurors say that Geoffrey did not disseise him as the writ says. So it is adjudged that Richard is to take nothing by this assize and is in mercy for a false claim, by the surety of Richard Earl of Belstead[1] (*amercement*). Richard [is] without day.

[1] The clerk wrote *Bested* but as the plea is a Samford plea, I think this place is Belstead which is in Samford hundred. The amercement section also indicates '*Belstede*'.

248. (*Lothingland*) William of Hevingham[1] and Grace, his wife, in whose place[2] [an attorney comes] etc claim against Herbert of Hoveton twenty acres of land with appurtenances in Browston, Hobland and Wheatcroft[3] and against Edmund Woodcock twenty acres of land with appurtenances in the same vills, as the right of the same Grace.

Herbert and Edmund come and claim a view (in respect thereof[i]). They are to have [it] and they are to come on a Friday etc [**484** and **980**].

[1] There is a Hevingham in South Erpingham hundred in Norfolk and a Heveningham in Blything hundred. It is not possible to determine which it is. The clerk wrote *Hevingham*.
[2] This looks like a standard phrase that indicates that Grace was represented by an attorney.
[3] Hobland and Wheatcroft are not much more than farms. There is a Hobland Hall, possibly a manor house, still in existence.

249. (*Mutford, age*) Hawise of Hopton (claims[i]) against Roger de Colville six shillings and two penceworth of rent with appurtenances in Carlton [Colville] and Henstead, which she claims to be her right and marriage portion, and in which the same Roger does not have entry except by Robert de Colville to whom Geoffrey of Sandon,[1] the former husband of the said Hawise, demised that [rent], whom she in his lifetime could not contradict.

Roger comes and says that his father died seised of the said rent, and that he is under age and claimed his age and he has [it]. So the plea is without day until [he comes] of age.

[1] There is a Sandon in a number of counties of which the nearest to Suffolk is in Essex. Others are in Berkshire, Hertfordshire and Staffordshire. It is also possible the clerk meant Santon, which is in Lackford hundred.

250. William the Ewer appoints as his attorney Walkelin of Holbrook against Agnes de *Bromford*[1] concerning a plea of land.

[1] Probably Bramford in Bosmere hundred. But it could also be *Bruniford* as there are a number of pleas with Agnes de *Bruniford*.

251.[1] Robert de Wykes and Amice his wife appoint as their attorney Ralph Marshall against Roger Rain[2] and his wife Agnes concerning a plea of dower. [**470**]

[1] There is no paragraph mark at the start of this attorney. However, all other attorneys have a separate mark.
[2] In **470** he is shown as 'Roger Train'.

Membrane 9

252. A jury comes to declare whether fifty acres and one rood of land[1] with appurtenances in Willingham are free alms pertaining to the church of Master Robert de
Saintes in Willingham or the lay fee of Waleran de Muncy, William Holdman, Geof-
frey Oldman, Henry the clerk, Geoffrey of Weston, William his brother, William
de Bosco, Laurence Wade, Robert of Shadingfield, Alice his wife, Philip the son
of Robert, the widow Gunnilde, Dunstan the son of Wuner,[2] Geoffrey the son of
Godwin, Macelina the daughter of the widow Lettice, Philip the palmer and William
Huntman, in respect whereof the said Waleran holds twelve acres [of land], William
Holdman one rood, Henry the clerk one and a half acres, Walter[3] one rood, Geoffrey
Oldman one acre, Geoffrey of Weston and William his brother five roods, William
de Bosco half an acre, Laurence, Robert and Alice his wife two acres, the widow
Gunnilde one and a half acres, Philip the son of Robert one acre, Dunstan six acres,
Alice half an acre, Geoffrey the son of Godwin eight acres, Macelina two acres,
Philip the palmer three acres and William Huntman two acres. Waleran and all
the others have come and Waleran acknowledged that three [of the] acres, which
he holds from the twelve acres, which are called *Aylwardesdale*[4] are the free alms
pertaining to the said church. Robert, the parson, grants that he may hold the said
three acres by service of three pence per year, and concerning the nine acres, he
says that they are not the demesne nor fee of the church, but his ancestors gave to
the same church twelve penceworth of rent and they granted that if the said rent is
in arrears at any time those nine acres may be distrained for that rent. Afterwards,
he grants that he may hold in peace as he held it previously. Waleran gives to the
parson one mark. William Oldman acknowledges that he owes to the said church
one halfpenny per annum but his land is not [held] in fee nor [is in] the demesne of
the church. Henry the clerk, concerning one and a half acres, vouches (to warranty[i])
Walter Cobbe, who is present and is under age. So let the said Henry hold his land
in peace until the boy is of age. Geoffrey Oldman acknowledges that he holds his
land from the church by the service of two and a half pence per annum. Geoffrey of
Weston and (William[i]) his brother acknowledge that they hold from the church by
the service of three pence per annum. William de Bosco acknowledges that he holds
from the church by the service of one penny per annum. Laurence Wade, and Robert
of Shadingfield and Alice his wife acknowledge that they hold their land from the
church by two and a half pence per annum. Gunnilda acknowledges that she holds
from the church by four pence per annum. Philip, the son of Robert, acknowledges
that he holds from the church by two pence per annum. Dunstan [acknowledges
that he] holds from the church by twenty six pence per annum. Geoffrey, the son of
Godwin, acknowledges that he holds from the church by two shillings per annum.
Mascelina acknowledges that she, similarly with Leticia her mother, hold from the
church by five pence per annum. Philip the palmer acknowledges that he holds from
the church by nine pence per annum. William Huntman acknowledges that he holds
from the church by five pence per annum.

The same Robert afterwards has granted that everyone of the said tenants is to
hold as he has acknowledged for as long as he lives. Meanwhile, he acknowledged
that the widow Avelina, Henry Cogger, Avelina the daughter of Godwin, Ralph the
son of Maricite, Alexander his son, the widow Mascelina, who are named in the
writ, have not come and given [him] satisfaction.[5]

[1] I calculate it as up to 48 acres of land.

2   It looks as though the clerk was going to put in *Willelmi* as an 'l' looks as though it is rubbed out in the middle of the name.
3   This name does not appear in the original list.
4   This place cannot be found near Willingham in Wangford hundred.
5   This Mascelina must be a different one from that named above in the original list; for all these additional names in the writ there is no indication of what they own in the plea. If this Mascelina was the one in the plea it would mean the clerk has made a mistake.

253. (*Blything, half a mark*) Alexander the son of [Swaine][1] gives half a mark for licence (to agree[i]) with Susanna his mother concerning a plea of warranty of charter by the surety of John de Brook of Beeston. [*chirograph* CP 25(1) 213/15/40][2]

1   This name has a matronymic ending but I can find no woman's name like this, unless it is a form of 'Susanna'. In the agreement section of this roll [**1661**] he is shown as 'Alexander the son of Susanna'. However, as 'Swain' is a recognised name for a man I have kept the name in the translation. However I have cross-referenced them in the index of people and places.
2   In the chirograph Alexander is shown as the son of Warren, not Swain or Susanna.

254. (*Norfolk*) Beatrice who was the wife of Robert Sorel claims against Geoffrey Raynard half of two acres of land with appurtenances in North Lynn as her dower, and in respect whereof Robert her former husband dowered her etc.

Geoffrey comes and vouches to warranty William Sorel who is present and he warrants him and he gives satisfaction to the said Beatrice so she is to have her seisin. Beatrice appoints as her attorney William de Munescedon or Ralph Aeremund and others in the writ concerning the plea of dower.

255. (*Essex*) Hugh de Hodden and Thomas de Lascelles claim by their attorneys against Idonea de Beche a third of two carucates of land and one messuage with appurtenances in Great Maplestead as their right, in which the said Idonea did not have entry except by Wynda de Wyndeshover, who held that [land] in dower from the gift of Walter de Wyndeshover, her husband, and cousin of the said Hugh and Thomas, who are his heirs.

Idonea de Beche comes and denies force and injury and such entry, and she says that in fact the said Wynda held that land in dower, so namely that after the death of the said Walter, her husband, who died without heirs from her, William de Freyney, her father [Idonea's] and brother to the said Walter, assigned the said land to the said Wynda as her dower as the rightful heir of Walter himself, his brother, for all the tenements which he William held. The same William had two daughters, a certain Margery, the first born, and this Idonea the later born. After the death of William, Robert Aguillon came, who married the said Margery, and he placed himself in all the inheritance of William so that same Idonea pleaded them in the court of the lord king for her share. As a result she at length proved title to that same land which is claimed against her by a fine made in the same court. And because from the said Margery there issued three daughters, namely (a certain[i]) Isabella, Ella and Margery, and from Isabel issued Adam, her son, who is present and [who is] under age and her parcener, it does not seem to her that she ought to answer them concerning the said land until Adam will be of full age nor also without her [other] parceners, namely: Thomas of Poynings, the said Ella his wife, Giles de Argentan and the said Margery his wife, who by their attorneys are present, unless the court gave judgement.

(*on Thursday*) Afterwards, they have come to terms.[1] They are to have a chirograph.

1   See **488** for some of the detail of the agreement.

256.[1] Alice, who was the wife of Robert Aylwy, acknowledged that the abbot of Sibton and all the others named in the writ against whom she claimed her dower have given her satisfaction concerning her dower. So all [are to be] without day.

1   There is gap of 4.9 cm between this plea and the previous one.

257. Macelina, who was the wife of Alan the son of Richard, of whom she claimed dower against Simon Osman and many others in the writ, came and acknowledged that all have given satisfaction. So she is to have her seisin.

258. (*Blything*) An assize comes to declare if Thomas le Latimer unjustly disseised the prior of Wangford of his free tenement in *Hatheburfeud*[1] etc and in respect whereof the prior complains that he disseised him of five shillings and four pence-worth of rent and four cocks per annum etc (from the four tenants in the same vill namely: Philip Curlew forty pence, Dene Brid twenty pence and four hens[i]), Alan the son of Godwin two pence and one salt pan, and Andrew the son of Presberi two pence and two hens, who[2] are present and it is said to them that henceforth they must answer to the said prior and [his successors][3] for their services from their tenements as [their] lord.

Thomas comes and by licence renders to him his seisin. So the prior is to have his seisin.

1   This might be Bramfield in Blything hundred, which is shown as 'Burifelda' in Domesday Book, but more likely is an unidentified vill called *Hatheburgfelda* which is shown in *Domesday Book Suffolk*, Part One, section 4, no. 33 etc. in Wangford hundred.

2   The clerk has this part of the sentence at the end of the plea with a mark after *gallinas*, 'hens', and another before *qui* to indicate that the rest of this sentence should be placed here.

3   Normally when there is a case involving services to a prior there is the phrase indicating that it also relates to his successors in the role of prior, so I have inserted it here.

259. (*Blything*) An assize comes to declare if [Thorald][1] Bert unjustly etc raised a dyke in Henstead to the nuisance of the free tenement of Margery of Poynings in the same vill etc.

The same assize comes to declare if William Ore, Ralph Spirard and William Berewer unjustly etc disseised the same Margery of common pasture in Benacre which pertains to her free tenement in Wrentham after the first etc.

Thorald and the others have not come, but Simon de Pierpont comes and says that they are his villeins and he answers for them, and says nothing to stay the assize.

The jurors say that the said William, Ralph and William disseised Margery of common pasture, which pasture[2] [she placed] in their view, except [for] around four acres, which had been cultivated since olden times. So it is adjudged that she has recovered her seisin, and they [are] in mercy for disseisin (*amercements*). Because the said Margery placed more in their view than was disseised therefrom, so [she is] in mercy. They say, furthermore, that Thorald raised the dyke as the writ says. So it is adjudged that he is in mercy, and by view of the recognitors the nuisance will be levelled. Note: that Simon Pierpont is the surety of his men.

Damages: for pasture six pence.

Damages: for ditch fifteen pence.

1   The clerk originally wrote *Thorardus* but the name later changes to *Thoraldus*, which is probably correct. In the amercement section of this roll he is shown as 'Thomas'; see **1642**, the last entry.

2   The clerk wrote the Latin word for 'pasture'. He should have written *pasturam* to agree with *quam*.

45

260. (*Samford*)[1] An assize comes to declare if William Gerald the father of Michael was seised in his demesne as of fee of one messuage and forty acres of land with appurtenances in Sutton on the day that he died, and if he died etc and if the said Michael [is his nearest heir] etc which land Flora Iovenal holds. She comes and by licence renders [it] to him, saving her pasture in the same land until the festival of St Michael, so however that the same Michael will be able to fallow that land within that term if he wishes. He is to have his seisin.

1   I think the clerk should have put Wilford as Sutton is in Wilford hundred, unless he made a mistake in the text as there is a Stutton in Samford hundred.

261. Gervase of Bradfield[1] appoints as his attorney ... [unfinished]

1   This is Bradfield Combust, Bradfield St Clare or Bradfield St George in Thedwestry hundred.

262. Philip of Flegg appoints as his attorney Raymond of Hickling against Andrew of Hingham concerning a plea to hear judgement. [**178** and **1114**]

Membrane 9d

263. (*Kent*) Alice, who was the wife of John of Cuddington, by her attorney claims [against] the abbot of Lesnes[1] half of twenty-four acres of land with appurtenances in Chiselhurst as her dower etc.

The abbot by his attorney comes and then claims a view. Let him have it. A day is given to them at Chelmsford in the county of Essex in the octave of Holy Trinity [Sunday 17 June] etc. (*Chelmsford*). In the meanwhile etc.

1   Lesnes was an abbey of Augustinian canons in Kent founded in 1178 by Richard de Lucy.

264. (*Blything*) Robert de Grimilies, Richard Cook and Nigel, his groom, were attached to answer William the Breton concerning a plea why they entered into his rabbit warren by force and arms in Sternfield and beat his serjeant against the peace of the lord king.

Robert comes and gives one hundred shillings for licence to agree by the surety of Simon de Pierpont and William de Auberville (*one hundred shillings*). The same Robert recognises that he owes to the same William twenty marks of which he shall pay to him ten marks at the feast of St Michael [29 September] in year twenty-four [of King Henry III etc]; and ten marks at the next Easter following the beginning [of year] twenty-five.[1] If he does not do [this] etc he grants that he may be distrained by[his] land [and chattels] etc until etc and as regards to the cost etc. [*chirograph* CP 25(1) 213/17/83][2]

1   That is on 31 March 1241 after the start of year 25, which began on 28 October. See Cheney 1996, p.19.
2   The agreement only indicates that 20 marks would be paid; the payment schedule is not mentioned.

265. (*Blything*) The jury comes to declare by command of the lord king by means of Baldwin of Mellis, Alan de Money, Walter of Cove, John Blench, Hugh of Cotton, Robert of Easton, Henry de Enepol, Robert of Wissett, Michael of Bungay, Robert the son of Adam, John de Hechede, Edmund de Wymundhall, Adam de Suthall, whether the wreck of the manor of Wrentham was accustomed to belong to the lords of the same manor of Wrentham, so that our beloved and faithful Simon de Pierpont and his predecessors have had hitherto that [wreck], or to us [the king] so that we were accustomed to have that [wreck]. They [the jurors] say on their oath that the predecessors of that Simon always have had wreck as long as the land was theirs as pertaining to their manor in Wrentham. As a result the same Simon, for all his time until one and a half years ago, was in seisin of the said wreck when the lord king took the wreckage there. Therefore the lord king, or his ancestors, never previously had wreck in the land of that manor, until the said time[1] (*coram rege*).

[1] Wreck is the right to seize objects cast on the shore. See Plucknett 1948, pp.422–423. Instead of giving judgement against the king in line with the jury's verdict, he adjourns the case *coram rege*. I have not found any record of it there.

266. (*Blything*) The abbot of Leiston was summoned to answer Robert de Blaueny[1] concerning a plea that he render to him four charters which he unjustly withholds from him etc.[2]

The abbot comes and acknowledges that he lent to Michael de Blaueny, the brother of Robert, a certain chest at his religious house of Leiston where the same Michael placed certain[3] [charters], but he readily affirms that he does not know whether he placed the charters or other things in there and closed the chest and carried off the key. He readily grants that the same Robert may come there and open that chest and see if his charters can be found there or not. He may come on Thursday[4] (*on Thursday*). Afterwards, the abbot comes and renders to him three charters because more are not found in that chest. So [he is] without day.

[1] There is some rubbing out below the name, which has obscured the tail of the 'y'.
[2] This is a plea of detinue of charter.
[3] This is the place where the something rubbed out and interlined should be placed. It is difficult to read but could be *carte* for charters. If this is correct then this should be accusative and should be *quasdam*. In which case *carte* is also wrong and should be *cartas*. Perhaps this is why it was rubbed out but the clerk forgot to correct it all.
[4] This could be Thursday 3 or 10 May as these are the Thursdays when the eyre was at Ipswich.

267. (*Norfolk, half a mark*) Henry of Henstead gives half a mark for licence to agree with Richer of Cawston and Juliana his wife concerning a plea of land by the surety of Richer of Cawston etc. The agreement is as follows: that two acres of land with appurtenances in Henstead,[1] which the same Richer [and] Juliana claimed against Marriota the daughter of John of Matlask and Henry her son remain to the same Richer and Juliana and to the heirs of that Juliana.

[1] I have not been able to locate a Henstead in Norfolk. There is one in Blything hundred. There is a Hempstead in Happing hundred and also one in Holt hundred in Norfolk. I have assumed the one in Suffolk because of the spelling of the place name and the also the name of one of the litigants. It is possible that this plea started in Norfolk and the agreement was completed here.

268.[1] (*Norfolk*) William of Reedham and Matthew his son and Ralph the rector of the church of Reedham (have acknowledged[s])[2] that they have granted to Stephen of Reedham, knight, that he and his heirs henceforth can hunt freely and without hindrance of others in the warren of Reedham whenever they wish and with whomsoever they wish and as often soever as regards to hares and other beasts of the chase and birds to be captured when they are there. If they are not it has been readily allowed to them to send in those whomsoever [they] wish. Meanwhile they have granted that all the other things contained in the chirograph, duly established between them in the agreement, remain valid.

[1] There is a new hand for this plea and the next one; thereafter it reverts back to the original clerk for this membrane.
[2] The clerk wrote *convoverunt*; this should be *cognoverunt*, 'have acknowledged'.

269. John of Brantham appoints as his attorney Ralph de Flay against Agnes de *Bruniford* concerning a plea of debt etc. [**353**]

270. (*St Etheldreda*) Isolda, who was the wife of Walter le Deynes,[1] presented herself on the fourth day against Roger de Mohaut concerning a plea for a third part of fifteen shillings with appurtenances in Cretingham, and concerning a plea of half of two shillingsworth of rent with appurtenances in Ipswich, and against Adam the son of Roger concerning a plea of half of eleven acres of land with appurtenances in Framsden which she claims in dower against them. They have not come and were summoned. Judgement: the half and the third part may be taken into the lord king's hand. The day for confiscation [is told to the justices] etc and they are to be summoned to be at Cattishall on the morrow [of the feast] of the Ascension (*Cattishall*).

> [1]   See **576** for what I believe is a continuation of part of this plea but the name of Isolda is shown as the wife of 'Walter de Deneys' in that plea.

271. (*Bosmere, half a mark*) Roger of Ketteringham gives half a mark for licence to agree with John le Bret concerning a plea of land and a plea of ward by the surety of John himself and William Malerbe from the county of Norfolk. [*chirograph* CP 25(1) 213/17/86][1]

> [1]   The chirograph mentions the land is in *Handleye*. There is a Henley in Claydon hundred.

272. (*Wangford*) An assize comes to declare if Ralph the son of Basil unjustly disseised Agnastas the daughter of Moraud[1] (Pentok[i]) of her free tenement in Mettingham after the first [crossing into Brittany] etc and in respect whereof she complains that he disseised her of one acre of land with appurtenances in the same vill.

Ralph comes and says nothing to stay the assize.

The jurors say that the said Ralph disseised her as the writ says. So it is adjudged that she is to recover her seisin and Ralph [is] in mercy for disseisin (*amercement*). He is remanded in custody. The surety [is] Richard of Elmham.

Damages: one mark (*one mark*).

> [1]   The clerk may also have written *Morandi*. It is difficult to determine which, but I have never come across Morand as a Christian name.

273. (*Norfolk, forty shillings*) Robert Byl gives forty shillings for having an inquest to recognise whether he had any other entry into the sixteen acres of land and two acres of marsh with appurtenances in Rollesby, which John of Waxham claims against him as his right other than by Agnes of Rollesby to whom Warren of Waxham, the brother of that John whose heir he is, has demised [it] for a term etc as the same Robert says or by the same Agnes as the same John says by surety.

Afterwards, they have agreed and John gives half a mark for licence to agree by the surety of the knight Walter of Ingham (*half a mark*). [*chirograph* CP 25(1) 156/67/840][1]

> [1]   Robert won the plea but gave John half the land and marsh for a rent and his homage to him and his heirs.

274. (*Cattishall, at the ascension of the lord, -------*),[1] *Lothingland*) An assize comes to declare if Edmund Woodcock unjustly etc disseised William Fers of his free tenement in Little Yarmouth after the first crossing etc and whence the same William complains that the same Edmund disseised him of a certain dwelling in the same vill.

Edmund comes and says nothing to stay the assize.

The jurors say that Warner Engaine has tenure in Lothingland by the lord king who says (----il) at the same place his certain brother who took that land into the hands of the lord king. Besides (---- ----il) Edmund for twelve pence per year where the said William whose land it was not accustomed to pay except [for] (----il) pence per year. To judgement: (----il) and if he may be able to [recover] against (----il) of Edmund or another (----il) twelve pence … [possibly unfinished] (*to judgement*).

> 1 This marginal note is written above the start of this plea but there appears to be a line from the end of this element of the marginalia to it.

Membrane 10

275.[1] A jury comes to declare whether thirty-three and a half acres of land and one and a half acres of meadow with appurtenances in Thurleston and Whitton are free alms pertaining to the church of Gilbert the parson of the church of St Nicholas of Ipswich or the lay fee of Baldwin Loth and of the others who are named in the writ, in respect whereof Baldwin holds two acres of land, Alan Prest and Robert Prest one acre, Robert Gull two acres, Geoffrey Gull one acre, John and Galiena, his wife, one and a half acres, John de Beumis two and a half acres, Roger de *Brunton*[2] half an acre, William Golle one acre, Beatrice Golle one acre, Geoffrey Cotewine one and a half acres, William Red one and a half acres, Roger Liw five and a half acres, John of Westerfield one and a half acres, William Pannel one acre, Edmund Hahene half an acre, Robert Gunter half an acre, Daniel one and a half acres of meadow, Robert de Bosco half an acre, William de Blauncheville one messuage and three acres of land, Clara of Thurleston one acre of land, John Crice one acre of land, William de Alneto one acre of land, Thurstan del Clay one acre, William the son of Hahene half an acre of land and Adam the merchant one acre of land they hold.

> 1 This utrum plea is spread over **275–285** inclusive. It appears that the clerk has taken a different approach to other clerks by writing the section signs at the start of each section within the plea, whereas the usual routine is for paragraph signs to be placed at the start of each plea or essoin. This clerk's handwriting is larger than that of other clerks and is quite distinct. I have decided to treat these separate sections with a separate item number and cross reference them. There are totals of twenty-seven separate people and twenty-five parcels of land involved in the plea.
> 2 Possibly 'Bruntuna' in Domesday Book, which was unidentified but also in Claydon hundred. See *Domesday Book Suffolk*, Part Two, section 41, no. 15.

276. Baldwin, Alan and Robert Prest have come and acknowledged that they are the villeins of William le Rus. So they [are] without [day] and Gilbert [is] in mercy and he may proceed against William le Rus if he wishes (*amercement*). William Pannel acknowledges that he is the villein of Daniel the parson. So [he is] without day and Gilbert [is] in mercy (*amercement*).

277. John de Beumis comes and acknowledges the land which he [the parson] claims against him to be the right of the said church and Gilbert grants it to him to hold that land from him in perpetuity by renting [at] five pence per year.

278. Daniel Cuer and Roger Lyw come and vouches to warranty William the son and heir of Adam de Blauncheville who is under age. So they are to wait [his coming of] age (*age*).

279. John of Westerfield vouches to warranty the abbot of St Osyth[1] by aid of the court. He is to have him on the morrow of the Ascension at Cattishall (*Cattishall*).

Afterwards, John comes and acknowledges that it is the fief of the church on payment of three pence per year rent.

John and Galiena come and say that they hold that land in dower from the said heir Adam and they vouch [him] to warranty and because he is under age they are to wait [his coming of] age (*age*).

¹   This house of Augustinian canons in Essex, founded in 1121, became an abbey in 1161.

280. William Red and Robert Gunter, Edmund and Beatrice Golle and Geoffrey Cotewine, concerning one acre, come and say that they hold from the dower of the said John and Galiena who come and vouch to warranty the said heir of Adam concerning everything. So they are to wait [his coming of] age (*age*).

281. Robert de Bosco comes and acknowledges that land to be the right of the church and Gilbert the [parson]¹ grants to hold from him for a payment of five pence annually. William de Blauncheville is under age (*age*).

John Crick [and] William Hahene² come and acknowledge that land to be alms and they render [it] to the prior.

¹   The clerk has made a mistake here as he wrote *prior*. This would suggest a different Gilbert from 'Gilbert the parson' who is claiming free alms in **275**.
²   This defendant was William the son of Hahene in **275**.

282. Thurstan comes and vouches to warranty John de Beumis who is present and he warrants and he acknowledges [him] and the prior grants Thurstan to hold [the land] by two pence [per annum].

283. Adam (the Merchant¹) comes and vouches to warranty William de Blaueny by aid of the court. He is to have him on the morrow of the Ascension [at] Cattishall (*Cattishall*).

Afterwards, Adam comes and acknowledges that it is the free alms of the said church that he [Adam] holds from the church by service of two pence per annum.¹

¹   The clerk has squeezed in this paragraph between the first paragraph and the next plea.

284. Robert Gull, Geoffrey Gull, Roger de *Brunton* [and] William Golle put themselves on a jury. So let them have a jury.

Similarly¹ William de Alneto whenever he comes on a account of a default.

¹   *Willelmus de B-l'* was crossed out.

285. The jurors say that the land, which Robert, Geoffrey, Roger and William hold, is not free alms pertaining to the said church having this [land] in demesne, because the ancestors of William de Blauncheville had held that land similarly with the other lands of the said church for three shillings per year and one feast and boon service. The said William made a fine for that feast on payment of two shillings, so that he renders in all five shillings. The said Robert, Geoffrey, Roger and William hold that land from the heir of William de Blauncheville. So it is adjudged that they may hold in peace and the [parson]¹ [is] in mercy and he may distrain his fief for his service if he wishes (*amercement*). Afterwards, William Golle comes and acknowledges that land, which he claims against him, is free alms of the said church. The prior grants that he [William Golle] may hold of the said church for service of six pence per (year¹).

¹   The clerk has used *prior* again in this item, whereas in **275** he indicates that the plaintiff is a parson of the church.

CONCERNING THE TOWN OF IPSWICH

286. (*Ipswich*) A jury comes to declare whether three perches of land with appurtenances in Stoke are free alms pertaining to the church of William the parson of the church of Stoke or the lay fee of John le Mestur.

John comes and (then vouches to warranty[r]) John the son of Rolland who is present and he warrants him and says nothing to stay the jury.

The jurors say that the said land is not free alms pertaining to the said church nor did he ever take from it except two pence per year. So it is adjudged that the said John may hold [that land] in peace and render to the church two pence per year and William [is] in mercy for a false claim (*amercement*).

287.[1] (*Samford*) An assize comes to declare if Gerard Richaud, William of Badley, Ralph Grehund and Richard the son of Osbert unjustly etc disseised Osbert the son of John Grubbe and Clarice his wife of their free tenement in Sproughton after the first etc and in respect whereof Osbert and Clarice complain that the said Gerard and the others disseised them of three and a half acres of land in the same vill.

Gerard and the others come and say nothing to stay the assize.

The jurors say that … [unfinished]

Afterwards, Gerard comes and by licence of the court he freely renders to them the chief messuage and half of all the land facing the east. They are to have their seisin, and they are satisfied.

[1]   There is a change in hand here back to the original hand.

288. The abbot of Leiston acknowledges that he owes to Alpesia, who was the wife of William the son of Theobald, four silver marks of a fine made between them, which he will pay to her at the feast of St Peter in Chains [1 August] in year twenty-four [of the king's reign]. If hc does not do [this] he grants [that he may be distrained] etc until [it is paid in full] etc. [*chirograph* CP 25(1) 213/15/24][1]

[1]   See **202** for the making of the agreement, but note in the chirograph that it indicates five marks, not four.

289. (*Bosmere*) An assize comes to declare if the prior of the Hospital of St John [of Jerusalem] in England, Peter the son of Walter, Gilbert of Baylham, and Walter the carter unjustly etc disseised Richard Best of his free tenement in Hemingstone and Barham after the first crossing etc.

The prior comes and says nothing to stay the assize.

The jurors say that in fact they have not disseised the said Richard of any tenement but they said that they uprooted certain shoots which the same Richard had planted in his messuage. So it is adjudged that Richard is in mercy for a false claim (*amercement*). Peter and Gilbert and Walter [are] in mercy (because[i]) it is established that they uprooted and carried off his shoots, in respect whereof he has damages to the value of half a mark (*amercements*). The sureties of Peter [are]: Robert Hovel, knight, and Peter Cook de Huledon.

290. (*Hoxne*) The prior of Norwich by his attorney[1] claims against Richard le Newman three roods of land with appurtenances in Hoxne as the right of his church, and in which the same Richard has no entry except by William de Gilkin, a monk of Norwich, who demised[2] those [lands] to him, without agreement etc Richard comes and by licence he renders [it] to him. So he is to have his seisin.

51

291. (*Blything*) An assize comes to declare if Warren Starboc the uncle of Anketill the son of Robert Starboc was seised in his demesne as of fee of one carucate of land with appurtenances in Ilketshall[1] on the day that etc and if etc which land Nicholas de Stuteville and Alice his wife hold. They come and vouch to warranty William the son and heir of Richard de Blunville and he is under age. So he is to await [his] age (*age*). So the plea [is] without day.

   1   The Ilketshalls are in Wangford hundred, not Blything as the clerk has indicated in the marginalia.

292. (*Blything*) An assize comes to declare if William Fukelin, the brother of Adam, was seised in his demesne etc of thirty acres and twenty shillingsworth of rent with appurtenances in *Rendeshal*[1] on a day etc and if etc which land and whose rent Henry de *Boclering* holds. He comes and then vouches to warranty Agnes and Matilda, daughters of William Fukelin, who are present, and they warrant him and say that the assize in respect thereof should not be taken because they are the daughters and heirs of William Fukelin, and Adam is not able to deny this. So it is adjudged that Agnes and Matilda are to go without day, and Adam [is] in mercy (*amercement*). The sureties of Adam [are] William of Middleton and John Sordebel.

   1   I cannot find this place in Blything hundred or elsewhere in Suffolk.

293. Warren of Bassingbourne and Agnes his wife and Parnel the wife of Geoffrey of Swaffam appoint as their attorney that Geoffrey against Robert of Hereford and Cecilia his mother concerning a plea of the assize of mort d'ancestor. **[586]**

294. Robert de Grimilies appoints as his attorney Walter de Boville against John Cordebof concerning a plea of land.[1]

   1   The clerk has erased *etc* here.

Membrane 10d

295. (*Stow*) Beatrice, who was the wife of Robert Sorel, claims against William the dean of Stow [Stowmarket] one eighth of a rood of land with appurtenances in Stowmarket as her dower etc. William comes and then vouches to warranty William the son of Robert Sorel, who is present and he warrants him and by licence [of the court] he renders [it] to her. She is to have her seisin.

296. (*St Etheldreda', one mark*) Ralph, the parson of the church of Martlesham gives one mark for licence to agree with Robert de Aguillon (and William[i]) of Loose and Beatrice his wife, and Roger de la Bruera and Simon de la Bruera concerning a plea of utrum, by the surety of Roger de la Bruera of Martlesham and Simon his brother. The agreement is such that William of Loose and Beatrice his wife renders to him six acres which he [the parson] has claimed against them. They are to have a chirograph. Roger and Simon similarly have rendered to him one acre of land which he claimed against them. Robert de Aguillon holds two and a half acres of wood for eight pence per year.

297. (*Norfolk*) Roger the son of Richard was attached to answer Adam Falro of Shouldham and Emma his wife concerning a plea that he holds to his fine made in the time of King Richard, uncle of the present King Henry, in his court before his justices at Ipswich between Ingonald of Shouldham and Elmed his wife, the aunt of the said Emma whose heir she is, demandants, and Peter the provost, the grandfather of the said Roger whose heir he is, tenant, of fifty acres of land with appurtenances in Shouldham, in respect whereof a chirograph [was made] etc. The same Adam and Emma complain that whereas by that fine the same Richard ought to hold from them half of the said fifty acres of land by the service of two shillings and six pence per year, the same Richard kept back from them the said rent for sixteen years wherefore they have suffered and have damage to the value of forty shillings.

Roger comes and he readily grants the fine and whatsoever is contained in the fine and says that the prior of Shouldham is in seisin of the said rent. The same prior is to come to Cattishall on a day five weeks after Easter [Monday 21 May] to show what right he claims in the said rent. The same day is given to the parties and Emma appoints as her attorney her husband Adam etc.

(Afterwards, at Cattishall the same prior comes and says that the said Richard is his villein and Richard is present and agrees with this (*Cattishall*). So Roger [is] without day and Adam [is] in mercy and he may proceed against the prior if he wishes.[i]).[1]

[1]   This has been added in after the following plea had already been written and is written alongside the end of the previous paragraph.

298. (*Bosmere, half a mark*) William the son of Hugh le Rus gives half a mark for licence to agree with Gundreda who was the wife of Edmund of Tuddenham concerning a plea of rent.

299. (*Blything, half a mark*) Thomas le Primur gives half a mark for licence to agree with Hugh le Lamer concerning a plea for an assize of mort d'ancestor by the surety of William de *Rothenhale*.

300. (*Blything*) Agnes, who was the wife of Adam the son of Robert, claims against Waleran de Muncy one messuage with appurtenances in Cove, which she claims to be her right and marriage portion, and in that the same Waleran does not have entry except by Ralph de Muncy to whom the said Adam demised that for a term etc.

Waleran comes and says that he claims nothing in that messuage except only of the wardship through Robert de Muschamp whose bailiff he is and whose escheat it is because Adam her husband, of whose inheritance she held that messuage, has been outlawed So Waleran [is] without day.

The same [Agnes] claims against Camilla of Willingham half of one messuage with appurtenances in the same vill, and against Waleran de Muncy half of one messuage with appurtenances in the same vill.

Camilla comes and vouches to warranty Waleran, who is present, and he warrants her and answers for all and readily grants that the said messuage is the marriage portion of the said Agnes, and he readily grants that he had entry by the said Ralph since the said Adam her husband etc. So it is adjudged that she is to recover her seisin against him and Waleran [is] in mercy for an unjust detention. Waleran will make an exchange with the said Camilla to the value [of that holding].

301. (*Bosmere*) An assize comes to declare if John the son of Brian unjustly etc disseised William the son of Brian of his free tenement in Battisford and Ringshall after the first crossing etc and in respect whereof the same William complains that the said John disseised him of fourteen acres of land with appurtenances in the same vill. John comes and says nothing to stay the assize.

The jurors say that he [John] did not disseise him as the writ says. So it is adjudged that William is to take nothing by this assize, and he is in mercy for a false claim. It has been remitted for poverty.

302. (*Hartismere*) Robert de Perrers and Leticia, his wife, who brought an assize of mort d'ancestor against Andrew Kempe concerning nine and a half acres of land and three and a half acres of wood with appurtenances in Westhorpe, are themselves and their sureties in mercy because the said Leticia, his wife, does not prosecute with him, namely: Robert the son of the carpenter of Finningham [and] Stephen le Dormur of the same (*amercements*).

303. (*Lothingland*) John the son of Adam and Alice his wife, who brought a writ concerning the dower of that Alice, have not prosecuted against Stephen Spurne-water and many others named in the writ. So they and their sureties for prosecuting [are] in mercy, namely: Alan the son of the reeve of Carlton and Adam the son of Ordwine de Alencon (*amercements*).

304. (*Blything*) An assize comes to declare if Stephen Illeiur and John Illeiur, Roger the son of Botild and Hugh the son of Camilla unjustly etc raised a certain dyke in Henham to the nuisance of the free tenement of Ellen de Rufford in the same vill after the first etc.

Stephen and Roger and Hugh come and say nothing to stay the assize. John has not come nor was he attached because he was not found, so let the assize against him proceed by default.

The jurors say that the said Stephen and the others unjustly etc raised the said dyke to the nuisance of the free tenement of the same Ellen. So it is adjudged that the dyke be levelled and is to be as it ought and is accustomed to be. Stephen and the others [are] in mercy (*amercements*). The sureties of Stephen [are]: Walter of Henham and William of the same [vill]. The surety of Hugh [is] Wymer of Carlton.

Damages: sixteen pence.

305. (---*mere*[il]) Robert of Newburgh presented himself on the fourth day against Roger de (Cri--eham[il]) concerning a plea that he keeps his fine made in the court of the lord king before the itinerant justices at Ilchester[1] between that Roger, plaintiff, and the said Robert, tenant, concerning two carucates of land with appurtenances in *Conirsuston*[2] in respect whereof a chirograph was made etc. Roger has not come etc and he was attached by Ralph Letort and Ranulf de Pentir. So he is to be put on better sureties [and] that he be before the itinerant justices at Chelmsford in County Essex on a day three weeks from Holy Trinity [Sunday 1 July]. The first [sureties are to be summoned likewise].

[1] According to Crook 1982a, p.93 this was on 7 January 1236.
[2] I cannot find this place in Suffolk or in Somerset.

306. (*Lothingland*) An assize comes to declare if Geoffrey the son of Guy of Yarmouth (Pelerin of Yarmouth[i]), Thomas Ringebell and John Ketel have unjustly etc raised a certain dyke in Burgh to the nuisance of the free tenement of William de Badham in the same vill after the first etc.

The same assize comes to declare if Ralph of Burgh, Roger Codman, Ralph the son of Joscelin, Nicholas the son of William the parson of Burgh and Walter of Newton unjustly etc levelled a certain dyke in Burgh to the nuisance of the free tenement of the same William in the same vill.

Geoffrey the son of Guy and Pelerin of Yarmouth come and say nothing to stay the assize. The others have not come nor were they attached. So Robert of Yarmouth and (----[i, ii])[1] Henry, his brother, serjeants of the hundred, [are] in mercy.

The jurors say that the said Geoffrey and the others have raised the dykes as the writ says to the nuisance etc. So the dyke is to be levelled by view of the recognitors, and they [are] in mercy. They say also that the said Ralph and the others levelled the said dyke as the writ says. So it is adjudged that the dyke be erected by view [of the recognitors] etc and [those] who [are] in mercy through levelling the dyke, two shillings.[2]

Damages concerning the raising [of the dykes] twenty pence, in respect whereof Pelerin [is to pay] two pence, Geoffrey six pence [and] John twelve pence. [**311** and **368**]

1   This is illegible. It might be *alias*. See **311**. One other possibility is *Philip*.
2   There is no legible designation of this amercement or the following damages in the margin.

Membrane 11

307. (*Norfolk*) William Malherbe acknowledges that he owes to Ranulf of Cringleford ten marks of silver concerning a fine made between them, concerning which he will pay to him five marks on the day of Holy Trinity and five marks at the feast of St Michael [29 September]. If he does not do [this] he grants [that he may be distrained] and concerning the cost etc. [**241** and **242**] [*chirograph* CP 25(1) 156/67/836]

308. (*Bosmere, half a mark*) John the son of Walter of Stonham gives half a mark for licence to agree with Hugh Wastinel concerning a plea of rent by the surety of Hugh. The agreement is such that the same John pays to the same Hugh the said rent, which he claimed against him.

309. (*Norfolk*) A day is given to John of Gaywood to hear his judgement against the Earl Warenne and others named in the writ of novel disseisin taken before R[obert] de Lexington, at the first appearance of William of York, the provost of Beverley, and his fellows at the court *coram rege*[1] (*coram rege*). Note: that neither the earl nor any other appeared at court in front of the justices etc.

1   That is to say at the court *coram rege* where William of York and his fellow justices sat after their participation in this eyre.

310. (*Hartismere*) An assize comes to declare if William Sturmey, Robert the son of Adam,[1] Richard de Farnley, Katherine Sturmey, Nicholas the baker and Ralph the friar unjustly etc disseised Richard the Fleming of his free tenement in Buxhall[2] after the first etc and in respect whereof he complains that they disseised him of two acres of land with appurtenances in the same vill.

William and all the others, except for Katherine and Ralph, come and say nothing to stay the assize. Katherine was attached by William the son of Peter and Robert de Hill[3] of Buxhall. So [they are] in mercy. Ralph was not attached because he was not found and Hugh of Badley, one of the jurors has not come. So [he is] in mercy (*amercements*).

The jurors say that the said William and the others, except Katherine and Nicholas, disseised the said [Richard][4] of the said two acres as the writ says. So it is adjudged that [Richard] has recovered his seisin and William and the others [are] in mercy (*amercement*). He made a fine for himself in return for half a mark by the surety of Roger Sturmey, knight (*half a mark*). [Richard][5] is in mercy for a false claim by the surety of William Herbert.

Damages: four shillings.

¹ The clerk should have indicated *Ade* not *Ada* abbreviated.
² Buxhall is in Stow hundred, not Hartismere as shown in the margin.
³ The clerk has written *de Hel* whereas the clerk in the amercement section has indicated *de Hil*. I have assumed *de Hill*.
⁴ The clerk wrote *Ranulfum* but this should be *Ricardum* unless the clerk made a mistake in the initial paragraph.
⁵ As the clerk is persistent with *Ranulfus* it looks as though he made a mistake early on when he was describing the initial disseisin in the first paragraph. However, I will keep 'Richard' in the English translation. He is also shown as 'Ranulf' in the list of amercements in **1645**. However under the agreements in **1662** he is shown as 'Richard'.

311. (*Lothingland*) An assize comes to declare if Oliver the son of Sampson unjustly etc disseised William de Badham of his free tenement in Burgh after the first etc. The same assize comes to declare if Pelerin of Yarmouth, Edmund his son, Geoffrey [the son of] Guy, John Past, Richard King, John the tanner, William de Brolkendon, Simon the son of Alan and Roger, his brother, unjustly etc disseised him of his free tenement in Burgh after the first crossing [of the king into Brittany]. William, asked of what free tenement he complains, says that they have newly made a certain right of way through half his meadow.

Oliver comes and Geoffrey the son of Guy and Richard King come and seek judgement, in as much as the same William is in seisin of the same tenement in respect whereof he claims as he has acknowledged. Pelerin and others have not come nor were they attached, and because it has been attested that Robert of Yarmouth and Henry his brother, the serjeants of the hundred of Lothingland, have seen them after they have obtained the writ and they have not attached them, so to judgement concerning them (*to judgement*). Because William de Badham acknowledged that he is in seisin of the tenement in respect whereof a view was made, it is adjudged that the assize does not apply, and he is in mercy for a false claim, and the others [are] without day (*amercement*). [**306** and **368**]

312. Felicity who was the wife of Simon de Blogate appoints her son Henry as her attorney against Gilbert the son of William of Carlton concerning a plea of land etc.

313. (*Samford*) An assize comes to declare if Peter de *Pridington*, Henry Pykesumer and Matilda the daughter of William, and Geoffrey Pogell and Avice his wife disseised Richard of Erwarton of his free tenement in Erwarton after the first crossing etc and in respect whereof he complains that they disseised him of six acres of land with appurtenances in the same vill.

Peter and the others come and say that the assize should not be taken on this because that land of which he complains remained to the same Peter by a fine made in the court of the lord king between them. Richard, asked if they disseised him of any tenement now contained in that fine of which he had seisin by that fine, says no. So it is adjudged that the assize is not to be taken between them. Richard [is] in mercy for a false claim. It is pardoned because [he is] poor.

314. (*Claydon*) Robert the son of Richard de *Brunton* acknowledges that he owes every year to Parnel his sister four quarters of corn at the four terms in the year until he has married her off, namely: at the feast of St John the Baptist [24 June] one quarter, and at the feast of St Michael [29 September] one quarter, and at the feast of St Andrew [30 November] one quarter, and at the feast of the Annunciation of the Blessed Mary [25 March] one quarter. If he does not do [this] he grants that he may be distrained by the court until etc and concerning the cost etc.

315. (*Bosmere*) An assize comes to declare if John de Hauville unjustly etc raised a certain dyke in *Benekecretring*[1] to the nuisance of the free tenement of Alice, who was the wife of Gilbert de Mara after the first etc.

The bailiff of John comes and he answers for him and says nothing to stay the assize.

The jurors say that the said John did not raise any dyke as the writ says. So it is adjudged that Alice is to take nothing from the assize and is in mercy. She is pardoned for poverty.

    1   This might be Creeting All Saints in Bosmere hundred.

316. (*Bosmere*) An assize comes to declare if Matilda Hayl the mother of Brian Hayl was seised in her demesne etc of three roods of land with appurtenances in Blakenham on the day on which she died etc and if etc and if she died after etc and in respect whereof Robert of Durnford holds two roods, Ralph Haliday half a rood, and Geoffrey Justin half a rood of land. They come and say that he cannot claim the right in the said land from them, because after the death of his mother he was in seisin of the said land and he sold it to that Geoffrey Justin, and then they put themselves on the jury. Brian comes and says that his mother did not die seised of the said land which he sold to Geoffrey nor has he claimed anything in that land, on the contrary, he claims that land whereof his mother died seised and that it is not that land[1] [for which] he puts himself on the jury.

The jurors say that the said Matilda did not die seised as of fee because she held that land in purparty with a certain Alberr', her sister, so that land never was divided in her life. So it is adjudged that Brian is to take nothing by this assize, and he is in mercy for a false claim (*amercement*). He is remanded in custody.

    1   That is the land Brian's mother sold to Geoffrey Justin before she died.

317. (*Mutford*) An assize comes to declare if Adam the cooper and Matilda his wife, Robert le Muner and Matilda his wife, Sewal the son of Andrew and Warren the son of Robert unjustly etc disseised Roger Swift of his free tenement in Kirkley after the first crossing etc and in respect whereof he complains that they disseised him of three acres of land with appurtenances in the same vill.

Adam and all the others come, except Sewal, and they say nothing to stay the assize. Sewal was not found nor was he attached, so nothing.

The jurors say that they did not disseise him as the writ says because he had no free tenement there. So it is adjudged that he is to take nothing by this assize and he is in mercy for a false claim by the surety of Henry the son of the reeve of Carlton and Roger de Colville (*amercement*).

318.[1] William of Crepping who brought an assize of novel disseisin against Loretta of Gedding concerning a tenement in Stutton has not prosecuted. So his sureties for prosecuting [are] in mercy, namely: Robert the son of Ralph of Stutton, Geoffrey the merchant [of] the same (*amercement*).[2]

(+)[3] Furthermore, they say on their oath that the said William died seised and after the term of the said messuages and three roods of land, which Mena holds. And similarly concerning the three and a half acres of land, which the said Robert holds, and that the said John is the nearest heir. So it is adjudged that he is to recover his seisin against them, and they [are] in mercy for an unjust detention (*amerce-*

ments). The surety of Robert [is] Edmund de Wymundhall. But, they say that the said William did not die seised of one and a half roods, which he claimed against Roger and Matilda, his wife, because it was from the dower of her sister. So they may hold in peace. John [is] in mercy for a false claim by the surety of William of Whitton (*amercements*^s).⁴

¹ This plea at first sight appears to be a mishmash of all sorts of pleas from novel disseisin, mort d'ancestor, and possibly dower etc. There is a change of clerk for the first paragraph of this plea, whereupon it reverts back to the original clerk. The process mark is opposite the change of clerk. The second paragraph does not belong to the first and there is another paragraph in the roll where the initial part of this plea is shown. See below for when this occurs.

² This paragraph is written in different ink and writing from what follows.

³ This process mark indicates the start of the paragraph that belongs to **329** and is the final paragraph of that plea. The English translation has been included after this paragraph and not after the end of **329** in keeping with what the clerk has done.

⁴ The clerk has made a mistake here as only John the son of William is being amerced, so the marginal note for the amercement should be singular, not plural.

319. Agnes of Cretingham appoints as her attorney John de Medendon or Adam Snow against Stephen of Stratton and Anna his wife concerning a plea of covenant. [**1008**]

320. Agnes of Cretingham appoints as her attorney Adam Snow against (----^{il, e}) [unfinished].

Membrane 11d

321. Margery, who was the wife of John the son of Ralph presented herself on the fourth day against John Bordewater concerning a plea of half of one messuage with appurtenances in Little Yarmouth which she claimed in dower against him. John has not come etc and was summoned etc. Judgement: the half messuage is to be taken into the king's hand and the day [of caption told to the justices] etc and he is to be summoned to be at Cattishall on the nearest Monday after the Ascension of the Lord etc. [28 May] (*Cattishall*).

322. (*Lothingland*) Margery, who was the wife of John the son of Ralph, claims against Henry Bacon half of ten acres of land with appurtenances in Repps as her dower, and in respect whereof the said John, her late husband, dowered her etc.

Henry comes and to say he does not know anything why she should not have her dower. So it is adjudged that she has recovered her seisin against him. Henry [is] in mercy for an unjust detention by the surety of William de *Routhenhale* (*amercement*).

323. (*Lothingland*) Alice, who was the wife of Roger of Burgh, claims against Oliver of Burgh one acre of land with appurtenances in Burgh, in which the same Oliver has no entry except by Phillip the clerk who held that land from the said Alice in villeinage as she says.

Oliver comes and says that he does not hold that land because William Chauceden holds that land and he held it before the writ was sought and Alice cannot deny this. So [she is] in mercy for a false claim, by the surety of Ralph of Reedham, and she may proceed [by another writ] against the same William if she wishes (*amercement*).

324. (*Lothingland*) Richard of Hopton and Avelina his wife and Mabel the sister of Avelina who brought an assize of mort d'ancestor against Henry the son of Winerys and Hawise[1] [his sister] concerning six acres of land with appurtenances in Belton, have not prosecuted. So [they are] in mercy. They had no surety except [their good] faith for [they are] poor. **[110]**

    [1]   In **110** Hawise is shown as Henry's wife.

325. (*Essex*) Joan de Westwar' presented herself against James de Westwal' concerning a plea as to why he has removed[1] from the wardship of Joan, Gilbert Bacon the son and heir of Roger Bacon. James has not come and was summoned etc. Judgement: he is attached to be at Chelmsford at the arrival of the justices at the first assize etc. (*Chelmsford*)

    [1]   There is a gap in the text at this point, but it appears to carry on in reasonable Latin and nothing is rubbed out.

326. (*Mutford*) A jury comes to declare whether five and a half acres with appurtenances in Carlton are free alms pertaining to the moiety of the church of Carlton [Colville] of which Robert of Carlton is the parson or the lay fee of Henry de Colville and Wymer of Carlton, and in respect whereof Henry holds five acres and Wymer half an acre. They come and Henry says that they have entry in that land by a certain parson. Because he shows nothing concerning the endowment from the ordinary of the place, nor does he show any other warrant, it is adjudged that the said Robert has recovered his seisin against him. He [Henry de Colville] is in mercy for an unjust detention by the surety of Wymer of Carlton. Wymer says that he claims nothing in the said land except only the term and that he does not hold that land. On the contrary, that land is the right of Robert the son of Niker, so he may proceed against him if he wishes. Robert [of Carlton] is in mercy for a false claim. The amercement is pardoned because he is a scholar.

327. (*Lothingland*) An assize comes to declare if Henry Red unjustly etc disseised Robert the son of John of his free tenement in Corton,[1] and in respect whereof he complains that he disseised him of three roods of land with appurtenances in the same vill.

Henry comes and acknowledges that he disseised him [Robert] as the writ says. So it is adjudged that he has recovered his seisin against him and he is in mercy for the disseisin, by the sureties of John de Wymundhall and Master Walter of Blundeston (*amercement*). He has given satisfaction to the same Robert concerning damages.

    [1]   The clerk has written *Cotton* with an abbreviation sign, which is probably there for the ending. There is a Corton in Lothingland hundred and a Cotton in Hartismere hundred. As the clerk has indicated Lothingland I have assumed that Corton is correct.

328. (*Bosmere*) Natalina, who was the wife of Edmund de *Brunton*, claims against Ralph de Blunville a half of one acre and a half and half of one acre of pasture with appurtenances in Hemingstone,[1] and against Robert Welaund half of two acres of land with appurtenances in Henley, and against the same half of one hundred and seven acres of land with appurtenances in Hemingstone, and against Richard the son of Edmund half of one messuage and of one acre and a half of land with appurtenances in the same vill as her dower etc and in respect whereof the same Edmund, by the agreement and wish of Agnes his mother, dowered her etc and of what etc.

Ralph and the others come and Ralph by licence renders to her a third part because it is held by serjeanty. She is to have her seisin. Richard the son of Edmund similarly by [his] permission renders to her the half [in question]. She is to have her seisin. Robert says that she cannot claim against him in the name of dower concerning the said land because Edmund, her husband, never was seised of the said land that he could dower her thereof because Agnes the mother of that Edmund in her free widowhood, before the said Edmund married her [Natalina],[2] sold to him that land by her charter, which he proffers, and which attests to this. She cannot deny this, so [she is] in mercy for a false claim, and Robert [is] without day.

The same [Natalina] presented herself on the fourth day against the prior of the Hospital of St John of Jerusalem in England concerning a plea of half of twenty-eight (acres of land and eight acres[i]) of wood with appurtenances in Hemingstone, which halves she claims in dower against him. The prior has not come and [was] summoned etc. Judgement: the halves are to be taken into the hands of the lord king and the day etc and he is to be summoned to be at Chelmsford on the octave of Holy Trinity [Sunday 17 June] (*Chelmsford*). [*chirograph* CP 25(1) 213/17/97][3]

[1] *Hemmigested* is what the clerk has written here. There is a Hemingstone in Bosmere hundred and there is a Hempstead in Happing hundred in Norfolk, but it is more likely to be in Bosmere because there is another plea contained in this plea which also has a claim for a dower in Hemingstone below.

[2] This chirograph indicates the settlement at Chelmsford with the prior of the Hospital of St John of Jerusalem in England, but in that it indicates Natalina is claiming one third of 46 acres of land and the 8 acres of wood in Hemingstone.

329. (*Mutford*) An assize comes to declare if William Dosi the father of John the son of William was seised in his demesne etc of one messuage and five acres of land with appurtenances in Mutford[1] on the day that he died, and if he died etc, and if etc which land Mena of Yarmouth, Roger Habanc and Matilda his wife, Richard the son of Simon, Henry and Robert his brothers and Robert the son of Henry hold. Richard the son of Simon, Henry and Robert his brothers come, and the others have not come and they were resummoned. So let the assize be taken against them by default, namely, concerning one acre and a half rood and one messuage.[2] Richard the son of Simon[3] says that the assize should not be taken because [at] another place, before Robert de Lexington and his fellow itinerant justices, the same Richard recovered the same land by an assize of mort d'ancestor against Richard the son of William and Mena of Yarmouth. Richard asked what right Simon his father had, on whose death he brought that assize. He says that [it was] through Edith,[4] the mother of Richard, whose inheritance and right the land was and who enfeoffed him. He then puts himself on the assize. Richard says that the said Edith has had nothing in that land except only the dower, and that the land was the right and inheritance of his father Simon, and in respect whereof he died seised. He then puts himself on the assize. Robert, the brother of the said Richard, answered for three and a half acres and vouches to warranty for two acres Ralph Muriel, and for one and a half roods the said Mena. He is to have them. Afterwards, they come and freely put themselves on the assize.

The jurors say that a certain Woolvin held the said land, which Richard holds, [and] died seised of it, and had a certain daughter named Edith who was his heir. Whilst the said Edith was under age after the death of her father, the same Simon, father of this Richard, bought that land from a certain Simon the lord of this fief, and moreover, because he [Simon] knew the said Edith to be the heir he took her as his wife and begot this Richard from her. After the death of Simon her first husband, the said William Dosi, father of this John, bought the land from the said Edith and from a certain Henry her husband, who married her after the death of her first husband [and] who was in seisin and died seised.

Turn the roll and seek at the cross at the end of the roll.[5]

60

1   The clerk wrote *Morford*. I think the clerk has made a mistake and this should be Mutford, which is in Mutford hundred. I have found no such place as Morford.

2   There is a large space after this word and there is evidence of something rubbed out. I can identify a *d* and possibly an *a*. The Latin continues to read in a reasonable manner.

3   The clerk has crossed out *Henricus et Robertus fratres eius* at this point.

4   *per* is written very lightly, which suggests it may have been rubbed out, also *Edehiwam* appears to be split into *Ede* and *Wam* with some other letters rubbed – *hi* in the middle of the name. Later it looks as though the clerk may have changed her name to *Editha*, but I believe *Ediwa* and *Editha* are the same person.

5   This statement is at the bottom of the membrane – there is a large gap between this statement and the last line of the plea proper but it refers to this case. The end of the plea is in fact at the end of membrane 11 and appears to form part of **318**. The statement indicates the form of the process mark, that is a cross, but there is no similar process mark here to indicate pictorially what a reader should look for at the end of membrane 11.

Membrane 12

330. (*Norfolk*) Richard the son of William of Langham, whom William of Bures and Eugenia his wife have claimed as their naif and fugitive, came and William and Eugenia have not prosecuted against him, nor sureties found. So he [is] without day.

331. (*Samford*) Adam the son of Hubert, who brought an assize of mort d'ancestor against Adam the son of Roger concerning thirty acres of land with appurtenances in Bentley, has not prosecuted. So he and his sureties for prosecuting [are] in mercy namely: William le Muner[1] and Geoffrey of Hackford[2] concerning the same (*amercements*).

1   In the amercements section, **1644** below, this person is shown as William the miller of Ipswich.
2   There are two Hackfords in Norfolk, in Eynsford and Forehoe hundreds.

332.[1] (*Mutford*) Thomas Haldherring was summoned to answer the prior of Weybourne concerning a plea that he do him the customs and right services which he ought to do to him etc. The same prior complains whereof that though the same Thomas ought to make to him the customary feudal aid per year, and to give merchet for his daughters and sisters to be married, and six shillings of rent per year, and one hen at Christmas, and five eggs at Easter, and three ploughings in the winter[2] at his own food[3] and twelve carrying services in the autumn at his own food, as his villein, the same Thomas withdrew from the same prior the said customs and services for two years and more whereon he has suffered damage to the value of one hundred shillings etc.

Thomas comes and says that he is a free man, and he firmly denies that he owes to the same (prior[i]) the said services and villein customs, because William of the household of Warren enfeoffed Nicholas, his father, of the land, which he holds in Kessingland by his charter for eight shillings per year for all services, to be held by himself and his heirs, from the same William and his heirs, from which land and tenement the same prior claims him [Thomas] as naif and the said services. And that neither Nicholas, his father, nor his grandfather Ralph, nor the same Thomas made to the same prior, or to any of his predecessors, any villein customs for the said tenement or for any other [tenement], he offers to the lord king one mark that it is inquired into by the country, and it is accepted by the surety of Thomas Jeremy (*one mark*).

The prior says that that charter ought not to harm him because that charter was made in the time when the said William disseised a certain Roland, his predecessor, but he affirms that his house was in seisin of the said customs and services in the time of the said Ralph. As a result the same Ralph made to his predecessors the said services and villein customs; and Nicholas, similarly, after the death of his father, Ralph made the same services and customs. And this Thomas, similarly, after the death of his father made to the current prior the same services[4] and customs as his villein. That this may be inquired into he offers to the lord king one mark and it is being accepted[5] by the surety of William of Loose (*one mark*). So let there be a jury thereon, whether Ralph, the grandfather of this Thomas, did for all the time of the predecessors of those priors the said services and villein customs and [whether] Nicholas, the father of that Thomas, after the death of the said Ralph did the same services and villein customs, and this Thomas, similarly, did to that prior the same services and customs as his villein as the prior says or not (or whether the same Thomas and his said ancestors have always held that tenement by the free service of eight shillings per year[i]) as the same Thomas says.

The jurors, chosen by consent of the parties, say on their oath that neither the said Thomas nor his ancestors ever made to the priors and the house of Weybourne any service other than the service of the said eight shillings per year for every service, nor ever made to the same house any villein service. So it is adjudged that the said Thomas may hold in peace the said tenement for the said service so that neither the said prior nor his successors hereafter will be able to demand from him or his heirs any service other than the said eight shillings per year. The prior is in mercy for a false claim (*amercement*).

1   See **131** for the appointment of attorneys in this plea.
2   Although this indicates three ploughings in winter it is likely they were probably performed on the Ember Days at the end of winter (7, 9, 10 March) when the ploughing for the year's crop would begin.
3   That is Thomas has to supply his own food while doing the work.
4   There is a damaged section here, which looks as though it was in the original as the clerk has written around it.
5   There is more damage in the membrane here but no obvious text is missing.

333.[1] (*Samford*) An assize comes to declare if Thomas de Meulinghes and Olive his wife unjustly etc disseised Stephen, the son of William, of his free tenement in Brantham after the first etc and in respect whereof he complains that they disseised [him] of a certain part of a meadow, namely twenty feet in length and four in width.

Thomas and Olive come and say nothing to stay the assize.

The jurors say … [unfinished] (*age*).[2]

1   There is a gap of 8 cm between this plea and the previous one. This plea is probably unfinished because it is the same as **429**.
2   It is possible that the plea may have been adjourned to await the age of the defendant. This is very unusual as normally there were very few instances of adjournment of a novel disseisin plea. See Sutherland 1973, pp.19–20 and 129–133. There is a gap of 3.5 cm after this plea.

334. (*Samford*) An assize comes to declare if Stephen Hente and John Smalthing unjustly etc disseised William the son of John of his free tenement in Brantham after the first crossing etc and in respect whereof the same William complains that they disseised him of fifteen acres of land with appurtenances in the same vill.

Stephen comes and says nothing to stay the assize. John has not come nor was he attached because he was not found. So let the assize be taken against him by default.

The jurors say that the said Stephen and John did not disseise the said William of his free tenement as the writ says because he had no free tenement there nor furthermore has his father held that land only for a term. So it is adjudged that William is to take nothing by this assize and he is in mercy for a false claim by the surety of Thomas de Mading.[1] Stephen [is] without day. The amercement is pardoned because he [William] is under age.

   [1]   This might also be Melding, which could be Milden in Babergh hundred.

335. (*Samford*) An assize comes to declare if Stephen Hente unjustly etc raised a dyke in Brantham to the nuisance of the free tenement of William the son of John in the same vill after the first etc.

Stephen comes and says nothing to stay the assize.

The jurors say that the said Stephen did not raise any dyke to the nuisance of William as the writ says. So it is adjudged that William is to take nothing by this assize and is in mercy for a false claim. The amercement is pardoned.

336. (*Lothingland, one mark*) Henry of Cuddington gives one mark for licence to agree with William the son of Hardwin concerning a plea of mort d'ancestor by the surety of Robert of Cuddington and Abraham the son of Godfrey. [*chirograph* CP 25(1) 213/15/31[1] and CP 25(1) 213/15/32][2]

   [1]   In the chirograph a Robert de Cudington is also part of the agreement with William.
   [2]   This chirograph is between 'William the son of Hardwin' and 'Abraham the son of Godfrey'. There is no mention of this in the roll.

337. (*Blything*) An assize comes to declare if Camilla, who was the wife of Ralph de Money, and Ralph de Money unjustly etc disseised Alexander Bailie and Matilda his wife of their free tenement in Henham after the first crossing etc.

Camilla and Ralph come and say that the assize should not be taken on this because Alexander is the villein of William de Money, who is present and he [Alexander] is not able to deny this. So it is adjudged that he is to take nothing by this assize and he is in mercy for a false claim. It is pardoned because [he is] poor. Camilla and Ralph [are] without day.

338. (*Wangford, twenty shillings*) Hubert of Braiseworth gives twenty shillings for licence to agree with Edmund of Sotterley concerning a plea of waste by the surety of William of Cotton, knight, and Richard Beard. The agreement is such that the same Hubert and Sarah his wife grant that henceforth they will not make waste there. For this [chirograph] etc.

339. A jury, chosen by consent of the parties, comes to declare, by William of Reedham, Ranulf of Blickling, Roger de Wymples, John Blench, William of Darsham Walter of Henham, Andrew de *Henepol*, Walter de *Ingesford*,[1] Benedict de *Dufford*, Thomas Chevere, Thomas Russel and Richard de *Haldhag*, if Adam of Poynings the grandfather of Thomas of Poynings in the time of the reign of King Richard held a certain marsh in Wrentham named *Wavesey*[2] in his severalty,[3] so that neither Alice of Frostenden nor her ancestors have had any common in the same place as pertaining to her tenement in Frostenden as the said Thomas says, or if she, Alice, and her ancestors have always had right of pasture in all of it from the conquest of England as pertaining to her tenement in Frostenden as the same Alice says. And, if the said Alice and her ancestors have had right of common there, from what time and by what manner they have had that right of common. They come and say on their oath that the said Alice and her ancestors have always had right of common in the said marsh which is called *Wavesey* from the conquest of England until a certain Wulwin, who for a small amount of time held it outside that common, and instantly enclosed it, [and] a certain Herbert,[4] against whom Alice recovered her seisin by an assize of novel disseisin, and thus her seisin was always [to continue]. So it is adjudged that Alice and her heirs forever may have that right of common. Thomas [is] in mercy (*amercement*). All the jurors [are] in mercy for a false declaration (*amercements*).

1 The amercement section of this roll indicates *Walter de Iokesford* or 'Yoxford' in Blything hundred. The following person in the plea, 'Benedict de *Dufford*', is also shown as being of 'Yoxford' in the amercement section.

2 I cannot find this marsh, or moor, near Wrentham on the Ordnance Survey map.

3 In legal terms this means in her own right.

4 The clerk may be referring, in a condensed fashion and with something omitted, to two distinct breaks in seisin, one as a result of Wulwin and the other by Herbert.

340. (*Wangford*) Roger the son of Gilbert claimed against William of Redisham three roods of land with appurtenances in *Upredisham*[1] as his right, and which he does not have entry etc.

William comes and says[2] nothing why the said Roger is (not[i]) to have his seisin. So it is adjudged that he is to recover his seisin against him and he is in mercy for an unjust detention by the surety of Waleran[3] de Muncy.

1 I presume this should be Upper Redisham. There is no such place in Suffolk on any map I have found. There is a reference to Upredesham in *Cal. Feet of Fines, Suff.*, pp.230 and 239. However these are very late feet of fines in Edward III's reign. There is the village of Redisham in Wangford hundred, but I cannot find any reference to a part of the village called Upper Redisham or even a separate village close to Redisham that had once been called *Upredisham*.

2 The membrane is damaged here but there is sufficient to determine the words.

3 The membrane is damaged here in the middle of the name but the clerk looks as though he has written around it.

341. (*Colsandr'*[il]) who was the wife of Roger the son of Geoffrey, who claims her dower against John le Enveyse and others named in the writ comes and acknowledges that all have given her satisfaction concerning her dower. So [they are] without day.

342. Alan de Wymundhall appoints as his attorney William de *Rodenhall*[1] against William Talebot and Richard his brother concerning a plea of land, and against Herbert the parson of Pakefield concerning a plea of utrum.

1 This is a place listed in Mutford hundred in Domesday Book but not existing now: see *Domesday Book Suffolk*, Part One, section 4, no. 36. However, there is a William de *Rothenhall* who appears in a number of pleas in this roll. See **410** where he is also appointed as an attorney. One other possibility is Redenhall in Earsham hundred, Norfolk.

Membrane 12d

343. (*Samford, half a mark*) The jury comes to declare whether four acres of land with appurtenances and a half and one acre of meadow[1] with appurtenances in Raydon and *Sturmed*[2] are free alms pertaining to the church of Raydon in respect whereof Nicholas of Raydon is the parson or the lay fee of William Lotun and Geoffrey de Brademere and Alice, his wife, concerning which William holds two acres of land and half an acre of meadow and Geoffrey and Alice, his wife, two acres of land. They come and Geoffrey and Alice vouched to warranty William himself, who warrants them, and he answered for all, and he says that the said land and meadow never was in free alms of that church and then he puts himself on a jury.

The jurors say that the said four acres [of land] and the half acre of meadow with appurtenances never were free alms of the said church as Nicholas says. On the contrary, they hold the said land in chief from the lord king. So it is adjudged that Nicholas is to take nothing from this jury and is in mercy for a false claim. He made a fine for half a mark by the surety of Gilbert de Bircheye of Belstead. William and the others may hold in peace.

1 There is only a mention of half an acre of meadow later in the plea.
2 This is possibly Sturmer in Risbridge hundred near Haverhill or it could relate to a named meadow near Raydon.
3 The clerk wrote *Albr* but the name was definitely Alice earlier in the plea, so I have assumed this name throughout the translation.

344. (*Hartismere*) The jury comes to declare whether three acres and one rood of land with appurtenances in Bacton are free alms pertaining to the church of Bacton in respect whereof Richard is the parson or the lay fee of Simon Athlard, Ralph the son of Ascelin, Herbert Folet, Simon the son of Geoffrey, Alvina Thedam, Wymark her sister and Mabel Sparrow and Richard of Bures, and concerning which Simon [Adlard] holds half an acre of land, Ralph half an acre, Herbert half an acre, Simon one acre, Alvina and Wymark one rood, Mabel one rood and Richard of Bures one rood. Richard and Olwyn come and Olwyn says that she is a villein of Earl Richard,[1] so then [she is] without day. Richard [the parson] may proceed against him [Earl Richard] if he wishes. Richard says nothing to stay the jury. All of the said above who have not come [are] in mercy[2] [and] they were resummoned. So let a jury be taken against them by default.

The jurors[3] say that the half an acre which Simon Athlard, the half acre Ralph the son of Ascelin and the half acre Herbert Folet each hold are free alms to the said church. It [the church] is then to have its seisin. Concerning the land, which Mabel Sparrow holds they say that the parson can have nothing except one penny per year by the hand of Geoffrey Gausel. Concerning the land, which Simon the son of Geoffrey holds they say that it is not pertaining to the aforesaid church, so let him hold in peace, and Mabel similarly. Richard the parson, similarly, [is] in mercy for a false claim (*amercement*). He has made a fine of half a mark by the surety of Jordan of Shelton. Simon Athlard, Ralph the son of Ascelin and Herbert Folet are in mercy for an unjust detention.

1 Presumably Earl Richard of Cornwall who held the honour of Eye in Hartismere hundred.
2 There is no mention in the margin of the amercement, nor is there one in the amercement section of this roll below.
3 There is a change of hand here as though the first clerk stopped after *dicunt* and some other clerk resumed later and completed the result of the jury.

345.[1] (*Bosmere*) William the son of Robert claims against John of Hatfield half an acre of land with appurtenances in Henley as his right, in which the same John does not have entry except by William who demised that [land] to him while he was under age etc.

John comes and grants the entry and by licence renders [it] to him. He is to have his seisin.

1 There is a gap of 4.4 cm between the start of this plea and the end of the previous one. There is a fault in the membrane, which is probably the reason why the clerks did not write in this area.

346.[1] (*Samford*) An assize comes to declare if Roger Dodemer, brother of Seyna the daughter of Osbert Dodemer was seised in his demesne as of fee of six acres of land in Wherstead on the day he died, and if etc and if etc which land Roseret the daughter of Hamo de Ramis holds. She comes and says that she does not hold said six acres in their entirety because Alice, who was the wife of the said Roger, holds in respect thereof two acres in dower. So it is adjudged that Seyna is to take nothing by this assize and is in mercy for a false claim. It is pardoned because [she is] poor.

¹ See **1148** where Seyna has tried to sue for the four remaining acres.

347. (*Mutford*) An assize comes to declare if William Muriel and Geoffrey Muriel unjustly etc disseised Ralph Muriel of his free tenement in Carlton [Colville] after the first crossing etc and in respect whereof he complains that they disseised him of four acres of land with appurtenances in the same vill.

William and Geoffrey come and acknowledge that they are the villeins of Thomas de Hemmegrave and they say that the said tenement is land held by villein tenure and that the assize should not be taken on this and that the said Ralph is a villein. Ralph says that he is a free man and he holds freely and thereupon he puts himself on the assize whether the tenement is free or not.

The jurors say that they have not disseised Ralph of any free tenement because he had no free tenement because he is a villein of Thomas de Hemmegrave. So it is adjudged that he is to take nothing by this assize and is in mercy for a false claim by the surety of Thomas de Hemmegrave (*amercement*).

348. (*Lothingland*) An assize comes to declare if Henry of Belton, John de Ponte, John the son of Benjamin, Bartholomew Amaund, William Gillemyn,¹ Robert Gunnild, Simon Assert, Robert Wykeman, Humphrey of Norton, Rainer Cristin, William Flacke, John the son of Woolvin, Gerard Brictmer, John Farman, Robert de Rydeby, Humphrey the son of Woolvin, John Puteforby, Robert Gare, Robert Mannin, Roger Bert, Nicholas le Neir,² Geoffrey Nokedam, Henry de Vere and Letitia Elger unjustly disseised Robert Figge and Avelina his wife of their common pasture in Belton, which pertains to their free tenement in the same vill after the first crossing etc.

Henry of Belton, Humphrey of Norton, Rainer Cristin, John the son of Woolvin, Gerard Brictmer, Humphrey the son of Woolvin, Thomas Puteforby,³ Robert Gare, Robert Mannin, Roger Bert, Nicholas le Neir [and] Geoffrey Nokedam, come and say nothing to stay the assize. John de Ponte and the others have not come nor were they attached. So the serjeant of the hundred [is] in mercy (*amercement*).

The jurors say that Henry of Belton, John de Ponte, Bartholomew Amaund, William Gillemyn, Robert Gunnild, Simon Assert, Rainer Cristin, Gerard Brictmer, John Farman, Thomas Puteforby, Robert Gare, Geoffrey Nokedam, Henry de Vere [and] Letitia Elger⁴ disseised Robert and Avelina of their common pasture in Belton as the writ says, because they have newly raised certain dykes in the same pasture. So it adjudged that the dykes be levelled by view of the recognitors, and that Robert and Avelina have recovered their seisin. They [i.e. the 14] [are] in mercy. They say also that the others [that is the other 10] named before have not disseised them after the term, so Robert⁵ [is] in mercy for a false claim against them by the surety of John de Wymundhall (*amercement*). Stephen the son of William de *Hatcetorp*⁶ is the surety of the said Henry, John and their fellow disseisors.

(*to the clerks*) Damages: forty pence.

¹ This is the name Gillman. See Reaney 1997, p.191.
² This is probably Nicholas the Black. In Reaney 1997, p.319 the name is also shown as 'Nares'.
³ Shown as John above but as Thomas below and also in the amercement section of this roll. See **1645**, last entry. I have taken Thomas to be correct and that the clerk made a mistake above in the original list of defendants.
⁴ That is fourteen out of the original twenty-four names are in mercy.
⁵ This must be Robert and the clerk has made a mistake here. The clerk wrote *Radulfus* for Ralph.

⁶   It is probably Akethorpe in Lothingland hundred.

349.[1] (*Bosmere*) The jury comes to declare by William de Ciresy, Geoffrey the son of John, Robert[2] de Sancto Claudo and Robert de *Pirho* witnesses named in the charter which John de Hauville proffers under the name of Alice who was the wife of Gilbert de Mara, and moreover, Hubert Gernegan, Robert de Wleden,[3] Richard of Newton, Walter of Stonham, John de Bradestrete and Robert the butler to ascertain if the said Alice, after the death of Gilbert her husband, quitclaimed to the said John all right and claim that she had in half of thirty acres of land, of one messuage, of one acre and one perch of meadow, of one acre of marsh, of one acre of pasture and of twelve penceworth of rent with appurtenances in Creeting in respect of dower or not. They [the jurors] come and say on their oaths that the said Alice on the seventh day after the death of her husband, in the presence of all the parishioners of Creeting, quitclaimed by her charter all right and claim that [she had] in the said land, meadow, marsh and twelve pence rent with appurtenances according to contents of her charter. So it is adjudged that John may hold in peace, and Alice [is] in mercy for a false claim. The amercement is pardoned because [she is] poor.

¹   See **233** for appointment of attorney.
²   The clerk wrote *Robertus* in the nominative instead of *Robertum* in the accusative, which is the case in which all the other witness names are written.
³   This might be Wilden, Welden or Ulenden for *Olden*.

350. (*Lothingland*) An assize comes to declare if William Sauvage, Master Henry of Yarmouth, Robert of Yarmouth and Simon Esman unjustly etc disseised Roger Pere-bourne of his free tenement in Gorleston after the first etc and in respect whereof he complains that they disseised him of eighty acres of marsh. Robert and Simon came and Robert answered for himself and Master Henry, as his bailiff. William has not come nor was he attached, so the bailiff of the hundred [is] in mercy (*amercement*). Robert and Simon say nothing to stay the assize. William de Capeton, one of the recognitors, has not come. So [he is] in mercy (*amercement*).

The jurors say that the said William and the others have not disseised the said Roger of any free tenement because in fact they say that the same Roger held the said marsh once on payment of forty-one shillings per year and afterwards he increased his farm and has paid seven marks, afterwards eight marks. So it is adjudged that Roger is to take nothing by this assize and is in mercy for a false claim and the others [are] without day. The surety for Roger [is] Wanier of Carlton [Colville]. He made a fine by Roger by the surety of the same Wanier.

351.[1] Simon of Gorleston give half a mark for licence to agree with Stephen the son of Roger and Margery his wife concerning a plea [of land],[2] [by the surety of] Roger Perebourne of Yarmouth.

¹   See **204** for the appointment of an attorney. There is a gap of about 2.5 cm between this plea and the previous one. It looks as though the clerk was using up spare space for something not very long.
²   There is an illegible part of the plea roll here but **204** provides the plea type.

Membrane 13

352. (*Stow*) An assize comes to declare if Roger Thurst, Brian his brother, Nicholas Cavet [and] Roger his brother unjustly disseised Emma of Finesford, Matilda and Denise her daughters of their free tenement in Finborough after the first etc and in respect whereof they complain that they disseised them of one acre and one rood of land in the same vill.

Roger and the others come and concede the disseisin. So they [are] in mercy. They are pardoned for poverty. They are to have their seisin and he [Roger Thurst] is to satisfy them for their damage by two shillings.

353. (*Samford, half a mark*) Agnes de *Bruniford* give half a mark for licence to agree with John of Brantham concerning a plea of debt by the surety of Alan de *Bruniford*. The agreement is such that the same Agnes remitted to the same John the said debt by licence etc. The same John remits to the same Agnes eighty acres of land with appurtenances in Wenham which the same John had at farm from the same Agnes saving to the same John the crop of that year only.

354. (*Norfolk*) Roger the son of Adam presented himself on the fourth day against Henry Folcard concerning a plea for half an acre of (meadow[i])[1] with appurtenances in Mellis.[2] Henry has not come etc and was summoned etc. Judgement: the said land is to be taken into the hands of the lord king, and the day etc. He is to be summoned that he be at Cattishall on the nearest Saturday after the Ascension of the Lord [26 May] (*Cattishall*).

  1   The clerk had crossed out *terre* and inserted *prati* above the line.
  2   In Hartismere hundred, but this may have been a plea originally taken in the Norfolk eyre because of the marginal note.

355. (*Norfolk*) William le Fort and Mabel his wife presented themselves on the fourth day against Ralph de Koma concerning a plea that he keeps the fine made with them in the court of the king before the eyre justices at [King's] Lynn between the said William and Mabel, plaintiffs, and the said Ralph, defendant, concerning one messuage with appurtenances in Lynn[1] in respect whereof a chirograph [was made]. Ralph has not come and he was not attached. So the sheriff has been ordered that he does not omit, on account of the liberty of Freebridge, to have his body at Cattishall on the nearest Saturday after the Ascension of the Lord [26 May] (*Cattishall*).

  1   It is uncertain to which vill of Lynn the clerk refers.

356. (*Norfolk*) Hamo of Narborough presented himself on the fourth day against John Grim of Terrington, who he claimed as [his] naif and fugitive with all his chattels and all his family household etc. John has not come. It was commanded to the bailiff of Freebridge that he was to summon him to be [here] on this day. The bailiff did nothing thereon. So the sheriff has been ordered that he does not omit, on account of the liberty of Freebridge, to have his body at Cattishall on the nearest Saturday after the Ascension of the Lord [26 May] (*Cattishall*). [**982** and **1017**]

357. (*Mutford*) An assize comes to declare if Roger the son of Richard, Adam the cooper and Matilda his wife, Robert le Muner and Matilda his wife, Agnes the daughter of Richard and Gunnild her sister unjustly etc disseised Benedict the son of Hugh, John of Kirkley and Juliana his wife of their free tenement in Kirkley after the first etc and in respect whereof they complain that they disseised them of four acres of land with appurtenances [in] the same vill.

Roger and the others come and say nothing to stay the assize. Benedict the son of Hugh has not come, so he and his sureties for prosecuting [are] in mercy namely: Master Walter of Blundeston, and Richard the son of Robert of Trowse (*amercements*).

The jurors say that they have not disseised them as the writ says, because they are villeins and they do not have any free tenement. So it is adjudged that they are to take nothing by this assize and they are in mercy for a false claim, by the surety of Simon the priest[1] of Kirkley and Master Walter of Blundeston (*amercements*).

> 1 The clerk wrote *le Prestre*, which looks like an early form of French. It is used for Simon's surname throughout the roll.

358. (*Mutford*) An assize comes to declare if Wymer of Carlton unjustly disseised Agnes, the daughter of Andrew, of her common pasture in Gisleham, which pertains to her free tenement in the same vill.

Wymer comes and says nothing to stay the assize.

The jurors say that he (disseised[i]) the same Agnes of common pasture as the writ says. So it is adjudged that she has recovered her seisin against him. Wymer [is] in mercy for disseisin of land by the surety of William de Rothene.

359. (*Exning*) Malina, who was the wife of Henry Mody (claims[i]) against Geoffrey Beivin a third part of fifteen acres and one messuage with appurtenances in Exning as her dower.

Geoffrey comes and then vouches to warranty Edmund Kemesec. He is to have him by the aid of the court at Cattishall on the nearest Tuesday before the Ascension of the Lord [22 May] (*Cattishall*).

360. (*Half a mark*) Peter of Gisleham gives half a mark for licence to agree with Alan the son of Roger concerning a plea of land by the surety of Geoffrey de Biskel and William la Pays. It is agreed such that the same Alan claimed against the same Peter and Alice his wife three acres with appurtenances in Stoke by an assize of mort d'ancestor. Peter and Alice render to him two acres with appurtenances and retain one acre in respect of the dower of Alice.

361. (*Blything*) Thomas the son of Edward who brought an assize of novel disseisin against Camilla of Henham and Hugh her son has not prosecuted. So he and his sureties for prosecuting [are] in mercy namely: William the son of Richard of Reydon and William (the son[r]) of Alexander (*amercements*).

362. (---*rford*) An assize comes to declare if Benedict de Cawe, the father of Thomas, was seised in his demesne [as of fee] etc of one acre of land with appurtenances in Bosmere[1] on the day he died etc and if etc and if etc which land Andrew de Ripis holds. He comes and says that the assize should not be taken on this because he [Thomas] is a villein and then he puts himself on the assize.

The jurors say that the said Thomas is a free man and he held freely and his father Benedict was a free man and held freely and that the same Benedict died seised of the said land as in his demesne etc and after the term etc and that this Thomas is the nearest heir etc. So it is adjudged that he has recovered his seisin and Andrew [is] in mercy by the surety of Wymer of Carlton (*amercement*).

> 1 Bosmere is actually in Bosmere hundred in Domesday Book but it no longer exists as a vill. See *Domesday Book Suffolk*, Part Two, section 21, no. 47. So it appears the clerk made a mistake in the margin for the hundred entered.

363. (---*thing*--)[1] An assize comes to declare if Geoffrey the son of Guy unjustly etc disseised Alice, who was the wife of Roger of Burgh, of her free tenement in Burgh after the first etc and in respect whereof she complains that he disseised her of one rood of land with appurtenances in the same vill.

Geoffrey comes and says nothing to stay the Assize.

The jurors say that he disseised her of her free tenement as the writ says. So it is adjudged that Alice has recovered her seisin against him. Geoffrey [is] in mercy for disseisin.

Damages: two pence.

[1] Probably Lothingland hundred in the margin as the hundred where Burgh is located, not Thingoe hundred. See **323** where I believe the same person is pursuing another plea.

364. (----il)[1] An assize comes to declare if Ralph of Burgh unjustly etc disseised Alice, who was the wife of Roger of Burgh, of her free tenement in Burgh after the first crossing etc and in respect whereof she complains that he disseised her of one acre of land with appurtenances in the same vill.

Ralph has not come and he was attached by John Benjamin and Gerard, the son by the priest. So they [are] in mercy.[2] Let the assize be taken against him by default.

The jurors say that the said [Ralph][3] disseised her as the writ says. So it is adjudged that she has recovered her seisin against him. Ralph [is] in mercy for disseisin.

Damages: twelve pence.

[1] I believe this should also be Lothingland hundred for the same reasons as in the previous note.
[2] There is no indication in the margin of the amercement to indicate to the estreat that a sum of money could be claimed, although the amount of damages is inserted.
[3] The clerk wrote *Ricardus* instead of *Radulfus*, unless the original name in this plea was wrong.

365. An assize comes to declare if Andrew the son of Richard, William of Stuston, Robert le Reytur[1] and Robert the son of Aylward unjustly etc disseised Thomas the son of Richard of his free tenement in Sibton, Yoxford and Bulcamp after the first crossing etc. Geoffrey Laurette one of the recognitors has not come, so [he is] in mercy.

Andrew comes and says that the assize should not be taken on this because if he [Thomas] ever had or was able to have any right in the said tenement, that right he quitclaimed from himself and his heirs in perpetuity, to Andrew and his heirs, by his charter, which he proffers and which attests to this and then he puts himself on the assize. The others have not come, nor were they attached because they were not found, so nothing.

The jurors say that [neither] the said Andrew nor the others disseised him of the said tenement as the writ says because he [Thomas] quitclaimed to him all right that he had, or could have, by his charter in the said land. So it is adjudged that he is to take nothing by this assize and he is in mercy for a false claim. It is pardoned because [he is] poor.

[1] The man's profession might be 'the ratter'; or 'the net maker' from the Old French word *retour*.

Membrane 13d

366. (*Blything*) An assize comes to declare if Agnes Eligraunt, the mother of Alice, was seised in her demesne etc of three acres of land with appurtenances in Stone [Street] on the day she died etc and if she died etc and if etc which land Alan de Monay holds. He comes and then vouches to warranty Roger de Colville who is under age. So she is to await his age (*age*).

367. (*Blything*) Alan de Hemesdon, who brought an assize of mort d'ancestor against Thomas de Furnell concerning one messuage and three acres of land and two roods of turf pit with appurtenances in Theberton, comes and acknowledges that the bailiffs of that Thomas have given him satisfaction. He is poor, so nothing.

368. (*Lothingland*) An assize comes to declare if Geoffrey the son of Guy, Pelerin of Yarmouth, Thomas Ringebell, John Ketel and John the son of Robert unjustly etc raised five dykes in Burgh to the nuisance of the free tenement of Richard the beadle in the same vill after the first etc. Pelerin and Thomas have not come and Pelerin was attached by Geoffrey the son of Guy and John the son of Benedict. So all [are] in mercy (*amercements*).

Geoffrey and the others come and say nothing to stay the assize.

The jurors say that the said have raised the said dykes to the nuisance etc. So it is adjudged that the dykes be levelled by view of the recognitors. All [are] in mercy. Surety for Geoffrey [is] Alexander Allan of Yarmouth. Surety for John of Burgh [is] William the son of Osbert of Yarmouth. Surety for John Ketel ... [unfinished]

Damages: twelve pence. [**306** and **311**]

369.[1] (*Norfolk*) Baldwin Rede, Agnes Gye, Richard the son of Gunnild claim against Richard Puleyn fourteen acres of land with appurtenances in Wereham as their right, and in respect whereof a certain Thirkill their ancestor was seised in his demesne as of fee and right in the time of King Henry [II] grandfather of the present king, taking profits to the value of half a mark. From the same Thirkill descended the right of that land to a certain Beatrice, Gunnild, and Agnes who now claim as daughters and heirs and from the same Beatrice to that Baldwin as [her] son and heir, and from that Gunnild to that Richard, who now claims, and that such is their right they offer [to prove] etc.

Richard comes concerning eight acres [and] vouches to warranty Richard the English. He is to have him by aid of the court.

Concerning the six acres of land with appurtenances he [Richard Puleyn] denies their right and the seisin of the said Thirkill and everything etc and puts himself on the grand assize of the lord king and seeks a recognition be made whether he has the greater right in the said six acres of land with appurtenances, or the said Baldwin, Agnes and Richard. Hugh Burt, William de Bacon, Baldwin of Mellis and Alan de Money four knights, selected to choose etc to make a recognition of the grand assize between the said Baldwin, Agnes and Richard, plaintiffs, and the said Richard, defendant, whether he has the greater right in the said six acres or the said Baldwin, Agnes and Richard, have come and chosen these: Adam le Kaly, Thomas Rivit, John of Runham, William Luvel, Samson Thalebot, Andrew of Hingham (Sicth----[ii])[2] de Chervill, Richard the butler of Rougham, Robert the son of Ralph of Thorpe,[3] Hugh the son of Robert of Massingham, John of Walpole, Geoffrey of Gasthorpe, Robert of Scole, Roger of Clare, Richard de la Rokele and Thomas of Babingley. Agnes and Richard the son of Gunnild appoint as their attorney Baldwin le Rus.

Later they are agreed concerning the six acres whereof they had put themselves on the grand assize and Richard Puleyn gives half a mark for licence to agree by the surety of Richard Angot (*half a mark*). [*chirograph* CP 25(1) 156/66/812][4]

1   See **820** for their claim for the other 8 acres.
2   There is a large stain here which has obscured the writing and it cannot be read with ultraviolet light.
3   There is a Thorpeland in the same hundred as Wereham.
4   On the reverse of the chirograph there is a note that 'William de Meyse lays a claim to the fine because he says that Richard Pulleyn is his villein'. See **820** for a William de Meysi being vouched to warranty.

370.[1] (*Blything*) Ranulf de Becling,[2] William de Ciresy, Stephen of Stratton and

William the son of Robert of Reydon four knights, summoned to choose twelve etc to make a recognition of the grand assize between William Bullok and Rose his wife, plaintiffs, and Richard of Brantham, defendant, concerning half of forty shillingsworth of rent with appurtenances in Westleton, in respect whereof the same Richard, who is the tenant, puts himself on the grand assize of the lord king and seeks a recognition be made whether he or the said William and Rose have the greater right in the said rent, have come and chosen these: John of Brantham,[3] Baldwin of Mellis, Alan de Muney,[4] William de Colville of Aspall, William of Cotton, Hubert of Braiseworth, Hasebert of Bawdsey, Adam of Mendham, John Cordebof, Philip of Winston, John the son of Robert of Ubbeston, John of Stonham, Matthew of Peyton, William of Ha--legh,[5] William the son of Rainer and Roger Sturmey (*on Tuesday*).

Later[6] they have agreed and William Bullok gives one mark for licence to agree by the surety of Richard of Tuddenham (*one mark*). [*chirograph* CP 25(1) 213/17/106]

1   There is a gap of 5.2 cm between this plea and the end of the previous one.
2   This is probably Ranulf of Blickling which is in South Erpingham hundred in Norfolk. He appears as a juror in a number of pleas in this roll but the spelling of Blickling is more obvious than this.
3   The clerk mixes his Latin nominative and accusative cases in this list of names.
4   Alan de Muney is probably the same knight as Alan de Money. I have kept the spelling but cross-referenced them in the index of people and places.
5   This is probably Haughley in Stow hundred.
6   There is a separate section mark in the margin for this paragraph but it relates to this plea. The marginal note also includes the money for the licence.

371.[1] (*Norfolk*) William the son of Richard of Thrigby claims against Thomas Darnel one acre of land and one messuage with appurtenances in Thrigby as his right etc. Thomas by his attorney comes and then vouches to warranty Roger of Clare and Alice his wife.

Later by licence they are agreed. They are to have a chirograph. [*chirograph* CP 25(1) 156/66/817]

1   There is a gap of 8.2 cm between this plea and the previous one.

372. (*Blything, amercement*) An assize comes to declare if Hugh of Stoven, the father of Simon, was seised in his demesne etc of one and a half acres of meadow with appurtenances in Stoven on the day he died, and if he died, and if etc which meadow John the son of Waleran holds. He comes and vouches to warranty Alan de Money, who is present, and he warrants (him and says[il])[1] that the said Hugh about five years before his death gave the said meadow to him, so that he did not (die[il]) seised and then he puts himself on the assize.

The jurors say that the said Hugh died seised [and] after the term and that Simon (is the nearest heir[il]). So it is adjudged that the said Simon has recovered his seisin against him. Alan [is] in mercy for an unjust detention. He is to make an exchange to the value [of his holding] etc.

1   There are a number of illegible parts to this plea and the words in brackets are the likely words used by the clerk.

Membrane 14

373. (*Lothingland*) Alice, who was the wife of John le Rus, and Robert her son, who brought an assize of novel disseisin against Richard del Clif concerning a tenement in Ruston,[1] have not prosecuted. So they and their sureties for prosecuting [are] in mercy, namely Walter the son of John the clerk of Blundeston and Robert the son of Richard of Little Yarmouth (*amercements*).

¹ This is really a foreign plea. Ruston is in Happing hundred in Norfolk, not in Lothingland hundred.

374. (*Wangford*) An assize comes to declare if Bartholomew the son of Alan, Thomas his brother, Warren the carpenter, Alan Osmund, Richard the son of Roger of Thurston, Peter the son of William, William the son of John, William the son of Henry and Alexander the son of John unjustly etc disseised Henry de Gosenhall of his free tenement in Sotterley after the first etc and in respect whereof he complains that they disseised him of one acre and three roods of land. Bartholomew comes and says nothing to stay the assize. The others have not come nor were they attached, except Alan Osmund and Alexander the son of John. Alan was attached by Richard the son of Roger and Alexander the son of John, and Alexander was attached by John Osmund and Richard de Haberfeud.¹ So they and their sureties [are] in mercy (*amercements*).

The jurors say that the said Bartholomew and all the others disseised the said Henry of his free tenement as the writ says. So it is adjudged that Henry will recover his seisin and Bartholomew and all the others [are] in mercy.

Damages: 4 shillings.

Henry de Gosenhall acknowledged that after the said land was his escheat and he was seised thereof, he had given to Henry the son of Mascelin one rood. So he is to have his seisin to the value of the buildings.²

The same assize, by the same recognitors, comes to declare if the said Bartholomew and the others mentioned above unjustly etc disseised Andrew the son of Roger de Hapelingfeud of his free tenement in Sotterley after the first etc and in respect whereof he complains that they disseised him of half an acre.

The jurors say that they disseised him as the writ says. So he will recover his seisin. Bartholomew and the others [are] in mercy (*amercements*).

¹ This is probably Haverfield, which is a Suffolk name.
² It looks as though Henry de Gosenhall had given to Henry the son of Mascelin one rood of the land before he was disseised by Bartholomew and the others, and therefore Henry the son of Mascelin was to receive back his one rood to the value of the property.

375. Agnes the daughter of Agnes Finning who brought an assize of mort d'ancestor against William Brumham concerning a tenement in *Cressingland*¹ has not prosecuted and she has not furnished sureties for prosecuting except faith.

¹ This might be Cressingham in Norfolk or Kessingland in Mutford hundred. It is probably the latter as there is no mention of a Norfolk plea in the margin or of a Suffolk hundred. See **332** where the clerk has indicated the hundred in the margin.

376. (*Blything*)¹ An assize comes to declare if Oliver of Burgh unjustly etc disseised Alan of Pakefield of his free tenement in Burgh after the first etc and in respect whereof he complains that he disseised him of one acre. Oliver comes and says nothing to stay the assize.

The jurors say that the said Oliver did not disseise the said Alan of any free tenement as the same Alan has claimed. So it is adjudged that Oliver [is] quit and Alan [is] in mercy by the surety of [Simon] Ashman² and William of Carlton (*amercements*).

¹ The clerk has probably made a mistake in the marginal note and should have put Lothingland and not Blything as there is no Burgh in Blything hundred. This is either Burgh in Carlford hundred, or Burgh Castle in Lothingland hundred. The two protagonists have place names in their names,

which are also located in Lothingland hundred. As Carlford hundred is in the liberty of Ely I would have expected a marginal note of 'Ely' or 'St Etheldreda' as written by the clerk in other pleas for the liberty of Ely.

2 The clerk has missed out the surety's first name, *Simon*, as shown in the amercement section in **1647**. His name is therefore Simon Ashman.

377. (*Hoxne*) An assize comes to declare if William de Chantelu, the father of William,[1] was seised in his demesne etc of two acres of wood with appurtenances in Mendham on the day etc and if etc which wood Alan of Withersdale holds. He comes and says that the said William, father of that William did not die seised of the said wood in demesne etc and then he puts himself on the assize, and William also.

The jurors say that William de Chantelu, father of William, who brought this assize, did not die seised of the said wood, as of fee, because for a year before the death of that William, the father of this William, the said Alan was in seisin. So it is adjudged that William is to take nothing by this assize and he is in mercy for a false claim, by the surety of John de Arthes and William Turgis. Alan [is] without day (*amercement*).

1 This might well be the William de Cantilupe who became Henry III's regent while he was in France in 1242–1243.

378. (*Samford*) Wymer the son of Edmund, who brought an assize of mort d'ancestor against John Cabelot concerning the tenement in Bentley, has not prosecuted. So he and his sureties for prosecuting [are] in mercy namely, Est of [East] Bergholt, Richard Moraunt de Questeden (*amercements*).

379.[1] (*Hoxne*) An assize comes to declare if Roger Trussebut, John of Stradbroke, Hugh of Bedingfield and Robert Maloisel[2] unjustly etc disseised Robert of Dereham of his common pasture in Denham which pertains to his free tenement in the same vill after etc. (*on Tuesday*).

Roger and all the others come and acknowledge that they disseised him as the writ says. So it is adjudged that he has recovered his seisin and all the others [are] in mercy. It[3] is pardoned for poverty.

1 See **388**, as that is a repeat of this plea.
2 This is a nickname meaning 'bad bird'. See Reaney 1997, p.296.
3 That is the amercement is pardoned.

380.[1] (*Bosmere*) An assize comes to declare if Alexander Bat[2] was seised in his demesne etc concerning three roods of land with appurtenances in Helmingham on the day etc and if etc which land William de Monte holds. He comes and by licence renders [it] to him. So he is to have his seisin.

1 There is a gap of 4.8 cm between this plea and the previous one.
2 It looks as though the clerk has missed out the person actually bringing the plea as this is a mort d'ancestor plea but there is no relation of Alexander Bat mentioned as bringing the plea. Whoever it was, he or she won.

381. (*Hoxne*) An assize comes to declare if Thomas of Withersdale uncle of Walter Punit was seised in his demesne etc of twelve acres of land with appurtenances in Withersdale the day etc and if etc which land Alan the son of Alan holds. He comes and says that the said Walter is a bastard and could not claim the inheritance (*bastard*). So Alan [is] without day. The bishop of Norwich is ordered to convene [before him those who know the truth] etc [and] diligently inquire into [the matter] etc [and make known the results of] the inquest [to the justices by his sealed letters] etc.

382.[1] (*Blything*) An assize comes to declare if Robert of Badingham and Agnes his wife, William of Stuston, John Teuteis, William Richard, William de Bonhawe, Roger Bonvalet, Alexander Page, Harvey Shacel and Robert Sheriff unjustly etc disseised Adam the son of William of his free tenement in Knodishall after the first etc and in respect whereof he complains that they disseised him of sixteen acres of land. None of them comes except Robert of Badingham, who says nothing to stay the assize. Robert Sheriff was attached by Alexander Page and John the palmer of Buxlow, and Harvey Shacel by Rainer of Sternfield and William Burd',[2] and Alexander Page by John Gunels and Walter Burdun. So all [are] in mercy (*amercements*).

The jurors say that the said Robert and the others unjustly etc disseised the said Adam of the said sixteen acres as the writ says. So it is adjudged that Adam has recovered his seisin and Robert and the others [are] in mercy by the surety of Herbert [de] Alicon (*amercements*).

(*to the clerks*) Damages: five shillings and six pence.

[1] There is a further gap of 5 cm before this plea as though the clerk was anticipating the results of the inquiry by the bishop of Norwich in the previous plea.

[2] This might be William Burdun given this abbreviation. There is such a person in **551**.

383. Thomas Darnel, by his attorney, acknowledges that he owes to William the son of Richard two marks of silver, concerning which he will pay to him half a mark at the feast of St John the Baptist [24 June] and half a mark at the Nativity of the Blessed Mary the Virgin [8 September] and one mark on the octave of St Michael [6 October]. If he does not do [this the sheriff is ordered] etc that he will distrain [by all his lands and chattels] until [the value of the debt is paid] etc. [*chirograph* CP 25(1) 156/66/817][1]

[1] This plea gives the payment detail whereas the agreement in the chirograph relates the land detail.

384. (*Hoxne*) An assize comes to declare if Richard of Fressingfield, the father of Richard, was seised in his demesne etc of six acres of land with appurtenances in Fressingfield on the day he died, and if he died, etc which land William le Rus holds. He comes and says that the assize should not be taken on this because that Richard[1] after the death of his father was seised of the said land for one year and more and he sold that land to Hugh le Rus, his father. Richard cannot deny this. So [he is] in mercy by the surety of William de Evingham (*amercement*). He may proceed [against] him by a writ of entry if he wishes. William [is] without day.

[1] That is the one bringing the claim, not the father.

Membrane 14d

385. (*Hoxne*) An assize comes to declare if Walter of Mendham, father of Reynold, was seised in his demesne etc of two acres of land with appurtenances in Mendham on the day he died etc and if etc which land John Snelling holds. He comes and admits that he is a villein of the prior of Mendham[1]. So it is adjudged that Reynold is to take nothing by this assize and is in mercy for a false claim. He is poor.

[1] A Cluniac house founded in 1155.

386. (*Hoxne*) An assize comes to declare if Thomas le Gosewold, Peter the son of William of the same[1] unjustly etc disseised Robert the son of William of his free tenement in Dennington after the first etc and in respect whereof the same Robert complains that they disseised [him] of twenty-seven acres of land with appurtenances in the same vill.

Peter (and William[s])[2] comes and says nothing to stay the assize. Thomas has not come and he was attached by Hubert of Tannington and William Gosewold, so [they are] in mercy.

The jurors say that … [unfinished]

Afterwards, Robert and Thomas came and placed themselves in the mercy of the lord king. Robert the son of William gives ten shillings for his fine by the surety of Peter the son of William (*ten shillings*). The same Peter gives ten shillings for the same by the surety of Robert the son of William (*ten shillings*).

> 1   There is no place mentioned prior to this in the plea.
> 2   The clerk wrote 'Peter and William' but I think the clerk has made a mistake here. He probably should be indicating 'Peter the son of William' has come to the court or possibly 'Peter and Robert' have come to the court.

387. (*Hoxne*) An assize comes to declare if Henry of Pontefract uncle of Roland the son of Herbert was seised in his demesne etc of one messuage and sixteen acres of land and four shillings and sixpenceworth of rent and half an acre of meadow with appurtenances in Tannington on the day he died etc and if etc and if the same Roland etc which messuage, land[1] and meadow Godfrey the Parker of Brundish holds. He comes and says nothing to stay the assize.

The jurors say that the said Henry died seised of the said land as of fee and that that Roland is his nearest heir. So it is adjudged that Roland has recovered his seisin. Godfrey [is] in mercy by the surety of Thomas of Shotford and William de Childerhus (*amercement*).

> 1   The clerk wrote *terra*. He should have written *terrram* in the accusative case and not the nominative.

388. (*Hoxne*) An assize comes to declare if Roger Trussebut, John of Stradbroke, Hugh of Bedingfield and Robert Maloisel unjustly etc disseised Robert of Denham of his common pasture in Denham which pertains to his free tenement in the same vill after the first etc.

Roger and all the others come and acknowledge that they disseised him as the writ says. So it is adjudged that he has recovered his seisin and all the others [are] in mercy. It is pardoned for poverty.[1]

> 1   This is almost word for word the same as **379**, so it looks as though the clerk has repeated himself here.

389. (*Surrey*) Roger de Bavent and Sarah his wife in whose place [an attorney comes] claim against Amabil de Waterville one sixth part of two knights fee with appurtenances in Morden, Chessington and Pisley Farm except for three virgates of land with appurtenances in the same vills as the right of Sarah etc.

Amabil comes and then claims a view. She has it. A day given to them at Chelmsford in the octave of Holy Trinity [Sunday 17 June] and meanwhile etc (*Chelmsford*).

390. (*Hoxne, on Wednesday*) Richard of Cransford claims against Thomas Balaunc fifteen acres of land with appurtenances in Mendham as his right etc.[1]

> 1   This plea is obviously unfinished and the clerk has left a large gap after it of 15.5 cm in the roll. See **474** for its continuation.

391.[1] (*St Etheldreda, amercement*) Robert de Hay [is] in mercy because he has not prosecuted his writ of grand assize against William de Colville concerning six acres of land with appurtenances in *Assted* and *Thwaite*. Note: that William has not come.

> [1] There is a gap of 15.4 cm between this plea and the previous one.

392. (*St Etheldreda*) Robert Jordan [is] in mercy because he has not prosecuted his writ of grand assize against William Bulloc and Rose his wife of ten acres of land and one mill with appurtenances in Tuddenham. Note: that William and Rose have not come.

393.[1] (*Hoxne*) An assize comes to declare if the prior of Mendham, Robert the son of Alan, Walter le Rolund, Reynold (de[r])[2] Brunchil,[3] Walter Hodard, Thomas Stumbevilt and William de Thawe unjustly etc disseised the same Alan of Semer of his free tenement in Weybread after the first etc and in respect whereof the same Alan complains that the prior and the others disseised him of one acre of meadow with appurtenances in the same vill.

The prior comes and replies for all the others and he says nothing to stay the assize.

The jurors say that they did not disseise him as the writ says. So it is adjudged he is in mercy for a false claim by the surety of Thomas of Shotford, and the prior [is] without day (*amercement*).

> [1] There is a new hand here which is totally different from that of the rest of membrane 14, suggesting that a gap was left here and then the plea inserted later by a different clerk. There is a gap of 3.8 cm between this plea and the previous one.
> [2] This is partially erased by the clerk.
> [3] This might be 'Brownhill'.

Membrane 15

394. (*Wangford*) An assize comes to declare if Hugo of Cove, the father of Robert, was seised in his demesne etc of four acres of land with appurtenances in Cove on the day etc and if etc in respect whereof Hugh the son of Osbert holds one and a half acres, Alan de Wymundhall half an acre and William de Haberfeud two acres etc. They come and say that the assize should not be taken on this because a certain brother of his, the first born, was in seisin of the said land after the death of his father [and] who sold that [land]. Robert cannot deny this. So it is adjudged that Hugh and the others [are] without day. Robert [is] in mercy. He is poor.

395. (*Mutford*) The jury comes to declare whether twenty-six acres of land with appurtenances in Pakefield is the free alms pertaining to the church of Pakefield, in respect whereof William and Herbert are the parsons[1] or the lay fee of Richard of Chediston and of others, concerning which the said Richard holds four and a half acres, Amabil of Chediston eighteen acres, John of Chediston four and a half acres, Roger le Latimer one acre, Ralph of Semer[2] one acre and one rood, Hugh Wulfric one and a half acres, Andrew Branch one rood, John Argus one and a half acres, John the son of Alan two acres (and Richard Hay one acre[i]).[3]

Richard of Chediston, John of Chediston, Ralph of Semer, Alan the clerk, John Argus and Richard Hay come. John Argus says that he does not hold that land because his mother holds that land in dower. Richard Hay says that he did not hold that land when the writ was sought, nor after, because Herbert the parson holds one rood, William de *Rothenhale* half an acre and Alan de Satermere half an acre. The parsons cannot deny this, so they [are] without day and the parsons [are] in mercy (*amercement*).

Alan comes and renders now and because he has not rendered previously, so [he is] in mercy (*amercement*). Surety for the amercement [is] Edmund de Wymundhall. Richard, John and Ralph come and say that the said church was never in seisin of the said land and then put themselves on the assize. Amabil of Chediston, Hugh Wulfric, Andrew Branch and John the son of Alan have not come and they are to be resummoned etc. So let the assize proceed against them by default.

The jurors say that the said church of Pakefield was never in seisin as of free alms of the land, which Richard of Chediston and Amabil and John hold, and the land which John the son of Alan holds, except only concerning service. So it is adjudged that Richard and the others may hold in peace and the parsons [are] in mercy (*amercements*). Meanwhile they say that the said church was never in seisin of the land which Ralph holds nor of the land of Hugh, nor of the land of Andrew, nor of the land of Roger except only concerning the service. So it is adjudged that they may hold in peace and the parsons [are] in mercy. They have made a fine for half a mark by the surety of William de *Rothenhale* (*half a mark*).

1   Note that there are two parsons.
2   The clerk wrote *Radulfus de Sotimere* but he is shown as 'Ralph of Semer' later in the plea.
3   This actually adds up to 35.5 acres not 26.

396. (*Blything*) An assize comes to declare if Margery the daughter of John, sister of Agnes the wife of Robert of Peasenhall was seised in her demesne etc of five acres of land with appurtenances in Knodishall on the day etc and if she died etc and if etc which land the abbot of Leiston holds. He comes and says that the assize should not be taken on this because the said Agnes had a certain brother William, the first born of the father and mother, who had two daughters who still live and Agnes cannot deny this. So the abbot [is] without day and Robert of Peasenhall [is] in mercy by the surety of Jordan Nepot[1] of Yoxford (*amercement*).

1   His surname might be Nephew, which is not uncommon in Norfolk.

397. (*Lothingland*) An assize comes to declare if William of Newton unjustly etc disseised Ralph of Gorleston of his common pasture in *Newton*[1] which pertains to his free tenement in *Reyston*[2] after the first etc. William has not come but William de *Routhenhale*, his bailiff, is present and answered for him and he says nothing to stay the assize.

The jurors say that the said William of Newton has not disseised the said Ralph of any common pasture in Newton which pertained to his free tenement in *Reyston* because he has no common there. So it is adjudged that William [is] without day and Ralph [is] in mercy by the surety of Roger Perebourne (*amercement*).

1   This place can no longer be found in Lothingland hundred. *Domesday Book Suffolk*, Part Two, maps and map keys, appears to place it north of Lowestoft and Corton but south of Hopton.
2   This place cannot be found in Lothingland hundred either.

398. Matilda, the daughter of Alan, and Geoffrey de Cadamo[1] and his wife who brought an assize of mort d'ancestor against Henry de Bakeling concerning a tenement in Knodishall and Leiston have not prosecuted. So they and their sureties for prosecuting [are] in mercy, namely: John Ivor of Middleton and Aylward le Despencer of Saxmundham (*amercements*).

1   This is probably Caen in Normandy.

399. (*Hoxne*) An assize comes to declare if Peter, the prior of Butley,[1] and Ralph the son of Ernulf unjustly etc disseised Ralph the son of Ralph of his free tenement in

Denham after the first etc and in respect whereof he complains that they disseised him of twelve acres of land with appurtenances in Denham.

The prior and Ralph and Ralph[2] come and say nothing to stay the assize.

The jurors say that the said prior and Ralph have not disseised the said Ralph the son of [Ralph][3] of any free tenement. So it is adjudged that the prior and Ralph [are] without day and Ralph the son of Ralph [is] in mercy for a false claim, by the surety of Ernulf of Kettleburgh and Roger of Carlton (*amercement*).

[1]   Ranulf de Glanvill, Henry II's justiciar, founded Butley priory in 1171 for Augustinian canons.
[2]   That is the plaintiff and the defendant.
[3]   The clerk wrote *Ernulf* but he has made a mistake.

400. (*Hoxne*) Basilda, who was the wife of William Red, claims against Andrew the tailor half of two acres of land with appurtenances in Framlingham[1] as her dower and in respect whereof William her former husband dowered her etc. Andrew comes and then vouches to warranty William Austin, who is present, and he warrants him and then vouches to warranty Peter the son of William Red. Let him come on Tuesday [1 or 8 May] (*on Tuesday*).

[1]   The clerk wrote *Framingham*. There is no Framingham in Hoxne hundred. This is almost certainly Framlingham in Loes hundred. There is a Framingham in Norfolk in Henstead hundred. However Framlingham is considerably nearer to Hoxne hundred.

401.[1] (*Hoxne*) An assize comes to declare if Adam Bule and Isabel, his wife, unjustly etc disseised Henry the son of Selot of his free tenement in Brundish after the first etc and in respect whereof he complains they disseised him of three acres. Adam and Isabella come and say nothing to stay the assize.

The jurors say that the said[2] Adam and Isabella did not disseise the said Henry of any free tenement. So it is adjudged that Adam and Isabel [are] without day and Henry [is] in mercy (*amercement*). He is remanded in custody.

[1]   There is a gap of 4.8 cm between this plea and the previous plea.
[2]   The clerk wrote *predictus*. I would have expected to see *predicti* because he is indicating more than one person.

402. (*Blything, one mark*) William of Kerdiston gives one mark for licence to agree with Roger of Kerdiston concerning a plea of warranty of charter by the surety of Roger of Boyland. The agreement is such that the said William gives to the same Roger all the service of Hugh of Kerdiston that the same Hugh was obliged to do to the same William for one carucate of land with appurtenances in Stratford,[1] namely; twenty shillings per year, and besides the service of half a knight's fee. Hugh, who is present, acknowledges that he claims nothing in the said land except for the term of his life, and that henceforth he will do service to the same Roger according to what is contained in the charter of that Roger, which he holds as a gift of that William.

[1]   There is no Stratford in Blything hundred, so this is probably the Stratford in Plomesgate hundred as that is the nearest to Blything hundred. The marginal note by the clerk is therefore wrong.

403. (*Norfolk*) Matilda of Leverington by her attorney presented herself on the fourth day against Jordan de Ros and Margery his wife concerning a plea of two acres of land with appurtenances in Emneth which she claims as her right etc. Jordan and Margery have not come and they have defaulted elsewhere before the eyre justices in the county of Norfolk, so that the sheriff was ordered that the land was to be taken into the hands of the lord king and that a day etc and that they were to be summoned etc. The sheriff then did nothing. So as before the sheriff has been ordered that he does not omit, on account of the liberty of the earl of Arundel, to take [the land] into the hands of the lord king, and that the day etc and that they are to be summoned to be before the itinerant justices at Cattishall on Monday next after the Ascension of our Lord [28 May] (*Cattishall*). The sheriff is to be there to hear judgement on him.

404. Sarah the wife of Roger [de] Bavent appoints as her attorney Sampson of Battisford or Roger her son against William de Waterville and others named in the writ, and against John de Say concerning the same.

405. Matilda the wife of Philip the son of William appoints as her attorney her husband Philip against Matthew of Peyton and others named in the writ concerning a plea of novel disseisin. She appoints the same against the same in the county of Essex.[1]

> 1   This is the next county in the circuit by William of York and his fellow judges.

406. (The prior[il])[1] of Leighs appoints as his attorney Richard of Benley against Agnes de *Bruniford* concerning a plea of land and dower.

> 1   I think this is probably the prior of Leighs, Essex, shown in **635** pursuing a plea against Agnes de *Bruniford*.

Membrane 15d

407. (*Hoxne*) An assize comes to declare if William le Rus unjustly etc disseised Walter de Elsham and Godiva his wife and Matilda the daughter of Roger of their free tenement in Weybread after the first etc and in respect whereof they complain that he disseised them of one messuage and twenty acres of land with appurtenances in the same vill.

William comes and says nothing to stay the assize.

The jurors say that a certain William, the chaplain, and Edward his brother held the said messuage and land in common, and at length the same William demised his part to the same Edward. As a result the same William dowered (Botilda[i]), his mother and from ten acres of the same land. Afterwards, the same Edward was in seisin of the said messuage and land, by a certain dispute, which was moved between the same William and [Edward], the same William came and dispossessed the same Edward. He [then] sold that land and messuage to Hugh le Rus, the father of this William [le Rus], who then enfeoffed a certain Alan Wyn, who after he had held it [the land] for some time, the same Alan came and killed Edward. As a result after that death Alan was outlawed and the said land reverted to the said Hugh after a year and a day as his escheat, so that the same Hugh died seised of the said land and messuage. After the death of that Hugh, the lord Earl Warenne took that land into his hands together with all the lands, which the same Hugh held with this William [le Rus] his son, and he gave it to a certain Andrew, his tailor, until the said William came of age. The same Andrew demised the said land, until the same term, to the said Walter and the others, and when the said earl rendered to the same William his land, he returned to him the said land and messuage. But they [the jurors] said the said Hugh was never in seisin of the other said ten acres of land, which the said Botilda held in dower, neither in demesne nor in service, because in all her time the same Botilda was answerable to the said Edward concerning her dower as her warrantor. As a result after the death of Botilda, the said Walter and others, as the heirs of Edward, entered into that land and messuage, and they held it peacefully until the said William disseised them. It is adjudged that they have recovered their seisin against him concerning the ten acres of land and one messuage, and William [is] in mercy for disseisin (*amercement*). Because Walter and the others were claiming he disseised them of twenty acres of land and one messuage, and the jurors say that [he disseised them] of only the ten acres and one messuage, so [they are] in mercy for a false claim (*amercements*).

(*to the clerks*) Damages: twelve shillings.

408. (*Stow*) Matilda the daughter of William who brought an assize of mort d'ancestor against John Gagge concerning a tenement in Chilton, and Hawise the daughter of John who brought an assize of mort d'ancestor against James the son of Richard concerning a tenement in Suddon, and John the son of Wibert who brought an assize of mort d'ancestor against Geoffrey the son of Clemence concerning a tenement in Thorney, and William le Franceys who brought an assize of mort d'ancestor against Katel Galagell concerning a tenement in Combes have not prosecuted. They have agreed to prosecute.

409. (*Bosmere*) William the son of Mar' who brought an assize of novel disseisin against Geoffrey of Stonham concerning a tenement in Little Stonham has[1] not prosecuted. So he[2] and his sureties for prosecuting [are] in mercy namely: Roger de *Goseleford* and Adam Burting concerning the same (*amercements*).

[1] The clerk made a mistake here and indicated the third person plural when only one person is indicated as prosecuting.

[2] The clerk persisted with the mistake by putting the plural *illi* here.

410. Henry de Colville appoints as his attorney William de *Rothenhale* against Hawise de Hocton concerning a plea of dower etc. [**485**]

411. (*Hoxne*) The jury comes to declare whether one acre and one rood of land with appurtenances in Fressingfield are free alms pertaining to half of the church of Alexander the parson of the same vill, or the lay fee of Matilda of Fressingfield and Robert the son of Hubert, concerning which Matilda holds one acre and Robert one rood. Robert comes and by licence renders [it] to him. Matilda has not come and was re-summoned. So let a jury be taken against her by default.

The jurors say that the said acre of land with appurtenances in Fressingfield is the free alms pertaining to half of the said church. So it is adjudged that the said Alexander has recovered his seisin of the said acre with appurtenances and Matilda [is] in mercy (*amercement*). He is to have his seisin.

412.[1] (*Norfolk*) The abbot de Savigny[2] by his attorney claims against Alan de Cruce one acre of land with appurtenances in Saxlingham[3] as the right of his church of Savigny in which the same Alan has no entry except by John the scribe[4] who held that land in villeinage from the said abbot.

Alan comes and acknowledges entry but he says that the said John was a free man and held freely that land and sold it to him by his charter, and whereon he puts himself on the country.

The same abbot by his attorney claims against William the son of Peter half an acre of land with appurtenances in Saxlingham as the right of his church, and which the same William has no entry except by Peter of Hoe to whom the said John demised it [the land] [and] who held it in villeinage from the said abbot.

William comes and acknowledges entry but he says that the said Peter is a free man and held freely so that he could give and sell and he sold that [land] to him and then he puts himself on the country, and the abbot similarly.

81

The same abbot, by the same attorney, claims against the said Alan one toft and three and a half roods of land with appurtenances in Saxlingham, and against Thomas Peyvere[5] one rood of land in the same vill, and against Peter Gerond half a rood of land with appurtenances in the same vill as the right of his church of Savigny, and in which they do not have entry except by Emma Kiriel, which she held in villeinage from the said abbot etc.

Alan and the others come and acknowledge entry and say that the said Emma was free and held freely that land. They put themselves on the country, and the abbot similarly. So let there be a jury thereon.

(*at Cattishall*) The jurors, chosen by consent of the parties, say that John the Scribe and [Emma] Kiriel held freely and were free so that they could give and enfeoff [that land]. So it is adjudged that William and the others may hold in peace and the abbot [is] in mercy (*amercement*).

[1] There is a gap of 6.25 cm between this plea and the previous one.
[2] Savigny was now a Cistercian house in Normandy.
[3] There is a Saxlingham in Henstead and in Gallow hundreds in Norfolk. I suspect this is the one in Henstead.
[4] The clerk has written *Scriptorem*. Later he writes *Scriveyn* for the same man. By 1240 Scrivener is another name for a clerk.
[5] He is probably a paver.

413. (*Hoxne*) An assize comes to declare if William le Rus unjustly etc disseised Richard of Manston of his free tenement in Stradbroke after the first crossing etc and in respect whereof he complains he disseised him of fifteen acres in the same vill.

William comes and says nothing to stay the assize. Afterwards, Richard came and withdrew [from the plea]. So he and his sureties for prosecuting [are] in mercy, namely: Hugh the carpenter and Roger the Smith of Bedingfield of [Monk] Soham (*amercements*).

414.[1] (*Hoxne*) Geoffrey Batley, Richard Frebern, Adam Rowe and Richard Alleyn who brought an assize of novel disseisin against William le Rus of his free tenement in Stradbroke have not prosecuted. So they and their sureties for prosecuting [are] in mercy, namely: Robert of Bedingfield and Hubert the carpenter of [Monk] Soham (*amercement*).

[1] There is a gap of 4.2 cm between this plea and the previous one.

415. (*Norfolk, five marks*) Hamo Chevere gives five marks for licence to agree with Arnulf de Mounteney concerning a plea of land by the surety of (C. ... .[il]) de Mounteney. Arnulf acknowledges that he owes the same Hamo forty-five marks concerning a fine made between them. He will pay to him twenty-five marks at the feast of St John the Baptist [Sunday 24 June] and twenty marks at the feast of St Michael [Saturday 29 September] by the surety of Ralph de Camoys and Ernulf de Mandeville who grant that if he does not pay they may be distrained until (etc ... [il]) and concerning the cost etc in the twenty-fourth year ... [unfinished] [*chirograph CP 25(1) 156/66/806*][1]

[1] On the reverse of this chirograph it indicates *Radulfus de Ginges apponit clamium suum in quinquaginta acris terre.*

Membrane 16

416.[1] (*Hartismere*) An assize comes to declare if Roger the fuller of Bacton unjustly disseised Hubert of Braiseworth of his free tenement in Cotton after the first etc and in respect whereof he says that he disseised him of half an acre of land. Roger comes and says nothing to stay the assize.

The jurors say that the said Roger disseised him as the writ says. So it adjudged that the said Hubert is to recover his seisin. Roger [is] in mercy for disseisin. He is poor.

To the clerks. Damages: eighteen pence.

[1] There is a change of clerk here, who uses very small writing, division sign for *est* etc.

417. (*Hartismere, half a mark*) Walter Freschese gives half a mark (by the surety of William of Onehouse and Sampson of Battisford[i]), for licence to agree with Henry the son of Hugh concerning one and a half messuages and one acre and one rood in *Stowes*, in respect whereof the same Walter holds half an acre, Nicholas the tailor half an acre, Walter de *Brumscrede* one messuage and one rood, Robert Cudde holds half a messuage etc. The agreement is such that the said Henry remised and quit-claimed etc concerning him etc with the said Walter and the other tenants etc all the right etc that he had in the said land and messuage with appurtenances in perpetuity etc. For the licence etc the others give to him etc three shillings and six pence.

418. (*Hartismere*) An assize comes to declare if Alexander the son of Margery was seised in demesne as of fee of twenty acres of land with appurtenances in Buxhall on the day etc and if he died etc and if etc in respect whereof Ralph Hulin holds ten acres and Stephen Caliz holds ten acres of land. Ralph comes and says that the assize in respect thereof ought not to proceed because he and the said Margery are the brother and sister of one father and mother. Stephen comes and says that he claims nothing in the said land by way of right, except by Hulina his wife, whose dower that land is and he then vouches her to warranty, and she is present and warrants him. She answered with her husband and says that in fact they hold the said ten acres of land in dower and do not wish to answer her unless the court considers [thcy should]. The said Margery cannot deny that she is not the sister of the said Ralph of one father and one mother, nor that the said Stephen and Hulina hold in dower. So it is adjudged that the assize is not valid between them, and so Ralph and Stephen [are] without day and Margery [is] in mercy for a false claim. She is poor.

419. (*Hartismere*) An assize comes to declare if Walter of Westhorpe brother of Roger of Westhorpe was seised in demesne as of fee of two parts of one knight's fee with appurtenances in Westhorpe on the day that etc and if he died after the latest return etc and if etc which two parts (Robert[i]) Hovel holds. He comes and then vouches to warranty William de Hanley by aid of the court, who is present and he warrants him. He says, in fact, that Walter, his brother, died seised of the said land as of fee and after the term, and that the said Roger is the nearest heir. But the said Walter a long time before his death demised the same land to the said William, to hold [it] for twenty years after the death of bishop Thomas de Blunville,[1] and he claims nothing of right in the said land except the said term. Robert Hovel gives twenty shillings for licence to agree by the surety of Ralph de Arderne (*twenty shillings*). [*chirograph* CP 25(1) 213/15/6]

[1] Thomas de Blunville died on 16 August 1236, so William had the land until 1256.

420. (*Hartismere*) An assize comes to declare if William the parson of Buxhall, John Page, Robert Kelle unjustly etc disseised Nicholas of Buxhall of his free tenement in the same vill after the first crossing etc and in respect whereof he complains that they disseised him of two parts of a certain meadow. William and Robert come and say nothing to stay the assize. John Page has not come and he was attached by William Copinger of Buxhall and Robert del Hill. So [they are] in mercy (*amercement*).

The jurors say that the said William and the others have not disseised the said Nicholas of any free tenement because he did not hold that tenement except for a term. So William and the others [are] without day and Nicholas [is] in mercy for a false claim by the surety of Ranulf the Fleming of Buxhall and Ranulf the son of Alice of the same (*amercement*).

421. (*Hartismere*) An assize comes to declare if Ralph the Fleming[1] unjustly etc disseised Katherine de Sturmyn of her free tenement in Buxhall after the first crossing etc and in respect whereof she complains that he disseised her of a strip of meadow. Ralph comes and says nothing to stay the assize.

The jurors say that the said Ralph has not disseised her as the writ says. So Ralph [is] quit and Katherine [is] in mercy for a false claim by the surety of Roger le Sturmyn (*amercement*).

   [1]   See **420** where possibly this person acted as a surety.

422.[1] Ralph de Furnaus who brought a writ of novel disseisin against Roger de Furnaus and others named in the writ has not prosecuted. So he and his sureties [are] in mercy, namely: Martin the son of Robert of Bacton and Roger the son of Adam of the same (*amercement*).

   [1]   There is a small gap between this plea and the previous one of 1.9 cm with a surplus paragraph mark.

423. An assize comes to declare if Alice the daughter of Hamelin, the sister of Edith wife of Richard Blundel, was seised in demesne as of fee of one messuage and six acres of land with appurtenances in Finborough on the day that etc and if etc and if she died after the last etc which land and messuage Richard the son of Geoffrey holds. Richard Blundel and Edith his wife come and acknowledge that they are the villeins of Ralph de Arderne. So it is adjudged that they are to take nothing by this assize but that they are in mercy for a false claim by the surety of Richard the son of Geoffrey of Finborough (*amercement*).

424. Thomas the barker of Eye who brought a writ of mort d'ancestor against Thomas the tailor concerning half of one messuage with appurtenances in Eye has not prosecuted. So he and his sureties for prosecuting [are] in mercy, namely: Hugh de Blogate of Yaxley and Roger de Ripa de *Spirwelton* (*amercement*).

425. Nicholas the son of Manser, Ralph and Bartholomew and [Ralph][1] his brothers who brought a writ of mort d'ancestor against the prior of Broomholm and others concerning one messuage and forty-one acres of land, five acres of wood, ten shillings and four penceworth of rent and one acre of meadow with appurtenances in Brockford [and] in Worlingworth have not prosecuted. So they and their sureties for prosecuting [are] in mercy, namely: Rich[aud] of Sproughton [and] Walter the son of Roger de Eys (*amercement*).

   [1]   The clerk has probably made a mistake here and meant Richard, unless he was a half brother.

426. (*Hartismere*) Andrew Tabbard and Avice his wife who brought a writ of mort d'ancestor against Walter de Launcs and Christine his wife concerning one messuage and one acre of land with appurtenances in Eye have not prosecuted. So they and their sureties [are] in mercy, namely: Roger Auket of Yaxley and Gilbert the carpenter de Raudeston (*amercement*).

427. (*Samford*) An assize comes to declare if Roger de Ripa and Roger Grubbe unjustly etc disseised William of Badley of his free tenement in Sproughton after the first crossing etc and in respect whereof he complains that they disseised him of three and a half acres of land. Roger de Ripa comes and says nothing to stay the assize. Roger Grubbe has not come because he was not (attached[i]).

The jurors say the said Roger de Ripa and Roger Grubbe disseised him as the writ says. So it is adjudged that William is to recover his seisin by view of the recognitors. Roger de Ripa and Roger Grubbe [are] in mercy (*amercement*). Sureties of Roger de Ripa: Osbert Grubbe of Sproughton and Henry Wicher of the same [place].

Damages: half a mark. To the clerks forty pence.

428. (*Samford*) An assize comes to declare if Roger de Ripa unjustly etc disseised Walter the merchant of his free tenement in Sproughton after the first crossing etc and in respect whereof he complains that he disseised him of three acres of land. Roger comes and says nothing to stay the assize.

The jurors say that the said Roger disseised him as the writ says. So it is adjudged that the said Walter is to recover his seisin and Roger [is] in mercy (*amercement*). Sureties of Roger [are] as shown above.

To the clerks. Damages: twelve pence. [**427**]

429. (*Samford*) An assize comes to declare if Thomas de *Meldinghes*[1] and Olive his wife and William the son of John unjustly etc disseised Stephen the son of William of his free tenement in Brantham after the first etc and in respect whereof he complains that they disseised him of eight feet of meadow in length. Thomas de *Meldinghes* and Olive his wife (and William the son of John[i]) come and say nothing to stay the assize.

The jurors say that the said Thomas disseised him of one foot of land and not of the (eight[il]) feet which he placed in their view. So it is adjudged that Thomas is in mercy for disseisin by the surety of Adam of Brantham and Alexander the clerk of Stutton. Stephen [is] in mercy for a false claim by the surety of Alan of Brantham and Alexander the clerk of Stutton.

   1   It is spelt *Medlinges* later in this plea. This could be Milden in Babergh hundred. Almost certainly the same Thomas and Olive occur in **333**.

430. (*Bosmere*) William the son of Geoffrey of Hemingstone who brought an assize of mort d'ancestor against Ralph de Blunville concerning a tenement in Hemingstone has not prosecuted. So he and his sureties for prosecuting [are] in mercy, namely: Henry de *Bucermande* and John the son of Gilbert of Tuddenham (*amercement*).

431. Robert the son of Osbert who brought an assize of novel disseisin against Geoffrey the parson of Copdock has not prosecuted. So he and his sureties [are] in mercy, namely: Gerard Richend of Sproughton and Robert of Stanstead of Copdock (*amercement*).

432. (*Bosmere*) Nicholas the son of Micah who brought an assize of mort d'ancestor against Geoffrey de Bosco concerning a tenement in Nettlestead has not prosecuted.

So he and his sureties [are] in mercy, namely: Austin of Blakenham and Albert Pigaz de la Hone (*amercement*).

433. (*Samford*) An assize comes to declare if Adam Mittebotes father of Isabella wife of Golding of Ipswich and Christine wife of Ralph le Leu and Rose the sister of Isabella and Christine was seised in his demesne etc of five acres of land with appurtenances in Wherstead on the day that etc and if the said Isabella and the others etc which land Richard the son of John holds. He comes and he says that the assize should not be taken on this, because the said Adam died before the term named in the writ. Isabella and the others do not deny [this]. So it is adjudged that Richard[1] [is] without day and the others[2] [are] in mercy. They are poor.

[1] The clerk actually wrote *Rogerus*.
[2] The clerk wrote *alii* instead of *alie* as all the 'others' are female. Had there been a mixture of male and females or only males that are to be amerced the clerk would have been correct.

434. Agnes de Bruera appoints as her attorney William de la Bruera against John of Kirkton concerning a plea of mort d'ancestor. [**538**]

435. Robert de (B-efeud[il]) (plaintiff[r]), appoints as his attorney Ranulf his son against Geoffrey de Burnaville concerning a plea of an assize of novel disseisin.

Membrane 16d

436. (*Samford, half a mark*) Roger of Sproughton gives half a mark for licence to agree with Geoffrey de Bosco concerning a plea of assize of mort d'ancestor (namely concerning one acre of land[i]), by the surety of Geoffrey de Bosco. The agreement is such that Roger of Sproughton acknowledged the (land[i]) to be the right of Geoffrey. For this acknowledgement etc the same Roger grants to the same Geoffrey the said land to be held etc by service of four pence per year.

437. (*Bosmere*) Thomas the chaplain, who brought a writ of mort d'ancestor against John of Barking and Joan his wife and others in the writ, has not prosecuted. So he and his sureties for prosecuting [are] in mercy, namely: William le Veutrer[1] of Brantham and Robert the son of Andrew (*amercement*).

[1] That is the greyhound keeper of Brantham. It might also be *Ventrer*, the adventurer.

438. (*Samford, amercement*) An assize comes to declare if William of Ladbroke the father of Robert de Rothe was seised in his demesne of one acre of land with appurtenances in Raydon on the day that etc and if etc which land Robert of Northwold holds. He comes and says that the said William did not die seised as in demesne.

The jurors say that the said William did not die seised as in demesne, because he held that land only for his lifetime. So it is adjudged that Robert is to take nothing by this assize and he is in mercy for a false claim by the surety of John of Chattisham and John the son of John of the same. Robert [is] without day.

439. (*Bosmere*) An assize comes to declare if Robert of *Olden*[1] unjustly etc raised [the level of] a certain pond in Coddenham to the nuisance of the free tenement of Ernulf the son of Ranulf of Coddenham after the first crossing etc. Robert comes and says nothing to stay the assize.

The jurors say that the said Robert has raised [the level of] a certain pond as the writ says to the nuisance of the said Ernulf. So it is adjudged that the raising is to be lowered and is to be as it ought to be and is accustomed [to be]. Robert [is] in mercy by the (surety[r]) of Philip of Winston (*amercement*).

Damages: twelve pence.

1   *Olden* is shown in *Domesday Book Suffolk*, Part One, section 1, no. 5 etc. It is in Coddenham in Bosmere hundred. Also see *VCH* i, p.419, n.2.

440. (*Samford*) An assize comes to declare if Walter of Shelfhanger, uncle of John the son of William, was seised in demesne etc of five acres of land in Badley on the day that etc and if etc and if etc which land Robert of Blakenham holds. He comes and vouches to warranty Geoffrey of Badley. He is present and he warrants him and he [Geoffrey] says that the assize should not be taken on this because the said Walter had a certain brother Ralph from the same father and mother, and from the (same[i])[1] Ralph issued a certain Nicholas who is still alive. He [also] says etc that the said William, father of that William, who brought the assize, was in fact the brother of his father Walter, from one father but of a different mother.

John says that Walter died seised of the said land as of fee and that he is the nearest heir and then he puts himself on the assize, and Geoffrey similarly.

The jurors say that Walter died seised of the said land as of fee and that this John is the nearest heir. So it is adjudged that John is to recover his seisin, and Geoffrey [is] in mercy. He will make an exchange to Robert to the value [of that land] (*amercement*).

1   The clerk had also crossed out *quo* to read 'from whom'.

441. (*Samford*) Thomas the son of Joscelin and Beatrice his wife who brought an assize of mort d'ancestor against the prioress of Wix[1] concerning a tenement in Chattisham have not prosecuted. So they and their sureties [are] in mercy namely: John the son of Richard of Chattisham and John the son of John of the same (*amercement*).

1   Wix was a priory of Benedictine nuns in Essex, founded 1123–1133.

442. An assize comes to declare if Robert of Erwarton and Roger of Kirkton unjustly etc disseised William the son of William of his free tenement in Kirkton after the first etc and in respect whereof he complains they disseised him of sixteen acres.

Robert and Roger come and they say nothing to stay the assize.

The jurors say that the said Roger and Robert have not disseised the said William (of[i]) any tenement. So it is adjudged that they may go without day and William [is] in mercy. He is poor and under age (*poor*).

443. (*Bosmere, half a mark*) Beatrice de Rubroc gives half a mark for licence to agree with Roger the son of Henry concerning a plea of assize of mort d'ancestor by the surety of Geoffrey Carbunel.

444. (*Samford*) An assize comes to declare if Margery the wife of John Andrew unjustly etc disseised Richard of Erwarton of his free tenement in Sproughton after the first etc and in respect whereof he complains that she disseised him of eight acres of land. Margery comes and says nothing to stay the assize.

The jurors say that the said Margery disseised him as the writ says. So it is adjudged that the said Richard is to recover his seisin and Margery [is] in mercy. It is pardoned because [she is] poor.

To the clerks. Damages: two shillings.

445. (*Bosmere*) An assize comes to declare if Ralph Blund the father of Robert Blund was seised in his demesne of six acres of land and half an acre of meadow with appurtenances in Little Blakenham on the day etc and if etc and if etc in respect whereof Brian le Pervit holds two acres, Austin of Blakenham three acres, Robert Wighe one acre and Geoffrey Carbonel half an acre of meadow. They all come. Robert [Blund] does not wish to proceed, against Austin nor against Geoffrey.[1] So he and his sureties [are] in mercy for a false claim by the surety of Austin of Blakenham (*amercement*).

Robert Wighe comes and he says nothing to stay the assize.

The jurors say that the said Ralph died seised of the said acre as of fee and after the term etc and that the said Robert is his nearest heir. So it is adjudged that the said Robert Blund is to recover his seisin of the said acre of land and Robert Wighe [is] in mercy for an unjust detention. It is pardoned because [he is] poor.

1   As Brian no longer appears in the plea I suspect that the clerk has missed him out.

446. (*Samford*) An assize comes to declare if William de Floxford uncle of Roger the son of Gilbert was seised in demesne etc of six acres of land and one messuage and one acre[1] of meadow with appurtenances in Sproughton on the day that etc and if etc and if he Roger etc in respect whereof the prior of St Peter's of Ipswich[2] holds six acres and the one messuage and half an acre of meadow [and] William Godescalc holds half an acre of meadow. They come and then vouch to warranty Roger de *Bruniford*, who is present, and he warrants them and he says nothing to stay the assize.

The jurors say that the said William de Floxford had married a certain Alice, the mother of Roger de *Bruniford*, who held in dower the said land in respect whereof the assize has been brought, and after he had married her she came to the said Roger, her son, and warrantor of her dower, and handed the said land over to the said Roger. The same Roger afterwards enfeoffed the said William de *Floxford* of the said land by his charter to be held by him and his heirs etc from the said Roger and his heirs etc and thus he [William] died seised. After the death of the same William de Floxford the same Alice remained in seisin of that land and she died seised. After the death of Alice, Roger de *Bruniford* came and gave the said land to the said prior by his charter. (*to judgment*) The jurors also say that the same Roger de *Bruniford* had no seisin of the said land after the said William and Alice de Floxford had handed it over to the said Roger.[3] Afterwards, they are agreed by licence and Robert remised all for twenty shillings.

1   The clerk mistakenly indicated *unam acram* (accusative) when it should have been in the ablative, *una acra*. All the other elements are in the ablative, that is the six acres of land and one messuage.
2   Actually St Peter and St Paul, an Augustinian house founded in the time of Henry II and dissolved in 1528 for Cardinal Wolsey's college at Ipswich.
3   That is the plaintiff, Roger the son of Gilbert.

447. (*Hoxne*) An assize comes to declare if Thomas Russel unjustly etc disseised Matilda the daughter of Richard of her free tenement in Mendham after the first etc and in respect whereof Matilda complains that the same Thomas disseised her of six acres of land with appurtenances in the same vill.

Thomas comes and says nothing to stay the assize.

The jurors say that the said Thomas disseised the said Matilda of the said six acres of land unjustly etc So it is adjudged that she has recovered her seisin. Thomas [is] in mercy by the surety of Roger of Shotford and the knight Adam of Mendham (*good amercement*).

Damages: twenty-five shillings.

448. (*Hoxne*) An assize comes to declare if William le Rus unjustly etc disseised Richard the son of Brictmer and Thomas the son of Ernald (and Roger[1] the son of Geoffrey[i]) of their common pasture in Stradbroke which pertained to their free tenement in the same vill after the first crossing etc.

William comes and says nothing to stay the assize, but William gives forty shillings for having a 'good' jury by the surety of William de Stuteville (*40 shillings*). Afterwards, Roger came and withdrew [from the plea]. So he and his sureties for prosecuting [are] in mercy, namely: Richard of Wingfield and Walter Mervin of Wingfield (*amercement*).

The jurors say that the said Richard and Thomas and their ancestors, in the time of Ernulf le Rus great grandfather of this William, and in the time of (Bernard[i]) his grandfather, and in the time of Hugh his father, and in the time in which the same William was under age and in the custody of Roger of Huntingfield, and also in the time of this William until the said year, have always given aid at will, sometimes more, sometime less. They say also that they never gave merchet nor ought to give [it]. Because of this the services and customs are not villein, so it is adjudged that they are to recover their seisin and William [is] in mercy (*amercement*).

1   The clerk mistakenly put *Rogerus* in the nominative case instead of the accusative.

Membrane 17

449. (*Wiltshire*) Master William de la Wyke[1] by Nigel de Moldburn, his attorney, acknowledges that he owes to Waleran of Blunsdon 100 shillings concerning which he should pay fifty shillings at the feast of St John[2] in the 24th year, and fifty shillings at the feast of St Peter in Chains [1 August]. If he does not do [this] he grants that he may be distrained [by his land and chattels] until etc and the cost etc. Unless the same Richard[3] has paid, Nigel grants that he may be distrained [by his land and chattels] etc. [*chirograph* CP 25(1) 282/6/78[4] and CP 25(1) 250/11/14]

1   This is almost certainly an agreement to pay from a Wiltshire plea as the two protagonists almost certainly come from Wick and Blunsdon in Wiltshire. It is possible that this was a leftover from the Wiltshire eyre of 1236 or from a plea at the Curia Regis.
2   This must be the feast of the Nativity of St John the Baptist on 24 June.
3   Richard de la Wyke and Waleran of Blunsdon appear in a number of pleas in the Wiltshire eyre of 1249, which may suggest that the clerk made a mistake and put in William of Wick instead of Richard. See *1249 Wilts Civil Pleas*, pleas 161, 162, 176, 260, and 425.
4   This is the left-hand chirograph of CP 25(1), 250/11/14 according to Crook 1982a, p.101, n.1. The chirographs also indicate that the two litigants were Master Richard de la Wyke and Waleran of Blunsdon. The attorney is also mentioned and he is shown as Nigel of Medbourne, Leicestershire.

450.[1] (*Hartismere*) Katelina the daughter of William le Waleys[2] and Alice her sister claim against Robert de Hirdel[3] five acres of land with appurtenances in Wortham, and against William de Belecumbre five acres of land with appurtenances in the same vill, and against Richard Bishop one acre of land with appurtenances in the same, and against Robert de Aldewood and Saina[4] his wife four acres of land with appurtenances in the same, and against William Darnel twenty acres of land with appurtenances in the same, and against Odo Kat and Simon his brother four acres of land with appurtenances in the same vill, and against Walter the son of William the priest two acres of land with appurtenances in the same, and against Roger le Breton eight acres of land with appurtenances in the same, and against Roger Heved seven acres of land with appurtenances in the same, and against Henry of Northwold four acres of land with appurtenances in the same, and against Walter the Reeve three acres of land with appurtenances in the same, and against John de Salerne two (and a half[1]) acres of land with appurtenances in the same as their right etc in[5] respect whereof a certain William, their ancestor, was seised in his demesne as of fee and right and in the time of King Richard [I] uncle of the present king by taking profits therefrom to the value of half a mark. From the same William the right of that land descended to a certain John as son and heir, and from the same John descended the right of that land to a certain Alan as brother and heir because he died without a direct heir, [and] from the same Alan, [the right of that land descended to] Matilda, Katelina and Alice as the daughters[6] [of William],[7] and because Matilda died without heirs the right descended to those who now claim, and that such is their right they offer [to prove].

Robert[8] and all the others come and Richard Bishop, Odo Kat, Simon his brother and Roger Heved and Walter the Reeve say that they cannot answer them because they are villeins. Because the said Richard acknowledges himself to be the villein of John de Crammaville,[9] and Odo Kat and Simon his brother acknowledges themselves to be the villeins of the abbot of Bury St Edmunds, and Roger Heved acknowledges himself to be the villein of Richard of Crepping, and Walter the Reeve acknowledges himself to be the villein of Giles of Wattisham, so [they are] without day, and Katelina and Alice [are] in mercy (*process mark,[10] amercement*). They may proceed against the said etc [if they wish]. But Robert de Hirdel, William de Belecumbre,[11] and William Darnel, Walter the son of William the priest and Henry of Northwold then vouch to warranty Thomas of Gedding. He is to come on the morrow of the Ascension at Cattishall by aid of the court (*Cattishall, on the morrow*). Robert de Aldewood[12] and Saina his wife then vouch to warranty Henry Folcard. John de Salerne says that he claims nothing in the said land save only in the name of the wardship of Adam the son of John who is under age. So let him await [his] coming of age (*age*). Afterwards, Henry Folcard comes and he vouches to warranty the said Thomas of Gedding. He is to have him by aid of the court at the same term.

Roger le Breton denies their right and the seisin of the said William and everything etc. He puts himself on the king's grand assize and he seeks a recognition be made whether he has the greater right in that land, as for that which a certain Robert le Waleys their grandfather gave to a certain Robert de Breton his grandfather as a marriage portion with a certain Sabina[13] his stepdaughter, or the said Katelina and Alice as for that land from which the said William their ancestor died seised as of fee in the time of King Richard [I]. Roger [le Breton] gives half a mark to have an inquiry, concerning a year and a day etc by the surety of John of Stanton (*half a mark*). Hugh Burt, Baldwin of Mellis, William of Cotton and Walter of Cove four knights, selected to choose etc to make a recognition of the grand assize between Katelina the daughter of William le Waleys and Alice her sister, plaintiffs, and Roger le Breton, defendant, of eight acres of land with appurtenances in Wortham in respect whereof the same Roger, who is the tenant, placed himself on the grand assize of the lord king, and sought a recognition to be made whether he has the greater right in that land as in that which a certain Robert le Waleys, grandfather of the said Katelina and Alice, gave to a certain Robert le Breton, his grandfather, in marriage portion with a certain Sabina his stepdaughter, or the said Katelina and Alice as in that [land] from which the said William their ancestor died seised, etc have come and chosen these, namely: Robert de Wykes, Roger Sturmey, Ralph of Weston, William de Ciresy, Michael Gernegan, John Cordebof,[14] John de Crammaville, John of Stonham, Phillip of Winston, John de Hodeboville, James le

Enveyse, Robert le Envoyse, William of Stratford, Adam of Welnetham, Adam de Bylce and Osbert of Bawdsey.

Afterwards, they have agreed by licence, for God and for poverty.[15]

(*process mark*)[16] Afterwards[17] on the day Thomas comes and he warrants them as is shown in the roll of Cattishall. [*chirographs* CP 25(1) 213/17/111[18] and CP 25(1) 213/17/98][19]

1 See **1096** and **1097** for the continuation of this plea.

2 This is a Celtic name. There were a number of Bretons that came over after the conquest and settled in Norfolk. The modern name is shown as 'Wallis'. See **835** and Reaney 1997, p.474.

3 This name might be hurdler, a maker of hurdles, but I would expect *le* rather than *de Hirdel*. I cannot find a place with this name in Suffolk or Norfolk.

4 *Sainam* is inserted at this point but later in the membrane *Sarram* is shown; I have assumed Saina in this English translation as in the chirograph she is also shown as Sayna.

5 The remainder of the paragraph was very squashed as the clerk was trying to squeeze it into a small gap.

6 As Alan died without a direct heir the clerk may have left something out here or is indulging in a bit of shorthand, as he should be saying that the right of the land descended to William le Waleys and then to the three women as daughters of William le Waleys, and who may also have been sisters of John and Alan.

7 Although the transcription appears to imply that they are the daughters of Alan, they are in fact the daughters of William le Waleys. It looks as though the clerk has left out a line indicating that the right passed to William from Alan.

8 There is a gap of 1.2 cm between the start of this paragraph and the previous one. This lends credence to the clerk fitting in the last part of the previous paragraph.

9 There is a crease in the membrane at this point but *Crammavil* is definitely what is shown in the text.

10 This is shown as three dots on the left of the margin.

11 *Belencumbe* is written by the clerk. *Willelmum de Benecumb* is what the clerk wrote at the start of this plea. In the chirograph he is shown as *Willelmus de Belecumbre* which is the name I have used consistently in this English translation.

12 *Ailwode* is what the clerk originally wrote in the first paragraph for this person but here he is Robert de Aldewood and in **186**, where he is appointed as the attorney of his wife Selena, he is Robert of Alderwood; see note 4 above for his wife's name used in the chirograph.

13 The clerk wrote *Katerina*. Later in the plea she becomes *Sabina*. I have assumed that she is Sabina in this English translation.

14 There is a Cordebef family in Suffolk according to *Feudal Aids 1284–1431* v, p.57.

15 This probably means that no charge was made for the licence.

16 This looks like a 'Q' with a long tail and with 4 dots, two on each side of the tail. It is used as a pointer to a clerk to find a similar sign on the later item, **1096**, where the plea is shown as continuing.

17 There is a substantial gap of 2.6 cm between the two last lines of this plea. It looks as though the clerk has added this statement in after an agreement was made at Cattishall. See **1096** where Thomas of Gedding makes his appearance for the others in the plea.

18 This chirograph is made at Chelmsford on the octave of St John the Baptist. I presume that the licence to agree for 'God and for poverty' is the reason why the two plaintiffs were also not amerced. This was made with the vouchee Thomas of Gedding for the others involved in the plea.

19 Between Roger le Breton and Katherine and Alice her sister who remised and quitclaimed their right for one mark of silver from Roger.

451. (*Samford, half a mark*) Reynold de Stanho gives half a mark for licence to agree with William Dionis concerning a plea of warranty of charter by the surety of the same William. [*chirograph* CP 25(1) 213/15/26][1]

1 On the reverse of the chirograph is the following: *Clamium Rogeri le Bigod Comes Norf' et Florie Juvenal quia Willelmus Dionis columpniatus est pro villano.* William was challenged as a villein at the time the fine was made.

452. The prior of Norwich by his attorney presented himself on the fourth day against Richard Carpenter concerning a plea that he should restore to him two acres of land with appurtenances in Chickering[1] which he claims to be the right of his church etc. Richard has not come and [was] summoned etc. Judgement: the land is to be taken into the king's hand and he is to be summoned to be at Cattishall on the Thursday next after the Ascension of the Lord [31 May] (*Cattishall*).

[1] There is very little left of this vill except a few farm buildings, private houses and a nursing home. It is located between Stradbroke and Hoxne.

453. (*Lothingland*) Hawise of Hopton claims against Edmund de Wymundhall four acres of land and three shillings and six penceworth of rent with appurtenances in Hopton, and seven and a half acres of land with appurtenances in Boyton[1] which she claims as her dower, which she had from the free tenement that was of Osbert of Hopton her first husband in the same vills, and in which the said Edmund has no entry except by Geoffrey of Sandon the second husband of Hawise who demised that [land etc] to him whom [she could not contradict] etc. Edmund comes and concerning the seven and a half acres vouches to warranty Roger the son of Osbert, and concerning the four acres and rent vouches to warranty Mabel and the heirs of the said Osbert. He is to have them by aid of the court at Cattishall on the morrow of the Ascension [Friday 25 May] (*Cattishall*).

Afterwards, Roger comes and he says nothing why she should not [have] the dower. So it is adjudged that she has recovered her seisin and Roger [is] in mercy (*amercement*). He will make an exchange to the said Edmund to the value [of the land and rent Edmund held]. Edmund comes and by licence renders to her the said four acres of land and the said three shillings and six penceworth of rent. So she is to have her seisin.

[1] There is a Boyton Farm in Lothingland hundred, which is relatively close to Lound. Hopton, which is where the plaintiff probably came from and where the other land is located, is very close to Boyton Farm.

454. William de Gosewolde who brought a writ of entry against Hugh Capell and others named in the writ has not prosecuted. So he and his sureties for prosecuting [are] in mercy. He made a fine for himself and his sureties for ten shillings by the surety of Roger de Breton[1] (*Ten shillings*).

[1] This is probably the same Roger the Breton in **450**. This is what he is named in the amercement section.

455. (*Lothingland, Cattishall*) Matilda who was the wife of Thomas of Boyton claims against Henry the son of John half of five acres of land, and of three roods of land with appurtenances in Boyton,[1] and against Warren Blench half of one acre of land with appurtenances in the same vill, and against Edmund de Wymundhall eighteen penceworth of rent with appurtenances in the same vill as her dower.

Henry, Edmund and Warren, by Warren's attorney, come and then vouch to warranty Henry, son and heir to the said Thomas, who is in the wardship of Matilda. She is to have him at Cattishall on the morrow of the Ascension [Friday 25 May]. On that day the same Henry comes and he is under age and in the wardship of Matilda with all his land. Because they [the three defendants] proffer charters of enfeofment it is adjudged that they may hold in peace and she may have from the land of Henry [the heir] to the value [of the land and rent Matilda held].

[1] See **453**.

456. Thomas Bacon acknowledges that he owes to the abbot de Savigny one mark of the arrears of his relief from the tenement that he holds from him in Dallinghoo. [*chirograph* CP 25(1) 156/61/694]

457.[1] (*Hoxne*) Gillian de Skeling, who brought a writ of entry against John the clerk concerning a tenement in Rishangles,[2] has not prosecuted. So she and her sureties for prosecuting [are] in mercy. namely: Robert Stasarcher of Rickinghall and Edmund the son of Robert of Mellis (*amercements*).

[1] The next four pleas are in a different hand on this membrane.
[2] Rishangles is actually in Hartismere hundred.

458. (*Hartismere*) Roger the son of Hugh de *Raudeston*, who brought a writ of detinue of charters etc against Safrid the chaplain of Palgrave, has not prosecuted. So he and his sureties for prosecuting [are] in mercy namely: Geoffrey the son of William de Raudeston and Humphrey le Neir (*amercements*).

459. (*Hartismere*) Roger the son of Hugh de *Raudeston*, who brought a writ of covenant against the abbot of Bury St Edmunds concerning a tenement in Palgrave, has not prosecuted. So he and his sureties for prosecuting [are] in mercy, namely: Thomas the son of Oselina de Raudeston and Geoffrey the son of Matilda of the same (*amercements*).

460. (*Norfolk, forty shillings*) Roger de Cressy gives forty shillings for licence to agree with William de Stuteville concerning a plea of land in respect whereof a trial by battle.
The same William gives forty shillings for the same with the same (*forty shillings*).

461. Juliana,[1] who was the wife of Richard le May, appoints as her attorney John Cordebof against William Seman, and against Roger Wilsy concerning a plea of land etc.

[1] The membrane now reverts back to the original clerk from this plea.

462. Matilda the wife of Ralph de Tyely appoints as her attorney Ralph her husband against Hugh Burt and Margery his wife respectively concerning a plea of the assessment of dower, and against Simon Bold concerning a plea of land etc. [*chirograph* CP 25(1) 213/15/7][1]

[1] See the essoin in **46**. The rest of this case does not appear in the roll but the chirograph concerns the plea with Hugh Burt and Margery his wife on the plea of the measurement of the dower. Matilda in effect wins because Hugh and Margery rent back from her the agreed dower in Fressingfield for 4s. a year payable at four terms. It does look as though Matilda lost her plea concerning her dower in Laxfield, which they agreed was the dower of Margery. There is no mention of the plea with Simon Bold, but see **477** where there is a plea against a Simon Bolt.

463. Ralph de Arderne appoints as his attorney Robert Mynyot against Isabella who was the wife of Nicholas of Clopton concerning a plea of land etc. [**985**]

Membrane 17d

464.[1] (*Lothingland*) Mabel who was the wife of Thomas of Browston claims against Laurence of Newton a third part of eleven acres of land, a third part of one and a half acres of meadow and a third part of one and a half acres of wood with appurtenances in *Newton* as her dower.

Laurence comes and then vouches to warranty the said Henry at the said term by aid of the court (*Cattishall*).

    1   There is a new clerk for this and the next two pleas. The membrane then reverts back to the last clerk at the end of the previous side of this membrane.

465. (*St Etheldreda*) Roger the son of William claims against Robert the taberer and Margery his wife eight acres of land with appurtenances in Blaxhall as his right. They have agreed by licence and the agreement is such that Roger remises all for half a mark.

466. (*Bosmere*) A day is given to Geoffrey the son of Geoffrey and Hugh of Badley, plaintiffs, and William de Ciresy concerning a plea of debt at Cattishall at the arrival of the judges by prayer of the parties. [**970**]

467. (*Norfolk*) Avice who was the wife of Eustace of Kimberley by her attorney claims against Thomas de Gelham half of fourteen acres of land with appurtenances in Carlton and Kimberley, and against Thomas the son of Eustace half of one carucate of land with appurtenances in the same vill, Wicklewood, as her dower etc and in respect whereof the said Eustace her former husband dowered her etc on the day etc. Thomas de Gelham and Thomas [son of Eustace] come and Thomas de Gelham then vouches to warranty Thomas, who is present and he warrants him, and he answered for all and he knows nothing to declare why she ought not to have her dower. So it is adjudged that she has recovered her seisin and Thomas [is] in mercy. It is pardoned because [he is] under age.

468. (*half a mark*) Robert de Freney gives half a mark for licence to agree with Basilia Potekin concerning a plea of land by the surety of Robert de *Burnaville*.
The same Basilia by her attorney gives half a mark for licence to agree with the same concerning the same by the surety of Robert de Freney (*half a mark*). [*chirograph* CP 25(1) 213/17/84][1]

    1   The chirograph provides the information that the plea was for over 20 acres of land in Erwarton in Samford hundred.

469. (*Blything*) William the son of Geoffrey claims against Walter the son of Geoffrey half of sixteen acres of land with appurtenances in Stoven as his right, and in respect whereof Geoffrey their father was seised etc in the time of King John by taking profits therefrom to the value of half a mark etc. From the same Geoffrey the right to that land descended to a certain Adam, their brother, and to themselves (as[i]) sons and heirs because that land is partible, and because Adam, their brother, died without heirs from his body the right to that land descended to William and Walter, and that such is his right he offers [to prove].

Walter comes and denies his right and he says that that land was never divided, nor is partible, and that this might be inquired into by the jury he offers to the lord king half a mark (*half a mark*). They are received by the surety of Adam le Pays de Hoppechare. So let there be a jury thereon.

The jurors say that the said land was never divided nor was ever partible. So it is adjudged that the said William is to take nothing by this jury, and is in mercy for a false claim (*amercement*). Walter is to hold in peace.

470.[1] (*Blything*) Roger Traine and Agnes his wife claim against Robert de Wykes and Amice his wife and William de Blunville half of one carucate of land with appurtenances in Cove as the dower of Agnes because a certain Richard the palmer her former husband dowered her etc on the day etc.

Robert and the others come and say that they cannot answer to this writ because they hold nothing in the said land, because a certain Sybil de Blunville holds that land. Roger cannot deny this. So [they are] in mercy (*amercement*). She may proceed against her [Sybil] if she wishes and the others [are] quit.

¹ See **251** for the appointment of an attorney. There is a large gap of 11.4 cm between this plea and the previous one.

471. (*Hoxne*) Simon of Sheering claims against Avice of Mendham and Robert her son half an acre of land with appurtenances in Mendham in which the said Avice and Robert have no entry except by Nicholas Crowe to whom the said Simon demised that [land] for a term which has passed etc.

Avice and Robert come and readily grant the entry and they cannot deny that the said land is the right of Simon. So it is adjudged that the said Simon is to recover his seisin and they [are] in mercy (*amercements*).

472. (*Half a mark, Hoxne*) John the son of Robert of Metfield gives half a mark for a licence to agree with Gilbert of Mendham by the surety of William the son of Thomas of Metfield concerning a plea of land. [*chirograph* CP 25(1) 213/15/34]

473. Gilbert the son of John of Metfield presented himself on the fourth day against John Esot concerning a plea of two acres of land with appurtenances in Metfield, which he claims as his right against him. John has not come and was summoned etc. Judgement: the land is to be taken into the hands of the lord king, and the day etc and they are to be summoned etc that they be at Cattishall on the morrow of the Ascension of the Lord (*Cattishall*).

474. (*Hoxne*) Richard of Cransford claims against Thomas Balaunc fifteen acres of land with appurtenances in Mendham as his right etc. Thomas came and by licence they have agreed. The agreement is such that the said Thomas acknowledges the said land to be the right of Richard. For this etc the same Richard grants that Thomas and his heirs may hold the said land from the same Richard and his heirs forever, rendering annually one mark, and performing the service of one twentieth part of a knight's fee etc. [*chirograph* CP 25(1) 213/17/82]¹

¹ The feet of fines indicates the place as being Metfield in Hoxne hundred and not Mendham as in the plea. Note that there is no mention of the agreement in the agreement section at the end of this roll, probably because no mention is made of payment for the chirograph in the plea.

Membrane 18

475. (*Norfolk*) Geoffrey de Say and Alina his wife, by the attorney of Alina, claims against Simon Peche and Agnes his wife seventy-two shillings and six pennyworth of rent with appurtenances in Cringleford as the dower of Alina etc.

And against William Mauclerc ten acres of land with appurtenances in the same vill.

And against William Stute twelve acres of land with appurtenances in the same vill as the dower of Alina etc.

Simon and all the others come and then claim a view. They are to have [it]. A day is given to them at Cattishall on the Monday before the Ascension of the Lord [21 May] etc (*Cattishall*). This is void because [it is] elsewhere afterwards in the roll of Cattishall. [**727**]

476. The prior of Bricett was summoned to answer Robert de Alneto concerning a plea that he warrant him two acres of land with appurtenances and one acre of wood with appurtenances in Buxhall which he holds etc. He says that the same John Sturmey impleads him concerning the said land in the county of Suffolk. The prior is present and he says that he willingly warrants him. So it is said to him that he is to go to the county court.

477. Ralph de *Trelly* and Matilda his wife claim against Simon Bolt three roods of land with appurtenances in Fressingfield as the right of Matilda etc and in which she does not have entry except by Hubert de *Ryveshall*.[1] Simon comes and vouches to warranty Hubert who is present and by licence renders [it] to them. So Ralph and Matilda are to have their seisin. Hubert will make an exchange to the said Simon to the value [of his holding] etc.

> [1] Either Ringshall in Bosmere hundred or Rishangles in Hartismere hundred, which is closer to Fressingfield.

478. (*St Etheldreda*) An assize comes to declare if Matthew of Peyton, Roger his brother, Hugh Galston and Simon the ploughman unjustly etc disseised Philip of Horkesley and Matilda his wife of their free tenement in Peyton after the first etc and in respect whereof they claim that they disseised them of thirty acres of marsh and a third part of sixty acres of heath and in a certain place in the same vill one portion of land, containing in length thirty-seven feet and in width forty-seven feet, and besides of a certain pasture in respect whereof he was accustomed to receive nineteen pence a year for pasture.

Roger has not come and was attached by William the son of Peter of Peyton and John of Barford concerning the same. Hugh was attached by Ranulf, knight of Peyton, and Robert de Buskes concerning the same. So all [are] in mercy (*amercements*).

Simon was not attached because he was not found. Matthew comes and he says nothing to stay the assize.

William of Littlecross one of the recognitors has not come. So [he is] in mercy (*amercement*).

The jurors say that the said Matthew and the others did not disseise them of any marsh nor of heath because their writ speaks of a free tenement and they never had any free tenement there because they have never enjoyed their separate possession nor is there any free tenement in the marsh and pasture because it is common pasture. So it is adjudged that Philip [is] in mercy and Matilda [is] in mercy for a false claim (*amercements*). But they [the jurors] say that they disseised them of the certain portion of land,[1] so Matthew and the others [are] in mercy for disseisin. Philip and Matilda have recovered their seisin (*amercements*). Surety of Philip: William de *Bromeshaft*.

> [1] That is the particular area of land measuring 37 feet by 47 feet.

479. (*St Etheldreda*) An assize comes to declare if Adam the son of Edulf the father of Thomas was seised in his demesne etc of one acre of land with appurtenances in Rendlesham on the day that he died etc and if etc which land John the son of Grimward holds. He comes and says that he is the villein of Roger Clerenbaud. So then [he is] without day and Thomas [is] in mercy by the surety of Thomas the son of Ivetta of Rendlesham and William Snelling of the same (*amercements*).

480.[1] (*Norfolk, Cattishall*) The sheriff is commanded that he has the body of Robert de Bosco of Stalham at Cattishall on the morrow of the Ascension of the Lord [Friday 25 May] to reply to Simon of Sheering concerning a plea of annual rent which the same Simon demands from him concerning the tenement that he holds from him in Hilborough.

> 1   This plea contains a different place from the chirograph mentioned in **806**. The chirograph shows *Glosbrigge*, a place I cannot find in Norfolk.

481. (*Blything*) William the son of Thomas claims against the prior of Blythburgh sixteen acres of land with appurtenances in Halesworth as his right etc and in respect whereof a certain Edrich his ancestor was seised in demesne[1] [as of fee and right] etc in the time of King Henry II grandfather of King Henry III by taking profits therefrom to the value of half a mark. From the same Edrich descended the right of that land to a certain William as son and heir, and from the same William to a certain Thomas as son and heir, and from the same Thomas to this William who now claims as son and heir, and that such is his right he offers [to prove].

The[2] prior comes and then vouches to warranty Roger the son of Osbert who is present by his attorney and he warrants him. He denies his right[3] and the seisin of the said Edrich and all etc. He puts himself on the grand [assize][4] of the lord king, and he seeks a recognition be made [as to] which of them has the greater right of them in the said land.

(*half a mark*)[5]

(*half a mark*) Afterwards,[6] they are agreed and William the son of Thomas gives half a mark for licence to agree by the surety of Master Walter of Blundeston *spilletause*.[7] [*chirograph* CP 25(1) 213/16/81]

> 1   There is something erased at this point which is illegible.
> 2   There is a gap of 1.4 cm prior to this paragraph. Nothing appears to have been rubbed out.
> 3   That is William son of Thomas.
> 4   The clerk missed out the word *assisam* at this point.
> 5   This marginal note is located within the gap between the previous paragraph and the final paragraph that follows. It does not appear to relate to any part of the plea. The scribe has rubbed out a sentence, none of which is legible. The marginal note may have related to this rubbed out sentence and the scribe has forgotten to rub it out.
> 6   Before this is a space of 2 cm in the middle of which, in the margin, is placed one of the *dimidia marca*.
> 7   I cannot translate this satisfactorily. It might be a description of his profession, perhaps a skinner or pill maker. He might also be a crossbowman or a maker of the bolts for a crossbow, but I think this unlikely given that he is a master. It might also be a nickname.

482.[1] (*Stow*) Hamelin the son of Brian who brought a writ to take homage against the prior of Butley has not prosecuted. So he and his sureties for prosecuting [are] in mercy, namely: Siger Benesoth of Buxhall and William Richold from the same [vill].

> 1   There is a gap of 9.8 cm between this plea and the previous one.

483.[1] (*Bosmere, ten shillings*) Thomas the son of Roger of Naughton and Humphrey the son of Osbert give ten shillings for licence to agree with William Talebot concerning a plea of naifty by the surety of Roger de Holdham. [*chirograph* CP 25(1) 213/17/116][2]

> 1   See **12** for the essoin of Humphrey. These are almost certainly one and the same person.
> 2   There is no mention of Thomas the son of Roger of Naughton in the agreement, but Humphrey is to be considered a free man for certain services, including some ploughings and four hens at Christmas, also for money rent for William Talebot.

Membrane 18d

484. (*Lothingland*) William of Hevingham and Grace his wife claim against Osbert[1] of Hopton twenty acres of land with appurtenances in Browston and against Edmund Woodcock twenty acres of land with appurtenances in the same vill as the right of the same Grace.

Osbert and Edmund come and then vouch to warranty William the son of Bartholomew. They are to have him at Cattishall on the morrow of the Ascension of the Lord [Friday 25 May] etc by aid of the court (*Cattishall*). Osbert appoints Master Walter of Blundesdon etc.

[1] See **248** where it is Herbert, not Osbert, the clerk has written.

485.[1] (*Lothingland*) Hawise who was the wife of Geoffrey of Sandon claims against William Schule half of four acres of land and five acres of marsh with appurtenances in Flixton, and against Henry de Colville half of two acres and one rood of land with appurtenances in the same vill as her dower etc.

William Schule comes and by licence he renders to her the half of all the land and marsh[2] that he holds in the same vill. She is to have her seisin. Henry comes and then vouches to warranty Roger de Colville who is present and by licence renders to her the half of all the land, which he holds. She is to have her seisin.

The same [Hawise] presented herself on the fourth day against Walter the son of Philip concerning a plea that he render to her half of three roods of land with appurtenances in Flixton which she claims in her dower against him. Walter has not come and [was] summoned etc. Judgement: the half is to be taken into the hands of the lord king etc and the day etc and he is to be summoned that he be at Cattishall on the morrow of the Ascension of the Lord [Friday 25 May] (*Cattishall*).

Afterwards, it is attested at Cattishall that the land was taken into the hands of the lord king and he has not come as he was summoned, and he has not claimed that land. So it is adjudged that she is to have her seisin.

[1] See **410** for the appointment of an attorney.
[2] The clerk indicated a 'meadow' at this point but there is no mention of a meadow in the opening paragraph of this plea. It should probably be the marsh mentioned above, which is what I have given.

486. (*St Etheldreda*) William Russel was summoned to reply to William de Auberville concerning a plea wherefore without the licence of William de Auberville he hunted and took hares in the free warren of William [de Auberville] in Benhall, *Keleton* and Farnham. He complains that whereas he has free warren there, so that nobody ought to enter into that warren nor hunt hares or any other beast without his licence, the same William Russel against the peace of the lord king came into his said warren and took his hares. He has suffered damage in respect whereof to the value of forty shillings etc.

William (Russel[i]) comes and firmly denies that he ever hunted in his warren in [Benhall][1] and *Keleton* nor does he claim anything in the said warren, but he readily acknowledges that he hunted in his own land in Farnham as in that [land] in which he and his ancestors were accustomed to run, because his land in Farnham is of the honour of Eye, so that it pertains not at all to his[2] land in Benhall and *Keleton*.

William de Auberville says that he and his ancestors always had from the time of King Henry, grandfather of the present king, free warren in Farnham, both in the land of William Russel and in his own as well as in the lands of Benhall and *Keleton*, so that neither William nor his ancestors ran there nor could they run without the licence of William de Auberville or his ancestors or by the straying of animals.[3] That this might be inquired into by a jury, he offers the lord king five marks (*five marks*). They are received by the surety of Herbert [de] Alicon. So let there be a jury thereon in the said form. It is to come on the morrow of the Ascension of the Lord [Friday 25 May] at Cattishall (*Cattishall*).

The jurors, elected by consent of the parties, come and say on their oath ... [unfinished]

Afterwards, they are agreed and William Russel gives five marks for licence to agree by the surety of John Cordebof and William de Colville (*five marks*). [*chirograph* CP 25(1) 213/16/76][4]

1   The clerk wrote Belton, but that vill is in Lothingland hundred and this plea is all about the free warren in these three vills, not Belton.
2   That is William de Auberville's land.
3   The sense here appears to be that the Russels cannot enter the Auberville warren, even in pursuit of escaped animals.
4   As far as the plea is concerned William de Auberville wins his plea but gives up his claim for damages. Note: in the feet of fines numbered CP 25(1), 213/16 in TNA there is no chirograph number 75. This is obviously a mistake in the numbering at TNA. Instead there is a chirograph numbered 81 in this feet of fines and another numbered 81 in CP 25(1), 213/17.

487.[1] (*St Etheldreda*) An assize comes to declare if Roger of Carlton unjustly etc disseised William of Cotton and Joan his wife of their free tenement in Rendham after the first etc and in respect whereof they complain that he disseised them of fifteen acres.

Roger comes and says nothing to stay the assize.

The jurors say that the said Roger disseised the said William and Joan of their free tenement as the writ says. So it is adjudged that they have recovered their seisin against him. Roger [is] in mercy by the surety of Arnulf of Kettleburgh.

To the clerks.

Damages: half a mark.

1   There is a gap between this plea and the preceding one of 7.1 cm.

488. Robert de Aguillon acknowledges that he owes Hugh de Hoddeng and Thomas de Lascelles thirty marks on the fine made between them, concerning which he will pay to them ten marks at the feast of St John the Baptist [Sunday 24 June] in the year twenty-four, and ten marks at the feast of St Michael [Saturday 29 September] next following, and ten marks on the morrow of Epiphany [Monday 7 January 1241]. If he does not do [this] he grants that he may be distrained by means of [his] lands etc until etc and concerning the cost etc. [**255**]

489. (*Norfolk, half a mark*) The prior of Weybourne gives half a mark for licence to agree with Richard de Grey and Lucia his wife concerning a plea of pasture by the surety of Robert de Twybot.

Membrane 19[1]

1   There is stitching on the membrane at the bottom and in the middle of the membrane. The clerk has avoided the stitching on both sides of the membrane.

490. (*Bosmere*)[1] An assize comes to declare if Robert of *Olden*[2] unjustly etc disseised Nicholas Pie of his free tenement in Darmsden[3] after the first etc and in respect whereof he complains that he disseised him of one and half acres of meadow. Robert comes and says nothing to stay the assize.

The jurors say that the said Robert disseised the said Nicholas Pie of one and a half acres of meadow as the writ says. So it is adjudged that Nicholas is to recover his seisin and Robert [is] in mercy for disseisin (*amercement*). He has other good sureties.

(*to the clerks*) Damages: two shillings.

1   There is a new clerk at this point. He has very small writing.
2   The clerk wrote *Ulenden*. This vill can no longer be found on a modern Ordnance Survey map; however it probably relates to 'Olden' as shown in Domesday Book. It is also shown in Domesday Book as *Uledana*. This is now a lost village in Suffolk but is believed to lie near Gosbeck, which appears to have been mentioned for the first time in 1179. See Ekwall 1960, p.153.
3   Darmsden is now part of Barking parish but there is still a Darmsden Hall and a hamlet of Darmsden, which contains a few farms.

491. (*Bosmere, one mark*) Loretta of Gedding and Wynnesia Visdelu gives one mark for licence to agree with William le Rus concerning a plea of an assize of mort d'ancestor by the surety of William. [*chirograph* CP 25(1) 213/15/29][1]

1   This was for land in Akenham and Whitton in Claydon hundred.

492. (*Bosmere*) An assize comes to declare if Robert the son of Gilbert of *Olden*, Ralph de Ponte, Gilbert de Ory and Alexander Wanger[1] unjustly etc disseised Ralph of Boyland, William le Focchere and Amaberlia his wife of their free tenement in *Olden* after the first etc and in respect whereof they claim that they disseised them of five acres of land and one messuage. Robert comes and acknowledges the disseisin. So he is remanded in custody (*remand in custody*). Ralph and the others have recovered their seisin.

The jurors say without an oath that the damages [are] one mark. The sureties of Robert concerning the amercement [are]: Robert de Bucellyer and Robert de Srubelund.

Damages: one mark.

1   This means he is a carter.

493. (*Bosmere*) An assize comes to declare if Stephen Smith father of Matilda the wife of Peter de Hagenet was seised in his demesne of two and a half acres of land with appurtenances in Creeting on the day that etc and if etc and if etc which land Robert of *Olden* and Rose his mother and Thomas Coteman holds. They come and say that the assize should not be taken on this because the same Peter at another time brought an assize of mort d'ancestor before the last justices itinerant[1] against the same Robert concerning the same tenement, so that the assize was taken between them and that land was passed to the said Robert by the said assize. He then puts himself upon the rolls of the same eyre justices. Peter and Matilda [do] likewise.

Afterwards,[2] the rolls have been examined and it has been found that Stephen the father of Matilda was a villein. So Robert [is] without day and they are to take nothing by this assize.

1   10 November to 14 January 1234/1235 were the dates of the last Suffolk eyre according to Crook 1982a, p.90. Unfortunately no plea rolls survives.
2   From here to the end of this plea looks like a later addition. The colour of the ink is different from the rest of the plea.

494. (*Wangford, half a mark*) Adam of Herringfleet gives half a mark for licence to agree with Robert Weynpin and Gunnild his wife concerning a plea of land by the surety of William of Mettingham. [*chirograph* CP 25(1) 213/16/45][1]

1   This chirograph was made at Cattishall but this plea in the roll is in the Ipswich section. Given the gaps around the plea it is possible the clerk put it into an empty space while at Cattishall.

495. (*Stow*) A jury comes to recognise whether one acre and one rood of land with appurtenances in Buxhall are free alms pertaining to the church of Buxhall, in respect whereof William is the parson or the lay fee of Katherine de Sturmyn. She comes and then vouches to warranty Roger de Sturmyn, who is present and he warrants her, and he then vouches to warranty Nicholas of Buxhall, who is present and he warrants him, and he then vouches to warranty Ranulf the Fleming, who is present and he warrants him, and he then vouches to warranty William the Fleming. He is to come at Cattishall (*on the morrow*).

Afterwards, he comes and warrants him and by licence renders [it] to him [the parson]. He is to have his seisin. He [William the Fleming] will make an exchange to the said Katherine.

496. (*Samford*) An assize comes to declare if William of Freston the father of William the son of William was seised in [his] demesne etc of nineteen acres with appurtenances in Freston on the day etc and if etc and if etc in respect whereof Adam Bulloc holds seventeen acres [and] William Spinc two acres. William has not come and he [was] resummoned. So let the assize be taken against him by default. Adam comes and then vouches to warranty Micah of Freston who is present and he warrants him, and he says that the said William did not die seised of the said land as of fee and then he puts himself on the assize and Micah similarly.

The jurors say that the said William of Freston did not die seised of the said land as of fee. So it is adjudged that Adam Bulloc and William Spinc may hold in peace and William [is] in mercy. It is pardoned because he is poor.

497. (*Hartismere*) Joan of Wetherden claims against William Blundun one acre of land with appurtenances in Wetherden,[1] which she claims to be her right and inheritance and in which the same William does not have entry except by Ralph Pakerel her former husband who demised that [land] to him [and] whom [she could not contradict in his lifetime] etc. William comes and by licence renders [it] to her. She is to have her seisin.

[1] I think the clerk has made a mistake, possibly with the marginalia, as Wetherden is in Stow hundred.

498. (*one mark*) Hamo of Felsham gives one mark for licence to agree with Adam the son of Walter concerning a plea of land by the surety of Herbert de Alencon.

499. (*one mark*) The same Adam gives one mark for licence to agree with the said Hamo concerning a plea of land by the surety of the same Hamo.

500. (*Bosmere*) John the son of Robert and Matilda his wife who brought an assize of mort d'ancestor against Richard of Brantham concerning a tenement in Stonham have not prosecuted. So he and their sureties [are] in mercy, namely: Thomas Garneys and Geoffrey the son of Robert of Ulverston. Surety of John concerning the amercement is John the parker of Ubbeston (*amercement*).

501. (*Bosmere*) Agnes, who was the wife of Hugh de la Grene, who brought a writ of entry against Roger Leu concerning a tenement in Thurleston, has not prosecuted. So she and her sureties [are] in mercy, namely: Stephen Sott of Ipswich and William Marese of the same (*amercement*).

502. (*Bosmere*)[1] Robert Blund claims against Ranulf Haliday one and a half acres of land with appurtenances in Little Blakenham as his right etc. Ranulf comes and by licence renders [it] to him. He is to have his seisin.

[1] There is a line from this plea to the next plea indicating it is also a Bosmere plea.

503. (*Bosmere*) A day is given to Geoffrey the son of Geoffrey and Hugh of Badley, plaintiffs, and William de Ciresy concerning a plea of debt at Cattishall at the arrival of the justices there by prayer of the parties (*Cattishall*).

504. (*Stow*)[1] Ralph[2] Sweyn [is] in mercy because he has not prosecuted his writ for a grand assize against William of Onehouse concerning fifteen acres of land with appurtenances in Finborough and Onehouse. Note: that William comes, so he is to (go[i]) without day.

[1] The clerk had originally written *Blything* but erased it.
[2] The clerk had originally written *Willelmus* but erased it.

505. (*Hoxne*) Basilia, who was the wife of William Red, claims against John de Colville, chaplain, four and a half acres of land with appurtenances in Hacheston[1] as her right, and in which the same John does not have entry except by Philip le Messager[2] to whom William, her former husband, demised those [lands and] whom [she could not contradict in his lifetime] etc.

John comes and then vouches to warranty the said Philip, who is present, and he warrants him and acknowledges that the said land is the inheritance and right of the said Basilia and by licence he renders [it] to her. So she is to have her seisin and he [Philip le Messager] will make an exchange to the said John to the value [of his holding] etc.

[1] This vill is in Loes hundred. It looks as though the clerk has made a mistake here in the margin-alia.
[2] According to Reaney 1997, p.307 he is a messenger.

506. (*Hoxne*) An assize comes to declare if Alan of Semer, Thomas and John, his sons, unjustly etc disseised William de Tykebroc of his free tenement in Weybread after the first etc and in respect whereof he complains that they disseised him of a certain part of land where they are accustomed to hold commonly, so that no one enjoyed his separate possession and [each] one [of them] appropriates[1] all the land.

Alan and the others come and say nothing to stay the assize.

The jurors say that they disseised him as the writ says. So it is adjudged that he is to recover his seisin against them and Alan and the others [are] in mercy (*amercements*). They are remanded in custody.

[1] That is, each person holds all the land.

507.[1] (*Hoxne*) An assize comes to declare if Adam of Westwood and Seman his son unjustly etc disseised Margery the daughter of Adam of her free tenement in Worlingworth after the first crossing etc and in respect whereof Margery claims that they disseised her of one and a half acres with appurtenances in the same vill.

Adam and Seman have not come and they were attached by Henry Ballard and Osbert the miller. So [they are] in mercy, and the assize is to be taken against them by default.

The jurors say that the said Adam and Seman unjustly etc disseised the said Margery of the said one and a half acres. So it is adjudged that she has recovered her seisin and Adam and Seman [are] in mercy.

Damages: eighteen pence.

[1] The margin is damaged here. I would have expected some reference to an amercement.

508.[1] (*two marks*) Roger de Cressy gives two marks for licence to agree with Robert of Boyton concerning a plea of land. [*chirograph* CP 25(1) 213/15/23][2]

[1] A different clerk writes this plea. It may have been added later.
[2] On the reverse of the chirograph it indicates the following: *Episcopi Norwici apponit clamium suum et Robertus filius Ufford apponit clamium suum.* So it looks as though these two may also have had a claim on Roger de Cressy.

Membrane 19d

509. (*Hoxne*) Philip the son of Richard (of Braiseworth[i]) who brought an assize of mort d'ancestor has not prosecuted against John de *Brunstanshagh* and others named in the writ. So he and his sureties for prosecuting [are] in mercy namely: Richard the son of Hubert of Yaxley and Joss the son of Richard of the same [vill] (*amercements*).

510. (*Hartismere*) Hugh of Cotton who brought an assize of novel disseisin against William of Cotton and others named in the writ has not prosecuted. So he and his sureties for prosecuting [are] in mercy, namely: John of Otley and William de *Wenekeston*[1] (*amercements*).

[1] This might be Wenhaston in Blything hundred.

511. (*Blything*) William the son of Conie who brought an assize of novel disseisin against John le Coe has not prosecuted. So [he is] in mercy. He pledged his faith.

512. (*Hoxne, half a mark*) Gilbert Maunce[1] gives half a mark for licence to agree with Hubert the carpenter concerning a plea of mort d'ancestor (concerning a tenement in [Monk] Soham[i]) by the surety of the same of Hubert.

[1] This is probably 'Manche', the name for a sleevemaker.

513. (*Stow*) Thomas the son of Walter Folet who brought an assize of mort d'ancestor against Edmund de Beauchamp and others named in the writ concerning a tenement in Wetherden has not prosecuted. So [he is] in mercy. He pledged his faith.

514. (*Hoxne*) Edmund the son of William of Brundish gives half a mark[1] for licence to agree with William of Peasenhall and Roger de *Rockam*[2] concerning a plea of land by the surety of the same Roger. The agreement is such that William of Peasenhall acknowledges that the three acres of land, which he claimed against him, is the right of Edmund. For this etc the same Edmund grants that the same William is to hold the said three acres by service of four pence per annum. Meanwhile Roger acknowledges similarly the four acres of land, which he claimed against him to be the right of Edmund. For this etc the same Edmund grants that the same Roger may hold the said four acres by service of twelve pence per annum for all service.

[1] No mention is made of the amount in the margin.
[2] This might be Rougham in Thedwestry hundred, although it is usually written as *Rucham*.

515. (*Blything*) Cecilia de Uvigton[1] who brought an assize of mort d'ancestor against Thomas de *Pirho* concerning a tenement in Yoxford has not prosecuted. So she and her sureties for prosecuting [are] in mercy, namely: Ralph Grim of Soham and Roger of Markshall (*amercements*).

[1] This is probably Ovington in Wayland hundred in Norfolk.

516. (*Blything*) John the son of Robert and Matilda his wife claim against Richard of Brantham ten marks, which he owes to them and unjustly withholds. Afterwards,

John and Matilda come and seeks licence to withdraw from their writ and they have [it].

517.[1] (*Blything*) An assize comes to declare if Richard Burghard, the father of Margery [and] the wife of William de Bosco, and Sarah the sister of that Margery was seised in his demesne etc of twenty-four acres of land with appurtenances in Flixton[2] on the day he set out on pilgrimage to the [Holy] Land etc and if the said etc which land Robert Bucett holds. He comes and says nothing to stay the assize.

The jurors[3] say the said Richard was not seised of the said land on the day he set out on the journey as of fee because the said land is the marriage portion of a certain Juliana the mother of [Margery and Sarah] who still lives and who now holds eighteen of the acres. So it is adjudged that they are to take nothing by this assize.

William de Bosco [is] in mercy (*amercement*). He is poor.

1   There is a gap of 3 cm between this plea and the previous one, in the middle of which the clerk has entered a paragraph mark but no plea details.
2   Flixton is in Wangford hundred not Blything although in *Feudal Aids 1284–1431* v, p.38, Blything hundred is shown as *Blithinge et Waynford* hundred. I discount it being the Flixton in Lothingland hundred.
3   There is either a change of clerk here or there is a change of ink, either of which would suggest a later insertion. I suspect the former, as there are a few differences in the formation of the letters. The style continues in some of the later pleas on this membrane.

518. (*Hartismere*) Katherine le Walesch and Alice her sister claim against John of London and Katherine his wife three acres of land with appurtenances in Stanton, and [against] Adam [and] his wife two acres of land with appurtenances in the same vill. John and his wife, and John of Stanton and his wife in whose place [an attorney comes] etc come.

Katherine and Alice remise all for four shillings.

519. (*Wangford*) An assize[1] comes to declare if Alexander de Scenges etc raised a certain dyke in South Elmham to the nuisance of the free tenement of John de Northam in the same vill after the first crossing etc.

Alexander comes and he says that the assize should not be taken on this because the same John is the villein of John of Middleton. The same John acknowledges this. So he and his sureties for prosecuting [are] in mercy,[2] namely: Henry the son of Geoffrey de Enepol and Warren the son of William Barnard of Spexhall.

1   There is no start of paragraph mark here, but it is a new plea.
2   The clerk has not indicated this amercement in the margin.

520. Robert the son of Edward and Matilda the wife of Hamo of Copdock and Christine the wife of Benedict and William the son of Hugh appoint Benedict of Copdock as their attorney against Robert the son of Ivo and his parceners concerning a plea of land.

521. Master Benedict the parson of Abberton appoints William de Medham against Thomas Russel concerning a plea of land, in respect whereof [is] a grand assize.

522. (*Bosmere*) Cecilia who was the wife of Adam de Boloyne[1] was summoned to reply to Ralph of Mickfield concerning a plea that she render to the same Ralph the wardship of the land and the heir of Adam de Boloyne which belongs to him etc. They have agreed by licence. The agreement is such that the same Ralph granted to the same Cecilia the marriage of Hamo, the son and heir of the said Adam, for forty shillings. Besides, he granted to the same Cecilia the third part of all the land, which the same Adam has held from him, in dower. Note: that the same Hamo was aged one year, in the twenty-fourth year of the reign of King Henry [III].[2]

¹   This is probably Boulogne in France.
²   That is 28 October 1239 to 27 October 1240.

523. Agnes the wife of Ralph Crabbe appoints Roger[1] her husband as her attorney against Robert de Wykes and Amice his wife concerning a plea of dower.

¹   Could this be because Roger is her current husband, and *Radulfus* her previous husband, now dead, was the one that dowered her; or did the clerk make a mistake? I suggest the latter is the case.

524. Lettice the wife of John the son of Robert appoints her husband John as her attorney against Robert of Peasenhall and others named in the writ concerning a plea of the assessment of dower etc.

525.[1] (*Ipswich*) Thomas le Latimer and Robert Malet acknowledge that they owe to William of York,[2] the provost of Beverley, one hundred shillings which he lent to them at Ipswich, and which they will pay to him at Bury St Edmunds on the octave of the Ascension of the Lord [Thursday 31 May]. If they did not do [this] they grant that the sheriff may levy [the amount] from their lands etc. Concerning the cost etc.

¹   There is a gap of 2.8 cm between this plea and the previous plea. This is probably because of a fault in the membrane.
²   William of York was the senior justice on the Suffolk eyre. This shows that he used the rolls as a record of his transaction and as a means for its payment.

526. (*Hoxne*) Geoffrey de Say and Alina his wife claim against Thomas the son of Thomas of Moulton[1] and Matilda his wife one and a half carucates of land[2] and forty shillingsworth of rent with appurtenances in Denham and the advowson of the church of Denham as the dower of Alina[3], and in respect whereof Hubert de Vallibus her former husband dowered her etc [on the day on which][4] etc by the assent and wish of Robert de Vallibus, the father of Hubert. She produces a charter of Robert, which proves that the same Robert gave and granted all his land of Surlingham[5] to the said Hubert with the advowson of the church and the knight's fees and the free tenants and all the other appurtenances [belonging] to the said land, within the said land and beyond without any reservation to dower the said Alina. As a result the said Hubert dowered her of the appurtenances [belonging] to the said manor of Surlingham, so that she was immediately in seisin [of the property in Denham] as pertaining to the manor of Surlingham and then they put themselves on the jury.

Thomas and Matilda by Matilda's attorney come and they readily concede the charter and whatsoever is contained in the charter, and they say that the said Alina has her full dower according to the contents and purport of that charter, because they firmly say that the manor of Denham is not of the appurtenances of the manor of Surlingham nor ever was, nor [did] the said Hubert and Alina have seisin by a gift of Robert [de Vallibus] of the said manor as pertaining to the manor of Surlingham when they had seisin of the manor of Surlingham. They put themselves on the country, and she similarly. So let there be a jury thereon [to see] whether or not the said manor of Denham pertains to the manor of Surlingham, so that the manor of Denham always used to answer to the manor of Surlingham as a portion of the manor of Surlingham and pertaining to it, [and] as a result when Robert de Vallibus gave the manor of Surlingham to the said Hubert with all its appurtenances, the same Hubert had seisin of the manor of Denham as pertaining to the manor of Surlingham. Because both [parties put themselves on the inquest] etc.

The jurors, chosen by consent of the parties, come and say that a certain Edward de Vallibus the ancestor of Matilda was enfeoffed of the manor of Denham for a long time before he [Hubert] was enfeoffed of the manor of Surlingham. (*d*)[6] They say that the manor of Denham does not pertain to the manor of Surlingham nor ever did, because it is a chief manor. So it is adjudged that Thomas and Matilda may hold in peace and Geoffrey and Alina [are] in mercy (*amercement*).

[1]   See **13** for the essoin of Thomas of Moulton.
[2]   That is 180 acres of land.
[3]   The clerk wrote *Alicie*. This should be Alina, as surely this is the dower of Alina, Geoffrey's wife.
[4]   The clerk wrote *dis qua* but this is written at the end of a line and is rather indistinct. I would have expected *die quo* and that is what I have used in this translation.
[5]   A Margery de Say is shown as the principal holder of the vill of Denham in the Risbridge hundred. See *Feudal Aids 1284–1431* v, p.45. The de Say family is shown as still in evidence in the Risbridge 'Denham' in 1346.
[6]   This letter is used by the clerk to indicate a carry over from the previous line; it is the first letter of the word *dicunt* on that line. The remainder of the word is on the next line.

Membrane 20

527. (*Bosmere*) Clianus, the son of Olive de *Bruniford*, whom Thomas de Greley claimed as his naif and fugitive with all his household, comes and acknowledges that he is his villein and he is handed over to him with all his household. Thomas immediately gave the same Clianus with all his household to Peter de *Bruniford*, who is present and he is committed to him with all his household.

528. (*Norfolk*) Bartholomew of Mellis, Hugh Burt, Gilbert of Walsham[1] and Ranulf de Becling four knights, selected etc to choose twelve etc to make a recognition of the grand assize between Roger the son of Richard, plaintiff, and John Folcard, tenant, concerning three acres of land with appurtenances in Brampton[2] in respect whereof the same John, who is the tenant, placed himself on the grand assize of the lord king and seeks a recognition be made [as to][3] which of them has the greater in that land, have come and chosen these, namely: Thomas le Latimer, Robert de Grimilies, William of Catton, Hubert of Braiseworth, Alan de Money, John the son of Robert, Jordan of Shelton, Osbert of Bawdsey, Robert le Envoyse, William the son of Rainer, John de Crammaville, William de Alneto, Robert de Wykes, Ranulf[4] de Blything and Baldwin of Mellis.

Afterwards, they have agreed by licence. The agreement is such that the same John acknowledges all the said land with appurtenances to be the right of Roger. For this etc the same Roger grants to him one and a half acres of the same land holding from him for three halfpence per year for all service etc.

[1]   This is probably North Walsham in Tunstead hundred in Norfolk as it is the nearest to a Brampton in South Erpingham hundred and the knights in a grand assize are supposed to be reasonably local to the land in dispute. However, given that 'Baldwin of Mellis' presumably comes from Mellis in Hartismere hundred it is conceivable that Gilbert comes from the Walsham in Blackbourn hundred.
[2]   This is either Brampton in South Erpingham hundred or Bramerton in Henstead hundred in Norfolk. Also, given the place shown in the next plea, it is possible that this plea refers to Brampton in Blything hundred and that this plea started in the Norfolk eyre, which is maybe what the clerk is drawing reference to in the marginalia.
[3]   The clerk wrote *utrum* but I believe it should be *uter*.

4   The clerk wrote *Rany* but this is probably Ranulf. This knight appears in a number of pleas. See **151**.

529.[1] (*Blything*) The same four knights,[2] selected to choose etc to make a recognition of the grand assize between Roger the son of Richard, plaintiff, and Richard the son of Osbert, tenant, concerning four acres of land with appurtenances in Brampton, and in respect whereof the same Richard, who is the tenant, placed himself on the grand assize of the lord king and seeks a recognition be made whether he or the said Roger has the greater right in that land, have come and chosen all the above named [as jurors].

(*half a mark*) Afterwards, they have agreed and Roger the son of Richard gives half a mark for licence to agree by the surety of Richard the son of Osbert. The agreement is such that the same Roger acknowledges the said land to be the right of Richard. For this etc the same Richard grants to him half an acre of the same land holding from him by the service of one halfpenny per year for all service.

1   The clerk has left a gap of 7.2 cm between this plea and the previous one, presumably in case he had to enter the names of the jurors and the four knights.

2   There are lines on the membrane between the previous plea and this one and from this plea to the next one, **530**, and from **530** to **532**. I believe it indicates that the same four knights chose the jury and the same jurors decided the pleas. The jurors are not named in this plea or in **530** or **532**, but agreements are made in the pleas.

530. (*Hoxne*) The same four knights, selected to choose twelve etc to make a recognition of the grand assize between Thomas Russel, plaintiff, and Richard Picot, tenant, concerning six acres of land with appurtenances in Metfield, and in respect whereof the same Richard, who is the tenant, puts himself on the grand assize of the lord king and seeks a recognition be made [as to] which[1] of them has the greater right in that land, have come and chosen all the above named [as jurors].

(*one mark*) Afterwards, they are agreed and Thomas gives one mark for licence to agree by the surety of Richard Picot and Adam of Mendham. (*half a mark*) Richard gives half a mark for the same by the surety of Hugh Burt. [*chirograph* CP 25(1) 213/17/94][2]

1   The clerk wrote *utrum*, which usually translates as 'whether' but does not translate well here. I think the clerk should have written *uter*.

2   The chirograph gives a different amount of land in dispute, that is 13 acres in Mendham and 12 acres in Metfield. The roll gives no other pleas between these two to make up the shortfall. The fine is in the list of agreements at the end of the roll in **1664**.

531. (*half a mark*) Robert the son of Adam of Worlingworth gives half a mark for licence to agree with Basilia who was the wife of William Red, by the surety of William de Childerhus. The agreement is such that the said Robert renders to the same Basilia eight acres which she claimed against him for two marks, which the same Basilia gives to him.

532. (*Hoxne*) The same four knights, selected to choose the twelve etc to make a recognition of the grand assize between Robert de Latimer, plaintiff, and Richard of Manston, tenant, concerning twenty-one acres of land with appurtenances in Stradbroke, and in respect whereof the same Richard who is the tenant puts himself on the grand assize of the lord king and seeks a recognition be made [as to] which of them has the greater right in that land, have come and chosen all the above named [as jurors].

Membrane 20d

533.[1] (*Hoxne, two marks*) Hugh Burt, Gilbert of Walsham, Bartholomew of Mellis and Ranulf of Blickling[2] four knights, selected etc to choose the twelve etc to make a recognition of the grand assize between Roger of Shotford, plaintiff, and Margery de Bleville, tenant, concerning forty acres of land and one messuage with appurtenances in Weybread, whereof Margery de Bleville, who is the tenant, placed herself on the grand assize of the lord king and she seeks a recognition be made whether she or the said Roger has the greater right in the said land and messuage, have come and chosen these, namely: Richard of Ixworth, Osbert of Bawdsey, Hubert of Braiseworth, Philip of Winston, Gilbert de St Clare, William of Cotton, William de Alneto, Richard of Narford, William of Stratford, John of Gedding, Roger Sturmey, Richard the butler, Matthew of Peyton, Gilbert de Colville, John son of Robert and Walter of Cove.

Afterwards, they are agreed and Margery de Blevill' gives two marks for licence to agree by the surety of William de Tykebrom[3] and Robert le Blund of Stonham. Roger of Huntingfield and Joan his wife lay their claim.[4]

1   See the essoin in **7** for the essoin of Margery de Bluville, or Bleville as shown here, with the same plaintiff.
2   See **528** where a clerk has the same four knights and the name is shown as *Ranulf de Becling*. This is probably the same person.
3   There is a *Thicchebrom* shown in Domesday Book in Wangford hundred: see *Domesday Book Suffolk*, Part One, section 6, no. 295. However I suspect that this is the same person as William de Tykebroc in **506**.
4   This separate claim against Margery can be a feature of the plea but it is usually shown on the back of the chirograph.

534.[1] (*St Etheldreda,*) An assize comes to declare if Nicholas Haliday, the brother of Ranulf Haliday, was seised in his demesne etc concerning three acres of land with appurtenances in Ashfield (and [Earl] Soham[i]) on the day that etc and if etc and if etc which land Richard de Ribos holds. He comes and says nothing to stay the assize.

The jurors say that the said Nicholas did not die seised. So it is adjudged that he is to take nothing by this assize and Richard [is] without day. Ranulfus [is] in mercy for a false claim by the surety of Jordan of Shelton and Simon Fernlard (*amercement*). (*forty shillings*) Afterwards, Ranulf comes and gives forty shillings to have a jury of twenty-four to attaint the twelve by the surety of William the son of Robert of Helmingham, Geoffrey of Bocking and Adam Bullok and Thomas de Hildere.

1   There is a gap of 5.8 cm between this plea and the previous one. In **537** Ranulf withdraws from the attaint but the clerk in **1019** provides the jury of twenty-four and then indicates that Ranulf still withdrew from the plea. The clerk has also indicated that **534** and **537** are linked by drawing a line between them in the margin.

535. (*St Etheldreda, half a mark*) An assize comes to declare if Richard the goldsmith unjustly etc disseised Geoffrey of Brockdish of his free tenement in Kettleburgh after the first crossing etc and in respect whereof he complains that he disseised him of two acres of land.

Richard comes and says nothing to stay the assize.

The jurors say that the said Richard has not disseised the said Geoffrey of his free tenement as the writ says. So it is adjudged that he [Geoffrey] is to take nothing by this assize and he is in mercy for a false claim. He [Geoffrey] makes a fine for half a mark by the surety of Hugh Burt.

536.[1] (*Norfolk*) Walter de Evermue, who appointed William Alicton[2] or Adam de Blakeville[3] [as his attorneys] against William of Reedham concerning a plea of land in respect whereof a trial by battle [follows], came before the justices and removed the said [attorneys] and wishes to proceed in [his] own person.

1   There is a paragraph mark between this plea and the previous one. This was adjourned to Chelmsford in **81** [essoin] and to Cattishall in **158**.
2   This is shown as Ditton in **158**.
3   This is shown as Blukevill in **158**.

537.[1] (*Ely*) Ranulf Haliday who summoned a jury of twenty-four to attaint the twelve came and withdrew [from the plea]. (*One hundred shillings*) He [made] a fine for himself and his sureties for one hundred shillings, by the surety of William of Holbrook and Geoffrey of Barham, the serjeant of the prior of Ely, Roger of Hoo[2] and Nicholas of Easton.

1   See **534** for the mort d'ancestor case and **1019** for the attaint itself. **534** and **537** are shown to be connected by a line joining the two pleas in the margin. There is also no paragraph mark at the start of this plea.
2   Probably the one in Loes hundred, but there is also a Hoo in Wilford hundred both of which had the prior of Ely as their lord.

538. (*St Etheldreda*) An assize comes to declare if Roger the father of John was seised etc of eight acres of land with appurtenances in Kirkton[1] on the day that etc and if he died after etc and if the same John etc and in respect whereof (Alexander[i]) de Canerio holds six acres, Richard the chaplain of Kirkton one and a half acres, and William Boneyt one rood and Agnes[2] de Bruera and William, her son, one rood. They come and say nothing to stay the assize.

The jurors say that the said Roger did not die seised of the said land. So it is adjudged that he [John] is to take nothing by this assize and he is in mercy for a false claim (*amercement*). [**434**]

1   In Samford hundred, which was not in the liberty of Ely.
2   The clerk wrote *Angnes* but in **434** she is shown as Agnes.

539. (*St Etheldreda*) Alice who (was[i]) the wife of William of Otley claims against William Fairfax two acres of land with appurtenances in Stratford as her right and marriage portion, and in which the same William does not have entry except by the said William of Otley, the former husband of Alice, who demised that [land] to him whom in life [she could not contradict].

William comes and then vouches to warranty Walter the son of William who is present. He says that the said land was not the marriage portion of Alice. On the contrary it was an acquisition of William his father and he was enfeoffed thereof. But, because he did not show [evidence] concerning the feoffment, and Alice brought the best suit that it was her marriage portion, so it is adjudged that she has recovered her seisin against him. He [is] in mercy, by the surety of William of Holbrook (and Luke the parson of *Micceleye*[i, ii])[1] (*amercement*). Walter will make an exchange to the said William to the value etc.

1   I cannot locate this place in Suffolk. It might be Mickelgate in Colneis hundred, now a lost village according to Arnott 1946, p.39.

540. (*St Etheldreda*) John Musard[1] of Tuddenham who brought a writ of an assize of mort d'ancestor against Roger the chaplain of Tuddenham concerning a tenement in Tuddenham has not prosecuted. So he and his surety[2] for prosecuting [are] in mercy, namely Osbert the son of John of Sproughton (*amercements*).

[1] The name was divided into two words *mu* and *Sard*; I believe they belong together to give the name Mussard, or somebody absent-minded according to Reaney 1997, p.318. Why the clerk divided the name it is not possible to say. There is no obvious defect in the roll at this point.

[2] The clerk wrote the plural *plegii* but only one surety is named.

541. (*St Etheldreda*) An assize comes to declare if Hugh of Naughton and Robert Camelot unjustly etc disseised Roger of Littlecross of his free tenement (in[r]) *Hallesne*[1] after the first etc and in respect whereof he complains that they disseised him of a certain piece[2] of land.

Hugh and Robert come and say nothing to stay the assize.

The jurors say that they disseised him as the writ says. So it is adjudged that he has recovered his seisin against them and they [are] in mercy by the surety of Richard of Woodbridge and Henry of Naughton (*amercement*).

Damages: eight shillings.

[1] I cannot find this place in Suffolk, Norfolk or Cambridgeshire where the liberty of Ely had its principal lands. It might be Hollesley in Wilford hundred, which was in the liberty of Ely.

[2] The clerk had originally written *parte* but had then erased it.

542. (*St Etheldreda*) An assize comes to declare if Richard the goldsmith unjustly etc disseised Joan of Burston of her free tenement in Kettleburgh after the first etc and in respect whereof the same Joan complains that the same Richard disseised her of one acre of land with appurtenances in the same vill.

Richard comes and says nothing to stay the assize.

The jurors say that the said Richard has not disseised her as the writ says. So it is adjudged that she is to take nothing by this assize and is in mercy for a false claim. It is pardoned for poverty.

543. (*Bosmere, half*[1] *a mark*) The dean of Claydon gives half a mark for licence to agree with Adam the son of Matilda concerning a plea of land by the surety of Roger de *Brunton* etc. [*chirograph* CP 25(1) 213/16/72]

[1] A clerk wrote '½' here. This sign looks more modern and may have been inserted over the usual *di* by somebody who updated it from the text alongside.

544. (*St Etheldreda*) An assize comes to declare if Roger the son of Adam brother of Richard was seised in his demesne etc of one messuage and four acres of land with appurtenances in *Redisham*[1] and of one acre of land with appurtenances in Ash on the day that he died, and if etc which land and messuage William Herthenbaud holds. He comes and says nothing to stay the assize.

Afterwards, they are agreed and William Herthenbaud gives half a mark for licence to agree by the surety of Richard the son of Adam. [*chirograph* CP 25(1) 213/16/51]

[1] This is classed as a lost village in Beresford 1983, p.387. However, there is a Redisham in Wangford hundred according to Domesday Book and there is one on the modern Ordnance Survey map but possibly not in the same place. There are two places, Great and Little Redisham, in the *Book of Fees*, p.40 in Wangford hundred. There does not appear to be a Redisham in the liberty of Ely and I can find no reference to the liberty holding the one in Wangford.

545. (*Ely*) An assize comes to declare if Roger the son of William and Ranulf Alyday unjustly etc disseised Robert the son of William of his free tenement in Charsfield after the first etc and in respect whereof the same Robert complains that Roger and Ranulf disseised him of three acres of land with appurtenances in the same vill.

Roger and Ranulf come and say nothing to stay the assize.

The jurors say that the said Roger and Ranulf did not disseise him as the writ says. So it is adjudged that he is to take nothing by this assize and he is in mercy for a false claim. It is pardoned because [he is] poor.

546. (*Ely*) Alexander the parson of Winston who brought a writ to ascertain whether etc against Nicholas the son of (---- ----[il]) [has not prosecuted. So] he and his sureties for prosecuting [are] in mercy, namely Geoffrey Bernard of Winston and William Bughe of the same (*amercement*).

Membrane 21

547. (*Ely*) An assize comes to declare if Herbert [de] Alicon, Gervase of Bradfield, Adam his brother, Acellus the priest and Roger de Valonyes unjustly etc disseised Tristram of Rendham of his free tenement in Rendham after the first crossing etc and in respect whereof the same Tristram complains that they disseised him of one and a half acres of land and four penceworth of rent with appurtenances in the same vill.

Herbert (and the others[i]) come and say nothing to stay the assize. Robert de Grimilies one of the recognitors has not come, so [he is] in mercy (*amercement*).

The jurors say that the said Herbert and the others did not disseise the said Tristram of any free tenement. So it is adjudged that Herbert and the others [are] without day. Tristram [is] in mercy by the surety of Stephen de Colville and Walter his brother (*amercement*).

548. (*Ely*) A jury comes to declare whether two acres and one messuage are free alms pertaining to the church of Levington in respect whereof Jordan is the parson, or the lay fee of William Trenchmer. He comes and he declares himself to be the villein of the earl Roger le Bigod. So [he is] without day. Jordan [is] in mercy. He is poor.

549. (*Blything*) Roger the son of Gilbert claims against Henry Prat and Avelina his wife one and a half acres of land with appurtenances in Redisham,[1] and against William of Redisham half an acre of land with appurtenances in the same vill by a writ of right, and against Richard the son of Osbert by a writ of mort d'ancestor two acres of land with appurtenances in the same vill, and against the same Henry one and a half acres of land with appurtenances in *Upredesham*, and against the said William half an acre of land with appurtenances in the same vill by [the writ] *precipe* as his right etc.

They all come and by a licence they render [the lands] to him. He is to have his seisin.

The same Roger presented himself on the fourth day against Richard Schec concerning a plea that he render to him one acre of land with appurtenances in Redisham which Alan the tailor held from Gilbert of Redisham the father of the said Roger whose heir he is, and which ought to revert to him as his escheat because the said Alan died without an heir. Richard has not come and [was] summoned etc. Judgement: the land is to be taken into the king's hands, and he is to be summoned to be at Chelmsford on the octave of the Holy Trinity [Sunday 17 June] (*Chelmsford*).

1   Redisham is in Wangford hundred not Blything hundred.

550. (*Ely, amercement*) An assize comes to declare if Gervase of Bradfield, Adam his brother, Roger of Rendham and Alice who was the wife of Hugh Smith unjustly etc disseised Walter de Colville of his free tenement in Rendham after the first etc and in respect whereof he complains that they disseised him of one rood of land with appurtenances in the same vill.

Gervase and the others come and say nothing to stay the assize. Afterwards, the same Walter came and withdrew [from the plea]. So he and his sureties for prosecuting [are] in mercy namely: Geoffrey the son of Hamon of Titsey and Thurstan of Rendham (*amercements*). The surety of Walter concerning the amercement [is] Gilbert de Colville, knight (*amercement*).

551.[1] (*Blything, amercement, half a mark*) John the son of Robert was summoned to reply to John the parker concerning a plea that he allow Thomas Garneys, Elias the son of William and Ediwa his wife, Walter the son of John, Robert de Bukestoc, William Malse, Robert Hare and Matilda his wife, Austin the son of Henry and Agatha his sister, William Sirich, Henry the clerk and Muriel his wife, Robert Alwin, Roger Galewer, Robert Bloc, Simon Beadle, Richard Aveline, Robert le Cove, William Prat, William Richeward, Gunnild Ryen, William the merchant, Hubert Gosezun, Richard le Waleys, Walter Edger, Roger Ailith, William Edward, William the son of Geoffrey and Basilia his mother, Joscelin the son of Peter and Roger the son of John, Letitia Goseron, Saxlena the widow, Alice Triton, Geoffrey the carpenter, Jordan le Siker, John Saxfield, Philippa his wife, Herbert le Sutur,[2] John the son of Roger, Edelma Hathebrend, Richard le Neaivit[3], William the Templer, Richard le Swayn, Richard Barker,[4] William Cook and Isabella his mother, William Burdun, Thomas Edger and Richard Dodd, his [John the son of Robert's] men from Ubbeston to do a suit to him at his mill of Ubbeston, which they ought to make to him. He says in respect whereof that a certain Agatha, namely his mother, who still lives was in possession of the suit of the aforesaid [men of Ubbeston] concerning the said mill. Because John was enfeoffed and never was in seisin concerning the said suit, and the said Agatha lives concerning whose seisin he speaks, it is adjudged that John can claim nothing in the said suit as long as the same Agatha survives. John the son of Robert [is] without day and John Parker [is] in mercy for a false claim.

He made a fine for half a mark by the surety of Herbert [de] Alicon.

1   There is a gap between this plea and the previous one of 3.1 cm.
2   This is probably the name Suter, a shoemaker, according to Reaney 1997, p.418.
3   He might be a Richard Knevit or Nevitt according to Reaney 1997, p.268.
4   Possibly he is a tanner.

552. (*Ely*) Richard the son of Walter of Carlton and John and Thomas his brothers claim against Reynold the son of Walter of Carlton three parts of ten acres of land with appurtenances in Rendham as their reasonable portion, which befalls them from the inheritance, which was of [Walter] of Carlton, the father of the said Reynold, Richard and Thomas of Rendlesham whose heirs they are and who recently died etc and in respect whereof they say that a certain Alueric, their ancestor, held twenty acres. There issued from the same Alueric a certain Walter and a certain Godwin between whom that land was divided, and there issued from Walter a certain Robert, and from the same Robert a certain Walter the father of those who now claim, and from Godwin a certain Roger, and from Roger, Robert, and from Robert a certain Walter who lives and he holds ten acres as his reasonable portion. And that the land is divisible and was so divided, they produce suit etc.

Reynold comes and denies their right and everything and he says that that land is not divisible nor ever was divided. On the contrary he holds that land by knight's service. And that it is so he puts himself on [the verdict of] the country, and they [do] likewise. So let there be a jury thereon.

The jury says that ... [unfinished]

(*half a mark*) Afterwards, they have agreed and Reynold of Carlton gives half a mark for licence to agree by the surety of Richard Erchenbaud. The agreement is such that the same Reynold gives to the said Richard and his brothers seven acres of land by means of twenty-four feet measure of land[1] and half an acre of moor, and two shillingsworth of rent from the service of Roger Wytolf whom they say is a villein, with the villein himself and all his household.

> [1] This probably means that the 7 acres of land was divided up in 24-foot strips of land between the brothers.

553. (*Ely*) Geoffrey of Titsey who brought an assize of novel disseisin against Gervase of Bradfield and others in the writ concerning a tenement in Rendham has not prosecuted. (*ten shillings*) He has made a fine for himself and his sureties for ten shillings by the surety of Ernulf of Kettleburgh.

554. (*Ely*) An assize comes to declare if Ralph Buck father of Juliana was seised in his demesne of four acres of land with appurtenances in Snape on the day etc and if he died after the last etc and if etc which land Hugh the son of Eudo holds. He comes and then vouches to warranty Walter de Dufford[1] who is present and he warrants him and he says nothing to stay the assize.

The jurors say that the said Ralph died seised of the said land as of fee etc.

Afterwards, they have agreed by licence. The agreement is such that the said Walter grants to the same Hugh all the said land in marriage with Juliana to [be held by] them and their heirs begotten by Juliana for the service of sixteen pence [per year], where before it was customary to render for the same land twenty-six pence per year, on condition that if the same Hugh at another time contracted to marry or gave his faith, so that by an ecclesiastical judgement they are divorced, all the said land will revert to the same Juliana and her heirs without any claim of anyone for the said service (*marriage portion*).

> [1] Probably Ufford in Wilford hundred.

555. (*Ely*) An assize comes to declare if Rainer the son of Toke[1] father of Robert of Butley was seised in his demesne etc on the day that [etc] and if etc and if etc which land Wymarca, who was the wife of Roger Picot, holds. She comes and says that the assize should not be taken[2] on this because Rainer died five years and more before the term, and Robert cannot deny this. So it is adjudged that he is to take nothing by this assize and he is in mercy for a false claim. It is pardoned because [he is] poor. Wymarca ...[3] [unfinished]

> [1] This is a Viking name.
> [2] The membrane is damaged here by what appears to be a tear, which has been badly put together so that some of the text is illegible, but ultraviolet light provides the answer.
> [3] The text below the written membrane number is unreadable even with ultraviolet light.

556.[1] [A jury][2] comes to declare whether ten acres of land and one rood of meadow with appurtenances in Tuddenham[3] are the free alms pertaining to the church of Tuddenham whereof Elias is the parson or the lay fee of Robert Jordan and of others. Harvey Hok in respect whereof holds half an acre, Robert Jordan and his wife Matilda two and a half acres and one rood of land, Roger Godman and Alice his wife one (----[il]), John the son of Jocelyn half an acre, Walter Golb half an acre, John le Sture[4] half an acre, Sarah de Smalemedewe[5] and (----[il]) rood, Constantine Pader one and a half acres, Robert de Laus three roods, Elias le Stalun one acre (----[il]) All come, except Harvey Hok, who crossed the sea before the writ came. Robert

Jordan and Matilda his wife and Constantine Pader come and vouch to warranty Richard the son of Osbert concerning one acre and concerning the remainder the jury [will decide]. Richard is present and he warrants them and they put themselves on the jury. John the son of Jocelyn and Walter Golb vouch to warranty Roger Godman and Alice his wife, who are present and they warrant them and they say that the said church never [held the land in] demesne except only by service, and then they put themselves upon the jury. Elias [le Stalun] comes and vouches to warranty Robert de (----il) who is present and he warrants him and similarly puts himself on the jury. All of the others come and say that the said church never [was seised of] the said lands in demesne except only by service, and then they put themselves on the jury, and the parson similarly. So they are (----il) the said church (----il) which he makes to be seised with the said lands in demesne except only the service (----il) the parson is to nothing by this assize except only the service (----il) [by the surety] of Henry Puniel.

1   This plea is written on a piece of parchment that has been stitched on to the end of the membrane, which suggests that the parchment was torn at some time and then stitched on to the appropriate membrane. The state of the additional piece is very poor and much remains illegible. Also the left-hand edge looks as though it has worn away or been cut off. There are no marginalia as a result. There is nothing written on the other side of the stitched-on parchment.

2   I have assumed this, as the left-hand edge is missing.

3   Probably the one in Carlford hundred. The other Tuddenham is in Lackford hundred. Their pleas would probably have figured at Cattishall, not Ipswich.

4   This may be a reference to the river Stour.

5   This is probably the name Small Meadow, but I can find no such place.

Membrane 21d

557. (*Ely*) A jury comes to declare whether two acres of land and a half acre of meadow with appurtenances in Parham are free alms pertaining to the church of Parham in respect whereof the prior of Hickling is the parson, or the lay fee of the prioress of Campsey [Ash]1. She comes and says nothing to stay the assize.

The jurors say that this is void2 because it is elsewhere in the rolls for Cattishall3 (*on the morrow*).

1   This place is in Loes hundred. The priory was founded in 1195 and had twenty-one nuns in the thirteenth century.

2   From this position to the end of this plea the writing is in lighter ink or there has been some rubbing to make it lighter. This also might mean it was added later. There is also a gap after this sentence, which suggests the clerk was going to complete it later. This suggests the clerks put in these headings and expected to fill them up later. No wonder so many are crammed in if they do not leave sufficient space.

3   See **932**.

558.1 (*Ely*) Robert de Freyney was summoned to reply to Gilbert Altebon concerning a plea that he render to him eighteen marks which he owes to him and unjustly withholds etc. Robert comes and acknowledges that he owes him the said debt. So the sheriff is ordered to levy the said eighteen marks from the lands and chattels of the said Robert.

1   Prior to this plea there is a gap of 2.8 cm, as though the clerk had left a space to write in the fact that the previous plea was elsewhere in the rolls in the pleas taken at Cattishall.

559. (*Ely, one mark*) An assize comes to declare if Robert de Agnell uncle of Henry de Agnell was seised in his demesne etc of one knight's fee with appurtenances in Moulton and of half a knight's fee with appurtenances in Cretingham on the day that he died, and if he died after the latest etc and if etc that half a [knight's] fee Ralph de Iveni holds. He comes and gives one mark for licence to agree by the surety of Herbert [de] Alicon. The agreement is such that the same Ralph acknowledges the said one and a half fees to be the right of Henry. For this etc the same Henry remises to the same Ralph all the right and claim that he had or could have in the one knight's fee with appurtenances in Moulton. For this etc the same Ralph grants that the same Henry may hold forever the half of a knight's fee with appurtenances in Cretingham from the chief lord of that fee. This agreement was made saving to Herbert [de] Alicon one marksworth of rent in the same vill, which he will hold from Henry. [**771**]

560. (*Ely*) The prior of Snape[1] claims against William Hacon five acres of land with appurtenances in Benhall as the right of his church, and in which the same William has no entry except by Osbert Grim who holds that [land] in villeinage. [[who] is not present, that William never had nor holds [that land]. So the prior [is] in mercy and William [is] without day[e, i]].[2]

The same prior claims against Ralph Swan five acres of land with appurtenances in the same vill, and in which the same Ralph does not have entry except by William Hacon to whom Osbert Grim, who held that land from the said prior in villeinage, demised that [land] etc. Afterwards, it was proved that William holds nothing of the said five acres of land, which is being claimed (against him. So he [is] without day and the prior [is] in mercy[i]) (*amercement*).

William and Ralph come and Ralph then vouches to warranty William, who warrants him and answers for all and they say that the said Osbert was a free man and he held that land freely, so that he could enfeoff as a free man and that he was not a villein. That this may be inquired into by a jury, he offers to the lord king half a mark (*half a mark*). They are received by the surety of Ralph, and the prior similarly puts himself on the jury.

The jurors say that the said Osbert held his land for four shillings per year for all services and that the same prior never had any service except only those four shillings. So it is adjudged that William Hacon [is] without day and the prior [is] in mercy (*amercement*).

1.   Snape priory was founded in 1155, originally dependent on Colchester Abbey and had at most twelve Benedictine monks.
2.   I have left the erased text here because it sheds some light on the plea.

561. (*Stow*) Margery de Glanvill by her attorney claims against Robert de Alneto nine acres with appurtenances in Buxhall, which she claims to be her marriage portion, and in which the same Robert has no entry except by Roger de Glanvill, the former husband of the said Margery, who demised that [land] to him whom she in her life etc.

Robert comes and then vouches to warranty Geoffrey the son of Roger de Glanvill who is under age. Margery, his mother, grants that she wishes to await his age, so [he is] without day.

562. (*Ely*) Robert of Clopton, who brought an assize of mort d'ancestor against Robert de Colville concerning half a marksworth of rent with appurtenances in Parham, Framsden and Helmingham, has not prosecuted. So he and his sureties for prosecuting [are] in mercy, namely: Richard Baron of Clopton and Alan Compel of the same (*amercements*).

563. (*Ely*) William the son of Adam and Rose his wife, who brought an assize of mort d'ancestor against Robert the son of Jordan concerning one acre of land with appurtenances in Tuddenham, have not prosecuted. So he and his sureties for prosecuting [are] in mercy, namely: Bullar of Holbrook and Hastings Moyse of Chelmondiston (*amercements*).

564. (*Ely*) Richard Edger who brought an assize of mort d'ancestor against William the son of Robert concerning sixteen acres of land with appurtenances in Monewden, has not prosecuted. So he and his sureties for prosecuting [are] in mercy, namely: Robert Kamere of Ash and John de Cosinere of Oakley (*amercements*).

565. (*Ely*) Geoffrey de Haringford, who brought an assize of mort d'ancestor against Henry Herthnitte concerning one messuage with appurtenances in Debenham, has not prosecuted. So he and his sureties for prosecuting [are] in mercy namely: James the son of Thomas of Gedding and John the son of Osbert of Henfield (*amercements*).

566. (*Ely, amercements*) John of Farnham who brought an assize of mort d'ancestor against Henry the son of Erburg concerning three roods of land with appurtenances … [unfinished]

567. (*Ely*) Roger Sturmey who brought an assize of novel disseisin against John of Yarmouth concerning a tenement in Iken has not prosecuted. So he and his sureties for prosecuting [are] in mercy namely: William Smith of Buxhall and William Coppinger of the same (*amercements*).

568. (*Ely*) Ralph Fidling who brought an assize of novel disseisin concerning a tenement in Butley against the prior of Butley has not prosecuted. So he and his sureties for prosecuting [are] in mercy. He had no sureties except [his] faith.

569. (*Ely*) Walter the son of William who brought an assize of novel disseisin against Roger de Mohaut concerning a tenement in [Earl] Soham has not prosecuted. So he and his sureties for prosecuting [are] in mercy namely: Roger of Brockford and Robert de Beaufoy (*amercements*).

570. (*Ely*) William de Colville who brought a writ to attaint the twelve against Agnes of Cretingham concerning a tenement in Cretingham has not prosecuted. So he and his sureties for prosecuting [are] in mercy namely: Thomas de Hemmegrave and John of Gaddesden (*amercements*).

571. (*Ely*) William [le][1] Daveys who brought an assize of mort d'ancestor against Ranulf Haliday concerning a tenement in Cretingham has not prosecuted. So he and his sureties for prosecuting [are] in mercy namely: Thomas de Loges of Brandeston and Geoffrey Bene of Cretingham (*amercements*).

[1]   The clerk has missed out *le*. William appears in a number of other pleas and in the amercement section as *William le Daveys*.

572. (*Ely*) Robert the son of William who brought an assize of mort d'ancestor against Alice the daughter of William concerning a tenement in Eyke has not prosecuted. So he and his sureties for prosecuting [are] in mercy namely: Roger the son of the dean of Sutton (*amercements*).

Membrane 22

573. (*St Etheldreda*) An assize comes to declare if Robert Aguillon,[1] William of Gravely and Walter le Venur unjustly etc disseised Henry de Biccermede of his free tenement in Seckford after the first etc and in respect whereof he complains that they disseised him of two shillingsworth of rent.

Robert and the others come and they say nothing to stay the assize.

The jurors say that the said Robert and the others did not disseise him of any of his free tenement because he is a villein of the prior of Ely. So it is adjudged that he is to take nothing by this assize and he is in mercy for a false claim, by the surety of William of Holbrook (*amercement*). Robert and the others [are] without day.

[1] See **255** and **488** for other pleas involving Robert.

574. (*St Etheldreda*) An assize comes to declare if Richard de Ribos unjustly etc disseised Ranulf Haliday of his free tenement in Ashfield after the first crossing etc and in respect whereof he complains that the said Richard disseised him of one acre of meadow and one acre of land with appurtenances in the same vill.

Richard comes and says nothing to stay the assize.

The jurors say that the said Richard disseised the said Ranulf of a certain headland and not of one acre of land nor of one acre of meadow. So it is adjudged that Ranulf has recovered his seisin and Richard [is] in mercy (*amercement*). Ranulf [is] in mercy for a false claim by the surety of Jordan of Shelton and Simon Fulyard (*amercement*). Richard de Ribos made a fine for half a mark (*half a mark*).

575.[1] (*St Etheldreda*) An assize comes to declare if Roger de Berneshege father of Roger was seised in his demesne as of fee etc of one messuage, and twenty-five acres of land and one (acre[i]) of meadow and four shillings and ten penceworth of rent with appurtenances in Clopton and Grundisburgh on the day that etc and if etc and if etc and concerning which Roger de Berneshege holds one messuage, twenty acres of land, one acre of meadow and three shillings and sixpenceworth of rent, William le Chappelle one acre of land and sixteen penceworth of rent, Robert Viben one acre of land, and Richard de Borneswall two acres of land, Gerard the son of Medusa and William his brother half an acre and Gerard the son of Ralph half an acre. They come and say nothing to stay the assize.

The jurors say that in fact the said (Ralph[s])[2] died seised but this Roger after his death was then in seisin. So it is adjudged that he is to take nothing by this assize and he is in mercy for a false claim, and the others [are] without day (*amercement*).

[1] See **1011** which sheds a bit more light on this confusing situation.
[2] It is not certain where this person fits into the plea. It is probable that he is Ralph de Berneshege the father of Roger de Berneshege, one of the defendants. If it was Roger, the plaintiff, in seisin after the death of Roger de Berneshege, then why was he bringing the plea? Was he trying to regularise his illegal position? The only reason why the plaintiff did not win his case is that the descendants of Ralph should be in seisin.

576. Isolda who was the wife of Walter de Deneys acknowledges that Adam the son of Roger against whom she has claimed in dower in Framsden, has satisfied her for the forty shillings which the same Adam owed to her, namely: at the feast of St Botulf [17 June] in the twenty-fourth year [of King Henry III] one mark, and at the next Assumption of the Blessed [Virgin] Mary [15 August] following, one mark, and at the feast of St Michael [29 September] one mark. If he does not do [this] he grants etc until etc and concerning the cost etc. Note: that he paid her half a mark cash down. The same acknowledges that Roger de Mohaut and all the others against whom she claimed dower similarly satisfied her. So [they are] without day.

577. (*St Etheldreda*) A jury comes to declare whether one messuage and nine acres of land with appurtenances in Wickham [Market] are the free alms pertaining to the church of Wickham [Market] of which Godfrey is the parson or the lay fee of Rainer the son of Nigel. He comes and by a licence renders [it] to him. So he is to have his seisin.

578. (*St Etheldreda*) An assize comes to declare if the prior of Hickling, Brother Richard of Hacheston, John le Lung,[1] John Hereward, William Wymark, William Denger, John Batley and Robert Schireward unjustly etc disseised Agnes of Glevering of her free tenement in Glevering after the first etc.

The prior and the others come and say nothing to stay the assize.

The jury says that the said prior and the others did not disseise Agnes as the writ says. So it is adjudged that she is to take nothing by this assize and is in mercy for a false claim. It is pardoned because [she is] under age.

> [1] This means tall or long. See Reaney 1997, p.271.

579.[1] (*St Etheldreda*) An assize comes to declare if Roger de Bavent, uncle of Geoffrey de Bavent, was seised in his demesne etc of fifty-seven acres of land and one messuage with appurtenances in Sutton on the day that he died, and if he died etc and if etc and in respect whereof William Osmund holds thirty-six acres, Bartholomew Osemund six acres, (Aldr[ed] de Saxfield[i]) three acres, Robert de Wood two acres, Rosa de Wood one acre, Alice of Aldeburgh half an acre, Bertha de Swestermere half an acre and Agnes de Wood one messuage.[1]

William and Bartholomew come, and Bartholomew acknowledges that he is the villein of William (so Geoffrey [is] in mercy for a false claim[i]) (*amercement*). William vouches to warranty Richard of Whitwell who is present and he warrants him, and then he vouches to warranty John the son of William the son of Rocelin. He is to have him by aid of the court on the morrow of the Ascension [Friday 25 May] at Cattishall.

Afterwards, it was proved by the jury taken below on those who defaulted that Roger died before the term. The warrant is to stand over.

Robert[3] and the others have not come and they were resummoned, so let the assize be taken against them by default.

The jurors say that in fact the said Roger died seised of the said land, and that this Geoffrey is his nearest heir. But they say in truth that Roger died before the term. So it is adjudged that Geoffrey is to take nothing by this assize and he is in mercy for a false claim, and he may proceed by a writ of right against all the above named if he wishes. The amercement is pardoned because [he is] poor.

> [1] There is a gap of 2.6 cm between this plea and the previous one. This plea is also a good illustration of a person who had died before the start of the term for the assize of mort d'ancestor. Therefore the plaintiff lost the case. In this case the term starts with the time of King John's last return from Ireland into England. See **94** for reference.
>
> [2] The claim is calculated as 57 acres and one messuage but only 49 acres and one messuage are noted by the clerk.
>
> [3] There is a space of 3.9 cm between this sentence and the preceding one. Maybe the clerk expected to put in a lot more. There is also a line connecting this paragraph with the preceding one in the margin.

580. (*St Etheldreda*) Alice who was the wife of William of Otley claims against Robert the son of Richard half a rood of land with appurtenances in Stratford as her right and marriage portion etc. Robert comes and by licence renders [it] to her. So she is to have her seisin.

581. (*St Etheldreda*) John of Culpho gives half a mark for licence to agree with John of Tuddenham concerning a plea of land by the surety of the same John. [*chirograph* CP 25(1) 213/17/119]

582. (*St Etheldreda*) An assize comes to declare if Roger of Flixton[1] the father of John Escot was seised in his demesne etc of twelve acres of land with appurtenances in Alnesbourn on the day that etc and if etc whose land Adam Symund holds. He comes and says that he cannot answer to him because he is under age (*age*). So let him await [his] age.

> [1] In Lothingland or Wangford hundred.

583. (*St Etheldreda*) An assize comes to declare if Walter Curteys, Gilbert of Brinklow,[1] John of Brinklow[2] and Gilbert Farma unjustly etc disseised Richard Plaice of his common pasture in Blaxhall, which pertains to his free tenement in the same vill after the first etc.

Afterwards, Richard comes and he does not wish to proceed, so he and his sureties for prosecuting [are] in mercy, namely: William the son of Seman of Boyton and Walter the son of Simon of the same. It is pardoned because of poverty.

> [1] In Warwickshire.
> [2] There is evidence of some repair to the membrane at this point with some obvious stitching. The clerk has worked around the stitching. This has erased the *nn* in *Bri[nn]kelawe*. However, I have assumed this is the same name as *Gilbertus de Brinnkelawe*.

584. (*St Etheldreda, half a mark*) Robert the parson of [Earl] Soham gives half a mark for licence to agree with Godfrey of Brundish concerning a plea of land by the surety of the same Godfrey. [*chirograph* CP 25(1) 213/15/27][1]

> [1] **387** gives the full name of Godfrey Parker of Brundish, whereas the chirograph only gives Godfrey Parker. This plea concerns a plea of utrum.

585. (*Ely, half a mark*) The abbot of St Osyth gives half a mark for licence to agree with Richard of Tuddenham concerning a plea of assize of mort d'ancestor concerning a tenement in Tuddenham and Westerfield. [*chirograph* CP 25(1) 213/16/63]

586.[1] (*St Etheldreda, twenty shillings*) Warren of Bassingbourne and Geoffrey of Swaffham give twenty shillings for licence to agree with Robert of Hereford concerning a plea of land by the surety of William de ... . [*chirograph* CP 25(1) 213/16/50]

> [1] This was a significant plea if they are giving such a large amount of money. It was for two parts of a carucate of land. Robert also gives 24 marks of silver to these two and their respective wives for the quitclaim etc. See **293**.

587.[1] Roger de Cressy acknowledges that he owes to Nicholas of Lynn fifty marks, of which he will pay to him on the feast of St Michael [29 September] in the twenty-fourth year, twenty-five marks, and on the Easter term twenty-five marks. Nicholas grants that if the same Roger is able to gain the grace of the king that the outlaws may return it will readily please him.[2]

> [1] This is an odd plea but there may be a connection between it and **460**.
> [2] There is an entry in *Cal. Pat. Rolls, 1232–47*, p.391 which may have a bearing on this part of the case. It is dated '18 August 1243 at Bordeaux', and says '... pardon to Ralph Luvel of his flight

and outlawry for a trespass committed against Nicholas de Lenn by the said Ralph and others of the men of Roger de Cressy with the usual condition'. So it looks as though Roger de Cressy obtained the pardon for his men.

Membrane 22d

588. (*St Etheldreda*) Beatrice, who was the wife of Adam Evielot, claims against Simon Suliard half of one messuage and seven acres of land with appurtenances in Cretingham as her dower, and in respect whereof the said Adam dowered her on the day etc.

Simon comes and says that she could not claim dower because the said Adam her husband on the day that he married her or ever afterwards [never][1] was in seisin of the said land and messuage, so that he could dower her. He then puts himself on the country, and she similarly.

The jurors say that the said Adam was a villein and never held that land and messuage, so that he could dower her thereof. So it is adjudged that she is to take nothing by this assize, and is in mercy for a false claim. It is pardoned because [she is] poor.

   [1] The clerk has missed out *numquam*, 'never', which makes more sense given the verdict.

589. (*Ely*) An assize comes to declare if Eustace the son of Jul'[1] unjustly etc disseised Roger the son of Ralph of his free tenement in Blaxhall after the first etc and in respect whereof Roger complains that the same Eustace disseised him of one acre of land with appurtenances in the same vill.

Eustace comes and says nothing to stay the assize.

The jurors say that he did not disseise him as the writ says. So it is adjudged that he is to take nothing by this assize, and he is in mercy for a false claim. The amercement is pardoned because [he is] poor.

   [1] This might be Juliana or Julius.

590. (*Ely*) An assize comes to declare if William de *Prauteston* unjustly etc raised a certain dyke in Cretingham to the nuisance of the free tenement of John of Monewden in the same vill after the first crossing etc.

William has not come and he was attached by Roger Pylhar and Amys Cake of the same, so all [are] in mercy. The assize is to be taken against them by default.

The jurors say that the said William raised a certain dyke as the writ says to the nuisance of the free etc. So it is adjudged that that dyke be levelled by a view of the recognitors and that it is as it ought to be and is accustomed [to be], and William [is] in mercy (*amercement*).

Damages: four pence.

591. (*Ely*) An assize comes to declare if Turgis of Charsfield father of William was seised in his demesne of three acres of land with appurtenances in Charsfield[1] on the day that he died and if etc and if the same William etc which land Adam the son of Matilda of Debach holds. He comes and then vouches to warranty the prioress of Campsey [Ash]. He is to have her at Cattishall on the morrow of the Ascension of the Lord by the aid of the court. Afterwards, the prioress comes and warrants him and then she vouches to warranty Brian of Hickling. She is to have him by the aid of the court at Cattishall on the next Saturday after the Ascension of the Lord [Saturday 26 May] (*Cattishall*).

The prioress appoints as her attorney Hamo de Valoines[2] or Thomas de Plesseto. [*chirograph* CP 25(1) 213/15/12][3]

1   The clerk wrote *Cattefeud*. This may be the Sussex Catsfield, which means it is a foreign plea. However, as far as I am aware Ely did not have any lands in Sussex. There is also a Catfield in Norfolk but there is no indication that Ely had any lands in this part of Norfolk. Ely held Charsfield in Loes hundred, which is another possibility. The chirograph below answers the question, which indicates Charsfield is the vill in this plea.

2   The de Valoines family founded the priory in 1195 according to Knowles and Hadcock 1971, p.279.

3   Note: there is no mention of Brian in the chirograph. There is also no further indication of this plea in the pleas taken at Cattishall.

592.[1] *(Ely)* An assize comes to declare if Seman the son of Ranulf and Roger Woolnoth unjustly etc disseised Richard Mariot of his free tenement in Tunstall after the first crossing etc and in respect whereof the same Richard complains that they disseised him of one third part of one rood with appurtenances in the same vill.

Seman comes and says nothing to stay the assize. Roger has not come and he was attached by Ralph Woolnoth of Blaxhall and Theobald Tyring of the same, so [they are] in mercy *(amercements)*.

Afterwards, Richard comes and acknowledges himself to be a villein of Roger Bigod the earl of Norfolk and he is committed to him, and he [Roger Bigod] does not prosecute the case, so he and his sureties for prosecuting [are] in mercy, namely: Roger the son of John of Wantisden and Alexander Siward of Tunstall *(amercements)*.

1   There is a gap of 2.7 cm between this plea and the previous one.

593. *(Ely)* An assize comes to declare if Robert Ostheberne the father of Hugh was seised in his demesne etc of twelve acres of land with appurtenances in *Curf*[1] on the day that he died, and if he died (after the last return[i]) etc and if the next etc which land John le Bracur and Botilda the daughter of Henry holds. They come and say nothing to stay the assize.

The jurors say that the said Robert died seised thereof and that this Hugh is the nearest heir, and that he died after the term. So it is adjudged that Hugh has recovered his seisin against him. John [is] in mercy *(amercement)*.

(half a mark) Afterwards, they are agreed and John le Bracur gives half a mark for licence to agree by the surety of Hugh the son of Robert. [*chirograph* CP 25(1) 213/16/52][2]

1   This place cannot be located in Suffolk. It might be Culpho in Carlford hundred which was part of the liberty of Ely in Suffolk. The chirograph indicates a different place – Walton, which is in Colneis hundred and is also part of the liberty of Ely. The chirograph also indicates that the father of Hugh was *Robert de Grangia*. There is no mention of *Ostheberne*. I am reasonably confident that this chirograph made at Ipswich, one month after Easter in this eyre, is the correct one because of the name of the defendant and the fact this defendant does not appear again in the roll. A personal surname of *Ostheberne* is still possible if the clerk making the chirograph did not write this into the chirograph at the time but only indicated the place of his origin.

2   On the reverse of the chirograph it indicates that *Radulfus le Bigod apponit clamium suum*.

594. *(Ely)* An assize comes to declare if Nigel Smith unjustly disseised John Biring of his common pasture in Trimley,[1] which pertains to his free tenement in the same vill.

Nigel comes and says nothing to stay the assize.

The jurors say that the said Nigel disseised him of his common pasture as the writ says. So it is adjudged that he has recovered his seisin, and Nigel [is] in mercy, by the surety of Walkelin of Norton and Robert Fizal the priest *(amercement)*.

1   This is either Trimley St Martin or Trimley St Mary in Colneis hundred.

595. (*Ely*) An assize comes to declare if Gervase of Bradfield, Adam his brother, Roger de Valoines and Alice, who was the wife of Hugh Smith, unjustly etc disseised Stephen de Colville of his free tenement in Rendham after the [first][1] crossing etc and in respect whereof he complains that they disseised him of one acre. Gervase and all the others come and say nothing to stay the assize.

The jurors say that the said Gervase[2] and the others have not disseised the said Stephen of any free tenement, because they say that when the said Alice enfeoffed the said Stephen of one acre she was mad and (that[1]) she was neither in possession of her [faculties] nor indeed of memory, so they say that the said Gervase and the others have made no disseisin. So [they are] without day and Stephen [is] in mercy (*amercement*).

[1]   The clerk missed this out from the usual formula.
[2]   From this point onwards the script is different from the rest of the plea.

596. (*Ely*) The same assize comes to declare by the same recognitors if Gervase of Bradfield, Adam his brother, Roger of Rendham and Alice, who was the wife of Hugh Smith, unjustly etc disseised Tristram of Rendham of his free tenement in Rendham after the first crossing etc and in respect whereof the same Tristram complains that they disseised him of five[1] acres of land with appurtenances in the same vill.

Gervase and all the others come and say nothing to stay the assize.

The jurors say that Gervase and all the others have not disseised the said Tristram, because they say that when the said Alice made a charter to him, and placed him in seisin of the said land, she was out of her mind and that she was neither in possession of her [faculties] nor indeed of memory, because the same Tristram made her drunk, so that she did not know what she did for two days, in respect whereof they say that they have not disseised him. So it is adjudged that he is to take nothing by this assize, and he is in mercy for a false claim (*amercement*). He is remanded in custody.

[1]   The stitched tear mentioned earlier obviously affected the clerk, so the tear must have happened around the time of writing as the clerk has deliberately avoided the area of stitching. See **583**.

597. (*Ely*) Alice of Stanstead who brought a writ of novel disseisin concerning a tenement in Monewden against John of Stoke[1] has not prosecuted. So she and her sureties for prosecuting [are] in mercy, namely: William Sylvester of Monewden (*amercements*).

[1]   There are three possibilities: Stoke-by-Nayland in Babergh hundred, Stoke-by-Clare in Risbridge hundred and Stoke in Ipswich borough.

Membrane 23

598. (*Ely*) An assize comes to declare if Tristram of Rendham, Geoffrey of Titchwell, William Capun and Roger of Blaxhall unjustly etc disseised Agnes the daughter of Elias of her free tenement in Rendham after the first crossing etc and in respect whereof she complains that they disseised her of one acre of land with appurtenances in the same vill.

Tristram and the others come and acknowledge the disseisin. So she is to have her seisin, and they are to be remanded in custody, and Agnes remits her damages.

599. (*Ely*) An assize comes to declare if the same Tristram, Geoffrey and William unjustly etc disseised Elias of Rendham and Loretta his wife of their free tenement in Rendham after the first crossing etc and in respect whereof they complain [that] they disseised them of two acres of land with appurtenances in the same vill.

Tristram and the others come and acknowledge the disseisin. So let them be remanded into custody. The others are to have their seisin. They are to be remanded in custody.

600. (*Ely*) Tristram of Rendham who brought an assize of novel disseisin against Elias of Rendham concerning a tenement in Rendham has not prosecuted. So he and his sureties for prosecuting [are] in mercy, namely Geoffrey of Titsey of Rendham and Stephen de Colville of Parham (*amercements*).

601.[1] (*Loddon*)[2] Margery the daughter of Laur'[3] claims against Richard the son of Ralph three acres of land with appurtenances in Kirstead as her right and inheritance, into which he has no entry except by William le Trucerse while the said Margery was under age and in his wardship.

Richard comes and says that he ought not answer her because only six years have elapsed since she demised the said land to the said William, and then she was forty years [of age] and not under age as she says. So it is adjudged that she is to take nothing by this writ and she is in mercy for a false claim. The amercement is pardoned for poverty and Richard [is] without day.

[1] This plea is written in the hand of the same clerk who wrote part of **595**.
[2] This is Loddon hundred in Norfolk, so is really a foreign plea.
[3] This might be Laurence or Loretta.

602. (*Mutford*) Thomas de Hemmegrave seeks Thomas de *Wychesfield* as his naif and fugitive with all [his] chattels and all his household. Thomas comes and acknowledges that he is his villein. So he is committed to him etc.

603. (*Ely*) Richard the son of Siward Heyhare, who brought an assize of mort d'ancestor against Alice de Prato[1] concerning a tenement in Gooderstone,[2] has not prosecuted. So his sureties for prosecuting [are] in mercy, namely: William the son of Robert of Gooderstone and Alexander the son of William of the same. The amercement of Richard is pardoned.

[1] This is the name Pray according to Reaney 1997, p.360.
[2] This is Gooderstone in Norfolk in South Greenhoe hundred but again there is no obvious connection with Ely. This would also make this a foreign plea.

604. (*Ely, ten shillings*) Stephen of Loudham gives ten shillings for licence to agree with Edward Yepheye and Robert de Wynderville concerning a plea of an assize of mort d'ancestor by the surety of William of Holbrook. [*chirograph* CP 25(1) 213/17/96][1]

[1] In the chirograph *Edward Ghepeghe* is shown as vouching Stephen to warranty. Stephen is also shown as being vouched to warranty by *Reyner de la Grene*.

605. (*Ely, half a mark*) Richard Smalprud gives half a mark for licence to agree with John Audr[ey] concerning a plea of land by the surety of William (and[i]) Robert the brothers of Richard. The agreement is such that Richard de la Brenthalle,[1] whom John vouches to warranty and who, warrants him, and he acknowledges that the five acres of land with appurtenances in Clopton are the right of Richard and of his brothers. He returned that [land] to them. He will make an exchange to the said John to the value etc.

[1] This is possibly Burnt Hall.

606. (*Ely*) An assize comes to declare if Matthew de Valoines uncle of Robert de Valoines was seised in his demesne etc of six acres of land with appurtenances in Rendham on the day that he died, and if he died after the last return etc and if etc which land the prioress of Campsey [Ash] holds. She comes and then vouches to warranty Huelma, who was the wife of Matthew de Valoines. She is to have her at Cattishall on the nearest Saturday after the Ascension of the Lord [Saturday 26 May] by the aid of the court (*Cattishall*).

607.[1] (*Ely*) An assize comes to declare if Thomas Tyrel unjustly etc raised [the level of] a certain pond in Foxhall to the nuisance of the free tenement of Walter the son of Ernulf after the first etc.

Thomas comes and says nothing to stay the assize. Thomas Winter, one of the recognitors, has not come, so [he is] in mercy (*amercement*).

The jurors say that the said Thomas has raised the [level of] the said pond unjustly etc to the nuisance of the free tenement of the same Walter. So it is adjudged that the unjust raising be lowered and that it is as it ought to be and is accustomed [to be]. He is in mercy by the surety of Philip of Winston (*amercement*).

Damages: forty pence.

1   There is a flaw in the membrane in this plea which the clerk has worked around. There is a gap of 3.7 cm between this plea and the previous one.

608. (*Ely*) An assize comes to declare whether eight acres of land with appurtenances in Rendham are the free alms pertaining to the church of Rendham whereof Anselm is the parson, or the lay fee of William of Rendham, Alice who was the wife of William Cuiccing,[1] Tristram the son of Elias, William Bernard, Agnes his wife and William Trywy. William of Rendham, in respect thereof, holds one and a half acres, Alice half an acre, Tristram one and a half acres, William and Agnes four acres and William Trywy half an acre. William of Rendham and Tristram have (not[i]) come and [they were] resummoned. So let the assize be taken against them by default.

The jurors say that the said land is free alms pertaining to the church of Rendham. So it is adjudged that the said Anselm has recovered his seisin against them. They [are] in mercy (*amercement*).

1   This might be the name Quicking.

609. (*Ely*) An assize comes to declare if William the son of William Edward uncle of Amis,[1] the daughter of Baldwin, was seised in his demesne etc of three roods of land with appurtenances in Moulton[2] on the day [he took] the religious habit etc and (if[i]) he took that habit after the last return, and if the said Amis etc which land Richard Rugband holds. He comes and says nothing to stay the assize.

The jurors say that the said Amis is a villein. So it is adjudged that she is to take nothing by this assize and is in mercy for a false claim (*amercement*).

1   The clerk makes no distinction between the genitive at this point and the nominative later in the plea. She is probably named Amisia.
2   This is probably the Moulton in Risbridge hundred, although there is no obvious connection with the liberty of Ely. Moulton in Risbridge hundred was considered to be in the hands of the Beauchamp family: see *Feudal Aids*, v, p.45. One other possibility is Melton in Wilford hundred where the liberty of Ely had held lands since Saxon times. See Arnott 1946, p.79.

610. (*Blything*) Richard the son of Osbert and Michael of Ringsfield were summoned to reply to Roger the son of Gilbert (concerning[i]) a plea that they would allow him to have common pasture in *Upredisham* concerning which Gilbert of Redisham, the father of Roger, whose heir he is, was seised [of the common pasture] as pertaining to his free tenement in the same vill.

Richard and Michael come and they readily grant that he is to have common pasture as his father had. So he is to have his seisin and the others [are] without day.

611. (*Ely*) Elias the son of Robert, who brought an assize of novel disseisin against John the son of Robert concerning a tenement in Easton, has not prosecuted. So he and his sureties for prosecuting [are] in mercy, namely: Roger the son of William of Hoo[1] and Roger the son of Ralph of Easton (*amercements*).

[1]   Probably the Hoo in Loes hundred, but there was also a Hoo in Wilford hundred; both had the prior of Ely as their lord.

612. (*Ely*) John the son of Manerius, who brought an assize of mort d'ancestor against Hingulf the parson of Sternfield concerning a tenement in Sternfield, has not prosecuted. So he and his sureties for prosecuting [are] in mercy, Henry the son of Ranulf of Blickling and Geoffrey the son of Wareys de Calafina (*amercements*).

613. (*Ely*) Agatha, who brought an assize of mort d'ancestor against Ralph the son of Geoffrey and Gunnild his wife concerning nine acres of land with appurtenances in Grundisburgh, comes and acknowledges that she is a villein and she does not prosecute. They [are] without day. She and her sureties for prosecuting [are] in mercy, namely: Gilbert the son of Warren of Grundisburgh [and] William the son of Reynold of Culpho (*amercements*).

614. Warren the son of Henry of Wenham appoints as his attorney Milo his son against Benedict of Copdock and Christine his wife and of another named in the writ concerning a plea of land etc.[1]

[1]   The clerk had written in the margin that an amercement was due, but there would not normally be an amercement in the appointment of an attorney.

615. Thomas of Metfield appoints as his attorney William of Metfield against Master Benedict of Mendham concerning a plea of land, and against Richard Picot concerning a plea to receive his chirograph. [*chirograph* CP 25(1) 213/17/94]

616. A day is given to Robert de Blaueny by his attorneys, plaintiff, and Roger Bigod, earl of Norfolk, deforciant, concerning a plea of covenant at Chelmsford in the octave of Trinity [Sunday] by prayer of the parties (*Chelmsford*).

Membrane 23d

617. (*Bosmere*) Brian of Ringshall claims against Matilda of Ringshall thirty acres of land with appurtenances in Ringshall as his right etc and in respect whereof a certain William the son of Hamelin his predecessor was seised in his demesne as of fee and right in the time of King Henry grandfather of the present lord king by taking profits therefrom to the value of half a mark. From the same William descended the right of that land to a certain Hamelin as son and heir, and from the same Hamelin to a certain Anselm as son and heir, and from the same Anselm to this Brian who now claims as son and heir, and that such is his right he offers [to prove].

Matilda[1] comes and denies his right and all etc and she says that it does not seem to her that she ought to answer him, because whereas the said land with appurtenances had remained to her by the fine made before (R.[i])[obert] de Lexington and his colleagues in the last eyre at Ipswich[2] between Roger of Aldham whose heir she [Matilda] is, the plaintiff, and Laurence de Horshangham and Matilda his wife whose heir he [Brian] is, tenants, and the same Brian was of full age and in the court and did not lay his claim, she claims a judgement if she ought to answer him.

Afterwards, they are agreed by licence and Brian remised all right and claim for two marks.[3]

1   There is a gap of 1.4 cm prior to the start of this paragraph.
2   Robert de Lexington apparently led the circuit for Suffolk at Ipswich on 10–20 November 1234. There is no plea roll for this but according to Crook 1982a, p.90 there are 147 feet of fines. The agreement could not be found.
3   The clerk has not put this in the margin nor in the list of agreements at the end of this roll.

618. (*Norfolk*) Walter the son of Bernard acknowledges that he remitted and quit-claimed from himself and his heirs to the nuns of Carrow[1] sixty shillings of annual rent, which the said nuns [are accustomed] to pay to him in the name of Thomas la Velye for a tenement that Roger la Velye gave to the said nuns in Norwich, Trowse and Newton. The same Walter and his heirs will acquit [and] defend the said tenement for the said nuns against all [others]. [*chirograph* CP 25(1) 156/66/810]

1   St Mary of Carrow was a house of Benedictine nuns in Norwich founded in 1146.

619. (*Norfolk*) The grand assize between William the Earl Warenne, plaintiff, and John of [Horsham] St Faith, tenant, concerning 34[1] acres of land (and one messuage[i]) with appurtenances in Edingthorpe is to be adjourned until the quindene of Holy Trinity[2] at Chelmsford for the lack of knights. The sheriff is ordered that he has the knights on that day.

1   In plea **144**, there were only 33 acres.
2   Holy Trinity in 1240 was on Sunday 10 June. According to Crook 1982a, p.101, the eyre in Essex started on the octave of Trinity, that is Sunday 17 June. The quindene of Trinity was Sunday 24 June, but see the introduction, p.xiii for the argument on courts sitting on a Sunday.

620.[1] (*Norfolk*) An assize comes to declare which patron in time of peace presented the last parson, who is dead, to the church of Ringstead which is vacant, which advowson Humphrey de Wyneless and Matilda his wife say pertains to them and which advowson Geoffrey de Siri withholds from them. They say in respect whereof that a certain Emma le Estraunge, who held the tenement of Ringstead and the advowson of the same church, presented a certain clerk, named William the Bastard, who on her presentation was admitted and in the same instituted and who finally died in the same [church]. After she had presented the said William, that Emma gave the same land with the advowson of the said church to the said Matilda by her charter, which she proffers and which attests to this.

Geoffrey comes and readily grants (that[il])[2] the said Emma presented the said William, who on her presentation was admitted and instituted in the same, and he died finally in the same, but he firmly states that the charter which they proffer ought not to harm him, because before the making of that charter the said Emma gave by her charter to a certain Ralph, her son, the rent with all her tenements in the same vill together with the advowson of the church, so that nothing remained to the same Emma except sixty acres of land in the same vill, which he proffers and which attests this. Upon this afterwards in the court of the lord king a final concord was made between the prior of Lewes, plaintiff, and the said Ralph, tenant, concerning the advowson of the church of Burnham Thorpe, so that by that fine the said advowson remained to the said Ralph. For this etc the same Ralph gave to the said prior two marksworth of rent from the said tenants saving to the same

Ralph that remaining rent in the same vill with the advowson of the same church [of Ringstead], so that the said Ralph died seised of the said [tenement], and Philip his brother and heir after him similarly. From the same Philip descended that rent and advowson to a certain Cecilia as daughter and heir, who is under age and in wardship.

A[3] day is given to them to hear their judgement at Chelmsford in the octave of Holy Trinity [Sunday 17 June]. Geoffrey appoints as his attorney Roger Senges or Thomas le Sire.

[1] There is a gap of 3.4 cm between this plea and the previous one.
[2] It looks as though a hole in the membrane was originally located here but has subsequently been filled in by somebody as the clerk has worked around it. The *q* of *quod* for 'that' has been lost, possibly as part of the remedial work, or possibly just by the passage of time.
[3] There is a large blank space on the membrane before this paragraph but it relates to the plea in question. The clerk has inserted a separate paragraph mark at the beginning of this paragraph as though it started a new plea but it does not.

Membrane 24

621. (*Ely, twenty shillings*) Ranulf Haliday gives twenty shillings for licence to agree with William le Daveys concerning a plea of mort d'ancestor by the surety of William Holbrook.

622. (*Ely, half a mark*) The same William gives half a mark for the same by the surety of Ranulf Haliday.

623. (*Ely*) Gilbert Pelerin who brought an assize of mort d'ancestor against Elias of [Earl] Soham concerning one messuage with appurtenances in *Atherton* has not prosecuted. So he and his sureties for prosecuting [are] in mercy, namely: faith. So nothing.

624. (*Ely*) Richard of Mendham and Eva his wife, William of Weybread and Beatrice his wife, Walter of Thorpe and Eda his wife and Richard Fulger and Christine his wife who brought an assize of mort d'ancestor against Sabina the daughter of Ivo de Senton[1] concerning three acres of land with appurtenances in Thorpe have not prosecuted. So they and their sureties for prosecuting [are] in mercy, namely: Leofric of Westgate[2] of Thorpe and William his son (*amercements*).

[1] The only possibility is Santon Downham in Lackford hundred. There is also a Santon in Norfolk, which is just across the border from Santon Downham, and the two are now associated together as one village. I have not seen it spelt as indicated above in any other source.
[2] This is probably Westgate in Ipswich. The construction of the name usually means that this person, or one of his ancestors, was originally from Ipswich and moved to Thorpe.

625. (*Ely*) Alexander the son of William who brought a writ of entry against Roger Trussebut concerning three acres of land with appurtenances in Hasketon has not prosecuted. So he and his sureties for prosecuting [are] in mercy, namely: Seman the son of William of Creeting and Hervey the son of William of the same (*amercements*).

626. (*Ely*) Gilbert de Miners who brought a writ against Adam Bulloc and Margery his wife concerning thirty acres of land with appurtenances in Martley has not prosecuted. So he and his sureties for prosecuting [are] in mercy, namely: William de *Hemsted*[1] and Richard of Stonham (*amercements*).

[1] It looks like the clerk has made a mistake here and it should be Henstead, although there is a 'Hempstead' in Essex and two 'Hempsteads' in Norfolk.

627. (*Ely*) John the son of Andrew who brought a writ of warranty of charter against Robert the son of Philip concerning five acres of land with appurtenances in Clopton has not prosecuted. So he and his sureties for prosecuting [are] in mercy, namely: Alan of Thorpe and Guy of Barkestone (*amercements*).

628. (*Ely*) Roger le charpenter[1] who brought a writ of warranty of charter against John Batley[2] concerning one and a half acres of land with appurtenances in *Hiketon*[3] has not prosecuted. So he and his sureties for prosecuting [are] in mercy, namely: William de *Hemsted*[4] and Stephen the son of William of Barkestone (*amercements*).

[1] This is Old French for a carpenter.
[2] This could be Badley although the clerk has written 'Batalye'. Batley tends to be a name in Yorkshire rather than Suffolk, but Badley is a Suffolk name. See *Feudal Aids 1284–1431* v, p.338.
[3] This is either Ickleton or Hinxton in Wittlesford hundred in Cambridgeshire, but I cannot find these vills in the liberty of Ely.
[4] This surety is not shown in the amercement section of this roll. See **1650**.

629. (*Ely*) Nicholas Chaplain de *Sucling* who brought a writ of warranty of charter against Adam the son of Richard concerning half an acre of land with appurtenances in *Sucling*[1] has not prosecuted. So he and his sureties for prosecuting [are] in mercy, namely: Richard de Ribos and Robert the chaplain of Wymondham (*amercements*).

[1] This place cannot be found. The only place that comes close is Suckley in Worcestershire.

630. (*Ely*) Augustine Mole who brought a writ of warranty [of charter] against John of Tuddenham concerning two acres of land and three roods of land with appurtenances in Tuddenham, and Robert the son of Austin who brought the same writ against the same concerning the same have not prosecuted. So they and their sureties for prosecuting [are] in mercy, namely: Richard Sewale and Augustine Guthelbert[1] (*amercements*).

[1] This could be either Godbert or Godlebert.

631. (*Ely*) Robert Bastun who brought a writ of warranty of charter against Stephen of Stratton concerning one acre of land with appurtenances in *Gancheston*[1] has not prosecuted. So he and his sureties for prosecuting [are] in mercy, namely: John Bures of Grimston and Stephen Gunter of the same (*amercements*).

[1] The clerk may have made a mistake here. This is possibly Grimston Hall in Colneis hundred, which is part of the liberty of Ely, because the place names of the people named in the plea, that is Stratton and Grimston, are both in Colneis hundred. The only other place it could be is Garveston in Mitford hundred in Norfolk, which is also part of the liberty of Ely, – unless the clerk has written the place wrongly and he was meaning Hacheston which is in Loes hundred and is part of the liberty of Ely.

632. (*Ely*) Alexander the son of William claims against Roger Trussebut three acres of land with appurtenances in Hasketon and against William le Rus four acres of land and a half an acre of meadow with appurtenances in the same vill as his right etc.

Roger and William come and say that he has never impleaded them in the County [Court], and he cannot deny this. So it was said to him that he is to go to the County [Court].[1]

[1] This is interesting procedurally but unfortunately no county court rolls survive with this case.

633. (*Ely*) Henry the son of Eva who brought a writ of covenant against John the son of Norman concerning three acres of land with appurtenances in Sternfield has not prosecuted. So he and his sureties for prosecuting [are] in mercy, namely: John the son of William of Sternfield and John the son of [Robert][1] of the same (*amercements*).

> [1] In the roll this person is shown as also being the son of William of Sternfield but in the amercement section he is shown as 'John the son of Robert of the same', which is more likely to be correct because otherwise there would be two sureties called by the same name.

634.[1] (*Ely*) Stephen of Stratton and Anna[2] his wife claim against Ralph de Colville and Idonea his wife half of nine acres of land and twelve penceworth of rent with appurtenances in Clopton, and against William de Spina half of two acres of land with appurtenances in the same vill, and against the said Ralph and Idonea a third part of two and a half acres of land and eight penceworth of rent with appurtenances in the same vill, and against the said William de Spina a third part of two acres of land with appurtenances in the same vill, and against Gilbert de Bosco a third part of two acres of land with appurtenances in the same vill, and against Mabel, who was the wife of Walter Levegar, a third part of one acre of land with appurtenances in the same vill, and against Brother[3] Norman a third part of one acre of land with appurtenances in the same vill as her dower etc and in respect whereof William de Colville, her first husband, dowered her etc and on the day etc.

Ralph and all the others come and Ralph and Idonea then vouch to warranty Henry de Colville, son and heir of William de Colville, who is under age and in the wardship of John of Gaddesden. William, Gilbert and Norman then vouch to warranty the said Ralph and Idonea, who are present and they warrant them, and then they [Ralph and Idonea] vouch to warranty the said Henry. So John of Gaddesden, the guardian of the said Henry is to be summoned that he be at Chelmsford on the octave of the Trinity, and he is to have the said Henry there. Mabel then vouches to warranty Alexander her son who is in her wardship and is under age. She is to have him at the said term.[4]

The same Stephen and Anna presented themselves on the fourth day against William Gage concerning a plea of a third part of half an acre of land with appurtenances in Clopton, which third part they claim as the dower of Anna. William has not come, and [was] summoned etc. Judgement: the third part is to be taken into the hands of the lord king, and the day etc and he is summoned to be at (----ᵉ)[5] [the term] named before (*Chelmsford*).

> [1] There is a change of clerk and ink at this point.
> [2] See **28** as there the clerk has written Stephen's wife as *Alina*. Below in this same plea the clerk reverts to *Alina*. But in **319** and **1008** she is shown as Anna. I have assumed Anna in this translation.
> [3] The clerk wrote *Normannum fratrem* and there is nothing written after it. So, this could be 'Brother Norman' or 'Norman the brother [of *****]' I have decided on the former because there is no obvious space for something to be written in later or any attempt at interlining anything.
> [4] That is at Chelmsford on Monday 18 June.
> [5] There is something rubbed out after *ad*. It is impossible to see what it is, even under ultraviolet light.

635. (*Samford*) Agnes, who was the wife of William de *Bruniford*, claims against the prior of Leighs half a rood of land with appurtenances in *Brentewentham*[1] as her right, and in which the same prior does not have entry except by Ralph Gernun[2] to whom the said William, the former husband of the said Agnes, demised that [land] to him, whom she in his lifetime [could not contradict] etc.

The prior comes and vouches to warranty that Ralph. He is to have him at Chelmsford on the octave of Holy Trinity [Sunday 17 June] by aid of the court (*Chelmsford*).

The same [Agnes] claims against the same prior a third part of forty acres of land with appurtenances in *Berewhonc* as her dower, and in respect whereof she has nothing etc.

The prior comes by his attorney and says that he ought not to answer her on this writ, because he says she has been dowered in the same vill, and she cannot deny this. So she is in mercy[3] for a false claim, and she may proceed by a writ of right if she wishes. The prior [is] without day.

The same [Agnes] claims against William le Wentrer[4] eight acres of land with appurtenances in Wenham as her right and inheritance, and in which William does not have entry except by the said (P[e])[5] William de *Bruniford*, her former husband, who demised that [land] to him whom she in her lifetime etc.

William comes and denies such entry and says that he had entry by William his father to whom Geoffrey de Mandeville, the father of Agnes, gave that land by his charter which he proffers and which attests this.

Agnes says that after the said William, father of this William [le Wentrer], was enfeoffed by Geoffrey her father, the right of that land descended to a certain Ralph his first born son, [and] the brother of this William, as heir, who was in seisin until he lost that land through felony. As a result the land was the escheat of the said Geoffrey, who afterwards gave that [land] as the marriage portion to the said William, her husband, who demised that [land] to this William etc. And that it is so she puts herself on the country, and William similarly. So let there be a jury thereon.

The jurors, chosen by consent of the parties, come and say on their oath ... [unfinished]

[*chirograph* CP 25(1) 213/17/81][6]

1 I cannot find this place in Samford hundred or anywhere else. It might be just plain Wenham or Brantham. As there is another plea by the same woman for land in Wenham it is probably the former. In Samford there is a Great and Little Wenham. I think the likelihood is that it is Great Wenham which is nearer to East Bergholt.
2 This may be a relation to the patron of the priory of Leighs in Essex, who founded it *c.*1200.
3 There is no mention of the amercement in the margin – possibly because the plea is unfinished.
4 This might be *Ventura* or the Adventurer. See Reaney 1997, p.466.
5 Possibly the clerk was in a rut and he was going to write the 'prior' again when he realised his mistake.
6 Although some of this plea indicates it went to Chelmsford the chirograph indicates that the last part of this plea with William le Wentrer was completed at Cattishall. However there is no mention of it under the Cattishall pleas. It looks as though Agnes won as William acknowledged her right to the land. He received it back from her for a rent of 3s. a year payable at two terms on the feast of St Michael and at Easter. He is also to pay scutage when necessary and he also gave to Agnes 30s. sterling.

Membrane 24d

636. (*Ely*) Richard the son of Osbert and Anastasia his wife claim against the prior of Snape half of eighteen acres of land and eighteen acres of pasture with appurtenances in Aldeburgh as the dower of Anastasia.

The prior comes and says that he cannot answer her, because he only claims wardship in the said land, which he has through Philip of Eye. So the prior [is] without day.

PLEAS[1] AND ASSIZES OF THE TOWN OF IPSWICH[2]

[1]   There is a paragraph mark after the last plea and before this heading, possibly to indicate the end of a section from the start of the previous heading, or that a plea was intended for here but has either been missed or that no more pleas were found by the clerk to insert.

[2]   There has been some rubbing out under the heading. The only words decipherable are *vill* and *Gypewicy*. There may also be a section mark at the start of this, so it may have been the start of a plea and then rubbed out. The use of ultraviolet light throws no light on this.

637. (*one mark*) Matthew de Luveyn gives one mark for licence to agree with Adam the son of William concerning a plea of land. [*chirograph* CP 25(1) 213/17/124]

638. (*half a mark*) Alexander the son of William gives half a mark for licence to agree with Hugh of Langstone concerning a plea of covenant by the surety of the same Hugh. [*chirograph* CP 25(1) 213/16/73]

639. An assize comes to declare if John of St George unjustly etc disseised John Hane of his free tenement in the suburb of Ipswich after the first etc and in respect whereof he complains that he disseised him of two acres of land with appurtenances. John comes and says nothing to stay the assize.

The jurors say that he did not disseise him as the writ says, because he never had a free tenement there because he did not have [anything] except for a term. So it is adjudged that he is to take nothing by this assize and he is in mercy for a false claim by the surety … (*remand in custody, amercement*).

640. An assize comes to declare if Gilbert the prior of St Peter's[1] of Ipswich, Richard the dean of Coddenham, William Godescalc unjustly etc disseised Master Robert of Coddenham of his free tenement in Ipswich after the first etc.

The same assize comes to declare by the same if the prior of Holy Trinity[2] of Ipswich, Thomas the butler, Richard the seller and Seman le Lung unjustly etc disseised Robert of his free tenement in the same vill.

They all come and Master Robert came and withdrew [from the plea], so [he is] in mercy. The amercement is pardoned. For this etc the same Master Robert granted that all may always hold in peace whatsoever they hold, so that he will never be able to claim against them any messuage that his father gave to them.[3]

[1]   This was the Augustinian priory of St Peter and St Paul in Ipswich.

[2]   The priory of Augustinian canons founded in 1133 under a charter of Henry I.

[3]   This looks like a plea where Master Robert's father gave lands and messuage in Ipswich to the priories etc. and he is trying to get them back.

641.[1] An assize comes to declare if Robert Kinc, Gilbert Karila, Augustine Reading, John Erne, Hawise del Saler and Margery her sister unjustly etc disseised Geoffrey de *Teyden*[2] and Agatha his wife of their free tenement in Wix after the first etc and in respect whereof they claim that they disseised them of one acre of land.

They all come, except Robert Kinc, and they say nothing to stay the assize.

The jurors say that they did disseise them as the writ says. So it is adjudged that [they] have recovered their seisin and all [are] in mercy (*amercement*).

Damages: on Robert six shillings and on the others two shillings.

[1]   There is no paragraph mark for this plea but it is a totally different case from that which has gone before so it has been given a separate item number.

[2]   This might be Theydon in Ongar hundred in Essex.

642. An assize comes to declare if Robert Blundel unjustly etc disseised Stephen Sot and Matilda his wife, Richard the carter and Cecilia his wife of their free tenement in Ipswich after the first etc and in respect whereof they complain that he disseised them of one messuage.

Robert comes and says nothing to stay the assize.

The jurors say that he did not disseise them as the writ says. So it is adjudged that Robert may hold in peace, and that they are to take nothing by this assize and they are in mercy[1] for a false claim.

1 This is not shown in the margin.

643. An assize comes to declare if Peter le Muner unjustly etc raised [the level of] a certain pond in the suburb of Ipswich to the nuisance of the free tenements of John Prikehert and Rose Golhouck in the same vill after the first etc Peter comes and acknowledges that he unjustly raised [the level of the pond] etc. So it is adjudged that the nuisance be lowered by a view etc and Peter [is] in mercy. He has nothing.

644. An assize comes to declare if Robert the parson of the church of St Matthew of Ipswich unjustly etc disseised Roger Kepere[1] of his free tenement in the suburb of Ipswich after the first crossing etc.

Roger came and withdrew [from the plea]. So he and his sureties for prosecuting [are] in mercy, namely: William Margery of Ipswich and Roger the son of Ranulf (*amercements*).

1 This person may well have been employed at a keep, perhaps as a jailer. See Reaney 1997, p.261.

645. Benedict of Blakenham who brought a writ of entry against Robert of Blakenham for sixteen shillingsworth of rent with appurtenances in Ipswich has not prosecuted. So he and his sureties for prosecuting [are] in mercy, namely: Robert Cook of Ipswich and Thomas of Clavering (*amercements*).

646. Golder Hagen the son of Edmund and Bella his wife claim against Clement the son of Roger a third part of one messuage with appurtenances in Ipswich which they claim to be the right of Bella, and in which the same Clement has no entry except by the said Bella, who without the agreement and wish of the said Golder her husband [Clement], had demised that [messuage] to him.[2]

Golder and Bella come and do not wish to proceed. So they [are] in mercy. They are poor and they did not have sureties except faith. So nothing.

1 The clerk wrote *cui* after *viri sui* as though he wanted to write the stock phrase *cui in vita sua contradicere non potuit*, which would normally be used after her husband had died. In this case, however, her husband was very much alive.

647. (*half a mark*) Henry the son of Gilbert and Robert the son of Agnes of Clare give half a mark for licence to agree with Hugh the son of Hawe (Vilder[i]) concerning a plea of one messuage by the surety of Hugh.

648. (*half a mark*) Roger le Lung gives half a mark for licence to agree with Geoffrey of Langston concerning a plea of land by the surety of Geoffrey.

649. Louis de Giradville and Parnel his wife in whose place [an attorney comes] claim against Richard of Stonham half of eleven pence rent with appurtenances in Ipswich, and against Seyna the daughter of William half of two shillingsworth of rent with appurtenances in the same vill, and against Cecilia, who was the wife of Henry de la Grene, half of two shillingsworth of rent with appurtenances in the same vill, and against Godwin the merchant half of twenty penceworth of rent with appurtenances in the same vill, and against William Pygel half of eighteen penceworth of rent with appurtenances in the same vill, and against Edmund de Marisco half of four penceworth of rent with appurtenances in the same vill, and against William Spendeluve half of three shillingsworth of rent with appurtenances in the same vill, and against Andrew Piper half of five shillingsworth of rent with appurtenances in the same vill as the dower of Parnel etc and in respect whereof Thomas of Blakenham her first husband dowered her etc on a day when etc.

Richard and all the others come and say that she cannot have the dower because [neither] on the day the said Thomas espoused her nor ever after was he seised of the said rent, so that he could dower her. They then put themselves on the men of the town, and they similarly. So let there be a jury thereon.

The jurors say that the said Thomas was never seised of the said[1] rent, so that he could dower the said Parnel. So it is adjudged that the said may hold in peace and [Louis] and Parnel [are] in mercy. They are pardoned.

    [1]   The membrane is damaged at this point and it looks as though it has been torn off.

650.[1] (----[il]) John of St (----[il])[1]

    [1]   There is a gap of 3.6 cm between this scrap of a plea and the previous one. It is in the bottom right-hand corner of this side of the membrane.

Membrane 25

651. (*Ipswich*) The prior of Holy Trinity of Ipswich was summoned to answer Alice Biccernut concerning a plea that he warrant her one messuage with appurtenances in Ipswich that she [holds] from him etc and in respect whereof a charter [was made] etc and in respect whereof the same [Alice] complains that, whereas by her charter she holds the said messuage with appurtenances for twenty-eight pence per year for all service, the same prior unjustly,[1] against her charter, exacted payments of four shillings from her tenants, who hold messuages pertaining[2] to her messuage, whereof she has suffered damage etc.

The prior comes and readily acknowledges the charter and says that concerning the said messuage that she holds he demands nothing from it except the said twenty-eight pence, and that the tenants whom he distrained for the said four shillings she does not hold from it,[3] nor is [she] in seisin of the said messuages, which she says pertain to her messuage, in demesne nor in service, nor ever was. Because she does not hold the said messuages, which she says pertain to her messuage and she says in her writ that she does not hold[4] nor has another impleaded her, so it is adjudged that she is to take nothing by this writ and is in mercy for a false claim.[5] The amercement is pardoned for the Queen.[6]

    [1]   The clerk has erased and crossed out a word here; it is so illegible that it could not be determined. However, as it was crossed out it does not affect the plea.

    [2]   The clerk made a mistake here because this word qualifies the messuages and it was put in the singular instead of the plural form.

    [3]   That is Alice's chief messuage and the prior is also saying that she does not hold the tenants' messuages as subordinate to her chief messuage, which she holds from the prior. So the prior is saying she has no subordinate tenants who hold messuages that are subordinate to her messuage. This is the best interpretation that I can make from the text but it is by no means certain that this is a reasonable interpretation given the lack of suitable signposts by the clerk. I think what the clerk is also trying to convey here is that Alice has a charter which indicates that she has a messuage which she holds from the prior for 28d. a year but there is no mention in the charter of the other messuages which she claims to hold by virtue of her holding her current messuage. So the prior is claiming that she does not hold these messuages, nor have seisin etc of these messuages, nor ever had.

    [4]   It looks as though Alice has also not indicated in her writ of warranty any mention of these other

messuages that supposedly pertain to her messuage, so she loses her plea accordingly as a false claim.

5 This is a very confusing plea but this is the best translation that I can give, with this text. It is possible that the clerk has omitted some text or made some other errors, other than those noted, but I am unable to detect what they should be.

6 Eleanor of Provence and queen to Henry III.

652. Robert the son of Hervey and Richard his brother claim against William Ruter and Juliana his wife three acres of land with appurtenances in Wix, and against Alice the daughter of Juliana and Agatha her (sister[i])[1] three acres of land with appurtenances in the same vill, and against Saer'[2] Gall one acre of land with appurtenances in the same vill, and against Geoffrey Blundel one acre and one rood of land with appurtenances in the same vill, and against Siward the merchant three roods of land with appurtenances in the same vill as their right. Etc.

William and all the others come and William and Juliana vouch to warranty the said Alice and Agatha. Agatha is under age and she has claimed her age (*age*). She has [it]. Saer' and Geoffrey and Siward come and then claim a view. They are to have [it]. They are to come to Cattishall on Tuesday[3] (*Cattishall*).

1 The clerk had crossed out 'wife' here.
2 This name might be Sarah but in the Latin on the membrane it has masculine endings, so it is unclear what name should be put in here.
3 I assume this is the first Tuesday the court is held at Cattishall, that is Tuesday 22 May.

653.[1] (*Ipswich*) Nigel Erchenbaud claims against Ralph le Muner and Matilda his wife one messuage with appurtenances in Ipswich as his right etc.

Ralph and Matilda come and then vouch to warranty Wymund the son of Humphrey and William and Matthew his brothers, who are present. Matthew is under age and he has claimed age, and he has [it]. So the age is to be awaited (*age*).[2]

1 There is a gap of 12.3 cm between this plea and the previous one.
2 This is where the pleas taken at Ipswich end and following this plea is a section mark to suggest the end of this section. There follows a gap of 3.4 cm where the heading for the essoins from Cattishall starts.

Membrane 25 continued

ESSOINS[1] OF SICKNESS PREVENTING TRAVEL AT CATTISHALL ON THE NEAREST SUNDAY BEFORE THE ASCENSION OF THE LORD [20 MAY][2] BEFORE WILLIAM OF YORK PROVOST OF BEVERLEY AND HIS FELLOWS.

1 This is shown with a normal paragraph mark in the membrane.
2 It probably means that they took the essoins on Sunday 20 May which is the Sunday prior to the start of the session at Cattishall. See below at the start of membrane 26, where the pleas taken at Cattishall start.

654.[1] (*Norfolk*) Robert Blund against H[ugh de Vere] the earl of Oxford concerning a plea of land by William the son of Adam in the octave of the Trinity at the Chelmsford. He pledged his faith.

The same day is given to Ralph Blund whom the said Robert vouches to warranty. Note: that both are now essoined.

1 See **83**, which is the same as this essoin. Either they all essoined again at Cattishall or the clerk made a mistake and inserted the essoin twice.

655. (*Norfolk*) W.[1] The bishop of Norwich against Walter the son of Robert concerning a plea of an assize of mort d'ancestor by Andrew the summoner, on the quindene of Holy Trinity [Sunday 24 June] at Chelmsford by the surety of Roger of Boyland.

[1] This is William de Ralegh who was appointed bishop of Norwich in 1239 and translated to Winchester in 1244.

656. (*Suffolk*) Matthew de Luvayne against the abbot of Bury St Edmunds and others named in the writ of replevin by William Gernegan.

The same Matthew against Adam of Reading concerning a plea of mort d'ancestor by Gilbert the son of Osbert.

Muriel his wife against the same concerning the same by William the son of Richard.

657. John de Beauchamp against the prior of St Anthony[1] and others named in the writ concerning a plea of land by Walter de Wal.[2]

Nesta, his wife, against the same, concerning the same by Robert the son of Eustace. [**1046**]

[1] There are four possibilities. Two are in Cornwall: St Anthony-in-Meneage, and St Anthony in Roseland. The former is a Benedictine house and the latter a house of Augustinian canons. The third possibility is the priory of St Anthony of Vienne in France. It was one of the few institutions licensed to solicit alms throughout England. The fourth possibility is the priory of St Mary and St Anthony in Kersey in Cosford hundred. I suspect it is the latter considering the agreement in **1047** where the priory is described as the priory of St Anthony in Kersey.

[2] This is probably Wall. See Reaney 1997, p.473.

658. (*Suffolk*) Robert Darnel against Sarah Burnel concerning a plea of land by Gilbert the parker.

659. Gerard the constable against Martin the son of Simon and Barbot his wife concerning a plea of a fishpond in the octave of Holy Trinity[1] [Sunday 17 June].

1. This is actually at Chelmsford.

660. Richard Belensaunt against the same concerning a plea of land by William de Vastur.

661. William Marshall against the same concerning a plea of land by John of Tarring.

Membrane 25d

662. Thurston del Pont against the same concerning the same [plea] by Robert le Donerd.

663. Edrich de Bosco against the same concerning the same plea of land by Thomas the son of Edmund.

664. (*Norfolk*) Agnes the wife of William Cokerel against Matilda the daughter of Alice concerning a plea of land by Richard April etc.

665. William de Oddingseles[1] against Gerard his brother concerning a plea of land by Walter Ferling. [*chirograph* CP 25(1) 213/17/91.[2]]

[1] The Oddingswell family comes from the Solihull area and inherited the barony of Limesy, including lands in Bedingfield and Cavendish in Hoxne and Babergh hundreds respectively. The family may be Flemish from Oudinghesels.

[2] This was completed at Canterbury on Sunday 30 October 1240.

666. Alan of Heckingham against Hamo Chevere concerning a plea of covenant by John the son of Geoffrey. **[1091]**

667. Adam of Bedingfield against Gerard de Oddingseles concerning a plea of rent by William of Horning.

668. (*Southampton*)[1] Sampson de Puteo[2] of Southampton versus Eva de Clinton concerning a plea why she prosecuted by Ralph of Hampton. **[136, 669, 730]**

[1] This is shown as Hampshire and also Southamptonshire in the *Book of Fees* iii, pp.563 and 583.
[2] This probably translates as 'of the Well'.

669.[1] (*Southampton*) William Fottyn of the same against the same concerning the same by Henry Petit of Hampton.

[1] There is a line from the marginal note to the previous item, to indicate that the note covers both pleas.

670.[1] (*Suffolk*) Amabil of Narford versus Alice la Petite and Sarah her sister concerning a plea of land by Henry Hanboys.

[1] See **739** for the appointment of an attorney for Amabil. There she is shown as the wife of Peter of Narford who is essoining in **671**.

671.[1] (*Suffolk*) Peter of Narford against the same concerning the same by Alan the son of Robert of Stanningfield.

[1] There is a line drawn from the marginalia above to this plea.

672. (*Suffolk*) The abbot of Warden[1] against William of Wordwell concerning a plea of a fishpond[2] by John the son of Robert. [*chirograph* CP 25(1) 213/15/13][3]

[1] Warden (near Bedford) was a Cistercian abbey and hospital founded by Rievaulx and had a daughter house at Sibton. See **116**.
[2] Possibly taking fish from the pond or making a pond for the nuisance of his common fishery. See note below.
[3] Although there is a chirograph for this plea there is no plea itself in the roll. It is also shown in the chirograph as common fishery and not a fishpond.

673. Walter the son of Lettice against Arnulf the Fleming concerning a plea of land by William the son of William of Clare.

674.[1] (*It does not lie because John is under age*) (Thomas le Sauvage and Cecilia his wife against John de Murihaus and Katherine^c) his wife concerning a plea of covenant by Nicholas the son of Adam.

[1] The first line is largely crossed out. I have translated it because not all is crossed out for some reason.

Membrane 26

THE PLEAS AND ASSIZES TAKEN AT CATTISHALL ON THE NEXT MONDAY BEFORE THE ASCENSION OF THE LORD[1] IN THE TWENTY-FOURTH YEAR OF THE REIGN OF KING HENRY BEFORE WILLIAM OF YORK PROVOST OF BEVERLEY AND HIS FELLOWS.

¹ Monday 21 May. See Crook 1982a, p.101.

675.[1] Sarah of Hawkedon appoints Roger the son of William of Hawkedon as her attorney against the prior of Chipley[2] concerning a plea of land.

¹ Note that on this plea and **676** the writing is different from the rest of this side of the membrane and is written in different coloured ink. See **950** for the agreement.

² Chipley was an Augustinian priory near Stoke-by-Clare in Risbridge hundred, which appears to have only been founded around 1235, that is only five years prior to the eyre in Suffolk. It appears to have been a small priory and did not last to the Dissolution.

676.[1] Agnes the wife of John Ilger appoints John as her attorney against the same prior concerning a plea of land etc.

¹ See **950**. Although Agnes is not mentioned in the plea, she is included in the chirograph shown there.

677.[1] (*Babergh*) Robert of Layham, Adam of Eleigh,[2] John de Hodeboville and Gerbert of St Clare four knights, [selected to choose] the twelve [jurors] etc to make a recognition of the grand assize[3] between John of Gravely, plaintiff, and Flavian of Lawshall,[4] tenant, concerning eighteen acres of land with appurtenances in Lawshall,[5] and in respect whereof the same Flavian, who is the tenant, placed himself on the grand assize of the lord king, and seeks a recognition be made as to which of them has the greater right in that land, have come and chosen these: Richard Marshall, Stephen of Stratton, William del Auney, Adam of Welnetham, Robert de Wykes, Hugh of Polstead,[6] Gilbert of Walsham, John of Brantham, Richard de *Higkebache*,[7] William of Stuston, Richard of Glemham [and] Nicholas Peche.

(*Fifty shillings*) Afterwards, they have agreed. John of Gravely gives fifty shillings for licence to agree by the surety of Flavian de Rowenhoge and William the cook of Bury St Edmunds. [*chirograph* CP 25(1) 213/16/56]

¹ In this plea and in **679** the agreement is noted in a different hand, but the same hand in both cases, to that of the plea itself. It looks as though these were put in later by a different clerk.

² This might be Ilger or possibly Monks Eleigh in Babergh hundred. There is a reference to a John Ilger in Suffolk in the *Book of Fees*, p.78. Also, in the *Book of Fees*, pp.28, 43 and 68 there are references to Illegh.

³ It looks as though the case may have started earlier, possibly in the Norfolk eyre, as the text starts with the grand assize and not the beginning of the plea.

⁴ In the chirograph and in the agreement shown in the plea he is shown as Flavian de Rowenhoge.

⁵ The manor of Lawshall belonged to the abbey of Ramsey.

⁶ See **160** where Hugh is a defendant.

⁷ I can find no reference to such a place in Suffolk or elsewhere.

678.[1] (*Babergh, half a mark, half a mark*) The same four knights, summoned to choose the twelve etc to make a recognition of the grand assize between William the son of Ralph, plaintiff, and Adam the son of Godfrey le Gos, deforciant, concerning customs and services which the same William demands from the aforesaid Adam as regards to one messuage and three (and a half acres[i]) of land with appurtenances in Waldingfield. And in respect whereof the same Adam, who is the tenant, placed himself on the grand assize of the lord king, and he seeks a recognition whether he

137

owes to the said William concerning the said messuage and the said land eighteen pence per year only as he acknowledges to him or the same service, and besides three pence for the sheriff's aid and two ploughings, and the work of two men for one day in the harvest in return for food provided by William, as the same William demands from him. They [the four knights] have come and chosen these … [unfinished]

Afterwards, they have agreed, and William the son of Ralph gives half a mark for licence to agree by the surety of Henry de Linholt.

Adam le Gos gives half a mark for the same with the same by the surety of William.

[1]　There is a large gap of 5.2 cm between this plea and the previous one. It looks as though the clerk expected the previous plea to contain the result of the jury.

679.[1] (*Babergh*) The same four knights, summoned to choose the twelve etc to make a recognition of the grand assize between Thomas Bertel, plaintiff, and William the son of Walter, tenant, concerning thirty acres of land with appurtenances in Assington, and in respect whereof the same William who is the tenant places himself on the grand assize of the lord king, and seeks a recognition be made whether he has the greater right in the said land, or the said Thomas, have come and chosen these:[2] Giles of Wattisham, William de Hambli, Walter of Wissett, Richard Marshall,[3] Richard Applegard,[4] Gilbert of Walsham, Matthew of Mendham, John de Crawil, William de Alneto, Robert de Wykes, Adam de Wellbecham, Julian de la Hay, John of Gedding, John of Brantham [and] John de la Londe.

(*two marks*) Afterwards, they have agreed, and William gives two marks for licence to agree by the surety of Gilbert the son of Warren of Edwardstone and Robert the son of Geoffrey Polkat. [*chirograph* CP 25(1) 213/17/107][5]

[1]　There is a gap of 6.8 cm between this plea and the previous one.
[2]　The names following are written by a different clerk and in different ink.
[3]　This is probably the same Richard Marshall as in **677**.
[4]　See **1067** for this same knight and he is shown as Applegard.
[5]　This chirograph was made at Cattishall on the morrow of the Ascension, Friday 25 May.

680.[1] (*Blackbourn*) An assize comes to declare which patron in time of peace presented the last parson, who is dead, to the church of Barningham, which is vacant etc whose advowson Eustace of Barningham says pertains to him, which Walter the son of Robert withholds from him. He says in respect whereof that Adam of Barningham, his father whose heir he is, presented a certain William Gernun, who at his presentment was admitted and instituted in the same and died the last parson in the same.

Walter comes and says that the assize should not be taken on this because at another time, before Martin Pattishall[2] and his fellow itinerant [justices] at Cattishall, Robert the son of Walter, his father, brought an assize of darrein presentment against Adam of Barningham, the father of this (Eustace[i]), so that by that assize that presentment remained to the same Robert, so that he presented a certain Roger of Barningham who at his presentment etc. Afterwards, after the death of Roger, a dispute between the said Robert and this Eustace on the said presentment was moved before Thomas Heyden[3] and his fellow justices assigned for this, so that before them the assize of darrein presentment was taken and by that assize, as previously, that presentment similarly remained to the same Robert, but while the dispute was pending between them William Gernun was presented to the same church [and] who died as the last parson.

Eustace says that Humphrey, his grandfather, presented a certain Roger of Walsingham who at his presentation etc who in all of the time held that church, so that immediately after the death of Roger the same Adam presented the said William Gernun who at his presentment etc and who died last etc and then he puts himself on the assize.

Afterwards,[4] it was found by the court in the Rolls of the lord king that Robert the son of Walter presented Roger of Barningham, who died as last parson, whom at the presentation of the same Robert in the same church [was admitted], and that the same Robert in the court of the lord king recovered his seisin by the assize of darrein presentment taken before Martin [Pattishall by the father of the said][5] Robert, and the said Eustace. So it is adjudged that Walter is to recover his seisin to the presentment in that [church and Eustace is in mercy] by the surety ... [unfinished] (*amercement*)

<ol>
<li>There is a gap of 6.9 cm between this plea and the previous one.</li>
<li>This is Martin Pattishall who was one of the major judges in thirteenth-century England, much praised by *Bracton*. Pattishall's last circuit in Suffolk was in 1228 so Walter is saying that the case was sorted out then. The plea rolls for this Suffolk eyre still exist, JUST 1/819. See Crook 1982a, p.83.</li>
<li>A fellow justice of Martin Pattishall in Suffolk in 1228, but presumably this was at a different assize.</li>
<li>This paragraph appears to be written in a different hand and in different ink.</li>
<li>The membrane is damaged at this point but enough remains to deduce the text.</li>
</ol>

Membrane 26d

681. (*Blackbourn*) A jury comes to declare whether twelve acres of land with appurtenances in Assington are free alms pertaining to the church of Assington whereof Peter de Rivall is the parson, or the lay fee of William de Beaumont. He came and they have agreed by licence. The agreement is such that Peter grants to the said William the land to be held on payment of four shillings per year, where before he was accustomed to pay two shillings. For this etc the same William will give to the same Peter ten marks of which he will pay to him five marks at the Feast of St John the Baptist [24 June], and five marks at the Feast of St Nicholas [6 December] in the twenty-fourth year [of King Henry III]. If he does not do [this] he grants that he may be distrained [to do so] etc and concerning the cost etc.

682. (*Blackbourn*) An assize comes to declare if Richard the son of Gunnild unjustly etc disseised Richard le Cornur[1] of his free tenement in Boxford[2] after the first crossing etc and in respect whereof the same Richard complains that he disseised him of one rood of land with appurtenances in the same vill.

Richard comes and he says nothing to stay the assize.

The jurors say that he has not disseised him as the writ says. So it is adjudged that he is to take nothing by this assize and is in mercy for a false claim (*amercement*). He is remanded in custody.

<ol>
<li>He may be a hornblower according to Reaney 1997, p.110.</li>
<li>This is also in Babergh hundred in the thirteenth century, not Blackbourn. Later it was part in Babergh and part in Cosford hundred. The clerk is obviously having a blind spot between Babergh and Blackbourn hundreds. In the *Feudal Aids 1284–1431* v, p.43 it is shown as Boxford cum Grotene, which is only shown as Groton in *Domesday Book Suffolk*, Part One, section 4, no. 16.</li>
</ol>

683. (*Blackbourn*) Roger the son of Hermer who brought an assize of novel disseisin against Roger de Albo Monasterio[1] concerning the free tenement in Hartest has not

139

prosecuted. So he and his sureties for prosecuting [are] in mercy, namely: Roger the son of Henry of Boxted and Robert the gardener of Hartest (*amercements*). Sureties of Roger concerning the amercement [are]: Michael of Hartest and Ralph Volant of the same etc.

¹ This is possibly Whiteparish in Wiltshire. See *Feudal Aids 1284–1431* v, p.454.

684. (*Thedwestry, half a mark*) Thomas of Bradfield gives half a mark for licence to agree with William the son of Geoffrey concerning a plea of land by the surety of Robert his brother. [*chirograph* CP 25(1) 213/17/117]

685. (*half a mark*) Robert de Theye gives half a mark for licence to agree with John of Essex and Isabella his wife concerning a plea of land by the surety of Henry of Hempnall. The agreement is such that the same John and Isabella render to the said Robert and Omphale his wife and Matilda, the sister of Omphale, their reasonable part, which falls to them from the free tenement that was of Thomas the arblaster[1] on the day he was alive and dead in Clare and Chipley saving to the same John and Isabella the elder.

¹ A crossbowman or maker of crossbows.

686. (*Ely*) John of Essex and Isabella his wife, Omphale and Matilda, the sisters of Isabella, who brought an assize of novel disseisin against Walter de *Haffeud*[1] and others named in the writ, have not prosecuted. So they and their sureties for prosecuting [are] in mercy, namely: Richard Tripodas and William of Swineford[2] (*amercements*).

¹ I think this may be Hatfield. There is no such place in Suffolk, but there are three in Essex.
² There are a number of Swinefords according to *Feudal Aids 1284–1431* v, p.379, in Leicester, Staffordshire and Worcester, but none in Suffolk.

687. A day is given to Warren the son of Bartholomew, Walter the son of Bartholomew and William of Mettingham,[1] plaintiffs (Roger le Bigod, earl of Norfolk[i]), and Ralph le Bigod, deforciants, concerning a plea of fishery at Chelmsford on the quindene of Holy Trinity [Sunday 24 June] by prayer of the parties (*Chelmsford*). [*chirograph* CP 25(1) 213/16/71][2]

¹ The clerk has erased the name *Ralph*. Perhaps he was going to write Ralph le Bigod here.
² The agreement was actually made at Hertford where the judges went after Essex.

688. William Brun who brought an assize of novel disseisin against William Schanke concerning his free tenement in Bardwell has not prosecuted. So he and his sureties for prosecuting [are] in mercy, namely: Warren the son of William of Bardwell and Gilbert Thedred of the same (*amercements*).

689. (*Thedwestry*) William the son of Elias who brought an assize of novel disseisin against John de Prisseny and others concerning his free tenement in Stanningfield has not prosecuted. So he and his sureties for prosecuting [are] in mercy, namely Simon Lambert of Stanningfield and Adam Freman (*amercements*).

690. (*Blackbourn*) An assize comes to declare if Roger del Estur father of William del Estur was seised in [his] demesne etc of two messuages with appurtenances in Stoke [by Nayland] on that day on which he died, and if he died after the term and if etc which messuages Henry the chaplain of Stoke holds [and] who comes and says nothing to stay the assize.

The jurors say that the said Roger died seised of the said messuages as the writ says and that the said Roger died after the term, and that the said William is his

140

nearest heir. So it is adjudged that the said William has recovered his seisin and Henry [is] in mercy. It is pardoned.[1]

1   Poverty is the obvious reason, or possibly because he is a chaplain.

691. Gilbert the son of Thomas appoints Robert de Strete as his attorney against Walter of Shipmeadow concerning a plea of covenant. **[724]**

692. (*Blackbourn*) An assize comes to declare if Robert le Franceys unjustly etc disseised William the son of Baldwin of his free tenement in Worlington after the first crossing etc and in respect whereof he complains that he disseised him of thirty acres of land and one messuage with appurtenances in the same vill.

Robert comes and he says nothing to stay the assize.

The jurors say that the said Robert disseised him as the writ says. So it is adjudged that he has recovered his seisin against him, and Robert [is] in mercy for disseisin by the surety of Robert of Hastings (*good amercement*).

Damages: one mark.

693. (*Norfolk, half a mark*) Robert of Shelfhanger gives half a mark for licence to agree with Walter of Shelfhanger concerning a plea of land by the surety of Hubert of Semere. The agreement is such that Robert gives to Alice of Frostenden, the guardian of Walter, fifteen shillings. Alice warrants to the said Robert twelve acres of land with appurtenances in Shelfhanger which the same Walter claimed against him for six complete years from the feast of St Michael in the twenty-fourth year [of King Henry III].[1]

1   29 September 1240 and the term will end on 28 September 1246.

694. (*Norfolk*) Godfrey de Miliers claims against Thomas of Whimpwell[1] thirty acres of land with appurtenances in Happisburgh, and against Agatha the mother of the same Thomas fifteen acres of land with appurtenances in the same vill, and against Roger Bennet four acres of land with appurtenances in the same vill, and against Peter the son of Andrew one acre of land with appurtenances in the same vill as his right, which he claims pertain to his free tenement in the same vill and in Wymondham.

Thomas and all of the others come and then claim a view. They may have [it] and they may come on Wednesday (*on Wednesday*). Andrew is to pursue [the case] for Peter who is under age and he is to answer for him because he was enfeoffed under age.

1   The clerk wrote *Pympewell* but in **33** and **1029** he is known as Thomas of Whimpwell and he is shown as such in the chirograph in **937**.

695.[1] (*Blackbourn*) An assize comes to declare if Ralph de Cruce and Matilda his wife and Robert of Dunmow unjustly etc disseised Cecilia[2] de Cruce of her free tenement in [West] Stow after the first crossing etc in respect whereof she complains that they disseised her of two acres. Ralph and Matilda come and say that Matilda and Cecilia are sisters of one father and one mother, and Ralph and Matilda grant that of the fifteen acres of land with appurtenances in [West] Stow, which Thomas de Cruce, the father of Matilda and Cecilia, held, Cecilia is to have her reasonable part saving to the same Ralph and Matilda[3] the chief messuage. Cecilia is to answer to the same Ralph and Matilda concerning her part as to the chief lord.

1   There is a gap of 5.9 cm between this plea and the previous one.
2   From after this name to the end of this plea the writing is in a different hand and ink.
3   The clerk wrote *capl*. Could it be he started to write *capitali*, for 'chief', realised he had made

a mistake then forgot to cross it out? Also the hand and ink revert to that at the start of the plea from this point to the end of the plea.

696. Henry of Livermere who brought an assize of novel disseisin against Master Hamo de *Rodenhall* concerning a tenement in Livermere has not prosecuted. So he and his sureties for prosecuting [are] in mercy, namely: Ralph the son of Gilbert de Mara and William his brother (*amercement*). The surety of Henry concerning the amercement [is] Roger of Boyland.

Membrane 27

697.[1] (*Norfolk*) Hugh the son of Robert, John of Runham, Adam of Burlingham and Andrew of Shernborne, four knights sent to Joan, the wife of William Mauduyt, to see whom she wished to appoint in her place in the plea, which is between William and Joan, the plaintiffs, and Robert de Bosco, the tenant, concerning a tenement in Kirby, come and say that she appoints Roger de Cauz.

   [1]   This plea appears to be written in a different hand to the rest of this side of the membrane.

698. (*Babergh, amercement*) An assize comes to declare if Gilbert (the[i]) Serjeant, Henry de Curtes, Walter the son of Alexander and Hervey the son of John unjustly etc disseised Richard le Legristr' of his free tenement in Acton after the first etc and in respect whereof the same Richard complains that they disseised [him] of a certain ditch etc.

Gilbert and the others come and say nothing to stay the assize.

The jurors say that they have not disseised him because he is a villein and he has no free tenement. So it is adjudged that he is to take nothing by this assize. He is in mercy for a false claim. He is remanded in custody by the surety of Roger of Melford [Culing']]¹ and Hugh the son of Maurice of Melford.

   [1]   The clerk did write this but I suspect he may be referring to a *[Rogeri de] Culing* as well as a *Rogeri de Meleford*. However, *Roger de Culing* does not appear in the amercement section of this roll in **1652**. Cowlinge is in Risbridge hundred, which is next to Babergh hundred. No part of Long Melford itself contains a Cowlinge or Culing as far as can be discovered.

699. Ralph le Bigod appoints William of Raveningham or Thomas del Estre as his attorney against Hugh the son of Ralph and many others by many writs concerning a plea of fishery. [*chirograph* CP 25(1) 213/17/89]¹

   [1]   This chirograph is not shown in Crook 1982a, p.101. It was made at Canterbury. See note 3 in **908** for the problems surrounding these chirographs made at Canterbury.

700. (*Thedwestry*) Bartholomew Thormod who brought an assize of novel disseisin against Thomas Casse concerning a tenement in Rattlesden has not prosecuted. So he and his sureties for prosecuting [are] in mercy, namely: William the son of Osbert of Gedding and James Thomas¹ of the same (*amercements*).

   [1]   I suspect that the clerk has missed out *filius* because in **565** there is a James the son of Thomas of Gedding.

701. (*Thedwestry*) An assize comes to declare if Thomas the son of William unjustly etc disseised Thomas the son of William of his free tenement in Langham after the last return etc and in respect whereof he complains that he disseised him of twelve (penceworth[i]) of rent (etc[i]) with appurtenances in the same vill.

Thomas comes and says nothing to stay the assize.

The jurors say that the said Thomas the son of Master William has not disseised the said Thomas of the said rent. So it is adjudged that he is to take nothing by this assize and he is in mercy for a false claim (*amercement*). [*chirograph* CP 25(1) 213/15/14. and CP 25(1) 213/17/102 and CP 25(1) 213/15/9][1]

1 In these chirographs there is also a mention of 12 acres of land and 6d. rent in Pakenham as well as 6d. rent in Langham.

702. (*Blackbourn*) An assize comes to declare if Nicholas of Bury St Edmunds unjustly etc raised a certain ditch in Wyken[1] to the nuisance of the free tenement of Thomas de Wykes in the same vill after the first crossing etc.

Nicholas comes and says nothing to stay the assize.

The jurors say that he raised that ditch as the writ says. So it is adjudged that by a view of the recognitors that ditch is to be levelled, and Nicholas [is] in mercy (*amercement*).

Damages: one pence.

1 Wyken no longer exists as a vill, but there is a Wyken Hall.

703. (*Blackbourn*) An assize comes to declare if Walter the son of Bernard unjustly etc disseised Nicholas of Bury St Edmunds of his free tenement in Wyken after the first crossing etc.

Walter comes and says nothing to stay the assize.

The Jurors say that he disseised him as the writ says. So it is adjudged that he has recovered his seisin against him, and Walter [is] in mercy (*amercement*).

Damages: twenty shillings.

704. (*Thedwestry*) An assize comes to declare if Godman the son of Jordan, Roger le Suur[1] and Gilbert the son of Susanna unjustly etc disseised Nicholas the chaplain of his free tenement in Stanningfield after the first crossing etc and in respect whereof he complains they disseised him of three roods of land, half an acre of wood and one acre of pasture with appurtenances in the same vill.

Godman comes and the others have not come but he answered for them and he says nothing to stay the assize.

The jurors say that they have not disseised him as the writ says. So it is adjudged that he is to take nothing by this assize and he is in mercy for a false claim (*amercement*).

1 Reaney 1997, p.402 provides three possibilities of occupation: a shoemaker, an attendant at table, or a sewer/tailor.

705. (*Ely*) The prior of Ely appoints Brother William his monk, or Nicholas his clerk as his attorney against Walter de Haffeud and Matilda his wife concerning a plea of land, and against the abbot of Bury St Edmunds concerning a plea of liberties.

706. (*Babergh*)[1] Alice,[2] who was the wife of Richard Angot,[3] and Angod her [son or daughter][4] were summoned to answer Robert of Mendham concerning a plea that they render to him chattels to the value of twenty-nine shillings which they unjustly withhold from him.

Alice and Angod come, and Alice says that she has a husband without whom she cannot answer. Robert cannot deny this. Alice and Angod [are] without day and Robert [is] in mercy. He has nothing, so nothing.

1 The clerk put *Balberg*. This is the spelling of Babergh hundred in the hundred rolls. See Cam 1930, p.279.

2 I will call her Alice throughout the plea. In the second paragraph the clerk has written her name as *Avicia*.

3 This is probably Angood or Osgood. See Reaney 1997, p.332.

⁴ I do not know whether this person is a son or daughter. I suspect this is her son as I think Richard
    Angod is the same as Richard of Cornard in **907** and there is only one person in the roll with a
    first name of Angod with a father called Richard.

707. (*amercements*) William the son of Anselm who brought an assize of novel
disseisin against Thomas the son of Master William of Pakenham¹ of his free tenement in Pakenham has not prosecuted. So he and his sureties [are] in mercy, namely:
Thomas the son of William of Pakenham and John the son of Ralph of Whatfield.

¹ Thomas the son of Master William of Pakenham failed to sue again in **967**. He comes from
    Pakenham in Thedwestry hundred. He is also shown in the amercement section of this roll in
    1652.

708. (*five marks, Norfolk*) Brian the son of Alan gives five marks for licence to agree
with Warren de Montchensy concerning a plea of land, whereupon a trial by battle,
by the surety of Robert de Curton.

709. (*Blackbourn*)¹ An assize comes to declare if Robert the bailiff of the Thedwestry
hundred unjustly etc disseised Amice de *Horsec* of her free tenement in Timworth
after the first crossing etc and in respect whereof she complains that he disseised her
of a certain mill and one messuage with appurtenances in the same vill.
    Robert comes and says nothing to stay the assize.
    The jurors say that he has not disseised her as the writ says. So it is adjudged that
she is to take nothing by this assize and is in mercy. It is pardoned.

¹ I think the clerk has this wrong: it should be Thedwestry hundred as Timworth was in Thedwestry
    hundred.

710. Henry of St Albans claims against Hamo Passelewe nine marks which he owes
to him etc. Hamo comes and acknowledges that he owes to him nine marks, and he
paid him three marks. Concerning the residue of six marks, he will pay to him three
marks at the feast of St Michael [29 September], and three marks at Christmas. If
he does not do [this] he grants etc while etc and concerning the cost etc.

711. An assize comes to declare if Alexander the son of William (the palmerⁱ)
unjustly etc disseised Robert of Waldingfield of his free tenement in Waldingfield¹
after the first crossing etc and in respect whereof he complains that he disseised him
of a certain quickset hedge.
    Alexander the son of William the palmer comes and says nothing to stay the
assize.
    The jurors say that he disseised him as the writ says. So it is adjudged that he
has recovered his seisin against him, and Alexander [is] in mercy for disseisin, by
the surety of Roger de Ponte of Waldingfield and Gilbert Childer (*amercements*).
    Damages: two pence.

¹ This is either Great or Little Waldingfield in Babergh hundred.

712. (*Norfolk, six marks*) Warren Sax made a fine for many trespasses of six marks,
by the surety of Adam de Kaly, John de Helgeton and Robert del Hill of Thetford.

713.¹ Agnes the wife of John Hereman and Alice her sister appoint as their attorney
this John against Thomas de Gelham and Beatrice his wife concerning a plea of *de
fine facto*.

¹ This plea and the next start in the margin because there is a large torn off piece in the membrane
    and the clerk has obviously worked around it.

714. Louis de Gerardville and Parnel his wife appoint as their attorney Simon the son of Robert or Matthew of Wickham[1] [Market] against Henry de Capella concerning a plea of waste.

> [1] This is probably Wickham Market in Wilford hundred, but it could be any of the other Wickhams in England. One other possibility is Winchester. See **764**.

Membrane 27d

715. (*Thingoe*) An assize comes to declare if Thomas the son of John de Hemmegrave,[1] Adam Gulberd and Walter of Flempton unjustly etc disseised Peter de Grenville and Isabella of Saxham of their free tenement in Saxham after the first crossing etc and in respect whereof they complain that they disseised them of ten acres of land with appurtenances and a certain meadow.

Thomas and the others come and say nothing to stay the assize.

The jurors say that they have not disseised them as the writ says. So it is adjudged that they are to take nothing by this assize and are in mercy for a false claim, by the surety of Walter of Hepworth (*amercements*).

> [1] The Hemmegrave family in Thingoe hundred is shown as the main landowner in Hengrave and Flempton in *Feudal Aids 1284–1431* v, p.44.

716. (*Stow*) A jury comes to declare whether two acres of land with appurtenances in Buxhall are free alms pertaining to the church of William the parson of Buxhall, or the lay fee of Ranulf the Fleming. He comes and vouches to warranty William the Fleming, who is present, and he warrants him, and says nothing to stay the jury. Afterwards, he comes and he cannot deny that it is indeed the free alms of the said church and he renders [it] to him, and he is in mercy for an unjust detention (*amercement*). He [William the parson] is to have his seisin, and he [William the Fleming] will make an exchange to the value, and he made a fine for half a mark (*half a mark*).

717. (*Norfolk*) A day is given to Robert de Curton the plaintiff, whom Simon of Whatfield vouched to warranty at Chelmsford in the octave of Holy Trinity [Sunday 17 June] by prayer of the parties (*Chelmsford*). The same day is given to Margery de Rivers, by Adam Woodcock her attorney, whom the same Simon vouched to warranty by a writ of the lord king.

718. (*Blackbourn*) A jury comes to declare whether twenty-four acres of land with appurtenances in Langham are the free alms pertaining to the church of John the parson of Langham, or the lay fee of William Gilbert and Joan his daughter. They came and have agreed. John gives half a mark for licence to agree by the surety of William (*half a mark*). William gives half a mark by the surety of the same John (*half a mark*). The agreement is such that, concerning the same land, the same William gives to the same John six sown acres of land saving to the same William the crop of three acres. For this [concession] etc the same John remises to the same William all right and claim that he has or that he could have in all the remaining [land] etc.

719. (*Stow*) Master William of Beccles acknowledges that he holds half an acre in Finborough[1] [from Robert][2] de Mucegros[3] for twelve pence per year, namely: six pence at Easter and six pence at the feast of St Michael [29 September].

> [1] There is a Little and a Great Finborough in Stow hundred.
> [2] See the next two pleas.

3   The de Mucegros or Musgroves originally came from Mussegros in Normandy and subsequently
     held lands in Charlton Musgrove in Somerset and Boddington in Gloucester, as well as Great
     Finborough. This information was provided by Edward Martin of the Suffolk County Archaeo-
     logical Service.

720. Robert de Alneto was summoned to answer the same Robert [de Mucegros] concerning the plea that he do to him the customs and rightful services which he should do to him for his free tenement that he holds from him in Finborough. He says in respect whereof that whereas he holds from him eleven acres of land with appurtenances in Finborough for four shillings per year, the same Robert has already kept back from him two shillings for three years, namely in each separate year [two shillings]: whereupon he has suffered and has damage to the value etc.

Robert comes and he says that he holds nothing from him nor claims to hold anything from him. On this Robert de Mucegros came by his attorney and he claimed licence to withdraw from his writ, and he has [it].

721. Ranulf the Fleming acknowledges that he holds from the said Robert [de Muce-gros] ten acres of land with appurtenances in Finborough for three shillings per year, in respect whereof he will pay to him eighteen pence at Easter, and eighteen pence at the feast of St Michael [29 September]. He grants that if anything is in arrears of the said service that he will freely render [it] back to him.

722. (*Hartismere*) An assize comes to declare if the abbot of Bury St Edmunds unjustly etc disseised William de Stanilaund of his free tenement in Wortham after the first crossing etc and in respect whereof the same William complains that he disseised him of thirty acres of land (and one messuage[i]) with appurtenances in the same vill.

The abbot comes and says nothing to stay the assize. Adam of Gravely one of the recognitors has not come, so [he is] in mercy (*amercement*).

The jurors say that the abbot has not disseised him of any free tenement because he has no free tenement because he is a villein. So it is adjudged that he is to take nothing by this assize and he is in mercy for a false claim (*amercement*). The abbot [is] without day. The amercement is pardoned.

723. (*Blackbourn*) Martin the son of Simon and Barbot his wife claim against Walter the Constable[1] six acres of land with appurtenances in Stoke[2] [by Nayland], and against William the constable one fishpond and nine acres of land with appurtenances in the same vill, as the right of Barbot, and in which etc.

Both [defendants] come and vouch to warranty Gerard the constable. They are to have him by aid of the court in the octave of Holy Trinity [Sunday 17 June] at Chelmsford (*Chelmsford*).

1   Constables could hold office in a castle, borough, hundred, shire or village. The most likely is the
     village in these cases.
2   This is probably Stoke by Nayland in Babergh hundred; or possibly Stoke Ash in Hartismere
     hundred or Stoke-by-Clare in Risbridge hundred. I have not found a Stoke or Stokes in Black-
     bourn hundred. As the clerk mixes up Blackbourn and Babergh hundreds I have assumed that it
     is Stoke-by-Nayland in Babergh hundred.

724. (*one mark*) Walter of Shipmeadow gives one mark for licence to agree with Gilbert the son of Thomas concerning a plea of land by the surety of William the son of Ralph of Hackford. **[691]** [*chirograph* CP 25(1) 213/15/18]

725. (*Essex*) Nicholas the son of Thomas the constable claims his land on the eve of the Ascension of the lord [Wednesday 23 May], by a replevin, which was taken into the hands of the lord king (for default[i]), which he made against Alice who was the wife of Alan Gundwy, and he has [it].

726. (----[e, il]) (----d ----s ----[e, il])[1]

>   [1] There is a plea here that has been rubbed out by the clerk. It is totally indecipherable, even under ultraviolet light.

727.[1] (*Norfolk*) Geoffrey de Say and Alina (his wife[i]), by the attorney of Alina, claim against Simon Peche and Agnes his wife seventy-two shillings and six penceworth of rent with appurtenances in Cringleford, and against William Mauclerc ten acres of land with appurtenances in the same vill, and against [William] Stute twelve acres of land with appurtenances in the same vill, and against the abbot of Langley nine acres of land in the same vill[2] as her dower etc.

Simon and all the others come and then claim a view. (Let them have it[i]). A day is given to them at Cattishall on the nearest Monday before the Lord's Ascension.[3] Afterwards, Simon and all the others came and Simon and Agnes then vouch to warranty Alexander de Vallibus, who is present, and he warrants them, and then he vouches to warranty Thomas the son of Thomas of Moulton and Matilda his wife. William Mauclerc and William[4] Stute then vouch to warranty the said Thomas and Matilda. The abbot (of Langley[i]) concerning six acres[5] then vouches to warranty Henry of Barford, who is to come on Tuesday.[6] Concerning the [other] three acres he vouches to warranty the said Thomas and Matilda. Thomas is present and says that he cannot answer without the said Matilda, nor furthermore was she summoned to warrant. So it is said [to him] that he is to be at Chelmsford in the octave of Holy Trinity [Sunday 17 June] and he is to have the said Matilda there to warrant (*Chelmsford*). The same day is given to Geoffrey and Alina and all the others. The abbot appoints Brother Stephen of Ashby,[7] his monk, as his attorney, and Alexander de Vallibus appoints Robert of Bungay as his attorney.

>   [1] See **63** for Thomas Stute, and **153** and **475** for those named in the first paragraph of this plea. They must all be connected with this plea although the abbot is in **153** only and has claimed a view. The first paragraph has been written by a different hand and in different ink.
>   [2] In **153** it mentions Rockland as the vill where Geoffrey and Alina claim the land, unless it is a separate claim.
>   [3] Monday 21 May. This is odd as according to Crook 1982a, p.101 the eyre started at Cattishall on Monday 21 May. I presume the clerk is indicating the details from the day given to them at Ipswich.
>   [4] The clerk wrote *Thomas*. This should be William Stute rather than Thomas, unless the other clerk wrote the wrong name by mistake earlier in the plea. There is a Thomas Stute mentioned in essoin **63** against the two plaintiffs, but **475** definitely mentions William as the defendant for the 12 acres of land in dispute.
>   [5] Out of the nine acres.
>   [6] Presumably Tuesday 22 May.
>   [7] This is either Ashby in Lothingland hundred or more likely one of the three Ashbys in Norfolk, probably the one in Loddon hundred, Ashby St Mary, which is in the hundred where the abbey is located.

728.[1] Richard the barber appoints Basilia his wife as his attorney against Robert Bulsi and others named in the writ concerning a plea of land.

>   [1] There looks as though there is a licence to agree erased in the middle of this gap of 6.5 cm. Ultraviolet light indicates a few words only. This appointment of an attorney is tucked in the right-hand corner of this side of the membrane after the large torn-off portion taken out of the membrane, and also after a gap of 6.8 cm from the previous plea.

Membrane 28

729. (*Blackbourn*) An assize comes to declare if Basilia de Oddinges',[1] the mother of Gerard de Oddinges',[2] was seised in her demesne etc of one messuage and twenty acres of land in *Havendis*,[3] and if etc which land the prior of Hertford[4] holds. He came and they have agreed. (*one mark*) Gerard gives one mark for licence to agree by the surety of Richard Makerell. The agreement is such that the prior renders all to him. So he is to have his seisin.

1. This is almost certainly Oddingseles. See **665**.
2. See **66** for Gerard's essoin.
3. This might be Cavendish in Babergh hundred. I cannot find such a place in Blackbourn hundred.
4. This is the priory of Benedictines at Hertford.

730. (*Southampton*) Eva de Clinton presented herself on the fourth day against Stephen the sacristan of Southampton concerning a plea why he prosecuted a plea in Court Christian for chattels [which do not relate to a will or a marriage] etc against [the king's] prohibition etc and against the Dean of Southampton why he held the same plea etc, against the prohibition etc. They have not come etc and they have defaulted many times, so that the sheriff was ordered that he should place them on better sureties [and] that they be [here] on this day. The sheriff reports that they have no lay fee and that he cannot distrain them etc. Because it has been attested that the Dean has five messuages in the town of Southampton, and Stephen a lay fee, the sheriff was ordered that he does not omit, on account of the liberty of the town of Southampton, but that he takes into the hands of the lord king all lands, messuage and tenements, so that they are not to lay a hand [on them], and that he is to have their bodies before the justices (at Chelmsford[i]) in the octave of Holy Trinity [Sunday 17 June] to answer [to the pleas] and to hear their judgement concerning the many defaults. [**136, 668, 669**]

731. (*Cosford*) An assize comes to declare if Ailbreda of Whatfield the mother of John the son of Ralph was seised in her demesne etc of six and a half acres of land with appurtenances in Whatfield on the day she died, and if she died after the term etc and if etc which land Simon of Whatfield holds. He comes and says nothing why he ought not to have his seisin. So he is to have his seisin, and Simon [is] in mercy for an unjust detention (*amercement*). [*chirograph* CP 25(1) 213/17/122][1]

1. The agreement was made at Westminster in front of William of York and Henry of Bath on the octave of St Martin, that is probably 19 November 1240. In this chirograph there is no mention of Ailbreda, but there is a mention of Nicholas their brother who appears to be the chief lord of the land and in effect Simon recovers his seisin for a payment of 20s.

732. (*half a mark*) Robert Mauduyt gives half a mark for licence to agree with Gerard de Oddingesel' concerning a plea of customs and services by the surety of Gerard. The agreement is such that the said Robert and Margery his wife acknowledge that they hold from the said Gerard one carucate of land with appurtenances in Cavendish by the service of a tenth part of one knight's fee. [**68**]

733. (*Blackbourn*) An assize comes to declare if Richard the son of Ralph, brother of Constance was seised in his demesne etc of one acre of land with appurtenances in Boxted[1] on the day that he died, and if he died after the term etc and if etc which land Roger the son of Henry holds. He comes and says nothing to stay the assize. The jurors say that the said Richard died in seisin, but after the death of this Richard a certain Roger, his brother, who held that land, sold it to a certain William who holds that [land], and they say that this Roger does not hold that [land]. So it is adjudged that she is to take nothing by this assize and she is in mercy for a false claim. It is pardoned because [she is] poor.

> 1   Boxted is in Babergh hundred, not Blackbourn hundred as the marginal note suggests.

734. (*half a mark*) Gerard de Oddingesel' gives half a mark for licence to agree with Thomas the son of Geoffrey of Cavendish. The agreement is such that the same Thomas remises to him two acres of land and one acre of meadow, which he claimed against him, and he has returned them to him.

735. (*Babergh*) An assize comes to declare if John de Beauchamp and Richard the miller unjustly etc disseised Lucy the wife of Thomas Crowe of her free tenement in Cornard after the first crossing etc. Afterwards, Thomas came and withdrew [from the plea].[1] So she and her sureties for prosecuting [are] in mercy, namely: John the son of John of Cornard and Alexander the son of Robert of Sutton (*amercement*). The surety of Thomas concerning the amercement [is] Andrew the son of William of Assington.

> 1   It looks as though Thomas stepped in to withdraw his wife from the plea after the action had started. However, it is also possible that Thomas and Lucy started the action but it was for Lucy's land, possibly her *maritagium*, but he had the right to withdraw from the case and his wife could do nothing about it.

736. (*Blackbourn*) An assize comes to declare if Peter Ferling unjustly etc disseised Walter Ferling of his free tenement in Boxted after the first crossing etc and in respect whereof he complains that he disseised him of three acres of land with appurtenances in the same vill.

Peter comes and he says that a certain Roger, their brother, was enfeoffed of the said land and he died seised without an heir of his [body]. Because he died thus seised without an heir, Peter the son and heir of this Peter put himself into that land as his heir, so that the said Walter has [no][1] seisin of the said land. So it is adjudged that Walter is to take nothing by this assize and he is in mercy for a false claim. It is pardoned because [he is] poor.

> 1   The clerk has missed out the *non* if the amercement is to make any sense.

737. (*Blackbourn*) An assize comes to declare if Loretta the daughter of William mother of Robert the English was seised in her demesne etc of five acres of land with appurtenances in Great Waldingfield on the day that she died, and if she died after the term etc and if etc which land Henry the son of Walter holds. He comes and then vouches to warranty William his brother who is present and he says nothing to stay the assize.

The jurors say that ... [unfinished]

(*half a mark*) Afterwards, they have agreed. Robert gives half a mark for licence to agree by the surety of Robert the son of Martin.

738. (*Risbridge*) An assize comes to declare if Walter the palmer the father of Ranulf was seised in his demesne etc of one messuage and eight acres of land with appurtenances in Haverhill on the day that he died etc and if etc and if etc in respect whereof Alice de Heliun holds one messuage and four acres of land, Geoffrey de Capella three acres [and] Ediwa de Cornhill one acre of land. They come and Alice and Geoffrey then vouch to warranty Andrew de Heliun. They are to have him at Chelmsford in the octave of Holy Trinity [Sunday 17 June] by the aid of the court (*Chelmsford*). Ediwa acknowledges herself to be the villein of the said Andrew. So

Ranulf [is] in mercy, and she [is] without day. The amercement is pardoned because [he is] poor. Alice appoints Richard Hikelingham as her attorney. [*chirograph* CP 25(1) 213/16/58][1]

> [1] This agreement made in Essex shows 'Randulf the son of Walter' but Alice and Geoffrey are mentioned as the original defendants. It also indicates that Andrew was the vouchee. However, the amount of land and the messuage in Haverhill are shown as the same as this plea. I think the clerk has probably made a mistake here as to the name of the plaintiff. Also see *Cal. Feet of Fines, Suff.* p.43, no. 89 which has named the plaintiff as 'David the son of Walter', but I think that it is mistaken.

739. Amabil who was the wife of Peter of Narford appoints her son Peter as her attorney against Alice the daughter of William le Petit and Sarah her sister concerning a plea of land.

Membrane 28d

740. (*Lackford*) Henry of Brandon acknowledges that he has attorned Stephen Alex[ander] of Brandon to the abbot of Warden[1] to pay to him [the abbot] five shillings per year when previously they were paying to the same Henry the said five shillings. So it said to the same Stephen that he is to answer to the same abbot henceforth.

> [1] See **672**.

741. (*Blackbourn*) An assize comes to declare if Robert of Shelton, Roger, the reeve of Richard de Harencurt, Martin Albot, Martin Aylward, Adam de Cuku,[1] Gilbert the carpenter, Geoffrey Brill, Adam Brune and Roger de Bosco unjustly etc disseised Walter Drageswerd[2] and Christine his wife of their free tenement in Eleigh after the first crossing etc and in respect whereof they complain that they disseised them of one acre of land with appurtenances in the same vill.

Robert and the others have not come, but the bailiff of Robert comes and says nothing to stay the assize. All the said were attached by Hugh le Caliere,[3] John Woodcock, Walter the Franklin,[4] Martin de Brook, Robert Smith, John Aylward and Adam the son of David, so all [are] in mercy (*amercements*).

The jurors say that they have not disseised them because the said Christine is a villein, and she has no free tenement. So it is adjudged that they are to take nothing by this assize and they are in mercy for a false claim. They are pardoned because [they are] poor.

> [1] Cuckoo apparently. See Reaney 1997, p.120.
> [2] This name is probably Drawsword. See Reaney 1997, p.141.
> [3] Probably Callier, so he was probably a maker of cauls or coifs for the head. See Reaney 1997, p.81.
> [4] A freeman who held land.

742. (*Blackbourn*) An assize comes to declare if Alexander the son of William was seised in his demesne etc of one messuage and fifteen acres of land and one acre of meadow and forty penceworth of rent with appurtenances in [Long] Melford on the day that he died etc and if he died etc and if etc which messuage, land, meadow [and] rent William de Wyndebok and several others named in the writ hold. They come and seek a judgement if they ought to answer to this writ, inasmuch as they are not joint holders, and have not been named in his writ as to what or how much each one holds, nor also does he know to say. So it is adjudged that he is to take nothing by this assize and he is in mercy for a false claim (*remand in custody, amercement*).

743. (*Blackbourn*) An assize comes to declare if Gilbert the son of Wymund the father of Benedict was seised etc of half an acre of land with appurtenances in Edwardstone on the day that etc and if he died after the latest etc and if etc which land Robert Christmas holds. He comes and by licence they are agreed. The agreement is such that the land is to be divided between them, so that Robert has one rood, which was behind his court.[1] Benedict will have that rood, which is situated next to the king's highway.

> 1 The clerk wrote *cur'*, which I have expanded to *curia*, court. Court in this context is understood to mean his house and any surrounding buildings.

744. (*Thedwestry*) An assize comes to declare if Roger the son of Froda, the father of Alice, the wife of John of Pakenham, and Imenye, the wife of Hugh of Pakenham, was seised in his demesne etc of three acres of land (and one rood of meadow[i]) with appurtenances in Pakenham on the day etc and if etc which land James of Pakenham holds. He came and they have agreed by licence. The agreement is such that they remit [their claim] for one mark.

745. (*five marks*) Richard the bishop of Rochester gives five marks for licence to agree with the abbot of Bury St Edmunds concerning a plea *de fine facto*. [**199, 1117**]

746. (*half a mark*) Geoffrey the son of Ralph gives half a mark for licence to agree with Adam the son of William of Polstead concerning a plea of an assize of mort d'ancestor by the surety of the same Adam. The agreement is such that Adam renders to him six acres, which he claimed against him for one mark.

747. (*Blackbourn*) An assize comes to declare if William Ingenulf unjustly etc disseised Robert of Sudbury of his free tenement in Waldingfield after the first crossing etc and in respect whereof the same Robert complains that he disseised him of half an acre of land with appurtenances in the same vill.

William comes and says nothing to stay the assize.

The jurors say that he has not disseised him as the writ says. So it is adjudged that Robert is to take nothing by this assize and he is in mercy for a false claim. The amercement is pardoned.

748. (*half a mark*) Gilbert the miller gives half a mark for licence to agree with Gerard de Oddinges'[1] concerning a plea of customs and services by the surety of the same Gerard.

> 1 This is Oddingseles in **665**. Also, see his essoin for this plea in **66**.

749. (*Babergh*) An assize comes to declare if Katelina the daughter of Gilbert of Kelsale, sister of John, was seised in her demesne as of fee of one messuage and thirty acres of land with appurtenances in Newton on the day she died and if she died after the last etc and if etc that messuage and which land William of Newton holds. He comes and he renders [it] to him. He is to have his seisin and he [William of Newton] is in mercy for an unjust detention, by the surety of John of Kelsale (*amercement*).

750. The same John claims against Matthew of Sudbury three acres of land with appurtenances in the same vill by the same assize. He comes and by licence renders [it] to him. He is to have his seisin, and Matthew [is] in mercy for an unjust detention (*amercement*). He is remanded in custody.

751.[1] (*Blackbourn*) An assize comes to declare if Geoffrey of Thorpe and Peter of Beccles unjustly etc disseised John the chaplain of his free tenement in [Ixworth] Thorpe after the first crossing etc and in respect whereof he complains that they disseised him of forty acres of land and twenty-three acres of meadow and a third part of one mill. Geoffrey comes and he says nothing to stay the assize. Peter has not come nor was he attached.

The jurors say that they have not disseised him as the writ says. So it is adjudged that he is to take nothing by this assize and he is in mercy for a false claim. The amercement is pardoned.

[1]   There is a paragraph mark after this plea but nothing written.

Membrane 29[1]

[1]   There is a flaw in the membrane at the top so that the clerk has worked around it. There is also a great bite out of the membrane at the bottom, which the clerk has again worked around.

752. (*Essex*) Matthew of Peyton and Rose his wife claim against Henry de Merk a third part of two carucates of land with appurtenances in Bardfield[1] as the dower of Rose, and in respect whereof Henry de Merk her first husband dowered her at the [church] door etc on the day etc and then she produces suit.

Henry comes and he has nothing to say why she should not have her dower. So it is adjudged that she has recovered her seisin. She is to have her seisin and Henry [is] in mercy. (*half a mark*) He made a fine for half a mark, by the surety of Robert the son of Alexander de Theye.

[1]   This is either Great or Little Bardfield in Freshwell hundred in Essex.

753. (*Babergh, ten shillings*) John the parson of Shimpling gives ten shillings for licence to agree with Robert of Henham concerning a plea of an assize of mort d'ancestor, by the surety of Benedict of Shimpling. The agreement is such that Robert remises to the same John and his church all right and claim that he had in the said nine acres of land with appurtenances in the same vill, and for this [concession] etc the same John gives to the same Robert three acres of land from the land of the church.

754.[1] (*Cosford, four marks*) Roger de Bavent gives four marks for licence to agree with John de Say concerning a plea of an assize of mort d'ancestor, by the surety of Adam of Eleigh and Simon of Whatfield. [*chirograph* CP 25(1) 283/11/156]

[1]   A paragraph mark follows this plea, but no plea shown.

755.[1] (*Norfolk*) Roger de Mortimer claims against Hugh de Albanico[2] one messuage and one carucate of land with appurtenances except for eight acres of land in Wymondham as his right, and in respect whereof a certain Richard, his father, was seised in his demesne as of fee and right, in the time of King Henry grandfather of the lord king who now is,[3] by taking profits therefrom to the value of half a mark in time of peace. From the same Richard the right to that land descended to a certain Robert as the son and heir, and from the same Robert, who died without an heir from him, the right of that land descended to a certain William as brother and heir, and from the same William to this Roger who now claims as brother and heir, and that such is his right he offers to prove by the body of a certain free man of his, John Punchard, as according to the direction of his father,[4] and if, as regards him, [he shall fall ill] etc by another[5] etc

Hugh comes and denies his right, now and elsewhere, and the seisin of the said

Richard and everything etc He offers to deny [this] by the body of a certain free man of his, Adam the son of William (who is prepared for this etc[i]) and if, as regards him, [he shall fall ill] by another etc.[6] So it is adjudged that there be a trial by battle between them, and that Adam would give pledges for denying, and John would give pledges for proving (*trial by battle*). The sureties of Adam [are]: Thomas of Ingold-isthorpe[7] and Ralph de Waung. The sureties of John [are]: John de Hodeboville and Matthew de Manling.

A day[8] is given to them at Chelmsford on the morrow of the octave of Holy Trinity [Monday 18 June] and then let them come armed.

1   There is a gap of 2.4 cm. See the essoin at **30**.
2   As is shown in the essoin **30**, he is the earl of Arundel. Hugh died *c*.1243. The family is often known as d'Albini or d'Aubigny.
3   That is King Henry II.
4   I cannot explain why the clerk has used the phrase *ut de precepto patris sui* here as it literally translates into 'as according to the order of his father'. However, it is possible that his father gave this direction on his death bed. Richard was the father of Roger de Mortimer and Roger must have been the youngest son, and brother of the other two mentioned in the plea, and what this phrase may be trying to indicate is that Roger is aiming to fight the duel for his right to inherit according to the order of the inheritance outlined by him above and which Hugh is contesting.
5   The phrase *et si de ipso per alium* appears to be part of a formulaic phrase that the clerk has shortened. What it covers is the possibility that the champion may fall ill before the duel takes place and therefore his place can be taken by another. See *Lincs, Worcs Eyre*, pp.306–308, plea 643 for an example of this phrasing, with the addition of *male contigerit etc*. Also in *Glanvill*, p.23, where he covers trial by battle and the readiness to prove the matter by means of a named champion, there is another variant of this phrase, which is *et si quid de eo male contigerit per illum vel illum tertium etc*.
6   Again this is the formula in case a champion should fall sick.
7   This place is in Smethdon hundred in Norfolk. The chief lord was the countess of Arundel according to the hundred rolls.
8   There is a gap of 5.3 cm between the main body of the plea and this statement. It looks as though the clerk expected more to be inserted but nothing was forthcoming.

756. (*Thedwestry*) William the son of Thurgod and Lecia his wife who brought an assize of novel disseisin against Adam the son of Simon concerning a free tenement in Welnetham[1] have not prosecuted. So they and their sureties for prosecuting [are] in mercy, namely: Walter the son of Ralph of Welnetham and Robert the son of Geoffrey of Halstead (*amercements*).

1   There is a Great and a Little Welnetham in Thedwestry hundred.

757. (*Babergh*) A jury comes to declare whether five acres of land with appurtenances in Alpheton are free alms pertaining to the church of Alpheton in respect whereof John is the parson, or the lay fee of Walter of Barnham. He comes and he says nothing to stay the assize.

The jurors say that the said five acres of land with appurtenances are not free alms of the said church because he never held them in demesne nor was it vested except only of service, namely, six pence. So it is adjudged that he is to take nothing by this jury, but only service, and he is in mercy for a false claim. He is remanded in custody.

758. (*Blackbourn*) An assize comes to declare if Peter of Beccles unjustly etc disseised Geoffrey of Thorpe of his free tenement in [Ixworth] Thorpe after the first crossing etc and in respect whereof he complains that he disseised him of eighty acres of land with appurtenances in the same vill.

Peter comes and he says nothing to stay the assize.

The jurors say that he disseised him as the writ says. So it is adjudged that he has recovered his seisin against him. Peter [is] in mercy for disseisin by the surety of[1] Matthew of Layham and Gerard de Oddinges' and William the son of Robert de Rendon.[2] *(five marks)* Afterwards, the same Peter comes and offers to the lord king five marks to have a jury of twenty-four to attaint the twelve and they are admitted by the surety of the above. Note that all [are] similarly the sureties for prosecuting. Afterwards, Peter came and withdrew [from the appeal]. So he and his sureties [are] in mercy. He is remanded in custody. *(twenty marks)* Afterwards, he made a fine for twenty marks, by the surety of Richard Marshall, John de Crammaville, Daniel of Beccles [and] Ralph de la Cressunere.

[1] The clerk has crossed out *Martin of Rockland* but left in the *et* after *Rokelund* by mistake.

[2] This is probably Raydon in Samford hundred as William the son of Robert of Reydon appears in quite a number of pleas (see **145, 146** etc.) but it may also be Rendham in Plomesgate hundred.

759. *(Norfolk, Suffolk)* Robert de *Pirho*, William le Blund and Robert le Blund by their attorneys acknowledge that they owe to Bartholomew of Creake, each year for the maintenance of his wife as long as they held the manors of Creake, Helmingham, Hillington and Flixton, fourteen pounds sterling for payment to the same namely: in the octave of St John the Baptist seven pounds at Fundenhall, and on the day of St Hilary or on the morrow in the same place seven pounds. If they do not do so they grant that they may be distrained etc until etc and concerning the cost etc.

760. *(Babergh, one mark)* Gilbert of Polstead gives one mark for licence to agree with Thomas the son of Nicholas and Emma his wife by the surety of Sampson of Groton.

Judgement to be given against Walter of Groton because he has not come *(to judgement)*. *[chirograph CP 25(1) 213/17/112]*[1]

[1] The chirograph indicates that this was an assize of mort d'ancestor. There is no mention of Walter of Groton in the chirograph, so it may be assumed that he was either a voucher to warranty or a juror. I suspect the latter.

761. *(Risbridge)* An assize comes to declare if William Aylwy the father of Alice was seised in his demesne etc of one messuage and three acres of land and three roods with appurtenances in Stansfield on the day that he died, and if he died after the last etc and if etc which land and that messuage Richard the son of Aylwin holds. He comes and then vouches to warranty Ralph of Waldingfield. He comes and he says nothing to stay the assize.

The jurors say that the said William died seised after the term, and that she is his nearest heir. So it is adjudged that she has recovered her seisin against him and he [is] in mercy by the surety of Richard Aylwin de *Predington* and Ralph de la Kessuner *(amercement)*. Ralph will make an exchange to the value etc.

762. *(half a mark*[r]*)*[1] Robert of Necton gives half a mark for licence to agree with Thomas the son of William of Pakenham by the surety of the same Thomas. *[chirograph CP 25(1) 213/15/11]*

[1] The marginal note is repeated, I presume, because the clerk puts the first in the normal margin position but because of the large torn off portion out of the end of the membrane this plea is moved to the right of the membrane and so the clerk has repeated it to the immediate left of the plea.

Membrane 29d

763.[1] *(Lackford)* An assize comes to declare if Robert des Eschaleres and Martin of Middleton unjustly etc disseised Emma the daughter of Geoffrey of her free tenement in Worlington after the first crossing etc and in respect whereof the same Emma complains that they disseised her of twenty-two acres of land with appurtenances in the same vill.

Robert and Martin come and say[2] nothing to stay the assize.

The jurors say that they disseised her as the writ says. So it is adjudged that she recovered her seisin against them. Robert and Martin [are] in mercy for disseisin by the surety of John of Dunham (*amercements*).

Damages: two marks.

1   There is a large fault in the membrane, which the clerk has largely worked around in this plea.
2   The first two letters of *dicunt* have been eroded over time from the remaining portion of the membrane from where the tear occurred.

764.[1] (*Corsford*) Louis de Gerardville and Parnel his wife were summoned to answer Benedict of Blakenham[2] concerning a plea why they made waste, sale and exile of the lands and woods, which they hold in the dower of Parnel from the inheritance of the said Benedict in Chelsworth against the prohibition [of the king] etc. The same Benedict, by Henry de la Chapel his guardian, complains that they cut down one hundred trees of oak, ash, and apple and they have given them away at their will and have sold [them], in respect whereof he has suffered damage, and he has damage to the value etc.

Louis and Parnel come and denies force and injury and everything, and they say that they never cut down any trees, nor made anything waste, nor sale as he says, but they wish to tell the truth. They say that in fact they cut down the trees in the same place to maintain her houses and to the repair of a certain pool and a certain mill that they hold in the dower of Parnel, and that they made no sale, nor exile nor wasted anything. They put themselves on the country.

The jurors say that they made waste of the said wood to the value of one mark. So it is adjudged that henceforth they must not make waste in the said wood and that they should satisfy him of the said mark.

(*note concerning the ----*)[3]

1   There is a gap of 6.8 cm between the end of the main body of the plea and the next plea. The second marginal note is also some 4.9 cm below the final line of the plea. Did the clerk miss something out of the list of items in question? See **714** for the appointment of an attorney.
2   This is either Great or Little Blakenham in Bosmere hundred.
3   The clerk wrote *memorandum de cayspas*. The marginal note is approximately 4.9 cm below the last line of this plea, which suggests it might refer to a missing plea. As I have been unable to translate the last word it is difficult to tell. It might be just a marginal reminder to the clerk himself but *de cayspas* might also be the last part of a proper name. I have been unable to locate a place with this name.

765. (*Blackbourn*) An assize comes to declare if Thomas de Hay unjustly etc disseised Henry the son of Peter of his free tenement in Little Livermere after the first [crossing] etc and in respect whereof he complains that he disseised him of a certain part of a marsh.

Thomas comes and he says nothing to stay the assize.

The jurors say that he disseised him as the writ says. So it is adjudged that he has recovered his seisin against him. Thomas [is] in mercy for disseisin by the surety of Matthew of Layham[1] (*amercement*).

1   This place is in Corsford hundred.

766. (*Blackbourn*) Henry of Livermere who brought and assize of novel disseisin against Thomas de Hay concerning his free tenement in Little Livermere has not prosecuted. So he and his sureties for prosecuting [are] in mercy, namely: Richard the son of Woolmer of Livermere and Ralph the son of Gilbert of Livermere (*amercement*). The surety of Henry concerning the amercement [is] Roger of Boyland.

767. (*Blackbourn*) An assize comes to declare if Stephen of Glemsford the brother of Mabel the daughter of Hubert and Helen the wife of Goldwin of Glemsford was seised in his demesne etc of seven acres of land with appurtenances and half of one messuage with appurtenances in Glemsford on the day that etc and if he died after the last etc and if etc which land and that messuage Robert of Glemsford holds. He comes and says nothing to stay the assize.

The jurors say that when the said Stephen started on his journey[1] he demised that land and messuage to this Robert for a term of four years, under this condition that if he does not return within four years that the said land would pass to him in fee, and because the same Robert says that he believes him to be more likely alive than dead, and six years have already elapsed since he started the journey, so it is adjudged that the said sisters who are his nearest heirs are to have their seisin, and Robert [is] in mercy.[2] It is pardoned.

[1] He is likely to have been going on a crusade.
[2] I would have expected Robert to win here as the four years were already up. I can only reason that the justices believed that if a person was still alive such a condition should not apply.

768. (*Blackbourn*) Thomas de Hay who brought a writ of covenant against Henry the son of Peter of Little Livermere has not prosecuted. So he and his sureties for prosecuting [are] in mercy, namely John le Baron of Copdock.

769.[1] (*half a mark*) Roger of London gives half a mark for licence to agree with Solomon the goldsmith concerning a plea of *de fine facto* by the surety of Solomon.

[1] This is probably a plea with a Jew. It might be a foreign plea as there is no mention of it at Ipswich, so it is likely it was heard at Norwich. Norwich had a sizeable Jewish population.

770. (*Hartismere*) Roger the tailor and Avice his wife claim against Hervey Flegg one messuage with appurtenances in Haughley [Green] as the right of Avice. Hervey came and by licence they have agreed. The agreement is such that they remise and quitclaim the said messuage with appurtenances to the same Hervey for half a mark,[1] which he gave to them.

[1] There is no marginal note for this value.

771.[1] (*Ely*) Henry de Agius the son of Thomas de Agius acknowledges that he remised in perpetuity and quitclaimed from him and his heirs all right and claim that he had or could have in the one knight's fee with appurtenances in Moulton to Master Ralph de Agius and his heirs in perpetuity, so that neither he nor any of his heirs will be able henceforth [to have] any right or claim in the said land of Moulton. For this written grant etc the said Ralph gave to the same Henry all his lands with all its appurtenances without any reservation which he has in the vill of Cretingham etc as is more fully contained in the charter which the same Ralph has from the said Henry.

[1] See **559**. This plea might be the same litigants writing their further agreement in the roll concerning the reciprocal rights in the two vills.

772. (*Thedwestry*) Robert of Hoo claims against Katherine of Gedding whom Hamo Peche vouches to warranty and she warrants him the eighteen acres of land with

156

appurtenances in Felsham, concerning which, Thorold Sprunt, his kinsman whose heir he is, was seised in his demesne etc.

Katherine came and they have agreed by licence. The agreement is such that he remised all for forty shillings and one talent[1] for which she gave immediately to him one mark, cash down, and one talent. At the feast of St Michael [29 September] he will bring his brothers[2] and he will have [them] make to her the quitclaim, when she will give to him the two marks. If he does not do [this] she is quit of those two marks etc.

[1] I have not been able to find a value for this. According to Latham 1965, p.475 it could just be a sum of money. At a later time than this eyre it came to be interchangeable with a bezant, which also appears to vary in value from a shilling to a florin.

[2] It is likely that his brothers are there to quitclaim as well, as part of the deal, and only when they have done that will she pay the final instalment of the quitclaim.

773. Richard le Chanunye acknowledges that Joan Noel paid to him twenty marks concerning a certain fine made between them.

Membrane 30

774.[1] (*Norfolk*) A jury of twenty-four to attaint the twelve comes to declare by Richard the butler, Hamo Chevere, Thomas of Babingley, James[2] le Envoyse, Geoffrey of Toft, Hugh de Dunedal, Geoffrey of Gasthorpe, Nicholas de Stuteville, Robert the son of Ralph, William of Gimingham, John of Dunham, Hubert Hacon, Robert de Bosco, Gilbert of Hoe, Roger de Mustroyl, Richard of Narford, Jordan de Shelton, John de Curton, Thomas de Bavent, Hugh Burt, William de Senges, Andrew of Shernborne whether Roger the son of Hermer unjustly etc disseised the prior of Shouldham of his common pasture in Wereham, which pertains to his free tenement in Shouldham after the first crossing etc and in respect whereof the same Roger complains that the jury of the assize of novel disseisin, which was summoned (and[i]) taken before the eyre judges at Norwich, made a false oath. They come and say on their oath … [unfinished]

(*three marks*) Afterwards, they have agreed and the prior gives three marks for licence to agree by the surety of Stephen of Stoke and William Luvel. (*three marks*) Roger the son of Hermer gives three marks for the same by the surety of Richard of Dereham and Nicholas of Lynn. The agreement is such that the prior may remain in his seisin, which he has recovered by the assize of novel disseisin, so namely that if the abbot of Dereham wishes to agree to a perambulation [of the boundary] being made between the marsh of Wereham and Shouldham as to the digging of turf it shall be done so that the common pasture is to remain on either side as it is accustomed to be and the ditches, which have been raised anew, are to be levelled, so that on either side his animals may freely exit as it was accustomed to be. If however, he does not wish to agree then he may remain in the same seisin. Thomas Burt, Walter de Manerio, Robert Banyard, Andrew of Hingham, Stephen of Brockdish, Sampson Talebot, John the Breton, Thomas de Charneles and Robert of Hellington knights summoned to attaint the twelve etc have not come, so [they are] in mercy (*amercements*).

[1] There is a line in the margin from **774** to **776** to indicate that the same jury of the twenty-four to attaint the twelve is being used in this plea.

[2] The clerk wrote *Jacobus*, which I have translated as James and not Jacob.

775. (*Norfolk, twenty shillings*) Thomas of Grimston, who brought a writ of twenty-four to attaint the twelve concerning an assize of novel disseisin against John of

Congham concerning common pasture in Grimston, gives twenty shillings for licence to agree by the surety of Reynold of Gayton and Adam of Rockland.

(*twenty shillings*) The same John gives twenty shillings for the same by the surety of Richard of Docking, knight. The agreement is such that the same Thomas grants for himself and his heirs that the same John and his heirs of Congham have henceforth common pasture in the marsh of Grimston as pertaining to his tenement in Congham. For this etc the same Thomas and his heirs will have from each villein of the same John and his heirs one mowing in the harvest work in return for food provided by Thomas. Moreover the same villeins will give one 'russia'[1] to the hayward[2] of Thomas.

1   This could be either a *ruschia* or *ruisa* for which there are a number of possibilities: a firkin of butter, a measure of rosin or possibly a bed of rushes. See Latham 1965, p.414 for these definitions.
2   This is the office of hayward in the vill; the hayward looks after the field strips when they are with hay.

776.[1] The same jury of twenty-four to attaint the twelve comes to declare whether William Skett unjustly etc disseised Agnes and Lecia of Hainford of their free tenement in Hainford after the first etc.

(*one mark*) Afterwards, they are agreed, and William Skett gives one mark for licence to agree by the surety of Richard Turnel of Rackheath.

1   There is a line in the margin from **774** to this plea to indicate that this is also a Norfolk plea and has the same jury of the twenty-four to attaint the twelve that was used in **774**.

777. (*Norfolk, half a mark*) David of Crimplesham gives half a mark for licence to agree with Richard Angod concerning a plea of land by the surety ... [unfinished] [*chirograph* CP 25(1) 156/67/835][1]

1   The chirograph indicates that Richard Angood is in fact the attorney and that David was in fact the tenant and named by John son of Ralph who was the plaintiff.

778.[1] (*Bury St Edmunds*) Know, men present and future, that I Anselm the son of Roger of Boyton[2] have granted and by this, my present charter, confirmed to Thomas the son of Michael of Rushbrooke[3] one toft with buildings and their appurtenances in the town of Bury St Edmunds lying in the street called Reymer Street beside the toft of Adam of Stoke, to be held and to be had from me and my heirs by the said Thomas and his heirs or his assignees and their heirs freely and peacefully etc [and] paying twelve pence a year for all services. The same Anselm and his heirs will warrant etc. Note: that the same Anselm was present in the court and acknowledged the gift and charter.

1   This is a deed. It is very unusual to see one in this form in an eyre plea roll, particularly as it is in the first person. It is as if Anselm wanted this to be included in the rolls for security purposes. He or his heirs could call upon any future court for redress by indicating the deed in this roll.
2   I presume this is the Boyton in Risbridge hundred as the abbot of Bury St Edmunds is the chief lord there and the other two Boytons are in hundreds in the liberty of Ely.
3   There are two Rushbrooks, one in Cosford hundred and one in Thedwestry hundred. I suspect it is the latter as the former is now nothing more than a farm, although it might have been larger in 1240. Thedwestry hundred is borne out by *Feudal Aids 1284–1431* v, pp.43–44 where there is no mention of a Rushbrook in Cosford hundred.

779.[1] (*Stow, one mark*) Richard Caiphas gives one mark for licence to agree with Ralph the chaplain of Stonham concerning a plea of a jury of twenty-four to attaint the twelve by the surety ... [unfinished]

1   See **244** which I believe is the result of this plea.

158

780. (*Norfolk, one mark*) John of Burgh the son of Beatrice of Burgh who brought a writ concerning the raising of a certain dyke has not prosecuted. He made a fine for himself and his sureties by one mark by the surety of J[ohn] the sheriff.

781. Marsilia of Welnetham acknowledged that she remised and quitclaimed to Richard, the rector of the church of Welnetham and his successors as rector of the same church, two and a half acres of arable land and two acres of wood with one messuage and one acre of meadow, for seven acres of land which the said Marsilia took in exchange from the fief of the aforesaid church. Marsilia and her heirs will warrant to the said church and Richard and his successors the said land, wood and messuage in unconditional and perpetual alms etc as is more fully contained in the chirograph made between them.

782. (*Risbridge*) Thomas the son of William le Bigod gives one mark[1] for licence to agree with William of Bures concerning a plea of debt by the surety of Henry of Kirtling. The agreement is such that of the forty marks which he had claimed against him he remised to the same Thomas twenty marks, and of the other twenty marks the same Thomas will pay to the same William ten marks at Pentecost [3 June] in the twenty-fourth year [of King Henry III], and at Pentecost [19 May 1241] in year twenty-five, ten marks. If he does not do so, he grants that he may be distrained [by his lands and chattels] etc. Note: that the same William hands over to the same Thomas a charter concerning the forty marks.

The same Thomas acknowledged that he owes to Roger the son of Thomas of Creake sixteen shillings, which he will pay in the feast of St Matthew the Apostle [21 September] in the autumn. If he does not do [this] he grants etc as long as etc and concerning the cost etc.

> [1] There is normally a marginal note for these agreement amounts. Also, I have not found it in the agreement lists at the end of the roll.

783. (*Cambridgeshire*)[1] Alda, who was the wife of Geoffrey [de] Arsik, claims against Richard le Mervelius a third part of one hundred and forty acres of land with appurtenances in Silverley, and against John le Rus a third part of twenty-four acres of land with appurtenances in the same vill, and against Roger de Buscy a third part of twenty acres of land with appurtenances in the same vill, and against the prior of Spinney[2] a third part of forty-five acres of land in the same vill, and against Ralph de Gogeshal[3] and Joan his wife a third part of twenty-eight acres of land with appurtenances in the same vill, and against William the son of Nicholas a third part of ten acres of land with appurtenances in the same vill, and against German of Ashley a third part of fifteen acres of land with appurtenances in the same vill, as her dower etc and in respect whereof the said Geoffrey her former husband dowered her etc on the day etc.

Richard and all the others come and then vouch to warranty Roger de Arsik. They are to have him at Chelmsford on the quindene of Holy Trinity [Sunday 24 June] by the aid of the court.

The same Alda presented herself on the fourth day against Roger de Arsik concerning a plea of a third part of one hundred and forty acres of land with appurtenances in Silverley, and against Thomas de Kemesek concerning a plea of a third part of eighty acres of land with appurtenances in the same vill, and against the prioress of Thetford[4] concerning a plea of a third part of twenty acres of land with appurtenances in the same vill, and against Edmund of Elveden concerning a plea of a third part of twenty acres of land with appurtenances in the same vill, and against Baldwin de Gernell concerning a plea of a third part of six acres of land with appurtenances in the same vill. These third parts she claims in dower against them. They have not come etc and [were] summoned etc. Judgement: let the third parts be taken into the king's hands and the day etc and they are to be summoned to be at Chelmsford on the quindene of Holy Trinity [Sunday 24 June] etc. Joan appoints Ralph her husband as her attorney etc and Alda appoints John the Poitevin as her attorney.

1   Silverley is fairly close to Suffolk. It appears that Alda could not wait until the eyre reached Cambridgeshire in September 1240 when she could have obtained redress in her own county.
2   This is the Benedictine priory of Spinney in Cambridgeshire, and also one of Augustinian canons founded in 1227–1228.
3   This might be Coggeshall in Essex.
4   There was a priory of Benedictine nuns in Thetford from 1160.

784. (*Norfolk, Chelmsford*) A grand assize between Roger of Thirkelby and Letta his wife, plaintiffs, and Thomas of Walcott, deforciant, concerning the advowson of the church of Walcott is placed in adjournment until the quindene of Holy Trinity[1] by prayer of the parties and then the assize may proceed.

1   The quindene of Holy Trinity was Sunday 24 June in 1240 and occurred during the Essex eyre. There is no evidence of an agreement in this eyre nor has the plea roll survived to check the result.

Membrane 30d

785. (*twenty shillings*) Walter of Bradfield gives twenty shillings for licence to agree with Thomas of Bradfield concerning a plea of warranty of charter by the surety of Henry of Livermere. [*chirograph* CP 25(1) 213/17/103]

786. (*Blything*) Agnes the daughter of Walter, who brought an assize of novel disseisin against Richard the son of Ralph concerning her free tenement in Mettingham,[1] has not prosecuted. So she and her sureties for prosecuting [are] in mercy, namely: William de Ullecote[2] and Thomas of Battisford (*amercements*). They have agreed. The agreement is such that the said Agnes remises and quitclaims from herself and her heirs in perpetuity to the same Richard and his heirs all right and claim that she had or could have in all the said land with appurtenances which she had claimed against him by the assize of novel disseisin, and which land, John Austin her uncle, gave to her, for twenty-three silver marks. He[3] will pay to her five marks at Pentecost [3 June] in the twenty-fourth year [of King Henry III], and at the feast of St Michael [29 September] following five marks, and at the feast of the Purification of the Blessed [Virgin] Mary [2 February 1241] six marks, and at the following Easter [31 March 1241] six marks, and if not etc.[4]

The same Agnes appoints William Austin as her attorney against the same Richard concerning a plea of covenant.

1   Mettingham is actually in Wangford hundred, not Blything.
2   I cannot find this place. It might be Walcott in Norfolk. The sheriff at this time was John de Ullecote, so William might be his brother.
3   This is Richard who will pay the 23 marks to Agnes so that she quitclaims on the land her uncle gave her. That is she is selling the land to Richard.
4   The clerk has made a mistake here as these separate amounts add up to 22 marks.

787. Henry the son of Robert who brought an assize of mort d'ancestor against Ralph the son of Geoffrey concerning one messuage and one acre of land with appurtenances in Pakenham has not prosecuted. So he and his sureties for prosecuting [are] in mercy, namely: Ralph the son of William of Pakenham and Hugh the palmer (*amercements*). The amercement of Henry is pardoned because [he is] poor.

788. (*Blackbourn*) Anselm the son of Odo, who brought an assize of mort d'ancestor against Henry the son of Peter and many others concerning four and a half acres of land with appurtenances in Hepworth, has not prosecuted. So he and his sureties for prosecuting [are] in mercy,[1] namely: Stephen the son of Ralph of Hepworth and Gilbert the son of Jordan de Haverhill Sprot.[2]

> [1]   There is no mention of the amercement in a marginal note.
> [2]   This must be Haverhill in Risbridge hundred. I assumed that the name Sprot might apply to some part of Haverhill, but I cannot find it on any map. According to the Reaney 1997, p.422 there is a Sprot which looks as though it has something to do with shoots or a twig. Also see Sweet 1973, p.159.

789. (*Ely*) John Bennet, who brought an assize of novel disseisin against the prior of Ely concerning a tenement in Stoke, has not prosecuted. So he and his sureties for prosecuting [are] in mercy, namely: Gerard Richaud and Richard the son of Robert de Ailwarton. John is poor.

790. Ailsilda the daughter of Roger, who brought an assize of mort d'ancestor against Agnes Bonnard concerning a tenement in Chevington, has not prosecuted. She had no sureties for prosecuting except faith. So nothing.

791. (*Blackbourn*) An assize comes to declare if Alan the son of William [and] Nicholas Trussebot unjustly etc disseised Elias the son of William of his free tenement in Norton after the first etc and in respect whereof he complains they disseised him of one garden.

Alan and the other come and they say nothing to stay the assize.

The jurors say that the said Alan and Nicholas disseised him of the said garden as the writ says. So it is adjudged that Elias has recovered his seisin against them. They [are] in mercy for disseisin (*amercement*).

Damages: two shillings.

792. (*Blackbourn*) Matilda de *Longestotf*,[1] who brought an assize of novel disseisin against Richard of *Langetoft*,[2] has not prosecuted. So she and her sureties for prosecuting [are] in mercy, namely: William Claviger[3] of Thurston[4] and Robert Peche of Mendham (*amercements*).

> [1]   The clerk has obviously made a transcription error here.
> [2]   I believe that Matilda and Richard are related and they belong to the same family, Langetoft, which according to Watts 2004, p.330 gave its name to Stowlangtoft in Blackbourn hundred.
> [3]   According to Reaney 1997, p.99 a claviger was the keeper of the keys or the mace bearer.
> [4]   This is either the Thurston in Risbridge hundred or the Thurston in Thedwestry hundred.

793. (*Blything*) Alan the son of William, who brought an assize of mort d'ancestor against Thomas de Furnell concerning half a knight's fee with appurtenances in *Thelington*[1] has not prosecuted. So he and his sureties for prosecuting [are] in mercy, namely: Henry the son of Richard de *Sprotteshall*[2] and William Mapeleneheved[3] (*amercements*).

> [1]   This vill cannot be found Suffolk. It might be Theberton or Thorington in Blything hundred.
> [2]   I cannot find this place or surname. It might be Spexhall in Blything hundred.
> [3]   I cannot find this surname, but it might be Maplehead. See **1128** for this same person.

794. (*Lackford*) An assize comes to declare if Henry the abbot of Bury St Edmunds, Thomas of Whepstead, Alexander the steward, Otinell the reeve of Edmund de Sudhec,[1] Richard the son of Joscelin, William Arbureg,[2] Walter Freman, Nicholas de Aussingeburn,[3] Stephen de Haringesworth,[4] Thomas Joscelin Urry,[5] Adam Scot, William Carpenter, William Puttok, Walter Puttok, Richard Putok, Richard Brid,[6] Joscelin Flurard [and] Ranulf Standard unjustly etc disseised John de Hirsteston[7] and Thomas Ailgar of their common pasture in Tuddenham which pertains to their free tenement in the same vill after the first crossing etc.

The abbot came and answered for them because they are his men and he says that they are in seisin of the same pasture, and they acknowledge the same. So it is adjudged that the abbot and the others [are] without day. John and Thomas [are] in mercy, by the surety ... [unfinished] (*amercements*).

1   This may be Southey according to Reaney 1997, p.418.
2   This might be Arbury, a dweller by the earthwork, according to Reaney 1997, p.13.
3   This might be Osborne, but it is not obvious.
4   I cannot find this place in Suffolk. It might be Herringswell in Lackford hundred or Harringworth in Northamptonshire.
5   There is a surname of Urry in Reaney 1997, p.245. This means that the clerk has given three names for this person, or he has missed the surname of Thomas.
6   This name is probably Bird. See Reaney 1997, p.45.
7   This might be Hunston in Blackbourn hundred, but this is not obvious from any other source.

795. (*Lackford*) An assize comes to declare if John of Cottenham,[1] Thomas Ailgar, Thomas the son of Richard, John de Mauveys, Norman the palmer, Peter Verape, Adam de Molendino, Peter Hawis, Rygan the son of Roger, Richard the son of Ralph, Gervase of Tuddenham, John the miller, Peter Geoffrey Jaye,[2] Gilbert Bulle, William Goderhele,[3] William Baron, Peter le Wicher, Thomas the son of Norman, Gilbert Smith, Roger the son of the Widow,[4] Roger the son of Leffled, Baldwin the carter, Seman Gage, William Billing, Robert Berker, Alan Hayt,[5] Clement the son of Walter, Thomas the son of Roger, John of Risby, Thomas of Badmondisfield, Roger the son of William, Roger Wyat, Thomas the son of Thomas, Stephen the tailor, Walter Scot, Alan de Cludesdal,[6] Thomas Prat, William the son of Robert, Thomas the berker, Sarah of Knapwell, Thomas the son of Joscelin, William the son of Richard, Clement the son of Walter,[7] Woolmer Pikesalt, Sired the son of Gilbert, Erald the son of Adam, William Bernard, Alan the son of Alice, Richard Billot, Peter the son of Norman, Thomas Bule, Ralph the Bailward, Roger Fassard, Richard the son of William, Robert Way, Wigan the son of Robert, Thomas the son of William, Thomas Baghat, William the son of Adam and Thomas the son of Roger[8] unjustly etc disseised John de la More and Adam de Araz[9] of their common pasture in Tuddenham which pertains to their free tenement in Herringswell after the first crossing etc.

John of Cottenham and [Thomas] Ailgar[10] come and say nothing to stay the assize. The others have not come and they were attached mutually[11] because the men of the whole vill are contained in the writ.

The jurors say that they have not disseised them as the writ says. So it is adjudged that they are to take nothing by this writ. They are in mercy for a false claim by the surety of John le Blund of Herringswell and Ranulf Wiseman of the same (*amercements*).

1   This is either Cottenham in Cambridgeshire or Coddenham in Babergh hundred, probably Cottenham as it is nearer to Tuddenham and Herringswell. See later in this plea.
2   This might be Peter and Geoffrey Jaye or it might be a person with a middle name. The membrane shows no obvious second person.

162

3 This might be the name Goodheal.
4 The clerk does not name the widow, but the name may be Widowson. See Reaney 1997, p.491.
5 This might be Hake for a hook or crook or it could be Height, Hight or Hite.
6 This might be Cloudsdale, but I cannot find such a place.
7 The clerk may be repeating a name here, or they might be two different people.
8 A total of sixty names for a common of pasture case.
9 This might be Arras in France.
10 The clerk wrote *Richard*. I assume the clerk should have written Thomas Algar as then this would
   be the first two names in the plea as defendants. Otherwise he is new and is not in the list of
   alleged disseisors.
11 This means that the other fifty-eight defendants attached each other to appear at the eyre.

796. (*Cosford*) An assize comes to declare if Henry of Gedding the father of Thomas of Gedding was seised in his demesne etc of three acres of land with appurtenances in Brettenham on the day that he died and if he died after the last return etc and if etc which land Jolan[1] de Nevill and John of Pulham[2] hold. They come and by licence they are agreed. The agreement is such that the same Thomas remises to them all [the land] etc for six shillings etc.

1 This might be the diminutive of Joscelin or a form of Joel. See Reaney 1997, pp.256–257.
2 There are two Pulhams, Pulham Market and Pulham St Mary, both in Norfolk in Earsham
   hundred.

797. (*Norfolk*) A day is given to Brian the son of Alan, plaintiff, and Warren de Montchensy concerning a plea of land at Chelmsford on the quindene of Holy Trinity [Sunday 24 June] (*Chelmsford*). The sheriff is commanded that he attends in his own person at Clare,[1] and by the oath of twelve etc cause the whole land to be valued and appraised, which William Blund held in Clare on the day that the trial by battle was fought, except for the advowson of the church, the chief messuage with gardens and a close with appurtenances in the meadows, pastures, rents, mills and all things pertaining to the same land immediately. And he is to assign and cause the said Brian to have a third part in everything to be assigned to Brian, according to what has been said before that he has. He is to notify that valuation, and what, and how much, and where and by which items he assigns to the same Brian etc at the said term by his sealed letters and by [four or six][2] of those by whose oath he shall make that valuation etc.

1 Clare is in Risbridge hundred, so this plea must have started in Norfolk, the previous eyre county,
   but the land in question is in Suffolk. Presumably the sheriff is attending at Clare in the honorial
   court. There was a *Clareia* in Domesday Book in Tunstead hundred in Norfolk but it cannot be
   found in Beresford 1983.
2 There is a break in the membrane here which has made one or two words illegible. I think that it
   should read *iiij vel sex*; that is 'by four or six'.

Membrane 31

798.[1] (*Norfolk*) An assize comes to declare which patron in time of peace presented the last parson, who is dead, to the church of Rollesby which is vacant etc, the advowson of which Isabella of Caister[2] says pertains to herself, which advowson Robert Byl withholds from her. He comes and says that he claims nothing in the said presentation but he claims the advowson of the said church as his right etc. So the bishop of Norwich is ordered that notwithstanding the claim of the said Robert, at the presentation of Isabella,[3] he is to admit a suitable parson etc.

1 There is a chirograph for this advowson of Rollesby but, although Robert Byl is present in the
   chirograph, Isabella is not. Its number is CP 25(1), 156/66/822.
2 She is *Isabella de Castris* in the text. The surviving castle at Caister is fifteenth-century.

3   It looks as though Isabella will present this time but will thereafter revert to the normal patron. The bishop is being asked to affirm the parson selected by Isabella. This was apparently fairly common in the later Middle Ages.

799. (*Thedwestry*) Martin the son of Warren, who brought an assize of mort d'ancestor against Richard with the beard and many others, has not prosecuted. So he and his sureties for prosecuting [are] in mercy, namely: Ralph the son of the chaplain of Barton[1] and Simon the son of John of the same (*amercements*).

1   This is probably Great Barton in Thedwestry hundred, where Cattishall lies.

800. (*Babergh*) An assize comes to claim if William of Necton the father of Henry was seised in his demesne etc of two shillingsworth of rent with appurtenances in [Long] Melford on the day that the died, and if he died after the latest etc and if etc which rent Robert the son of Ralph holds. He comes and says that he ought not answer to this because he is a bastard. Because the inquiry of this case [belong to an ecclesiastical court] etc the bishop of Norwich is ordered that he convene [before him those who know and ascertain] the truth of the matter etc and that in respect thereof etc make known by his sealed letters [the finding of the inquest] etc. (*bastardy*).

801. (*one mark*) James[1] le Envoyse, gives one mark for licence to agree with Benedict of Copdock and others.

1   The clerk wrote the modern version of the name. In other pleas he is indicated by the clerk as *Jacobus.* See **774.**

802. (*Norfolk*) A jury comes to declare whether five acres of land and two acres and one rood of marsh are the free alms pertaining to the church of Kirstead whereof Ralph is the parson or the lay fee of James le Envoyse who holds that land, and he comes and then vouches to warranty John le Envoyse, who is present, and he warrants him and then vouches to warranty Milo de Verdon. He is to have him at the arrival of the justices at the first assize when they come to those districts (*at the arrival of the justices*). **[11]**

803. (*One mark*) Nicholas of Bury St Edmunds gives one mark for licence to agree with Walter the son of Bernard concerning a plea of covenant by the surety of Walter. **[703]** [*chirograph* CP 25(1) 213/16/48]

804.[1] [The clerk has put a paragraph mark and has left a space but there is no plea placed here.]

1   I have given this a plea number compared with the previous section marks standing alone because the other ones are at the end of a particular section and probably an indication of such by the clerk. This cannot be such an occasion. It is also possible that the clerk indicated that there is now no more to come on the previous item when the clerk had originally expected to insert the details of the agreement.

805. (*Suffolk*) Master Robert de L'Isle claims against Henry of Caldecott[1] sixty acres of land with appurtenances in Caldecott, Fritton and Belton as his right etc.

Henry comes and then claims a view. He is to have [it] and he is to come on Tuesday.

1   See **75** for his essoin *de malo lecti* and **10** for *de malo veniendi.*

806.[1] (*Norfolk, ten shillings*) Robert de Bosco of Saham gives ten shillings for licence to agree with S. of Sheering concerning a plea of rent by the surety of Simon of Saham. [*chirograph* CP 25(1) 156/66/823]

164

¹   This plea may follow on from **480** but the place named in this chirograph is different from that in **480**.

807. (*one mark*) Richard de *Meleburne* made a fine for ten shillings because he withdrew [from the plea] by the surety of Ivo [of] Knettishall and Walter the son of Bernard.

808.¹ (*Hoxne*) Simon of Sheering claims against Nicholas Crowe whom Thomas of Shotford vouched to warranty, and who [has claimed] a third part of five acres of land with appurtenances in Mendham etc. Nicholas comes and by licence he renders [it] to him. He is to have his seisin. He is to make an exchange to the value etc.

¹   This looks as though it is a plea of dower but this is not evident from the text. See **471** as they may be connected.

809. (*Risbridge*) Roger of Hawstead claims against Robert of Cockfield one carucate of land with appurtenances, excepting thirty acres of land and one messuage in Moulton, and against the prioress of Thetford thirty acres of land and one messuage in the same vill as his right etc.

Robert and the prioress come by their attorneys. Robert then vouches to warranty Richard de Grenville. He is to have him at Chelmsford on the quindene of Holy Trinity [Sunday 24 June] by the aid of the court (*Chelmsford*). He is to be summoned in the county of Gloucestershire. The prioress comes and then vouches to warranty the said Robert. She is to have him at the said term by the aid of the court. He is to be summoned in the county of Norfolk.

810.¹ (*Norfolk*) William the son of Gerberga by his attorney presented himself on the fourth day against Robert Hauteyn² concerning a plea to take his chirograph concerning two mills with appurtenances in Hellesdon. Robert has not come, and he had a day on this day by the order of the justices. And so the sheriff was commanded that he distrain him by lands and chattels so that he is at Chelmsford on the octave of Holy Trinity [Sunday 17 June] etc. (*Chelmsford*).

¹   This plea is as a result of a writ *Venire facias* being made to the defendant to make him bring the chirograph to the court so that the truth of the matter of the two mills can be sorted out. The chirograph may have been a fine made earlier. No doubt the original plea was made at the Norfolk eyre.
²   This name could be Hawtayne and is a name in Suffolk and Norfolk meaning hall thane. See Reaney 1997, p.222.

811. (*Norfolk*) Avelina, who was the wife of Adam of Lynn, claims against John of [Burnham] Deepdale half of one messuage and sixteen acres of marsh with appurtenances in [Burnham] Deepdale, and against Eudo the son of Adam of Lynn half of thirteen acres of land with appurtenances in the same vill, and against Walter Paunfelec half of one messuage and five roods with appurtenances in the same vill, and against the abbot of West Dereham half of one hundred acres of marsh and one messuage and two and a half acres with appurtenances in the same vill as her dower etc. John and the others come and vouch to warranty the said Eudo, who is present, and he warrants them and renders to her the dower of her land. So she is to have her seisin and the others are to hold in peace.

812. (*Babergh*) An assize comes to declare if Hugh Webbe, Margaret his wife, Simon Mariot, Isabella his wife and Margery the daughter of Richard unjustly etc disseised John the son of Baldwin of his free tenement in Acton after the first crossing etc and in respect whereof he complains that they disseised him of five acres.

Hugh and the others come and say nothing to stay the assize.

The jurors say that they disseised him as the writ says. So it is adjudged that he has recovered his seisin against them. They [are] in mercy for disseisin by the surety of Geoffrey of Melford (*amercements*).

Damages: six pence.

813. (*Blackbourn*) An assize comes to declare if Henry the son of Durand unjustly etc disseised Griman the son of Durand, Robert Helyam, Adam and Ranulf the brothers of Griman of their free tenement in Rickinghall [Inferior] after the first crossing etc and in respect whereof they complain that he disseised each of four acres of land and of his part of one messuage.

Henry comes and acknowledges the disseisin, so [he is] in mercy. It is pardoned because [he is] poor. They are to have their seisin. Damages: are remitted for poverty.

814. (*Babergh*) An assize comes to declare if Alexander of Sudbury the father of William was seised in his demesne etc of one acre of meadow with appurtenances in Cornard on the day that he died, and if he died after the last return, and if he William etc which meadow Henry the son of John holds. He comes and says that he claims nothing in the said meadow because his mother holds that meadow. So it is adjudged that he is to take nothing by this assize and is in mercy for a false claim; by the surety of Robert de Melun (*amercements*).

815. (*Blackbourn*) An assize comes to declare if Richard de *Sudlington* the father of Adam the son of Richard was seised in his demesne etc of one messuage and thirty acres of land with appurtenances in Barningham on the day that he died, and if he died after the last return, and if etc which messuage and land Maria, who was the wife of Richard, holds. She comes and says nothing to stay the assize.

The jurors say that the said land and messuage are the marriage portion of Maria and that the said land and messuage were never of the inheritance of Richard nor even of his acquisition. So it is adjudged that he is to take nothing by this assize. He is in mercy for a false claim, by the surety of Walter of Hepworth, and Maria may hold in peace (*amercement*).

The same Adam who brought an assize of mort d'ancestor against Thomas Sorell concerning two acres and one rood of land with appurtenances in Barningham has not prosecuted. So he and his sureties for prosecuting [are] in mercy, namely: (William[i]) Overfen of Bardwell and William Breton of the same.

816. (*Cambridgeshire, forty shillings*) Ralph of Soham gives forty shillings for licence to agree with Stephen Turpin concerning a plea of *de fine facto* to make a fine by the surety of Everard of Trumpington. The [agreement is such that][1] the same Ralph renders to him a half of three virgates[2] with appurtenances [in] Whaddon as his right (----[il]) saving with the men who have sowed that land half of the [corn][3] (----[il]) [unfinished]

[1] There is a large chunk of the membrane missing at this point, which looks as though it has been torn off. From what remains this is the best guess.

[2] A virgate varies from place to place but was considered to be a quarter of a carucate; in Suffolk it would be about 30 acres. The amount in question here would be about 45 acres. As far as I am aware the virgate in Cambridgeshire is of the same size as in Suffolk.

[3] This is a guess but the letters *blad* are visible.

817. (----[il])[1] The prior of (----[il])[2] against Hugh of Hundon and others named in the writ.

1   The marginal note is unreadable, even with ultraviolet light.
2   This is unreadable because a large chunk of the parchment is missing here because of rodents. It is possible that this item and the next one are the appointment of attorneys.

818. (----il)[1] Essex concerning a plea of warranty of charter. (----il)[2] Walter of Parham against William de Garlesle.

1   There is a marginal note here but unreadable, even with ultraviolet light.
2   I suspect the missing words are *ponit loco suo* here for the appointment of an attorney.

Membrane 31d

819. (*Blackbourn*) An assize comes to declare if Henry the abbot of Bury St Edmunds, Robert de Shardlow[1] and Robert le Eschot and Cecilia the wife of Thomas unjustly etc disseised Ralph de Cruce and Matilda his wife of their free tenement in Stow[2] after the first crossing etc.

The abbot and the others come and they say that he[3] disseised him, and he cannot deny this. So he [is] in mercy. The others [are] without day and Ralph [is] in mercy. It is pardoned for poverty.

1   There is a Shardlow in Derbyshire. However, the Shardlow family appears in Suffolk in a number of feet of fines and they also appear to own land around Cowlinge in Risbridge hundred: see *Feudal Aids 1284–1431* v, pp.31 and 77–79; also see **1070**. Master Robert of Shardlow was an important royal clerk and justice in the 1220s and 1230s but he was disgraced in the 1232 Cambridge eyre with Master Roger Cantelupe for complicity in agitating against foreign clerks. See Crook 1982a, pp.86–88. He was also involved in the fall of Hubert de Burgh in 1232: see Carpenter 1996, p.55.
2   This is either West Stow or Stowlangtoft in Blackbourne hundred.
3   It is not totally clear from what the clerk has written but I believe what the others and the abbot are saying is that only the abbot disseised Ralph; then it would be the case that the abbot would be amerced and the others would be without day. Ralph would also be amerced for a false claim against the other defendants on the side of the abbot, as is shown.

820.[1] (*Norfolk*) Baldwin Rede, Agnes Geye and Richard [son of] Gunnild[2] by his attorney claims against Richard Puleyn eight acres of land with appurtenances in Wereham as their right etc.

Richard comes and then vouches to warranty Richard the English, who is present, and he then vouches to warranty William de Meysi. He is to have him at Chelmsford on the octave of Holy Trinity [Sunday 17 June] by aid of the court (*Chelmsford*).

1   See **369** for the other 6 acres and the chirograph for the agreement for the 6 acres.
2   In **369** there is an Agnes Gye. In the same plea there is a Richard son of Gunnild whom I believe is the same person.

821.[1] [There is only a paragraph/section mark here.]

1   Paragraph mark only. There is a gap as though for a later insertion but the clerk has not inserted anything.

822. (*Blackbourn*) Agnes who was the wife of Stephen le Blund claims against Robert de Shardlow[1] half of one hundred acres of land with appurtenances in Herringswell,[2] and against John le Blund half of one messuage and thirty acres of land with appurtenances in the same vill as her dower etc. John comes and he renders to her the half of that messuage and of that thirty acres of land. Master Robert gives to her thirty acres of land from the same land, which she claims against him, and he is to give to her one messuage. She then holds herself to be content.

1   This is the same Robert de Shardlow as in **819**.
2   This is Herringswell in Lackford not Blackbourn hundred.

823. (*Bosmere*) A plea, which is between Roger of Westleton, Richard of Tuddenham, John the son of Osbert, the plaintiffs, concerning the common fishery of Bosmere [Hall],[1] and Hugh the bishop of Ely, is being adjourned until the octave of Holy Trinity [Sunday 17 June] at Chelmsford (*Chelmsford*). All except John appoint as their attorney Richard of Tuddenham. [*chirograph* CP 25(1) 213/17/100][2]

1   There is a Bosmere Hall near Needham Market and Creeting St Mary, beside the river Gipping.
2   In the chirograph completed at Chelmsford John the son of Osbert is shown as John the son of Edmund. The bishop wins the plea as the others remise and quit claim their right forever in the common fishery and the waters of Bosmere. For this the bishop gives them 6s.

824. (*Norfolk*) Ralph de Koma was attached to reply to William le Fort and Mabel his wife concerning a plea that he keep the fine made before the eyre justices at King's Lynn between that William and Mabel, demandants, and that Ralph, tenant, concerning one messuage with appurtenances in Lynn[1] in respect whereof a chirograph [made between them was proffered] etc. And in respect whereof the same complain that since by that fine he owes to them per year for the said messuage thirty-one shillings at four terms,[2] the same Ralph has kept back from them concerning the said rent for many terms, forty-three shillings, whereon they have suffered damage to the value etc.

Ralph comes and grants the fine and whatsoever is contained in the fine and he readily denies that he ever contravened the fine, but readily acknowledges that he owes to them thirty-one shillings for one year and that it is not through him that the foresaid money has not been paid, but it has occurred through them because they did not wish to come to Lynn for the said money, nor to send [for it]. He says that the money was always ready and he is prepared to pay [it], and he says that the residue of the said forty-four shillings that was in arrears to them for the said year he has paid to them.

Afterwards, they have agreed by licence. The agreement is such that the said William and Mabel remise the said arrears for forty shillings concerning which he has paid to them twenty shillings (and[i]) at the feast of St John the Baptist, twenty shillings. If he does not do [this] he grants etc. Ralph acknowledges that he gave the said tenement to W.[3] the bishop of Norwich and his successors, or to his assignees, making to the same William and Mabel and their heirs the said services each year as is more fully contained in the charter, which the same bishop has. [355]

1   This could be King's, North, South or West Lynn in Norfolk.
2   This might mean that he owes 124s. a year payable at 31s. at each of the four terms, or that he pays 31s. for the year, that is he pays 7s. 9d. at each of the four terms. I think it is likely to be the latter but it is not certain.
3   This would be William de Ralegh, who was made bishop of Norwich in 1239.

825. (*Lothingland*) Hawise of Hopton[1] ... [unfinished]

1   Hopton is in Lothingland hundred. The rest is missing and the clerk has left a gap. It is possible that the clerk realised a mistake in that this lady had already settled all her pleas, but he had entered her name here, then realised his mistake in duplicating one of her pleas. See **453**.

826. (*Risbridge*) Warren the son of William de Wadeshill claims against Heloise, who was the wife of Warren de Wadeshill, one messuage and five acres of land and two acres of wood with appurtenances in Little Thurlow into which the same Heloise has no entry except by intrusion in which she did [enter] after the death of the said Warren her husband [and] the grandfather of the said Warren whose heir he is.

Heloise comes and then vouches to warranty Macy of Cowlinge, who is present,

168

and he warrants her and says that if anyone were to implead him for the said land he would be obliged to warrant them, because Warren, his grandfather, enfeoffed him of the said land and wood by his charter, which he proffers and which attests to this. As a result he was in seisin of the said land and wood and messuage for a long time before his death and he still is in seisin, because the said Heloise does not have [entry] except only for a (term[i]) of the said land. He then puts himself on the country. Warren (says[i]) that that charter ought not to harm him because he never had seisin by means of the said gift and charter in the life of the said Warren and then he puts himself on the country. So let there be a jury thereon.

The jurors say that the said Warren [husband of Heloise] gave the said messuage, land and wood to the said Macy and he placed him in seisin, so that he had full seisin for about eight days. Afterwards, the same Macy came and he gave the said messuage, land and wood to the said Heloise for her lifetime. As a result the same Warren and Heloise put themselves in that land, and they enjoyed together their seisin until the same Macy, about eight days before the death of Warren, intruded on that land until Heloise expelled him. So it is adjudged that Macy's seisin [is] null, and that Warren [the plaintiff] has recovered his seisin. Macy [is] in mercy,[1] and he will make an exchange to Heloise for her lifetime.

[1]   There is no mention of this amercement in the margin.

827. (*Risbridge*) Heloise, who was the wife of Warren de Wadeshill was attached to reply to Warren the son of William concerning why she has made waste, sale and disposal from the woods and orchards which she holds in dower from the inheritance of the said Warren in Great and Little Thurlow against the prohibition [of the king] etc and in respect whereof he complains she cut wood in his woodland whereon he has suffered damage [to the value of] etc.

Heloise comes and cannot deny that she has made waste etc and she has built elsewhere with the said wood than in her dower. So it is adjudged that she must make satisfaction to him concerning his damages. She is in mercy for trespass by the surety of Macy of Cowlinge. Damages are being assessed at twenty shillings, by the surety of the same Macy. (*half a mark*) She made a fine for half a mark for the amercement.

828. (*Norfolk*) John the son of Alexander and Matilda his wife claim against Richard Akeman and Grecia his wife three acres of land with appurtenances in Wiggenhall as the right of Matilda, and in which the same Richard and Grecia have no entry except by Ralph [the son of][1] Ketelbern the first husband of Matilda who [demised] that [to them] etc [and] whom she [Matilda] could not contradict in his lifetime.

Richard and Grecia come and deny such entry, and they say that the father of Matilda and Grecia died seised of all the land which John, Matilda, Richard and Grecia hold, so that after the death of this Alan[2] (all[i]) the land was divided between them, so that half of all [the lands] passed to Ralph and Matilda, and the other half to Grecia. Whereon they say that the said three acres fell due to them on her [Grecia's] behalf. She then puts herself on the jury, and they similarly. So the sheriff is commanded that in the full county he summon and make a jury of twelve etc and by whom [the truth can best be known] etc and who neither [have any affinity with either party] etc and by their oath [to declare] etc if the said Richard and Grecia have had entry in the said three acres of land with appurtenances by Ralph the son of Ketelbern, the first husband of the said Matilda, who demised that [land] to them, whom she could not contradict in his lifetime etc as the same John and Matilda say, or if they had entry in the said three acres of land as in that [land], which was appertaining to Matilda in the purparty of Grecia and Matilda from the inheritance of the said Alan their father. The inquiry, which he will carry out, he shall make known etc on the nearest Saturday after the quindene of Holy Trinity [Saturday 30 June] by letters etc and by two etc who so much etc. Grecia appoints her husband Richard as her attorney. Afterwards,[3] on that day the inquiry comes, which says that Richard and Grecia did not have entry by Ralph the son of Ketelbern, but they had entry in the land of Alan as in the inheritance of that Grecia.[4] So it is adjudged that they may hold in peace and the others [are] in mercy (*amercement*).

[1] Later in the plea it is shown that Ralph is the son of Ketelbern.
[2] This is the name of the father of Matilda and Grecia, as shown later in the plea.
[3] There is a change in ink and writing here as though some clerk has put in the result from the Essex eyre court, which is the next one after Suffolk for William of York and his fellow judges. The same writing continues on to the next membrane.
[4] That is in the 3 acres Grecia received as her share of the land on the death of Alan, her father. It appears that her sister was trying to obtain all the land by saying that her first husband demised the land to Grecia and Richard when in fact it was Matilda's. What Matilda appears to be trying to do is to obtain Grecia's land from the division after their father's death.

Membrane 32[1]

[1] There is a long tear in this membrane towards the bottom, which has been stitched up, possibly by the maker, as the clerk has worked around the tear. What may have happened here is that a parchment tie was torn off the membrane at this point. The script on this side is similar to the addition made on the last plea. The clerk also makes many mistakes on the number of amercements to take. He often cites only one when there should be more. What is also interesting is that the number '32' is written above **840** and may be part of the Agarde numbering system put in place c.1600. There is also another number '33' crossed out next to the PRO stamp, indicating that the torn off bit had gone by the time these two marks were made.

829. (*Cosford*) An assize comes to declare if Robert of Layham unjustly etc disseised William of Bures of his free tenement in Layham after the first crossing etc and in respect whereof he complains that he disseised him of one rood of land. Robert comes and he says nothing to stay the assize. Robert Walranc, one of the recognitors, has not come. So [he is] in mercy (*amercement*).

The jurors say that the said Robert disseised him of half a rood of land and not of one rood of land. So William is to recover his seisin and Robert [is] in mercy (*amercement*). Because Robert has not disseised him of one rood of land as he claims, so William [is] in mercy (*amercement*).

Damages: six pence.

830. (*Cosford*) An assize comes to declare if Thomas de Ponde unjustly etc disseised Matilda Godrich and Matilda her daughter of their free tenement in *Lafham*[1] after the first crossing etc and in respect whereof they complain that he disseised them of half an acre. Thomas comes and he says nothing to stay the assize.

The jurors say that the said Matilda and Matilda were in seisin of the said land before the term contained in the writ, but in fact they say that they were never in seisin of the said land after the term. So Thomas [is] quit, and Matilda and Matilda [are] in mercy. They are pardoned for poverty.

[1] This might be Layham as there is no *Lafham* in Cosford hundred. I think it is unlikely to be the unidentified place *Lafham* in Risbridge hundred in Domesday Book. See *Domesday Book Suffolk*, Part Two, section 73, no. 1. One other possibility is that it is Lavenham, but that was in Babergh hundred. See Watts 2004, p.216.

170

831.[1] (*Cosford*) An assize comes to declare if Simon de Skerninghe, Roger of Chilton and Osbert his brother unjustly etc disseised Thomas de la Hide of his free tenement in Kettlebaston after the first crossing etc and in respect whereof he complains that they disseised him of three acres of land. Simon, Roger and Osbert have not come, and so let the assize be taken by default. Simon was attached by William de Kauewrde[2] and Robert of Rushbrooke, so [they are] in mercy (*amercement*). Roger was attached by Richard the son of Alexander of Hitcham and Geoffrey le Chevalier of the same, so [they are] in mercy (*amercement*). Osbert was attached by William of Groton and William of Groton,[3] so [they are] in mercy (*amercement*).

The jurors say that Simon, Roger and Osbert disseised him as the writ says. So it is adjudged that Thomas is to recover his seisin, and the others [are] in mercy (*amercement*).

(*to the Clerks*) Damages: half a mark.

1   See **974** and **1116** for other pleas of Thomas de la Hide.
2   See **1653** for a slightly different spelling of this name. It might be Chelsworth in Cosford hundred but it is not obvious.
3   This might be the same William of Groton repeated, or it might be the same name but a different person. I have assumed the latter. They are not shown in the amercement section of this roll below.

832. (*Cosford*) An assize comes to declare if Simon of Pattishall unjustly etc disseised Hugh Ravel of his free tenement in Whatfield after the first crossing etc Simon comes and he says nothing to stay the assize.

The jurors say that the said Simon has not disseised him as the writ says. So Simon [is] without day, and Hugh [is] in mercy by the surety of Ralph de Hauville of Bildeston and Robert of Semer (*amercement*). [*chirograph* CP 25(1) 213/17/120][1]

1   Although this is a novel disseisin case they came to an agreement in Chelmsford in which Hugh acknowledged the 15 acres in dispute to be the right of Simon and he gave him an additional 3 roods of meadow, and the rent from three tenants who will now pay Simon their rent. For this and his other tenements Simon holds from Hugh he gave 10s. 1d. payable annually at two terms and also the service of one knight's fee and the service of watch and ward at the castle of Norwich. For this Hugh will warrant this agreement to Simon and his heirs. For the agreement Simon is to give Hugh a male sparrowhawk.

833. (*Cosford*) An assize comes to declare if Austin of Blakenham unjustly etc disseised Matilda who was the wife of Herbert of Aldham of her free tenement in Whatfield after the first crossing etc and in respect whereof she complains that he disseised her of two acres of land.

Austin has (not[i]) come because he was not attached nor found, so let the assize be taken against him by default.

The jurors say that the said Austin disseised her as the writ says. So it is adjudged that she is to recover her seisin, and Austin [is] in mercy (*amercement*).

(*to the clerks*) Damages: four shillings.

834. (*Risbridge*) Isabella the daughter of Godwin, who brought a writ of novel disseisin against Richard of Rattlesden concerning her free tenement in Little Bradley, came and withdrew [from the plea]. So she and her sureties for prosecuting [are] in mercy, namely Walter the son of William of Bradley and William the son of William de Bradford[1] (*amercement*).

1   Apart from the obvious places in Yorkshire and Wiltshire, I cannot find a place in Suffolk with this name; perhaps the clerk has made a mistake and meant Bradley or Bradfield.

835. (*Risbridge*)[1] An assize comes to declare if William the son of Walter unjustly disseised Ralph the son of Lettice[2] of his common pasture in Great Bradley after the first etc. [William][3] comes and he says nothing to stay the assize.

The jurors say that the father of the said Ralph was a villein and that this Ralph is a villein. So it is adjudged that he is to take nothing by this assize and he is in mercy for a false claim, and William [is] without day (*amercement*). The sureties of Ralph for the amercement [are]: Roger the clerk of Bradley and Henry Walles[4] of the same.

[1] There is an arrow pointing to *Risbrigge* in **834**, indicating that the place in this plea is also in Risbridge hundred.
[2] In the amercement section of this roll he is shown as *Radulfo Letice* in **1653**.
[3] The clerk wrote *Radulfus* by mistake. He should have written William if he was following the normal formula for a novel disseisin.
[4] This is 'the Welshman'. See **450**, note 2.

836. (*Risbridge*) An assize comes to declare if Robert Darnel unjustly etc disseised Robert the carpenter of his free tenement in Stansfield after the first etc. Robert Darnel has not come and he has fled. [He was] attached by John Ilger de *Pridington* and Roger the son of William of Hawkedon, so he and his sureties [are] in mercy, and the assize is to proceed against him by default (*amercement*).

The jurors say that a certain parcel of land, namely that land in respect whereof the assize has been brought, is a certain common pasture pertaining both to the free tenement of Robert [the] carpenter and to the free tenement of Robert Darnel, concerning which neither of them holds it [the common pasture] separately.[1] So it is adjudged that Robert is to take nothing by this assize and he is in mercy for a false claim (*amercement*). Robert Darnel [is] quit. The sureties of Robert [the] carpenter [are]: William Wyburg of Stansfield and Roger the son of Odo of Stradishall.

[1] This indicates that neither of the parties to the dispute holds it as their own private property and can exclude the other from pasturing their animals on the pasture, but that the pasture in effect belongs to both of them because of the tenements they occupy.

837. (*Risbridge*) An assize comes to declare (if[1]) Gilbert of Clare, Walter le Waleys, James the son of Maurice, Everard de Wadeshill, Roger the son of Aubert [and] Warner the son of Ralph unjustly disseised Alexander of Walpole and Robert his son of their free tenement in Little Thurlow after the first crossing etc. Gilbert and Warner come and they say nothing to stay the assize. Walter le Waleys and the others have not come nor were they attached because they were not found. So the assize is to proceed against them by default. The same Alexander and Robert in respect whereof complain that they disseised them of one and a half roods of land and half an acre of meadow.

The jurors say that the said Gilbert and the others have not disseised him of the said meadow because he never had that except for the crusader's term. Concerning the land they say that in fact he was at some time in seisin of the said land and he gave that land to a certain man in exchange, who still holds that land, and he has the exchange. So it is adjudged that he is to take nothing by this assize and he is in mercy for a false claim (*amercement*). Gilbert and the others [are] quit. The sureties of Alexander [are]: Thomas of Alby in Withersfield and Thomas of Bradley.

838. (*Risbridge*) An assize comes to declare if William the son of Nigel and Sarah his wife unjustly etc disseised Stephen the son of Nigel of his free tenement in Thurston after the first crossing etc and in respect whereof he complains that they disseised him of seven acres of land, half an acre of wood and one messuage with appurtenances. William has not come [and] he was not attached because he was not found. His [sister or wife][1] Sarah comes and she says nothing to stay the assize.

The jurors say that, in fact, the father of the said Stephen, in his full power of disposition for a long time before his death, gave the said tenements, in respect whereof the assize has been brought, by the said Stephen, his son, and in respect thereof he made his charter to him, and in the presence of the whole parish of Thurston placed Stephen in his seisin. Afterwards, he returned to the messuage that was on that land and he handed over to him the hasp of the door of the house[2] in respect of the seisin. Then the said Nigel went from that house, so that the said Stephen [made] a certain Adam Darnel his attorney to take care of it and he went elsewhere about his business where he made a sojourn for eight days. They say that on the same day that the said Nigel had made his seisin over to the said Stephen, as said beforehand, Nigel came in the evening at vespers and claimed from Adam, the attorney of Stephen, that he should provide him hospitality and then he [Adam] provided him [with] hospitality, and thus he [Nigel] remained in that house for the eight days until Stephen, his son, returned. When Stephen returned he asked what his father was doing in his house. Adam replied to him that he provided him [with] hospitality because he was his father. He [Stephen] then allowed him to remain for all his life [and] the same Nigel had his estovers from the said land and the said Nigel and Stephen cultivated the land together, and together they had the profits in respect thereof so that there never was heard a dispute[3] between them. They say also that in the last year that Nigel was alive he [Stephen][4] handed over half [of] that land to be sowed. The half, which belonged to him, he [Nigel] bequeathed for his soul. When the said Nigel was dead the same Stephen came and put himself in seisin of the said tenements. He sent for the said William, his brother, who was the elder [and] then in Ireland. Thus the same Stephen remained in seisin for fifteen days. Afterwards, the said William, his brother, came and he wished to receive homage for that land, but he went to Thomas of Moulton the lord of the fee and did homage to him for the lands of his father, and afterwards the same William came and ejected the said Stephen from it because he did not accept the deed of his father, and so to judgement. Because it has been proved incontestably that Nigel always, by the gift that he made to the said Stephen, was in seisin of the said land and he died in seisin, it is adjudged that Stephen is to take nothing by this assize,[5] and he is in mercy for a false claim (*amercement*). Sarah [is] without day.

[1]   The clerk wrote *soror* here for sister. She must be acting for William in his absence, probably as an attorney. This means she is also the sister, or half sister, of Stephen. William also has a wife called Sarah according to the first line in the plea, so it is possible that the clerk has made a mistake here or in the first line of the plea. If she is William's wife it is interesting that she is the one appearing and saying nothing to stop the assize, even if he could not be found.

[2]   See Clanchy 1993, p.260 for the symbolism of this action.

[3]   There is a fault in the membrane, which has been stitched and the clerk has worked around. It continues to the middle of the next plea.

[4]   He is in effect indicating that Nigel, his father, now controls this half of the land which he has handed over.

[5]   It looks as though Stephen received the land as a gift from his father but that Nigel could not do away with the obligations to his elder son, who had a legal entitlement to the land and which he obtained from his lord Thomas of Moulton.

839. (*Risbridge*) An assize comes to declare if Marcellus the parson of Dalham unjustly etc disseised Adam le Grant of his free tenement in Moulton after the first crossing etc and in respect whereof he complains that he disseised him of one rood of land. Marcellus has not come nor was he attached because he had no lay fee.

So the assize is to proceed against him by default. Thomas Orpedeman[1] one of the recognitors has not come, so [he is] in mercy (*amercement*). Afterwards, Thomas comes and he is a poor little man (*poor*).

The jurors say that he disseised him of a certain tenement that he holds around three feet.[2] So it is adjudged that he is to recover his seisin against him. Marcellus [is] in mercy (*amercement*). Adam le Grant (similarly[i]) [is] in mercy for a false claim against Marcellus because he has not disseised him of one rood of land (*amercement*). Sureties of Adam for the amercement: Simon le Franceys of Moulton and Edmund of Barnardiston.[3]

Damages: four pence

[1]   See Reaney 1997, p.331, under Orpet, which indicates that this person may have been stout.
[2]   This plea sounds like some modern cases where people move boundaries of land.
[3]   There are a number of Bernardistons in the *Book of Fees*, p.920 and in *Feudal Aids 1284–1431* v, p.76, but not an Edmund. Barnardiston is in Risbridge hundred.

840. (*Risbridge*) William of Stoke,[1] who brought a writ of an assize of novel disseisin against William the chaplain of Polstead and Gregory the parson of the same for two ditches in Brockley[2] [raised to] the nuisance of his free tenements in the same vill, came and sought licence to withdraw from his writ (----[il]) Bath.[3]

[1]   This is probably Stoke-by-Clare in Risbridge hundred.
[2]   There is considerable rubbing of the membrane here. The only possibility is Brockley in Risbridge hundred. I have managed to obtain some of this by using ultraviolet light.
[3]   This might be by the surety of Henry of Bath, the justice, but as there is a piece of the parchment missing it is impossible to say.

Membrane 32d

841. (*Risbridge*) An assize comes to declare if William the son of Walter unjustly etc raised two ditches in Bradley to the nuisance of the free tenement of Ralph the son of Lettice in the same after the first etc. William comes and he says nothing to stay the assize.

The jurors say that the father of the said Ralph was a villein and that this Ralph is similarly a villein. So it is adjudged that he is to take nothing by this assize and he is in mercy for a false claim. William [is] quit. The sureties [are] elsewhere within the roll. [835]

842. (*Risbridge*) An assize comes to declare if Roger of Hingham and John le Fevre[1] unjustly etc disseised William of Ely and Matilda his wife of their free tenement in Cowlinge after the first etc and in respect whereof the same William and Matilda complain that they have been disseised of six pence rent coming from a certain messuage, so that he who holds that messuage is being distrained to pay the said rent and to perform the customs and services which pertain to it. Roger and John come and say nothing to stay the assize.

The jurors say that the said Roger and John have not disseised the said William and Matilda because a certain Godfrey Smith holds a certain messuage in respect whereof this assize has been brought. And a servant of a certain Geoffrey of Bottisham came, whose daughter William took to wife, together with a servant of the said Godfrey, in order that she might render to him the service that she owed to his lord for that tenement that he held from him, and she handed over to him three pence. Then at the same time the servant of the said William and the servant of Godfrey departed, but they did not know whether he handed over to him [the lord] the said money or not. But, of the other seisin which the said [William][2] and Matilda have,

174

they knew nothing. So it is adjudged that William and Matilda are to take nothing by this assize and they are in mercy for a false claim (*amercement*). Roger and John [are] quit. The sureties of William are: Thomas of Bures [and] Adam le Grant of Moulton.

¹ This is old French for a smith, the Latin for which is *faber*.
² The clerk has made a mistake here as he wrote *Gilbertus*. This must be William.

843. (*Risbridge*) An assize comes to declare if Adam Buzun, Walter le Rus and Robert le Cat unjustly etc disseised Gilbert de Brook of his free tenement in Withersfield after the first etc and in respect whereof he complains that they disseised him of one rood of land. Adam and all the others come and they say nothing to stay the assize.

The jurors say that the said Adam and the others have not disseised the said Gilbert. So Gilbert is to take nothing by this assize and he is in mercy for a false claim (*amercement*). Adam and the others [are] without day. The sureties of Gilbert for the amercement are: John of Bealings of Haverhill and William the carter of Wratting.

844. (*Risbridge*) An assize comes to declare if Humphrey of Cowlinge, Hugh Picot, Godiva the widow and Richard the granger unjustly etc disseised William of Ely and Matilda his wife of their free tenement in Cowlinge after the first etc and in respect whereof they complain that they handed over a certain open space of land to a certain Reynold la Cat to be held in villeinage, so that he would keep their wood, and would do them other customs. He says also that the said Hugh Picot and Godiva the widow were holding from him in villeinage and the said Humphrey distrained them to do to him the customs which they have been accustomed to do to the said William and Matilda, by which they can have nothing from either tenement and they claim their assize. Humphrey and the others come and they say nothing to stay the assize.

The jurors say that the said Humphrey and the others have not disseised them. So William and Matilda are to take nothing by this assize and they are in mercy for a false claim (*amercement*). Humphrey and the others [are] quit. Sureties of them [are] above. **[842]**

845.¹ (*Risbridge, amercement*) An assize comes to declare if Warren the son of William de Wadeshill, Walter the son of Wibert, Warren le Bude,² Reynold Lardn[er],³ Alexander of Walpole and Warner the son of Walter Sutor⁴ unjustly etc disseised Heloise who was the wife of Warren de Wadeshill of her free tenement in Little Thurlow after the first etc. Warren the son of William and all the others come and they say nothing to stay the assize. She complains in respect whereof that they disseised her of two acres of land.⁵

The jurors say that the said Warren and all the others except Alexander of Walpole disseised the said Heloise as the writ says. So it is adjudged that she is to recover her seisin. Warren and the others [are] in mercy (*amercement*). Heloise similarly [is] in mercy against Alexander (*amercement*). The steward of Bury St Edmunds is commanded that he cause her to have seisin by the view of the recognitors. Damages: five shillings.

¹ See **826** and **827**. It looks as though Heloise has won one at last.
² This might be the name Booth, a cow or herd man.
³ The clerk ran out of parchment and this may be a shortened version of lardner, an officer in charge of the larder. See Reaney 1997, p.272. The clerk has not indicated a suspension, for which there is room.

175

⁴   Walter may have been a shoemaker.
⁵   This sentence is not in its normal place in the formulary for the assize. It would normally come
    after the place where the vill is mentioned as to how much land etc has been disseised.

846. (*Risbridge*) William Woolmer who brought an assize of novel disseisin against
Richard de Colville concerning his free tenement in Wratting came and withdrew
[from the plea]. So he and his sureties [are] in mercy (*amercement*). He has no sureties except faith because [he is] poor. The sureties of William for the amercement:
William the carter of Wratting and William Berard of the same.

847. (*Risbridge*) An assize comes to declare if Richard of Dalham unjustly etc
disseised Roger the son of William of his free tenement in Dalham after the first
etc and in respect whereof he complains that he disseised him of a certain spinney.
Richard comes and he says nothing to stay the assize.

   Afterwards, Roger of Dalham came and acknowledged that the tenement he
claims is in Cowlinge and not in Dalham, and that he claims nothing in Dalham by
this writ. So Richard [is] without day. Roger [is] in mercy, by the surety of Peter de
Pridington and John Ilger of Stansfield (*amercement*).

848. (*Risbridge*) An assize comes to declare if Walter of Bradfield the father of
William the son of Walter was seised in his demesne etc of one acre of meadow
with appurtenances in Bradley on the day that etc and if etc which meadow Roger
the son of Ranulf holds. He comes and says nothing to stay the assize. Note: that
the same jurors were in this assize that were in the assize between Thomas le Bigod
and William the son of Walter.

   The jurors say that the said Walter did not die seised of the said meadow as the
writ says because a long time before his death he gave that meadow to Ranulf the
father of the said Roger so that the same William is still in seisin as regards the said
exchange. So it is adjudged that Roger [is] without day, and William [is] in mercy
for a false claim (*amercement*).

849. (*Risbridge*) Gilbert Sprot, who brought a writ of an assize of mort d'ancestor
against William Sprot for two and a half acres in Haverhill, came and withdrew
[from the plea], and so he and his sureties [are] in mercy, namely: Anselm the son
of Odo of Hepworth and Stephen the son of Ralph of the same (*amercement*). The
sureties of Gilbert for the amercement namely: William the clerk of Hundon, Hubert
de Lea in Haverhill.

850. (*Risbridge, amercement*) An assize comes to declare if Nicholas the son of
Renier, the brother of Malger the son of Renier was seised in his demesne etc of
half an acre of meadow and one rood of land with appurtenances in Withersfield on
the day [he died] etc and if etc which land and that meadow Hugh the son of Walter
holds. He comes and he says that the said Nicholas did not die seised of the said
meadow. Concerning the land he says that in fact the said Nicholas died seised in
respect thereof as of fee, but he had a certain son by reason of which he had that land
in wardship as long as the boy lived. After he¹ died, he held that land in his hands
until the rightful heir should come and pay [homage] to him for the land which he
ought to do, and he readily grants that the said Nicholas died seised of the said land
as of fee and after the term. Because he cannot deny this that the said Malger is the
nearest heir of the said Nicholas, it is adjudged that the said Malger is to recover his
seisin of the said rood of land and Hugh [is] in mercy for an unjust detention, and
that the assize is to proceed concerning the said meadow (*amercement*).

The jurors say that the said Nicholas died seised of the said meadow as the writ says and that Malger is his nearest heir. So it is adjudged that Malger has his seisin by view of the recognitors, and Hugh [is] in mercy, by the surety of Walter Ruffus of Withersfield and Guy Grut of Haverhill (*amercement*).

> [1] Presumably the boy.

851. (*Thedwestry*) An assize comes to declare if Alan the father of Matilda and Maria the daughters of Alan the son of Roger was seised in demesne as of fee of half an acre of land with appurtenances in Hessett on the day that [he died] etc and if etc which land Rery of Hessett holds and he has not come etc and he was resummoned. So the assize is to proceed against him by default.

The jurors say that the said Alan died seised of the half acre of land as the writ says. The said Matilda and [Maria][1] are his nearest heirs. So they are to have their seisin by view of the recognitors. Rery [is] in mercy (*amercement*).

> [1] The clerk wrote *Sarah*, but I assume this is his mistake and that Maria the sister of Matilda is the correct name.

852. (*Risbridge*)[1] Gilbert the parson of Withersfield, who brought a writ of free alms against Adam Buzun and Sarah his wife concerning the land in Withersfield, came and acknowledged that they have satisfied him. So [they are] without day.

> [1] There is a line from this name in the margin to the next plea implying that the next plea is also for land in Risbridge.

853.[1] (*Risbridge*)[2] An assize comes to declare if Anselm the baker father of Mabel the daughter of Anselm was seised in his demesne etc of six acres of land and a half acre of meadow with appurtenances in Bradley[3] on the day etc and if etc and after the term etc whereof Thomas le Bigod holds four acres of land and the half acre of meadow and Thomas of Bures two acres of it.

Thomas le Bigod has not come and he was seen in the court, so let the assize be taken against him by default.

Thomas of Bures comes and he says that the assize should not be taken (against him[i]) on this because a certain Gilbert the son of Anselm [and] brother of the said Mabel after the death of their father was seised of the said land, so that he sold four acres to the father of the said Thomas Bigod and two acres he sold to Thomas of Bures and then he puts himself on the assize, and he readily grants that if the said Gilbert was (not[i]) seised of the said land after the death of his father she would recover her seisin. So then the inquest is to be made.

The jurors say that the said Gilbert was seised of the said land for a long time after the death of his father so that a certain part he sold to William le Bigod, the father of the said Thomas le Bigod, and a certain part to the said Thomas of Bures. Afterwards, Thomas of Bures came and he gave to the said Mabel two shillings and she remised all etc.

> [1] This plea is one of those most seriously affected by the stitched up tear. The clerk has worked around it.
> [2] Although there is no name against this plea there is a line from the marginal note against the previous plea. I have therefore repeated it here as it looks as though this is the intention of the clerk.
> [3] This is Bradley in Risbridge hundred.

854. (*Thedwestry*)[1] Thomas of Gedding, who brought an assize of mort d'ancestor against Matthew de Luveyn concerning five and a half acres of land with appurtenances in Bradley,[2] came and withdrew [from the plea], so he and his sureties [are] in mercy, namely: Henry of Livermere and Thomas the son of Geoffrey de Haffeud (*amercement*).[3]

1   This impinges into the body of the text but the ¶ sign for a new section follows it so it must be a marginal note.
2   Bradley is in Risbridge hundred not Thedwestry. The clerk has probably made a mistake in the marginal note.
3   The clerk has written the Latin for only one amercement when he should have indicated the plural.

Membrane 33[1]

1   The membrane is damaged at the end, where a piece is missing and it has affected the last plea on this side.

855. (*Risbridge*) An assize comes to declare if Thomas le Bigod unjustly etc disseised William the son of Walter of his free tenement in Great Bradley after the first crossing etc and in respect whereof he complains that he disseised him of half a rood of land. Thomas comes and he says nothing to stay the assize.

The jurors say that the said Thomas has not disseised the said William of any tenement. So Thomas [is] without day, and William [is] in mercy (*amercement*). The sureties of William: John of Samford and Thomas of Alby of Withersfield.

856. (*Risbridge*) The same assize, by the same recognitors, comes to declare if the same Thomas unjustly etc disseised William of his common pasture in the same vill after the same term. Thomas comes and he says nothing to stay the assize.

The jurors say that the said Thomas disseised the said William of his common pasture as the writ says, namely in a certain assart that is called *Westwood*[1] in which he ought to have his common for his cattle with the cattle of the said Thomas, and that the same Thomas made a certain park before his portion[2] [of land], where he enclosed a certain part of the pasture in which William was accustomed to have a common. So he is to have his seisin by view of the recognitors. Thomas [is] in mercy (*amercement*).

Damages: two shillings.

1   This name does not appear on the Ordnance Survey map of Great Bradley. See **855**.
2   What the clerk is trying to say here is that Thomas has enclosed a park on a portion of his own land but it incorporates a portion of the common pasture on which William is allowed to graze his cattle.

857. (*Risbridge*) An assize comes to declare if Thomas le Bigod unjustly etc disseised Richard of Rattlesden, Alice de Hauville, Hugh de Ponte, Walter Mauveysyn[1] and John of Samford of their common pasture in Great Bradley which pertains to their free tenement in Little Bradley after the first etc. Thomas comes and he says nothing to stay the assize. Note: that the same jurors are in this assize who were in the assize between Thomas le Bigod and William the son of Walter.

The jurors say that the said Thomas disseised the said Richard and all the others as the writ says. So it is adjudged that they are to have their seisin by view of the recognitors. Thomas [is] in mercy (*amercement*).

Damages: twelve pence. They are pardoned.

1   This means he was a bad neighbour in old French. See Reaney 1997, p.303.

858. (*Risbridge*) An assize comes to declare if Aylmer, the father of Robert the son of Aylmer, was seised in his demesne etc of eight acres of land with appurtenances in Little Bradley on the day that etc and if etc which land Alice de Hauville holds.

She comes and says nothing to stay the assize. Thomas de Ponte of Thurlow, one of the recognitors, has not come, so [he is] in mercy (*amercement*).

The jurors say that Aylmer was a free man and he died seised of the said land as the writ says. So Robert is to have his seisin by view of the recognitors, and Alice [is] in mercy by the surety of Henry of Cowlinge and Roger the son of Ranulf of Bradley (*amercement*).

859. (*Risbridge*)[1] An assize of novel disseisin, which William de Blunville holds against William Buttevyleyn[2] concerning a tenement in Mildenhall remains without day from him because William Butlin died.

₁ There is a line from this marginal note to the next plea indicating the same hundred for **860**.
₂ This is the name Butlin according to Reaney 1997, p.76.

860. (*Risbridge*) An assize comes to declare if Rose the daughter of Robert, the mother of William the [son][1] of John Ruffus was seised in her demesne as of fee of six acres of land with appurtenances in Withersfield and in Hanchet[2] on the day that etc and if etc and if after the term etc which land Thomas of Alby holds. He comes and readily acknowledges that the said Rose died seised as the writ says and that William is her nearest heir. So William is to have his seisin by view of the recognitors and Thomas [is] in mercy for an unjust detention, by the surety of Robert the son of Adam de *Talworth*[3] and Thomas of Hanchet (*amercement*).

₁ The clerk wrote *fuit*, 'was'. I think this should be *filii*.
₂ This is Hanchet in Risbridge hundred, which is now totally incorporated into the town of Haverhill, except for Hanchet Hall and Hanchet End.
₃ The Talworth family were amongst the chief landowners in Great Wratting which has sometimes been called Talworth Wratting. Also see Copinger 1905–11 v, p.316.

861.[1] (*Lackford*) An assize comes to declare if John of Coddenham[2] unjustly etc disseised William of Tuddenham of his free tenement in Tuddenham after the first crossing etc and in respect whereof he complains that he disseised him of sixty acres of land.[3] John comes and he says that the assize should not be taken on this because the land in respect whereof the assize has been held is land held by villein tenure and that the said William is a villein. He then puts himself on the assize.

The jurors say that William is a free man and that from the sixty acres he held twenty-three acres by the service of six shillings per year, and all the residue of the land[4] he holds by the customs written underneath, namely: by making four plough services in return for food from the said John, namely: two at the summer sowing and two at the winter sowing, and he must make each week in the harvest, on Mondays, two harvest services by two men and similarly two harvest services on each Wednesday in return for food from the said John as long as the said John had anything for reaping, and to sow for one day and to load hay as long as the same John had anything to load, and similarly [reap] the corn at harvest-time and all in return for food from the said John. And he owes ten shillings per year for two feasts. They also say that no ancestor of the said William gave merchet for his daughter until the time that a certain agreement was made between Gilbert the father of Juliana, who was the wife of the said John, and John the brother of the said William. By a certain agreement it was agreed between them that whenever the said John (*process mark*)[5] (*process mark*) would wish to marry his daughter he would place twelve pence in the hands of the said Gilbert, and the same Gilbert immediately ought to pay the said twelve pence to the daughter of the said John to be married, but it never happened after that agreement that the said John or William had any daughter to marry. Because it has been proved by the jury that the said William held a certain portion of the said land by a certain service of money and a certain portion by doing certain customs in return for food from the said John⁶ without any of his ancestors giving merchet for their daughters to marry, it is adjudged that William is to recover his seisin and John [is] in mercy, by the surety of William of Cotton and Thomas the son of Richard of Tuddenham (*amercement*).

(*to the clerks, one mark*) Damages: six marks.

¹ This plea is split in two with the next plea intervening. It looks as though there were two clerks, one of whom left a gap for this plea, but not large enough, and then the other clerk wrote the next plea leaving a larger gap but for which he did not need all the space, so the first clerk compromised and split up this plea with **862** sandwiched between the two parts. The other possibility is that the second clerk came and added this in later between the gaps left by the first clerk.

² There is a Coddenham in Bosmere hundred and also one in Babergh hundred.

³ It was probably in or near Tuddenham as described above as his free tenement, as William is from there and there is a Tuddenham in Lackford hundred.

⁴ That is 37 acres.

⁵ There is a circle symbol with two parallel lines through it to indicate that the text continues at the place on the membrane where there is a similar symbol. The split takes place here and the remainder of the plea follows after **862**. However I continue it here.

⁶ The clerk uses a small 'i' at the beginning of *Johannis*.

862. (*Lackford*) An assize comes to declare if John of Coddenham unjustly etc disseised Matilda, who was the wife of Peter of Tuddenham, of her free tenement in Tuddenham after the first crossing etc and in respect whereof she complains that he disseised her of thirty acres of land. John comes and he says that the assize should not be taken on this because the said Peter, the husband of Matilda, was a villein and his tenement, in respect whereof Matilda has brought this assize, is land held by villein tenure. He then puts himself on the assize.

The jurors say that the said Matilda never had the land in her separate possession, but always she held jointly with her son, so that she did not enjoy her separate possession. But they readily say that her husband was a free man and he held freely. Because she never enjoyed her separate possession it is adjudged that she has not been disseised of any tenement, and so John [is] quit, and Matilda [is] in mercy.

¹ John is written with a small 'i' again.

863. (*Lackford, twenty shillings*) Henry Canevaz gives twenty shillings for licence to agree with Henry of Stoke and Ivetta his sister concerning a plea of land and rent by the surety of the said Henry of Stoke and John le Blund de Hagwell. [*chirograph* CP 25(1) 213/17/123]

864. (*Lackford*) An assize comes to declare if Richard the son of Astil, Henry his brother and Walter Greneknyct unjustly etc disseised Robert the son of Richard and Christine his wife of their free tenement in Mildenhall after the first crossing etc and in respect whereof they complain that they disseised them of three roods of land. Henry and the others....,¹ except Richard who has not been (--ᶜˏ ᵉˏ ⁱˡ)² found, come and they say that the assize ought not to proceed because the said Robert is a villein and the land in respect whereof the assize has been held is land held by villein tenure of the abbot of Bury St Edmunds. They then put themselves on the assize, and the assize is being taken against Richard by default.

The jurors say that the said Robert is the villein of Henry Canevaz.³ So it is adjudged that they have not been disseised of any free tenement. So Richard and the others [are] without day, and Robert [is] in mercy. He is poor.

¹ There are dots here, probably to indicate the remains of an erasure over which these words have been written.

2   I cannot decipher it but it looks crossed out. Also there are more dots, which might mean that
    this is a continuing erasure from the previous one. The Latin seems to be fine and there appears
    to be nothing missing.
3   See **863**.

865. (*Risbridge*) Cecilia the daughter of Gilbert, who brought a writ of novel disseisin
against William the son of William concerning her free tenement, namely of one
messuage in Clare, has not prosecuted. So she and her sureties for prosecuting [are]
in mercy, namely: William of Lynn in Cowlinge and Alexander the son of Richard
of Walpole (*amercement*).

866. (*Babergh, one mark*) Richard the son of Payn of Cornard gives one mark for
licence to agree with William the son of Alexander and many others concerning
a plea of land by the surety of William the son of Alexander and Seman de Nort-
strete.

867. Robert the son of Woolward who brought a writ of mort d'ancestor against
Alan de Sture[1] concerning one acre of land with appurtenances in Cornard has not
prosecuted. So he and his sureties [are] in mercy, namely: Hubert the son of Joss of
Sudbury [and] Walter the son of Robert of Cornard (*amercement*).

1   This name probably derives from the river Stour. There is no such vill in Suffolk.

868. (*Babergh*) Richard the son of Ralph of Boxford and Alice his wife who brought
a writ of mort d'ancestor against Geoffrey Blund concerning two acres of land with
appurtenances in Boxford have not prosecuted. So they and their sureties for prosecuting [are] in mercy, namely: Richard the son of William of Hadleigh, Reynold the
son of Roger of the same (*amercement*). Note: that Richard[1] has started on a journey
towards the Holy Land about one year before the eyre of the justices.

1   The clerk unfortunately does not indicate whether this is the plaintiff or the surety. Either way
    the king will not get his full money for some time.

869. (*Babergh*) Henry Gerewy, who brought a writ of novel disseisin against Adam
the fisher concerning a tenement in Stoke [by Nayland], came and withdrew [from
the plea]. So he and his sureties for prosecuting [are] in mercy, namely: John the
son of John of Cornard, and Richard the son of Thomas de *Lafham* (*amercement*).
Sureties of Henry for the amercement [are]: Robert Gerewy and Richard the son of
Vivian of Layham.

870. (*Babergh*) Gervase de Meulinghes, who brought a writ of novel disseisin
against Walter the son of Robert concerning a tenement in Waldingfield, came and
withdrew [from the plea]. So he and his sureties [are] in mercy, namely: Gilbert the
son of Warren of Edwardstone and Adam his brother (*amercement*).

871. Robert de Alneto, against whom Geoffrey the son of Ralph brought a writ of
novel disseisin concerning a tenement in Westacre, came and acknowledged that he
disseised the same Geoffrey of one acre of land. So Geoffrey is to have his seisin
by view of the recognitors and Robert [is] in mercy, by the surety of John Marshall
of Stoke and Philip de *Hunelegh*[1] (*amercement*).

1   There is a mention of a *Honilega* in Babergh hundred in Domesday Book, but it is now unidentifi-
    able. See *Domesday Book Suffolk*, Part Two, section 34, no. 2.

872. (*Babergh, ten shillings*) Henry the son of William de Helmeswell gives ten
shillings for licence to agree with Hugh the son of Maurice concerning a plea of

land and meadow, by the surety of the same Hugh. The agreement is such that the said Hugh remises all claim for twenty shillings.

873. (*Babergh*) John the son of Ralph, who brought a writ of novel disseisin against John de Grey in Cornard[1] and others named in the writ concerning a tenement in Great Cornard, has not prosecuted. So he and his sureties [are] in mercy, namely: William Testepin[2] [and] John the son of Richard of Chattisham (*amercement*).

[1] This must have been at a special assize of novel disseisin at one of the Cornards, presumably Great Cornard.

[2] The Testepin family appear to have had lands around Hintlesham in Samford hundred. They were involved in two cases approximately a hundred years apart, one in 1220 and one in 1315 according to *Cal. Feet of Fines, Suff.*, pp.21 and 136. The early one was by a William Testepin. I have been unable to find out what the name means.

874.[1] (*Thedwestry*) William the son of Walter who brought a writ of novel disseisin against Matthew Smallwood and William Tesegod concerning a free tenement in Hessett has not prosecuted. So [he and his sureties are in mercy], namely: Thomas the son of Elud of Hessett and Roger de Mora (*amercement*).

[1] This plea is affected where part of the end of the membrane has been torn off. This leaves a few words missing from the plea, which have been supplied from the context.

Membrane 33d

875. (*Cosford*) An assize comes to declare if Alan Stanhard unjustly etc disseised Hugh the parson of Kettlebaston of his free tenement in the same vill after the first crossing etc and in respect whereof he complains that he disseised him of one and a half roods.

Alan comes and he says nothing to stay the assize.

The jurors say that Alan has not disseised the said Hugh of any free tenement. So Alan [is] without day and Hugh [is] in mercy (*amercement*).

876. (*half a mark*) Thomas of Hanchet gives half a mark for licence to agree with John the son of Robert and his brothers concerning a plea of land by the surety of John the son of Robert of Hanchet and Roger his brother. The agreement is such that the said John and his brothers remise all to the said Thomas and his heirs in perpetuity.

877. (*Cosford*) Walter Smith and Emma his wife who brought a writ of mort d'ancestor against William de Aumbly[1] and Geoffrey the son of Alexander concerning land in Elmsett came and withdrew [from the plea], so they and their sureties for prosecuting [are] in mercy, namely: William de Brook in Elmsett and Peter Marshall of Bury St Edmunds (*amercement*). The amercement of Walter is pardoned for poverty.

[1] This is almost certainly a member of the de Ambli family who had lands in Emsett and Somersham in Cosford and Bosmere hundreds.

878. Matilda of Eleigh who brought a writ of novel disseisin against Henry the son of Alured and Hugh Gril concerning her free tenement in Eleigh has not prosecuted. So she and her sureties [are] in mercy (*amercement*).[1] She did not find a surety except faith because she is a poor little woman.

[1] The clerk is going to amerce the plaintiff only, even though she is poor and has no sureties to amerce. There is no evidence that she was amerced in the amercement section of this roll.

879. (*Blackbourn*) An assize comes to declare if William the son of Eustace the uncle of Walter the son of Heloise was seised in his demesne as of fee etc of one

182

messuage and twelve acres of land with appurtenances in Troston on the day that [he died] etc and if etc which land Robert the son of William holds. He comes and says that he is the villein of the abbot of Bury St Edmunds and he holds that land, in respect whereof the assize has been held, in villein tenure from David Cumyn.[1] So it is adjudged that Robert [is] without day and Walter [is] in mercy by the surety of William of Troston and Henry of Livermere (*amercement*).

> [1] See *Book of Fees*, pp.592, 911 for Suffolk. The name appears to be of French origin. The family of that name may be related to the Comyns in Scotland. See Reaney 1997, p.120

880. (*Thedwestry*) Matilda, the daughter of Richard the miller, Avice and Beatrice, her sisters, who brought a writ of novel disseisin against Henry the son of Roger of Rede and Simon his brother concerning their free tenement in Hessett, have not prosecuted. So they and their sureties for prosecuting [are] in mercy, namely: Thomas the son of Aylmer of Hessett and Roger de Mora of the same (*amercement*).

881. (*one mark*) Geoffrey the son of Ralph (de Leyland[i]) gives one mark for licence to agree with Richard the son of Thomas concerning a plea of land by the surety of Gilbert Warner. [*chirograph* CP 25(1) 213/15/39][1]

> [1] The chirograph indicates that this was a plea of mort d'ancestor for 7 acres of land in Layham in Cosford hundred.

882. An assize of mort d'ancestor which Hugh the son of Alexander, Godfrey and William his brothers have brought against Thomas de la Ponde concerning land in *Lafham* remains without day because Godfrey has died.

883. An assize comes to declare if Thomas de *Lafham* the father of Richard de *Lafham* was seised in his demesne etc of seven acres of land with appurtenances in Hadleigh on the day that [he died] etc and after the term etc which land John the son of William and Agnes Slag hold. They come and say nothing to stay the assize.

The jurors say that the said Thomas did not die seised of the said land as of fee. So Richard is to take nothing by this assize and he is in mercy for a false claim (*amercement*). John and Agnes [are] without day. The surety of Richard for the amercement [is] Henry Gerwy.

884.[1] (*Samford*) Geoffrey the son of Geoffrey who brought a writ of entry against Baldwin[2] the son of Robert concerning a tenement in Belstead has not prosecuted. So he and his sureties for prosecuting [are] in mercy, namely: William Testepin of Hintlesham and Edmund the son of Richard of Sutton (*amercements*).

> [1] The plea is written by two different hands and in a different colour ink for each hand. Even the marginal note is split between the two hands. It must have been started by one clerk and completed by another.
> [2] It is at this point that the second hand takes over and continues to the end of this membrane.

885. (*Bosmere*) William le Rus claims against Matilda de Merk[1] and Alice her sister twelve acres of land with appurtenances in Coddenham as his right etc. Matilda and Alice come and by licence they render [it] to him, so he is to have his seisin.

> [1] This might be Mark in Somerset, Mark Hall, Marks Tey or Markshall in Essex or Mark Cross in Sussex.

886.[1] Gerard de Oddingseles was attached to answer Nicholas de *Sanford*[2] concerning a plea why by force and arms against the peace of the lord king he felled and devastated the timber of Nicholas, that he felled in his wood in Cavendish etc and in respect whereof the same Nicholas complains that the said Gerard felled and devastated thirty oaks of the value of ten marks, whereon he has suffered damage to the value etc.

Gerard comes and denies force and injury and everything and denies that he ever felled and devastated any timber of Nicholas as the same Nicholas says. Because the same Nicholas accused the same Gerard that against the peace of the lord king by force and arms etc it is adjudged that it be inquired into by the country concerning the said trespass. So then the inquiry is to be made.

The jurors, chosen by consent of the parties, say on their oath that the said Gerard has not felled or devastated the timber of Nicholas as the same Nicholas says, nor has he come there with force and arms, because they say those oaks did not belong to Nicholas but they belonged to certain men who bought those oaks from the servant of William de Oddingseles. So it is adjudged that Gerard [is] without day. Nicholas [is] in mercy (*amercement*).

1   This is a case of trespass. See **69** for the essoin of Gerard.
2   This is either the name of Samford hundred or of a place called *Sanford'*, which I am unable to locate.

887.[1] [There is a paragraph/section mark but no plea inserted.]

1   There is a paragraph/section mark but no plea follows. There is a large gap of 5.3 cm between the previous plea and the next as though a reasonable size plea would be inserted here; but the clerk either misjudged the size of the plea or missed a plea out. I have given this a plea number whereas I have not numbered those previous section marks that stand alone at the end of a particular section and probably mark the end of a section. This cannot be such an occasion.

888.[1] (*Blything, one mark*) Robert the son of Reynold gives one mark for licence to agree with John Blench and Alice his wife by the surety of Hamo de Valoines.

(*one mark*) The same John gives one mark for licence to agree with the same by the surety of Robert of Wissett and Henry of Spexhall. [*chirograph* CP 25(1) 213/16/53][2]

1   See **913** for the appointment of the attorney of the Alice in this plea.
2   The chirograph indicates that this was an action of right with a grand assize. The chirograph indicates that the plea was heard at Dunwich on 11 June, but no plea for the litigants has been found in the pleas heard at Dunwich in this roll. As this section deals with cases made at Cattishall then it is obvious that the clerk was probably scratching around for space on the roll to put this case. Note that the appointment of the attorney of *Alice* is later than this plea; so this agreement is not in chronological order.

889. (*Blackbourn*) Ralph of Fakenham was attached to answer David the engineer concerning a plea that he keep the fine made in the king's court before the justices at Westminster between that David, the plaintiff, and the said Ralph, the defendant, concerning one hundred and eighty acres of land with appurtenances in Little Fakenham, Euston, Sapiston, Barningham, Thelnetham, and Wattisfield, Bury St Edmunds and Thetford in respect whereof a chirograph was made. The same David complains that whereas by that fine half of that land with appurtenances ought to remain to him in the lifetime of Ralph, the same Ralph deforces him of half of twenty-eight acres of land with appurtenances in Little Fakenham, and half of twenty acres of land with appurtenances in Sapiston, and half of one mill with appurtenances in Euston, and half of one messuage with appurtenances in Thetford and half of one market stall with appurtenances in the town of Bury St Edmunds, and of half a silver mark for the annual rent and of half of three acres of land with appurtenances in Wattisfield, whereon he has suffered damage to the value of ten marks.

Ralph comes.

They have agreed. They are to have a chirograph. [*chirograph* CP 25(1) 213/16/44][1]

1 This chirograph was presumably a replacement for the one made at Westminster. It looks as though this case was originally pleaded in 1238/1239 as there is a chirograph shown for that date in *Cal. Feet of Fines, Suff.*, p.39.

Membrane 34

890. (*Risbridge*) An assize comes to declare if John Pepper the father of Beatrice the wife of Gikel was seised in his demesne etc of twenty acres of land and of a half of three and a half acres of meadow and three acres of wood and one messuage with appurtenances in Stansfield on the day that he set out on his crusade etc and if he journeyed after the first crossing etc and in respect whereof Hugh Wigge and Alice his wife hold ten acres, Richard the clerk three acres and one rood of meadow, William Syburt one acre of land and a half acre of meadow, Ernald of Chipley one acre of land, Warren Grapinel three roods of land, Richard Pocok one rood of land, Austin the son of Alice one acre of land and three roods of wood, Gilbert Aungel and Rose his wife two and a half acres of land and three roods of wood. They come and then vouch to warranty Hugh Wigge and Alice his wife, who are present, and they warrant them and they say nothing to stay the assize.

The jurors say that the said John did not die seised of the said land as of fee because that land was the inheritance of the said Alice, the wife of Hugh Wigge. So it is adjudged that Gikel and Beatrice are to take nothing by this assize, and they are in mercy for a false claim (*remand in custody, amercement*). Hugh [is] without day.

891. (*Lothingland*) Nicholas de Crew, plaintiff, who brought an assize of novel disseisin against Geoffrey the son of Guy and many others, has not prosecuted. So he and his sureties for prosecuting [are] in mercy, namely: Alan Godrich of Herringfleet, and John the son of the parson of Somerleyton (*amercements*).

892. (*Lothingland*) An assize comes to declare if Robert Crevquor[1] the father of Nicholas Crevquor was seised in his demesne etc of four messuage with appurtenances in South Yarmouth and North Yarmouth on the day that he died, and if he died after the last return and if etc and in respect whereof Robert Pate holds one messuage, Richard of Bing two messuages and the prior of Broomholm[2] one messuage. They have not come and they were resummoned, so the assize is to be taken against them by default.

The jurors say that the said Robert died seised of the messuages, which he [Nicholas] claimed against [Robert][3] and Richard, and that the same Nicholas is the nearest heir, and that he died after the term. So it is adjudged that he is to recover his seisin against them. They are in mercy for an unjust detention (*amercements*). They say also that he did not die seised of that messuage which he claimed against the prior. So it is adjudged that he is in mercy for a false claim. (*half a mark*) He made a fine for half a mark. The prior [is] without day.

1 A French name from Crèvecoeur in the Calvados region of Normandy.
2 Broomholm priory is on the north Norfolk coast in Tunstead hundred. This is the place where supposed relics of the Holy Cross resided. The pilgrimage of Henry III to Bromholm was probably instrumental in the downfall of Hubert de Burgh. See Carpenter 1996, pp.50–54.
3 The clerk wrote *Radulfus*. However, this must be Robert.

893. ((*Norfolk (day----*il, e))[1] Eudo of Moulton claims against John of Morley one twenty-fifth of one knight's fee[2] with appurtenances in Beeston[3] as his right, and in which the same John has no entry except by William the Earl Warenne and Matilda his wife, who have entered into the same fifth part after the death of Emma de Beaufoy, who held that land in dower by the gift of Gilbert of Norfolk her former husband [and] uncle of the said Eudo whose heir he is.

John comes and he denies force and injury and everything. He says that he ought not to answer to this writ because the prior of Broomholm in respect [of the property sought] thereof holds twelve acres, and Nicholas the parson of Felbrigg[4] two shillingsworth of rent with appurtenances.

Afterwards, Eudo (came[i]) and sought licence to withdraw from his writ, and he has [it].

1 It looks as though the clerk has rubbed something out here, perhaps *die lune* but it is illegible.
2 Literally a fifth part of a fifth part as expressed in Latin.
3 There are three places called Beeston in Norfolk, Beeston Regis in North Erpingham hundred, Beeston St Andrew in Taverham hundred and Beeston St Lawrence in Tunstead hundred.
4 Felbrigg is in North Erpingham hundred, which suggests that the vill of Beeston is probably Beeston Regis.

894.[1] (*Lothingland*) An assize comes to declare if William the son of Alan unjustly etc disseised Margery the daughter of Robert of Burgh concerning her free tenement in Gapton[2] after the first crossing etc and in respect whereof she complains that he disseised her of two acres of land with appurtenances in the same vill.

William comes and says nothing to stay the assize.

The jurors say that Alan the father of the said William gave to the said Margery the said two acres, in the lifetime of Herbert her husband, so that she was in full seisin. After the same Herbert had committed a certain felony, on account of which he abjured the realm, a certain bailiff of Lothingland came and took the said land into the king's hands and immediately handed it over to that William. Because it has been attested by the jury that the said land was given to that Margery and that she was in seisin, it is adjudged that she is to recover her seisin and William [is] in mercy. He is poor.

1 There is a gap of 5.9 cm before this plea. It is a good case of a woman winning against the odds, even though the land was hers from the grandfather of the defendant, as once a person is outlawed their lands are normally forfeit to the crown or they revert to the lord of the person outlawed. However, it looks as though the bailiff of Lothingland was too quick off the mark, took the land into the king's hands and subsequently took the decision to give it to the defendant, rather than finding the truth of the matter. It looks as though the defendant and the bailiff may have been working together to get some of his grandfather's land back into the family.
2 Gapton is in Lothingland hundred but it now appears to have been subsumed into the vill of Bradwell. The only reference to Gapton on the modern Ordnance Survey maps is Gapton Marshes.

895. Joan, who was the wife of Robert Leydeyt, claims against the prior of Leighs a third part of fifty-five acres of land with appurtenances in *Bercot*[1] as her dower, and in respect whereof Robert her former husband dowered her etc on the day that he married her etc.

The prior comes and then vouches to warranty Geoffrey the son of William de *Bruniford*. He is to have him by aid of the court at Chelmsford in the octave of Holy Trinity [Sunday 17 June].

1 I cannot find this place in Suffolk or Norfolk. East Bergholt is a possibility according to Watts 2004, p.51.

186

896. (*Hartismere*) Beatrice, who was the wife of Robert Sorel, presented herself on the fourth day against Agnes the daughter of Robert of Newton concerning a plea for half of three acres of land with appurtenances in Newton which she claims in her dower against her. She has not come and [was] summoned etc. Judgement: the half is to be taken into the hands of the lord king etc and the day [of caption told to the justices] etc and she is to be summoned to be at Chelmsford in the octave of Holy Trinity [Sunday 17 June] (*Chelmsford*).

897. (*Samford*) Cecilia, who was the wife of Reynold the carpenter, claims against the prior of Leighs half of twelve acres of land with appurtenances in Wenham as her dower.

The prior comes and then vouches to warranty Ralph Gernun. He is to have him at Chelmsford in the octave of Holy Trinity [Sunday 17 June], and he is to be summoned in the county of Essex (*Essex*). [*chirograph* CP 25(1) 213/16/42][1]

[1]   This chirograph was made at Chelmsford on the octave of Holy Trinity.

898. (*Norfolk, twenty pounds*) John of Colkirk gives to the lord king thirty marks for a trespass by the surety of Richard de St Denis,[1] Richard de *Langetoft*, knight, Adam of Mendham, Alan of Withersdale, Gilbert of Walsham and Ranulf de Roseyc.

[1]   In the pipe roll he is shown as John de St Denis. See Appendix H(iii).

899. (*Hartismere*) Roger the son of Adam claims against Henry Folcard, whom Agnes Crasschepanne vouched to warranty, and who [claims] etc half an acre of land with appurtenances in Mellis as his right. Henry comes and he renders to him that half an acre for half a silver mark. He is to make an exchange to the said Agnes to the value etc.

900. (*Ely*) William de Glanvill presented himself on the fourth day against Ranulf Main concerning a plea for two acres of turf pit [*turbaria*] in Benhall, in respect whereof Ranulf, who is the tenant, puts himself on the grand assize of the lord king. He has not come and [was] summoned etc. Judgement: the turf pit is to be taken into the king's hands and the day etc and he is to be summoned to be at Chelmsford in the octave of Holy Trinity [Sunday 17 June] etc. (*Chelmsford*).

901.[1] (*half a mark*[r])[2] Master Nicholas of Layham[3] gives half a mark for licence to agree with William his brother concerning a plea of customs and services by the surety of William. [*chirograph* CP 25(1) 213/16/80]

[1]   This plea is indented into the body of the text area of the membrane and has included the marginal note alongside it as well. It is not certain why the clerk did this as given the length of the plea it could easily have been fitted in as normal.
[2]   There are two references to *dimidia marca*: one in the normal margin and one alongside the indented plea before the section/paragraph mark.
[3]   The chirograph indicates that Nicholas and his brother are 'of Layham' and not 'Leighs', which *Legh* implies from what the clerk has written.

Membrane 34d

902. (*Samford*) Richard de Bordesho claims against Roger de Rivers forty acres of land with appurtenances in Sproughton as his right etc. Roger comes and then vouches to warranty Henry Wicher. He must have him by aid of the court at Chelmsford in the octave of Holy Trinity [Sunday 17 June] (*Chelmsford*). Henry is to be summoned in the county of Suffolk.

903. (*Blything*) The prioress of Campsey [Ash] presented herself on the fourth day against William the Fleming concerning a plea that he discharge her from services and customs which Roger le Bigod the earl of Norfolk demanded from her concerning her free tenement that she holds of the said William in Hacheston, in respect whereof the same William who is the mesne tenant between them ought to discharge her etc.

William has not come and [was] summoned etc. Judgement: he is attached to be at Chelmsford on the quindene of Holy Trinity [Sunday 24 June] (*Chelmsford*).

904. (*Samford, one mark*) Godwin the son of Geoffrey claims against William the son of Robert ten acres of land with appurtenances in *Thurkelton*[1] and Kirkton as his right etc and in respect whereof Godwin his ancestor was seised in his demesne as of fee etc in the time of King Henry the grandfather of the present king, by taking profits therefrom to the value of half a mark etc. From the same Godwin the right to that land descended to a certain Geoffrey as the son and heir, and from the same Geoffrey the right to that land descended to this Godwin who now claims as the son and heir, and that such is his right he offers [to prove] etc.

William comes and denies his right and the seisin of the said Godwin and everything etc and he puts himself on the king's grand assize. He seeks a recognition be made as to which of them has the greater right in that land. Hugh Burt, James le Enveyse, Adam of Eleigh, William of Stratford four knights, summoned to choose etc the twelve etc to make a recognition of the grand assize between the said etc have come and chosen these, namely: William of Cotton, Hubert of Braiseworth, John Cordebof, Stephen of Stratton, Osbert of Bawdsey, Robert le Enveyse, William the son of Reyner, William de Alneto, John the son of Robert de *Oppeston*,[2] John of Stonham, Jordan of Shelton, Robert of Layham, Robert de Wykes, Walter of Cove, Walter of Hatfield, Richard Marshall.

Afterwards, they have agreed. William the son of Robert gives one mark for licence to agree by the surety of Godwin. [*chirograph* CP 25(1) 213/16/62]

[1]   This place is unidentified. It appears as *Turchetlestuna* in Domesday Book and is shown as being in Samford hundred. See *Domesday Book Suffolk*, Part Two, section 36, no. 6.

[2]   This place cannot be identified. There is a John the son of Robert of Ubbeston in **370** and this might be the same person because this list of jurors contains the usual suspects.

905.[1] The same four knights, selected to choose twelve etc to make a recognition of the grand assize between Thomas of Metfield, demandant, and Benedict of Acton, tenant, concerning four acres of land with appurtenances in Metfield, in respect whereof the same Benedict, who is the tenant, placed himself on the grand assize and seeks a recognition be made as to which of them has the greater right in that land, have come and chosen ... [unfinished]

(*two marks*) Afterwards, they have agreed and Thomas of Metfield gives two marks for licence to agree by the surety of Adam of Mendham.

[1]   There is a gap of 6.8 cm between the previous plea and this one and another gap of 6.5 cm between this plea and the next. The first part of the plea is written in another hand and in different ink; it is very elegant and its style almost suggests a later time. The final part of the plea reverts to the hand on the rest of this side of the membrane. It is obvious that a gap was left for one or more pleas but only this small one was inserted.

906. (*Blything*) Joan who was the wife of Peter Tregoz claims against Parnel the daughter of Peter a third part of one marksworth of rent with appurtenances in Peasenhall as her dower etc.

Parnel comes and then vouches to warranty Richard Tregoz.[1] She is to have him by aid of the court at Chelmsford on the quindene of Holy Trinity [Sunday 24 June]. He is to be summoned in the county of Essex (*Chelmsford*). She appoints as her attorney Walter the son of Bernard or Gilbert of Hastings.

> ¹ The Tregoz family probably originated in Normandy. See Reaney 1997, p.453. It appears that some of the family were located around Billingford vill in Norfolk.

907. (*Samford*) Richard de Auvilers claims against Adam the son of Geoffrey six acres of land with appurtenances in Kirkton, and against Geoffrey the son of William six acres of land with appurtenances in the same vill as his right etc.

Adam and Geoffrey come and then vouch to warranty Angod the son of Richard of Cornard, who is under age, and he claimed his age (*age*). He has [it].

908. Master Robert de L'Isle claims against Henry of Caldecott sixty acres of land with appurtenances in Caldecott, Belton and Fritton as his right by *precipe in capite*,¹ and in respect whereof a certain Osbert his ancestor was seised in his demesne as of fee and right in the time of Henry² the old king taking profits therefrom to the value of half a mark. From the same Osbert the right of that land descended to a certain Robert as son and heir, and from the same Robert to a certain Roger as son and heir, and from the same Roger to a certain Robert as son and heir, and from that Robert, who died without an heir from him, to a certain Richard as the brother and heir, and from the same Richard to this Robert as son and heir, and that such is the right he offers [to prove] etc.

Henry comes and denies his right and seisin of the said Osbert and everything etc. He says that it does not seem to him that he ought to answer him because no right can descend to the said Richard, the father of this Robert, from the second Robert, namely the brother of this Richard, because the same Robert had a certain espoused wife from whom he begot three daughters, namely: Matilda, Agnes and Woolvina, who are still living. He claims a judgement, as they are from the first born brother, and this Robert from the younger, and in his narrative he made no mention of the said sisters, who are surviving, whether as they are alive he ought to answer to him. So it is adjudged that they are summoned to be at Chelmsford on the quindene of Holy Trinity [Sunday 24 June], to show (byⁱ) what right they claim in the said land (*Chelmsford*). The same Henry says this, saving to himself if he wishes to say anything else. [*chirograph* CP 25(1) 213/17/87]³

> ¹ This is the writ by which the plea is called. See *Early Register of Writs*, p.2 for an example of this type of writ. For a good description of its working and importance to the tenants-in-chief in the courts see Holt 1992, pp.173–178.
> ² This could either be Henry II or Henry I. The clerk normally describes the relationship of Henry II to Henry III in the roll as *tempore Henrici Regis avi domini Regis*. See **486**. As the clerk has indicated 'Henry the old King' I think this might just refer to Henry I. Also there are a considerable number of mentions of ancestors having sons and heirs, which would indicate a reasonable amount of time had passed since Osbert had the land, which might just point to Henry I rather than Henry II.
> ³ The feet of fines indicate that the judgement was made at Canterbury, not Chelmsford. It also indicates that the judgement was made on the octave of St Michael [7 October], which means that the judgement was not made on the eyre as Kent was completed in June 1241. The other odd thing is that the judges are the usual list except for the abbot of Ramsey, who is also shown as being present and whom Crook indicated did not judge in Essex or Kent. I think the clerk who did the feet of fines either made a mistake on the time the chirograph was made or the plea was settled at a special assize. Crook does not include this in his list of the feet of fines relevant to this roll. See Crook 1982a, p.101. Basically Henry of Caldecott won here, as Robert in certain parts of the property became the tenant and owed money at certain times. Other parts of the property were in the hands of other tenants who owed to Henry. Also see **9**, **21**, **75** and **805**.

Membrane 35

909. (*Blything, ten shillings*) William of Gimingham gives ten shillings for licence to agree with Daniel [the son of][1] Odo concerning a plea of land by the surety of John of Gayton.

The same William has claimed against Philip of Ingate three acres with appurtenances in Ingate,[2] and against John the son of Osbert Alden, his brother, and Ralph del Hill one messuage and seven perches of land with appurtenances in Beccles[3] as his right. They have agreed. The agreement is such that the same William grants that Philip may hold the said three acres on payment of seven pence per year and for three hens at Christmas for all services. The same William also grants that John and the others may hold the said messuage and seven perches on payment of seven pence per year for all service. [*chirograph* CP 25(1) 213/16/77][4]

1   See the note 4 below on the chirograph shown at the end of this translated plea as to why I have indicated that Daniel is the son of Odo.
2   Ingate or Endegate is part of the town of Beccles according to *Feudal Aids 1284–1431* v, p.40.
3   Both Beccles and Ingate are in Wangford hundred. The only possibility for the clerk to be correct is if the land in the first part of the plea here was in Blything hundred, but the clerk does not name it. However, the chirograph indicates the land is in Endegate again so the clerk has definitely made a mistake with his marginal note.
4   The chirograph indicates that it is 'Daniel the son of Odo' who makes the agreement. This indicates that the clerk has probably made a mistake here. This agreement is only for that with Daniel. For the remainder of the plea the agreement is enrolled in the membrane.

910. (*Blything*) An assize comes to declare if Turgis of Darsham, William le Chen, Roger the son of Oger and Ida the widow unjustly etc disseised Alexander of Darsham, the chaplain, of his free tenement in Darsham after the first crossing etc and in respect whereof he claims that they disseised him of one acre of marsh.

John the son of Turgis, their bailiff, came and answered for them and he says nothing to stay the assize. Robert of Easton and Walter de Bononia[1] two of the recognitors have not come, so [they are] in mercy (*amercements*).

The jurors say that they have not disseised him as the writ says. So it is adjudged that he is to take nothing by this assize. He is in mercy for a false claim. (*half a mark*) He made a fine for half a mark by the surety of Geoffrey Laurence of Middleton and William Kane of Darsham.

1   This is *Boloyne* (Boulogne) in France. See **522**.

911. (*Thedwestry, amercements*) Peter the son of Wulfric who brought an assize of mort d'ancestor versus Ranulf Glede and many others for nine acres of land with appurtenances in Pakenham has not prosecuted. So he and his sureties for prosecuting [are] in mercy, namely: William the son of Robert of Tostock and Walter de Sudstrete.

912. (*Risbridge*) Ralph the parson of the church of Stanton[1] who brought a writ against Arskell the son of Theobald whether two acres of land with appurtenances etc has not prosecuted. So he and his sureties for prosecuting [are] in mercy,[2] namely: Harvey the son of John of Hitcham and … [unfinished][3]

1   Stanton is in Blackbourn hundred.
2   There is no mention of the amercement in the margin.
3   The clerk has not completed the list of sureties. There is a gap of 2.3 cm between the end of this plea and the next one as though there was to be an insertion here but it was not inserted.

913. (*Blything*) Alan de Money, William of Cotton, Baldwin of Mellis and Walter of Cove four knights sent to Alice, the wife of John Blench, to hear whom she was appointing as her attorney in the plea, which is between Robert the son of Reynold, the plaintiff, and John Blench and Alice, the tenants, come and say that she appoints John Blench her husband.

914. (*sickness*) The same four knights, sent to John of Freston at Freston to see whether the infirmity, of which the same John essoined himself for bed sickness against Master Robert[1] de L'Isle concerning a plea of land, [was sickness or not,] come and say that they saw him on the nearest Thursday before the feast of St Dunstan[2], and they have given him a day from that day until one year and a day at the Tower of London. The same day is given to Master Robert de L'Isle, the plaintiff, in the Bench.

[1] In the essoin in **21** he is shown as Master Ralph de L'Isle but here and in the essoin in **76** he is shown as Robert. I suspect it should be Robert, particularly as Robert appears in other pleas.
[2] That is Thursday 17 May. This is in the interim period from when the court stopped sitting at Ipswich and moved to Cattishall.

915. (*Blackbourn*)[1] Hugh of Cockfield, who brought an assize of novel disseisin against Ralph de Mara and others concerning a tenement in Newton has not prosecuted. So he and his sureties for prosecuting [are] in mercy, namely: Geoffrey the son of William of Thorpe and Richard Derquin[2] (*amercement*).

[1] The clerk has made a mistake here as the hundred should be Babergh hundred and not Blackbourn. Newton is in Babergh hundred.
[2] This may be for the modern Darkin. See Reaney 1997, p.126.

916. (*one mark*) Robert Borcy gives one mark for licence to agree with John Beri concerning a plea of warranty of charter by the surety of the same John and Thomas of Hundon. [*chirograph* CP 25(1) 213/16/61]

917. Hugh of Thetford and Basilia his wife who brought an assize of novel disseisin against David Cumyn has not prosecuted. So they and their sureties for prosecuting [are] in mercy, namely: Alexander le Teyturer[1] of Bury St Edmunds and Walter the son of Nigel of Hawkedon (*amercement*).

[1] This person maybe a dyer in the cloth industry.

918. (*Blackbourn*) Nicholas the son of William who brought an assize of mort d'ancestor against William the son of Adam concerning one acre of land with appurtenances and one messuage in *Great Hakenham*[1] has not prosecuted. So he and his sureties for prosecuting [are] in mercy, namely: Ivo of Knettishall and William the son of Simon Calin (*amercement*).

[1] This place cannot be found in Blackbourn hundred or anywhere else in Suffolk. It is possible that the clerk has made a mistake and that it really is Great Fakenham, which is in Blackbourn hundred.

919.[1] (*Risbridge*) Sarah of Hawkedon, John Ilger and Agnes his wife were summoned to reply to Roger of Essex concerning a plea that they warrant him twelve acres of land and one rood of meadow with appurtenances in *Dripton*,[2] which he holds and claims to hold from them, and in respect whereof he has the charter of Margaret, the daughter of Martin [and] the mother of Sarah and Agnes whose heirs they are.

Sarah, by her attorney, and John and Agnes, in place of whom [the same attorney comes,] come and warrant him and readily acknowledge that he should hold from them. So it is said to the same Roger that he is to make homage to the said Sarah, who is the elder etc.

[1] See **92** where attorneys are appointed for Roger of Essex.

920. (*Babergh*) Hugh of Cockfield who brought an assize of mort d'ancestor against William the priest and many others concerning ten acres of land with appurtenances in Newton has not prosecuted. So he and his sureties for prosecuting [are] in mercy, namely: Anselm the son of William of Rougham and William the son of Robert of Stanton (*amercements*).

921. (*Norfolk*) Hamon Mundy and Matilda his wife claim against William the son of Ralph one messuage and seventeen acres of land with appurtenances and five shillingsworth of rent with appurtenances in Whissonsett, which Emma the daughter of William held from them and which should revert to Hamon and Matilda as their escheat from her because the said Emma was a bastard and she died without an heir of her [body] etc.

William comes and he says that he ought not to answer to this writ because Hamon and Matilda hold the said five shillingsworth of rent, which they claim against him, and they cannot deny this. So William [is] without day and Hamon [is] in mercy by the surety of William of Helmingham.

922. (*Risbridge*) Richard the son of Reynold who brought an assize of novel disseisin against Mathias of Cowlinge concerning a tenement in Cowlinge has not prosecuted. So he and his sureties for prosecuting [are] in mercy, namely: Hugh the son of John of Rushbrooke and Thomas the son of Norman of Bury St Edmunds (*amercements*). Surety of Richard concerning the amercement: Macy of Cowlinge.[1]

1   This possibly should be the same name as the defendant and therefore could be Mathias of Cowlinge as that is what is shown in the amercement in **1656**. However, we have met a Macy of Cowlinge before in **827**. So the clerk may have made a mistake either here or in the amercement section.

923. (*Thedwestry*) Simon Gardener and William Stepere who brought an assize of mort d'ancestor against Adam the parson of Rougham concerning a tenement in Rougham have not prosecuted. So they and their sureties for prosecuting [are] in mercy, namely: Roger of Rougham of Bury St Edmunds and Robert le Neir (*amercements*).

924. (*Babergh'*) Thomas de *Horsage* who brought an assize of mort d'ancestor against Richard Wigge concerning a tenement in Hitcham[1] has not prosecuted. So he and his sureties for prosecuting [are] in mercy, namely: Robert Doget and William Nichole. Thomas is from the liberty of Ely[2] (*amercements*).

1   Hitcham is actually in Cosford hundred, not Babergh.
2   Presumably this is mentioned because the lord of the liberty can claim back the amercement of half a mark from the crown. See **1656**. See Pollock and Maitland 1968, i, p.583.

925. Walter the son of Gilbert claims against Hugh the son of Nicholas and Juliana his wife two acres of land with appurtenances in Lindsay by an assize of mort d'ancestor. They come and by licence they have agreed. The agreement is such that Hugh and Juli[an]a may hold in peace and they give to the same Walter one mark.

926. (*Babergh', amercements*) Robert the son of Geoffrey who brought an assize of novel disseisin against Thomas of Coddenham and many others concerning a free tenement in Coddenham have not prosecuted. So he and his sureties for prosecuting [are] in mercy, namely: Richard Pride de *Nutstede*[1] and Richard the son of Robert the parmenter[2] de Ernefeud.[3]

¹ Nutsted is mentioned in *Cal. Feet of Fines, Suff.*, p.53 etc. but I cannot find this place in Suffolk.
² This is a tailor according to Reaney 1997, p.338.
³ This place might be in the vill of Polstead. See Copinger 1904–1907, iv, p.310.

927. (*Lothingland*) James the son of Henry who brought an assize of novel disseisin against Ralph the son of Henry concerning his free tenement in Bradwell has not prosecuted. So he and his sureties for prosecuting [are] in mercy, namely Alan Sunnecrist and Alan Trencham.

928. (*Risbridge*) The prior of Chipley who brought an assize of novel disseisin against Roger Marshall and many others concerning a free tenement in *Pridington* has not prosecuted. So he and his sureties for prosecuting [are] in mercy. The amercement is pardoned because of the poverty of the prior.

Membrane 35d

929. (*Norfolk*) John the berker, William de la Pole and many others, against whom Walter of Lewes the parson of Caldecote brought a writ to recognise whether three messuages and thirty-six and a half acres of land with appurtenances in Caldecote are the [free] alms of that church or the lay fee of them, come and they all render [the lands] to him, except William de la Pole to whom one messuage remains behind for eight pence per annum, and except John of Oxborough who retains half an acre by the service of one penny and one hen per annum.

930. (*Norfolk*) Master Simon of Sheering and Geoffrey of Loddon are the sureties of Giles de Munpincon concerning the waging of his law against Thomas of Risby as is shown in the roll of Norwich. He is to come with his compurgators on Sunday. The sheriff is ordered that he cause to come, then the twelve etc.

931. (*Norfolk*) Roger of Repps and Emma his wife were summoned to answer to Adam of Rockland concerning a plea that they render to him William of Hockham, kinsman and heir of Wymer of Hockham, whose wardship pertains to Adam because the said Wymer held from him by knight's service.

Roger and Emma come and then vouch to warranty Warren de Montchensy. They are to have him by the aid of the court at Chelmsford on the quindene of Holy Trinity [Sunday 24 June] (*Chelmsford*). Emma appoints Roger her husband as her attorney. Warren is summoned in the county of Norfolk.

932. (*Ely*) A jury comes to declare whether two acres of land and half an acre of meadow with appurtenances in Parham are free alms pertaining to the church of the prior of Hickling in Parham or the lay fee of the prioress of Campsey [Ash] who holds that land and meadow. She comes and by a licence they have agreed. The agreement is such that all the land and meadow remains to the same prioress, and for this etc the same prioress gives to the same prior the meadow that Woollard held in Parham etc at *Ruphal*¹ etc.

¹ This place cannot be found in Suffolk or anywhere else.

933.¹ (*Thingoe*) Walter of Risby claims against Walter of Woolpit and Amice his wife twelve acres of land with appurtenances in Risby as his right etc.

Walter comes and denies his right and he says that he claims nothing in the said land because he says that the said Amice holds that land, who is not his wife neither has he cohabited with her for sixteen years nor has her for a wife. Amice is present and she acknowledged the same. So it is adjudged that Walter and Amice [are] without day. He may proceed against them [as to] when they will have been joined or separated by an ecclesiastical judgement.

The same Walter claims against William Seyne one acre of land with appurtenances in the same vill, and against William Braham half acre of land with appurtenances in the same vill, and against Robert the berker half an acre of land with appurtenances in the same vill as his right etc.

William and the others come and William Seyne[2] and William Braham acknowledge that they are the villeins of Amice. So [they are] without day. Walter [is] in mercy[3] for a false claim. Robert comes and then vouches to warranty the said Amice, who is present, and she warrants him. She says that she cannot answer until it is known whether she ought to stay with her husband by the ecclesiastical judgment or not. So a day is given to them at the arrival of the justices etc that meanwhile etc (*at the arrival of the justices*).

1 This is an example of a plea being stopped because the defendants are villeins. They go free and the plaintiff is amerced.
2 The clerk wrote *Selune* but it is presumed that this person is the same as 'Willelmus Seyne'.
3 No amercement is shown in the margin.

934. (*Bedfordshire*) A day is given to the prior of the Hospital of St John of Jerusalem in England by his attorney, plaintiff, and Richard Marshall, defendant, concerning the church[1] in Dean at the arrival of the justices at the first assize[2] etc. Richard undertook to have his wife Cecilia [there] etc.

1 It is uncertain from what we have whether this is a plea of utrum or of advowson. I have therefore included it under miscellaneous actions in the index of pleas.
2 Presumably at Chelmsford in Essex, although the justices also met at Dunwich for one day. It could also be at the first assizes in Bedfordshire.

935. (*Samford*) William Bullok who brought a writ of warranty against Robert de Ailwarton concerning a tenement in *Thurkelton* has not prosecuted. So he and his sureties for prosecuting [are] in mercy, namely: John de Belamies of Ipswich and Roger de Speletorp.[1]

1 It has not been possible to locate this place. There is a Spelthorn Wood near Long Melford, which is the nearest I can get to it. See Copinger 1904–1907, iv, p.117.

936. (*Exning*) Godiva, who was the wife of Manerius of Exning, claims against Alexander Steppere five and a half roods of land and one messuage with appurtenances in Exning as her right and marriage portion, and in which the same Alexander has no entry except by Osbert Steppere to whom the said Manerius, the former husband of Godiva, demised that [land] to him [whom she could not contradict] in his lifetime.

Alexander comes and he cannot deny such entry. So it is adjudged that she is to recover her seisin against him. He [is] in mercy for an unjust detention by the surety of William of Ely (*amercement*).

937. (*Norfolk*) Godfrey de Miliers claims against Thomas of Whimpwell thirty acres of land with appurtenances in Happisburgh, and against Agatha his mother fifteen acres of land in the same vill, and against Roger Bennet four acres of land with appurtenances in the same vill, and against Peter the son of Andrew one acre of land with appurtenances in the same vill as his right, and in respect whereof a certain (Roger[i]) his ancestor was seised in his demesne as of fee and right in the time of King Henry II, grandfather of the present lord king, by taking profits therefrom to the value of half a mark. From the same Roger the right of that land descended to a certain William as son and heir, and from the same William to a certain Roger as brother and heir, and from the same Roger to a certain Robert as brother and heir, and from the same Robert to a certain Humphrey as brother and heir, and from the same Humphrey to a certain William as son and heir, and from William to a certain Roger as brother and heir, and from the same Roger to this Godfrey who now claims as brother and heir,[1] and that such is his right he offers [to prove] etc.

Thomas and the others come and all then vouch to warranty this Thomas. Thomas warrants them and he answered for all, and he denies his right and the seisin of the said Roger and everything etc. He puts himself on the grand assize of the lord king, and he seeks a recognition be made whether he has the greater right of holding that land from Godfrey as a gift of the said Roger, his grandfather, or the same Godfrey of having that [land] in demesne.

(*one mark*) Afterwards, they have agreed. Thomas of Whimpwell gives one mark for licence to agree by the surety of William of Herringby. [**694**] [*chirograph* CP 25(1) 156/67/833][2]

1   So Godfrey had two brothers, now presumably dead, Roger and William, and he was the third generation since the original Roger in the time of Henry II, that is in at least fifty-one years.
2   Thomas de Pympewell obtains the right to the land. In the chirograph he is shown as *Thomas de Whimpewelle* which is probably more correct than Pympewell. Also see **33** and **694**, and **1029** for an additional part of the agreement, when payment will be made.

938. (*Hartismere*) William of Cotton was summoned to answer Hugh of Cotton concerning a plea that he warrant him twenty-one acres of land with appurtenances in Cotton and Bacton which he holds etc and in respect whereof he has his charter etc and he says that a certain Hubert of Braiseworth impleaded him in the court of Bury St Edmunds[1] concerning seven acres of land from the same land.[2]

William comes and readily acknowledges the charter and he says that he will freely warrant him. So it is told to the sheriff that he is to distrain him [so] that he goes to the said court and warrant him there.

1   Presumably the court of the abbot as the holder of the liberty.
2   That is part of the 21 acres.

939. (*Blything, half a mark*) Richard of Elmham gives half a mark for licence to agree with Agnes the daughter of Walter concerning a plea of land by the surety of Robert of Dunwich.[1] [*chirograph* CP 25(1) 213/17/118]

1   There was another plea shown after this which had been erased by the clerk. All that could be seen of the plea was (*Norf'ᵉ*) (*Matill' de Levington per attornatum suum* ----- -----ᵉ). The rest was indecipherable mostly because of a stamp badly placed by the PRO.

Membrane 36

940. (*Cosford*) Robert the son of Reynold of Layham claims against William of Bures sixteen acres of land with appurtenances in Layham as his right etc.

William comes and then vouches to warranty Margery, Emma and Agnes the daughters of Robert the son of Emma. He is to have them at Chelmsford on the quindene of Holy Trinity [Sunday 24 June] (*Chelmsford*).

941. (*Ely*) Norman the son of Baldwin who brought a writ to prove his liberty has not prosecuted. So he and his sureties for prosecuting [are] in mercy, namely: Simon de Crolelun and Walkelin of Norton (*amercement*).

942. (*Ely*) Robert of Kenton who brought a writ of entry against William Pictor concerning half an acre of land with appurtenances in Thorpe has not prosecuted. So he and his sureties for prosecuting [are] in mercy, namely: Jordan le Waleys and Hamo de *Blacfeud*[1] (*amercement*). Surety for the amercement [is] Robert the son of Ralph of Dunwich.

    [1]   I cannot find this place in Suffolk. There is a Blackfield in Hampshire near Fawley but it is a relatively modern estate.

943. Gilbert the son of William of Yaxley claims against Henry the son of [Simon][1] and Felicity his mother ten acres of land with appurtenances in Yaxley as his right etc and in respect whereof a certain Richard his kinsman was seised in his demesne as of fee and right in the time of King Henry III who is the current [king] by taking profits therefrom to the value of half a mark. From the same Richard the right of that land descended to a certain William as brother and heir, and from the same William to a certain Richard as son and heir, and from the same Richard to a certain Henry as brother and heir, and from the same Henry to this Gilbert who now claims as brother and heir, and that such is his right he offers [to prove] etc.

    Henry and Felicity come and deny the right and they say that if anyone [else] were to implead them he [Gilbert] would be obliged to warrant them because the said Richard his ancestor, of whose seisin he is speaking, about half a year before his death gave the said land with appurtenances to Simon the father of this Henry by his charter, which he proffers and which attests this, so that the same Simon was in full seisin before the death of this Richard.

    Gilbert says that that charter should not harm him because the said Richard was neither in possession of, nor of a sound mind when that charter was completed. Moreover, he says that he [Simon] never had seisin of the said land in the lifetime of that Richard. That (this[i]) may be inquired into by the country he offers to the lord king half a mark, and it is received by the surety of [Hugh de] Blogat'[2] (*half a mark*). So let there be a jury.

    The jurors say that ... [unfinished]

    (*half a mark*) Afterwards, they have agreed. Gilbert the son of William gives half a mark for licence to agree by the surety of Hugh de Blakate.[3]

    [1]   The clerk wrote Sampson here but later he indicates that Simon is the father of Henry on two separate occasions in the plea. I have therefore assumed that Simon is the name of the father.
    [2]   I suspect the clerk has missed out the Christian name and that this is only the surname of the person as in *xxxxx de Blogat*, possibly Hugh de Blogate as a surety for the money to have the agreement to this plea as shown below.
    [3]   See Copinger 1904–1907, i, p.204 for Hugh de Blogate.

944.[1] (*Babergh*) Robert the Forester was summoned to warrant Adam the son of Richard fifteen acres of land and one messuage with appurtenances in [Long] Melford which he holds and claims to hold from him, and in respect whereof he has his charter etc and he claims that Walter the son of William of Melford has impleaded him in the court of [the liberty] of Bury St Edmunds.

    Robert comes and warrants him. So he is told that he must go to the court of Bury St Edmunds [and warrant him there].

    [1]   There is a gap of 2.4 cm between this plea and the previous one. Someone in the PRO has written the membrane number '36' in this gap. See also **948**.

945. Thomas the son of Robert of Melford was summoned to warrant William the carpenter one messuage and one acre of land with appurtenances in [Long] Melford, in respect whereof he claims that Alan the son of Thomas impleaded him in the court of [the liberty] of Bury St Edmunds. Thomas comes and says that he freely warrants him. So he is told that he must go to the said court and warrant him [there].

946.¹ (*Babergh*) Legarda the daughter of Robert who brought a writ of a plea of land against William of Kentwell and many others has not prosecuted. So she and her sureties for prosecuting [are] in mercy, namely: Ralph the son of Fulk of Melford and Richard the son of Ralph Luke of the same. The amercement of Legarda is pardoned for poverty.

> ¹ This plea and the next six pleas are in two different hands. The first name, or part of the name, is in the hand of the original clerk on this membrane and the rest of the plea is in a different smaller hand, in black ink and possibly more modern formed letters judging from the capital and smaller letter *R*.

947.¹ Thomas the son of Robert of Melford was summoned to warrant William the carpenter one messuage and one acre of land with appurtenances in [Long] Melford, in respect whereof he claims that Alan the son of Thomas impleaded him in the court of [the liberty] of Bury St Edmunds. Thomas comes and says that he freely warrants him. So it is said [to him] that he is to go to the said court.

> ¹ This plea is virtually a duplicate of **945**. In terms of the essentials it is a duplicate: names, places, land and messuage details and that the case should go to the court at Bury St Edmunds. I have not shown it as a repeat because it has an intervening plea between the original and this plea.

948.¹ Robert the Forester was summoned to warrant Adam the son of Richard fifteen acres of land and one messuage with appurtenances in [Long] Melford which he holds from him and he claims to hold from him, and in respect whereof he has his charter etc and he claims that Walter the son of William of Melford has impleaded him in the court of [the liberty] of Bury St Edmunds.

Robert comes and warrants him. So he is told that he must go to the court of Bury St Edmunds [and warrant him there].

> ¹ This is a repeat of **944**. The new clerk appears not to have looked to see if this plea was already completed.

949.¹ (*Cosford*)² Thomas de la Ponde gives half a mark for licence to agree with Hugh the son of Alexander and William his brother concerning a plea of two parts of sixteen acres of land with appurtenances in *Lafham* by the surety of Hugh and William. [*chirograph* CP 25(1) 213/16/64]³

> ¹ See **882**.
> ² The clerk erased 'half a mark' in the margin.
> ³ This indicates a plea of mort d'ancestor was the type of plea actually made.

950.¹ (*Risbridge, half a mark*) The prior of Chipley gives half a mark for licence to agree with Sarah of Hawkedon and others named in the writ concerning a plea of land by the surety of Warren the son of Hugh. [*chirograph* CP 25(1) 213/17/108]

> ¹ See **675** for an attorney for Sarah and **676** for an attorney of Agnes the wife of John Ileger. The agreement in the chirograph is for Sarah, John Ilger and his wife Agnes with the prior. The prior wins the plea as they all acknowledge his right to the land, but they receive it back for a money rent.

951. (*half a mark*) Richard the son of William the clerk of Thurston gives half a mark for licence to agree with William of Stuston concerning a plea of land by the surety of William of Stuston. Note: that the same William of Stuston remised to Richard the son of William against whom he claims eight acres of land with appurtenances which are named in the writ and he was absent. [*chirograph* CP 25(1) 156/61/697]

952.[1] (*Babergh', amercement*) Richard of Eleigh[2] who brought a writ of warranty of charter against Christine who was the wife of John the son of Adam has not prosecuted. So he and his sureties for prosecuting [are] in mercy, namely: Anselm the son of Adam de *Teles'*[3] [and] Walter the son of Robert of the same.

[1] The original clerk in the dorsal side of the membrane is now back on this plea, although there are two different inks as though the end part of the plea was put in later.

[2] This could be Brent or Monks Eleigh in Babergh hundred.

[3] In the roll the clerk has definitely written *Teles* but in the amercement section he is shown as *Lelesheye*, which is probably Lindsey in Cosford hundred. See Watts 2004, p.374. It is possible that the clerk put a cross on the cursive 'l'. The remainder of the name is abbreviated.

953. (*Risbridge*) William of Ely and Matilda his wife by the attorney [of Matilda][1] presented themselves on the fourth day against Geoffrey of Bottisham concerning a plea that he keep the fine made with them in the court of the lord king before the eyre justices at Chelmsford[2] between Geoffrey, the plaintiff, and the said William and Matilda, the tenants, concerning seventy-five acres of land with appurtenances in Cowlinge, in respect whereof a chirograph [was made][3] etc. Geoffrey has not come and he was not attached because it has been attested that (he has nothing[i]) within the liberty nor also in the county of (Suffolk[i]) by which he can be distrained. So he may be distrained in the county of Cambridgeshire to be at Chelmsford in the quindene of Holy Trinity [Sunday 24 June] (*Chelmsford, Cambridgeshire*). **[842]**

[1] The clerk wrote *ipsam Agn*. This is surely wrong. Normally if an attorney is indicated in the roll it is stated for whom the attorney is acting. It should probably be Matilda's attorney that the clerk is indicating. I have translated it as Matilda's attorney. Also, the qualifying word *ipsam* should be in the genitive case, that is *ipsius*.

[2] As Essex is the next port of call for William of York after this Suffolk eyre this must relate to the previous eyre held at Chelmsford from 14 January to 9 February 1235, according to Crook 1982a, p.90.

[3] I cannot locate the chirograph.

954. Alice, who was the wife of Roger de la Sture, claims against Henry the chaplain half of sixteen acres of land with appurtenances, and six alder groves with appurtenances in *Stoke*,[1] and against William de la Sture half of four acres and one messuage with appurtenances in the same vill, and against John the son of Robert a third part of three acres of land and one messuage with appurtenances in *Leyland* as her dower etc and in respect whereof Roger her former husband dowered her etc on the day etc.

Henry and the others come and then vouch to warranty the said William by the charters of Roger his father, which they proffer and which attests to this, that Roger gave to him the said land and that he should warrant him. William, who is present, says that he ought to warrant him by these charters because though the said Roger gave to him the said land by these charters, yet he says that by these charters he never was in seisin of the said land, because the same Roger died seised. Afterwards, Henry comes and by licence renders [it] to her. She is to have her seisin. William comes and by licence renders [it] to her. She is to have her seisin. John the son of Robert vouches to warranty the said William who warrants him and he renders [it] to her. She is to have her (seisin[i]).

[1] Assuming this is a Suffolk plea then the place may be Stoke-by-Nayland in Babergh hundred or Stoke-by-Clare in Risbridge hundred. Both are close to the river Stour which is obvious from the names of two of the people named in the plea. It could also possibly be the village of Stoke, near Ipswich.

955.[1] (*Cosford*) William the son of Osbert claims against William Ednoch one and a half acres of land with appurtenances in Elmsett in which the same William has no entry except by Nicholas of Hadleigh to whom the said Osbert, father of the said William whose heir he is, demised that [land] for a term etc. William comes and then vouches to warranty Thomas the son of Nicholas, who is present, and he warrants him and then vouches to warranty William the son of Osbert by the charter of Osbert his father, which he proffers. William the son of Osbert cannot deny this. So William the son of Osbert [is] in mercy (*amercement*).

[1] There is yet a third clerk on this side of the membrane and he has written in a darker ink.

Membrane 36d

956. (*Thedwestry*) Walter Bance who brought a writ of warranty against Walter de Huni[1] concerning his free tenement in Rattlesden has not prosecuted. So he and his sureties for prosecuting [are] in mercy, namely: Richard Baron of Rattlesden and Godfrey the miller of the same (*amercements*).

[1] This might be Hunn or Hum. See Reaney 1997, pp.243–244.

957. (*Thedwestry*) Baldwin the son of William who brought a writ of warranty concerning one acre of land with appurtenances in Rougham has not prosecuted. So he and his sureties for prosecuting [are] in mercy, namely: Gilbert the son of Walter of Rougham and Gilbert the son of Richard of the same (*amercements*).

958. (*Babergh*) Rose the daughter of William of Waldingfield claims against Richard the son of Matthew one acre of land and wood with appurtenances in Waldingfield, and against Alexander the son of Matthew one and a half acres of land with appurtenances in Sudbury as her right etc and in which they do not have entry except by Philip of Sudbury her former husband, who demised that [land and wood] to them, and whom etc.

Richard and Alexander come and Alexander vouches to warranty this Richard and he answered for all and he denies such entry by Matthew his father. She cannot deny this. So it is adjudged that Richard [is] without day and Rose [is] in mercy. It is pardoned for poverty.

959. (*one mark*) William of Swaffham gives one mark for licence to agree with Hugh Revel concerning a plea of warranty by the surety of William the Breton.

960. (*Cosford*) John le Fevre, against whom Rose de Viner claims five acres of land with appurtenances in Wattisham by a writ of entry, comes and acknowledges himself to be the villein of Giles of Wattisham. So [he is] without day. She may proceed against Giles if she wishes.

961. Hugh Revel was attached to warrant Robert of Ashfield fifteen acres of land with appurtenances in Elmsett which he holds etc and in respect whereof he claims that Gamel[1] of Battisford impleaded him in the court of [the liberty] of Bury St Edmunds. Hugh comes and he says that he freely warrants him. So it is said to him that he is to go to the said court.

[1] This might be the name Gambell according to Reaney 1997, p.183, who indicates it can be used as a Christian name.

962. (*Cosford*) Robert of Layham was summoned to answer William of Bures concerning a plea that he keep the covenant made between them concerning two mills with appurtenances in Layham. He complains that [whereas] by the covenant made between them he ought to have the multure[1] of the family of Robert and his men of Layham, the same Robert, unjustly and contrary to this covenant, which he proffered, has detained from him that multure for five years, he has suffered damage to the value [unspecified].

Robert comes and readily acknowledges the covenant, and whatsoever is contained in the covenant, and he readily denies against him and his suit that in any way he acted against that covenant. So it is adjudged that he is to wage law, and defend himself twelve handed (*compurgation*). He is to come with his compurgators at Chelmsford on the quindene of Holy Trinity [Sunday 24 June] (*Chelmsford*). William appoints Walter the son of Bernard as his attorney. Afterwards, on that day Robert came with his compurgators and waged [his law]. So it is adjudged that Robert [is] without day and William [is] in mercy (*amercement*).[2]

[1] This was a payment in cash or grain or the flour made for the privilege of having the grain ground at the mill.

[2] The word *misericordia* and the last two sentences of this plea are in a different ink and by a different clerk. It is also clear that the additional sentences were written here after the judgement at Chelmsford.

963. (*Babergh*) Matilda the daughter of Alice claims against William Cokerel and Agnes his wife one acre of land and one messuage with appurtenances in Thetford[1] as her right etc and in which the said William and Agnes have no entry except by Avice of Thetford who held it in dower by the gift of John of Thetford her former husband [and] uncle of the said Matilda whose heir [she is].

William comes and says that she can claim nothing in that land and messuage because the said John had a certain brother, Alexander, of whom two daughters have issued, namely: Matilda and Hawise, who are still surviving. They say that the same Matilda[2] has issued from the said Alice, his sister[3], in respect whereof it does not seem to them that they ought to answer her as long as they are surviving. William says that she [Matilda] had no issue save an only daughter named Matilda who died without an heir. They say that he [Alexander] had two [daughters] who are still living. So a day is given to them [to be] at Chelmsford on the quindene of Holy Trinity [Sunday 24 June], under these terms that if they produce them they need not answer Matilda, if they do not produce them Matilda will recover her seisin against them (*Chelmsford*).

[1] Thetford is on the border with Suffolk and in many cases would appear in both the Norfolk and Suffolk eyre courts, probably for those people whose lands straddled the border, assuming anybody knew where it lay. Babergh hundred is a long way from Thetford, so I think the clerk has made a mistake here and he should have put Blackbourn hundred or Thetford *villata*.

[2] She is the original Matilda who brings the plea.

[3] I presume that Alice is the sister of John and Alexander if John is the uncle of this Matilda.

964.[1] On that day a certain Matilda, daughter and heir of Alexander, comes and she says that she ought to succeed to John who was the brother of Alexander, and Matilda cannot deny this. So it is adjudged that William and Agnes may hold in peace, and Matilda [is] in mercy.

[1] This is a continuation of **963**. The paragraph mark is in the original ink but the rest of the plea is written by a different clerk and in different ink. It is presumed that the clerk has written this after the day in Chelmsford.

965.[1] (*Babergh*) John of Willingham who brought a writ of warranty against Simon of Cockfield concerning three acres of land with appurtenances in Hartest has not prosecuted. So he and his sureties [are] in mercy, namely: John the son of Ralph of Hartest and Ranulf Smith of the same (*amercements*).

200

¹   There is a gap between this plea and the previous one of 4.3 cm.

966. (*Babergh*) Amabil who was the wife of William of Melford who brought a writ of entry against Geoffrey of Semer and many others has not prosecuted. So she and her sureties for prosecuting [are] in mercy, namely John the son of Thomas of Melford and Richard the son of Boydin of the same (*amercements*).

967. (*Thedwestry*) Thomas the son of Master William of Pakenham who brought a writ of warranty of charter against Thomas the son of William has not prosecuted. So he and his sureties for prosecuting [are] in mercy, namely: Nicholas the son of Albert of Pakenham and John the son of Edrich of Tostock (*amercements*).

968. Agnes of Lynn presented herself on the fourth day against Master Benedict the parson of Acton concerning¹ a plea that he return to her chattels to the value of twenty-four shillings which he owes to her and unjustly etc. Master Benedict has not come, and he was not attached. It is attested that he has no lay fee by which etc. So the bishop of Norwich is commanded that he is to make him come to Chelmsford on the quindene of Holy Trinity [Sunday 24 June] (*Chelmsford*).

¹   There is a large gap here but there is a line from the end of *de* to the next word *placito* as though the clerk was indicating that there should have been no gap here. However, there is also something illegible rubbed out.

969. (*Babergh*) Peter the son of William Baudre and Harvey his brother claims against John the chaplain of Stanton one messuage and two acres of land with appurtenances in Stanton¹ as his right etc by a writ of entry.

John comes and he says that he does not hold that land because his mother holds it in villeinage from Ralph of Bardwell.² So [he is] without day. They may proceed against Ralph if they wish.

¹   Stanton is in Blackbourn hundred and not Babergh. There is a Stanstead in Babergh, so it looks like the clerk either made a mistake in the marginal note or in the body of the text.
²   Bardwell is also in Blackbourn hundred.

970.¹ (*Bosmere*) Geoffrey the son of Geoffrey and Hugh of Badley by his attorney presented themselves on the fourth day against William de Ciresy concerning a plea that he pay to them twenty-two marks which he owes to them and has unjustly withheld etc. He has not come etc and [was] summoned etc. So he is to be placed on securities and reliable sureties etc that he is at Chelmsford on the quindene of Holy Trinity [Sunday 24 June] etc.

¹   This plea and the next two are written by a different clerk and in different ink. This looks like a set of afterthoughts possibly at the end of the eyre and inserted later. There is also a hole in the membrane, which the clerk has worked around. See **971** for the appointment of an attorney for Hugh of Badley.

971. Hugh of Badley appoints as his attorney Geoffrey the son of Geoffrey of Wetherden.

972.¹ (*Risbridge*) Walter Pichard who brought a writ against John Perunel² that he be attached to answer concerning robbery and the breach of the peace of the lord king has not come. So he and his sureties for prosecuting [are] in mercy, namely: Robert the son of Roger of Withersfield and Richard the son of Ralph of Wratting (*amercement*).

¹   This looks as if it should be in the crown pleas and the clerk has put it in here as an afterthought.
²   This might be Parnel or Perrell. See Reaney 1997, pp.338–339, and 347.

Membrane 37

973. (*Lackford*) An assize comes to declare if Harvey of Mildenhall and Walter Greneking unjustly etc disseised Cecilia who was the wife of Astil of Mildenhall of her free tenement in Mildenhall after the first etc and in respect whereof she claims that they disseised ... [unfinished][1]

Harvey and Walter come and they say that the assize ought not to proceed because the said Cecilia has a husband and she admitted this and so Harvey and Walter [are] without day and Cecilia is a poor little woman.

[1] The clerk does not tell us what they disseised.

974.[1] (*Cosford*) An assize comes to declare if Alan de la Hide the father of Thomas de la Hide was seised in his demesne etc of thirty acres [of land] with appurtenances in Kettlebaston on the day that etc and if etc which land Simon de Cherning[2] holds. He comes and then vouches to warranty Geoffrey Peche. He is to have him on the morrow (*on the morrow*[e]).[3] The sheriff is commanded to make him come. Afterwards, he comes and warrants him.

Afterwards, they have agreed. (*one mark*) Geoffrey Peche gives one mark for licence to agree by the surety of Geoffrey Crowe and Robert of Semer. [*chirograph* CP 25(1) 213/17/109]

[1] See **831** where there are some of the same players. It looks as though Thomas has tried a number of tacks to get his hands on the land.
[2] In **831** this is Simon de Skerninghe.
[3] I think the clerk has written *cras* for *crastino* in the margin, as has occurred previously in other pleas, but it looks as though the membrane has been cut at this point and the beginning of this marginal note cut off or worn away.

975. (*Babergh*) Walter the son of Bernard claims against David Cumyn and Isabella his wife one messuage and two carucates of land with appurtenances in Great Fakenham[1] as his right by [the writ] *precipe in capite*[2].

David comes and he says that he had no reasonable summons. This is attested. Because his wife is in Scotland and the summons has not reached her, a day is given to the same David at Chelmsford on the quindene of St John the Baptist [Sunday 8 July] (*Chelmsford*). It is said to the same David that then he is to have the said Isabella there. The same day is given to the same Walter. David appoints as his attorney Walter de Monasterio or John de Galeweya.

[1] Great Fakenham is in Blackbourn not Babergh hundred. I think the clerk has made a mistake here.
[2] See note 1 in **908**.

976.[1] (*Hoxne*) Adam of Bedingfield was summoned to answer Gerard de Oddingesel' concerning a plea that he do him the customs and rightful services which he ought to do to him concerning his free tenement that he holds from him in Bedingfield. The same Gerard in respect whereof complains that though from that tenement he owes the service of one knight's fee he has detained from him that service in respect whereof etc.

Adam comes and he says that he holds no tenement from him nor anything he claims to hold from him, because he holds that tenement from William de Oddingesel'. So it is adjudged that Adam [is] without day, and Gerard [is] in mercy (*amercement*). [*chirograph* CP 25(1) 213/17/91][2]

[1] See the essoin for Gerard in **68**.
[2] Adam is mentioned in this agreement for the knight's fee as Gerard obviously sued Adam again and this time vouched William de Oddingeseles to warranty. This agreement is between Gerard

and William. William in effect loses according to the agreement, so it looks as though Adam eventually did as well.

977. (*Thedwestry*) Ernulf of Oakley was summoned to answer John de Crammaville and Lucy his wife [concerning] the customs and services of his free tenement that he holds from them in Thurston. They say that the same Ernulf owes to them twenty shillings per year from the said tenement, and moreover a fourth part of one knight's fee. Ernulf comes and acknowledges the said service. Afterwards, they have agreed. (*half a mark*) John de Crammaville gives half a mark for licence to agree ... [unfinished] [*chirograph* CP 25(1) 213/15/36][1]

> 1   In the chirograph Ernulf is shown as *Ernald*.

978. (*Cosford*) Hubert de Montchensy who brought a writ of waste against William de Montchensy has not prosecuted. So he and his sureties for prosecuting [are] in mercy, namely: Richard the son of William of Stonham and John the son of William of Stanton (*amercements*). Hubert is under age, so nothing from him.

979. (*Blackbourn*) Walter the son of Bernard who brought a writ of right against Henry de Balliol and Lora his wife and their co-parceners for the tenement in Fakenham has not prosecuted. So he and his sureties for prosecuting [are] in mercy, namely: Simon of Watford and Thomas Crowe (*amercements*).

980. (*Lothingland, two marks*) William of Hevingham and Grace, his wife, claim against William the son of Bartholomew of Hopton whom Edmund Woodcock and Herbert of Hoveton[1] vouched to warranty and who warranted them forty acres of land with appurtenances in [Browston], Hobland and Wheatcroft[2] as the right of Grace, and in respect whereof the same Matilda, her ancestor, was seised in her demesne as of fee and right in the time of King John, the father of King Henry the current king, by taking profits therefrom to the value of half a mark. From the same Matilda the right of that land descended to a certain Alexander as son and heir, and from the same Alexander to this Grace[3] as the daughter and heir who now claims, and that such is her right she offers [to prove].

William comes and denies her right and the seisin of the said Matilda and everything etc and he puts himself on the king's grand assize. He seeks a recognition be made whether he has the greater right in the said land as in that which the said Matilda gave to William his grandfather, or the said Grace to hold it in demesne. Hugh Burt, James le Enveyse, Adam of Eleigh, and William of Stratford four knights, selected to choose the twelve etc to make a recognition of the grand assize between the aforesaid, have come and chosen these, namely: William de Colville, Hubert Gernegan, Alan de Money, Hubert of Braiseworth, Robert de Grimilies, Walter of Cove, William of Reedham, Baldwin of Mellis, Richard the butler, William the son of Reyner, Ranulf of Blickling, Gilbert de Colville, Gilbert of Walsham, Adam of Mendham, John Cordebof and William de Alneto.

Afterwards, they have agreed. William the son of Bartholomew gives two marks for licence to agree by the surety of William of Hevingham. [*chirograph* CP 25(1) 213/15/15][4]

> 1   Note that the clerk has 'Osbert of Hoveton' in **484** whereas here and in **248** he has 'Herbert of Hoveton'.
> 2   See **248** for the places mentioned and **484** for the preliminaries to this plea. The clerk wrote *Boxton*, which I think should be Browston as in **248** and **484**.
> 3   The real claimant is Grace, a woman, but she has to claim with her living husband.
> 4   William and Grace get the land and provide William the son of Bartholomew two and a half marks of silver.

981.[1] (*Sunday, Bosmere*) Clarice who was the wife of Godard de Surbeston, Edmund of Stonham and Matilda his wife, Alice and Avice her sisters have claimed against Ralph the butler one acre of land with appurtenances in Hemingstone as their right. Ralph came and they have agreed. They remise everything for half a mark.

[1] There is a gap of 4.8 cm between this plea and the previous one.

982. (*Liberty of Freebridge, half a mark*) Hamo of Narborough gives half a mark for licence to agree with John Grim concerning a plea of villeinage of John by the surety of that John. (*half a mark*) The same John gives half a mark for the same with the same by the surety of John Bernard of Gayton. [**356** and **1017**]

983. (*one mark*) Thomas the son of Geoffrey of [Badley][1] gives one mark for licence to agree with the same Geoffrey by the surety of Stephen of Sutton. [*chirograph* CP 25(1) 213/15/17][2]

[1] The clerk wrote *Balegh* which is Badley in Bosmere hundred but the clerk has missed out the 'd'. The chirograph shown indicates *Baddel*.
[2] The chirograph indicates that the plea was one of warranty of charter. Thomas really won here.

Membrane 37d

984. (*Cosford*) Harvey the son of John claims against Ranulf Wigge one messuage and twenty acres of land with appurtenances in Hitcham as his right. Ranulf comes and then vouches to warranty John the son of Ranulf. He is to have him at Chelmsford in the octave of Holy Trinity [Sunday 17 June] by the aid of the court (*Chelmsford*).

985.[1] (*Ely*) Isabella who was the wife of Nicholas of Clopton claims against Isabella de Beauchamp half of six acres with appurtenances and a sixth part of one mill with appurtenances in Clopton, and against John de Rivers[2] half of six acres of land with appurtenances in the same vill, and against Ralph de Arderne[3] and Alina his wife half of six acres of land (and a sixth part of one mill[i]) with appurtenances in the same vill as her dower, and in respect whereof the said Nicholas her former husband dowered her etc and on the day that [he married her] etc.

Isabella, Ralph, and Alina by their attorneys and John and Matilda come, and by licence render [the lands] to her. She is to have her seisin etc.

[1] See **463** for the appointment of an attorney for Ralph de Arderne.
[2] It looks as though the clerk has missed out his wife Matilda as a defendant to the plea by mistake. See the next plea.
[3] See *Book of Fees* ii, p.917 for this person.

986. (*Ely*) Isolda de Beauchamp,[1] John de Rivers and Matilda his wife, Ralph de Arderne and Alina his wife by their attorneys claim against Isabella who was the wife of Nicholas of Clopton one messuage with appurtenances in Clopton as the right and inheritance of Isolda, Matilda and Alina, in which the said Isabella has no entry except by the said Nicholas, her former husband, to whom the said Isolda, Matilda and Alina demised that [messuage] for a term, which has passed.

Isabella comes and says that she claims nothing in the said messuage except in the name of the wardship of William her son who is under age. So [she is] without day.

[1] I suspect the clerk is meaning the same woman as in **985**, that is Isabella. If not, it could be her sister.

987. (*Hartismere*) Hugh of Cotton who brought a writ of warranty against William of Cotton concerning fifteen acres of land with appurtenances and six roods of meadow in Cotton, and nine acres of land and three roods of meadow with appurtenances in Bacton has not prosecuted. So he and his sureties for prosecuting [are] in mercy, namely: Richard the son of Benedict of Mildenhall and Walter the son of Hugh de Wenakeston (*amercements*).

988.[1] (*Norfolk*) Matilda of Leverington by her attorney presented herself on the fourth day against Jordan de Ros and Margery his wife concerning two acres of land with appurtenances in Emneth, which she claims as her right etc. Jordan has not come and he made many defaults, so that the land was taken into the hands of the lord king. Now Margery comes and says that Jordan is in prison at Lincoln for the death of a man. So a day is given to them at Chelmsford on the quindene of Holy Trinity [Sunday 24 June] to hear their judgement. Matilda is to have a writ of the eyre justices[2] at Lincoln to certify to the itinerant justices at Chelmsford whether the said Jordan is in prison at Lincoln as the same Margery says or not (*Chelmsford*). The same day is given to Margery.

   1   See **403** for the first time that the sheriff is requested to get the two defendants.
   2   The clerk wrote *inter* which appears to be a slip for *itinerantium* to indicate 'a writ of the eyre justices'. For judicial writs see *Early Register of Writs*, pp.lxiv–lxxxvi, and in particular for their administrative nature see pp.lxxiv–lxxv etc.

989. (*Suffolk*) A day is given to Colin de Beauchamp the plaintiff and Richard de Cadamo concerning customs and services on the quindene of Holy Trinity [Sunday 24 June] at Chelmsford by prayer of the parties (*Chelmsford*).

990. (*Babergh*) Matilda, who was the wife of Engelin of Melford, presented herself on the fourth day against Amiot the marshall[1] of Balsham[2] concerning a plea of half of one messuage and one and a half acres of land with appurtenances in [Long] Melford which she claimed in dower against him. Amiot has not come and [was] summoned etc. Judgement: the half messuage and land is to be taken into the hands of the lord king etc and the day etc and he is to be summoned to be at Chelmsford on the quindene of Holy Trinity [Sunday 24 June] (*Chelmsford*).

   1   According to Reaney 1997, p.300 Amiot was a farrier by trade.
   2   Balsham is in Cambridgeshire in Radfield hundred.

991. (*Bosmere*) William the son of William claims against John le Bigod two acres of wood with appurtenances in Stonham as his right, and in which the same John does not have entry except by Henry de Walker to whom William de Ciresy the father of the said William whose heir he is demised that [land] for a term etc.

John comes and says that he and the church were in seisin of the said wood for fifty years and more and he claims a judgement whether he ought to answer to the writ of entry for so great a time,[1] and William cannot deny this. So it is adjudged that he need not answer to him on this writ and he[2] is in mercy for a false claim by the surety of Robert le Blund (*amercement*).

   1   This looks like a time limit on the ability of the plaintiff to claim against a defendant. I cannot find any limit for an entry plea in *Early Registers of Writs*, *Novae Narrationes* and *Brevia Placitata*.
   2   That is William the son of William de Ciresy.

992. (*Babergh*) Adam of Cosford and Nicholas his brother claim against Amice of Cosford and Sabina her daughter two acres and one rood of land with appurtenances in Hadleigh [Hamlet?][1] as their right, and in which they have no entry except by

Ralph of Hadleigh who in respect thereof has nothing except the wardship as long as the said Adam and Nicholas were under age and in his custody.

Amice and Sabina come, and Amice says that she claims nothing in that land except in respect of the wardship of Sabina who is under age. She claims age and she has [it] (*age*).

[1] There is a Hadleigh in Cosford hundred, not Babergh as stated in the margin. However there is also a Hadleigh Hamlet which is included in Boxford vill and part of it is included in Babergh hundred and part in Cosford hundred. There is a letter smudged or crossed out in the middle of the name and it may be that the clerk was trying to cross out this letter. The litigants are associated with Cosford hundred, rather than Babergh.

993. (*Babergh', one mark*) Ralph the son of Gilbert of Walsham gives one mark for licence to agree with Argentela of Walsham concerning a plea of land by the surety of Walter the son of Robert of Walsham. [*chirograph* CP 25(1) 213/17/114][1]

[1] In the chirograph Ralph is shown as 'Robert'.

994. Robert the son of Warren, Thomas … [unfinished]

995. (*Blackbourne*) Robert the son of Alice who brought a writ to prove his liberty against H[ugh de Vere] the earl of Oxford has not prosecuted. So he and his sureties for prosecuting [are] in mercy, namely: William the son of Osbert of Elmsett and Athelard the son of Robert Kachevache[1] (*amercements*).

[1] According to Reaney 1997, p.87 Kachevache means 'chase cow' and is also the name of a local officer who chases debt.

996. (*Thedwestry*) William the son of Robert, who brought a writ of attachment [against] William de Alneto to answer him concerning the peace of the lord king, has not prosecuted. So he and his sureties for prosecuting [are] in mercy, namely: Adam Trenchelaunce of Tostock and Fulk of Woolpit (*amercements*).

997. (*Lackford*) William the son of Simon de Twamill[1] was summoned to answer Benedict de Twamill concerning two messuage and fifteen acres of land with appurtenances in Mildenhall, which he holds and [claims to hold] from him etc and in respect whereof a charter of Roger de Twamill grandfather of the said William whose heir he is etc and the same Benedict says that a certain Thurston the son of Reynold impleaded him in the court of Bury St Edmunds concerning the same land.

William comes and he is under age and he cannot answer for any charter. So the Steward of Bury St Edmunds is forbidden to proceed in that plea until the same William is of full age (*age*).

[1] This might be a place called Wamil, close to Mildenhall in Lackford hundred.

Membrane 38

998.[1] (*Ely*) Harvey de Hill and Margery his wife against whom William the butler claims one acre of land, one and a half acres of wood and one acre and one rood of meadow with appurtenances in Carlton as his right etc and William comes and acknowledged himself to be the villein of the prior of Ely. So [he is] without day and Harvey [is] in mercy. It is pardoned.

[1] I think the clerk lost his way and it is difficult to see a proper sentence in this plea. If William the butler, the plaintiff, claimed the land and he was a villein, why should Harvey, the defendant, be amerced even though pardoned? If a plaintiff or defendant was proved to be a villein, the case ceased, as a villein could not sue for land. It is possible that the clerk inadvertently reversed the plaintiff and the defendant and that Harvey and Margery are the real plaintiffs and William the defendant. This would mean that Harvey would correctly be amerced for a false claim.

999. (*Ely*) Alan of Withersdale was summoned to answer James of Playford concerning a plea that he permit him to have common fishery in the water of *Nekemere*[1] of which John of Playford, the father of the said James whose heir he is, was seised in his demesne as of fee on the day that he died. And in respect whereof the same James complains that, since he and his predecessors always had fished in the same fishery and they should [continue to do so], the same Alan deforced him of the same fishery whereon he has suffered damage to the value of ten marks. (For this to be inquired into by a jury he offers the lord king half a mark by the surety of Roger of Glemham[i]) (*half a mark*).

Alan comes and denies force and injury and everything and he says that neither he nor his predecessors ought to have common fishery there, nor have they ever, and that this may be inquired into by the jury he offers to the lord king one mark and it is received by the surety of William le Rus (*one mark*).

The jurors, chosen by consent of the parties, come and say on their oath that the said John, the father of James, had his boat in the same fishery for all his time, and he lived for eighty years, and he always had fished in the same fishery as of right without anyone's permission, and that this James should similarly. So it is adjudged that he is to recover his seisin and Alan [is] in mercy, by the surety of Baldwin of Mellis (*amercement*).

[1] From the person who is the plaintiff I would suggest that the fishery is in Carlford hundred as that was probably where he had his lands. Unfortunately I cannot find him or his lands in the *Book of Fees*. There is a place called *Neckemara* in Carlford hundred according to Domesday Book, but it is now unidentifiable. See *Domesday Book Suffolk*, Part One, section 6, no. 113 etc.

1000. (*Ely*) Ralph de Colville who brought a writ of warranty against Henry de Colville has not prosecuted. So he and his sureties for prosecuting [are] in mercy, namely: Ambrose of Ash, Brian de Essend (*amercement*).

1001. (*Ely*) Alice Peche who brought a writ of warranty against Richard Pincernam … [unfinished]

1002. (*Ely*) Stephen of Stratton was summoned to reply to Walter Burich concerning a plea that he warrant him fifteen acres of land with appurtenances in Guston[1] and Stratton which he holds etc. Stephen comes and he readily says that he freely warrants him if anyone should implead him and the sheriff has been ordered etc.

[1] This is probably Guston, a lost village near Kirton in Colneis hundred. It is shown as *Guthestuna* in *Domesday Book Suffolk*, Part One, section 7, no. 89. Also see Arnott 1946, p.32. It is certainly not Guston in Kent.

1003. (*Ely*) William the son of Roger claims against Roger Burs one acre and one rood of land with appurtenances in Easton, and versus Roger Osmund four acres of land with appurtenances in the same vill as his right etc and in which they have no entry except by Roger his father who demised that to them for a term etc.

Roger Burs and Roger Osmund come and deny such entry and they say that the said Roger, the father of William, enfeoffed them by his charter which they proffer and which attests to this, and William cannot deny this. So it is adjudged that Roger and Roger go without day and William [is] in mercy. He is poor.

1004. (*Ely*) Ralph de Colville, who brought a writ of warranty against Henry de Colville concerning a tenement in Clopton, has not prosecuted. So he and his sureties for prosecuting [are] in mercy, namely: Geoffrey the son of Edrich of Debenham and Bartholomew the son of Stephen (of[r]) Charsfield (*amercement*).

207

1005. (*Ely*) Stephen of Glemsford who brought a writ of covenant against Robert de Frerres[1] has not prosecuted. So he and his sureties for prosecuting [are] in mercy, namely: William de Ullecote and William the son of Roger of Hoveton (*amercements*).

[1] This name might be the name Frears. See Reaney 1997, p.177.

1006. (*Ely*) Adam Bulloc and Margery his wife claim against Matilda who was the wife of Adam of Tuddenham five acres of land with appurtenances in Tuddenham in which the said Matilda has no entry except by the said Adam of Tuddenham, her husband, who held that [land] from the said Adam and Margery in villeinage etc.

Matilda comes and says that she cannot answer them because she claims nothing in the said land except only by wardship, which she has in the name of John the son of Adam, who is under age, and he is present and he has claimed his age, and he has it (*age*).

1007.[1] (*Ely*) Alice Peche, who brought a writ of warranty against Richard Pincernam and Matilda his wife, has not prosecuted. So she and her sureties for prosecuting [are] in mercy, namely: Guido de Verdun and Richard of Pulham (*amercements*).

[1] See **1001**. The clerk left this unfinished.

1008. (*Ely*) Agnes of Cretingham was summoned to answer to Stephen of Stratton and Anna his wife concerning a plea that she hold to the covenant made between Agnes and Anna concerning half of twelve acres of land, and one acre of meadow, and a third part of one mill, and of nine shillings and four penceworth of rent with appurtenances in Rendlesham.

Afterwards, it is proved that the said Stephen and Anna can claim nothing in the said land in respect of the covenant except only in respect of dower if she then wishes to plead. So it is adjudged that Agnes is to go without day on this and Stephen [is] in mercy by the surety[1] of Gerard Richaud (*amercements*).

[1] The clerk has erased something here but it is not legible.

1009. (*Ely*) William the son of Hervey and Baldwin de Ringeston against whom Matilda who was the wife of Harvey of Little Bealings brought a writ concerning a plea of land, come and acknowledge that they are the villeins of Robert Aguillon, and so [they are] without day. Matilda [is] in mercy. It is pardoned. She may proceed [against Robert Aguillon if she wishes] etc.

1010. (*Ely*) Austin the son of Wymer presented himself on the fourth day against John Wenstan concerning a plea that he render to him one messuage with appurtenances in Framlingham in which he has no entry except by Wulwina of Framlingham who held that in dower by the gift of Periman of Framlingham her former husband the father of the said Austin whose heir he is etc. John has not come and [was] summoned etc. Judgement: the messuage is to be taken into the hands of the lord king etc and he is to be summoned to be [there] at the arrival of the justices at the first assize[1] (*at the first assize*).

[1] Possibly at Chelmsford, or just possibly at Dunwich on the 11 June in this eyre, but more likely at an assize held at Framlingham after the eyre had been completed.

1011. (*Ely*) Roger the son of Ralph de Berneshege claims against Roger de Berneshege one messuage and twelve acres of land with appurtenances in Clopton and Grundisburgh as his right etc and in which the said Roger has no entry except by William the Earl Warenne, Roger de Mohaut, Edmund of Tuddenham, Robert

Michell and Merven--[1] Kekeston who in respect thereof have not had tenure except while the said Roger the son of Ralph was under age and in his wardship etc.

Roger de Berneshege comes and denies etc that the father of Roger did not die seised of the said land, and because it has been proved by an assize of mort d'ancestor taken between them at Ipswich[2] that the said Ralph died seised, and the same Roger de Berneshege says nothing (else[i]) as to why he [Roger son of Ralph] ought not to have his seisin, so it is adjudged that Roger the son of Ralph has recovered his seisin. He is to have his seisin and Roger [is] in mercy for an unjust detention, by the surety of William of Holbrook (*misericordia*).

1   The rest of the name is illegible.
2   See **575**.

1012. (*Ely*) Gilbert the son of John, Peter, Thomas, Richard and John his brothers presented themselves on the fourth day against Robert Fiket concerning a plea of five parts of twelve acres of land and one messuage with appurtenances in Rendlesham, which they claim as their right against him. Robert has not come, and [was] summoned etc. Judgement: the five parts of the twelve acres of land and one messuage are to be taken into the hands of the lord king, and he is to be summoned … [unfinished]

1013. Richard the son of Ralph of Hevingham who brought a writ to prove his liberty has not prosecuted. So he and his sureties for prosecuting [are] in mercy, namely: Robert Gumbel of Walpole and Reynold Ely of the same [place] (*amercement*).

1014. (*Babergh*) William the son of Aildith who brought a writ to prove his freedom against Agnes of Alpheton has not prosecuted. So he and his sureties for prosecuting [are] in mercy, namely: Gerard the son of Humphrey de Doventon and Richard Micchelboy of Tattingstone (*amercements*).

1015. (*Babergh*) Agnes the daughter of Ivo who brought a writ of warranty against Ralph the son of Ivo concerning a tenement in [Long] Melford has not prosecuted. So she and her sureties for prosecuting [are] in mercy, namely: Thomas the son of William (*amercements*).

Membrane 38d[1]

1   On this side of the membrane there is a change of clerk for the first plea and also another change from **1021** to the end of the membrane and they are in different inks.

1016. (*Ely*) Robert the son of William of Hoo[1] claims against Roger the son of William of Hoo three acres of land with appurtenances in Charsfield as his right and in which he does not have entry except by William his father to whom the said Robert demised for a term which has passed etc.

Roger the son of William comes and claims a view. He must come on Monday (*on Monday*).

(*half a mark*) Afterwards, they have agreed, and Robert gives half a mark for licence to agree by the surety of this Roger.

1   This is probably the Hoo in Loes hundred as Charsfield is also in Loes hundred.

1017.[1] (*Norfolk*) Hamo of Narborough and John Grim acknowledged the covenants, made between them according to the purport of the chirographs kept in their possession, concerning the naifty of John and all of his household, except Walter the younger son of John, who remains a villein of Hamo, and all his household. It is noted that the same John acknowledges that he owes to the same Hamo ten marks, concerning which he will pay five marks to him in the feast of St Peter in Chains, and five marks in the feast of St Michael [29 September]. If he does not do [this] he grants that he may be distrained etc. John of Gayton[2] gives half a mark to the clerks by the surety of Andrew the clerk (*half a mark*).

[1]   There is a gap of 6 cm prior to this plea. See **356** and **982**.
[2]   See **982** where John Bernard of Gayton was the surety of John Grim.

1018.[1] Daniel the son of Odo of Beccles acknowledges that he owes to William of Gimingham two and a half marks, which he will pay to him at the feast of St Margaret [20 July] in the twenty-fourth year [of King Henry III]. If he does not do [this] he grants etc. [*chirograph* CP 25(1) 213/16/77][2]

[1]   See **909** for the agreement entered into, but not the details.
[2]   It looks as though that they made the agreement in **909** and Daniel could only pay William one and a half marks at this time so they enrolled the balance to be paid.

1019.[1] (*Ely*) A jury of twenty-four to attaint the twelve comes to declare by Richard the butler, Osbert of Bawdsey, Matthew of Peyton, Stephen of Stratton, William of Cotton, Roger Sturmey, Ranulf of Blickling, Adam of [Mendham],[2] Hugh Burt, Nicholas of Easton, Robert de Aula Arsa, William Baldwin, Jordan de Mansted, John the son of Lettice de Hoc,[3] William le Deveneys of Cretingham, Luke le Petit of Oakley, Geoffrey of Bocking, Alan of Thorpe, Adam Fausebrun, Richard of Benhall, Guy of Barkestone, Bartholomew of Tuddenham, Walter de Glanville and Richard of Tuddenham if Nicholas Haliday the brother of Ranulf Haliday was seised in his demesne etc of three acres of land with appurtenances in Ashfield and [Earl] Soham on the day that he died, and if he died after the first coronation [of the king] etc and if the same Ranulf etc and in respect whereof the same Ranulf complains that the jurors of the assize of mort d'ancestor taken between Ranulf and Richard de Ribos at Ipswich came and made a false oath.

Afterwards, Ranulf came and withdrew [from the plea], [and] he is remanded in custody, and his sureties for prosecuting [are] in mercy, namely William the son of Robert of Helmingham, Geoffrey of Bocking, Adam Bullok and Thomas Hadleigh. Richard Mauduyt one of the knights [is] in mercy because he has not come (*amercements, amercement*).

[1]   See **534** for the initial mort d'ancestor plea, which Ranulf lost and for which he gave 40s. to have the appeal, and **537**, which is oddly out of sequence in the judicial process. In **537** Ranulf withdrew from the appeal and made a fine of 100s. for him and his sureties for prosecuting the appeal, whereas in this item he is shown as withdrawing from the appeal but is remanded in custody and his sureties for prosecuting are amerced. So it looks as though the clerk has made a mistake here by putting in the jury detail he should have put in **537** along with the detail of the amercements for withdrawing. Or did Ranulf continue the appeal and **537** was merely a pointer to the appeal later in the roll with the result as shown here and the payment for the fine written in later by the clerk? In **1664** in the amercement section there is shown the 40s. to have the appeal but none of the amercements in this plea or the 100s. fine in **537**.
[2]   The clerk wrote *Mundham*, which is in Sussex. However, it is likely that the clerk has made a mistake here and should have written Mendham which is in Hoxne hundred. There are also a number of references to Adam of Mendham in other pleas, e.g. **146**, **151**, **370**, **980** etc., as a juror. I have assumed a mistake has been made and I have translated it as Mendham.
[3]   Reaney 1997, p.237 appears to indicate that *hoc* is Old English for a hill.

1020.[1] (*Hartismere*) Matilda who was the wife of Reynold the carpenter claims against the prior of Bricett whom Alpesia,[2] who was the wife of William of Horringer, [vouched] to warranty and who warranted her a third part of one acre with appurtenances in Finningham as her dower etc.

The prior comes and by licence renders [it] to her. She is to have her seisin and Alpesia is to hold in peace and Matilda may have to the value [of her land] etc.

1   There is a gap of 3.4 cm between this plea and the previous one and what looks like a 7 written in the gap. It may be some form of process mark or some later number, or the Tironian *et*.
2   See **219** for the first part of this plea.

1021. (*Cosford*) Alice, who was the wife of William of Crepping, presented herself on the fourth day against John of Gedding concerning a plea that he render to her nineteen marks, which he owes to her and unjustly withholds as she says. John has not come etc and [was] summoned etc. So he is to be put on securities and reliable sureties that he is at Chelmsford on the quindene of Holy Trinity [Sunday 24 June] etc. (*Chelmsford*).

1022. (*Risbridge*) Hugh de Gardino was summoned to answer (----)[1] of Stoke concerning a plea that he render to him forty marks. He came and acknowledged that he has satisfied him. So he is to go without day on this.

1   The clerk has missed out the first name.

1023. (*Thingoe*) Adam the son of William who brought a writ against Roger Kaylstaf concerning four roods of land with appurtenances in Hencote has not prosecuted. So he and his sureties for prosecuting [are] in mercy, namely: William the son of Richard of Hencote and Richard the palmer of the same vill (*amercement*).

1024. (*Cosford*) Matilda, who was the wife of Herbert of Aldham, appoints as her attorney Hugh of Aldham against Robert Bolle concerning a plea of land in Aldham. [**1092**]

Membrane 39

1025. Peter the son of Gilbert presented himself on the fourth day against Matilda Sutereswyf concerning a plea that she render to him four acres of land with appurtenances in Caldecott which he claims as his right etc. She has not come and [was] summoned etc. Judgement: the land is to be taken into the hands of the lord king, and the day etc and she is to be summoned to be at Chelmsford on the quindene of Holy Trinity [Sunday 24 June] (*Chelmsford*).

1026. (*Norfolk, half a mark*) Alice the daughter of William gives half a mark for licence to agree with Robert the son of Ralph the marshall concerning a plea of land by the surety of Richard Angod. [*chirograph* CP 25(1) 156/67/834][1]

1   The chirograph names other persons that could have been named in this plea, that is Reyner of Shouldham and Katherine his wife.

1027. (*Babergh*) Avice who was the wife of William Atteford claims against Thomas de la Tye and Katherine his wife six acres of land with appurtenances in Lavenham as her right etc and in which the said Thomas and Katherine do not have entry except by William de Blacke to whom William Atteford the former husband of Avice demised that [land] whom [she could not contradict in his lifetime] etc.

Thomas and Katherine[1] come and deny such entry and they say that they had entry by Robert the son of John and the said Avice, Robert's sister, and by her charter which they proffer and which attests this. Avice says that that charter should not injure her because it was made in the time of the said William her husband, and

211

that this may be inquired into by the country she offers to the lord king half a mark by the surety of Gilbert le Venur (*half a mark*).

Thomas and Katherine say that it was made in her widowhood and not in the time of the said William and then they put themselves on the country and on the witnesses named in the charter. So let there be a jury thereon.

Afterwards, they have agreed by a licence. They may have a chirograph. [*chirograph* CP 25(1) 213/17/105][2]

[1] There have been a number of instances where the name has changed, in this case from Katerina to Katelina. I assume the clerk is either making a mistake here or the names are interchangeable. I have stuck to the name Katherine in this translation.

[2] Avice in effect won her case as Thomas and Katherine acknowledged her right to the land, but it cost Avice 20s.

1028.[1] (*Babergh*) [John][2] de Mariaws and Katherine his wife presented themselves on the fourth day against Cecilia the wife of Thomas le Sauvage concerning a plea that she keep to their covenant made between them, and Thomas le Sauvage and Cecilia his wife concerning eighty acres of land and twelve shillingsworth of rent with appurtenances in Alpheton. Thomas and Cecilia have not come and [were] summoned etc. On this the said[3] Thomas comes and he undertook to have her at Chelmsford on the day of Holy Trinity in three weeks [Sunday 1 July] (*Chelmsford*). The same day is given to the same John and Katherine.

[1] There is a gap of 2.9 cm between this case and the previous one.

[2] The clerk wrote *Johanna*, which is Latin for Joan. I have assumed this should be *Johannes* for John, if Katherine was his wife.

[3] The membrane has some rubbing out here as though the clerk has made a mistake and added some letters on to *predictus*, 'the said', or he made a mistake on the 's' at the end of *predictus* and he rubbed out sufficient to make it look like an 's'.

1029. (*Norfolk*) Thomas of Whimpwell acknowledges that he owes to Godfrey de Miliers twenty marks for a fine made between them, of which he will pay to him ten marks within the quindene of St John the Baptist in the year twenty-four [of the king's reign], and ten marks at the feast of St Michael [29 September] in the next following. If he does not do [this] he grants [that the sheriff may distrain the amount from his lands] until etc and concerning the cost etc. [*chirograph* CP 25(1) 156/67/833]

1030. (*Cosford*) Isabella the daughter of Edrich claims against Walter Edrich three and a half acres of land with appurtenances in Hadleigh as her right etc and in which the same Walter has no entry except by Richard the merchant etc to whom Edrich Croh, the father of the said Isabella whose heir she is, demised that [land] for a term etc.

Walter comes and then vouches to warranty Peter, Alexander and Adam the sons of Richard the merchant, who are under age and they claim their age. So she is to await their age (*age*).

The same [Isabella] claims against Robert the lord and Margery his wife two and a half acres of land with appurtenances in the same vill as her right etc and by the same entry.

They come and then vouch to warranty the said Peter, Alexander and Adam. She is to await their age (*age*).

1031. (*Cosford*) Thomas, William [and] Richard the sons of Warren were attached to warrant Peter the son of Reynold of Elmsett two and a half acres of land with appurtenances in Elmsett which he holds etc and in respect whereof a charter etc and he complains that Emma the mother of Thomas, William and Richard sued them in the court of Bury St Edmunds. They come and acknowledge the charter. So it is said to them that they are to go to the said court [and warrant him there].

1032. (*Thingoe*) Hugh the son of Edwin and Sibilla his wife, who brought a writ of entry against William Tarlham of Nowton, have not prosecuted. So they and their sureties for prosecuting [are] in mercy, namely: Geoffrey the son of William of Thorpe and Richard Derquen of Nowton (*amercements*).

1033. William King was attached to warrant William le Suur and Lettice his wife one acre of land with appurtenances in Barrow which he holds, and whereon etc and they claim that Ralph the berker and Matilda his wife impleaded them in the court of Bury St Edmunds.

William comes and he says that he freely warrants [them]. So it is said to him that he is to go to the said court [and warrant them there].

1034. (*Babergh*) Matilda of Glemsford presented herself on the fourth day against Robert the son of Ralph concerning a plea that he render to her two acres of land with appurtenances in Glemsford which she claims as her right etc against him. He has not come, and [was] summoned etc. Judgement: the land is to be taken into the hands of the lord king, and the day etc and he is to be summoned to be at Chelmsford on the quindene of Holy Trinity [Sunday 24 June] (*Chelmsford*). Matilda appoints Robert Carbonel as her attorney.

1035. (*Cosford*) William the son of Osbert claims against Thomas the son of Nicholas two acres of land with appurtenances in Elmsett as his right etc and in which the same Thomas has no entry except by the said Nicholas, his father, to whom the said Osbert the father of the said William, whose heir he is, demised that [land] to him for a term etc.

Thomas comes and he says that he does not have that land for a term from the said Nicholas but was enfeoffed of the same land by his charter, which he proffers and which attests to this, and William cannot deny this. So he is in mercy for a false claim by the surety of John of Brettenham (*amercement*).

1036. (*Babergh*) John de Gray claims against Alan the chaplain two messuages and three acres of land with appurtenances in Cornard as his right, and in which the same Alan has no entry except by Nicholas Bastard to whom John of Cornard the father of John [de Gray] whose heir he is demised it[1] for a term.

Alan comes and denies such entry and he says that he had entry by John the father of Alan to whom John the father of John gave [that land] fifty years ago. Then he puts himself on the country. John says that he had entry by the said Nicholas and not by Alan, and that this be inquired into by the country he offers to the lord king one mark, and it is received by the surety of John de Hodeboville. So let there be a jury thereon (*one mark*).

The jurors say that ... [unfinished]

Afterwards, they have agreed by licence. They are to have a chirograph.

1   That is the land and messuages.

1037. (*Babergh*) Matilda who was the wife of Alexander of Weston claims against Alexander the son of Ralph half of forty acres of land with appurtenances in Weston,[1] and a third part of ten acres of land in the same vill as her dower etc and in respect whereof the said Alexander her former husband dowered her etc on the day that etc.

Alexander came and they have agreed. (*half a mark*) Alexander gives half a mark for licence to agree by the surety of Robert the engineer. The agreement is such that the same Alexander is to render the third part throughout. She is to have her seisin.

> 1 There is no vill of Weston in Babergh hundred but there are two in Blackbourn hundred, Coney Weston or Market Weston, which might suggest the clerk was in a rut in writing *Balb* in the margin and just carried on. Neither of the two Westons are close to Babergh hundred.

Membrane 39d[1]

> 1 There is a change of clerk on this side. There is another clerk and change of ink for **1048** and **1049**.

1038.[1] (*Norfolk*) Henry of Barford presented himself on the fourth day against Geoffrey de Say and Alina his wife concerning a plea of six acres of land with appurtenances in Cringleford, which the same Geoffrey and Alina have claimed against the abbot of Langley as the dower of Alina, and in respect whereof the same abbot vouched to warranty this Henry against them. They have not come and they had a day in the Bench. So it is adjudged that the abbot and Henry [are] without day, and they [Geoffrey and Alina are] in mercy (*amercement*).

> 1 See **153, 475** and **727** for the sequence of events.

1039. (*Babergh'*) Parnel who was the wife of Hugh the son of William presented herself on the fourth day against Thomas de Hemmegrave concerning a plea of five acres of land with appurtenances in *Benham*,[1] which she claims as her right against him. Thomas has not come etc and [was] summoned etc. Judgement: the land is to be taken into the hands of the lord king, and the day etc and he is to be summoned to be at Chelmsford on the quindene of Holy Trinity [Sunday 24 June] (*Chelmsford*).

> 1 This place cannot be located in Babergh hundred. There is a Barnham in Blackbourn hundred and given his propensity to mix up these two hundreds it is possible that the clerk has made a double mistake, that is in the margin and missing out an 'r' from *Bernham*, which is what I would expect to see if the place was Barnham. One other possibility is that this relates to Banham in Guiltcross hundred in Norfolk, which is not too far from Blackbourn, or it might be Denham in Risbridge hundred and the clerk has made a mistake with the initial letter of the place.

1040. (*Process mark, he withdrew to ...*)[1] [Section mark only]

> 1 It looks as though there was going to be something written here but the clerk withdrew it, or possibly the litigants did. This is doubtful as the justices would have amerced them. Possibly it was going to be placed elsewhere but the clerk forgot to tell us where. I have looked through the membranes and I cannot find any other reference in the margin to indicate that it was moved. I don't know what *Juc* or *Iuc* is an abbreviation of, unless it is a name.

1041. (*Risbridge*) Ralph Cook was summoned to warrant Gilbert the son of Basil and Richard his son three roods of land with appurtenances in Stoke [by Clare] and to warrant William the clerk and Margery his wife three roods of meadow in Withersfield, which they hold etc and in respect whereof [charters] etc (and they claim that he has sued them for the same[i]) in the court of Bury St Edmunds. Ralph comes and acknowledges the charters, which they have proffered under his mother's name. So it is adjudged that they may hold in peace and he warrants them. He is in mercy. He is poor.

1042. (*Earsham,*[1] *Norfolk*) Warren of Redenhall presented himself on the fourth day against Roger Bigod, the earl of Norfolk, concerning a plea that he allows him to have certain liberties in the manor of Redenhall which he ought to have and was accustomed to have thus far etc. The earl has not come etc and [was] summoned etc. Judgement: he is to be put (on securities[i]) and reliable sureties that he is at Chelmsford on the quindene of Holy Trinity [Sunday 24 June] etc. (*Chelmsford*)

  1 Apparently the clerk has put the hundred in Norfolk in which county the place in the plea is situated. This is the first time this has happened in all the membranes in this roll.

1043. (*Babergh*) Alice the daughter of Adam claims against Ralph the son of Hugh of Groton three and a half acres of land with appurtenances in Waldingfield, and against Edward de la Brewer one acre of land with appurtenances in *Coppewaldingfield*[1] as her right, and in which the same Ralph and Edward have no entry except by Brian of Brandeston the former husband of Alice who demised that [land] to them, who [in his lifetime she could not contradict] etc.

Hugh and Edward come and then vouches to warranty William the son of Brian of Brandeston, who is under age and in the wardship of Sampson of Battisford, and she acknowledges this. So she is to await his age (*age*).

  1 It can only be assumed that this land is in or near Great or Little Waldingfield, given that the first part of the plea is concerned with land in Waldingfield in Babergh hundred. It may have been a local name for one of the Waldingfields, possibly Great Waldingfield as the old English 'Copp' can be translated as summit.

1044. (*Risbridge*) William Roscelin claims against Bartholomew de Wadeshill and Heloise who was the wife of Warren de Wadeshill half an acre of meadow with appurtenances in Great Thurlow as his right, and in which the same Bartholomew and Heloise have no entry except by the said Warren de Wadeshill, the former husband of the said Heloise, to whom the said William demised that [land] etc and in respect whereof Bartholomew holds one rood and Heloise one rood.

Bartholomew comes and he says that he does not hold that rood because a certain William le Mascecren[1] holds [it] and William cannot deny this. So [he is] in mercy for a false claim. It is pardoned for poverty.

Heloise comes and then vouches to warranty Warren de Wadeshill. He is to come on the morrow. Afterwards, Heloise comes and by licence she renders [it] to him. He is to have his seisin (*refer to the Roll of York*).[2]

  1 This is probably *Mascecraria*, a butcher. See Reaney 1997, p.301 for maskery or massacrier.
  2 This could be to the plea roll of William of York, the senior justice, or to the plea rolls of Yorkshire, which were about to take place in this eyre by Robert de Lexington's circuit according to Crook 1982a, p.98. I suspect the former is correct. It appears the clerk is indicating that in the roll of William of York there is something on this case which provides more information.

1045. (*Thingoe*) Lettice the daughter of John claims against William of Thurston the chaplain half an acre of land with appurtenances in Nowton as her right, and in which the same William has no entry except by Richard of Nowton the former husband of Lettice who demised that [land] to him whom she in his lifetime [could not contradict] etc.

William comes and he denies such entry and he says that he had entry by Robert his father who died seised [and] whose heir he is. And that it is so he puts himself on the country, and she similarly. So let there be a jury thereon.

The jurors say that the said William had entry by the said Robert his father and not by the said Richard. So it is adjudged that William may hold in peace. Lettice [is] in mercy. She is poor, so nothing.

1046.[1] (*Cosford*) The prior of St Anthony's who brought a writ of warranty of charter against John de Beauchamp and Nesta his wife has not prosecuted. So he and his sureties for prosecuting [are] in mercy, namely: Peter de *Bruniford* and John de Beaumes (*amercements*). [*chirograph* CP 25(1) 213/17/92][2]

[1] See the essoin in **657**. There is a gap of 3.4 cm between this and the previous plea.
[2] It is odd that the prior has not prosecuted as the feet of fines indicates he won against John and his wife. It is probable that they came to the private agreement outlined in the chirograph so no further action in the court was required. There is unfortunately no mention of the verdict or the details in this roll. On the reverse of the feet of fines chirograph there is a mention that Bartholomew of Creake, William de Beaumont, Henry the bishop of Ely, and the abbot of Bury St Edmunds also laid a claim, I presume either to the advowson of the church at Kersey or to the land in question, 14 acres of land, 4 acres of pasture and 12 acres of wood in Kersey and Lindsay, both in Cosford hundred.

1047. (*Cosford*) Geoffrey of Suffolk who brought a writ of warranty of charter against the same has not prosecuted. So he and his sureties for prosecuting [are] in mercy, namely: Robert de Nutested of Polstead and John Galyen of Ipswich [*amercement*). [*chirograph* CP 25(1) 213/15/16][1]

[1] It is odd that Geoffrey did not prosecute but still there is this chirograph, unless the chirograph relates to a different writ of the same type. On the reverse of the chirograph is the following: *Bartholomeus de Crek' et Willelmus de Bello Monte apponunt clameum.*

1048.[1] Robert the son of Adam and Geoffrey his brother who brought a writ against Richard the son of Adam concerning land and wood in Felsham have not prosecuted. So they [are] in mercy (*amercements*). Sureties are not found because [of] a writ of right, by [the writ] pone.

[1] There is a change of clerk here for this and the next plea. There is also a change of ink to black.

1049. (*Babergh*) Nicholas of Lawshall presented himself on the fourth day against Godiva of Lawshall concerning a plea that she returns to him chattels to the value of six marks, which she unjustly withholds from him as he says. Godiva has not come etc and [was] summoned etc. Judgement: she is attached to be at Chelmsford on the quindene of Holy Trinity [Sunday 24 June] (*at Chelmsford*).

1050.[1] (*Norfolk*) Elunia who was the wife of William Curreman presented herself on the day against Reynold Rusteyn concerning a plea of a third part of three acres of land with appurtenances in Buckenham,[2] which third parts she claims in dower against him. Reynold has not come etc and [was] summoned etc. Judgement: the third parts are to be taken into the hands of the king etc and the day etc and he is to be summoned to be at Chelmsford on the octave of Holy Trinity [Sunday 17 June] etc. (*Chelmsford*).

[1] The original clerk on this plea resumes here and continues until the end of the membrane.
[2] There are three Buckenhams in Norfolk, which are in Blofield, Grimshoe and Shropham hundreds.

1051. Thomas Russel of Metfield acknowledges that he owes to Richard Picot six marks from the fine made between them, of which he will pay to him two marks at the feast of St Peter in Chains [1 August], and within the octave of St Michael [6 October] two marks, and at the feast of the Purification of the Blessed [Virgin] Mary [2 February 1241] two marks. If he does not do [this] etc he grants [that he may be distrained to do so] while etc concerning the cost etc. [**530**] [*chirograph* CP 25(1) 213/17/94][1]

[1] This is additional information to what is in the chirograph on how the person will pay the six marks.

1052.[1] Robert Pyket claimed on the Monday on the morrow of Pentecost [Monday 4 June] his land by security, which was taken into the hands of the lord king by the default, which he made against Gilbert and the others, his brothers. He is to have [it].

1   There is a gap of 4.2 cm between this plea and the previous one.

Membrane 40[1]

1   There is a change of clerk for this membrane, possibly to the one in the previous membrane: see **1048** and **1049**.

1053. (*Blything*) The prioress of Bungay[1] by her attorney claims against Austin Colekin a certain messuage with appurtenances in Bungay, in which he has no entry except by William Colekin of Bungay the father of Austin to whom the said prioress demised that [messuage] for a term, which has expired as she says. Austin comes and denies her right, and he readily grants that he had entry by William his father, but he readily says that the said prioress never demised that land to him for a term as she says. On the contrary his father had entry into that land by a certain Geoffrey del Brook who enfeoffed him, and then he puts himself on the country, and the prioress similarly. So let there be a jury thereon. The sheriff is ordered to make the twelve come before the justices on the morrow of Holy Trinity[2] [Monday 11 June] at Dunwich etc to ascertain [on oath] etc whether Austin Colekin had entry in the said land by the prioress of Bungay for a term which has expired, or if he had entry by Geoffrey de Brook, who enfeoffed him. Because both [parties put themselves on the inquest] etc (*Dunwich*).[3]

(*half a mark*) Afterwards, they have agreed, and Austin gives half[4] a mark for licence to agree etc by the surety of William of Mettingham, as is shown in the roll of Dunwich.[5]

1   There was a priory of Benedictine nuns called St Mary and Holy Cross at Bungay, founded in 1183 by Roger de Glanville.
2   This was the only day that the eyre sat at Dunwich. See Crook 1982a, p.101.
3   There is a gap here of 1.6 cm as though the clerk was intending to insert the result of the jury, but it is missing.
4   The clerk repeated the word *dimidiam* and then crossed it out having realised his mistake.
5   See **1153** for the formal agreement made at Dunwich. This statement is placed in the middle of a large gap between this plea and the next one. Presumably the clerk left the space to await the result of the plea at Dunwich, but there are only the two lines of the agreement and the chirograph has not been located.

1054.[1] (*Blything*) Camilla of Wangford[2] was attached to answer Waleran de Muncy why she has made waste, sale and disposal of the wood which she holds in dower from the inheritance of Waleran in Willingham,[3] and he says that since she ought not to have [anything] in that wood, except housebote and haybote, she sold that wood and she has given [it] away and has laid waste, in respect whereof he has been injured and he has a loss to the value of twenty marks etc and in respect thereof he produces suit.

Camilla comes and denies waste, sale and disposal, and she says that she never has taken in respect thereof except housebote and haybote. So let there be a jury thereon. It is to come at Dunwich[4] on the morrow of Holy Trinity (*Dunwich*).

The jurors[5] say that the said Camilla sold certain alder timber for five marks, and from one ditch the willows and white poplars to the value of five shillings, and three oaks to the value of three shillings, and about sixty oaks and ash trees to make for [her] profit in the same court.[6] Afterwards, it was found by the same jurors that after the death of her husband, for a great need and to make good her ploughs, she sold the said alder timber for the said five marks. Whereon it is adjudged that she made no waste nor disposals, and so [she is] quit. She is forbidden henceforth to make a sale, waste [or disposal] etc and if [she does] etc.

1. There is a gap of 5.2 cm between this plea and the previous one.
2. The clerk wrote *Wangefeud*. I have found no such place as *Wangfield*. This should probably be *Wangforda*, Wangford, in Blything hundred.
3. Willingham is in Wangford hundred.
4. The clerk had originally written *Gypewic* for Ipswich and had then crossed it out and written *Dunwich*. He must have realised that they had already been to Ipswich.
5. The clerk having indicated that the plea would continue at Dunwich then proceeds to a conclusion. It certainly does not look like an addition from the proceeding at Dunwich. There is also no further mention of this plea in those actually taken at Dunwich.
6. This probably means for the maintenance of her court, that is the house and surrounding buildings.

1055. (*Blything*) Henry the son of Warren and Alice his wife and Christine the [sister][1] of [Alice] who brought a writ of entry against John the son William of Westhall concerning land in Westhall have not prosecuted. So they and their sureties for prosecuting [are] in mercy, namely: Geoffrey Gikel of Westhall and Adam the son of Geoffrey of the same (*amercement*).

1. The clerk had written *uxor*. I suspect it should be the 'sister' of Alice.

1056. (*amercement*) John the son of Hamo who brought a writ of entry against Richard of Elmham concerning land in Ilketshall came and withdrew [from the plea]. So he and his sureties [are] in mercy, namely: Robert de Bosco of Fersfield[1] and Sampson of Battisford the clerk.

1. Fersfield is in Diss hundred in Norfolk.

1057.[1] (*Blything*) John the son of Hamo claims against Richard of Elmham fifty acres of land and eight penceworth of rent with appurtenances in Ilketshall, Elmham and Spexhall,[2] in which he has no entry except by Maria, who was the wife of Geoffrey de Aenton, who held that [land] in dower from the gift of Geoffrey her former husband [and] grandfather of the said John whose heir he is, as he says.

Richard comes and denies his right and such entry and term because he says that in fact the said land was the marriage-portion of the said Maria and she with full power of disposition after the death of her husband gave the said land to the said Richard and enfeoffed him, and that it is so he puts himself on the [verdict of the] country. He gives half a mark to have the inquest by the surety of Edmund de Wymun(dhall[i]) (*half a mark*).

John comes and he says that she [Maria] held that land in dower and not as marriage-portion, and then he puts himself on the [verdict of the] country. (*half a mark*) He gives half a mark to the lord king to have an inquest (by the surety of Robert de Bosco[i]). So let there be a jury thereon. The sheriff is ordered to make the twelve come [before the justices] etc to ascertain [on oath] etc if the said Maria held that land in dower as the same John says, or if that land was the marriage-portion of the said Maria as the same Richard says, because both etc.

(*half a mark*) Afterwards, they have agreed and John gives half a mark for licence to agree by the surety of Robert de Bosco. The agreement is such that the said Richard acknowledges the said fifty acres of land and eight penceworth of rent with appurtenances to be the right of John and he renders [them] to him. For this acknowledgement etc the said John gave to the said Richard thirteen marks, concerning which he will pay to the same Richard half at the feast of St Michael [29 September] in the year twenty-four, and the other half at the next Easter following [Sunday 31 March 1241]. If he does not [do this he grants that the sheriff may distrain his land and chattels to the value] (etc.[i]) The said Richard grants that he will render to the same John all the land which he had beyond the said fifty acres, excepting the marriage-portion of the land from the dower of the said Maria according to what will be inquired into by the oaths of the good men. The sheriff is ordered that (he is to make an inquest[i]).

1   See **1160** for a repeat of the licence to agree.
2   Only Spexhall is in Blything hundred. The other two vills are in Wangford hundred.

1058. (*Lothingland*) Simon Aysman presented himself on the fourth day against William the son of William of Yarmouth concerning a plea that he return to him chattels to the value of fourteen marks which he unjustly withholds from him as he says. William has not come etc and [was] summoned etc. Judgement: he is attached to be at Chelmsford on the nearest Thursday after the octave of Holy Trinity [Thursday 21 June] (*at Chelmsford*).

1059. Robert de Gaudington presented himself on the fourth day against William le Sauvage concerning a plea that he pays to him eleven and a half marks which he owes to him and unjustly withholds as he says. William has not come and was summoned etc. Judgement: He is attached to be at Chelmsford on the nearest Thursday after the octave of Holy Trinity [Thursday 21 June] (*Chelmsford*).

1060. Richard the son of Osbert was summoned to answer Thomas the son of John concerning a plea that he holds to his covenant made between them for three and a half roods with appurtenances in *Upredisham*. Richard came and they have agreed by licence. The agreement is such that Thomas remises all his claim for ten shillings and one pennyworth of rent per year.

1061.[1] Simon the son of Robert and Amice his wife presented themselves on the fourth day against John the son of Richard and Matthew his brother concerning a plea (that they render to them[i]) twenty acres of land with appurtenances in Woolverstone, and against Isabella of Woolverstone concerning a plea that she render to them twenty acres of land with appurtenances in the same vill, and against Hamo de Petra[2] and John his brother concerning a plea that they render to them two acres of land with appurtenances in the same vill, which they claim against them as their right. They have not come etc and [were] summoned etc. Judgement: the land is to be taken into the hands of the king, and the day etc and they are to be summoned to be at Chelmsford on the quindene of Holy Trinity [Sunday 24 June] (*Chelmsford*).

1   There is a change of clerk here, who continues to the end of the membrane.
2   This might be 'Peters', or possibly he had been to Petra in what is now Jordan.

1062. Simon de Enepol who brought a writ of warranty against Roger the son of Aubern has not prosecuted. So he and his sureties for prosecuting [are] in mercy, namely: Henry Gikel of Brampton and Richard Wyard of Westhall (*amercements*).

1063. John the son of Alice presented himself on the fourth day against Osgood of Kalweton concerning a plea that he render to him thirty acres of land with appurtenances in Harkstead, and against Walter of Stonham and Matilda his wife concerning a plea that they render to him thirty acres of land with appurtenances in the same vill, which he claims as his right against them. They have not come etc and [were] summoned etc. Judgement: the land is to be taken into the king's hands, and the day etc and they are to be summoned to be at Chelmsford on the quindene of Holy Trinity [Sunday 24 June] (*Chelmsford*).

1064. (*Blything*) Robert the son of Reynold who brought a writ of warranty against Ralph of Cookley has not prosecuted. So he and his sureties for prosecuting [are] in mercy, namely: Robert the son of the clerk of Huntingfield and Elias the chancellor[1] of Walpole (*amercements*).

> [1] Chancellor, that is a learned man who kept the records of a law court or custodian of records. I have found no indication of a court that sat at Walpole. It is possible he might have been connected with the king's courts.

1065. Letencia who was the wife of Roger Bell who brought a writ for her dower against Walter Pelling and many others has not prosecuted. So she and her sureties for prosecuting [are] in mercy, namely: Hugh Welond of Elmham and Stephen Hacon of the same (*amercements*).

1066. (*half a mark*) Walter of Bradfield (gives half a mark[i]) for licence to agree with Ralph of Clopton and Agatha his wife. [*chirograph* CP 25(1) 213/16/46][1]

> [1] This chirograph indicates that it was made at Chelmsford. Either the clerk held over its completion until the eyre in Essex or the clerk made a mistake making the chirograph. It indicates that the plea was a warranty of charter for half of 26 acres in Bacton in Hartismere hundred.

Membrane 40d

1067. Peter de Grenville and Isabella of Saxham claim against the abbot of Bury St Edmunds six acres of land with appurtenances (in[r]) *Gramfornham*[1] as their right etc.

(*The abbot appoints R. of Boyland*) The abbot comes and denies their right and then he vouches to warranty Geoffrey the son of Luke who is present and he warrants him, and then he vouches to warranty Alan the son of Geoffrey of Dearsley. He is to have him at Chelmsford on the quindene of Holy Trinity [Sunday 24 June] by the aid of the court. He is to be summoned in the county of Cambridgeshire (*Cambridgeshire*).

The same claim against William Cook of Livermere fourteen acres of land with appurtenances in *Gramfornham* as their right, and in respect whereof a certain Hugh their ancestor was seised in his demesne as of fee and right in the time of King Henry the grandfather of the current king by taking profits therefrom to the value of half a mark. From the same Hugh the right to that land descended to a certain Norman as son and heir, and from the same Norman to a certain Juliana and Isabella, who is the plaintiff, as daughters and heirs, and from the same Juliana to this Peter who now claims as son and heir, and that such is her right she offers to prove etc. Isabella appoints Robert (her son[i]) as her attorney.

William comes and denies the right and seisin of the said Hugh and everything etc. He puts himself on the grand assize of the lord king, and he seeks a recognition be made whether he has the greater right in the said land or the said Peter and Isabella. Robert de Wykes, Gerbert de St Clare, Richard Marshall and John de Crammaville, four knights, selected to choose the twelve etc to make a recognition of the grand assize between the aforesaid, have come and chosen these: Richard of Ickworth, William de *Corston*,[2] Hugh Burt, Adam de *Welstetam*,[3] William del Auney, Adam of Eleigh, Robert de Bosco, William of Cotton, Hubert of Braiseworth, John de la Londe, Richard Applegard, Gilbert of Walsham, Eustace of Barningham, Thomas Crowe, John de Crammaville,[4] Robert de Wykes, Gerbert de St Clare, Richard Marshall.

Afterwards, they have agreed. (*one mark*) William Cook gives one mark for licence to agree by the surety of Peter de Grenville and Hervey de Great Fornham (*Chelmsford at the quindene of Trinity*).[5] [*chirograph* CP 25(1) 213/17/121][6]

1   Presumably one of the three Fornhams in Thingoe and Thedwestry hundreds: Fornham All Saints, St Genevieve and St Martin. This one may be St Genevieve. It is shown as *Genonefae Forham* in *Domesday Book Suffolk*, Part One, section 14, no. 53. I have not been able to indicate which of the Fornhams was *Magna Fornham*, which the chirograph also indicates.

2   This might be Coston in Forehoe hundred in Norfolk, but it seems unlikely as it is hardly local. It could also be Cotton in Lothingland hundred. However, William of Cotton appears later in the plea, also as a juror.

3   This place cannot be found in Suffolk or elsewhere. It probably should be Welnetham as there is an Adam of Welnetham shown in **677** as one of the knights elected to be part of a grand assize jury.

4   It looks as though the four knights chose themselves for the jury; or perhaps the clerk repeated the knights by mistake.

5   This marginal note is placed almost 5 cm after the end of the plea and it appears just prior to the next plea. But it does appear to relate to this plea and is probably connected with the plea against the abbot of Bury St Edmunds.

6   The chirograph only covers the claim against William Cook of Livermere. William acknowledges the said land to be the right of Peter and Isabella for a money rent of 20d. payable in four terms of 5d. each term, which is specified in the chirograph. It is also noteworthy that this chirograph is made at Cattishall, not Chelmsford.

1068. (*Lackford*) An assize comes to declare if Baldwin of Eriswell and Margery his wife unjustly etc disseised Agnes the daughter of Henry and Beatrice her sister of their free tenement in Eriswell after the first crossing etc and in respect whereof they claim that they have disseised them of four and a half acres of land.

Baldwin and Margery come and they say nothing to stay the assize.

The jurors say that they have disseised them as the writ says. So it is adjudged that they have recovered their seisin against them. So they [are] in mercy by the surety of Ralph Spurun and John Katerin (*amercement*).

Damages: four shillings.

1069. (*Babergh*) An assize comes to declare if Godfrey the son of William, Richard Cook, Richard Attebrigge, William the son of Odo and Thomas the son of Robert unjustly etc disseised Alexander the son of William of his free tenement in Lavenham after the first etc and in respect whereof he complains that they disseised him of ten acres of land and one messuage.

Godfrey and the others come and they say nothing to stay the assize.

The jurors say that they have not disseised him as the writ says. So it is adjudged that he is to take nothing by this assize and he is in mercy for a false claim. He is poor.

1070. (*Lackford*) Master Robert de Shardlow[1] was summoned to answer Henry the son of Roger and Ivetta his wife concerning a plea that he hold to their covenant made between them of a third part of one knight's fee with appurtenances in Herring-swell, and of a sixth part of a knight's [fee] in Barton [Mills]. And in respect whereof the same complain that [whereas] by that covenant the same Master Robert owes to them one hundred shillings per year for the dower of Ivetta in Barton [Mills], the same Robert held back from them nine marks and five shillings, whereon they have suffered damage to the value of forty shillings.[2]

Master Robert comes and he denies force and injury and readily concedes to the covenant and whatsoever is contained in that covenant. He readily grants that he detained from them the said nine marks and six shillings,[3] but justly, because he says that whereas they ought to warrant that dower against everyone, it has been distrained by Jews for twenty-two marks,[4] which the Jews claim from the said dower, because the said Ivetta has borrowed from them the said money. Because it cannot be established whether the Jews distrain the said dower for the said Ivetta a day is given to them at Chelmsford on the quindene of Holy Trinity [Sunday 24 June], Master Robert undertook that he will produce the Jews by whom she may be distrained under this form, that if the Jews are able to show that she borrowed from them the said cash and that she is being distrained for the said money through that dower, that they [Henry and Ivetta] are to satisfy the Jews themselves. If however, they are not able to show that they owe them the said money, that Master Robert must satisfy them for the said nine marks and six shillings and for the damages. Afterwards,[5] at Chelmsford on the quindene of Holy Trinity [Sunday 24 June] Master Robert essoined himself and had a day by his essoin from that day in fifteen days[6] (*Chelmsford*). Henry and Ivetta presented themselves on the fourth day against him. The same Robert has not come, nor has he brought the Jews as he undertook. So it is adjudged that Henry and Ivetta have recovered the said nine marks and six shillings against him and he is in mercy (*amercement*).

[1] See **819** and **822** for the other pleas involving Master Robert de Shardlow.
[2] If he has held back 9 marks and 5s. I make that 125s., not 40s. – unless this means that he has not paid them for over a year and the 40s. is what he owes to bring him up to date on his rent according to the terms of the covenant.
[3] The clerk in the previous paragraph indicated that he held back 9 marks and 5s. It was good of him to add a shilling!
[4] That is £14 13s. 4d.
[5] There is a change of hand here and this part has been added later after the case appeared at Chelmsford and shows the result.
[6] Master Robert and the others were due to appear on the quindene of Holy Trinity, or Sunday 24 June, but Robert has essoined and has a further fifteen days to appear, that is until Monday 9 July. The eyre court sat at Chelmsford until 15 July according to Crook 1982a, p.101.

1071.[1] Ailsilda claims against William Bonard and Agnes who was the wife of Roger Bonard six acres of land with appurtenances in Chevington by an assize of mort d'ancestor. They have come and have acknowledged themselves to be the villeins of the abbot of Bury St Edmunds. So [they are] without day. She may proceed against the abbot if she wishes.

[1] This plea indicates why she did not prosecute in **790**. However, in **790** Ailsilda is only suing Agnes whereas here she is also suing William Bonard.

1072.[1] The abbot of Bury St Edmunds appoints Roger of Boyland or Martin of Barton as his attorney against the bishop and prior of Ely concerning a plea of liberties and replevins, and against Astelma and her sisters concerning a plea of land etc and against Richard of Harlow concerning a plea of warranty of charter, and against Edward the miller concerning a plea of land.

[1] See **705** for the appointment of an attorney by the prior of Ely.

Membrane 41

1073. John the son of Hervey, who brought a writ against Ranulf Wigge and Matilda his wife concerning one messuage in Hitcham in respect whereof a grand assize, has not prosecuted. So [he is] in mercy (*amercement*).

1074.[1] (*Norfolk*) The jurors chosen by the consent of the parties, between Thomas of Risby, the plaintiff, and Giles de Monpincon, the deforcer, concerning the common pasture in *Westmoor* and *Eastmoor* in Ryburgh,[2] and in respect whereof Thomas complains that contrary to the fine made between them in the court of the lord king he took his pigs in the same pasture. And in respect whereof the same Giles says that no pig should enter in that pasture which is called *Rikenhale*[3] where he took his pigs from the day of the Holy Cross in May[4] up to the feast of St Peter in Chains.[5] They [the jurors] come and say on their oath that a certain covenant was made between the said Giles and his men of Ryburgh, that neither the pigs of the said Giles nor the pigs of his men should enter in his pasture in the said vill from the said time of the Invention of the Holy Cross up to the feast of St Peter in Chains, but they say that Thomas never consented to that covenant, so that his pigs always before that covenant, and afterwards, have entered into that pasture, and they should throughout, except for the cornfield and meadows of Giles. So it is adjudged that Thomas may use those pastures just as he has used [them] till now without any impediment from Giles. Giles [is] in mercy. (*one mark*) He made a fine for one mark by the surety of Roger of Boyland.

1   See **930** for the sureties and for the order that the sheriff gets the jury together.
2   This is either Little or Great Ryburgh in Gallow hundred or Brothercross hundred respectively in Norfolk. These places are across the hundred boundary from each other. I presume the pastures refer to East and West Moors near one or both of these places, but I cannot locate them on an Ordnance Survey map. I have located a West Wood close to Great Ryburgh.
3   This pasture cannot be found near the Ryburghs either.
4   3 May when there is the feast of the Invention of the Holy Cross.
5   What is meant here is that they can feed their pigs on the pasture from 3 May to 1 August each year.

1075. (*Lothingland*) Richard the son of Ranulf of Newton claims against William the son of Sefrid[1] twenty acres of land with appurtenances in *Newton*, and against Thomas of Newton twelve acres of land with appurtenances in the same vill, and against Nicholas of Corton and Matilda his wife two acres of land with appurtenances in the same vill (and against Odo of Newton one acre of land with appurtenances in the same vill[i]) as his right, and in respect whereof Ranulf his father, whose heir he is, was seised in his demesne as of fee and right in the time of the current king by taking profits therefrom to the value of half a mark etc.

William and the others come (Thomas for ten acres of land[i]). Nicholas and Matilda then vouch to warranty the said William and he warrants them. He answered for all and he says that that land, which the same Richard claims against him, has passed to him by a fine made between William, the [defendant],[2] and (the said[i]) Thomas of Newton the elder brother of the said Richard, in respect whereof a chirograph etc which he proffers and which attests to this. Thomas says that he is his elder brother of the [same] father and mother, so while he is alive [Richard] can claim no right in that land.

Richard says that that fine ought not to harm him because the same Thomas is a bastard. Moreover, the same Richard, when that fine was made before the justices in the Bench, was present and laid his claim in that fine. He says moreover that the same Thomas acknowledged himself to be a bastard (*to judgement*).

Afterwards, they have agreed. William the son of Sefrid gives half a mark for licence to agree by the surety of Edmund de Wymundhall. They are to have a chirograph (*half a mark*). [*chirograph* CP 25(1) 213/17/113][3]

1   There is a William the son of Sefrey de *Neuton* shown in *Cal. Feet of Fines, Suff.*, p.29. He is

also impleading Thomas the son of Ranulf in *Neuton*. Strangely, there is no mention of this plea in this book under this eyre, given the fact that according to the roll a chirograph was issued.

2   The clerk put *petentem*. However, he was the defendant not the plaintiff.

3   Richard obtains 3 acres of land and 3 acres of heath from William the son of Sefrid according to the chirograph in return for a rent of 6d. a year payable at four separate feast days.

1076. (*Lothingland*) Adam the son of Sefrid claims against William the son of Sefrid seven acres of land with appurtenances in *Newton* and Carlton [Colville], and against Edith the mother of the same William seven acres of land with appurtenances in the same vill as his right, in respect whereof Sefrid the father of Adam and William was seised etc in the time of King John by taking profits therefrom to the value of half a mark etc. From the same Sefrid the right of that land descended to this Adam and William as partible land.

Edith comes and then vouches to warranty the said William, her son, who is present and he answered for all, and he denies his right and everything etc. He says that he cannot claim a part in the said land, because he readily says that the land never was divided nor is it partible, and then he puts himself upon the jury of the country.

Adam says that a certain Aylmer, his ancestor, had two sons, namely Sefrid and Ranulf, between whom his inheritance was divided, so that twenty-eight acres of land has passed to the same Sefrid and twenty-eight acres to Ranulf his brother as their shares, and that it is so he puts himself on the jury. William says that the said Ranulf had nothing in the said land except only by an intrusion, because he says that he intruded into that land so that Sefrid brought a writ against him for that land and by consent, because he was of great power, the said land remained with the same Ranulf. So the sheriff was ordered that before him and before [his fellow justices] etc he must make the twelve come etc and by whom etc and who neither etc and by the oath of them etc [to decide] whether the said land was divided between the said Sefrid and Ranulf as partible land as the same Adam says. [*chirograph* CP 25(1) 213/17/101][1]

1   The chirograph indicates William won but granted to Adam 6 acres out of the 14 claimed for 18d. a year.

1077. (*twenty shillings*) Alan de *Bruniford* gives twenty shillings for licence to agree with Agnes de *Bruniford* concerning a plea of land by the surety of William of Layham and Sylvester of Bures. [*chirograph* CP 25(1) 213/17/95][1]

1   There is no other mention of this case in the roll. The details are in the feet of fine. The agreement was actually written down at Chelmsford. Alan wins the right to 80 acres of land in Wenham, but Agnes rents the land for 10 marks a year.

1078. (*Norfolk, ten shillings*) For Philip of Flegg for default and for contempt of court ten shillings.

Membrane 41d[1]

1   There is a change of hand for this half of the membrane.

1079. (*Cosford*) Seyna Doddemere claims against Roesia the daughter of Hamo four acres of land with appurtenances in Wherstead[1] from whom Reynold the son of Roger the cousin of Seyna whose heir she is was seised in his demesne as of fee on the day that he died etc.

[Roesia][2] came and claimed a view. She is to have [it]. They are to come at Dunwich on the morrow of Holy Trinity, and in the meantime etc (*Dunwich*). Roesia appoints Maurice Argent as her attorney. [**346**]

1   Wherstead is in Samford hundred not Cosford, so the clerk has made a mistake in the marginal note.
2   The clerk wrote *Reginaldus* for Reynold, but Reynold is dead! It should be *Roesia* who comes.

1080. (*Risbridge*) An assize comes to declare if Thurstan de Mentemore[1] and Margery his wife unjustly etc disseised Richard of Dalham of his free tenement in Gazeley and Needham after the first crossing etc and in respect whereof he complains that they disseised him of three and (a half[1]) acres of land and twelve penceworth of rent.

Thurstan and Margery come and they say the assize should not be taken on this because they have impleaded him in the court of Clare[2] by a writ of right, so that by a default, which the same Richard made in the same court after a view of the land, they have recovered seisin of the said land and rent by the judgement of the same court. And then they put themselves on the assize.

The jurors say that the said Thurstan and Margery have not disseised the said Richard of the said land and rent. So Richard is to take nothing by this assize and he is in mercy for a false claim. Thurstan and Margery [are] without day. The surety for the amercement [is] Thomas de *Hameheth*[3] (*amercement*).

1   Probably Mentmore in Buckinghamshire.
2   This is an example of the working of the honorial or burghal court.
3   This might be Thomas of Hanchet. See **860** and **876**.

1081. (*Cosford*) Richard of Fressingfield claims against Richard the chaplain of Kersey ten acres of land with appurtenances in Kersey as his right, and in respect whereof a certain William, his ancestor, was seised in his demesne as of fee and right in the time of King John by taking profits therefrom to the value of half a mark etc. From the same William descended the right of that land to certain daughters, namely: Emma and Alice; and from the same Emma to a certain Robert as son and heir, and from the same Robert to a certain Robert as son and heir, and from the same Alice descended the right of that Alice to a certain Fabian as son and heir. Because the same Fabian died without a direct heir, the right to the land reverted to the said Emma and her heirs, and that such is his right he offers [to prove] etc.

Richard comes and denies his right. He says that it does not seem to him that he should answer him because the said Fabian had a certain sister, namely Levina. He claims a judgement, inasmuch as he makes no mention of her in his statement of claim whether he ought to answer him.

Afterwards, Richard [the plaintiff] comes and claims licence to withdraw from his writ and he has [it].

1082. (*Norfolk*) Margery who was the wife of Charles of Yarmouth presented herself on the fourth day against Roger le May and Beatrice his wife concerning a plea of half of two rengates[1] of land with appurtenances in Yarmouth, and against William of Winchelsea concerning a plea of half of one rengate of land with appurtenances in the same vill, and against Simon de Fysh concerning a plea of half of one rengate of land with appurtenances in the same vill, and against Henry le Charpenter concerning a plea of half of one rengate of land with appurtenances in the same vill, which halves she has claimed in dower against them. They have not come [nor were they attached] etc and at other times they have made defaults. As a result the sheriff is ordered to take those halves into the hands of the lord king, and that the day etc and that they were to be summoned etc. The sheriff has done nothing thereon nor has he ordered a day etc. So as before the halves are to be taken etc and the day etc. They are to be summoned to be at Chelmsford on the quindene of Holy Trinity [Sunday 24 June] (*Chelmsford*).

> 1 A *rengata*, or range, is a strip of land of fixed length in Norfolk. The length is not known. My definition comes from Latham 1965, p.391.

1083.[1] (*Lothingland*) Hawise Katewis who brought a writ of dower against John Bonde has not prosecuted. So she and her sureties for prosecuting [are] in mercy, namely: Hugh Rocinale of Little Yarmouth (*amercements*).

> 1 There is a gap of 3 cm between this plea and the previous one.

1084. (*Blything*) Margery who was the wife of Karlon of the Wardrobe by her attorney presented herself on the fourth day against William of the Wardrobe concerning a plea of half of thirty acres of meadow with appurtenances in Darsham, which half she claims in dower against him etc. William has not come etc and [was] summoned etc. Judgement: the halves are to be taken into the hands of the lord king etc and the day etc and he is to be summoned to be at Chelmsford on the quindene of Holy Trinity [Sunday 24 June] (*Chelmsford*).

1085. (*Mutford*) Hugh the chaplain who brought a writ against Warren Buchard concerning land in Kessingland has not prosecuted. So he and his sureties for prosecuting [are] in mercy, namely: Thomas the son of Nicholas Oldhering[1] and Adam the son of John of Kessingland (*amercements*).

> 1 This is almost certainly the same man as the one involved in a plea of customs and services with the prior of Weybourne in **332**.

1086. (*Samford*) John the son of Robert and Matilda his wife who brought a writ *de fine facto* against Richard of Brantham have not prosecuted. So they and their sureties for prosecuting [are] in mercy, namely John Godsweyn of Felmingham and Robert de Hospic of Stalham (*amercement*).

1087.[1] (*Babergh*) An assize comes to declare if Robert Soylard the brother of Isabella was seised in his demesne etc of three acres and one rood of land with appurtenances in Fenstead on the day [he died] etc and if etc after etc which land William the son of Philip holds. He comes and says that the assize should not proceed because the said Isabella has a certain surviving husband named Nigel without whom she should not answer. Isabella cannot deny this. So William [is] without day and Isabella [is] in mercy. She is poor.

> 1 There is a change of clerk here. The writing is in a smaller script as though the clerk tried to fit this in.

1088.[1] (*Suffolk*) Henry de Balliol[2] appoints Reynold de Sesselin or Joscelin of Hindley against Richard the son of Robert and Eustace of Barningham concerning a plea of *quare impedit* and of an assize of darrein presentment.

> 1 There is another change of clerk here from that in **1087** but not to the same as the one who wrote the rest of this side of the membrane.
> 2 This could be Bailleul-en-Vimeu in Picardy.

1089. (*twenty shillings*) John of Coddenham gives twenty shillings to have a jury by the surety of Thomas of Tuddenham the clerk and Thomas the son of Richard. Note: that Everard of Trumpington is the surety for prosecuting.

Membrane 42

1090. (*half a mark*) Richard the son of Robert of Groton gives half a mark for a licence to agree with John de Beauchamp and Nesta his wife concerning a plea of land by the surety of Walter of Groton. [*chirograph* CP 25(1) 213/15/10]

   ¹ This chirograph indicates that the plea was a warranty of charter for 20 acres of land. On its reverse is *Bartholomeus de Crek et Willelmus Bello Monte apponunt clameum.*

1091.¹ (*Risbridge*) Alan of Heckingham was summoned to answer Hamo the son of Hamo Chevere concerning a plea that he holds to his covenant made between them concerning two parts of the manor of Wixoe with appurtenances except the advowson of the church of the same vill. And in respect whereof the same Hamo claims that whereas by that covenant the same Alan ought not to have the power to tallage the men (belonging¹) to the said manor neither to cut the wood, nor to give, sell, mortgage, waste [or] in any other way to alienate the said manor or anything pertaining to it, whereby the condition of Hamo the son of Hamo could deteriorate, the same Alan coming unjustly [and] contrary to that covenant sold that wood and taxed the said men, whereby he has suffered damage to the value of twenty marks² etc. And in addition the same Hamo complains that [whereas] by that covenant he owes to the same Hamo, six pounds and seventeen shillings per year for the said manor, he has deprived him [of] the said rent etc for three years to the value of twenty pounds, twelve shillings, ten pence. and concerning which he produces suit etc (*on Monday*).

    Alan comes and denies force and injury and everything and he readily concedes the covenant and denies waste and everything etc and he does not show a deed or any tally nor produces suit that he has paid to him the said arrears. So it is adjudged that he must satisfy him concerning the said arrears of twenty pounds, twelve shillings [and] ten pence. Alan [is] in mercy. He is poor.

   ¹ See **666** for an essoin.
   ² That is £13 6s. 8d.

1092.¹ Matilda who was the wife of Herbert of Aldham claims against Robert Bolle half of five acres and one messuage with appurtenances in Lavenham as her dower etc. Robert comes and he knows nothing to say why she should not have the dower, and he is in mercy for an unjust detention. It² is pardoned because [he is] poor.

   ¹ See **1024** for an appointment of an attorney. There is a gap of 9 cm between this plea and the previous one.
   ² The amercement was erased in the margin as well.

1093. (*Thedwestry, amercement*) John the son of Osbert [is] in mercy because he has not prosecuted the grand assize.

1094. (*Blackbourn, forty shillings*) Robert the son of Richard de *Langetoft* gives forty shillings for licence to agree with Richard his father by the surety of Robert de Bosco and Geoffrey of Badley. [*chirograph* CP 25(1) 213/16/57]

1095. (*Thedwestry*) An assize comes to declare if Maria of Whatfield the aunt of Simon of Whatfield was seised in her demesne as of fee of four and a half acres of land with appurtenances in Little Livermere¹ on the day she died, and if she died after the last etc and if the same etc and in respect whereof Abel the son of Walter holds one acre, Richard Bule one acre and one rood and Robert the son of Walter two acres and one rood. They come and then vouch to warranty Walter of Groton, who is present, and he warrants them, and then he vouches to warranty John the son of Ralph of Whatfield. He is to have him on Monday and the jury is to come then (*on Monday*). Afterwards, John comes and he warrants him and he answered for all and he says that the assize should not be taken on this because they are of one descent, and they are nephews, so that one [is] from a brother and the others [are] from a sister and that the said Maria was his aunt and the aunt of Simon. Simon says the same to this. So it is adjudged that the assize is not to be taken between them. John [is] without day, and Simon [is] in mercy by the surety ... [unfinished] (*amercement*).

¹ Little Livermere is actually in Blackbourn, not Thedwestry, hundred, unless the clerk has made a mistake here. Great Livermere is in Thedwestry hundred.

1096. (*Hartismere, Process mark*)¹ Thomas of Gedding was summoned to warrant Robert of Hinderclay, William de Belencombe² and William Darnel, Walter the son of William the priest, and Henry of Northwold and Henry Folcard. He [Thomas of Gedding] comes and warrants them and he answered for all and he upholds³ the right of them and the seisin of the said William and everything etc. He puts himself on the grand assize of the lord king and he seeks a recognition be made whether he has the greater right in that land as in that which the said William quitclaimed to him, or the said Katelina and Alice. Gilbert of Walsham, William of Stratford, John de Cordebof and Walter of Cove four knights, selected to choose the twelve etc to make a recognition of the grand assize between the aforesaid, have come and chosen these, namely: Hugh Burt, William de Ciresy, Adam of Eleigh, Hubert of Braiseworth, Robert de Wykes, Gerbert de St Clare, John of Stonham, William of Henley, William the son of Rainer, William de Boville, Richard of Glemham, Ranulf de Blything, Robert of Layham, Richard Marshall and Osbert of Bawdsey.

Afterwards, they have agreed by licence, in God's name and for poverty. They are to have a chirograph.

A day⁴ is given to them to take his chirograph in the octave of St John the Baptist at Chelmsford and Thomas appoints John of Gedding as his attorney. [**450** and **1097**] [*chirograph* CP 25(1) 213/17/111]⁵

¹ The process mark looks like a tadpole with four dots, two on each side of the tail. It looks as though this is a pointer for a clerk to show where this plea follows on from **450**, as there is a similar mark at **450**.
² This might be the same William de Belencumbre who is shown as William Bellchamber in Reaney 1997, p.38. He is spelt Benecumb in **450**.
³ Normally the clerk uses the Latin word *deffendit* to deny the right of the plaintiff in this context but here I think he is using it in the sense of upholding the right of the defendants, otherwise Thomas would not be much good as a warrantor for these defendants.
⁴ There is a gap of 2 cm between the previous paragraph and this one.
⁵ This chirograph is made at Chelmsford on the octave of St John the Baptist. See **450** for the other plea and the initial stage of this plea.

1097. Sampson of Battisford pledged for security all his land that he will cause Katherine le Walesche and Alice her sister to have twenty shillings within the octave of St John the Baptist [Saturday 1 July] from which Thomas of Gedding [will pay] half a mark and Roger the Breton one mark. [**450, 1096**] [*chirograph* CP 25(1) 213/17/98 and CP 25(1) 213/17/111]¹

¹ See **450** for the agreements.

Membrane 42d

1098. (*Norfolk*) Ralph of Sibsey was summoned to answer Adam of Sibsey why he deforced him of the reasonable share which belongs to him from the inheritance that was of the mother of Adam and Ralph in Tilney, whose heirs they are and who recently died.

Ralph comes and denies his right and he says that he can claim no right in the said land as his share, because that land was given as a marriage-portion with a certain Estrilda to a certain Oncy, and from them the right of that land descended to a certain Mabel as daughter and heir and the mother of this Ralph, and it never was divided after it was given in marriage-portion. He claims a judgement (*to judgement*).

(*one mark*) Afterwards, they have agreed and Ralph gives half a mark for licence to agree by the surety of Nicholas of Lynn. [*chirograph* CP 25(1) 156/66/809][1]

> [1] According to the agreement Adam acknowledged the land to be the right of Ralph, his brother, and he hands it over for one mark of silver.

1099. (*Lothingland*) Margery, who was the wife of John the son of Ralph, presented herself on the fourth day against John Bordwater concerning a plea of half of one messuage with appurtenances in Little Yarmouth which she has claimed in dower against him. John has not come, and he has made a default [at another time], so that the land was taken into the hands of the lord king, nor was it sought, and the taking [of the land] has been attested. So it is adjudged that she has recovered her seisin against him. John [is] in mercy (*amercement*). [**321**]

1100. (*half a mark*) Thomas the son of Master William of Pakenham gives half a mark for licence to agree with Thomas the son of William by the surety of Thomas. [*chirograph* CP 25(1) 213/15/14 and CP 25(1) 213/17/102 and CP 25(1) 213/15/9][1]

> [1] These chirographs are identical. A chirograph was divided into three parts: one for the plaintiff, one for the defendant and one for the Chancery. It is unusual to have all three parts surviving.

1101. (*Norfolk*) Giles de Munpincon, who is to wage law against Thomas of Risby concerning a trespass, came and he did so. So [he is] without day. Thomas [is] in mercy for a false claim. (*one mark*) He made a fine for one mark by the surety of Richard of Oxwick. [**169, 930, 1074**]

1102. Warren de Wadeshill was summoned to warrant Bartholomew de Wadeshill sixteen acres of land with appurtenances in Little Thurlow which he holds and from him [he claims to hold] etc and in respect whereof he claims that he is being impleaded in the court of [the liberty] of Bury St Edmunds. Warren comes and he says that he freely warrants him. So he is told that he must go to the said court and warrant him [there] etc.

1103. Matthew de Meuling' presented himself on the fourth day against Thomas de la Pand concerning a plea that he returns to him a certain charter which he unjustly withholds from him etc. Thomas has not come, and [was] summoned etc. Judgement: he is attached to be at Chelmsford on the quindene of Holy Trinity [Sunday 24 June] (*Chelmsford*). Matthew appoints Laurence de Meulinges as his attorney.

1104.[1] Adam the son of Hervey was attached to answer Nicholas Felage concerning a robbery and the breach of peace of the lord king in respect whereof he has appealed him, and in respect whereof he says that he came to his house in Hopton and he has robbed him of seventeen sacks of barley at a price of forty shillings and he has badly beaten him and his wife, and he offers to prove that he did this wrongly and feloniously by his body as the court sees fit.

Adam comes and denies force and injury and robbery and everything [whatever is against the peace] etc. He says that the said Nicholas is the villein of the abbot of Bury St Edmunds, and because he was unwilling to withdraw from the land of the said abbot and has uprooted trees, the same abbot came and sent his serjeant to the said house and he took into his hands that house and crop and he demised it to this Adam. The serjeant is present and he testifies to this. Because he has not proceeded against him in the court of Bury St Edmunds before the coroner as he ought to have done, it is adjudged that the appeal [is] null, but for keeping the peace of the lord king it is to be inquired into by the country.

Afterwards, Adam comes and Nicholas does not wish to proceed. So he and his sureties for prosecuting [are] in mercy, namely: Laurence the son of Walter of Hepworth and John the son of Hervey of the same (*amercements*). Because it has been attested (by the jury[i]) that they have agreed concerning the removed crop, and that he has not broken his teeth, he [Adam the son of Hervey] is in mercy for making an agreement. [He made] a fine for ten shillings by the surety of Martin of Rockland (*ten shillings*).

¹ This is classed by the clerks as a trespass but it has certain aspects of a crown plea as well because of the appeal.

1105. (*Cosford*) Master William of Kentwell presented himself on the fourth day against Nicholas de Crevquore concerning a plea that he do him the customs and right services which he should do him from his free tenement which he holds from him in Brettenham as in the rent, arrears and other things. Nicholas has not come and [was] summoned etc. Judgement: he is attached to be at Chelmsford on the quindene of Holy Trinity [Sunday 24 June] (*Chelmsford*).

1106. William the son of Sefrey was attached to answer Thomas the son of Ranulf concerning a plea that he holds to his fine made in the king's court before the justices at Westminster between the said William, the plaintiff, and the said Thomas, the tenant, concerning thirty acres of land with appurtenances in *Newton* in respect whereof a chirograph [was made between them] etc. And the same Thomas claims that whereas by that fine there ought to remain to the same Thomas ten acres of land from the said thirty acres of land, the same William against that fine unjustly deforced him of eight acres of heathland which are pertaining to the said ten acres of land. He says that after that fine the same Thomas brought a writ *de fine facto* between them for the said eight acres of heath before Robert de Lexington and his fellow justices at the last eyre[1], [and] he has recovered his seisin against him, and then he puts himself on the rolls.

William comes and readily grants the fine and chirograph and whatsoever is contained in the fine. He says that he is in seisin of everything that is contained in the fine. Moreover, he says that he holds from the same land two acres more than is contained in that fine.

Afterwards, it was found in the rolls of the lord Robert de Lexington that the same Thomas recovered his seisin against the same William concerning his common pasture namely, that pertaining to the said ten acres and not of anything separate. So it is adjudged that he is in mercy for a false claim. He is poor. William readily acknowledges and wishes that he shall have that common as he ought to have it as pertaining to that land. William [is] without day.

¹ Robert de Lexington was the leading judge in the Suffolk eyre of November 1234 to January 1235. Unfortunately there are no plea rolls left for this eyre.

Membrane 43

1107. (*Blything*) Roger the son of Richard claims against Simon de Enepol two and a half acres of land with appurtenances in Brampton, and against Henry Gobel[1] three acres of land with appurtenances in the same vill, and against Richard Bacon three roods of land with appurtenances in the same vill as his right etc.

Simon and the others come. Simon and Richard then vouch to warranty Roger the son of Osbert. They are to have him at Chelmsford on the quindene of Holy Trinity [Sunday 24 June] by the aid of the court (*Chelmsford*). Henry comes and acknowledges that he is the villein of William the son of Hubert of Brampton. So Roger is in mercy. He may proceed against William if he wishes. He is poor.

[1] Henry could be a cup maker or seller of cups. See Reaney 1997, p.194.

1108. Hubert of Braiseworth claims Edmund the son of Robert the noble as his naif and fugitive. He says that a certain Gilbert who was a villein [and] his ancestor had two daughters, Clarice and Elvina. From Clarice issued Edric and Heloise who were villeins. From Edric issued two daughters, Alberr' and Juliana, who were villeins. From Juliana issued this Edmund, who is being claimed as a villein. Ailber' died without offspring. From Heloise issued Cecilia who was a villein, and from Cecilia a certain Richard, who is present, and he acknowledges himself to be the villein of Hubert. From Elvina issued a certain Robert the reeve who was a villein. From Robert issued two daughters, Agnes and Gunnilda, who were villeins. From Agnes a certain Hubert, who is present, and he acknowledges himself to be a villein. From Gunnilda issued a certain Stephen who is present and he acknowledges himself to be a villein.

Edmund comes and says that he is a free man and he readily grants that his mother Juliana was a villein, but he says that she was freed and (married[i]) to Robert his father who was a free man, and that he was born after the marriage contract. Hubert says that [it was] before the marriage and then he produces suit. Afterwards, Edmund grants the same. So it is adjudged that he be committed as a villein to him [Hubert of Braiseworth].

1109. William of Cotton and Joan his wife were summoned to answer Roger of Carlton concerning a plea that they hold to the covenant made between Roger and the said John concerning one carucate of land with appurtenances in Bruisyard, Cransford, Swefling, Rendham and Peasenhall.[1]

William comes and he says that he cannot answer without the said Joan. So he is told to have her at Chelmsford on the quindene of Holy Trinity [Sunday 24 June] (*Chelmsford*). The same day is given to the same Roger.

[1] All five of these places are in Plomesgate hundred except for Peasenhall, which is in Blything hundred.

1110. (*Babergh*) An assize comes to declare if Godfrey Prat the father of Leunie was seised in his demesne etc of nine and a half acres of land with appurtenances in Acton and Brandeston on the day that the died, and if he died after the last return etc and if she etc which land Nicholas and others named in the writ hold. They come and say that the assize should not be taken on this because she has three sisters, namely: Matilda, Rose and Selote without whom they cannot answer her. She cannot deny this. So they [are] without day. She [is] in mercy. She is poor.

1111. (*Babergh*) An assize comes to declare if Ralph the son of Adam the father of Constance was seised in his demesne etc of one acre of land with appurtenances in Boxted on the day that he died, and if after the last return etc and if the said etc which land William the son of Roger holds. He comes and he says nothing to stay the assize.

The jurors say that the said Ralph died seised, but after the death of Ralph a certain Richard the son of Ralph and brother of Constance was in seisin of the said land and he died seised thereof. So it is adjudged that she is to take nothing by this assize. She is in mercy[1] for a false claim.

[1] There is no mention of the amercement in the margin.

1112. Gerard Richaud claimed his land by replevin on the Tuesday in Whit Week[1], which was taken into the hands of the lord king for a default which he has made against Matilda the daughter of Hamo the Breton concerning a plea of land, and he has [it].

[1] Tuesday 5 June. This must have been at Cattishall but according to Crook 1982a, p.101 the eyre was completed at Cattishall on 4 June. So this transaction was taking place in the intervening period between closing down at Cattishall and opening at Dunwich on 11 June.

1113. (*Essex*) Thomas of Bildeston the essoiner of the dean of Colchester and Ernald de Dyham the essoiner of Master Geoffrey de Tywing presented themselves on the fourth day against Adam of Mildenhall and Agnes his wife, William Gamel and Simon the son of Ralph concerning a plea why they held a plea in Court Christian concerning the raising of the hue on the prior of Barnwell.[1] They have not come and they were the plaintiffs. So they [are] without day. The others [are] in mercy.[2] They have not found sureties.

[1] Barnwell in Cambridgeshire was a priory of Augustinian canons founded in 1092.
[2] There is no mention of the amercement in the margin.

1114. (*Norfolk*) Andrew of Hingham by his attorney presented himself on the fourth day against Philip of Flegg concerning a plea of hearing his judgement concerning the custody of twenty acres of land with appurtenances in Hockham, which pertains to Andrew because Walter of Bradcar[1] held that land from him by knight service etc. Philip has not come, and a day was given to him on this day. So the sheriff is ordered that he take the said custody into the hands of the lord king and that he keeps it safely etc and that he is to have his person at Chelmsford on the quindene of Holy Trinity [Sunday 24 June] (*Chelmsford*). [**178** and **262**]

[1] This indicates that this person is from the manor of Bradcar near Shropham in Norfolk. See Hudson 1901, pp.1–56.

1115. Baldwin de Charnell[1] claimed his land by replevin on the Tuesday in Whit Week, which was taken into the hands of the lord king for a default which he made against Alda who was the wife of Geoffrey de Arsik,[2] and he has [it].

[1] There is a Baldwin de Charneles shown in the feet of fines of 1205 for a property in Bruisyard in Plomesgate hundred. There are other references to the de Charneles family in 1222 and 1235 in the feet of fines: see *Cal. Feet of Fines, Suff.*, pp.22 and 35.
[2] This might be a Cambridge plea. See **783** where Baldwin had his land taken into the king's hands and where he is shown as *de Gernell*.

1116. Geoffrey Peche acknowledges that he owes to Thomas de la Hide nine and a half marks from which he will pay to him half at the feast of All Saints [1 November 1241] in the twenty-fifth year [of King Henry III], and the other half at the feast of the Purification of the Blessed Mary. If he does not do [this] he grants that the same Thomas is to have twenty acres of land with appurtenances in Kettlebaston to hold from him and his heirs for the service of one penny per year at Christmas. He grants also that if that land does not amount to the value he may be distrained by means of all his other lands elsewhere wheresoever they may be, and concerning the cost etc. [*chirograph* CP 25(1) 213/17/109]

1117.[1] (*Chelmsford*)[2] A day is given to the abbot of Bury St Edmunds, the plaintiff, and to the bishop of Rochester concerning a plea to levy their chirograph at Chelmsford on the quindene of Holy Trinity [Sunday 24 June].

    1   See the essoin in **40**, the attorney in **199** and **745** for a plea *de fine facto*. There is a gap of 14.7 cm between this plea and the previous one. This plea entry is probably an afterthought and the clerk intended to write the next plea on the other side of the membrane but realised it was too large to fit into the space left, so wrote it on the dorse side of the membrane. See **1118**.

    2   There is a marginal note here which has been a bit worn away. Using ultraviolet light provides the marginal note.

Membrane 43d[1]

    1   The whole of this side of the membrane is very squashed together as though the clerks wanted to get the completion of the pleas at Cattishall into this side without using another membrane.

1118.[1] (*Hoxne*) William le Rus was summoned to answer to Richard Bindedevel', Richard Hunipot, Thomas the son of Ernulf, John de Bircheholt,[2] William Therlewin, William Stopcroft, Thomas Sweyn and (William Mervyn[i]) concerning a plea why he exacts from them customs and other services other than those which they should do and have become accustomed to do in the time that the manor of Stradbroke was in the hands of the predecessors of the king, the kings of England. The same claim in respect whereof that from the conquest of England they were free sokemen[3] of the kings of England, until the said manor was given to the ancestors of William,[4] so that the ancestors of the lord king taxed them in common at their will, for more or for less when they have taxed their other manors. Moreover, in the time of the ancestors of the lord king they were accustomed [to pay] the pannage for their pigs, namely for each pig a price of ten pence and a further one penny when there was wood in the said manor. Moreover, in the time of the ancestors of the lord king it was a common custom to choose one from the said manor, by their common assent, who would carry the purse for the money collected in the manor. Despite all of this, the same William claims from them customary aid for each year at his will so that sometimes it is more, some time less, and though the wood is entirely devastated so that the land is arable and no pig food is able to exist there, he claims from them the pannage in full as if the wood was there. Moreover, at his will he distrains them for carrying the purse for the money collected in the manor. Moreover, though they do not owe suit to him at his court of Stradbroke except for afforcement of court, or for a writ of the lord king, he distrains them to pay suit at his court from quindene to quindene, in respect whereof they have suffered and have damage to the value of five hundred marks.[5]

William comes and he denies force and injury and everything and he says that the said manor never was the demesne of the predecessors of the king, the kings of England, because it is of the Honour of Eye, nor were they ever the sokemen of the predecessors of the king of England as they say, but he says that they and everybody from the manor are his villeins, so that all his ancestors[6] always took from them customary aid at their will, and rightly so. Moreover, he says that all who are from the said manor, excepting Richard Bindedevel, Thomas the son of Ernulf and William Stopcroft, gave merchet, for their daughters to marry, and rightly so. Moreover, he says that they were paying suit at his ancestors' (and[i]) his court, and rightly so (from quindene to quindene[i]), and that they should give pannage as they have always been accustomed to do, whether the pannage was there or not, and that he will appoint as purse carrier whoever he wishes, as all of his ancestors have always done, and that they ought to do all of these and other such customs and services, and that they are all villeins, he offers to the lord king five marks on condition (that[i]) it is inquired into, on the surety of Alan of Withersdale.

Afterwards, Richard Bindedevel, Thomas the son of Ernulf, John de Bircheholt, Thomas Sweyn William Stopcroft and William Mervyn came and they do not wish to proceed against him. Richard Hunipot and William Therlewin say that they are free [men], nor do they owe to him the villein customs, nor have any of their ancestors done customs of this kind to his ancestors or to him, and then they put themselves on the country. So let there be a jury thereon.

Afterwards, the same Richard and William come and they do not wish to put themselves on a jury of free men and knights, but on a jury of the sokemen. So it is said to William that he is to go without day on this.

1   See Appendix K for a full transcription and translation.
2   This is possibly East Bergholt in Samford hundred.
3   Free tenants who only do certain specified services. It looks as if the lord of the manor is trying to get them to do other services.
4   This suggests that William le Rus was the lord of the manor of Stradbroke.
5   The clerk wrote *d m* with abbreviation marks, which are not very helpful here. They might be *dimidie marce* for half a mark, or 10 marks (*decem*). Later in the plea the defendant spends 5 marks. It does not ring true to pay 5 marks for the plea to be heard and worry about half a mark, or even ten marks of damages, so it is probably 500 marks.
6   That is all lords of the manor before him.

1119.[1] (*Hartismere*) Ralph the merchant claims against Robert Clenchemere and Matilda his wife and Sarah Clenchemere two acres of land with appurtenances in Wetherden as his right.

Robert comes and he says that he cannot answer concerning the said [land] because he is the villein of Matilda de Beauchamp. So Robert, Matilda and Sarah [are] without day. Ralph [is] in mercy (*amercement*).

1   See the appointment of attorneys in **101** and **129**. There is a change of clerk here until the end of this membrane. There is also a change of ink except for the paragraph mark on this plea, which is in the same ink as for **1118**. It is a very distinct script but smaller than most of the others, making it difficult to read.

1120. (*Wangford*) Maria who was the wife of Henry the son of Hugh who brought a writ of entry against William[1] concerning one rood with appurtenances in Shipmeadow has not prosecuted. So she and her sureties for prosecuting [are] in mercy, namely: Peter de *Briham*[2] of Pulham and William of Soham[3] of the same (*amercement*).

1   The clerk has not put in a full name here.
2   I cannot find this place.
3   This is either Monk Soham in Hoxne hundred or Earl Soham in Loes hundred. Monk Soham is nearer Shipmeadow.

1121. (*Blything*) Alan of Stoven who brought a writ of waste and exile against Peter de Binseleham and Alice his wife has not prosecuted. So he and his sureties for prosecuting [are] in mercy, namely: Geoffrey de Briskele of Frostenden and Adam the son of Alan of Stoven (*amercement*).

1122. Clarice who was the wife of John the merchant who brought a writ of dower against Margery who was the wife of Wacer Winaun has not prosecuted. So she and her sureties for prosecuting [are] in mercy, namely: Robert Cook of Denton[1] and John Spines of the same.

> [1] Denton is in Earsham hundred in Norfolk.

1123. (*Wangford*) John de *Fome*[1] [who brought] a writ against Robert le Rus to take his homage has not prosecuted. So he and his sureties for prosecuting [are] in mercy, namely: Robert the son of Warren of Dereham and Hugh the son of Forgad of the same (*amercement*).

> [1] I cannot find this place.

1124. (*Blything*) Avelina who was the wife of Hamo Punchun who brought a writ of entry against Richard Clure has not prosecuted. So she and her [sureties] for prosecuting [are] in mercy, namely: Henry Pye of Reedham and William Sotman of the same (*amercement*).

1125. (*Blything*) Emma who was the wife of Nigel presented herself on the fourth day against Clement the son of David concerning a plea of one acre of land with appurtenances in Spexhall, which she claims as her right etc. He has not come etc. Judgement: the land is to be taken into the hands of the lord king etc and the day etc and he is to be summoned that he is at Chelmsford on the next Thursday after the octave of the Holy Trinity [Thursday 21 June] (*it[1] is to be taken, at Chelmsford*).

> [1] This is an order to the sheriff and relates to the land being taken into the king's hands, not the plea being taken at Chelmsford.

1126. (*Lothingland*) Thomas Stach who brought a writ of entry against Thomas and Agnes his mother has not prosecuted. So he and his sureties for prosecuting [are] in mercy, [namely]: John of Burgh and Richard the son of Serlon of Yarmouth (*amercements*).

1127. (*Samford*) [Agnes] de *Bruniford* presented herself on the fourth day against Henry de Merk that he discharge her from the services that Margery de Rivers demanded from her for her free tenement in *Brende Wenham*,[1] whereon the same Henry is the mesne tenant etc and Henry has not come and [was] summoned etc. Judgement: he is attached to be at Chelmsford on the next day after the octave of Holy Trinity [Monday 18 June] (*Chelmsford*). Agnes appoints Alan her [son or husband] as her attorney ... [unfinished]

> [1] I assume this to be *Brente Wentham* in Samford hundred although I cannot find such a place there. There is a Great or Little Wenham in Samford hundred. It is shown a great deal in this format in *Cal. Feet of Fines, Suff.*, e.g. p.42. See **635** for what is almost certainly the same place.

1128. (*half a mark*) William Mapelenheved gives half a mark for licence to agree with William Russ concerning a plea of land by the surety of Thomas Linsted. The agreement is that the said William Mapelenheved' acknowledges that land with his appurtenances to be the right of William Russ. He renders that [land] to him in the same court etc.

1129. (*Samford*) Henry the son of William who brought a writ of entry against Robert del Grene has not prosecuted. So he and the sureties for prosecuting [are] in mercy, namely: Gerard de Dunton[1] of Woolverstone and Simon Grenville de *Furstaft*[2] (*amercements*).

> [1] It is either Dunton in Norfolk or the one in Essex.
> [2] I cannot find this place.

1130. (*Hoxne*) Thomas the son of Ranulf who brought a writ of warranty of charter against Thomas Blund has not prosecuted. So he and his sureties for prosecuting in mercy, namely: Michael the son of Gerold of Elmham and John the son of Geoffrey of Polstead (*amercement*).

1131. (*Hoxne*) Basilia de Benour who brought a writ of entry against William de Roculf has not prosecuted. So she and her sureties for prosecuting [are] in mercy, namely: John the son of Robert of Carlton and Roger the son of Roger of the same (*amercements*).

1132. Maria who was the wife of Guthbert who brought a writ of dower against William of Holbrook has not prosecuted. So she and her sureties for prosecuting [are] in mercy, namely: Robert the son of Thurber of Ipswich and William Sprot of the same.

1133. (*Hoxne*) William Burnebusc who brought a writ of warranty of charter against William Russell has not prosecuted. So he and his sureties for prosecuting [are] in mercy, namely: John Cordebof and William Blench (*amercements*).

1134. (*Samford*) Richard Miners who brought a writ *de fine facto* against Robert the parson de *Byrry* has not prosecuted. So he and his sureties for prosecuting [are] in mercy, namely: John de Gramanvill[1] and Nicholas the son of Maurice of Harkstead. Afterwards, they attest that Richard has nothing. So nothing.

[1] This name is certainly Crammaville as shown in a number of pleas. He has appeared in many of the pleas as a juror or surety.

1135. (*Bosmere*) John of Stonham was summoned to warrant Alice of Stonham three acres of land with appurtenances in Stonham, which she holds [and claims to hold from him] etc and in respect whereof [she has] a charter of John Cholard grandfather of John whose [heir he is] etc and the same Alice says that a certain William May is impleading her in the county court. John comes and he warrants her and he freely warrants her where and when etc. So he is told that then he must go to the county court [and] warrant [her there]. Alice [is] without day.

1136. (*Hartismere*) Odo the son of Elias who brought a writ of warranty of charter against Richard de *Langetot*[1] has not prosecuted. So he and his sureties for prosecuting [are] in mercy, namely: Roger of Stow, Adam le Grant of Moulton. Afterwards, it has been attested that Odo died, and so nothing.

[1] This is the same Richard de Langetoft as is shown in **792, 819** and **1094**.

1137. William of Battisford who brought a writ of entry against Robert of Cattishall has not prosecuted. So he and his sureties for prosecuting [are] in mercy, namely: Ralph Hog of Wattisham and John Sefay of the same.

1138. (*Bosmere*) Isabel who was the wife of Adam le Blund, who brought a writ concerning her dower against William Serland has not prosecuted. So she and her sureties for prosecuting [are] in mercy, namely Ralph Marchaunt of Wetherden and Geoffrey the son of Geoffrey of Creeting.

1139. (----il)[1] Thomas the chaplain of Easton who brought a warranty of charter against Agnes the daughter of Gervase has not prosecuted. So he and his sureties for prosecuting [are] in mercy, namely: Sage of Coddenham and Peter Cook of the same.

[1] This marginal note cannot be ascertained even with ultraviolet light.

1140. (----*s*) Roger Fullo of Corton who brought a writ to prove his liberty against Hubert of Braiseworth has not prosecuted. So he and his sureties for prosecuting [are] in mercy, namely: Simon the son of Walter of Corton and Unnan[1] Sherefod[2] of the same.

1   This might be Hunn which is apparently an East Anglian name. See Reaney 1997, p.244.
2   I cannot find anything on this at all. There is a Shereford in Brothercross hundred in Norfolk but there would normally be a *de* to indicate that the person comes from there.

1141. William Gabet[1] who brought a writ of warranty of charter against Peter the son of Peter has not prosecuted. So he and his sureties for prosecuting [are] in mercy, namely: Ailneret of Battisford and Alexander Snod of Ash.

1   The 'G' is very faint and it might be a 'B', 'C' or 'T'. It might be 'Gabbett' as shown in Reaney 1997, p.181. It could also be 'Babet' (ibid., p.22). I suspect the former given the calligraphy of the way this clerk forms his capital 'G's.

1142. (----[il]) Ralph de Furneis who brought two writs of warranty of charter against Roger le Franceys has not prosecuted. So he and his sureties for prosecuting [are] in mercy, namely: Walter the son of Simon of Bacton and Simon the son of William de [unknown] and Walter the son of William of Hopton, if not (f----[il]) Adam of Fakenham.

Membrane 44[1]

1   There is a change of hand here. There is no indication of the usual wording here at the start of a new place where the travelling judges take pleas. It is also preceded by the bailiffs, electors and coroners as well as the ordinary jurors of the hundred. This is the only time in the civil pleas that the jurors are mentioned as one body, except in the individual pleas of the grand assize etc.

DUNWICH

1143.[1]   (*Bailiffs*)[2]   Robert the son of Reynold   Sworn
                            Lucas de Escot   Sworn
                            Edmund the son of Bernard.[3]

1   The start of this membrane is given to the officers and jurors of the hundred. I have split them up into four. The bailiffs' and electors' headings appear in the margin of the membrane, whereas the coroners and jurors appear as headings within the main body of the text. The jurors appear as two columns of six names in each column, which is how I have presented them in **1146**. The clerk uses the abbreviated word *Jur* for *juratores* from the last elector as the heading for the jurors with two lines from the word *Jur* to the top and bottom name of the first column of jurors. The officers and jurors of the hundred have strayed from the crown pleas, but none of the other hundreds etc. have their officers and jurors mentioned in the crown pleas or in any other part of the roll, but in some eyre rolls the jury 'calendar' does survive. See *1248 Berkshire Eyre*, pp.291–297.
2   The bailiffs are named here and there are two lines coming out of the marginal note here to the top and bottom bailiff. There are three bailiffs in total.
3   There is no 'Sworn' against this name. Was this a slip by the clerk, or was the bailiff new to the job and going to be sworn at the eyre, or was he dead before the eyre?

1144.   (*Electors*)[1]   John of Helmingham[2]   Sworn
                            Robert Bullok   Sworn.[3]

1   There are two lines coming from the heading to the top and bottom names of the two electors.
2   Helmingham is in Claydon hundred, which is a fair distance from Dunwich.

[3] This is where there are two lines coming from *Juratus* to the top and bottom names of the jurors.

1145.   (*Coroners*)   Gerard of Hazelwood[1]
Robert the clerk.

[1]   Hazelwood is in Plomesgate hundred and is near Aldeborough, where there is still a Hazelwood Hall and Marsh.

1146. (*Jurors*) Elias Jubbe   Sworn   Burghard Gikel   Sworn
Robert Freysel[1]   Sworn   Odo son of Stephen   Sworn
Robert of the Ford   Sworn   Stephen son of Ranulf   Sworn
Edmund son of Amabil   Sworn   Dionis son of William   Sworn
Reynold Cook   Sworn   Thomas son of Robert   Sworn
William Thedrich   Sworn   Nicholas Dionis   Sworn.

[1]   Fresel was a maker or seller of lace or ribbon.

1147. (*Cosford*)[1]

[1]   There is only the marginal note and the paragraph or section mark. There is no text here, just a space suggesting that something was expected but it never was put in by the clerk.

1148.[1] (*Cosford*) Seyna Doddemere claims against Roseta the daughter of Hamo four acres of land with appurtenances in Wherstead[2] from which Roger the son of Roger the kinsman of Seyna, whose heir she is, was seised in his demesne as of fee on the day that he died etc.

Roseta comes and she then vouches to warranty Gilbert de Reymes[3] by the aid of the court. She is to have him at Chelmsford on the octave of St John the Baptist etc. (*Chelmsford*).

[1]   See **346** where Seyna tried a mort d'ancestor plea to get 6 acres from Roseta (note the difference in name spelling) but she failed.
[2]   Wherstead is in Samford hundred, not Cosford as in the margin.
[3]   Gilbert held the manor of Wherstead and became a sworn burgess of Ipswich in 1239/40. See references to the Reymes family and Wherstead in Raimes 1937–1939, pp.89–115 and in particular to Gilbert on pp.98–99, 101. This could also be 'Raimes' or 'Rames', a vill in Normandy. See Reaney 1997, p.370.

1149. (*Lothingland*) Millicent the daughter of Alice claims against William Cholle and Margery his wife half of one messuage with appurtenances in Little Yarmouth as her reasonable share which falls to her from the inheritance of Alice Shire, the mother of Millicent and Margery, whose heirs they are and who has recently died as she says etc.

William and Margery come and deny her right etc. They say that the said half was never the right nor the inheritance of the said Alice, but they say that it was the inheritance of Wulfric, the father of the said Margery, and not the inheritance of the said Alice, and Margery is in seisin as the right heir of Wulfric. And that it is so she puts herself on the jury, and Millicent similarly. So let there be a jury thereon whether the said half of the said messuage with appurtenances is the right and inheritance of the said Margery as from the inheritance of the said Wulfric, or the right and inheritance of the said Millicent as from the inheritance of the said Alice, her mother etc.

Afterwards, they have agreed by licence for God and for poverty.[1] They are to have a chirograph. The agreement is such that the said Millicent quitclaimed to the said William and Margery all right etc for twenty shillings, concerning which they will pay to her ten shillings before the feast of St Peter in Chains, [before 1 August] and ten shillings within the quindene of [the feast of] St Michael [before Sunday 14 October] in the twenty-fourth year of the reign of King Henry. If she does not do so they grant etc and concerning the expense etc until etc. [*chirograph* CP 25(1) 213/16/55]

1   This indicates that they did not have to pay for the licence, because they were poor.

1150.[1] (*Lothingland*) An assize comes to declare if Geoffrey the son of Guy and Ralph of Burgh unjustly etc disseised Sibilia the daughter of Ralph of her free tenement in Burgh after the first etc and in respect whereof she claims that they disseised her of one messuage and seven acres of land with appurtenances in the same vill.

Geoffrey and Ralph come and they say nothing to stay the assize.

The jurors say that the said Ralph had promised the said land with appurtenances to the said Sibilia but he never put her in seisin nor made her a charter. So it is adjudged that the said Geoffrey and Ralph [are] without day. Sibilia [is] in mercy for a false claim. It is pardoned because [she is] poor.

1   There is a gap of 4.9 cm between this and the previous plea.

1151. (*Dunwich*) Edmund the son of Austin [who is] (under age[i])[1] [and] who brought a writ of novel disseisin against Robert le Riz[2] le Mester and the other named in the writ concerning a tenement in Dunwich has not prosecuted. So he and his sureties for prosecuting [are] in mercy,[3] namely: Philip the son of Adam of Lothingland and Robert the son of Richard de Brook.

1   This is written interlined between *Edmundus* and *filius* and is an obvious afterthought written in to indicate why, when the amercement section of this roll came to be compiled, the clerks should not to pick up the amercement shown in the margin and transfer it on to the amercement section.
2   This might be the name Rees or Rise: see Reaney 1997, pp.376 and 379. He might be a serjeant, reeve or bailiff, or possibly a ship's captain given the second name *Mester*. He is not shown as a bailiff of the town of Dunwich in the lists. See **1143–1146**.
3   The amercement was crossed out in the marginalia, presumably because Edmund was under age.

1152. (*Dunwich*) An assize comes to declare if Matilda Outell unjustly etc disseised Nicholas the son of Matthew of Kelsale of his free tenement in Dunwich after the first etc and in respect whereof he complains that she disseised him of one messuage with appurtenances in the same vill.

Matilda comes and she says nothing to stay the assize.

The jurors say that the said Matilda has not disseised him as the writ says. So it is adjudged that the said Matilda is to go without day on this. Nicholas (elsewhere[i]), [is] in mercy[1] for a false claim. He is remanded in custody.[2]

1   I cannot find him in the civil plea section of the roll or in the amercements section of this roll either.
2   The clerk has left in the text that Nicholas is to be remanded into custody but has crossed it out in the margin, perhaps because he was 'elsewhere' and therefore could not be found and the clerk forgot to cross it out in the text.

1153. (*Blything, half a mark*) Austin[1] Colekin gives half a mark for licence to agree with the prioress of Bungay concerning a plea of land by the surety of William of Mettingham. [**1053**]

1   The clerk wrote *Austinus*. In **1053** he is shown as Augustine, not Austin. Reaney 1997, p.19 indicates that this is the vernacular form of Augustine.

1154. (*Dunwich*) An assize comes to declare if Jack the son of Richard unjustly etc disseised Clarice the daughter of Bernard of her free tenement in Dunwich after the first crossing etc and in respect whereof she complains that he disseised her of one messuage with appurtenances in the same vill.

James comes and he says that she [can] claim nothing in the said messuage nor any he holds, and then he puts himself on the assize.

The jurors say that the said Jack has not disseised her as the writ says. So it is adjudged that the said James [is] without day. Clarice [is] in mercy for a false claim. It is pardoned because [she is] poor.

1155. [paragraph mark][1]

[1]   There is a paragraph or section mark placed after **1054** which is followed by a large gap, suggesting that something was planned for here but nothing was inserted by the clerk.

1156.[1] Roger the son of Osbert appoints Master Walter of Blundeston against Simon de Enepol and Richard Wyard concerning a plea of warranty of charter.

[1]   There is a gap of 4.5 cm between this plea and the previous one. Possibly the clerk realised that the first plea on membrane 44d could not fit into the space left here.

Membrane 44d

1157.[1] (*Dunwich, to judgement*) Clarice who was the wife of Gerard the son of Walter claims against Richard Pery half of one messuage with appurtenances in Dunwich, and against Constantine Woodmouse half of one messuage[2] with appurtenances in the same town as her dower etc.

Richard and Constantine come, and Richard says that she ought not to have the dower [she seeks], because Clarice, after the death of her husband, came to the court of Dunwich and in the same place quitclaimed all her right etc that she had in the said messuage for half a silver mark which he gave to her cash down. He then puts himself on the jury, and Clarice similarly.

Constantine says that the said Gerard, with the agreement and assent of the same Clarice for her great necessity, sold to him the said messuage, in respect whereof she cannot have dower according to the customs of the town of Dunwich. That such is the custom of the town he then puts himself on the town [jury],[3] which attests to this. It is adjudged she is to take nothing and they [are] without day.[4]

The jurors say that the said Gerard, the husband of Clarice, with the agreement and assent of the same Clarice sold to the said Richard the said messuage with appurtenances. After the death of Gerard, Clarice came and quitclaimed to the same Richard all right etc that she had in the said messuage for one coombe[5] of corn and two shillings and eight pence. So it is adjudged that Richard (and Constantine[i]) may hold in peace and Clarice [is] in mercy for a false claim. She is poor.[6]

[1]   It looks as though at some time a chunk of the margin was cut out and then some backing sheet put in its place to protect it. There may have been some writing missing here in this marginal note as a result.

[2]   Probably the same messuage.

[3]   Probably by the same jurors named in **1146**.

[4]   There is a separate line after this paragraph that has largely been erased. All I can make out are the letters shown as follows: (*Post venit-----Ph-----Aie----suam-----*[e, il]). Ultraviolet light provides no more information.

[5]   A coombe is a half quarter, or stone, or 14 pounds of weight.

[6]   There is something rubbed out after *Pauper est*. It is *Postea venit* but then nothing further.

1158. (*Dunwich*) Muriel who was the wife of Reynold the son of Bonde claims against Margaret the daughter of Gerard half of one messuage with appurtenances in Dunwich as her dower etc.

Margaret comes and says that the said Reynold, the husband of Muriel, sold to Gerard, the father of the said Margaret, the said messuage with appurtenances on the advice of Muriel for her great poverty, in respect whereof according to the customs of the town of Dunwich she ought not to have dower, and that such is the customs of the town she put herself on the town [jury].

Afterwards, it has been attested by the good men and bailiffs of the town, that the said Reynold sold to the said Gerard the said messuage etc as the same Margaret says. So to judgement (*to judgement*). Margaret appoints Nicholas the son of Matthew as her attorney. Afterwards,[1] at Chelmsford it is adjudged, because she has agreed to the said sale according to the customs of the town, that she is to take nothing from the said messuage in respect of the dower etc.

A day[2] is given to them at Chelmsford to hear their judgement in the octave of St John the Baptist (*Chelmsford*).

1   This sentence has obviously been inserted after the judgement at Chelmsford. It looks as though a different clerk wrote it. The clerk may not have wanted to place it after the date given to hear judgement because it may have overlapped into the next plea.
2   This is definitely by the original clerk who wrote the major part of this plea. So he originally left a small gap between the end of the plea taken at Dunwich and this sentence giving the date to hear the judgement, 1 July 1240.

1159. (*Dunwich*) Richard the son of Roger of Dunwich claims against Michael the son of Walter of Dunwich one messuage with appurtenances in the same town as his escheat and that it ought to revert to him [Richard] from him [Michael] because Robert Iorbbe held the said messuage from him and he died without an heir.

Afterwards, they have agreed by licence. The agreement is such that the said Michael acknowledged the said messuage with appurtenances to be the right of Richard. For this etc the said Richard granted to the same Michael to hold the said messuage from him and his heirs for nine pence per year and for ten shillings which he has given to him, and in respect thereof he took his homage etc.

1160.[1] (*Blything, half a mark*) John the son of Hamo gives half a mark for licence to agree with Richard of Elmham by the surety of Robert de Bosco.

1   See **1057** for the detail. This is a repetition of the agreement.

DUNWICH[1]

1   This heading is right at the bottom of the membrane and is in the centre.

Amercements and agreements

There are some unidentified pleas in the list of amercements. This could be because the clerk has included some crown plea amercement items or possibly he has named some people in this section but not in the plea text; the names included in this section could be for sureties for an amercement, for example 163 and 195.

The vast majority of the entries are amercements but there are one or two agreements incorporated in the amercement section of this roll and vice versa.

From membrane 61, which covers agreements, there are no sub-totals provided by the clerk at the end of each half membrane, or even membrane from then onwards. These totals have been calculated by the editor of the document.

Amercements

Membrane 59

AMERCEMENTS OF THE PLEAS OF THE ASSIZE OF THE COUNTY OF SUFFOLK.

1642.

	£	s.	d.
From Thomas de Punninges for a false claim, 20 shillings. [159]	1	0	0
From Richard de Elmham for trespass, 1 mark. [1057]	0	13	4
From Robert the son of John because he did not prosecute, ½ mark by the surety of Richard Berin and Roger Chapeleyn of Finningham. [119]	0	6	8
From Robert de la More for a disseisin, ½ mark by the surety of Nicholas Pik and William Pictsoft. [166]	0	6	8
From Alan of Semer for a false claim, ½ mark by surety of Thomas of Shotford. [393]	0	6	8
From Richard Fuscedame because he has not come, ½ mark. [190]	0	6	8
From William the reeve of Stonham because he did not have [Richard Fuscedame] for whom he stood surety, ½ mark. [190]	0	6	8
From Alan Bruncusaste[1] for the same, ½ mark. [190?]	0	6	8
From Hubert Gernagem for a disseisin, 1 mark. [190]	0	13	4
From Walter Badegrim for the same, ½ mark. [190]	0	6	8
(*Norfolk*) From Mathew of Waxham, John the son of Peter of Ingham, Bartholomew of Horsey, Goscelin the son of Peter of Waxham and William the son of Goscelin of Ingham by the surety of Geoffrey (le[i]) Despencer, 20 shillings. [213]	1	0	0
From Rainer de Langwode for a false claim, ½ mark by the surety of John de Langwode [and] Alexander (Cheppere[i]) of Exning. [218]	0	6	8
From Hugh of Polstead for a disseisin (----)[2] by the surety of Mathew of Layham, Robert de Noitstede, Roger de Ponz, Robert of Brampton, Robert le Enveyse, William le Enveyse, William of Polstead and Thomas de Caune. [160]	0	0	0
From George of Polstead for the same, 1 mark by the surety of Hugh of Polstead. [160]	0	13	4
From John of Polstead, Daniel le Franceys and his allies for disseisin, 1 mark by the surety of the same Hugh. [160]	0	13	4
From Robert the parson de Byri, 1 mark by the surety of Hugh de Arderne and William of Haughley, knight. [188]	0	13	4

From Nicholas of Fritton for a disseisin, ½ mark by the surety of Henry of Fritton and Constantine de *Reyston*[3]. **[196]**	0	6	8
From William de *Kunelesfeud* for the same, 10 shillings, by the surety of Henry of Fritton and Constantine de *Reyston*. **[196]**	0	10	0
From Ralph Swan for a false (claim[i]), ½ mark by the surety of William of Holbrook. **[201]**	0	6	8
From Thomas Berde, William Ore, Ralph Spirhard and William Barwere for a disseisin, ½ mark by the surety of Simon de Petraponte. **[259]**	0	6	8

[i]   I suspect the clerk missed out this second surety in the plea.
[2]   There is a blank space here where the clerk should have entered the money. This could be for 1 mark, given the others faced the same amercement value (below) or possibly the 8 marks that was given for the communal amercements.
[3]   These sureties are shown only once in the amercement section of this roll with a line from both this amercement and the next one below; that is they are sureties for both people amerced.

1643.

From Robert Malet for the same. **[195]**	0	10	0
From Margery of Poynings for the same,[1] ½ mark. **[259]**	0	6	8
From Roger the son of Osbert for many nuisances,[2] 1 mark. **[453]**	0	13	4
From William of Reedham for the same, ½mark. **[151]**	0	6	8
From Thomas de Valonyes for the same, ½ mark. **[151]**	0	6	8
From Geoffrey Tregoz for a false claim, 20 shillings. **[197]**	1	0	0
From Robert of Blundeston for an unjust detention, ½ mark by the surety of William de Leye of Wrentham. **[231]**	0	6	8
From Ralph the son of Basil of Mettingham for a disseisin, 1 mark by the surety of Richard the son of Ralph of Elmham. **[272]**	0	13	4
(*Gypewic*)[3] (*Ipswich*) From Mathew de Luveyn for licence to agree, 1 mark. **[637]**[4]	0	13	4
From Alexander the son of William for the same, ½ mark. **[638]**[5]	0	6	8
From John Hany for a false claim, ½ mark by the surety of Constantine Pader. **[639]**[6]	0	6	8
From Robert Knyot for a disseisin, ½ mark. **[641]**	0	6	8
From Gilbert Haryab, Augustine Reading, John Ernaud, Adewys' de Saler and Margery her sister for the same, 1 mark by the surety of (the bailiff of Ipswich[i]). **[641]**	0	13	4
From Roger Keperee because he did not prosecute, ½ mark. **[644]**	0	6	8
From William Margerie and Roger the son of Ranulf by surety, ½ mark. **[644]**	0	6	8
From Benedict of Blakenham because he did not prosecute. **[645]**	0	0	0
From Robert Coc because he did not prosecute. **[645]**[7]	0	0	0
From Thomas Clavering for the same. **[645]**	0	0	0
From Henry the son of [Gilbert][8], Robert the son of Agnes of Clare for licence to agree, ½ mark by the surety of Hugh Harvild'. **[647]**	0	6	8
From Roger le Lung for the same, ½ mark by the surety of Geoffrey of Langeston. **[648]**	0	6	8
From John Rouland for false and frivolous pleading, 1 mark. [no plea found]	0	13	4
From William Angot for the same, ½ mark. [no plea found]		6	8

1   In this amercement Margery is amerced for disseisin, but in the plea Margery appears as the plaintiff and she won. She was amerced in the plea because she made a false claim, not a disseisin.
2   I presume this is for the three items in the plea, two pieces of land and the rent.
3   From this amercement to the end of this plea number there are lines from one to the other suggesting all are Ipswich pleas.
4   This is an agreement in the middle of these amercements.
5   This is another agreement.
6   The surety is missing from the plea.
7   This person and the following are shown as sureties in the plea.
8   This is another agreement. In this section the clerk wrote *Henrici* here but in the plea he is shown as the son of Gilbert.

1644.

	£	s	d
From William the parson of Stoke for a false claim, ½ mark. [286]	0	6	8
From Peter the son of Walter de (-*nnidenton*'il) for trespass, 1 mark by the surety of Robert Hovel, knight, and Peter Cook de *Hulenden*. [289]	0	13	4
From Adam the son of Hubert of Bentley because he did not prosecute and William the miller of Ipswich and Geoffrey of Hackford of Ipswich for [acting as] the surety of Adam, ½ mark. [331]	0	6	8
From Waleran de Muncy for an unjust detention, ½ mark. [300]	0	6	8
From William of Redisham for the same, ½ mark by the surety of Waleran de Muncy. [340]	0	6	8
From Robert de Perer of Westhorpe because he did not prosecute, ½ mark. [302]	0	6	8
From Robert [the son of] the Carpentar of Finningham and Stephen le Dormur of the same, ½ mark for [acting as] sureties. [302]	0	6	8
From Geoffrey of Hickling because he did not prosecute, ½ mark. [245]	0	6	8
From William the son of Robert of Rishangles because did not have [Geoffrey of Hickling] for whom he stood surety, ½ mark. [245]	0	6	8
(*Norfolk*) From Hubert Hacun, knight, for the same, 10 shillings. [245]	0	10	0
From Richard Wygeyn for a false claim, ½ mark by the surety of Richard Erl of Belstead. [247]	0	6	8
From Thomas de Meuling' for a false claim, ½ mark. [333]1	0	6	8
From William of Reedham for a false declaration, ½ mark. [339]	0	6	8
(From Ranulf of Blickling for the same, ½ markc) elsewhere. [339]	0	0	0
From Roger de Wyples for the same, ½ mark. [339]	0	6	8
From John Blenc and William of Darsham for the same, ½ mark. [339]	0	6	8
From Walter of Henham and Andrew de *Enepol* for the same, ½ mark. [339]	0	6	8
From Walter of Yoxford2 and Benedict of the same for the same, ½ mark. [339]	0	6	8
From Thomas Chevere and Richard de *Haldehawe* for the same, ½ mark. [339]	0	6	8
De Thoma Russel pro eodem, di' m', – see From Thomas Russel for the same, ½ mark. [339]	0	6	8
From Stephen Illeior for disseisin, ½ mark by the surety of Walter of Henham and John of Henham.3 [304]	0	6	8

1. The case in the plea roll was not completed by the clerk in **333** but this is the only case where this name appears. In **334** it does have a *Thomas de Mading* as a surety also in a false claim. They may be the same person. I think this person is also shown in **429** where the plea is completed but it is not Thomas making the claim.
2. In plea **339** Walter is shown as coming from *Ingesford* and Benedict from *Dufford*.
3. In **304** the second surety is shown as William of Henham.

1645.

From Ranulf the Fleming[1] for a false claim, ½ mark by the surety of William Herberd. [**310**]	0	6	8
From Katherine Esturmy because she has not come, William the son of Peter and Robert de Hill of Buxhall because they did not have [Katherine Esturmy] for whom they stood surety, 10 shillings. [**310**]	0	10	0
[From Hugh of Badley for a false claim[2], ½ mark. [**310**]	0	6	8
From William the son of Ralph of Badham for the same, ½ mark. [**311**]	0	6	8
From Ralph Muriel for the same, ½ mark by the surety of Thomas de Hemmegrave. [**347**]	0	6	8
From Brian Hayl for the same, ½ mark by the surety of Augustine [Austin] of Blakenham and Ralph the son of Ailwin Hayl.[3] [**316**]	0	6	8
From Roger Swift for the same, ½ mark by the surety of Henry the reeve of Carlton and Roger de Colville. [**317**]	0	6	8
From Benedict the son of Hugh and Joan[4] of Kirkley for a false claim, ½ mark by the surety of Simon le Prestre and Master Walter of (Blundeston[i]). [**357**]	0	6	8
From Wymer of Carlton for disseisin ½ mark by the surety of William de *Rokenhal'*. [**358**]	0	6	8
From Thomas Geremy for false and frivolous pleading, ½ mark. [no plea found]	0	6	8
From William the clerk of Reydon[5] and William the son of Alexander, ½ mark because they did not have [Thomas the son of Edward] for whom they stood surety. [**361**]	0	6	8
From Andrew de Ripping' for a false claim[6], ½ mark by the surety of Wymer of Carlton. [**362**]	0	6	8
From Geoffrey Wy[7] of Yarmouth for disseisin and many nuisances, 20 shillings by the surety of Alexander Aleyn of Yarmouth. [**306, 311, 368**]	1	0	0
From John of Burgh of Norwich for the same, 10 shillings. [**368**]	0	10	0
From Pelerin of Yarmouth for the same, ½ mark. [**306, 311, 368**]	0	6	8
From Thomas Ringbelle for the same, ½ mark by the surety of Richard the Serjeant of Lothingland.[8] [**306, 311, 368**]	0	6	8
From Stephen de Bosco of Creeting and John Longinnyur of the same because they did not have [----] for whom they stood surety ½ mark. [no plea found][9]	0	6	8
From Robert Fige for a false claim, ½ mark by the surety of John de Wymundele and Stephen the son of William at *Hactorp*'[10]. [**348**]	0	6	8
From Henry of Belton and John de Ponte for disseisin, ½ mark. [**348**]	0	6	8
From Ranulf[11] Cristyn and Thomas Putforby for the same, ½ mark. [**348**]	0	6	8

¹ He is shown as Richard the Fleming in the plea and in the agreement in **1662**, but this plea is
   the correct one given the other names which follow; also the name of the surety is the same as
   the one in the plea. Also there is no plea in the roll where a Ranulf the Fleming is amerced for
   a false claim.
² Hugh was actually a juror who did not come to the eyre so the clerk has possibly made a mistake
   here in the reason for the amercement.
³ The two sureties are not shown in the plea.
⁴ In the plea she is shown as Juliana.
⁵ Shown in the plea as the 'son of Richard'.
⁶ Andrew was not the plaintiff but the defendant in a mort d'ancestor plea. He did lose the case
   but the reason should be for disseisin.
⁷ In **306** and **368** he is shown as Geoffrey the son of Guy.
⁸ This surety is not named in any of these pleas.
⁹ Possibly these are the sureties of John Ketel in **368**, which was an unfinished plea. It is note-
   worthy that John Ketel's name is not shown in the amercement section.
¹⁰ Stephen the son of William was not Robert Fige's surety but that of the disseisors in the plea.
¹¹ In the plea Ranulf is shown as Rainer by the clerk.

Sum Total 47 marks and 9 shillings¹

¹ This is the total shown on membrane 59. The amount calculated from the individual amounts
   found by the editor is as shown under the £ s. d. column below, whereas the amount given by the
   clerk on the membrane, as shown here, is calculated as £31 15s. 8d., a difference of £1 7s. 4d.,
   or 2 marks and 1s.

	Total	33	3	4

Membrane 59d

1646.

	£	s	d
From Geoffrey de *Nokedam* and Robert Gere for the same, ½ mark. [348]	0	6	8
From Ralph Smalemor for trespass, ½ mark. [no plea found]	0	6	8
From Gilbert of Browston, ½ mark. [no plea found]	0	6	8
From Robert Sudhaye for the same, ½ mark. [no plea found]	0	6	8
From Robert Bloure (Thomas Alric^c), Nicholas de Alneto for the same, 1 mark. [no plea found]	0	13	4
From Reynold Bloure, Richard Flemeng, Ralph Heigham for the same, 1 mark. [no plea found]	0	13	4
From Henry Bacon for an unjust detention, 1 mark by the surety of William de Rochenhall' [322]	0	13	4
From Alice, who was the wife of Roger of Burgh for a false claim, ½ mark by the surety of Ralph de Badham. [323]	0	6	8
From Geoffrey Laurence of Middleton because he did not come,¹ ½ mark. [910]	0	6	8
From Henry de Colville for an unjust detention, ½ mark by the surety of Wymer of Carlton. [326]	0	6	8
From Henry Red for disseisin, 10 shillings by the surety of John de Wymundhale and Master Walter of Blundeston. [327]	0	10	0
From Robert the son of Simon for an unjust detention, ½ mark by the surety of Edmund de Wimundhale. [329]	0	6	8
From John the son of William de Morford for a false claim, ½ mark by the surety of William of Whitton. [329 and 318]	0	6	8
From Nicholas of Buxhall for a false claim, 20 shillings by the surety of Ranulf le Flemeng. [420]	1	0	0

From Martin the son of Robert of Bacton and Roger the son of Adam of the same for [acting as] the surety, ½ mark. [422]	0	6	8
From Hugh de Blogate of Yaxley because he did not have [Thomas the barker of Eye] for whom he stood surety, ½ mark. [424]	0	6	8
From Andrew Toppard because he did not prosecute, Roger Duket[2] of Yaxley [and] Gilbert the carpenter de Raudeston because they did not have [Andrew Toppard] for whom they had stood surety (½ mark[i]). [426]	0	6	8
From Roger Grubbe for disseisin, ½ mark. [427]	0	6	8
From Roger de la Rivere in Sproughton for disseisin (½ mark[i]) by the surety of Henry Wicher in Belstead[3] and Osbert Grubbe. [427]	0	6	8
From Robert de Ulendon for the same, 1 mark by the surety of Philip de Wyleston. [490]	0	13	4

1   I think the clerk has given it the wrong reason. The plea indicates that Geoffrey was a surety for a fine made of half a mark. He might also be a surety for the amercement.
2   In the plea the clerk wrote Roger Auket of Yaxley.
3   In the plea he is shown as Henry Wicher of Sproughton.

1647.

From John the son of Richard of Chattisham because he did not have [Thomas the son of Joscelin and Beatrice his wife] for whom he stood surety, ½ mark. [441]	0	6	8
From Walter the son of John of Blundeston and Robert the son of Richard of Little Yarmouth because they did not have [Alice the wife of John le Rus and Robert her son] for whom they stood surety, ½ mark. [373]	0	6	8
From Bartholomew the son of Alan and his allies for disseisin, 1 mark by the surety of John Blench.[1] [374]	0	13	4
From Robert of Peasenhall for a false claim, 10 shillings, by the surety of Jordan le New of Yoxford and Henry of Brundish.[2] [396]	0	10	0
From Ralph of Gorleston for a false claim, 10 shillings by the surety of Roger Perebrun and Simon Aysman.[3] [397]	0	10	0
From Geoffrey de Chani because he did not prosecute, ½ mark. [398]	0	6	8
From John Iward of Middleton and Aylward le Despencer because they did not have [Geoffrey de Cadamo] for whom they stood surety, ½ mark. [398]	0	6	8
From Ralph the son of Ralph of Denham for a false claim, ½ mark by the surety of Ernald[4] of Kettleburgh and Roger of Carlton. [399]	0	6	8
From Roger de Godeford and Adam Bunting because they did not have [William the son of Mar'] for whom they stood surety, ½ mark. [409]	0	6	8
From Richard the son of Richard of Fressingfield for a false claim, ½ mark by the surety of William. [384]	0	6	8
From William de Gosewode and Hubert of Tannington because they did not have [Thomas le Gosewold] for whom they stood surety, ½ mark. [386]	0	6	8
From Alan de Sotmere for an unjust detention, ½ mark by the surety of Edmund de Wimundhale. [395]	0	6	8
From Alan of Pakefield for a false claim, ½ mark by the surety of Simon Asman and William of Carlton. [376]	0	6	8

From William the son of William de Chantelon for the same, ½ mark by the surety of John de Arthes and William Turgis. [377]	0	6	8
From Alexander Page and John the palmer of Buxlow because they did not have [Robert Sheriff] for whom they stood surety, ½ mark. [382]	0	6	8
From (Roger[c]) Rainer of Sternfield and Walter Burdun[5] for the same, ½ mark. [382]	0	6	8
From Robert of Badingham and his allies for disseisin, 1 mark by the surety of Herbert Alencon. [382]	0	13	4
From Henry the son of Seleder of Brundish for a false claim, ½ mark by the surety of Mundekin of Brundish.[6] [401]	0	6	8
From William Russo[7] for disseisin. [407]	0	0	0
From Walter de Esham for a false claim, ½ mark by the surety of William Bonhayt.[8] [407]	0	6	8

[1]   This surety is not shown in the plea.
[2]   This surety is not shown in the plea.
[3]   This surety is not shown in the plea.
[4]   In the plea he is shown as Ernulf.
[5]   The clerk has shown only one of the two attachees for two of the defendants named in the plea, that is Harvey Shacel and Alexander Page. The other two sureties for these two defendants are missing from the amercements.
[6]   The surety is not shown in the plea but it might be Edmund of Brundish who is mentioned elsewhere in the roll.
[7]   This is William le Rus in **407**. The amercements for the false claim by the plaintiff follow.
[8]   The surety is not shown in the plea.

1648.

From Geoffrey[1] the Parker of Brundish for an unjust detention, ½ mark by the surety of Thomas of Shotford. [387]	0	6	8
From Robert de Hay and Robert Jordan of Tuddenham, because they did not prosecute, ½ mark. [391, 392]	0	6	8
From Robert Blund of Blakenham for himself and his sureties because he withdrew[2] [from the plea], ½ mark by the surety Austin of Blakenham. [445]	0	6	8
From Albert Pigaz de la Hone because he did not have [Nicholas the son of Micah] for whom he stood surety 1 mark. [432]	0	13	4
From John the son of Robert of Ubbeston because he did not prosecute, ½ mark. [500]	0	6	8
From Stephen Sott of Ipswich because he did not have [Agnes wife of Hugh de la Grene] for whom he stood surety, ½ mark. [501]	0	6	8
From Thomas Garneys and John Norman of Elmham[3] because he did not have [John the son of Robert of Ubbeston and Matilda his wife] for whom they stood surety, ½ mark. [500]	0	6	8
From Mathew of Peyton for disseisin, 10 shillings. [478]	0	10	0
From Robert of Peyton and Hugh Godston[4] for the same ½ mark. [478]	0	6	8
From Philip of Horksley for a false claim, ½ mark. [478]	0	6	8
From Thomas of Rendlesham for the same, ½ mark by the surety of Walter Ivete of Mendlesham[5] and William Snelling. [479]	0	6	8
From Thomas Russel of Mendham for disseisin, 20 shillings by the surety of Adam of Mendham, knight, and Roger of Shotford. [447]	1	0	0

From Roger Thrumbald of Wingfield[6] because he did not have [Roger the son of Geoffrey] for whom he stood surety, ½ mark. [448]	0	6	8
From William Mervyn of the same for the same, ½ mark. [448]	0	6	8
(From Roger the son of Hugh de *Raudeston* because he did not have [----] for whom he stood surety, ½ mark.[s])[7] [458 and/or 459]	0	6	8
From Geoffrey (the son[i]) of William de *Raudeston* and Humphrey le Neyr[8] for the same, ½ mark. [458]	0	6	8
(+)[9] From Roger the son of Osbert for an unjust detention. [no plea found]	0	0	0
(+)[10] From Ranulf of Wymondham for the same. [no plea found]	0	0	0
From Roger Trainnes for a false claim, ½ mark by the surety of Henry de Enepol.[11] [470]	0	6	8
From Henry Bicceremede for the same, ½ mark by the surety of William of Holbrook. [573]	0	6	8
From Philip the son of Richard of Braiseworth because he did not prosecute, ½ mark. [509]	0	6	8

1   In the plea the clerk indicates Godfrey, not Geoffrey, but he also indicates another surety, William de Childerhus.
2   According to the plea he actually did not prosecute two cases but pursued the third and won. However, the person he prosecuted was pardoned the amercement.
3   This person is not shown in the plea as a surety. It is possible that the clerk made a mistake here or in the plea.
4   In the plea they are shown as Roger of Peyton and Hugh Galston.
5   In the plea he is shown as Thomas the son of Ivetta of Rendlesham.
6   The clerk in the plea has Richard of Wingfield.
7   The clerk here shows Roger as a surety whereas in these pleas he is the plaintiff and has not prosecuted. He does not appear in the rest of the roll.
8   These two are the real sureties for Roger the son of Hugh *de Raudeston.*
9   Cross in the margin. No plea found for this person for the reason given. He has already been amerced for 453 in 1643. One other possibility is 481 where Roger is vouched to warranty for the land by the prior of Blythburgh.
10   Cross in the margin. The clerk probably could not find a Ranulf of Wymondham in the roll to amerce.
11   This surety is not shown in the plea.

1649.

From Richard the son of William[1] of Yaxley and Joss of the same for [acting as] the surety, ½ mark. [509]	0	6	8
From John Musard of Tuddenham because he did not prosecute, ½ mark. [540]	0	6	8
From Osbert Grubbe the son of John Grubbe of Sproughton because he did not have [John Musard of Tuddenham] for whom he stood surety, ½ mark. [540]	0	6	8
From Hugh of Naughton for disseisin, ½ mark by the surety of Richard of Woodbridge and Henry of Naughton. [541]	0	6	8
From Walter de Colville[2] for the same, ½ mark. [547]	0	6	8
From William the son of Robert of Gooderstone and Alexander the son of William of the same for the same, ½ mark. [603]	0	6	8
From William the son of Seman of Boyton and Walter the son of Simon of the same for the same, ½ mark. [583]	0	6	8
From Roger Wyot because he has not come and Ralph Walnod of Blaxhall and Theobald Iring[3] because they did not have [Roger Wyot] for who they stood surety, ½ (mark[i]). [592]	0	6	8

From Richard Mariot for a false claim, ½ mark. [592]	0	6	8
From Roger the son of John of Wantisden and Alexander Styward [of Tunstall] because they did not have [Richard Mariot] for whom they stood surety, ½ mark. [592]	0	6	8
From Geoffrey Bernard of Winston and William Bughe of the same for the same, ½ mark. [546]	0	6	8
From William Silvester le Minden[4] and Roger de Prato for the same, ½ mark. [597]	0	6	8
From Geoffrey of Titsey of Rendham and Stephen de Colville [of Parham] because they did not have [Tristram of Rendham] for whom they stood surety, ½ mark. [600]	0	6	8
From Thomas Tyrel for disseisin, ½ mark. [607]	0	6	8
From William of Rendham and William Bernard for an unjust detention, ½ mark. [608]	0	6	8
From William Trilly and William Cuikyn[5] for the same, ½ mark. [608]	0	6	8
From Amis the daughter of Baldwin for a false claim and Robert of Clopton because he did not prosecute, ½ mark. [609 and 562][6]	0	6	8
From Richard Baron of Clopton for [acting as] the surety, ½ mark. [562]	0	6	8
From Alan Cumpot[7] for the same, ½ mark. [562]	0	6	8

1. In the plea he is shown as Richard the son of Hubert of Yaxley. The plea is definitely 509 because of the other surety.
2. In 547 Walter is a surety with his brother for Tristram of Rendham. The following two amercement entries are also for sureties and not disseisors.
3. Note the spelling of the names in comparison with the plea.
4. In the plea he is shown as William Sylvester of Monewden and the second surety is not shown.
5. In the plea it is William's wife, Alice, who is named as a defendant.
6. The clerk has combined the amercements of two totally separate pleas for no obvious reason.
7. In the plea he is shown as Alan Compel.

Sum Total 43 marks and 10 shillings[1]

1. The amount calculated from the individual amounts found by the editor is as shown under the £s.d. column below, whereas the amount given by the clerk on the membrane, as shown here, is calculated as £29 3s. 4d., a difference of 16s. 8d., or 1 mark and 3s. and 4d.

Total	**30**	**0**	**0**

Membrane 60

1650.

From Elias the son of Robert of Easton because he did not prosecute, ½ mark. [611]	0	6	8
From Roger the son of William of Hoo for [acting as] the surety, ½ mark. [611]	0	6	8
From Roger the son of Ralph of Easton for the same. [611]	0	6	8
From Gilbert the son of Warren of Grundisburgh and William the son of Reynold [of Culpho], ½ mark. [613]	0	6	8
From Roger Sturmy because he did not prosecute, ½ mark. [567]	0	6	8
From William[1] the son of William of Soham for the same, ½ mark. [569]	0	6	8
From William de Colville of Aspall for the same, ½ mark. [570]	0	6	8

(+)From Thomas de Hemmegrave for many trespasses. [**347**, **570**, **1039**][2]	0	0	0
From William le Daveys because he did not prosecute, ½ mark. [**571**]	0	6	8
From Thomas de Loges of Brandeston and John[3] Bene of Cretingham for [acting as] the surety, ½ mark. [**571**]	0	6	8
From Robert the son of William because he did not prosecute and Roger the son of the dean of Sutton and William Osmund[4] for [acting as] the surety, ½ mark. [**572**]	0	6	8
From Seman the son of William of Creeting and Hervey the son of William of the same for the same, ½ mark. [**625**]	0	6	8
From John the son of Andrew,[5] Alan of Thorpe and Guy of Barkestone because they did not have for whom they stood as surety, ½ mark. [**627**]	0	6	8
From Roger Carpenter[6] and Stephen the son of William of Barkestone for the same, ½ mark. [**628**]	0	6	8
From Richard de Rybos because he did not have [Nicholas Chaplain de *Sucling*][7] for whom he stood surety, ½ mark. [**629**]	0	6	8
From Richard Sewale and Augustine Gutheleburt for [acting as] the surety, ½ mark. [**630**]	0	6	8
From Robert Bast because he did not prosecute, ½ mark. [**631**]	0	6	8
From Stephen Gunter and John Burrich of Grimston for [acting as] the surety, ½ mark. [**631**]	0	6	8
From John the son of William of Sternfield and John the son of Robert of the same for the same, ½ mark. [**633**][8]	0	6	8
From Geoffrey Batley and Richard Frebern of Stradbroke because [they][9] did not prosecute, ½ mark. [**414**]	0	6	8

1. In the plea he is shown as Walter the son of William.
2. I can find these three occasions where Thomas de Hemmegrave was amerced in the text. The cross in the margin might be a note to the sheriff. It is possible that no amount was entered in the amercement section of this roll because the sheriff would pick up the amount from the pipe roll and he would collect from that. See the introduction, p.lvi, n.260.
3. Note that in the plea *Johanne Bene* is shown as *Galfridus Bene*.
4. William Osmund is not shown in the plea.
5. In the plea John the son of Andrew is shown as the plaintiff, not as a surety. The other two are the sureties.
6. Roger Carpenter is shown as the plaintiff in the plea, not a surety.
7. The plaintiff Nicholas and the other surety are not shown in the amercement section of this roll. See the plea for the others.
8. The plaintiff is not shown in the amercement section of this roll even though the plea indicates he was amerced.
9. The clerk wrote the singular here: *non est prosecutus*.

1651.

From Adam de Rowe and Richard Aleyn for the same, ½ mark. [**414**]	0	6	8
From Alan of Withersdale for an unjust detention, 1 mark by the surety of Baldwin of Mellis. [**999**]	0	13	4
From Roger de Bernesh' for the same, ½ mark by the surety of William of Holbrook. [**1011**]	0	6	8
From Richard Cook of Pulham for [acting as] the surety, ½ mark. [**1007**]	0	6	8
From Ralph de Colville because he did not prosecute, ½ mark. [**1000** or **1004**][1]	0	6	8

From Stephen of Brockdish for the same,[2] ½ mark. [774?]	0	6	8
From Robert of Farnham[3] for the same, ½ mark. [no plea found]	0	6	8
From Nicholas Gilcher' of Sternfield and John Culur of Kenton for [acting as] the surety, ½ mark. [no plea found]	0	6	8
From John the son of Walter de *Keleton* and Thomas the son of William of the same for the same, ½ mark. [no plea found]	0	6	8
From William the son of Hugh of Ramsholt and William the son of Ranulf of the same for the same, ½ mark. [no plea found]	0	6	8
From William del Hey because he did not prosecute, Roger Minetere of Tuddenham and Ralph Plasgere of Burgh for [acting as] the surety, ½ mark. [no plea found]	0	6	8
From Robert the son of Walter [of] Sudbury and William the son of Robert of the same for the same, ½ mark. [no plea found]	0	6	8
From Simon of Whatfield for an unjust detention, ½ mark. [731]	0	6	8
From Roger the son of Hermer because he did not prosecute. [683]	0	0	0
From[4] Roger the son of Hermer because he did not prosecute, ½ mark by the surety of Michael of Hartest and Ralph le Volant of the same. [683]	0	6	8
From Peter de Grenville for a false claim, ½ mark by the surety of Walter of Hepworth[5] and Norman of Saxham. [715]	0	6	8
From Henry of Livermere because he did not prosecute, ½ mark by the surety of Roger of Boyland. [696]	0	6	8
From Ralph de Mara of Livermere and William his brother, ½ mark by the surety of Henry of Livermere. [696]	0	6	8
(From Robert of Shelton because he has not come, 1 mark.c)[6] It is not. [741]	0	0	0
From Hugh [le] Caliere of Eleigh and John Woodcock of the same because they did not have [Robert of Shelton etc] for whom they stood surety, ½ mark. [741]	0	6	8

1 In both of these Robert de Colville did not prosecute.
2 I can find no plea in which Stephen of Brockdish did not prosecute the plea. There is the plea shown above where he is amerced for not turning up as a juror to attaint the twelve.
3 No plea found for Robert of Farnham but this could be for **566**. However, this plea shows a John of Farnham.
4 There is a gap between this amercement and the previous one, which is the same as this amercement except there are no sureties.
5 Only Walter is shown in the plea as a surety.
6 The clerk possibly realised his mistake that the bailiff answers for Robert and the others.

1652.

From Walter [the] Franklin of Eleigh and Martin del Brook of the same for the same, ½ mark. [741]	0	6	8
From John Ailward and Adam [the son of] David from the same for the same, ½ mark. [741]	0	6	8
From Richard le Legistre for a false claim, ½ mark by the surety of Roger of Melford and Hugh the son of Maurice of the same. [698]	0	6	8
From Bartholomew Thurment because he withdrew himself [from the plea], ½ mark. [700]	0	6	8
From William the son of Osbert of Gedding for [acting as] the surety, ½ mark. [700]	0	6	8

	£	s	d
From Thomas the son of William of Pakenham for a false claim, ½ mark. [701]	0	6	8
From Walter [the son of] Bernard[1] for disseisin, 20 shillings. [703]	1	0	0
From Nicholas the chaplain for a false claim, ½ mark by the surety of Martin of Rockland.[2] [704]	0	6	8
From William the son of Anselm of Pakenham because he did not prosecute, ½ mark. [707]	0	6	8
From Thomas the son of William of Pakenham and John the son of Ralph of the same[3] for [acting as] the surety, ½ mark. [707]	0	6	8
From Warren the son of Hugh of Bardwell[4] and Gilbert Thedred of the same for the same, ½ mark. [688]	0	6	8
From Alexander the son of William Palmer for disseisin, ½ mark by the surety of Roger de Ponte of Waldingfield and Gilbert Childer. [711]	0	6	8
From Simon Lambert of Stanningfield and Adam Freman of the same for they did not have [William the son of Elias] for whom the stood surety, ½ mark. [689]	0	6	8
From Robert Franceys for disseisin, ½ mark by the surety of William de *Holmereshey* and Henry of Exning.[5] [692]	0	6	8
From Thomas Crowe because he withdrew himself [from the plea], 1 mark by the surety of Andrew of Assington. [735]	0	13	4
From John the son of John de Cornhill[6] because he did not have [Thomas Crowe] for whom he stood surety, ½ mark. [735]	0	6	8
From Robert Walram de *Lopham*[7] because he did not come, ½ mark. [829]	0	6	8
From Robert of Layham for disseisin, 2 marks.[8] [829]	1	6	8
From William of Bures for a false claim, ½ mark. [829]	0	6	8
From Hugh Revel for a false claim, ½ mark by the surety of Robert de Hauville.[9] [832]	0	6	8

1   In the plea Walter is shown as *filius Bernardi*.
2   In the plea no surety is identified.
3   In the plea he is shown as being from Whatfield.
4   He is shown as Warren the son of William of Bardwell in the plea.
5   These sureties are not shown in the plea. Robert of Hastings is the one shown but it must be this one as this is the only plea that Robert le Fraunceys is accused of disseisin. There is a hole in the membrane, which the clerk has worked around.
6   In the plea this person is shown as from Great or Little Cornard. There is another surety not shown here, namely Alexander the son of Robert of Sutton. This appears to mean that the sheriff only collects from the one surety, who will be responsible for the collection of the debt and then pay the sum to the sheriff at the circuit.
7   This person is shown as *Robertus Walranc* in the plea and there is also no place name associated with the person. He is the recognitor who did not turn up.
8   This seems a bit excessive in comparison with other disseisins for far more land. It may be an example of fixing a penalty according to ability to pay.
9   In the plea there are two sureties, Ralph de Hauville of Bildeston and Robert of Semer.

1653.

	£	s	d
From William the son of Walter of Bradley[1] because he did not have [Isabella the daughter of Godwin] for whom he stood surety, ½ mark. [834]	0	6	8
From Ralph Letice[2] of Bradley for a false claim, ½ mark by the surety of Roger the clerk of Bradley and Henry Wastel[3] of (the same[i]). [835]	0	6	8

From Alexander of Walpole for the same, ½ mark by the surety of Thomas de Haleby and Thomas of Bures.[4] [837]	0	6	8
From William Woolmer because he withdrew himself [from the plea], ½ mark by the surety of William the carter of Wratting and William Berard (of the same[i]). [846]	0	6	8
From Roger the son of William for false claim, ½ mark by the surety of Peter de *Pridington* and John Ilger of Stansfield. [847]	0	6	8
From Thomas Bigod[5] for disseisin, 1 mark by the surety of John of Samford and Thomas de Aleby. [855–857]	0	13	4
From Gilbert Sprot because he withdrew himself [from the plea], ½ mark by the surety of : William the clerk of Hundon and Hubert de Lea in Haverhill. [849]	0	6	8
From Hugh the son of Walter of Withersfield for an unjust detention, ½ mark by the surety of Walter Ruffus of Withersfield (and Guy Grot[i]). [850]	0	6	8
From Rery the clerk for the same, ½ mark. [851]	0	6	8
From John le Breton[6] because he did not come, 10 shillings. [774]	0	10	0
Simon de Cherninges for disseisin, 1 mark. [831]	0	13	4
From Roger of Chilton and Osbert his brother for the same, 10 shillings. [831]	0	10	0
From William Causwrde and Ralph of Rushbrook because they did not have [Simon de Cherninges] for whom they stood surety, ½ mark. [831]	0	6	8
From Richard Alexander of Hitcham and Geoffrey le Chival[7] of the same for the same, ½ mark. [831]	0	6	8
From Robert Darnel because he did not come, ½ mark. [836]	0	6	8
From John Ilger de *Pridington*[8] because he did not have [Robert Darnel] for whom he stood surety, ½ mark. [836]	0	6	8
From Roger the son of William of Hawkedon[9] for the same, ½ mark. [836]	0	6	8
From Robert [the] carpenter of Stansfield for a false claim, ½ mark by the surety of William Wyburg of Stansfield and Roger (the son of Eudo of Stradishall[i]). [836]	0	6	8
From Gilbert [de] Brook for a false claim, ½ mark by the surety of John of Bealings of Haverhill and William the carter of Wratting. [843]	0	6	8
From Adam le Grant of Moulton for a false claim, ½ mark by the surety of Simon le Franceys of Moulton and Edmund of (Barnardiston[i]). [839]	0	6	8

1   Only one surety is shown here, the other being William the son of William of Bradford. Also the lady plaintiff, 'Isabella the daughter of Godwin', is not shown in the amercement section of this roll. In the plea this surety is shown as 'Walter the son of William of Bradley'.

2   Ralph is shown as the 'son of Lettice' in the plea roll.

3   The other surety in the plea is shown as Henry Walles of Bradley.

4   The clerk may have made a mistake here, or on the plea roll, as the second surety is shown in the plea as Thomas of Bradley.

5   Thomas Bigod is involved in the three writs as defendant. In **855** he is shown as winning but the two sureties are shown as these two named in the amercement for the plaintiff, but not in the other two pleas. Thomas loses the other pleas but the sureties are not shown. It is possible that the clerk has made a mistake here because of Thomas losing the other two pleas. However, he does not appear in the amercement section of this roll again, so it is probable that the sureties

are the same in all three pleas. The plaintiff in **855** is 'William the son of Walter' but he does not appear in the amercement section of this roll for this plea.

6   John is one of nine knights who did not come but there is no mention of the others. This was for an appeal of a novel disseisin.

7   These are the attachees for Roger of Chilton. Also Richard is shown as being the son of Alexander of Hitcham in the plea.

8   The first attachee for Robert Darnel in the plea.

9   The second attachee for Robert Darnel in the plea.

1654.

From Macy of Cowlinge for trespass, ½ mark. [826]	0	6	8
From Thomas de Ponte of Thurlow because he did not come, ½ mark. [858]	0	6	8
From Alice de Hauville for an unjust detention, ½ mark. [858]	0	6	8
From William the son of Alexander for a false claim, ½ mark by the surety of Robert de Melow. [814]	0	6	8
From Adam the son of Richard for the same, ½ mark by the surety of Walter [of] Hepworth and Adam de Horningsea.[1] [815]	0	6	8
From William Overfen[2] because he did not have [Adam the son of Richard] for whom he stood surety, ½ mark. [815]	0	6	8
From William of Newton for an unjust detention[3] by the surety of John of Kelsale. [749]	0	0	0
From Mathew of Sudbury for the same, ½ mark. [750]	0	6	8
From Robert[4] of Waldingfield for the same, 10 shillings. [761]	0	10	0
From Robert de Scales[5] for disseisin, 5 marks. [763]	3	6	8
From Martin of Middleton for the same by the surety of John of Dunham. [763]	0	0	0
From Maurice[6] the son of Warren of Pakenham because he did not prosecute, ½ mark. [799]	0	6	8

1   Adam is not named in the plea.

2   Only one surety is named here. The second surety was William Breton. These were the sureties in the second plea that Adam did not prosecute.

3   There is no amount shown for the amercement.

4   No plea found for this name but I believe that it relates to **761** where there is a Ralph of Waldingfield named who vouched to warranty the original defendant in a mort d'ancestor plea, so I think the clerk has made a mistake either here or in the plea in naming the individual.

5   No plea found for Robert de Scales but I believe that **763** as there is a *Robertus des Eschaleres* in the plea and I think this is likely to be him. Also, the next amercement is for the other person named as a defendant in the plea, Martin of Middleton, who along with Robert disseised the plaintiff. The surety for the amercement shown below is the same as that named in the plea.

6   The plea shows Martin the son of Warren [of Pakenham], which is probably correct. There is no Maurice the son of Warren in the roll.

Sum Total 54 marks, 3 shillings, 4 pence[1]

1   The amount calculated from the individual amounts found by the editor is as shown under the £ s. d. column bellow, whereas the amount given by the clerk on the membrane, as shown here, is calculated as £36 3s. 4d: a difference of 13s. 4d. or 1 mark. In membrane 60 there is one amercement of 1 mark crossed out. It is possible that the clerk has included in his total the 1 mark crossed out. There are four other entries where the clerk has not included an amercement value. Of these, one entry is a duplicate, which I have excluded in my calculations. One other entry is for Thomas de Hemmegrave who is shown in the membrane as having his amercement identified in the pipe roll. Of the other two entries, one is for two litigants that are named separately in this amercement section for the same plea but only one has an actual amercement present. It is presumed that of the two defendants amerced in **763**, one is responsible for the amount to be paid. It is not known why the clerk has shown no amercement in the other entry for **749**.

Total   35   10   0

Membrane 60d

1655.

From Ralph the son of the chaplain of Barton and Simon the son of John of the same because they did not have [Martin the son of Warren] for whom they stood surety, ½ mark. **[799]**	0	6	8
From Hugh le Webbe and Simon Mariot of Bacton for disseisin, 10 shillings by the surety of Simon of Lavenham and John (Christmas[i])[1]. **[812]**	0	10	0
From Thomas de Hay for disseisin, ½ mark by the surety of Mathew of Layham. **[765]**	0	6	8
From Richard the son of Woolmer and Ralph Gilbert of Livermere[2] for [acting as] the surety, ½ mark. **[766]**	0	6	8
From John Cappedale and Baldwin de *Kintewde* for the same, ½ mark. [no plea found][3]	0	6	8
From William Mapeleneheved because he did not have [Alan the son of William] for whom he stood surety, ½ mark. **[793]**	0	6	8
From Thomas Algar for a false claim, ½ mark. **[794]**	0	6	8
From John of Ubbeston for the same, ½ mark by the surety of Norman le Nuvelhume and Peter Nuvelhume. [no plea found][4]	0	6	8
From Robert of Easton and Walter Bonhaya because they did not come, ½ mark. **[910]**	0	6	8
From Geoffrey the son of William of Thorpe because he did not have [----] for whom he stood surety, ½ mark. **[915 or 1032]**	0	6	8
From Anselm of Rendham[5] for the same, ½ mark by the surety of Martin of Rockland. [no plea found]	0	6	8
From William the son of Robert of Stanton for the same, ½ mark. **[920]**	0	6	8
From Hamon Mundy for a false claim, ½ mark by the surety of William of Honingham.[6] **[921]**	0	6	8
From Robert the son of Geoffrey for the same, ½ mark by the surety of Richard Pride de *Nottsted*. **[926]**	0	6	8
From Alan Trencham and Alan Sunercist for [acting as] the surety, ½ mark. **[927]**	0	6	8
From William de Brook because he did not have [Walter Smith and Emma his wife] for whom he stood surety, ½ mark. **[877]**	0	6	8
From Walter the son of Adewis de Preston for a false claim, ½ mark by the surety of William of Troston and Henry of Livermere. **[879]**	0	6	8
From Richard the son of Thomas de *Lafham*[7] for the same, ½ mark by the surety of Henry Gerewy. **[869]**	0	6	8
From William the son of Robert of Tostock and Walter de Sudstrete for [acting as] the surety, ½ mark. **[911]**	0	6	8
From Ralph the parson of Stanton because he did not prosecute, ½ mark. **[912]**	0	6	8

1. The sureties are different to that shown in the plea but this is the only plea where these two litigants appear. The rest of the litigants are not shown in the amercements section.
2. The clerk has Ralph as the son of Gilbert in the plea.
3. This might be **768** but only one surety is shown there, and that is *Johannes le Barun de Coppedoc*.
4. It is possible that this amercement is also for **794**. The sureties were missing in the plea. However, the persons amerced were a John de Hirsteston as well as Thomas Algar above.

5   It is possible that this refers to **920** but there we have an Anselm of Rougham, not Rendham.
    Given the other surety in **920** follows it may be that the clerk has made a mistake on the vill
    and on the correct Anselm.

6   In the plea we have *Willelmi de Helingham*, which is Helmingham in Claydon hundred. There
    is a place called Honingham in Forehoe hundred in Norfolk, and note this is a Norfolk plea.

7   This person was one of the sureties for prosecuting and Henry Gerewy was the plaintiff. It looks
    as though Henry and his sureties for the amercement are in **1657**.

1656.

From Harvey of Hitcham for [acting as] the surety, ½ mark. [**912**]	0	6	8
From Hugh of Thetford in [the liberty of] St Edmund because he did not prosecute and Alexander le Teynturh' of the same and Walter the son of Nigel (of Hawkedon[i]) because they did not have [Hugh] for whom they stood surety, 10 shillings. [**917**]	0	10	0
From John of Coddenham for disseisin, 40 shillings[1] by the surety of William of Cotton and Thomas of Tuddenham. [**861**]	2	0	0
From Alan the son of William of Norton and Nicholas Trussebut because they did not have [----][2] for whom the stood surety, ½ mark by the surety of Walter de (Toppetoft[i]). [**791**]	0	6	8
From William le Claver of Thurston and Robert Peche for the same, ½ mark. [**792**]	0	6	8
From William the son of Walter of Livermere[3] because he did not prosecute, ½ mark by the surety of John the son of Laurence of Livermere and William Kenne (of the same[i]). [**874**]	0	6	8
From John de la More and Adam de Haraz for a false claim, 20 shillings, by the surety of John Blund of Herringswell.[4] [**795**]	1	0	0
From Alan Godrich of Herringfleet because he did not have [Nicholas de Crew] for whom he stood surety, ½ mark. [**891**]	0	6	8
From Nicholas the son of Godfrey of Bacton because he did not prosecute, ½ mark. [no plea found]	0	6	8
From Richard the son of Reynold of Cowlinge because he did not prosecute, ½ mark by the surety of Mathew of Cowlinge. [**922**]	0	6	8
From Roger of Rougham of Bury St Edmunds because he did not have [Simon Gardener and William Stepere] for whom he stood surety, ½ mark. [**923**]	0	6	8
From Robert le Blund of the same[5] for the same, ½ mark. [**991**]	0	6	8
From Thomas de *Horshawe*[6] because he did not prosecute, ½ mark. [**924**]	0	6	8
From William Testepin and Edmund the son of Richard because they did not have [Geoffrey the son of Geoffrey] for whom they stood surety, ½ mark. [**884**]	0	6	8
From John the son of William of Stanton[7] for the same, ½ mark. [**978**]	0	6	8
From Gerard de Hadingesele for a false claim, 1 mark. [**976**]	0	13	4
From Bartholomew the son of Stephen of Charsfield and William the son of (----[e]) de Oppeston[8] because they did not have [Ralph de Colville] for whom they stood surety, ½ mark. [**1004**]	0	6	8
From Robert of Kenton because he withdrew himself [from the plea], ½ mark by the surety of Robert the son of Reynold[9] of Dunwich. [**942**]	0	6	8

From Jordan le Waleys and Hamo de *Bladefeud* because they did not   0   6   8
have [Robert of Kenton] for whom they stood surety, ½ mark. **[942]**
From Stephen of Stratton for a false claim, ½ mark by the surety of   0   6   8
Gerard Richaut. **[1008]**

1   The amount shown for this amercement is the same as for the damages shown in the plea, that is 6 marks. This raises the question as to who gets the damages, the one who has suffered damage or the court and hence the crown.

2   The plea indicates that Alan and Nicholas are the defendants, the ones who lost the case and were amerced. Here they are shown as though they are the sureties and sureties are often amerced separately. I would normally put the amerced person(s) who had lost the case in here. What is also odd however is that they do have a surety for the amercement. It appears that the clerk was confused as to what role these people had in the plea.

3   This is the only plea where a *Willelmus filius Walteri* has a plea which he has not prosecuted but the sureties in the plea are not the same as these. In fact they cannot be found anywhere in the roll. It may be that they appeared in this plea, but because the plea is affected by the torn off parts of the membrane at this point it may be that they did appear here after all.

4   The second surety in the plea is not shown in the amercement section of this roll.

5   The amercement of this surety is repeated in **1657**.

6   In the plea this is shown as *Horsage*.

7   Only one of the two sureties is shown here.

8   The reason for the erasure may be that the other surety is different to that shown in the plea, but the clerk did not complete the erasure.

9   The surety for the amercement is shown as the 'son of Ralph' in the plea.

1657.

From William the son of William de Cyrici for the same, ½ mark by   0   6   8
the surety of Robert [le] Blund. **[991]**
From Ralph the son of Ivo of Melford[1] because he did not have [----]   0   6   8
for whom he stood surety, ½ mark. **[1015]**
From John de Beaumes of Ipswich for the same, ½ mark. **[1046]**   0   6   8
From Robert the son of Roger of Withersfield and Richard the son of   0   6   8
Ralph of Wratting for the same, ½ mark. **[972]**
From Adelard the son of Robert Kachevage for the same, ½ mark.   0   6   8
[995]
From Adam Trecheglace and Fulk of Woolpit for the same,   0   6   8
½ mark. **[996]**
From Anselm the son of Adam de *Lelesheye*[2] and Walter the son of   0   6   8
Robert of the same for the same, ½ mark. **[952]**
From William the son of Richard of Hencote and Richard the palmer   0   6   8
of the same for the same, ½ mark. **[1023]**
From Walter Bance because he did not prosecute, and Roger Barun   0   6   8
and Geoffrey the miller[3] for the same, ½ mark. **[956]**
From Nicholas the son of Albert of Pakenham and John the son of   0   6   8
Elias of Tostock for the same, ½ mark. **[967]**
From Henry Gerewy because he withdrew himself [from the plea], ½   0   6   8
mark by the surety of Robert Gerewy and Richard the son of William
of Layham.[4] **[869]**
From Gilbert the son of Warren because he did not have [Gervase de   0   6   8
Meulinghes] for whom he stood surety, ½ mark. **[870]**
From Gervase de Melhinges because he did not prosecute and Adam   0   6   8
the son of Warren de *Esriston* because he did not have [Gervase] for
whom he stood surety, ½ mark. **[870]**

From Robert de Alneto for disseisin, 20 shillings by the surety John Marshall of Stoke and Philip de *Hunileg*. [871]	1	0	0
From Geoffrey Gykel of Westhall and Adam the son of Geoffrey of the same because they did not have [[Henry the son of Warren and Alice his wife and Christine the [sister] of [Alice]] for whom they stood surety, ½ mark. [1055]	0	6	8
From Robert de Bosco because he did not have [John the son of Hamo] for whom he stood surety. [1056]	0	6	8
From Ralph the merchant for a false claim, ½ mark by the surety of Hugh of Badley and Geoffrey the son of Geoffrey of Wetherden.[5] [1119]	0	6	8
From Simon de *Herewell* in Burstall because he did not have [Thomas the son of Ranulf] for whom he stood surety and Thomas the son of Ranulf because he did not prosecute, ½ mark. [1130]	0	6	8
From Michael the son of Gerold of Elmham because he did not have [Thomas the son of Ranulf] for whom he stood surety, ½ mark. [1130]	0	6	8
From William of Battisford because he did not prosecute, ½ mark. [1137]	0	6	8

1   Ralph is shown in this plea as the defendant, not a surety. He is not shown anywhere in the roll as a surety. It looks as though this should be Agnes the daughter of Ivo who did not prosecute in **1015**.
2   See the plea for different spellings of this name.
3   The last two names are the sureties in the plea.
4   The second surety is shown as *Ricardus filius Viviani de Leyham* in the plea. Also this amercement may be duplicated in **1655**.
5   The sureties are not shown in the plea but this is the only plea where Ralph is identified as the plaintiff.

1658.

From Ralph Hog of Wattisham and John Sephore because they did not have [William of Battisford] for whom they stood surety, ½ mark. [1137]	0	6	8
Thomas the chaplain of Easton because he did not prosecute, ½ mark. [1139]	0	6	8
From Peter Cook de *Ulenden*[1] because he did not have [Thomas the chaplain of Easton] for whom he stood surety, ½ mark. [1139]	0	6	8
From Walter the son of William of Hepworth and Ralph the son of Adam (of[i]) Pakenham for the same, ½ mark. [no plea found]	0	6	8
From Adam of Cotton for an unjust hindrance, ½ mark by the surety of Edmund de Wymundhale. [no plea found]	0	6	8
From Hugh Weland of Elmham and Stephen Hacun of the same because they did not have [Letencia wife of Roger Bell] for whom they stood surety, ½ mark. [1065]	0	6	8
From Robert Cook of Denton and John de Spina of the same for the same, ½ mark. [1122]	0	6	8
From John (----e, i[l]) de Runie of Elmham because he did not prosecute, ½ mark. [no plea found][2]	0	6	8
From Robert the son of Warin and Hugh of Dereham for the same, ½ mark. [1123]	0	6	8

From Henry Pye of Reedham and William Sodman of Loddon[3] for the same, ½ mark. [1124]	0	6	8
From Richard of Dalham for a false claim, ½ mark by the surety of Thomas de *Hanethecy*. [1080]	0	6	8
From Thomas the son of Nicholas Oldhering because he did not have [Hugh the chaplain] for whom he stood surety, ½ mark. [1085]	0	6	8
From Elias le Franceys of Walpole and Robert the son of the clerk[4] for the same, ½ mark. [1064]	0	6	8
From Baldwin of Eriswell for disseisin, ½ mark by the surety of Ralph Espurun and Ralph Katerine. [1068]	0	6	8
From Richard Martin and John Catiwade by the surety of Richard of Brantham, ½ mark. [no plea found]	0	6	8
From Thomas the son of Henry of Brantham and Stephen de *Wytescrede*. [no plea found]	0	6	8
From Roger de *Poselingwrth*[5] because he did not come, ½ mark. [no plea found]	0	6	8
From Alan of Cowlinge for disseisin, ½ mark. [no plea found]	0	6	8
From Henry Busy for the same, ½ mark. [no plea found]	0	6	8
From Benedict of Bury St Edmunds and John his son for an unjust detention, ½ mark. [no plea found]	0	6	8

1　There is a Peter Cook as a surety in this plea, not from *Ulenden* but from Coddenham. The only other occasion in this roll where a Peter Cook is a surety is in 289, but that is not for somebody who had not shown or prosecuted. I suspect the clerk has made a mistake here because the amercement for 289 is in 1644 and Peter Cook de *Hulenden* is shown as being amerced there.

2　No plea found for this person but I think it may be 1123 as there is a John *de Fome* who is the person who did not prosecute and his sureties are certainly the ones present in the next amercement.

3　In the plea William is shown as coming from Reedham but here it is Loddon. They are probably the same person but which is correct? I have included them both in the index of people and places under the names shown in the plea and here.

4　In the plea he is shown as being the son of the clerk of Huntingfield.

5　This is possibly Poslingford in Risbridge hundred.

1659.

From the prior of Butley for a false claim, 1 mark. [no plea found]	0	13	4
From John the son of Walter for the same, ½ mark. [no plea found]	0	6	8
From William Franceys for the same, ½ mark. [no plea found]	0	6	8
From Andrew de Pirh' the clerk of Galsey for the same, ½ mark. [no plea found]	0	6	8
From Reynold de *Petr'*, Reynold the son of Ralph, John the son of Ralph, Geoffrey the son of Malerbe because they did not have [----] for whom they stood surety, 10 shillings. [no plea found]	0	10	0
From Ivo le Cava for an unjust detention, ½ mark. [no plea found]	0	6	8
From[1] Ralph Rasdiro of the same for the same, 20 shillings. [no plea found]	1	0	0
From William the son of Ralph of Bury St Edmunds for the same, ½ mark. [no plea found]	0	6	8
From Henry the son of Simon, Thur' the son of William for the same, ½ mark. [no plea found]	0	6	8
From Guy (Wes-soc[il]) for the same, 10 shillings. [no plea found]	0	10	0
From Joss the son of Richard of Yaxley for a false claim, ½ mark. [no plea found]	0	6	8

From Matilda of Freston for the same, ½ mark. [no plea found]	0	6	8
From Alan de *Mustere* for an unjust detention, ½ mark. [no plea found]	0	6	8
From Adam of Thetford for the same, ½ mark. [no plea found]	0	6	8
From Benedict King for the same, ½ mark. [no plea found]	0	6	8

1   From this point to the end of the membrane, apart from the last two entries, the clerk enters two amercements per line.

Sum Total 54 marks 10 shillings[1]

1   The amount calculated from the individual amounts found by the editor is as shown under the £ s. d. column below, whereas the amount given by the clerk on the membrane, as shown here, is calculated as £36 10s. 0d., which means there is a difference of 3s. 4d.

	Total	36	13	4

Agreements

Membrane 61

SUFFOLK

1660.

From Jordan Bunewastel for licence to agree with William Wyot, 1 mark by the surety of Stephen of Brockdish and Richard Berd. [107]	0	13	4
From Ernald de Munteny for licence to agree with Stephen of Brockdish concerning a plea of land, ½ mark by the surety of Roger of Boyland. [115]	0	6	8
From the abbot of Battle for licence to agree with Adam the Fleming concerning a plea of utrum, ½ mark by the surety of the same Adam. [120]	0	6	8
From William Garnoyse for licence to agree with John of Stradbroke concerning a plea of land, 2½ marks by the surety of Alexander of Chippenhall and Hubert of (Horam[i]). [122]	1	13	4
From John of Stradbroke for licence to agree with the same William of the same, 2½ marks by the surety of Adam of Bedingfield and Geoffrey of Barham. [123]	1	13	4
From Robert de Boys of Carlton for licence to agree with Roger the son of Thomas, ½ mark by surety of the same Roger. [126]	0	6	8
From Henry the son of William for licence to agree with the same Roger concerning a plea of land, ½ mark by the surety of Robert de Bosco. [127]	0	6	8
From the abbot of Bury St Edmunds for licence to agree with Theobald of Leiston concerning a plea of land, 1 mark. [140]	0	13	4
From Theobald of Leiston for licence to agree with the same abbot concerning the same, 1 mark by the surety of Philip of Freston. [141]	0	13	4
From the prior of Ely for licence to agree with Walter of Hatfield concerning a plea of land, 2 marks by the surety of Mathew Christian. [142]	1	6	8
From Alan of Withersdale for licence to agree with Roger of Shotford concerning a plea of the grand assize, 5 marks by the surety of Herbert de Alicon.[1] [145]	3	6	8

From William of Gislingham for licence to agree with Thomas le Buck concerning a plea of land, 1 mark by the surety of Sampson of Battisford. [157]	13	4
From Roger Bosse who withdrew himself [from the plea] against Roger the son of Bartholomew of Calthorpe concerning a plea of land, ½ mark by the surety of Roger of Calthorpe. [165]	0 6	8
From Thomas of Risby for licence to agree with Giles de Munpincon concerning a plea of trespass, 1 mark by the surety of the same Giles. [169]	0 13	4
From James of Playford for having a jury between himself and the prior of Eye concerning a plea of messuage and land, 20 shillings. [182]	1 0	0
From the prior of Eye for an unjust detention against Robert of Boyton. 1 mark. [182]	0 13	4
From William Grim for the appeal of Stephen of Reedham, 10 marks by the surety of William of Reedham and Robert of Stokesby. [192]	6 13	4
From Alpesia who was the wife of William the son of Theobald for licence to agree with the abbot of Leiston concerning a plea of land, ½ mark by the surety of the abbot. [202 and 288]	0 6	8
From the prior of Bricett for having a mention of a year and a day of Henry the old king between himself and Brian the son of Anselm, ½ mark. [146]	0 6	8
From the same Brian for licence to agree with the same prior concerning a grand assize, 10 shillings by the surety of the same prior. [146]	0 10	0

¹ In the plea Robert de Bosco is also shown as a surety.

1661.

From the prior of Bricett for licence to agree with the same Brian concerning the same, 10 shillings by the surety of the same Brian. [146]	0 10	0
From Robert the son of Reynold for a false claim against Oliver the son of Drogo, ½ mark by the surety of Robert of Bocking. [150]	0 6	8
From William Schec for having a jury of 24 to convict the 12 [original jurors], 40 shillings by the surety of William de Auberville and John the son of Robert of Ubbeston. [210, 776]	2 0	0
From Roger the son of Robert of Dereham for the same, 20 shillings by the surety of Nicholas of Lynn and Thomas of Grimston. [211]	1 0	0
From Thomas of Grimston for the same, 20 shillings by the surety of Adam of Rockland and Roger of Boyland. [212]	1 0	0
From Geoffrey le Despencer for a false appeal against John de Bosco, 1 mark by the surety of Walter of Ingham. [213]	0 13	4
From Baldwin de Freville because he did not prosecute against Alan Nodel and others, 1 mark by the surety of Thomas of Ingoldisthorpe. [215]	0 13	4
From Walter Craske for licence to agree with Thomas le Latimer, ½ mark by the surety of Simon le Daveys. [220]	0 6	8
From Peter of Burgate for licence to agree with Thomas of Gedding, 10 shillings by the surety of Adam of Tivetshall.¹ [227]	0 10	0

From Thomas of Gedding for licence to agree with the same Peter concerning the same, 10 shillings by the surety of the same Peter. [228]	0	10	0
From Geoffrey le Parker[2] for licence to agree with Theobald of Leiston concerning a plea of land, 40 shillings by the surety of Theobald of Leiston. [229]	2	0	0
From Peter of Pickenham for licence to agree with Simon the son of Ernald, ½ mark by the surety of the same Simon. [235]	0	6	8
From Roger of Carlton and his allies for disseisin against William of Cotton and Joan his wife, 40 shillings by the surety of Herbert [de] Alicon and Ralph le Bigot uncle of earl Roger Bigot. [236]	2	0	0
From William Malerbe for licence to agree with Ranulf of Cringleford, 1 mark by the surety of the same Ranulf. [241]	0	13	4
From the same Ranulf for licence to agree with the same William concerning the same, 1 mark by the surety of the same William. [242]	0	13	4
From William of Darsham for licence to agree with Robert Snow,[3] 20 shillings by the surety of William the son of Simon of Hempnall. [243]	1	0	0
From Richard Cayphas[4] for having a jury of 24 to convict the 12 [original jurors], 40 shillings. [244]	2	0	0
From Alexander the son of Susanna[5] for licence to agree with Susanna his mother, ½ mark by the surety of John de Brook of Beeston. [253]	0	6	8
From Robert de Grimilies for licence to agree with William the Breton, 100 shillings by the surety of Simon de Pierpont and William de Auberville. [264]	5	0	0
From Henry of Henstead for licence to agree with Richer of Cawston, ½ mark by the surety of Richer of Cawston. [267]	0	6	8

1 In the plea there is another surety named John Talchot.
2 In the plea he is shown as Godfrey Parker.
3 In the plea Robert Snow is also shown as a surety.
4 In the plea he is shown as Richard Ciaphas, so it is possible that the clerk made a transcription error here or in the plea.
5 In the plea he is shown as 'the son of Swaine'.

1662.

From Roger of Ketteringham for licence to agree with John le Bret, ½ mark by the surety of John himself and William Malerbe. [271]	0	6	8
From[1] Robert Byl for having an inquest between himself and John of Waxham, 40 shillings. [273]	2	0	0
From Richard the parson of Martlesham for licence to agree with Robert de Aguillon. 1 mark. [296]	0	13	4
From William le Rus for licence to agree with Gundreda who was the wife of Edmund of Tuddenham, ½ mark by the surety[2] ... [298]	0	6	8
From Thomas le Primur for licence to agree with Thomas le Latimer,[3] ½ mark by the surety of William de *Rothenhal'*. [299]	0	6	8
From John the son of Walter of Stonham for licence to agree with Hugh Wastinel, ½ mark by the surety of Hugh. [308]	0	6	8
From William Esturmy for disseisin against Richard the Fleming, ½ mark by the surety of Roger Esturmy. [310]	0	6	8

From Thomas Halharing for having a jury between himself and the prior of Weybourne, 1 mark by the surety of Thomas Jeremy. [332]	0	13	4
From the prior of Weybourne for the same against the same, 1 mark by the surety of William of Loose. [332]	0	13	4
From Henry of Cuddington for licence to agree with William the son of Hardwin, 1 mark by the surety of Robert of Cuddington and Abraham the son of Godfrey. [336]	0	13	4
From Hubert of Braiseworth for licence to agree with Edmund of Sotterley, 20 shillings by the surety of William of Cotton. [338]	1	0	0
From Nicholas the parson of the church of Raydon for a false claim against William Lotun and others concerning a plea of utrum, ½ mark by the surety of Gilbert de Burcheye of Belstead. [343]	0	6	8
From Simon of Gorleston for licence to agree with Stephen the son of Roger, ½ mark by the surety of Roger Petbru' of Yarmouth. [351]	0	6	8
From Agnes de *Bruniford* for licence to agree with John of Brantham, ½ mark by the surety of Alan de *Bruniford*. [353]	0	6	8
From Peter of Gisleham for licence to agree with Alan the son of Roger concerning a plea of land, ½ mark by the surety of Geoffrey de Biskel'. [360]	0	6	8
From Thomas le Gosewold (for licence to agree[r]) with Robert the son of William concerning a plea of land, 10 shillings by the surety of Peter the son of William. [386]	0	10	0
From Robert the son of William for the same with the same Thomas, 10 shillings by the surety of the same Thomas. [386]	0	10	0
From William and Herbert parsons of the church of Pakefield for a false claim against Richard of Chediston and others, ½ mark by the surety of William de *Rothenhal'*. [395]	0	6	8
From William of Kerdiston for licence to agree with Roger of Kerdiston, 1 mark by the surety of Roger of Boyland. [402]	0	13	4
From Hamo Chevere for licence to agree with Arnulf de Munteny concerning a plea of land, 5 marks by the surety of Arnulf himself. [415]	3	6	8
From Walter Freschese' for licence to agree with Henry the son of Hugh, ½ mark by the surety of William of Onehouse and Sampson of Battisford. [417]	0	6	8
From John of Waxham for the same with Robert Byl, ½ mark by the surety of the knight Walter of Ingham. [273]	0	6	8

¹ There are marks from *De* at the start of the agreement details. These may have been a couple of slips of the pen.
² The sureties are not shown here or in the plea.
³ In the plea he is shown as Hugh le Lamer but this is the correct agreement.

Total	**59**	**0**	**0**

Membrane 61d

1663.

From Richard Puleyn for licence to agree with Baldwin Rede, ½ mark by the surety of Richard Angod'. [369]	0	6	8
From William Bullok for the same with Richard of Brantham, 1 mark by the surety of Richard of Tuddenham. [370]	0	13	4

From Robert Hovel for the same with Walter of Westhorpe,[1] 20 shillings by the surety of Ralph de Arderne. [**419**]	1	0	0
From Roger of Sproughton for the same with Geoffrey de Bosco, ½ mark by the surety of the said Geoffrey. [**436**]	0	6	8
From Beatrice de Rubrok for the same with Roger the son of Henry, ½ mark by the surety of Geoffrey Carbunel. [**443**]	0	6	8
From William le Rus for having a good jury between himself and his men, forty shillings by the surety of William de Stuteville. [**448**]	2	0	0
From Roger le Breton for having a mention[2] of a year and a day between himself and Katelina the daughter of William le Waleys, ½ mark by the surety of John of Stanton. [**450**]	0	6	8
From Reynold de Stanho for licence to agree with William Dionis', ½ mark by the surety of the same William. [**451**]	0	6	8
From William de Gosevaude because he did not prosecute, 10 shillings by the surety of Roger le Breton. [**454**]	0	10	0
From Roger de Cresse for licence to agree with William de Stuteville, 40 shillings. [**460**]	2	0	0
From the same William for the same with the same, 40 shillings. [**460**]	2	0	0
From Robert de Frenay for the same with Basilia Potekin, ½ mark by the surety of Robert de *Burnaville*. [**468**]	0	6	8
From the same Basilia for the same with the same, ½ mark by the surety of Robert de Frenay. [**468**]	0	6	8
From John the son of Robert of Metfield for the same with Gilbert of Mendham, ½ mark by the surety of William the son of Thomas of Metfield. [**472**]	0	6	8
From Thomas the son of Roger of Naughton and Humphrey the son of Osbert for the same with William Talebot concerning a plea of naifty, 10 shillings by the surety of Roger de Aldeham. [**483**]	0	10	0
From William de Auberville for having a jury between himself and William Russel concerning the warren of Farnham, 5 marks by the surety of Herbert Alicun. [**486**]	3	6	8
From the prior of Weybourne for licence to agree with Richard de Grey, ½ mark by the surety of Robert de Thwibot. [**489**]	0	6	8
From Loretta of Gedding and Wyniesia Visdelu for the same with William le Rus, 1 mark by the surety of William. [**491**]	0	13	4
From Adam de *Heringfeud*[3] for the same with Robert Weinpin, ½ mark by the surety of William of Mettingham. [**494**]	0	6	8
From Hamo of Felsham for the same with Adam the son of Walter, 1 mark by the surety of Herbert de Alencon. [**498**]	0	13	4
From the same Adam for the same concerning the same, 1 mark by the surety of the same Hamo. [**499**]	0	13	4

[1] The clerk has made a mistake here or in the plea, because in the plea Walter was the brother of Roger of Westhorpe who had died seised and it should be Roger's name shown here.
[2] In the plea it is shown as an *inquisitione* for an inquest or inquiry rather than a *mencione*.
[3] In the plea he is shown as Adam of Herringfleet, which is almost certainly correct.

1664.

From Roger de Cressi for the same with Robert of Boyton, 2 marks. [**508**]	1	6	8

From Gilbert Mance for the same with Hubert the carpenter, ½ mark by the surety of the same Hubert. [512]	0	6	8
From Thomas Russel for the same with Richard Picot, 1 mark by the surety of the same Richard Picot. [530]	0	13	4
From the same Richard for the same with the same, ½ mark by the surety of Hugh Burt. [530]	0	6	8
From Robert the son of Adam of Worlingham[1] for the same with Basilia Red, ½ mark by the surety of William de Childerhus. [531]	0	6	8
From Ranulf Halidey for having a jury of 24 [to convict the 12 original jurors] etc, 40 shillings by the surety of William the son of Robert of Helmingham, Geoffrey of Bocking and Adam Bulloc and Thomas de Hilde. [534]	2	0	0
From Geoffrey of Brockdish for a false claim, ½ mark by the surety of Hugh Burd. [535]	0	6	8
From the dean of Claydon for licence to agree with Adam the son of Matilda, 1 mark by the surety of Roger de *Brunton*. [543]	0	13	4
From William Herthenbaud for the same with Richard the brother of Adam,[2] ½ mark by the surety of the same Richard. [544]	0	6	8
From John le Pacher for a false claim, ½ mark by the surety of Herbert Alicun. [551]	0	6	8
(*Ely*) From Roger[3] of Carlton for licence to agree with Richard the son of Walter, ½ mark by the surety of Richard Herchenbaud. [552]	0	6	8
From Geoffrey of Titsey because he did not prosecute against Gervase of Bradfield and others, 10 shillings by the surety of Ernulf of Kettleburgh. [553]	0	10	0
From Ralph [de] Iuvene for licence to agree with Henry de Agnell, 1 mark by the surety of Herbert Alicun. [559]	0	13	4
From William Hacun for having a jury between himself and the prior of Snape, ½ mark by the surety of Ralph Swan. [560]	0	6	8
From Richard de Ribos for disseisin, ½ mark. [574]	0	6	8
From John of Culpho for licence to agree with John of Tuddenham, ½ mark by the surety of the same John. [581]	0	6	8
From Robert the parson of Soham for the same with Godfrey of Brundish, ½ mark by the surety of the same Godfrey. [584]	0	6	8
From the abbot of St Osyth for the same with Richard of Tuddenham, ½ mark by the surety of the same Richard. [585]	0	6	8
From Warren of Bassingbourne and Geoffrey of Swaffham for the same with Robert of Hereford, 20 shillings. [586]	1	0	0
From John le Bracur for the same with Hugh the son of Robert, ½ mark by the surety of Hugh the son of Robert. [593]	0	6	8
From Stephen of Loudham for the same with Edward Wephege, 10 shillings by the surety of William of Holbrook. [604]	0	10	0

[1] In the plea this is shown as Worlingworth in Hoxne hundred. Worlingham is in Wangford hundred.

[2] In **544** Richard is shown as the brother of Roger the son of Adam, so I think the clerk has made a mistake here. The chirograph gives his name as Richard the son of Adam.

[3] In the plea this is Reynold, not Roger.

Total	**29**	**0**	**0**

Membrane 62

AMERCEMENTS OF THE ASSIZE[1]

> [1] This is the last membrane. Immediately preceding the civil assize pleas for Dunwich are the amercements for the Dunwich 'Pleas of the Crown' – hence the gap in the numbering. There is also a different clerk who has written the amercement section of this roll for Dunwich.

1666.

From Philip the son of Adam and Robert the son of Richard de Brook   0   6   8
by the surety of Edmund the son Austin,[1] ½ mark. **[1151]**
(*-aynes*[il, e]) From Austin Calkin as a fine for licence to agree,[2] ½ mark   0   6   8
by the surety of William of Mettingham. **[1153]**
(*Blithing'*) From John the son of Hamo for licence to agree with   0   6   8
Richard of Elmham, ½ mark by the surety of Robert de Bosco. **[1160]**

> [1] Edmund is shown as the plaintiff in the plea and the other two are his sureties for prosecuting.
> [2] Normally the agreement section would provide the name of the person who the agreement is with, in this case the prioress of Bungay.

Total   1   0   0

Total for all amercements and agreements from the civil pleas[1]   224   6   8

> [1] This is the sum total of all the individual amounts in the £ s. d. columns for the civil plea amercements and agreements as identified in membranes 59–62.

GLOSSARY

advowson: the right of presentation of an incumbent to a benefice or living.

amercement: money penalty due from a person who is in the king's mercy because of an offence. Shown as 'in mercy' in the pleas.

assize: the court and legal procedures which upheld the law and the justices who administered the four petty assizes.

attaint: the process of providing a jury of twenty-four to pronounce on the correctness of the first verdict, usually in an assize.

chirograph: written evidence of a legal agreement, a separate copy of which is kept by both parties and a further copy kept in the Exchequer.

co-parcener: one who shares equally with others in the inheritance of the estate of a common ancestor.

court Christian: ecclesiastical court in which canon law is applied.

darrein presentment: petty assize held to establish who presented the last incumbent of a benefice.

detinue: unlawful detention of a chattel or charter belonging to another person.

disseise: to remove someone by force and without a judgement from the seisin of their property.

distrain: to force a person by the seizure of a chattel and/or lands to perform some legal obligation or order of the court.

dower: the land to which a woman is entitled on the death of her husband according to feudal custom, amounting to one third of his land.

enfeoffed: put in the possession of the fee-simple of lands, tenements etc.

escheat: an incident of feudal law, whereby a fief reverts to the lord when the tenant dies seised without heir or is outlawed.

estovers: necessaries allowed by law, notably wood for repairs allowed to a tenant from off the landlord's estate.

essoin: to offer an allowable excuse on behalf of a person summoned to appear in court.

estreat: a true copy of the fines, amercements etc levied by the eyre court, which is subsequently sent to the Exchequer which would send details of those items to be collected to the sheriff of the county.

merchet: a fine paid by a bondsman to his overlord for liberty to give his daughter in marriage.

moiety: one of two (or more) parts into which something is divided.

mort d'ancestor: petty assize held to ensure that the rightful heir to a fief can obtain the fief if it had been possessed by another on the death of an ancestor.

murdrum: fine payable where proof of Englishry was necessary and a person had been killed whose Englishry had not been proved.

naifty: legal action concerning a claimant's right to have his naif, or villein, delivered to him by the sheriff.

novel disseisin: petty assize held to allow the speedy recovery of the seisin of a landholding or property.

on the country: plaintiff or defendant agree the matter in question is put to a jury.

purparty: a share in an inheritance.

quitclaim: a formal renunciation of a claim to an estate.

replevin: a legal action to restore goods or land distrained or taken from a person upon his giving security to have the matter tried in a court and to return it if the case is decided against him.

seisin: the exercise and enjoyment of rights of feudal possession, usually of land held as freehold, but not as leasehold or of a servile tenure.

serjeanty: a form of feudal tenure on condition of rendering some specified personal service to a lord.

utrum: petty assize held to determine whether land is lay or ecclesiastical.

villeinage: land held by villein service which a tenant, free or unfree, holds from a lord.

BIBLIOGRAPHY

ABBREVIATIONS

In addition to the following abbreviations, those used for the identification of printed primary sources are listed separately below.

Ec Hist Rev	*Economic History Review*
EHR	*English Historical Review*
EPNS	English Place-Name Society
HMSO	Her Majesty's Stationery Office
P&P	*Past and Present*
PRO	Public Record Office, now TNA
SRS	Suffolk Records Society
TCE	*Thirteenth Century England* (Woodbridge)
TNA	The National Archives
TRHS	*Transactions of the Royal Historical Society*
VCH	*Victoria County History: Suffolk*, 2 vols (London, 1911)

MANUSCRIPT SOURCES

The National Archives

Chancery:
C 60 (Fine Rolls)
CP 25(1) (Feet of Fines)
Patent Rolls – Meeking's Notes, in the shoebox in the strong room at TNA, 22 Henry III, C66/48, etc. These notes are Meeking's transcriptions of what is left of the Patent Rolls for 1238–1240 of the possessory assizes and gaol deliveries called during these years and which are shown on the dorse side of the Patent Rolls, but which were left out of the printed Patent Rolls published for the years 1232–1247.

Exchequer:
E159 (King's Remembrancer: Memoranda Rolls)
E163 (King's Remembrancer: Miscellanea of the Exchequer)
E368 (L.T.R. King's Remembrancer: Memoranda Rolls)
E372 (Pipe Rolls)
E401 (Receipt Rolls)

Judicial Records:
CP 40 (Common Bench plea rolls)
JUST1 (Eyre Rolls)

PRINTED PRIMARY SOURCES

Ann. Mon.   *Annales Monastici*, ed. H.R. Luard, 5 vols (Rolls Series, 1864–
1869): vol. i, *The Annals of Tewkesbury Abbey and Burton Abbey*;
vol. ii, *The Annals of Winchester Cathedral Priory and Waverley
Abbey*; vol. iii, *The Annals of Bermondsay Abbey and Dunstable
Priory*; vol. iv, *The Annals of Worcester Priory*

1248 Berkshire Eyre   *The Roll and Writ File of the Berkshire Eyre, 1248*, ed. M.T.
Clanchy, Selden Soc., 90 (1973)

Blythburgh Priory   *Blythburgh Priory Cartulary*, ed. C. Harper-Bill, 2 vols (SRS,
1980)

Book of Fees   *Liber Feodurum. The Book of Fees, commonly called Testa de
Nevill*, 3 vols (HMSO, 1920–1931)

Brevia Placitata   *Brevia Placitata*, ed. G.J. Turner with additions by T.F.T. Plucknett,
Selden Soc., 66 (1951)

Bury Chronicle   *Joceleyn of Brakelond's Chronicle of the Abbey of Bury St Edmunds*,
translated with an introduction and notes by D. Greenway and J.
Sayers (Oxford, 1989)

Bracton   *Bracton on the Laws and Customs of England*, ed. G.E. Wood-
bine, translated with revisions and notes by S.E. Thorne, 4 vols
(Cambridge, Mass., 1968–1977)

Bracton's Note Book   *Bracton's Note Book*, ed. F.W. Maitland, 3 vols (London, 1887)

Cal. Chart. Rolls   *Calendar of Charter Rolls*, 6 vols (HMSO, 1903–)

Cal. Feet of Fines, Suff. *Calendar of Feet of Fines for Suffolk*, ed. Walter Rye (Ipswich,
1900)

Cal. Inq.   *Calendar of Inquisitions 1219–1307*, 3 vols (HMSO, 1916–)

Cal. Inq. Post Mortem   *The Calendar of Inquisitions Post Mortem* (HMSO, 1904–)

Cal. Lib. Rolls   *Calendar of Liberate Rolls* (HMSO, 1916–)

Cal. Pat. Rolls   *Calendar of Patent Rolls* (HMSO, 1906–)

Casus Placitorum   *Casus Placitorum*, ed. W.H. Dunham, Selden Soc., 69 (1952)

Charters Med. Hosp. BSE *Charters of the Medieval Hospitals of Bury St. Edmunds*, ed.
Christopher Harper-Bill (SRS, 1994)

Chronica Majora   *Mattheai Parisiensis, Monachi Sancti Albani, Chronica Majora*,
ed. H.R. Luard, 7 vols (Rolls Series, 1872–1883)

Close Rolls   *Close Rolls, Henry III* (HMSO, 1902–) cited by dates

Curia Regis Rolls   *Curia Regis Rolls of the Reigns of Richard I, John and Henry III
preserved in the Public Record Office*, 20 vols (1922–2006); the
volumes cited are indicated by the years in the volume

DBM   *Documents of the Baronial Movement of Reform and Rebellion,
1258–1267*, ed. R.F. Treharne and I.J. Sanders (London, 1973)

1281 Derbyshire Eyre   *The Rolls of the 1281 Derbyshire Eyre*, ed. Aileen M. Hopkinson
with an introduction by David Crook (Derbyshire Rec. Soc.,
2000)

1238 Devon Eyre   *Crown Pleas of the Devon Eyre of 1238*, ed. H. Summerson, Devon
and Cornwall Record Soc., new series, 28 (1985)

Domesday Book Cambs   *Domesday Book: Cambridgeshire*, ed. Alexander Rumble (Chichester, 1981)

Domesday Book Essex   *Domesday Book: Essex*, ed. Alexander Rumble (Chichester,
1983)

Domesday Book Norfolk   *Domesday Book: Norfolk*, Parts One and Two, ed. Philippa Brown
(Chichester, 1984)

Domesday Book Suffolk   *Domesday Book: Suffolk*, Parts One and Two, ed. Alexander
Rumble (Chichester, 1986)

Early Registers of Writs	*Early Registers of Writs*, ed. Elsa de Haas and G.D.G. Hall, Selden Soc., 87 (1970)
EHD III	*English Historical Documents, 1189–1327*, III, ed. Harry Rothwell (London, 1975)
Eye Priory	*Eye Priory Cartulary and Charters*, ed. Vivien Brown, 2 vols (SRS, 1992, 1994)
Feudal Aids 1284–1431	*Feudal Aids 1284–1431*, 7 vols (HMSO, 1904)
Fleta	*Fleta*, ed. H.G. Richardson and G.O. Sayles, 3 vols (Selden Soc., 1955–)
Flores Historiarum	*Flores Historiarum*, ed. H.R. Luard, 3 vols (HMSO, 1896)
Gesta Regis	*Gesta Regis Henrici Secundi Benedicti Abbatis*, ed. W. Stubbs, 2 vols (Rolls Series, 1867)
Glanvill	*Tractatus de legibus et consuetudinibus regni Anglie qui Glanvilla vocatur*, ed. G.D.G. Hall (London, 1965)
Glouc, War, Staffs Eyre	*Rolls of the Justices in Eyre being the Rolls of Pleas and Assizes for Gloucestershire, Warwickshire and Staffordshire, 1221, 1222*, ed. D.M. Stenton, Selden Soc. 59 (1940)
Guide Contents PRO	*Guide to Contents of the Public Record Office* (HMSO, 1963)
Hoveden	*Chronica de Rogeri de Hoveden*, ed. W. Stubbs, 4 vols (Rolls Series, 1871)
Lay Subsidy Roll 1327	*Lay Subsidy Roll 1327*, ed. S.H.A. Hervey, vol. ii, Suffolk Green Books, IX (Woodbridge, 1906)
Letters Grosseteste	*Letters of Robert Grosseteste*, ed. H.R. Luard (Rolls Series, 1861–1863)
Liberate Rolls	*Calendar of Liberate Rolls: Henry III 1226–1240*, vol. 1 (HMSO, 1916)
Lincs, Worcs Eyre	*Rolls of the Justices in Eyre being the Rolls of Pleas and Assizes for Lincolnshire 1218–9 and Worcestershire 1221*, ed. D.M. Stenton, Selden Soc., 53 (1934)
1244 London Eyre	*The London Eyre of 1244*, ed. H.M. Chew and M. Weinbaum (London Rec. Soc., 1970)
1321 London Eyre	*Year Books of Edward II: The Eyre of London 14 Edward II A.D. 1321*, ed. Helen Cam, 2 vols, Selden Soc., 85–86 (1968)
Mirror of Justices	*The Mirror of Justices*, ed. W.J. Whittaker, Selden Soc., 7 (1895)
Monumenta Juridica	*Monumenta Juridica: The Black Book of The Admiralty*, ed. T. Twiss, 4 vols (Rolls Series, 1871–1876)
Novae Narrationes	*Novae Narrationes*, ed. Elsie Shanks (Selden Soc., 80, 1963)
Pipe Roll 31 Henry I	*Pipe Roll 31 Henry I*, ed. J. Hunter (Record Commission, 1833)
Pipe Roll 26 Henry III	*Great Roll of the Pipe for the 26th Year of the Reign of King Henry III*, ed. H.L. Cannon (Yale, 1918)
Red Book	*Liber Rubeus de Scaccario. The Red Book of the Exchequer*, ed. Hubert Hall, 3 vols (Rolls Series, 1896)
Rot. Litt. Claus.	*Rotuli Litterarum Clausarum 1204–27*, ed. T.D. Hardy, 2 vols (Record Commission, 1833)
St. Richard, Sources	*St. Richard of Chichester: The Sources of his Life*, ed. D. Jones, Sussex Record Soc., 79 (1993)
Sel. Cases King's Bench	*Select Cases in the Court of the King's Bench*, ed. G.O. Sayles, 7 vols (Selden Soc., 1937–)
Sel. Cases Manor. Courts	*Select Cases in Manorial Courts 1250–1550: Property and Family Law*, ed. L.R. Poos and Lloyd Bonfield, Selden Soc., 114 (1998)
Sel. Cases Proc. w/o Writ	*Select Cases of Procedure Without Writ Under Henry III*, ed. H.G. Richardson and G.O. Sayles, Selden Soc., 60 (1941)
Sibton Abbey	*Sibton Abbey Cartularies and Charters*, ed. Philippa Brown, 4 vols (SRS, 1985)

1256 Shropshire Eyre	*The Roll of the Shropshire Eyre 1256*, ed. Alan Harding, Selden Soc., 96 (1981)
Stubbs Select Charters	*Select Charters and other Illustrations of English Constitutional History: From the Earliest Times to the Reign of Edward the First*, ed. William Stubbs, revised by H.W.C. Davis (Oxford, 9th ed., 1951)
1235 Surrey Eyre	*The 1235 Surrey Eyre*, ed. C.A.F. Meekings, 3 vols (Surrey Record Soc., 1979, 1983, 2002)
1263 Surrey Eyre	*The 1263 Surrey Eyre*, ed. Susan Stewart (Surrey Record Soc., 2006)
William of Hoo	*The Letter-Book of William of Hoo, Sacrist of Bury St Edmunds 1280–1294*, ed. Antonia Gransden, SRS, v (Ipswich, 1963)
1249 Wilts Civil Pleas	*Civil Pleas of the Wiltshire Eyre, 1249*, ed. M.T. Clanchy (Wiltshire Record Soc., 1971)
1249 Wilts Crown Pleas	*Crown Pleas of the Wiltshire Eyre 1249*, ed. C.A.F. Meekings (Wiltshire Archaeological and Natural History Soc., Records Branch, 1961)

SECONDARY SOURCES

Arnott, W.G., 1946, *The Place-Names of the Deben Valley Parishes* (Ipswich)

Bailey, Mark, 1998, 'Peasant Welfare in England, 1290–1348', *Ec Hist Rev*, LI, 2, pp.223–251

Bennett, Judith M., 1987, *Women in the Middle English Countryside, Gender and Household in Brigstock before the Plague* (New York)

Beresford, Maurice, 1967, *New Towns of the Middle Ages* (London)

Beresford, Maurice, 1983, *The Lost Villages of England* (Gloucester)

Beresford, Maurice, and Finberg, H.P.R., 1973, *English Medieval Boroughs – a Handlist* (Newton Abbot)

Biancalana, Joseph, 1988a, 'For want of justice: Legal reforms of Henry II', *Columbia Law Review* (April), pp.433–536

Biancalana, Joseph, 1988b, 'Widows at common law: The development of common law dower', *Irish Jurist*, new series, 23, pp.255–329

Bolton, J.L., 1980, *The Medieval English Economy 1150–1500* (London)

Brand, Paul, 1992a, *The Making of the Common Law* (London)

Brand, Paul, 1992b, *The Origins of the English Legal Profession* (Oxford)

Brand, Paul, 2003, *Kings, Barons and Justices* (Cambridge)

Burt, Caroline, 2005, 'The demise of the general eyre in the reign of Edward I', *EHR*, CXX, pp.1–14

Cam, Helen M., 1921, 'Studies in the Hundred Rolls', in *Oxford Studies in Social and Legal History*, ed. P. Vinogradoff, vi (Oxford)

Cam, Helen M., 1930, *The Hundred and the Hundred Rolls* (London)

Cam, Helen M., 1963, *Liberties and Communities in Medieval England* (London)

Carpenter, D.A., 1990, *The Minority of Henry III* (London)

Carpenter, D.A., 1996, *The Reign of Henry III* (London)

Carpenter, D.A., 2003, *The Struggle for Mastery: Britain 1066–1284* (London)

Cheney, C.R., ed., 1996, *Handbook of Dates* (Cambridge)

Chrimes, S.B., 1966, *An Introduction to the Administrative History of Medieval England*, 3rd ed. (Oxford)

Clanchy, M.T., 1993, *From Memory to Written Record*, 2nd ed. (Oxford)

Copinger, W.A., 1904–1907, *Existing Records and other documents being Materials for ... the History of Suffolk*, 6 vols (London)

Copinger, W.A., 1905–11, *The Manors of Suffolk*, 7 vols (Manchester)

Crook, David, 1982a, *Records of the General Eyre* (HMSO)

Crook, David, 1982b, 'The later eyres', *EHR*, XCVII, pp.241–268

Darby, H.C., 1952, *The Domesday Geography of Eastern England* (Cambridge)

Denholm-Young, N., 1963, *Seignorial Administration in England* (London)

Dodwell, Barbara, 1967, 'Holdings and inheritance in medieval East Anglia', *Ec Hist Rev*, 2nd series xx, 1, pp.53–66

Douglas, D.C., 1927, *The Social Structure of Medieval East Anglia* (Oxford)

Dyer, C., 1996, 'Memories of freedom: attitudes towards serfdom in England, 1200–1350', in *Serfdom and Slavery: Studies in legal bondage*, ed. M. Bush (London), pp.277–295

Dyer, C., 1989, *Standards of Living in the Later Middle Ages: Social Change in England, c.1200–1500* (Cambridge)

Dyer, C., 2000, *Everyday Life in Medieval England* (London)

Dyer, C., 2002, *Making a Living in the Middle Ages: The People of Britain 850–1520* (New Haven and London)

Ekwall, E., 1960, *The Concise Oxford Dictionary of English Place Names* (Oxford)

Farrer, W., 1925, *Honors and Knights' Fees*, 3 vols (Manchester and London)

Faulkner, K., 1996, 'The transformation of knighthood in early thirteenth century England', *EHR*, CXI, pp.1–23

Gage, John, 1822, *History and Antiquity of Hengrave in Suffolk* (London)

Gallagher, E.J., 2005, 'An Introduction to and Edition of the Suffolk Eyre Roll 1240 – Civil Pleas', 3 vols (University of London, unpublished PhD thesis)

Green, J., 1986, *The Government of England under Henry I* (Cambridge)

Hanawalt, Barbara A., 1993, 'Remarriage as an option for urban and rural widows in late medieval England', in *Wife and Widow in Medieval England*, ed. S.S. Walker (Ann Arbor), pp.141–164

Harding, Alan, 1973, *The Law Courts of Medieval England* (London)

Harding, Alan, 1993, *England in the Thirteenth Century* (Cambridge)

Harriss, G.L., 1975, *King, Parliament, and Public Finance in Medieval England* (Oxford)

Hatcher, John, 1981, 'English serfdom and villeinage: Towards a reassessment', *P&P*, 90, pp.3–39

Hilton, R.H., 1965, 'Freedom and Villeinage in England', *P&P*, 31, pp.6–10

Hilton, R.H., 1969, *The Decline of Serfdom in Medieval England* (London and Basingstoke)

Holt, J.C., 1992, *Magna Carta*, 2nd ed. (Cambridge)

Howell, C., 1983, *Land, Family and Inheritance in Transition: Kibworth Harcourt, 1280–1700* (Cambridge)

Howell, Margaret, 1998, *Eleanor of Provence: Queenship in Thirteenth Century England* (Oxford)

Hudson, John, 1996, *The Formation of the English Common Law – Law and Society in England From the Norman Conquest to Magna Carta* (Harlow)

Hudson, W., 1901, 'Three manorial extents of the thirteenth century', *Norfolk Archaeology* xiv, pp.1–56

Hunnisett, R.F., 1961, *The Medieval Coroner* (Cambridge)

Hunnisett, R.F., 1977, *Editing Records for Publication* (British Records Association)

Hyams, Paul R., 1980, *Kings, Lords and Peasants in Medieval England: The Common Law of Villeinage in the Twelfth and Thirteenth Centuries* (Oxford)

Keefe, Thomas K., 1983, *Feudal Assessments and the Political Community under Henry II and his Sons* (Berkeley and Los Angeles)

Kitsikopoulos, Harry, 2000, 'Standards of living and capital formation in pre-plague England: a peasant budget model', *Ec Hist Rev*, liii, 2, pp.237–261

Knowles, David, and Hadcock, R. Neville, 1971, *Medieval Religious Houses: England and Wales*, 2nd ed. (Harlow)

Jessel, C., 1998, *The Law of the Manor* (Chichester)

Jones, A., 1979, 'Land measurement in England, 1150–1350', *Agricultural History Review*, xxviii, pp.10–18

Langdon, J., 1986, *Horses, Oxen and Technological Innovation: The Use of Draught Animals in English Farming from 1066–1500* (London)

Lapsley, G., 1935, 'The Court, record and roll of the county in the 13th Century', *Law Quarterly Review*, li, pp.299–325

Latham, R.E., 1965, *Revised Medieval Latin Word List* (London)

Loengard, J.S., 1993, '*Rationabilis Dos*: Magna Carta and the widow's "Fair Share" in the earlier thirteenth century', in *Wife and Widow in Medieval England*, ed. S.S. Walker (Ann Arbor), pp.59–80

McKinley, Richard, 1975, *Norfolk and Suffolk Surnames in the Middle Ages* (London)

Maddicott, J.R., 1984, 'Magna Carta and the local community', *P&P*, 102, pp.25–65

Maddicott, J.R., 1994, *Simon de Montfort* (Cambridge)

Maitland, F.W., 1897, *Domesday Book and Beyond* (Cambridge)

Maitland, F.W., 1898, *Township and Borough* (Cambridge)

Meekings, C.A.F., 1950, 'Six letters concerning the Eyres of 1226–8', *EHR*, LXV, pp.492–504

Meekings, C.A.F., 1956, 'The Rutland Eyre of 1253 – a correction', *EHR*, LXXI, pp.615–618

Meekings, C.A.F., 1957a, 'Roger of Whitchester (†1258)', *Archaeologia Aeliana*, 4th series, xxxv, pp.100–128

Meekings, C.A.F., 1957b, 'More about Robert Carpenter of Hareslade', *EHR*, LXXII, pp.260–269

Meekings, C.A.F., 1957c, 'The Pipe Roll Order of 12 February 1270', in *Studies presented to Sir Hilary Jenkinson*, ed. J. Conway Davies (Oxford), pp.222–253

Meekings, C.A.F., 1981, *Studies in 13th Century Justice and Administration* (London)

Miller, E., 1951, *The Abbey and Bishopric of Ely* (Cambridge)

Miller, E., 1964, 'The English economy in the thirteenth century: implications of recent research', *P&P*, 28, pp.21–40

Miller, E., and Hatcher, J., 1978, *Medieval England, Rural Society and Economic Change 1086–1348* (London)

Mills, A. D., 1998, *The Oxford Dictionary of English Place Names*, 2nd ed. (Oxford)

Milsom, S.F.C., 1969, *Historical Foundations of the Common Law* (London)

Milsom, S.F.C., 1981, 'Inheritance by women in the twelfth and early thirteenth centuries', in *On the Laws and Customs of England*, ed. M. Arnold *et al.* (Chapel Hill, North Carolina), pp.60–89

Morris, Marc, 2005, *The Bigod Earls of Norfolk in the Thirteenth Century* (Woodbridge)

Musson, Anthony, 2004, 'The local administration of justice: A reappraisal of the "Four Knights" system', in *English Government in the Thirteenth Century*, ed. Adrian Jobson (Woodbridge), pp.97–110

Palmer, R.C., 1982, *The County Courts of Medieval England 1150–1350* (Princeton)

Parsons, J.C., 1997, 'The intercessory patronage of Queens Margaret and Isabella of France', *TCE*, vi (Woodbridge), pp.145–156

Pitcairn, Ian, 2000, *The Story of Denham* (Denham Parish Council)

Plucknett, T.F.T., 1948, *A Concise History of Common Law*, 4th ed. (London)

Pollock, Frederick, and Maitland, Frederic William, 1968, *The History of English Law*, 2 vols, 2nd ed. (Cambridge)

Poole, Austin Lane, 1946, *Obligations of Society in the XII and XIII Centuries* (Oxford)

Postan, M.M., 1937, 'The chronology of labour services', *TRHS*, 4th series, xx, pp.169–193

Postan, M.M., 1973, *Essays on Medieval Agriculture and General Problems of the Medieval Economy* (Cambridge)

Postan, M.M., 1975, *The Medieval Economy and Society* (Harmondsworth)

Power, Eileen, 1975, *Medieval Women*, ed. M.M. Postan (Cambridge)

Powicke, F.M., 1947, *King Henry III and the Lord Edward*, 2 vols (Oxford)

Powicke, F.M., 1953, *The Thirteenth Century* (Oxford)

Pugh, Ralph B., 1968, *Imprisonment in Medieval England* (Cambridge)

Quick, J., 1986, 'The number and distribution of knights in thirteenth century England: The evidence of the grand assize lists', *TCE* i, ed. P.R. Coss and S.D. Lloyd (Woodbridge), pp.114–123

Raimes, A.L.1937–1939, 'The family of Raymes of Wherstead in Suffolk', *Proceedings of the Suffolk Institute of Archaeology and Natural History* xxiii, pp.89–115

Razi, Zvi, and Smith, Richard M., 1996, 'The origins of the English manorial rolls as a written record', in *Medieval Society and the Manor Court*, ed. Zvi Razi and Richard M. Smith (Oxford), pp.60–67

Reaney, P.H., 1997, *A Dictionary of English Surnames*, 3rd ed. revised by R.M. Wilson (Oxford)

Reedy, W.T., 1966, 'The origins of the General Eyre in the reign of Henry I', *Speculum*, xli, pp.688–721

Ridgeway, H., 1988, 'King Henry III and the aliens, 1236–72', *TCE*, ii (Woodbridge), pp.81–92

Rigby, S.H., 1995, *English Society in the Later Middle Ages: Class, Status and Gender* (London)

Shakar, Shulamith, 2003, *The Fourth Estate: The History of Women in the Middle Ages* (London)

Smith, R.M., 1986, 'Women's property rights under customary law: some developments in the thirteenth century', *TRHS*, 5th series, pp.165–194

Stacey, Robert, 1987, *Politics, Policy and Finance under Henry III, 1216–1245* (Oxford)

Stamp, L. Dudley, 1941, *The Lands of Britain, Parts 72–73, Suffolk (East and West)* (London)

Stenton, Doris M., 1965, 'King John and the courts of justice', in *English Justice between the Norman Conquest and the Great Charter* (London), pp.88–115

Stenton, Doris M., 1965, *English Justice between the Norman Conquest and the Great Charter* (London)

Summerson, H.R.T., 1979, 'The structure of law enforcement in thirteenth century England', *American Journal of Legal History*, xxiii, pp.313–327

Sutherland, D.W., 1963, *Quo Warranto Proceedings in the Reign of Edward I 1278–1294* (Oxford)

Sutherland, D.W., 1973, *The Assize of Novel Disseisin* (Oxford)

Sweet, Henry, 1973, *The Students Dictionary of Anglo-Saxon* (Oxford)

Tait, James, 1936, *The Medieval English Borough* (Manchester)

Thomas, H.M., 1993, *Vassals, Heiresses, Crusaders and Thugs: The Gentry of Angevin Yorkshire* (Philadelphia)

Titow, J.Z., 1969, *English Rural Society* (London)

Treharne, R.F., 1971, *The Baronial Plan of Reform* (Manchester, reprinted with additional material)

Turner, Ralph V., 1985, *The English Judiciary in the Age of Glanvill and Bracton c.1176–1239* (Cambridge)

Turner, Ralph V., 1988, *Men Raised from the Dust – Administrative Service and Upward Mobility in Angevin England* (Philadelphia)

Turner, Ralph V., 1994, *Judges, Administrators and the Common Law in Angevin England* (London)

Van Caenegem, R.C., 1959, *Royal Writs in England from the Conquest to Glanvill*, Selden Soc., 77 (London)

Van Caenegem, R.C., 1973, *The Birth of the English Common Law* (Cambridge)

Vincent, N.C., 1996, *Peter des Roches: An Alien in English Politics 1205–1238* (Cambridge)

Vinogradoff, Paul, 1892, *Villeinage in England* (Oxford)

Walker, S.S., 1993, 'Litigation as personal quest: Suing for dower in the royal courts, circa 1272–1350', in *Wife and Widow in Medieval England*, ed. S.S. Walker (Ann Arbor), pp.81–108

Ward, Jennifer C., 1992, *English Noblewomen in the Later Middle Ages* (London)

Ward, Jennifer C., 2002, *Women in Medieval Europe 1200–1500* (London)

Warner, Peter, 1996, *The Origins of Suffolk* (Manchester)

Warren, W.L., 1973, *Henry II* (London)

Warren, W.L., 1987, *The Governance of Norman and Angevin England 1086–1272* (London)

Watts, Victor, ed., 2004, *The Cambridge Dictionary of English Place-Names* (Cambridge)

Waugh, Scott L., 1983, 'Reluctant knights and jurors: Respites, exemptions and public obligations in the reign of Henry III', *Speculum*, lviii, pp.937–986

Waugh, Scott L., 1988, *The Lordship of England: Royal Wardships and Marriages in English Society and Politics 1217–1327* (Princeton)

Wilkinson, L.J., 1999, 'Thirteenth-century women in Lincolnshire' (University of London, unpublished PhD thesis)

Williamson, J., 1984, 'The peasant land market in Norfolk in the thirteenth century', in *The Peasant Land Market in Medieval England*, ed. P.D.A. Harvey (Oxford), pp.30–105

Youngs Jr., Frederic A., 1979, *Guide to the Local Administrative Units of England*, 1. *Southern England* (London)

Youngs Jr., Frederic A., 1991, *Guide to the Local Administrative Units of England*, 2. *Northern England* (London)

INDEX OF PEOPLE AND PLACES

Numbers in Roman numerals and in *italic* refer to pages in the introduction. Other numbers refer to entries in the translated text. Capital letters refer to the appendices to the introduction and are also in *italic*. Names like 'Robert son of John' are indexed under 'John'. A possible modern English name is sometimes shown within square brackets if known.

* signifies that the person in the plea was dead at the time of the eyre in April 1240, or had seisin of the land in question at some time in the past. Compound names are generally listed under both and cross-referenced.

Places are given the hundred (h) in which they are located. Unidentified places are italicised. For hundreds see index of selected subjects. For counties in foreign pleas, see Appendix F(iii) on p.lxxvii.

Abberton Abeton', Winstree h, Essex: Benedict, parson of, master, 521
Acr': Alice wife of William de, 19
Acton, Aketon', Babergh h: 698, 812, 1110:
 Benedict of, 905
 Benedict, parson of, master, 968
Adam: Alice daughter of, 1043
 Alice wife of John son of, 303
 Christine wife of John son of, 952
 Constance daughter of Ralph son of, 1111
 Erald son of, 795
 Geoffrey son of, 1048
 John son of, *xlv*; 303, 1006
 Nicholas son of, 674
 Ralph* son of, 1111
 Richard son of, 544, 1048, 1664
 Robert son of, juror, 265, 310, 1048
 Roger son of, 354, 544*, 899
 Rose wife of William son of, 563
 Thomas son of, 479
 Wife of, 518
 William son of, 1, 83, 563, 654, 795, 918
Aenton: Geoffrey* de, 1057
 Maria* wife of Geoffrey de, 1057
Aeremund: Ralph, attorney, 254
Ages: William de, knight, juror, 144, 149
Agius: Henry de, son of Thomas de, 771
 Ralph de, master, 771,
Agnell: Henry de, 559, 1664
 Robert* de, 559
Agnes: Agnes mother of Thomas son of, 1126
 Hubert son of, *xlvii*; 1108
 Thomas son of, 1126
Aguillon, Aguyliun, Aquiliun, Auguliun, Augulyun:
 Robert, 156, 255, 573, 1009
 Robert de, 296, 488, 1662
Aildith: William son of, 1014
Ailgar, Algar': Thomas 794, 795, 1655
Ailwarton: Richard son of Robert de, 789

Robert de, 935
Ailwode: *see* Aldewood
Ais, Ays: *see* Ash
Akeman: Grecia wife of Richard, 828
 Richard, attorney, 828
Akethorpe, Akethorc, Lothingland h: John brother of Stephen of, 61
 Richard of, 61
 Stephen of, 61
Aketon': *see* Acton
Alan: Alan son of, 381
 Bartholomew son of, 374, 1647
 Brian son of, *xxxii*, *li*; 70, 708, 797
 John son of, 395
 Matilda daughter of, 398
 Robert son of, 393
 Roger brother of Simon son of, 311
 Simon son of, 311
 Thomas brother of Bartholomew son of, 374
 William son of, 894
Albanico, Albunico [Aubeney, Aubigny]: Hugh de, earl of Arundel, *lin*, *H(iii)*; 30, 755
Albo Monasterio: Roger de, 683
Albot: Martin, 741
Alby, Aleby, Haleby, South Erpingham h, Norfolk: Thomas of, 860
 Thomas of, Withersfield, of Withersfield, 837, 855, 1653
Aldaring: *see* Oldherring
Aldeburgh, Aldburg', Audeburc, Plomesgate h: 636; Alice of, 579
Aldeham: *see* Holdman
Aldeyn [Alden]: John son of Osbert, 909
Aldewood, Ailwode, Aldewode: Robert de, attorney, 186, 450
 Saina wife of Robert de (Sarah, Sayna, Selena) 186, 450
Aldham, Audeham, Audham, Cosford h: 1024
 Hugh of, attorney, 1024
 Matilda wife of Herbert of, 833, 1024, 1092

281

John of, knight, juror, 145, 147, 159, 269, 353, 370, 677, 679, 1662
Richard of, 370, 500, 516, 1658, 1663
Thomas son of Henry of, 1658
William le Veutrer of, *see* Veutrer
William of, attorney, 104
Brautton: Roger de, 28
Brende Wenham, Brende Wenham, Samford h: 1127
Brenthalle: Richard de la, 605
Brentewentham, Samford h: 635
Bret: John le, 271, 1662
Bretmar: *see* Brictmer
Breton, Bretun: John the, knight, juror, 774, 1653
Matilda daughter of Hamo the, 1112
Robert* the, 450
Roger de, 454, 1663
Roger the, 450, 1097, 1663
Sabina* wife of Robert the, 450
William, of Bardwell, 815
William the, 264, 959, 1661
Brettenham Bretenham, Brethenham, Cosford h: 1105
John of, 1035
Brewer, Bruiwer': Edward de la, 1043
Brian: Hamelin son of, 482
John son of, 301
William son of, 301
Bricett: prior of, 146, 219, 476, 1020, 1660, 1661
Brickendon, Herts: 155
Brictmer, Bretmar: Gerard, 348
Richard son of, 448
Bricun: Agnes daughter of Ralph, 165
Botild daughter of Ralph, 165
Heloise daughter of Ralph, 165
Brid [Bird?]: Dene, 258
Richard, 794
Briham: Peter de, of Pulham, 1120
Brill: Geoffrey, 741
Brinklow, Brinnkelawe, Warwickshire: Gilbert de, 583
John de, 583
Briseworth', Brisewrth', Brisigwrth', Brysewrth': *see* Braiseworth
Briskele: Geoffrey de, of Frostenden, 1121
Brittany: *xxxv*
Broc: *see* Brook
Brockdish, Brokedis, Brokedish, Brokedys, Earsham h, Norfolk:
Geoffrey of, 535, 1664
Stephen of, 107, 115, 774, 1651, 1660
Brockford, Brocford', Hartismere h: 425
Roger of, 569
Brockley, Broc[kelagh], Risbridge h: 840
Brok: *see* Brook
Brolkendon: William de, 311
Bromeshaft: Philip de, 478
William de, 478
Bromford, Brumford: *see Bruniford*, Agnes de, 250

Brook, Broc, Brok: Geoffrey* de, 1053
Gilbert de, 843, 1653
John de, of Beeston, 253, 1661
Martin de, 741, 1652
Robert son of Richard de, 1151, 1666
William de, in Elmsett, 877, 1655
Broomholm: Bromholm, Tunstead h, Norfolk: prior of, 65, 425, 892, 893*
Browston, Brocston', Broxton, Broxston', Lothingland h: 248, 484, 980
Gilbert of, 1646
Mabel of, 205, 206, 207
Mabel wife of Thomas of, 464
Bruera [Heath]: Agnes de, 434, 538
Roger de la, of Martlesham, 296
Simon de la, of, Martlesham, 296
William de [la], attorney, 434, 538
Bruern, Oxfordshire: abbot of, 53
Bruisyard, Burierd', Buryesgerd', Plomesgate h: 236, 1109
Brumham: William, 375
Brumscrede: Walter de, 417
Brun, Brune [Brown]: Adam, 741
William, 688
Brunchil [Brownhill]: Reynold de, 393
Bruncusaste: Alan, 1642
Brundish, Burnedis, Burundis, Hoxne h: 401
Edmund of, 236
Edmund son of William of, 514
Godfrey of, 584, 1664
Godfrey the Parker of, *see* Parker
Henry of, 1647
Henry son of Selot' of, *see* Selot'
Mundekin de, 1647
Bruniford, Bromford', Brumford', Brunford' [Brownford]:
Agnes de, 269, 353, 406, 1077, 1127, 1662
Agnes wife of William de, *xlivn*; 635
Alan de, 353, 1077, 1662
Alan [son or husband] of Agnes de, attorney, 1127
Cliandus, Clianus son of Olive de, *xlvi*; 200, 527
Geoffrey son of William de, 895
Peter de, *xxxii*, *xlvi*; 1, 527, 1046
Roger de, 198, 446
William* de, 635
Brunman: Beatrice, 16
Brunstanshagh: John de, 509
Brunton: Agnes mother of Edmund de, 328
Natalina wife of Edmund de, 328
Parnell sister of Robert son of Richard de, 314
Robert son of Richard de, 314
Roger de, 275, 284, 285, 543, 1664
Bruse: Walter, attorney, 233
Brysewrth': *see* Braiseworth
Bucellyer [Buckler]: Robert de, 492
Buckenham, Bukenham, Grimshoe, Shropham or Blofield h, Norfolk: 1050
Bucermande: Henry de, 430

Coppinger, Copeng', Copinger: William, of
   Buxhall, 420, 567
Cordebof: John (de), knight, juror, attorney, 146,
   151, 294, 370, 450, 461, 486, 528–530, 532,
   904, 980, 1096, 1133
Cornard, Cornerd, Corenherde, Corenerde [Great
   or Little], Babergh h: 735, 814, 867, 873,
   1036
   Angod son of Richard of, 907
   John* of, 1036
   John son of John of, 735, 869, 1652
   Richard son of Payn of (Pagan), 866
   Walter son of Robert of, 867
Cornard, Great: Magna Corenherde, Babergh h:
   873
Cornhill: Ediwa de, 738
Cornur: Richard le, 682
Cornwall Cornub': foreign pleas from, *F(iii), xix*;
   125, 657
   Richard, earl of, *xviii*; 344
Corston: William de, knight, juror, 1067
Corton, Cortun', Cotton', Lothingland h: 327
   Matilda wife of Nicholas, 1075
   Nicholas of, 1075
   Roger Fullo of, *see* Fullo
   Simon son of Walter of, 1140
   Unnan Sherefod of, *see* Sherefod
Cosford, Corsford, Cosford h: 1147
   Adam of, 992
   Amice of, 992
   Nicholas brother of Adam of, 992
   Sabina daughter of Amice of, 992
Cosinere: John, of Oakley, 564
Costentin: Ismania wife of John, 232
Cote: possibly in Wangford h, 154
Coteman [Cotman]: Thomas, 493
Cotewine [Cotwin]: Geoffrey, 275, 280
Cotinton: Henry de, 17
   Robert de, 17
Cottenham, Chesterton h, Cambs: John of, 795
Cotton, Cottun', Hartismere h: 416, 938, 987
   Adam of, 1658
   Hugh of, juror, *xxx*; 265, 510, 938, 987
   Joan wife of William of, 236, 487, 1109, 1661
   William of, knight, juror, *xxx*; 146, 151, 158,
      236, 338, 370, 450, 487, 510, 533, 861,
      904, 913, 914, 938, 987, 1019, 1067,
      1109, 1656, 1661, 1662
Cove, Blything h: 300, 470
   Robert le, 551
   Walter of, knight, juror, 265, 450, 533, 904,
      913, 914, 980, 1096
Cove, Wangford h: 394
   Hugh* of, 394
   Robert of, 394
Coveneye: Richard de, attorney, 85
Cowlinge, Culing', Culinges, Kulling', Risbridge
   h: 842, 844, 847, 922, 953
   Alan of, 1658
   Henry of, 858
   Humphrey of, 844

Macy of, 826, 827, 922, 1654, 1656
Mathias of, 922
William of Lynn in, *see* Lynn
Crabbe: Agnes wife of Ralph, 523
   Roger [Ralph], attorney, 523
Crammaville, Cramavile, Cramavill', Crammavil',
   Crammavill', Gramanvill': John de, knight,
   juror, 145, 147, 450, 528–530, 532, 758, 977,
   1067, 1134
   Lucy wife of John de, 977
Cransford, Craneford', Cranesford', Plomesgate
   h: 1109
   Richard of, 32, 390, 474
Craske: Walter, 220, 1661
Crasschepanne: Agnes, 899
Cravene [Craven]: Matilda mother of Thomas
   de, 167
   Ranulf* de, 167
   Thomas de, 167
Crawil: John de, knight, recognitor, 679
Creake, Crek, Gallow h, Norfolk: 759
   Bartholomew of, knight, juror, 149, 759
   Thomas of, 782
Creding: Lauretta de, witness, 155
Creeting, Creting', Cretinge, Bosmere h: 162,
   163, 166, 349, 493
   Geoffrey son of Geoffrey of, 1138
   Hervey son of William of, 625, 1650
   Seman son of William of, 625, 1650
Creeting St Peter, Stow h: 223, 244
Crelingham: *see* Cretingham
Crepping, Creppinges, Lexden h, Essex:
   Alice wife of William of, 1021
   Richard of, 450
   William of, 318
Cressinghall: Robert son of Henry de, 214
Cressingland, Mutford h?: 375
Cressunere [Cresner]: Ralph, 758
Cressy, Cresse, Cressi, Cresy: Roger de, *H(iii)*;
   460, 508, 587, 1663, 1664
Cretingham, Crelingham, Loes h: 270, 559, 570,
   571, 588, 590, 771
   Adam of, attorney, 130
   Agnes of, 88, 319, 320, 570, 1008
   Geoffrey Bene of, *see* Bene
   Ivetta wife of Adam of, *xxxivn*; 130
   William le Deveneys of, *see* Deveneys
Crevquor, Calvados, Normandy: Nicholas (de),
   892, 1105
   Robert*, 892
Crew: Nicholas de, 891
Cri-eham: Roger de, 305
Crice [Crick]: John, 275, 281
Crimplesham, Clackclose h, Norfolk: David of,
   777
Cringleford, Cringelford', Humbleyard h,
   Norfolk: *xlii, xliii*; 153, 475, 727, 1038
   Ranulf of, 241, 242, 307, 1661
Cristin, Cristyn: Rainer, 348, 1645
Croh: Edrich*, 1030
   Isabella daughter of Edrich, 1030

Hickling, Hikeling', Hykeling', Ikeling', Happing h, Norfolk: Brian of, knight, juror, 144, 149, 591
Geoffrey of, 245, 1644
John chaplain of, 113
prior of, 203, 557, 578, 932
Raymond of, attorney, 262
Hide, Hyde: Alan* de la, 974
Thomas de la, 974, 1116
Higkebache: Richard de, knight, recognitor, 677
Hikelingham: Richard, attorney, 738
Hiketon: Unknown, 628
Hilborough, Ildeburwrth', South Greenhoe h, Norfolk: 480
Hildere, Hilde: Thomas de, 534, 1664
Hill, Hil', Hel': Harvey de, 998
Margery wife of Harvey de, 998
Ralph del, 909
Robert del, 420
Robert de, of Buxhall, 310, 1645
Robert del, of Thetford, 712
Roger de, attorney, 132
Hilling: Adam de, 155
Hillington, Freebridge h, Norfolk: manor, 759
Hinderclay, Hildercle: Robert of, 1096
Hindley, Hindelee: Joscelin of, attorney, 1088
Hingham, Hengham, Forehoe h, Norfolk: Andrew of, knight, juror, 144, 149, 178, 262, 369, 774, 1114
Geoffrey of, 35
Roger of, 842
Walter of, 167
William of, knight, juror, 144, 159
Hintlesham, Samford h: William Testepin of, *see* Testepin
Hirdel: Robert de, 450
Hirsteston: John de, 794
Hitcham, Hecham, Cosford h: 924, 984, 1073
Harvey son of John of, 912, 1656
Richard son of Alexander of, 831, 1653
Hobland, Habelund, Lothingland h: 248, 980
Hoc [Hook or Hill?]: John son of Lettice de, knight, juror, 1019
Hockham, Hocham, Hockam, Hokham, Shropham h, Norfolk: 1114
Emma of, 72
William of, 931
Wymer of, 931
Hocton: Hawise de, 410
Hodard: Walter, 393
Hodden, Hoddeng: *see* Heddeng
Hoddesdon, Hodeston', Hertford h, Herts: 155, 174
Hodeboville, Hodobovill', Odebovill', Oudebovile, in Acton, Babergh h: John de, knight, juror, *H(iii)*;145, 147, 450, 677, 678, 679, 755, 1036
Hoe, Ho, Launditch h, Norfolk: Gilbert of, knight, juror, 774, 776
Peter* of, 412
Hog [Hogg]: Ralph, of Wattisham, 1137, 1658

Hok [Hook]: Harvey, 556
Holbrook, Holebroc, Holebrok, Holebroke, Samford h: Bullar of, 563
Walkelin of, attorney, 250
William of, serjeant of prior of Ely, 198, 201, 537, 539, 573, 604, 1011, 1132, 1642, 1648, 1651, 1664
Holdham, Aldeham: Roger de, 483, 1663
Holdman: William, 252
Hole: Geoffrey, 224
Holmereshey: William de, 1652
Holy Trinity, Ipswich: prior of, 640, 651
Hone: Albert Pigaz de la, *see* Pigaz
Hoo, Ho, Loes or Wilford h: Robert of, 772
Robert son of William of, 1016
Roger of, 537
Roger son of William of, 611, 1016, 1650
William* of, 1016
Hoppechare: Adam le Pays de, *see* Pays
Hopton, Hoppetun', Blackbourn h: 1104
Hopton, Hopeton', Lothingland h: 453
Avelina, Avel' [Evelyn] wife of Richard of, 110, 324
Hawise of, 5, 249, 453, 825
Mabel sister of Avelina wife of Richard of, 324
Osbert of, 453* [Herbert of?] 484
Richard of, *xxvin*; 27, 110, 324
Walter son of William of, 1142
Walter, justice, rolls of, *xxin*
William son of Bartholomew of, 980
Horham, Hoxne h: Hubert of, 122, 1660
Horkesley, Horkel, Horkeleye, Lexden h, Essex: Matilda wife of Philip of, 478
Philip of, 478, 1648
Hornes, Horneye, Mutford h: Elias of, 37
Horning, Hornigge: William, 667
Horningsea, Flendish h, Cambs: Adam de, 1654
Horringer, [Horningsheath] Horingeshorth', Thingoe h: Alpesia wife of William of, 1020
Amabil wife of John of, 172
Henry son of John of, 172
Horsage, Horshawe: Thomas de, 924, 1656
Horsec: Amice de, 709
Horsey, Orseye, Happing h, Norfolk: Bartholomew of, 213, 1642
Horshangham: Laurence* de, 617
Matilda* wife of Laurence de, 617
Hosier, Hoezur: Geoffrey the, 236
Hospic: Robert de, of Stalham, 1086
Hovel: Robert, knight, 289, 419, 1644, 1663
Roger, attorney, 108, 727
Hoveton, Hovton', Tunstead h, Norfolk: Herbert [Osbert] of, 248, 980
William son of Roger of, 1005
Hoxne, Hoxene, Hoxne h: *A, K*; 290
Hubert: Adam son of, of Bentley, 331, 1644
Mabel daughter of, 767
Robert son of, 44, 411
Thomas son of, 193
Hubeston: *see* Ubbeston

Kirkton, Kirketon', Samford h: 442, 538, 904, 907
John of, 434
Richard chaplain of, 538
Roger of, 442
Kirstead, Kirkestede, Norfolk, Loddon h: 601, 802
Ralph parson of, 11, 802
Kirtling, Kerteling, Cheveley, h, Cambs: Henry of, 782
Knapwell, Cnapewell, Papworth h, Cambs: Sarah of, 795
Knettishall, Cnateshale, Gnateshall', Blackbourn h: Ivo of, 807, 918
Knodishall, Cnodeshal', Blything h: 382, 396, 398
Koke: *see* Cook
Kokerel: *see* Cokerel
Koma: Ralph de, 355, 824
Kumpenye: Henry de, 224
Kunelesfeud': *see* Camelesfeud

L'Isle: Insula: Osbert* ancestor of master Robert de, 908
Ralph de, 21
Richard de, 106
Richard* father of Master Robert de, 908
Robert* ancestor of Master Robert de, 908
Robert de, master, *xxxiiin*; 9, 75, 76, 805, 908, 914
Robert* uncle of Master Robert de, 908
Roger* great uncle of Master Robert de, 908
Lacell: *see* Lascelles
Ladbroke, Lodebroc, Knightlow h, Warwickshire: William* of, 438
Lafham, Cosford h: 830
Lafham, Laffam, Risbridge h: 882, 949
Richard son of Thomas de, 869, 883, 1655
Thomas* de, 883
Lagwode, Langwode [Langwood Fen, Cambs?]: Rainer de, 218, 1642
Lambert: Simon, of Stanningfield, 689, 1652
Lamer: Hugh le, 299
Launde: *see* Londe
Landegeith, Cornwall: *see* Landepar'
Godfrey parson of, 125
Landepar' Cornwall: *see* Landegeith
Godfrey parson of the church of, 105
Landwathe: John, 224
Langdon, Langedon' [Langdon Hills, Barstable h, Essex?]:
Alice wife of Stephen of, 78
Stephen of, 78
Langetoft, Langetot, Longestotf [Stowlangtoft?]:
Matilda de, 792
Richard de, 792, 898, 1094, 1136
Robert son of Richard de, 1094
Langetot: *see* Langetoft
Langham, Blackbourn h: 701, 718
John parson of, 718
Richard son of William of, 330

Langley, Langel', Langeleg', Lodden h, Norfolk: abbot of, *xliii–xliv, liii, liv*; 153, 727, 1038
Langstone, Langeston', Hampshire or Devon: Geoffrey of, 648
Hugh of, 638, 1643
Langwath, Langwode: John de, of Exning, 218, 1642
Lardn[er], Lardn': Reynold, 845
Lascelles, Lacell, Lascell': Thomas de, 37, 39, 255, 488
Latimer: Robert de, 532
Roger le, 395
Thomas [le], knight, juror, 145–147, 151, 158, 220, 258, 525, 528–530, 532, 1661, 1662
Launcs: Christine wife of Walter de, 426
Walter de, 426
Laur': Margery daughter of, 601
Laurence: Geoffrey, of Middelton, 910, 1646
Laurette: Laurett', Geoffrey, recognitor, 365
Laus: Robert de, 556
Lavenham, Laveham, Babergh h: 1027, 1069, 1092
Simon of, 1655
Lawshall, Laushill', Laweshull', Babergh h: 677
Flavian of, 677
Godiva of, 1049
Nicholas of, 1049
Laxfield, Lakafeud, Hoxne h: David of, 2
fine of vill of, *lviin*
Layham, Legham, Legyam, Leiham, Leyam, Cosford h: 829, 940, 962
Matthew of, 160, 758, 765, 1642, 1655
Nicholas of, master, 901
Richard son of Vivian of, 869, 1657
Robert of, knight, juror, 677–679, 829, 904, 962, 1096, 1652
Robert son of Reynold of, 940
William of, 1077
William, brother of Master Nicholas of, 901
Lea: Hubert de, in Haverhill, 849, 1653
Lech: Leye, William de, of Wrentham, 231, 1643
Leffled: Roger son of, 795
Legat: Walter, 231
Legristr: Richard le, 698, 1652
Leicestershire: *ix, xiii*
Leighs, Legh' [Leez]: prior of, 198, 406, 635, 895, 897
Leiston, Leeston', Leyston', Blything h: 266, 398
abbot of, 184, 202, 266, 288, 396, 1660
Aurelia of, 184
Theobald of, 140, 141, 229, 1660, 1661
Lelesheye: see *Teles*
Lenebaud: Roger son of William, 236
Thomas, 236
William, 236
Lenveise, Lenveyse: *see* Enveyse
Leonibus: Walter de, *H(iii)*
Lesnes: abbot of, 263
Letort: Ralph, 305
Lettice: Macelina daughter of the widow, 252,
Ralph son of, of Bradley, 835, 841, 1653

Wephege: *see* Yepheye
Wersted': *see* Wherstead
Wes-soc: Guy, 1659
West Stow: *see* Stow
Westacre, Freebridge h, Norfolk: 871
Westgate: Leveric of, of Thorpe, 624
  Richard of, *H(iii)*
  William son of Leveric of, of Thorpe, 624
Westerfield, Westrefeud, Westrifeud, Claydon h:
  585
  John of, 275, 279
  Ralph dean of, 65
Westhall, Westhal', Blything h: 151, 1055
  Adam son of Geoffrey of, 1055, 1657
  Andrew of, 151
  Geoffrey Gikel of, *see* Gikel
  John son William of, 1055
  Richard Wyard of, *see* Wyard
Westhorpe, Westorp', Hartismere h: 302, 419,
  420
  Roger of, 419, 1663
  Walter* of, 419
Westleton, Westlenon, Westleneton', Blything h:
  370
  Roger of, 823
Westminster, Westm', Westmonasterium: *ix, x*
  adjournments to, *xxix, xxxii, xxxiii, xliii, lii,*
    liii, lxiiin
  agreements at, *xxviii*
  justices on the bench at, *x, xiii, xxii, xxix,*
    lii
  pleas at, *xxxii, xxxiii, xliii, lii*; 889, 1106
Westmoor, Westmor', Brothercross or Gallow h,
  Norfolk: 1074
Weston, Blackbourn h: 1037
  Alexander* of, 1037
  Matilda wife of Alexander of, 1037
Weston, Wangford h, 154
  Geoffrey of, 252
  Ralph of, knight, juror, 146, 450
  William brother of Geoffrey of, 252
Westrefeud, Westrifeud: *see* Westerfield
Westwal': James de, 325
Westwar': Joan de, 325
Westwood: Adam of, 507
  Margery daughter of Adam of, 507
  Seman son of Adam de, 507
Westwood, Westwde: assart in Risbridge h, 856
Wetecroft: *see* Wheatcroft
Wetherden, Weterden, Wetheresden', Stow h:
  lviin; 497, 513, 1119
  Geoffrey of, attorney, 101
  Geoffrey son of Geoffrey of, attorney, 971,
    1657
  Joan of, 497
  Matilda (wife of Sarr' of?), 129
  Sarah Clenchemere of, *see* Clenchemere
Weybourne, Waberrun, Wabebrune, Wabrune,
  Holt h, Norfolk, 332
  prior of, 131, 332, 489, 1662, 1663
  Roland former prior of, 332

Weybread, Weybrede, Wybrede, Hoxne h: 145,
  147, 393, 407, 506, 533
  Beatrice wife of William of, 624
  William of, 624
Weynpin, Weinpin: Gunnild wife of Robert, 494
  Robert, 494, 1663
Whaddon, Waddon, Armingford h, Cambs: 816
Whatfield, Watefeud, Whateford, Cosford h: 731,
  832, 833
  Ailbreda* of, 731
  John son of Ralph of, of Pakenham, 707,
    1095, 1652
  Maria* of, 1095
  Simon of, 191, 226, 717, 731, 754, 1095, 1651
Wheatacre, Wetacrere, Clavering h, Norfolk: 75
Wheatcroft, Qwetecroft, Wetecroft, Lothingland
  h: 248, 980
  Thomas of, 206
Whepstead, Qwepsted', Thingoe h: Thomas of,
  794
Wherstead, Wersted', Samford h: 346, 433, 1079,
  1148
Whimpwell, Wimpewell, Pympewell, Happing h,
  Norfolk: Agatha mother of Thomas of, 694,
  937
  Thomas of, 33, 694, 937, 1029
Whissonsett, Wycangset, Launditch, Norfolk: 921
Whitchester,: Roger of, clerk of William of York,
  xvn, xvi
Whitton, Witenton', Wytton', Claydon h: 275
  William of, 329, 1646
Whitwell, Qwytewell, Eynsford h, Norfolk:
  Richard of, knight, juror, 144, 579
Wibert, Wybert: John son of, 408
  Walter son of, 845
Wicher: Henry, of Sproughton (in Belstead), 427,
  428, 1646
  Henry, 902
  Peter le, 795
Wickham Market, Wycam, Wycham, Wyk',
  Wilford h: 577
  Wilford of, 577
  Godfrey parson of, 577
  Matthew of, attorney, 714
Wicklewood, Wyclewde, Forehoe h, Norfolk: 467
Widow: Avelina the, 252
  Godiva the, 844
  Gunnilde the, 252
  Ida the, 910
  Leticia the, mother of Mascelina 252
  Mascelina the, 252
  Roger son of the, 795
  Saxlena the, 551
Wigge, Wikge: Alice wife of Hugh, 890
  Hugh, 890
  Matilda wife of Ranulf, 1073
  Ranulf, 984, 1073
  Richard, 924
Wiggenhall, Wygenhal', Freebridge h, Norfolk:
  H(iii); 828
  Adam of, 99
  Robert Russell of, *see* Russel

Walter of, 933

Woolverstone, Wlfreston', Wlvreston', Samford
h: 1061
Gerard de Dunton of, *see* Dunton
Isabella of, 1061

Woolvin, Wlvine: Humphrey son of, 348
John son of, 348

Woolward, Wlward:
Robert son of, 867

Wootton, Wodeton', Kinghamford h, Kent: 175
John of, 175

Worcester, Wygorn': Walter, bishop of, 51, 53,
54, 95, 114

Wordwell, Wridewell', Blackbourn h:
William of, 672

Worlingham, Wirlingh', Wangford h: 154
Alice wife of Thomas of, 117
Thomas of, attorney, 117

Worlington, Wridelington', Lackford h: 692, 763

Worlingworth, Wirlingwrth, Wyrlingwirth, Hoxne
h: 425, 507
Robert son of Adam of, 531, 1664

Wortham, Wrtham, Hartismere h: 450, 722

Wratting [Great or Little] Wrattinghe, Wratting',
Wreting', Risbridge h: 846
Richard son of Ralph of, 972, 1657
William Berard of, *see* Berard
William the carter of, *see* Carter

Wrentham, Wrantham, Wrentesham, Blything h,
x, xx, xxin; 159, 195, 259, 265, 339

Wulfric, Wlfric, Wlfryct: Hugh, 395
Peter son of, 911

Wuner: Alan son of, 27
Dunstan son of, 252
Henry son of, 27

Wyard: Richard, of Westhall, 1062, 1156

Wyat, Wyot: Roger, 795
William, 107, 1660

Wyburg: William, of Stansfield, 836, 1653

Wychesfield, Wychesfeud: Thomas de, 602

Wy de Lu: *see* Visdelu

Wygeyn, [Wigan]: Richard, 247, 1644

Wyke: Richard de la, master, 58, 449
William de la, master, 449

Wykeman [Wickman]: Robert, 348

Wyken, Wykes, Blackbourn h: 702, 703

Wykes, Wikes: Amice wife of Robert de, 251,
470, 523
Robert de, knight, juror, 145, 147, 159, 251,
450, 470, 523, 528–530, 532, 677, 679,
904, 1067, 1096
Thomas de, 702

Wymark, Wymarc: William, 578

Wymer: Austin son of, 1010
Hawise wife of Henry, 110
Henry, attorney, 110

Wymondham, Wymundh', Wymundham, Forehoe
h, Norfolk: 121, 694, 755
Thomas of, master, 121
Ranulf of, 1648
Robert the chaplain of, 629

Wymples, Wyples: Roger de, juror, 339, 1644

Wymund: Benedict son of Gilbert son of, 743
Gilbert* son of, 743

Wymundhall, Wymundhale: Alan de, 342, 394
Edmund de, attorney, *xxxivn*; 205–207, 265,
329, 395, 453, 455, 1057, 1075, 1646,
1647, 1658
John de, attorney, 172, 173, 327, 348, 1645,
1646

Wyn: Alan*, 407

Wyndebok: William de, 742

Wynderville: Robert de, 604

Wyndeshover [Windsor or Windover?]: Walter*
de, 255
Wynda* de, 255

Wyneless: Humphrey de, 620
Matilda wife of Humphrey de, 620

Wynesham: Christine aunt of Stephen de, 130
Matilda daughter of Stephen de, 130

Wyntermed: Henry de, 156

Wyples: *see* Wymples

Wytescrede: Stephen de, 1658

Wytolf: Roger, 552

Yarmouth, Gernem', Gernemue, Iernemue,
Iernemuth', East Flegg h, Norfolk: D, 1082
Alexander Allan of, *see* Allan
Edmund son of Pelerin of, 311
Geoffrey son of Guy of, 306
Henry brother of Robert of, sergeant, 306,
311
Henry of, master, 350
Hugh Rocinale of, *see* Rocinale
John of, 567
Margery wife of Charles of, 1082
Mena of, 329
Norfolk eyre at, 1240, *xiii*
Pelerin of, 306, 311, 368, 1645
Richard son of Serlon of, 1126
Richard the sergeant of, 1645
Robert of, sergeant, 306, 311, 350
Roger Perebourne of, *see* Perebourne
William son of Osbert of, 368
William son of William of, 1058

Yarmouth, Little, parva Gernemuth, Lothingland
h: *see* Gorleston, 274, 321, 1099, 1149
Richard of, 373
Robert son of Richard of, 1647

Yate, Yato, Henbury h, Gloucs, 95
Hugh of, essoiner, attorney, 54, 95

Yaxley, Iakele, Iakesl', Hartismere h: 208, 943
Gilbert son of William of, 943
Hugh de Blogate of, *see* Blogate
Henry* brother of Gilbert son of William of,
943
Joss son of Richard of, 509, 1649, 1659
Richard* brother of Gilbert son of William
of, 943
Richard* chaplain of, 208
Richard son of Hubert of, 509, 1649

INDEX OF PLEAS

The pleas are arranged under the twelve main headings adapted from those shown by Maitland's Index of Actions in *Bracton's Note Book* i, pp.177–187:

I. Actions of right	VII. Actions of darrein presentment
II. Actions of dower	VIII. Miscellaneous actions
III. Actions of entry	IX. Personal actions
IV. Assizes of novel disseisin	X. Crown pleas (not included in this volume)
V. Actions on limited descents	XI. Appellate proceedings
VI. Assizes utrum	XII. Prohibitions to courts Christian

Under each main heading the various types of plea are set out alphabetically in subsections Ia, Ib, Ic, etc. To find within which sub-section a particular type of plea or writ is classified, the index of subjects may be consulted. For example, under 'mort d'ancestor' in that index will be found the cross reference 'V(b)'. Where there are numerous references under a main heading or within a particular sub-section, the whole series of references is given first and then the references to pleas are listed again in detail, in such divisions as:

Procedure
Pleading by D
Court orders
*Conclude*d *by*

The layout is taken from *1248 Berkshire Eyre*, pp.565–585 and *1256 Shropshire Eyre*, pp.381–395.

Throughout the index *P* signifies the plaintiff, or demandant, who initiates the action, and *D* signifies the defendant, deforciant, impedient, or tenant, who opposes the plaintiff. References are to the numbers of the pleas in the text and not to the pages.

I. ACTIONS OF RIGHT

Ia. OF ADVOWSON, pleas, 149, 784

Ib. OF CUSTOMS AND SERVICES
      pleas, 177, 181, 193, 194, 197, 332, 618, 678, 719–721, 732, 748, 901, 976, 977, 989, 1105
    Procedure: action proceeds, 194, 197, 332, 678, 720, 976, 977
             default of *D*, 181,1105
             foreign pleas, 177, 181, 618
             grand assize, 678
             trial by jury, 332
    Pleading by D: acknowledges *P*'s right, 719, 721, 977
             freely warrants, 194
             non-tenure, 197, 720, 976
             enfeoffed by another, only services as a free man not villein, 332
    Counter pleading by P: *D* has withheld feudal dues, 332
    Court orders: attachment of *D*, 1105
                  D to go to county, 194
                  distraint of *D*, 181

Id. OF WARD

      pleas, 325, 522, 931

Procedure: action proceeds, 931

          attorney appointed, 931

          essoins, 60, 72

          foreign pleas, 60, 72, 325, 931

          military tenure, 931

Pleading by D: voucher to warranty, 931

Court orders: attachment of *D*, 325

Concluded by: adjournment – for production of defaulter, 325

          for production of vouchee to warranty, 931

          agreement, 522

          D rendering wardship to *P* by licence, 522

II. ACTIONS OF DOWER

IIa. *UNDE NICHIL HABET or* RIGHT OF DOWER

      pleas, 13, 14, 28, 46, 47, 74, 80, 88, 99, 102, 103, 108, 137, 153–155, 161, 172, 183, 187, 205–207, 219, 221, 222, 224, 225, 232, 233, 251, 254, 256, 257, 263, 270, 295, 303, 321, 322, 328, 341, 359, 400, 406, 410, 453, 455, 462, 464, 467, 470, 475, 485, 523, 524, 526, 576, 588, 634–636, 649, 727, 752, 783, 811, 822, 895–897, 906, 954, 985, 990, 1020, 1037, 1038, 1050, 1065, 1082–1084, 1092, 1099, 1122, 1132, 1138, 1157, 1158

Procedure: action proceeds, 153–155, 219, 221, 222, 224, 225, 232, 254, 256, 257, 263, 295, 322, 328, 341, 359, 400, 453, 455, 464, 467, 470, 475, 485, 526, 588, 634–636, 649, 727, 752, 783, 811, 822, 895–897, 906, 954, 985, 1020, 1037, 1084, 1092, 1157, 1158

          attorney appointed, 88, 102, 103, 108, 137, 155, 161, 172, 183, 187, 205–207, 224, 233, 251, 254, 270, 321, 406, 410, 462, 523, 524, 727, 783, 906, 1158

          charter proffered – by *D*, 328, 455

          by *P*, 526

          customs of Dunwich indicated on dower, 1157, 1158

          default of *D*, 225, 270, 321, 634, 783, 990, 1038, 1050, 1082, 1099

          of *P*, 1038

          essoins, 13, 14, 28, 46, 47, 74, 80

          foreign pleas, 74, 80, 99, 153, 155, 221, 232, 254, 263, 467, 475, 727, 752, 811, 1038, 1050, 1082

          land not petitioned by *D*, 1099

          land taken into king's hands, 1099

          liberty of prior of Ely, 588, 634, 636, 985

          verdicts detailed, 1157

Pleading by D: acknowledges disseisin, 1092

          acknowledges *P*'s right, 221, 256, 257, 752, 985

          attested at court of town, 1158

          charter provided by vouchee, 954

          D gives part of the claim only, 822

          knows no denial, 322

          land should be warranted, but husband died seised, 954

          non-tenure, 470

          P has land elsewhere as her dower, 635

          P already has dower, 526

          P can only claim a third as land is held in knight's fee and not socage 222

          P given satisfaction by all in writ, 341

          P never had seisin, 588

          P's husband never held in fee, 155, 328, 649

          P's husband sold messuage to *D*, 1157, 1158

          tenure as guardian of minor only, 636

          view claimed, 263, 475

          voucher to warranty, 99, 153, 219, 222, 225, 254, 295, 359, 400, 453, 455, 464, 467, 485, 634, 727, 783, 811, 895, 897, 906, 954

Counter pleading by P: *P* indicates content with what *D* offers, 822
Court orders: amercement pardoned because poor, 588, 649, 1092
            pardoned because under age, 467
            cape and summons, 225, 270, 321, 328, 485, 634, 783, 896, 990, 1050, 1082, 1084
            P may proceed against third party, 470
            P to have dower from ward's land, 455
            summons in county of Essex, 897
            trial by jury, 155, 526, 588
            vouchee to warranty to make exchange, 453, 1020
Concluded by: acknowledgement by *D*, 232
            adjournment – by command of the king to the next county, 99
                for jury trial, 155
                for production of defaulter, 270, 321, 328, 634, 783, 896, 990, 1050, 1082, 1084
                for production of vouchee to warranty, 153, 154, 219, 359, 400, 453, 464, 634, 727, 783, 895, 897, 906
                for view, 153, 224, 263, 475
                to hear judgment, 1038, 1158
            agreement, 221, 256, 257
            agreement by chirograph, 232
            D rendering dower to *P* by licence, 295, 453
            enrolled agreement, 576, 1037
            fine made by *D* on surety, 752
            judgement for *D*, 328, 455, 470, 526, 588, 635, 636, 649, 1038, 1157, 1158
            judgement for *P*, 222, 225, 232, 254, 322, 328, 467, 485, 752, 811, 822, 985, 1020, 1092, 1099
            non prosecution by *P*, 303, 1065, 1083, 1122, 1132, 1138
            poverty noted, 1157, 1158
            satisfaction made by *D*, 221, 254, 256, 257, 341
            by licence, 453, 954
            satisfaction made by voucher to warranty, 222, 225

III. ACTIONS OF ENTRY

IIIa. AD COMMUNEM LEGEM
    pleas, 255, 963, 964, 1010, 1057, 1160

IIIb. AD TERMINUM QUI PRETERIIT
    pleas, 157, 273, 300, 955, 958, 986, 991, 1003, 1016, 1030, 1035, 1036, 1044, 1053

IIIc. ALIENATION BY VILLEIN
    pleas, 323, 412, 560, 1006

IIId. CUI IN VITA
    pleas, 249, 497, 505, 539, 561, 635, 828, 936, 1027, 1043, 1045

IIIe. DUM INFRA ETATEM
    pleas, 175, 345, 601, 992, 1011

IIIf. PER INTRUSIONEM
    pleas, 826, 893

IIIg. SINE ASSENSU VIRI
    plea 646

IIIh. UNSPECIFIED
    pleas, 168, 214, 215, 290, 340, 454, 457, 477, 501, 645, 884, 960, 966, 969, 1032, 1055, 1056, 1120, 1124, 1126, 1129, 1131, 1137

IV. ASSIZES OF NOVEL DISSEISIN

IVb. FOR LAND, MESSUAGE, RENT ETC.

V. ACTIONS ON LIMITED DESCENTS

Va. COSINAGE

Vb. MORT D'ANCESTOR

amercement pardoned by lord, 124
assize cannot proceed, 94
enrolled agreement, 360, 436, 554, 559, 729, 743, 744, 746, 753, 796, 853, 925
error in fine roll, 329
fine made by *P* on surety, 892
judgement for *D*, 163, 167, 208, 209, 238, 292, 316, 329, 346, 377, 384, 385, 394, 396, 418, 423, 433, 438, 479, 493, 496, 517, 534, 538, 555, 575, 579, 609, 733, 742, 814, 815, 848, 853, 879, 883, 890, 1071, 1087, 1095, 1110, 1111
judgement for *P*, 223, 260, 362, 367, 372, 387, 440, 445, 446, 593, 690, 731, 749, 761, 767, 850, 851, 858, 860
    but *P* also amerced for excess claim, 892
no decision, 882
non prosecution by *P*, 302, 324, 331, 375, 378, 398, 408, 424–426, 430, 432, 437, 441, 445, 500, 509, 513, 515, 540, 562–565, 571, 572, 603, 612, 623, 624, 787, 788, 790, 793, 799, 815, 867, 868, 911, 918, 920, 923, 924
poverty noted, 324, 385, 394, 418, 433, 517, 1087, 1110
satisfaction made by *D*, 367
    by licence, 260, 380, 750
unfinished, 566
withdrawal by *P*, 849, 854, 877
after action has started, 613

Vc. NUPER OBIIT
    pleas, 552, 1098, 1149

VI. ASSIZES UTRUM

pleas, 11, 15, 120, 231, 239, 246, 252, 275–286, 296, 326, 342–344, 395, 411, 495, 548, 556, 557, 577, 608, 681, 716, 718, 757, 802, 852, 912, 929, 932
Procedure: action proceeds, 231, 239, 252, 276–283, 285, 286, 326, 343, 344, 395, 411, 495, 548, 556, 557, 577, 608, 681, 716, 718, 757, 802, 852, 932
attorney appointed, 342
default of *D*, 231, 284, 344, 395, 411, 556, 608
essoins, 11, 15
foreign pleas, 11, 802, 929
jury trial, 285, 286
liberty of prior of Ely, 548, 557, 577, 932
plea detailed, inclusive, one plea split up by *D*s, 275–284
verdict given, 286, 757
verdict detailed, 285
Pleading by D: acknowledges *P*'s right, 239, 277, 281, 577, 716
    D claims mother holds land in dower, *P* holds land, Church never had seisin – others did, 395
entry by third party, claims only term, 326
P never had seisin, 556
villeinage of *D*, 276, 344, 548
voucher to warranty, 231, 252, 278–280, 282, 283, 286, 343, 344, 495, 556, 716, 802
Counter pleading by P: acknowledges satisfaction given by *P*, 852
    P acknowledged that some of the *D*s may hold from him as before, 252
Court orders: amercement of *P*, 285
    pardoned because scholar, 326
assize to be taken by default, 231, 344, 395, 411, 608
D to have exchange from vouchee, 716
P may distrain for service, 285
P may proceed against third party, 344
remand in custody, 757
re-summons of *D*, 411
vouchee to warranty to make exchange, 495

Concluded by: acknowledgement by *D*, 285
adjournment – for jury trial, 284
for production of vouchee to warranty, 802
until next assize in that area, 802
until vouchee comes of age, 278–280
agreement, 277, 282,
by chirograph, 120, 246
D rendering free alms to *P* by licence, 577
enrolled agreement, 246, 296, 681, 718, 929, 932
fine made by *P* on surety, 343, 344, 395
judgement for *D*, 276, 286, 326, 343, 395, 548, 556, 757
judgement for *P*, 231, 239, 252, 277, 279, 281, 283, 326, 411, 495, 608
but *P* also amerced for excess claim, 344
damages for *P*, 716
non prosecution by *P*, 912
poverty noted, 548
satisfaction made by *D*, 252, 852
by licence, 932
void because elsewhere in rolls, 557

VII. ASSIZES OF DARREIN PRESENTMENT

pleas, 620, 680, 798, 1088

VIII. MISCELLANEOUS ACTIONS

There are some items in the roll for which a plea type cannot be determined. These have not been included in this section.

VIIIa. COMMON OF PASTURE (*QUOD PERMITTAT*)
plea, 610

VIIIb. COMMON OF PASTURE (*QUO JURE*)
plea, 131

VIIIc. ESCHEAT
on bastardy, plea 921,
on failure of heirs, plea 1159

VIIId. EXACTION OF SERVICES (*MESNE*)
plea, 903, 1127

VIIIe. EXACTION OF SERVICES (*MONSTRAVERUNT FOR ANCIENT DEMESNE*)
plea, 1118

VIIIf. FISHERY
attorney, 699
essoins, 24, 25, 659, 672
pleas, 687, 823, 999

VIIIg. FRANCHISE UNSPECIFIED (*DE PLACITO LIBERTATIS*)
attorney, 705, 1072
essoins, 43
pleas, 159, 1042

VIIIh. HOMAGE (*DE HOMAGIO CAPIENDO*)
pleas, 482, 1123

VIIIi. HUNTING RIGHTS (*DE LIBERA CHACIA*)
 plea, 268

VIIIj. LAND (FORM OF ACTION UNSPECIFIED)
 adjournment on plea of, 109, 114,191, 945, 947, 961, 1102
 agreement on plea of. 107, 115, 122, 123, 126, 127, 140–142, 202, 229, 235, 241–243, 267,
 351, 415, 460, 468, 472, 494, 498, 499, 508, 543, 581, 584, 586, 637, 647, 648, 684, 685,
 693, 724, 734, 762, 771, 777, 866, 872, 876, 881, 899, 939, 950, 951, 993, 1026, 1077, 1090,
 1128, 1153
 attorney appointed on plea of, 84–87, 92, 93, 96, 101, 104, 113, 118, 129, 133, 138, 139,
 143, 152, 170, 171, 184–186, 204, 234, 250, 294, 312, 342, 406, 461–463, 520, 614, 615,
 675, 676, 697, 705, 728, 739, 1024, 1072
 essoin on plea of, 1–5, 8–10, 20–22, 30–37, 39, 44, 45, 48–51, 53–55, 61, 63–67, 73, 75–79,
 83, 114, 654, 657, 658, 660–665, 670, 671, 673, 914
 judgment for *D*, 1009
 judgement for *P*, 605, 808, 885
 no decision, 1112, 1115
 non prosecution by *P*, 626, 946, 1023, 1048, 1085
 plea stayed because of death of *D*, 106

VIIIk. PERSONAL FREEDOM (*DE LIBERTATE PROBANDA*)
 pleas, 941, 995, 1013, 1014, 1140

VIIIl. PERSONAL FREEDOM (*DE NATIVO HABENDO*)
 essoins, 12, 16
 pleas, 200, 330, 356, 483, 527, 602, 982, 1108

VIIIm. SUIT (? OF COURT)
 essoins, 68, 668, 669
 plea, 551

VIIIn. WASTE
 attorney, 714
 pleas, 174, 338, 764, 827, 978, 1054, 1121

VIIIp. LEVY A CHIROGRAPH
 This is not part of Maitland's layout in *Bracton's Note Book* in the pages shown above but the
 plea to levy a chirograph is shown in *Early Registers of Writs*, p.195, writ 376.
 pleas, 180, 810, 1117

IX. PERSONAL ACTIONS

IXa. ANNUITY
 pleas, 204, 480, 740

IXb. COVENANT
 pleas, 57, 88, 96, 179, 189, 204, 319, 459, 616, 633, 638, 666, 674, 691, 768, 803, 962, 1005,
 1008, 1017, 1028, 1060, 1070, 1072, 1091, 1094, 1109
 Procedure: action proceeds, 189, 962, 1008, 1060, 1070, 1091, 1109
  attorney appointed, 88, 319, 691, 962, 1072
  damages claimed, 189, 962, 1070, 1091
  default of *D*, 179, 1028, 1109
  essoins on plea of, 666, 674, 1070
  foreign pleas, 179, 189, 1017
  liberty of prior of Ely, 633, 1005, 1008
  no deed or tally produced by *D*, 1091
 P complains that: *D* has held back money owed according to the covenant, 1070
   D has taxed men of the manor and sold wood, 1091
   D has withheld feudal dues, multure, 962

343

IXe. DETINUE
>
> of charters, 266, 458, 1103
> of chattels, 136, 706, 968, 1049, 1058

IXf. REPLEVIN
>
> pleas, 31, 42, 134, 656, 725, 1072, 1112, 1115

IXg. TRESPASS (IN CIVIL PLEAS)
>
> pleas, 169, 264, 486, 712, 886, 898, 972, 996, 1101, 1104

IXh. WARRANTY OF CHARTER
>
> pleas, 38, 62, 96, 98, 111, 112, 178, 220, 253, 402, 451, 627–631, 651, 785, 818, 916, 919, 935, 938, 944, 948, 952, 956, 957, 959, 965, 967, 983, 987, 997, 1000–1002, 1004, 1007, 1015, 1031, 1033, 1041, 1046, 1047, 1062, 1064, 1066, 1130, 1133, 1135, 1136, 1139, 1141, 1142, 1156

Procedure: action proceeds, 651, 919, 938, 944, 948, 997, 1002, 1031, 1033, 1041, 1135
> a plea previously heard in another court, 938, 1031, 1033, 1041
> attorney appointed, 96, 98, 111, 112, 1156
> charter proffered by *D*, 98, 944, 948, 1041
> foreign pleas, 38, 98, 176, 959
> land impleaded in court of liberty of St Edmund by another, 997
> liberty of Ely, 627–631, 944, 948, 1000–1002, 1004, 1007

Pleading by D: acknowledges charter by voucher, 1031
> *D* has never in anything gone against that covenant, 651
> *D* is a minor, cannot answer for charter, 997
> freely warrants, 919, 938, 944, 948, 1002, 1033, 1041, 1135

Court orders: amercement of *P* pardoned for Queen, 651
> *D* to go to county court and warrant there, 938, 944, 948, 1031, 1033, 1135
> *P* to make homage to the *D*, 919
> steward of liberty court ordered not to proceed with other plea, 997
> sheriff ordered to distrain *D*, 938

Concluded by: acknowledgement by *D*, 919
> adjournment by prayer of the parties, 176
> to another court to warrant there, 919, 944, 948, 1031, 1033, 1135
> until *D* comes of age, 997
> agreement by chirograph, 98, 220, 253, 451, 785, 916, 959, 983, 1066
> enrolled agreement, 402
> judgement for *D*, 651, 1041
> judgement for *P*, 938, 1002
> no decision, 818, 1001
> non prosecution by *P*, 627–631, 935, 952, 956, 957, 965, 967, 987, 1000, 1004, 1007, 1015, 1046, 1047, 1062, 1064, 1130, 1133, 1136, 1139, 1141, 1142
> poverty noted, 1041

XI. APPELLATE PROCEEDINGS

There are five other pleas involving appellate proceeding but their type is not known.

XIa. ATTAINT OF MORT D'ANCESTOR
> pleas, 534, 537, 1019

Xib. ATTAINT OF NOVEL DISSEISIN
> pleas, 244, 774–776, 779

XII. PROHIBITIONS TO COURTS CHRISTIAN

pleas, 71, 105, 125, 730, 1113

INDEX OF SELECTED SUBJECTS
IN THE INTRODUCTION AND APPENDICES

Small Roman numerals refer to pages in the introduction. Large Roman numerals in italics refer to the index of pleas, e.g. *I(a)*. Capital letters refer to the appendices in the introduction.

abbeys: *see* religious houses
abjuration of the realm: xx, lvii
adjournments: F(i), xviii, xix, xxi, xxviii, xxix, xxxiv, Table 3 xxxvi–xxxvii, xxxviii, xli, xlii, xlv, xlvi, li–lv, lxiii, lxvn
adjournment locations: Table 4 liii
advowson: *I(a)*, xviii, xlii, xliii, l
Agarde's Index: xxii
agreements: *see* chirographs
amercements: Dn, G, H, vii, x, xi, xiin, xivn, xvn, xvin, xix, xxn, xxi, xviiin, xxiii, xxiv, Table 1 xxv, Table 2 xxv, xxv–xxviii, xxxii, xxxiii, xxxix, xli, lii, liv–lvii, lviiin, lix, lx, lxi, lxii, lxiv, xcvii, c
ancient demesne: *VIII(e)*, K, xlviii–xlix
annuity, plea of: *IX(a)*
ante judicium: lviii
appeals: G, H(iii), xix, li
appellate proceedings: *XI*, B, F(i), Table 3 xxxvi–xxxvii, xl, lx
articles of the eyre: *see* eyres
assizes: Dn, x, xix, xx, , xxvii, xl, xli, Table 4 liii, lxi, lxiii, lxiv, lxv
   grand, I, xn, xivn, xv, xviii, xxixn, xxxiin, l, li, lviin
   possessory, x, xxxiv, xlviii, l, lvii, lxiv, *see darrein*
   presentment mort d'ancestor, novel disseisin, *utrum*
attachment: K, xx
attaint of juries: *XI*, G, xl, lx
attorneys: I, xi, xiv, xv, xxi, Table 2 xxv, xxxi, xxxiv, xlivn, xlv, livn, lv

bailiffs: H(iii), I(ii), K, xiv–xvi, xxiv, xxxviii, xlvii, xlviii
battle, trial by: xxxii, l, li
   champion in, I(i), li
boroughs: ix, xiv–xvi, xix, xxiv, lxiv; *see* Beccles, Bungay, Bury St Edmunds, Dunwich, Exning, Eye, Ipswich, Sudbury in index of people and places
Bracton: ixn, xn, xivn, xxxn, xxxi, xxxiin, xxxiiin, xxxivn, xxxviiin, xxxix, xln, xlin, xlivn, xlv, xlvi, xlviii, lvii

chancellor: I(ii), lxii
chancery: xvii, xix, xxx
charters: xvn, xxx, xlviii, lii
chattels: H(iii), x, xi, xxviiin, xxxix, lii, lvii
chirographs: Dn, E, H(iii), J, xi, xiin, xiii, xivn, xvii, xviii, xxi, xxiii, xxiv, Table 1 xxv, Table 2 xxv, xxv–xxviii, xxx–xxxiii, xxxv, xxxix–xlii, xlvi, xlvii, l–lii, liin, liii, lv, lvi, lviiin, lx, lxiii, lxviin, xcviii
churches named (references in index of people and places):
   elsewhere: Dean, Kenwyn, *Landegeith*, Landepar-', Savigny, *Trenery*, Worcester
   in Norfolk: Burnham Thorpe, Caldecote, Cringleford, Kirstead, Ringstead, Rollesby, Walcott
   in Suffolk: Alpheton, Assington, Bacton, Barking, Barningham, Burgh, Buxhall, Byry [Bury St Edmunds?], Carlton [Colville], Clare, Copdock, Denham, Dennington, Fressingfield, Henstead; Ipswich, Holy Trinity, St Matthew, St Nicholas; Langham, Levington, Martlesham, Pakefield, Parham, Raydon, Rendham, Shimpling, Snape, Stanton, Stoke, Stonham, Tuddenham, Welnetham, Weybread, Wickham [Market], Wixoe, Willingham
civil pleas: *see* common pleas
clerks, justices': I(ii), xiiin, xiv, xvn, xvi–xxi, xxiii–xxv, xxvii, xxxi, xxxviii, xxxix, lii, lv, lvi, lxi, xcvii–xcix
commissions: of assize, x, xix, xxvii, liii Table 4, lxi, lxiv
   of gaol delivery, x, lv, lxivn, lxv
   of knights, xn
common law: xlv, lxiii
common of pasture: xl
   novel disseisin, IV(a), xxxv, xxxix, xl, lii
   quod permittat, VIII(a)
   quo jure, VIII(b)
common pleas: *I–IX*, xix, xx, xxviii, lii
concords, final: J, xi, xiii, xiv, xvii, xxi, xxii, xxvi–xxviii, xxxivn, xlvii, xcvii, c
coroners: H(iii), I(ii), xiv–xv, xix–xx, xxiv, l

345